D1452929

INTERNATIONAL THEOLOGICAL COMMISSION

TEXTS AND DOCUMENTS, 1986–2007

INTERNATIONAL THEOLOGICAL COMMISSION

TEXTS AND DOCUMENTS
1986–2007

Edited by Reverend Michael Sharkey
and
Father Thomas Weinandy

IGNATIUS PRESS   SAN FRANCISCO

Cover photograph by istockphoto/Roberto A. Sanchez

Cover design by Roxanne Mei Lum

Published in 2009 by Ignatius Press, San Francisco
All rights reserved by the International Theological Commission
ISBN 978-1-58617-226-8
Library of Congress Control Number 2007928865
Printed in the United States of America ∞

CONTENTS

FOREWORD

The International Theological Commission is now in its fortieth year. It was first established by Paul VI in 1969 at the suggestion of the first Synod of Bishops in 1967. The cooperation between bishops and theologians during the council years had been so successful that many bishops wanted that cooperation to continue in an institutionalised manner. Suggestions for nominations to the membership of the Commission are sent in by Episcopal Conferences throughout the church. Thirty are then chosen and appointed for a period of five years. They are drawn from all over the world, represent the various branches of theology, and, indeed, the various approaches to theology. They are served by a General Secretary, and the Commission's President is *ex officio* the Prefect of the Congregation for the Doctrine of the Faith.

The Commission meets annually for a week's plenary assembly, whether to choose a new topic, advance one in progress, or to finalise it. Work on a topic is usually delegated to a sub-commission whose members share their draft texts (by email these days) and who meet on an *ad hoc* basis to improve and polish them. When the text is finalised, all the members vote on it: if it receives an absolute majority and is approved by the Prefect, it is published *in specific form*, which means that it can be taken as an authoritative presentation of the state of the question examined, even if some individual members would have liked to have gone further, but agree to the consensus; however, the Commission reserves the right to approve the text only *in generic form*, accepting the principal ideas of the document, the rest remaining the responsibility of individual author(s).

The theological method employed by the Commission is largely the one that emerged in Vatican II. Prior to the Council, students of theology were presented with theses explaining the teaching of the Church, illustrated by proof texts from the Scriptures. For example in the 1950's, students in Rome, following a four year course for a licence in theology (S.T.L.), completed the whole of moral theology at the end of the second year before even opening the Bible at the beginning of the third.

The Council changed all that. Sacred Scripture comes first: studied reverently, systematically and critically (in the academic sense); then the historical development so that the student can grasp the import of a decision or an idea in its historical context. In this way a student appro-priates the teaching of the Magisterium in a more profound manner. This is now the norm. It is what we expect; and it is what we get in the documents of the International Theological Commission.

Monsignor Michael Sharkey.
Lichfield, U.K., 18 October 2008.

15

FAITH AND INCULTURATION

INTRODUCTION

1. The International Theological Commission has had, on several occasions, the opportunity to reflect on the relationship between faith and culture.[1] In 1984 it spoke directly on the inculturation of faith in its study on the mystery of the Church, which it produced with a view to the extraordinary synod of 1985.[2] For its part, the Pontifical Biblical Commission held its 1979 plenary session on the theme of the inculturation of faith in the light of Scripture.[3]

2. Today the International Theological Commission intends to continue this reflection in a more profound and systematic manner on account of the importance assumed by this theme of the inculturation of faith throughout the Christian world and on account of the insistence with which the Church's magisterium has considered this theme since the Second Vatican Council.

3. The basis is furnished by the Conciliar documents and by the synod papers which have continued them. Thus, in the constitution *Gaudium et spes*, the council has shown what lessons and what tasks the Church has drawn from its first experiences of inculturation in the Greco-Roman world.[4] It then devoted an entire chapter of this document to the pro-

---

[1] See the documents of the International Theological Commission on theological pluralism (1972), human development and Christian salvation (1976), Catholic doctrine on the sacrament of marriage (1977), and selected questions on Christology (1979), in the collection of the Commission Théologique Internationale, *Textes et documents, 1969–1985* (Paris: Cerf, 1988) [English ed.: International Theological Commission, *Texts and Documents, 1969–1985* (San Francisco: Ignatius Press, 1989; repub. 2009 as vol. 1)].

[2] Commission Théologique Internationale, "Thèmes choisis d'ecclésiologie à l'occasion du 20ᵉ anniversaire de la clôture du Concile Vatican II" (1984), in the collection referred to in the previous note, pp. 336–40. [See "Select Themes of Ecclesiology on the Occasion of the Twentieth Anniversary of the Closing of the Second Vatican Council", chapter 13 of the English-language collection (pp. 267–304).]

[3] Pontifical Biblical Commission, *Fede e cultura alla luce della Bibbia / Foi et culture à la lumière de la Bible* (Turin: Editrice Elle di Ci, 1981).

[4] GS 44.

motion of culture ("*De culturae progressu rite promovendo*").[5] After describing culture as an effort toward a deeper humanity and toward a better plan for the universe, the council considered at length the relationships between culture and the message of salvation. It then enunciated some of the more urgent duties of Christians regarding culture: defense of the right of all to a culture, promotion of an integral culture and harmonization of the links between culture and Christianity. The Decree on the Church's Missionary Activity and the Declaration on Non-Christian Religions develop some of these positions. Two ordinary synods expressly treated the evangelization of cultures, that of 1974, on the theme of evangelization,[6] and that of 1977, on catechetical formation.[7] The 1985 synod, which celebrated the twentieth anniversary of the closing of the Second Vatican Council, spoke of inculturation as "the intimate transformation of authentic cultural values through their integration in Christianity in the various human cultures".[8]

4. Pope John Paul II himself has taken to heart in a special manner the evangelization of cultures: In his view, the dialogue of the Church and of cultures assumes a vital importance for the future of the Church and of the world. To assist him in this great work, the Holy Father has created a specialized curial body: the Pontifical Council for Culture.[9] It is moreover with this dicastery that the International Theological Commission is happily in a position to reflect today on the inculturation of faith.

5. Relying on the conviction that "the incarnation of the Word was also a cultural incarnation", the pope affirms that cultures, analogically comparable to the humanity of Christ in whatever good they possess, may play a positive role of mediation in the expression and extension of the Christian faith.[10]

6. Two essential themes are bound up with this view. First, that of the transcendence of revelation in relation to the cultures in which it finds expression. The Word of God cannot, in effect, be identified or linked in an exclusive manner with the elements of culture which bear it. The Gospel quite often demands a conversion of attitudes and an amendment of customs where it establishes itself: Cultures must also be purified and restored in Christ.

---

[5] GS 53–62.

[6] Paul VI, *Evangelii nuntiandi*, 18–20.

[7] John Paul II, *Catechesi tradendae*, 53; *Origins* 9, no. 21 (1979): 342.

[8] Extraordinary Synod for the twentieth anniversary of the closing of the Second Vatican Council, final report voted by the fathers, 7 December 1985, *Origins* 15, no. 27 (1985): 450.

[9] John Paul II, Letter of foundation of the Pontifical Council for Culture, 20 May 1982.

[10] John Paul II, Speech to the University of Coimbra, 15 May 1982; *Origins* 12, no. 2 (1982): 27.

7. The second major theme of the teaching of John Paul II revolves around the urgency of the evangelization of cultures. This task presupposes that one would understand and penetrate with a critical sympathy particular cultural identities and that, in the interest of a universality corresponding to the truly human reality of all cultures, one would favor exchanges between them. The Holy Father thus bases the evangelization of cultures on an anthropological conception firmly rooted in Christian thought since the fathers of the Church. Since culture, when pure, reveals and strengthens the nature of man, the Christian impregnation presupposes the surpassing of all historicism and relativism in the conception of what is human. The evangelization of cultures should therefore be inspired by the love of man in himself and for himself, especially in those aspects of his being and of his culture which are being attacked or are under threat.[11]

8. In the light of this teaching, and also of the reflection which the theme of the inculturation of faith has aroused in the Church, we first propose a Christian anthropology which situates, one in relation to the other, nature, culture and grace. We shall then see the process of inculturation at work in the history of salvation: in ancient Israel, in the life and work of Jesus and in the early Church. A final section will treat problems at present posed to faith by its encounter with popular piety, with non-Christian religions, with the cultural traditions in the young Churches and finally with the various characteristics of modernity.

I. NATURE, CULTURE AND GRACE

1. Anthropologists readily return to describe or define culture in terms of the distinction, sometimes even opposition, between nature and culture. The significance of this word *nature* varies moreover with the different conceptions of the natural sciences, of philosophy and of theology. The magisterium understands this word in a very specific sense: The nature of a being is what constitutes it as such, with the dynamism of its tendencies toward its proper ends. It is from God that natures possess what they are, as well as their proper ends. They are from that moment impregnated with a significance in which man, as the image of God, is capable of discerning the "creating hand of God".[12]

2. The fundamental inclinations of human nature, expressed by natural law, appear therefore as an expression of the will of the Creator. This

---

[11] Speech to the bishops of Kenya, 7 May 1980.
[12] Paul VI, *Humanae vitae*, 13.

natural law declares the specific requirements of human nature, requirements which are significative of the design of God for his rational and
free creature. Thus all that misunderstanding is avoided which, perceiving
nature in a univocal sense, would reduce man to material nature.

3. It is appropriate, at the same time, to consider human nature according to its unfolding in historical time: that is, to observe what man,
endowed with a fallible liberty and often subjected to his passions, has
made of his humanity. This heritage transmitted to new generations
includes simultaneously immense treasures of wisdom, art and generosity, and a considerable share of deviations and perversions. Attention
therefore, as a whole, revolves around human nature and the human
condition, an expression which integrates existential elements, of which
certain ones—sin and grace—affect the history of salvation. If, therefore, we use the word *culture* in a primarily positive sense—as a synonym of development, for example—as have Vatican II and the recent
popes, we will not forget that cultures can perpetuate and favor the
choice of pride and selfishness.

4. Culture consists in the extension of the requirements of human nature,
as the accomplishment of its end, as is especially taught in the constitution *Gaudium et spes*: "Man comes to a true and full humanity only through
culture, that is through the cultivation of the goods and values of nature. . . .
The word 'culture' in its general sense indicates everything whereby man
develops and perfects his many bodily and spiritual qualities." Thus the
domain of culture is multiple: "He strives by his knowledge and his labor,
to bring the world itself under his control. He renders social life more
human both in the family and the civic community, through improvement of customs and institutions. Throughout the course of time he
expresses, communicates and conserves in his works, great spiritual experiences and desires, that they might be of advantage to the progress of
many, even of the whole human family." [13]

5. The primary constituent of culture is the human person, considered
in all aspects of his being. Man betters himself—this is the first end of all
culture—but he does so thanks to the works of culture and thanks to a
cultural memory. Culture also still designates the milieu in which and on
account of which persons may grow.

6. The human person is a community being who blossoms in giving
and in receiving. It is thus in solidarity with others and across living social
relationships that the person progresses. Also, those realities of nation,
people, society, with their cultural patrimony, constitute for the development of persons a "definite, historical milieu which enfolds the man of

[13] GS 53.

every nation and age and from which he draws the values which permit him to promote civilization."[14]

7. Culture, which is always a concrete and particular culture, is open to the higher values common to all. Thus the originality of a culture does not signify withdrawal into itself but a contribution to the richness which is the good of all. Cultural pluralism cannot therefore be interpreted as the juxtaposition of a closed universe, but as participation in a unison of realities all directed toward the universal values of humanity. The phenomenon of the reciprocal penetration of cultures, frequent in history, illustrates this fundamental openness of particular cultures to the values common to all, and through this their openness one to another.

8. Man is a naturally religious being. The turning toward the absolute is inscribed in his deepest being. In a general sense, religion is an integral constituent of culture, in which it takes root and blossoms. Moreover, all the great cultures include, as the keystone of the edifice they constitute, the religious dimension, the inspiration of the great achievements which have marked the ancient history of civilizations.

9. At the root of the great religions is the transcendent movement of man in search of God. Purified of its deviations and disagreeable aspects, this movement should be the object of sincere respect. It is on this that the Christian faith comes to engraft itself. What distinguishes the Christian faith is that it is free adherence to the proposition of the gratuitous love of God which has been revealed to us, which has given us his only Son to free us from sin and has poured out his Spirit in our hearts. The radical reality of Christianity lies in the gift that God makes of himself to humanity, facing all the aspirations, requests, conquests and achievements of nature.

10. Therefore, because it transcends the entire natural and cultural order, the Christian faith is, on the one hand, compatible with all cultures insofar as they conform to right reason and good will, and, on the other hand, to an eminent degree, a dynamizing factor of culture. A single principle explains the totality of relationships between faith and culture: Grace respects nature, healing in it the wounds of sin, comforting and elevating it. Elevation to the divine life is the specific finality of grace, but it cannot realize this unless nature is healed and unless elevation to the supernatural order brings nature, in the way proper to itself, to the plenitude of perfection.

11. The process of inculturation may be defined as the Church's efforts to make the message of Christ penetrate a given sociocultural milieu, calling on the latter to grow according to all its particular values, as

[14] Ibid.

long as these are compatible with the Gospel. The term *inculturation* includes the notion of growth, of the mutual enrichment of persons and groups, rendered possible by the encounter of the Gospel with a social milieu. "Inculturation [is] the incarnation of the Gospel in native cultures and also the introduction of these cultures into the life of the Church." [15]

II. INCULTURATION IN THE HISTORY OF SALVATION

1. The relationships between nature, culture and grace shall be considered in the concrete history of the covenant between God and humanity that began with a particular people, culminated in a son of this people, who is also Son of God, and extending from him to all the nations of the earth, this history demonstrates the "marvelous 'condescension' of eternal wisdom". [16]

Israel, the People of the Covenant

2. Israel understood itself as formed in an immediate manner by God. And the Old Testament, the Bible of ancient Israel, is the permanent witness of the revelation of the living God to the members of a chosen people. In its written form, this revelation also bears the traces of the cultural and social experiences of the era during which this people and neighboring civilizations encountered each other. Ancient Israel was born in a world which had already given birth to great cultures and progressed together with them.

3. The most ancient institutions of Israel (for example, circumcision, the spring sacrifice, the Sabbath rest) are not particular to it. It borrowed them from the neighboring peoples. A large part of the culture of Israel has a similar origin. However, the people of the Bible subjected these borrowings to profound changes when it incorporated them into its faith and religious practice. It passed them through the screen of a faith in the personal God of Abraham (the free Creator and wise planner of the universe, in whom the source of sin and death is not to be found). It is the encounter with this God, experienced in the covenant, which permits the understanding of man and woman as personal beings and in consequence the rejection of the inhuman practices inherent in the other cultures.

---

[15] John Paul II, *Slavorum Apostoli*, 21; *Origins* 15, no. 8 (1985): 122.
[16] *DV* 13.

4. The biblical authors used, while simultaneously transforming, the cultures of their time to recount, throughout the history of a people, the salvific action which God would cause to culminate in Jesus Christ and to unite the peoples of all cultures, called to form one body of which Jesus is the head.

5. In the Old Testament, cultures, fused and transformed, are placed at the service of the revelation of the God of Abraham, lived in the covenant and recorded in Scripture. It was a unique preparation on the social and religious plane for the coming of Jesus Christ. In the New Testament, the God of Abraham, Isaac and Jacob, revealed at a deeper level and manifested in the fullness of the Spirit, invites all cultures to allow themselves to be changed by the life, teaching, death and resurrection of Jesus Christ.

6. If the pagans were "grafted onto Israel",[17] it must be emphasized that the original plan of God concerns all creation.[18] In fact, a covenant is made through Noah with all the peoples of the earth who are prepared to live in accordance with justice.[19] This covenant is anterior to those made with Abraham and Moses. Beginning from Abraham, Israel is called to communicate the blessings it has received to all the families of the earth.[20]

7. Let us also draw attention to the fact that the various aspects of the culture of Israel do not all maintain the same relationship with divine revelation. Some testify to the resistance to God's word while others express its acceptance. Among the latter, one must distinguish between the provisional (ritual and judicial prescriptions) and the permanent, universal in scope. Certain elements (in the law of Moses, the prophets and the psalms),[21] derive their signification from being the prehistory of Christ.

[17] Cf. Rom 11:11–24.
[18] Gen 1:1–2, 4a.
[19] Cf. Gen 9:1–17; Sir 44:17–18.
[20] Gen 12:1–5; Jn 4:2; Sir 44:21.
[21] Lk 24:44; cf. v. 27.

Jesus Christ, Lord and Savior of the World

1. The Transcendence of Jesus Christ in Relation to All Culture

8. One conviction dominates the preaching of Jesus: In Jesus, in his word and in his person, God perfects the gifts he has already made to Israel and to all nations, by transcending them.[22] Jesus is the sovereign light and true wisdom for all nations and all cultures.[23]

He shows, in his own activity, that the God of Abraham, already recognized by Israel as Creator and Lord,[24] is preparing himself to reign over all those who believe in the Gospel, and much more, through Jesus, God already reigns.[25]

9. The teaching of Jesus, notably in the parables, is not afraid to correct or, when the need arises, to challenge a good number of the ideas which history, religion as practiced and culture had inspired among his contemporaries concerning the nature and action of God.[26]

10. The completely filial intimacy of Jesus with God and the loving obedience, which caused him to offer his life and death to his Father,[27] show that in him the original plan of God for creation, tainted by sin, has been restored.[28] We are faced with a new creation, a new Adam.[29] Also, the relationships with God are profoundly changed in many respects.[30] The newness is such that the curse which strikes the crucified Messiah becomes a blessing for all peoples[31] and faith in Jesus as savior replaces the regime of the law.[32]

11. The death and resurrection of Jesus, on account of which the Spirit was poured out into our hearts, have shown the shortcomings of completely human wisdoms and moralities and even of the law (nonetheless given by God to Moses), all of which were institutions capable of giving knowledge of the good, but not the force to accom-

---

[22] Mk 13:10; Mt 12:21; Lk 2:32.
[23] Mt 11:19; Lk 7:35.
[24] Ps 93:1–4; Is 6:1.
[25] Mk 1:15; Mt 12:28; Lk 11:20; 17:21.
[26] Mt 20:1–16; Lk 15:11–32; 18:9–14.
[27] Mk 14:36.
[28] Mk 1:14–45; 10:2–9; Mt 5:21–48.
[29] Rom 5:12–19; 1 Cor 15:20–22.
[30] Mk 8:27–33; 1 Cor 1:18–25.
[31] Gal 3:13; Deut 21:22–23.
[32] Gal 3:12–14.

plish it; knowledge of sin, but not the power to extract oneself from it.[33]

2. The Presence of Christ to Culture and Cultures

A. *The Uniqueness of Christ, Universal Lord and Savior*

12. Since it was fully and historically realized, the incarnation of the Son of God was a cultural incarnation: "Christ [bound] Himself, in virtue of His Incarnation, to certain social and cultural conditions of those human beings among whom He dwelt."[34]

13. The Son of God was happy to be a Jew of Nazareth in Galilee, speaking Aramaic, subject to pious parents of Israel, accompanying them to the temple of Jerusalem where they found him "sitting among the doctors, listening to them and asking them questions".[35] Jesus grew up in a milieu of customs and institutions of first-century Palestine, initiating himself into the trades of his time, observing the behavior of the sinners, peasants and business people of his milieu. The scenes and countrysides on which the imagination of the future rabbi was nourished are of a very definite country and time.

14. Nourished by the piety of Israel, formed by the teaching of the law and the prophets, to which a completely singular experience of God as Father added an unheard-of profundity, Jesus may be situated in a highly specific spiritual tradition, that of Jewish prophecy. Like the prophets of old, he is the mouthpiece of God and calls to conversion. The manner is also quite typical: The vocabulary, literary types, the manner of address also recall the tradition of Elijah and Elisha—the biblical parallelism, the proverbs, paradoxes, admonitions, blessings, right up to the symbolic actions.

15. Jesus is so bound up with the life of Israel that the people and the religious tradition in which he shares acquire in virtue of this liaison a unique place in the history of salvation; this chosen people and the religious tradition which they have left have a permanent significance for humanity.

16. There is nothing improvised about the incarnation. The Word of God enters into a history which prepares him, announces him and prefigures him. One could say that the Christ takes flesh in advance with the people God has expressly formed with a view to the gift he would make

---

[33] Rom 7:16ff.; 3:20; 7:7; 1 Tim 1:8.
[34] *AG* 10.
[35] Lk 2:46.

of his Son. All the words uttered by the prophets are a prelude to the subsistent Word which is the Son of God.

17. Also, the history of the covenant concluded with Abraham and through Moses with the people of Israel, as also the books which recount and clarify this history, all together hold for the faithful of Jesus the role of an indispensable and irreplaceable pedagogy.

Moreover the election of this people from which Jesus emerges has never been revoked. "My brethren, my kinsmen by race," writes Saint Paul, "they are Israelites and to them belong the sonship, the glory, the covenants, the giving of the law, the worship and the promises, to them belong the patriarchs and of their race, according to the flesh, is the Christ. God who is over all be blessed forever. Amen." [36]

The cultivated olive has not lost its privileges to the wild olive, which has been grafted onto it.

B. *The Catholicity of the Unique Event*

18. However historically distinctive the condition of the Word made flesh may be—and consequently of the culture which receives, forms and continues him—it is not first this factor which the Son of God united to himself. It is because he became man that God has also assumed, in a certain way, a race, a country and a time.

"Since human nature as He assumed it was not annulled, by that very fact it has been raised up to a divine dignity in our respect too. For by His incarnation the Son of God has united Himself in some fashion with every man." [37]

19. The transcendence of Christ does not therefore isolate him above the human family but renders him present to all, beyond all restriction. He "cannot be considered foreign anywhere or to anybody." [38] "There are no more distinctions between Jew and Greek, slave and free, male and female, but all of you are one in Christ Jesus." [39]

Thus Christ is at one with us in the unity we form as in the multiplicity and diversity in which our common nature is realized.

20. However, Christ would not be one with us in the reality of our concrete humanity if he did not affect us as well in the diversity and the complementarity of our cultures. It is in fact cultures—language, history, general attitude to life, diverse institutions—which for better or worse receive us into life, form us, accompany us and survive our passing. If the

---

[36] Rom 9:3–5.
[37] GS 22.
[38] AG 8.
[39] Gal 3:28.

cosmos as a whole is, in a mysterious sense, the scene of grace and sin, do not our cultures have a similar role inasmuch as they are both fruits and seeds in the field of our human labors?

21. In the body of Christ, the cultures, insofar as they are animated and renewed by grace and faith, are moreover complementary. They permit us to see the multiform richness of which the teachings and energies of the same Gospel are capable, the same principles of truth, justice, love and liberty, when they are traversed by the Spirit of Christ.

22. Finally, is it necessary to recall that it is not in virtue of a self-interested strategy that the Church, bride of the incarnated Word, preoccupies itself with the fate of the various cultures of humanity? She wishes to animate from the inside, protect, free from the error and sin with which we have corrupted them these resources of truth and love which God has placed, as *semina Verbi*, in his creation. The Word of God does not come into a creation which is foreign to it. "All things were created through him and for him. He is before all things and in him all things hold together." [40]

The Holy Spirit and the Church of the Apostles

1. From Jerusalem to the Nations: The Typical Beginnings of the Inculturation of the Faith

23. On Pentecost day, the breaking in of the Holy Spirit inaugurates the relation of the Christian faith and culture as fulfillment in flower: The promise of salvation fulfilled by the risen Christ filled the hearts of believers by the outpouring of the Holy Spirit himself. "The marvels of God" will from now on be "preached" to all men of every language and culture.[41] While humanity was living under the sign of the division of Babel, the gift of the Holy Spirit was offered to it as the transcendent and now so human grace of the symphony of hearts. The divine unification (*koinonia*)[42] recreated a new humanity among people, penetrating without destroying the sign of their division: languages.

24. The Holy Spirit does not establish a superculture, but is the personal and vital principle which will vivify the new community in working in harness with its members. The gift of the Holy Spirit is not of the

---

[40] Col 1:16–17.
[41] Acts 2:11.
[42] Acts 2:42.

order of structures, but the Church of Jerusalem which he fashions is a *koinonia* of faith and of *agape*, communicating herself in many ways without loss of identity; she is the body of Christ whose members are united but with many faces. The first test of catholicity appears when differences of cultural origin (conflicts between Greeks and Hebrews) menace the communion.[43] The apostles do not suppress the differences but are concerned with developing an essential function of the ecclesial body: the *diakonia* at the service of the *koinonia*.

25. In order that the good news might be announced to the nations, the Holy Spirit awakens a new perception in Peter and the Jerusalem community, to wit,[44] faith in Christ does not require that new believers abandon their culture to adopt that of the law of the Jewish people; all peoples are called to be beneficiaries of the promise and to share the heritage entrusted for them in the people of the covenant.[45] Therefore, "nothing beyond the essentials", according to the decision of the apostolic assembly.[46]

26. Scandal for the Jews, the mystery of the cross is foolishness to the pagans. Here the inculturation of the faith clashes with the radical sin of idolatry which keeps "captive"[47] the truth of a culture which is not assumed by Christ. As long as man is "deprived of the glory of God",[48] all that he "cultivates" is nothing more that the opaque image of himself. The Pauline kerygma begins therefore with creation and the call to the covenant, denounces the moral perversions of blinded humanity and announces salvation in the crucified and risen Christ.

27. After the testing of catholicity among culturally different Christian communities, after the resistances of Jewish legalism and those of idolatry, the faith pledges itself to culture in Gnosticism.

The phenomenon begins to appear at the time of the last letters of Paul and John; it will fuel the majority of the doctrinal crises of the succeeding centuries. Here, human reason in its injured state refuses the folly of the incarnation of the Son of God and seeks to recover the mystery by accommodating it to the prevailing culture. Whereas, "faith depends not on human philosophy but on the power of God."[49]

---

[43] Acts 6:1ff.
[44] Acts 10 and 11.
[45] Eph 2:14–15.
[46] Acts 15–28.
[47] Rom 1:18.
[48] Rom 3:23.
[49] 1 Cor 2:4ff.

2. The Apostolic Tradition:
Inculturation of Faith and Salvation of Culture

28. In the "last times" inaugurated at Pentecost, the risen Christ, alpha and omega, enters into the history of peoples: From that moment, the sense of history and thus of culture is unsealed[50] and the Holy Spirit reveals it by actualizing and communicating it to all. The Church is the sacrament of this revelation and its communication. It recenters every culture into which Christ is received, placing it in the axis of the "world which is coming" and restores the union broken by the "prince of this world". Culture is thus eschatologically situated; it tends toward its completion in Christ but it cannot be saved except by associating itself with the repudiation of evil.

29. Each local or particular Church is called in the Holy Spirit to be the sacrament which manifests Christ, crucified and risen, enfleshed in a particular culture.

a. The culture of a local Church—young or old—participates in the dynamism of cultures and in their vicissitudes. Even if the Church is in the last times it remains subject to trials and temptations.[51]

b. The Christian "newness" engenders in the local Churches particular expressions stamped by culture (modalities of doctrinal formulations, liturgical symbolisms, models of holiness, canonical directives, etc.).

Nevertheless the communion between the Churches demands constantly that the cultural "flesh" of each does not act as a screen to mutual recognition in the apostolic faith and to solidarity in love.

c. Every Church sent to the nations witnesses to its Lord only if, having consideration for its cultural attachments, it conforms to him in the first *kenosis* of his incarnation and in the final humiliation of his life-giving passion. The inculturation of the faith is one of the expressions of the apostolic tradition whose dramatic character is emphasized on several occasions by Paul.[52]

30. The apostolic writings and the patristic witness do not limit their vision of culture to the service of evangelization but integrate it into the totality of the mystery of Christ. For them, creation is the reflection of the glory of God: Man is its living icon, and it is in Christ that the resemblance with God is seen. Culture is the scene in which man and the world are called to find themselves anew in the glory of God. The encounter is missed or obscured insofar as man is a sinner. Within

---

[50] Rev 5:1–5.
[51] Cf. Rev 2 and 3.
[52] 1 and 2 Cor passim.

captive creation is seen the gestation of the "new universe":[53] The Church is "in labor".[54] In her and through her the creatures of this world are able to live their redemption and their transfiguration.

III. PRESENT PROBLEMS OF INCULTURATION

1. The inculturation of the faith, which we have considered first from a philosophical viewpoint (nature, culture and grace), then from the point of view of history and dogma (inculturation in the history of salvation) still poses considerable problems for theological reflection and pastoral action. Thus the questions aroused in the sixteenth century by the discovery of new worlds continue to preoccupy us. How may one harmonize the spontaneous expressions of the religiosity of peoples with faith? What attitude should be adopted in the face of non-Christian religions, especially those "bound up with cultural advancement"?[55]

New questions have arisen in our time. How should "young Churches", born in our century of the indigenization of already-existing Christian communities, consider both their Christian past and the cultural history of their respective peoples? Finally how should the Gospel animate, purify and fortify the new world into which we have brought industrialization and urbanization?

To us it seems that these four question should be faced by anyone who reflects on the present conditions of the inculturation of faith.

Popular Piety

2. In the countries which have been affected by the Gospel, we normally understand by *popular piety*, on the one hand, the union of Christian faith and piety with the profound culture, and on the other with the previous forms of religion of populations. It involves those very numerous devotions in which Christians express their religious sentiment in the simple language, among other things, of festival, pilgrimage, dance and song. One could speak of vital synthesis with reference to this piety, since it unites "body and spirit, ecclesial communion and institution, individual and community, Christian faith and love of one's country, intelligence

---

[53] Rev 21:5.
[54] Cf. Rom 8:18–25.
[55] NA 2.

and affectivity".[56] The quality of the synthesis stems, as one might expect, from the antiquity and profundity of the evangelization, as from the compatibility of its religious and cultural antecedents with the Christian faith.

3. In the apostolic exhortation *Evangelii Nuntiandi*, Paul VI confirmed and encouraged a new appreciation of popular piety. "These expressions were for a long time regarded as less pure and were sometimes despised, but today they are almost everywhere being rediscovered. During the last Synod the bishops studied their significance with remarkable pastoral realism and zeal." [57]

4. "But if it is well oriented, above all by a pedagogy of evangelization", continued Paul VI, popular piety "is rich in values. It manifests a thirst for God which only the simple and poor can know. It makes people capable of generosity and sacrifice even to the point of heroism, when it is a question of manifesting belief. It involves an acute awareness of profound attributes of God: fatherhood, providence, loving and constant presence. It engenders interior attitudes rarely observed to the same degree elsewhere: patience, the sense of the cross in daily life, detachment, openness to others, devotion." [58]

5. Moreover the strength and depth of the roots of popular piety clearly manifested themselves in the long period of discredit mentioned by Paul VI. The expressions of popular piety have survived numerous predictions of disappearance of which modernity and the progress of secularity seemed to warn. They have preserved and even increased, in many regions of the globe, the attractions they exercised on the masses.

6. The limits of popular piety have often been condemned. They stem from a certain naivete [and] are a source of various deformations of religion, even of superstitions. One remains at the level of cultural manifestations without a true adhesion to faith at the level where this is expressed in service of one's neighbor. Badly directed, popular piety can even lead to the formation of sects and thus place true ecclesial unity in danger. It also risks being manipulated, be it by political powers or by religious forces foreign to the Christian faith.

7. The taking into account of these dangers invites us to practice an intelligent catechesis, won thanks to the merits of an authentic popular piety and at the same time duly shrewd. A living and adapted liturgy is equally called to play a major role in the integration of a very pure faith and the traditional forms of the religious life of peoples. Without any

---

[56] Third general conference of the bishops of Latin America, The Evangelization of Latin America in the Present and in the Future, 448.

[57] Paul VI, *Evangelii nuntiandi*, 48.

[58] Ibid.

doubt whatsoever, popular piety can bring an irreplaceable contribution to a Christian cultural anthropology which would permit the reduction of the often tragic division between the faith of Christians and certain socioeconomic institutions, of quite different orientation, which regulate their daily life.

Inculturation of Faith and Non-Christian Religions

8. From its origin, the Church has encountered on many levels the question of the plurality of religions. Even today Christians constitute only about one-third of the world's population. Moreover, they must live in a world which expresses a growing sympathy for pluralism in religious matters.

9. Given the great place of religion in culture, a local or particular Church implanted in a non-Christian sociocultural milieu must take seriously into account the religious elements of this milieu. Moreover, this preoccupation should be in accordance with the depth and vitality of these religious elements.

10. If we may consider one continent as an example, we shall speak of Asia, which witnessed the birth of several of the world's great religious movements. Hinduism, Buddhism, Islam, Confucianism, Taoism, Shintoism: Each of these religious systems certainly located in distinct regions of the continent [is] deeply rooted in the people and [shows] much vigor. One's personal life, as well as social and community activity, was marked in a decisive manner by these religious and spiritual traditions. In addition the Asian Churches consider the question of non-Christian religions one of the most important and most urgent. They have even made it the object of that privileged form of relation: the dialogue.

The Dialogue of Religions

11. Dialogue with other religions forms an integral part of Christian life; by exchange, study and work in common, this dialogue contributes to a better understanding of the religion of the other and to a growth of piety.

12. For Christian faith, the unity of all in their origin and destiny, that is, in creation and in communion with God in Jesus Christ, is accompanied by the universal presence and action of the Holy Spirit. The Church in dialogue listens and learns. "The Catholic Church rejects nothing that is true and holy in these religions. She regards with sincere reverence those ways of conduct and of life, those precepts and teachings which, though differing in many aspects from the ones she holds

and sets forth, nonetheless often reflect a ray of that Truth which enlightens all men." [59]

13. This dialogue possesses something original, since, as the history of religions testifies, the plurality of religions has often given rise to discrimination and jealousy, fanaticism and despotism, all of which drew on religion the accusation of being a source of division in the human family. The Church, "universal sacrament of salvation", that is, "sign and instrument both of a very close knit union with God and of the unity of the whole human race", [60] is called by God to be minister and instrument of unity in Jesus Christ for all men and all peoples.

The Transcendence of the Gospel in Relation to Culture

14. We cannot, however, forget the transcendence of the Gospel in relation to all human cultures in which the Christian faith has the vocation to root itself and come to fruition according to all its potentialities. However great the respect should be for what is true and holy in the cultural heritage of a people, this attitude does not demand that one should lend an absolute character to this cultural heritage. No one can forget that, from the beginning, the Gospel was a "scandal for the Jews and foolishness for the pagans". [61]

Inculturation which borrows the way of dialogue between religions cannot in any way pledge itself to syncretism.

The Young Churches and Their Christian Past

15. The Church prolongs and actualizes the mystery of the Servant of Yahweh, who was promised to be "the light of the nations so that salvation might reach the ends of the earth" [62] and to be the "covenant of the people". [63] This prophecy is realized at the Last Supper, when, on the eve of his passion, Christ, surrounded by the Twelve, gives his body and blood to his followers as the food and drink of the new covenant, thus assimilating them into his own body.

The Church, people of the new covenant, was being born. She would receive at Pentecost the Spirit of Christ, the Spirit of the Lamb sacrificed

[59] NA 2.
[60] LG 1, 48.
[61] 1 Cor 1:23.
[62] Is 49:6.
[63] Is 49:8.

from the beginning and who was already working to fulfill this desire so deeply rooted in human beings: a union the more intense with respect to the intense diversity.

16. In virtue of the Catholic communion, which unites all the particular Churches in one history, the young Churches consider the past of the Churches which give birth to them as part of their own history. However, the major act of interpretation which is the hallmark of their spiritual maturity consists in recognizing this precedence as originative and not only as historical. This signifies that in receiving in faith the Gospel which their elders announced to them, the young Churches welcomed the "initiator of the faith"[64] and the entire tradition in which the faith is attested, as also the capacity to give birth to new forms in which the unique and common faith would find expression. Equal in dignity, drawing life from the same mystery, authentic sister Churches, the young Churches manifest, in concert with their elders, the fullness of the mystery of Christ.

17. People of the new covenant: It is insofar as it commemorates the paschal mystery and ceaselessly announces the return of the Lord that the Church may be called an eschatology that began with the cultural traditions of peoples, on condition, of course, that these traditions had been subjected to the purifying law of death and resurrection in Christ Jesus.

18. Like Saint Paul at the Areopagus in Athens, the young Church interprets its ancestral culture in a new and creative manner. When this culture passes through Christ, "the veil falls".[65] At the time of the "incubation" of faith, this Church has discovered Christ as "exegete and exegesis" of the Father in the Spirit:[66] Moreover, it does not cease to contemplate him as such. Now it is discovering him as "exegete and exegesis" of man, source and destination of culture. To the unknown God, revealed on the cross, corresponds unknown man, announced by the young Church as the living paschal mystery inaugurated by grace in the ancient culture.

19. In the salvation it makes present, the young Church endeavors to locate all the traces of the God's care for a particular human group, the *semina Verbi*. What the prologue of the Letter to the Hebrews says of the fathers and the prophets may in relation with Jesus Christ be repeated, in an analogical manner of course, for all human culture insofar as it is right and true and bears wisdom.

---

[64] Heb 12:2.
[65] 2 Cor 3:16.
[66] Cf. Henri de Lubac, *Exégèse médiévale*, Théologie 41 (Paris, 1959), 1.1, pp. 322–24.

Christian Faith and Modernity

20. The technical changes which gave rise to the industrial revolution and subsequently the urban revolution affected souls of people in depth. They were beneficiaries and also, quite often, the victims of these changes. Therefore believers have the duty, as an urgent and difficult task, to understand the characteristic traits of modern culture, as also its expectations and needs in relation to the salvation wrought by Christ.

21. The industrial revolution was also a cultural revolution. Values until then assured were brought into question, such as the sense of personal and community work, the direct relationship of man to nature, membership in a support family, at home as at work, implantation in local and religious communities of human dimension, [and] participation in traditions, rites, ceremonies and celebrations which give a sense to the great moment of existence. Industrialization, in provoking a disordered concentrating of populations, seriously affected these age-old values without giving rise to communities capable of integrating new cultures. At a time when the most deprived peoples are in search of a suitable development model, the advantages as also the risks and human costs of industrialization are better perceived.

22. Great progress has been made in many areas of life: diet, health, education, transport, access to all types of consumer goods.

Deep misgivings, however, have arisen in the collective subconscious.

In many countries, the notion of progress has given way, especially since World War II, to disillusion. Rationality as regards production and administration operates against reason when it forgets the good of persons. The emancipation of communities from a sense of belonging has isolated man in the crowd. The new means of communication destroy to as great an extent as they create. Science, by means of the technical creations which are its fruit, appears simultaneously to be creator and destroyer. In addition some despair of modernity and speak of a new barbarism. Despite many faults and failings, one must hope for a moral uplift of all nations, rich and poor. If the Gospel is preached and heard, a cultural and spiritual conversion is possible. It calls to solidarity, in the interest of the whole good of the person, to the promotion of peace and justice, to adoration of the Father, from whom all good things come.

23. The inculturation of the Gospel in modern societies will demand a methodical effort of concerted research and action. This effort will assure on the part of those responsible for evangelization: (1) an attitude of openness and a critical eye; (2) the capacity to perceive the spiritual expectations and human aspirations of the new cultures; (3) the aptitude for cultural analysis, having in mind an effective encounter with the modern world.

24. A receptive attitude is required among those who wish to understand and evangelize the world of our time. Modernity is accompanied by undeniable progress in many cultural and material domains: well-being, human mobility, science, research, education, a new sense of solidarity. In addition, the Church of Vatican II has taken a lively account of the new conditions in which she must exercise her mission, and it is in the cultures of modernity that the Church of tomorrow will be constructed. The traditional advice applicable to discernment is reiterated by Pius XII. "It is necessary to deepen one's understanding of the civilization and institutions of various peoples and to cultivate their best qualities and gifts.... All in the customs of peoples which are not inextricably bound up with superstitions or errors should be examined with benevolence and if possible, preserved intact." [67]

25. The Gospel raises fundamental questions among those who reflect on the behavior of modern man. How should one make this man understand the radical nature of the message of Christ: unconditional love, evangelical poverty, adoration of the Father and constant yielding to his will? How should one educate toward the Christian sense of suffering and death? How should one arouse faith and hope in the event of the resurrection accomplished by Jesus Christ?

26. We must develop capacity to analyze cultures and to gauge their moral and spiritual indicators. A mobilization of the whole Church is called for so that the extremely complex task of the inculturation of the Gospel in today's world may be faced with success. We must wed to this topic the preoccupation of John Paul II: "From the beginning of my pontificate I considered that the dialogue of the Church with the cultures of our time was a vital area, whose stake is the fate of the world in this the end of the twentieth century." [68]

CONCLUSION

1. Having said that the important thing was "affecting and as it were upsetting, through the power of the Gospel, mankind's criteria of judgment, determining values, points of interest, lines of thought, sources of inspiration and models of life, which are in contrast with the Word of God and the plan of salvation", Paul VI asked that one "evangelize man's culture and cultures (not in a purely decorative way, as it were, by

---

[67] Pius XII, *Summi Pontificatus.*

[68] John Paul II, Letter on foundation of the Pontifical Council for Culture, 20 May 1982.

applying a thin veneer, but in a vital way, in depth and right to their very roots), in the wide and rich sense which these terms have in *Gaudium et spes*, always taking the person as one's starting point and always coming back to the relationships of people among themselves and with God."[69]

2. "In this the end of the twentieth century," as John Paul II affirmed for his part, "the Church must make itself all things for all men, bringing today's cultures together with sympathy. There still are milieus and mentalities, as there are entire countries and regions, to evangelize, which supposes a long and courageous process of inculturation so that the Gospel may penetrate the soul of living cultures, respond to their highest expectations and make them grow in the dimension of Christian faith, hope and charity. Sometimes cultures have only been touched superficially and in any case, to continuously transform themselves, they demand a renewed approach. In addition, new areas of culture appear, with diverse objectives, methods and languages."[70]

[69] Paul VI, *Evangelii nuntiandi*, 19–20.
[70] John Paul II, Discourse to the Pontifical Council for Culture, 18 January 1983.

16

THE INTERPRETATION OF DOGMA

INTRODUCTION

1. The State of the Question
2. The Work of the ITC
3. The Main Themes of the Document

1. If, for mankind, the interpretation of man's being, of history and of the world itself, has always been an important problem, we, today, are faced with the problem in a new phase of interpretation, and that is the hermeneutic circle: in reality, it claims, man in his concrete existence is not to be seen in a context of pure objectivity; reality is always found in a particular historical and cultural context. Now, this question of the subject-object relationship is studied by hermeneutics, whether of a positivistic or anthropocentric kind, and runs the risk of moving from a misconception of man's subjectivity to a downright subjectivism. Certain present-day theological currents deeply enmeshed in the hermeneutical approach concentrate on the meaning of dogmas without paying attention to their unchanging truth. For example, liberation theology and radical feminist theology interpret the faith in function of socio-economic and cultural factors. In such cases, social progress and the emancipation of women become the decisive criteria for interpreting the meaning of dogmas.

The present importance of the hermeneutical problem has led the ITC to this study in order to isolate the basic elements in the interpretation of dogma as conceived by Catholic theology.

This document of the International Theological Commission was prepared under the direction of His Excellency, Msgr. Walter Kasper, at the time Professor at Tübingen University and presently Bishop of Rottenburg-Stutgart, by a sub-commission consisting of Professors Ambaum, Columbo, Corbon, Gnilka, Leonard, Nagy, de Noronha Galvao, Peter, Schönborn and Wilfred. The document was discussed at the plenary session of 3rd to 8th October, 1988, and fully approved *in forma specifica* at the plenary session of October, 1989. In accordance with the statutes of the ITC, it is now published with the authorization of His Eminence Joseph Cardinal Ratzinger, the Commission's President. The basic text is in German.

2. As was the case with themes examined by the ITC in earlier five-year periods, the present theme was proposed from various quarters to the Commission at the opening of the fifth such period: Professor Walter Kasper, who was then Professor at the University of Tübingen, was made President of a sub-commission to study the problem and prepare the points for discussion at the eventual plenary session. With the agreement of the ITC's president, Cardinal Ratzinger, Professor Kasper picked the present sub-commission and each member was assigned a precise point to examine and then communicate. Professor Rasper's own contribution is called: "What Is a Dogma? Historical and Systematic Considerations". Our present publication is the result of the successive revisions of the initial work. The other preparatory submissions of the sub-commission addressed the following subjects: "The Interpretation of Dogma according to the Magisterium of the Church, from Trent to Vatican II" (Prof. Ambaum); "The Present Status of the Question of the Interpretation of Dogma" (Prof. Colombo); "Dogma in the Tradition and Life of the Church" (Prof. Corbon); "A New Testament Exegete Examines the Question of the Proper Interpretation of Dogma" (Prof. Gnilka); "Modern Hermeneutics: Its Philosophical Consequences and Bearing on Theology" (Prof. Leonard); "Present Problems in the Legitimate Interpretation of Dogma" (Prof. Nagy); "Hermeneutics of Faith in Liberation Theology" (Prof. de Noronha Galvao); "Unity and Plurality in Faith" (Prof. Peter); "Dogma and the Spiritual Life" (Prof. Schönborn); "Dogma and Inculturation" (Prof. Wilfred).

The members of the sub-commission made their respective contributions during the plenary session in 1988, and a week was spent on the discussion which arose. On the basis of the discussion and written submissions, Professor Kasper with the assistance of the sub-commission prepared a text, and this, after a series of corrections, was fully approved *in forma specifica* by the Commission at the plenary session of October, 1989.

3. In its first part the text underlines the importance of history, tradition that is, for the understanding of dogma. In the West today, the present is so valued as to cause the past to be considered as something alien. One kind of hermeneutic tries to bridge the gap between us and the past in various ways which are often reductionist. These must be left behind so that we attain to a metaphysical hermeneutics based on the fact that truth manifests itself in and through human intelligence. What then is the relationship between truth and history? In spite of all determinisms of human thought, we take it for granted that there is absolute truth and truths of an universal nature with their values intact.

As far as the theological problem of interpretation is concerned, the Church regards it as a first principle that the revealed truth which she teaches is universally valid and unchangeable in its substance. Still, difficulties arise when it is a question of passing on dogmatic truths to people who live in different cultural climates, as, for instance in Africa or Asia. How then does one "interpret" the faith? Some take a radical approach: the faith must be interpreted in a Marxist perspective; or, indeed, a particular idea about emancipation becomes the open sesame for interpreting the Bible.

The second part of the document shows how the Church, guided by the Holy Spirit, gives witness to revelation. The history of dogma highlights the unbroken continuity of tradition. This is followed by the presentation of the declarations of the Magisterium with regard to the interpretation of dogma (Trent, Vatican I, Pius X, Pius XII, Paul VI), with greater concentration on the doctrine of Vatican II. To this we may add the *praxis Ecclesiae* which, when new developments arise, interprets certain prior situations (for example such as concern religious liberty).

While presenting a systematic reflection on dogma as it lies at the heart of tradition, the document explains how it is that Tradition gives a more profound dimension to the words and images of human language as it uses these to express the faith. In the course of history the Church adds nothing new to the Gospel, but does present Christ in a new style. The place of dogma in evangelisation, and the theological import of dogma, must be understood according to such a rubric.

The use of and the interpretation of Scripture in this enterprise are examined in a third section under the title: "Criteria of Interpretation". The document underlines the unity of Scripture, Tradition and the life of the Church in maintaining an interpretation of dogma at the very heart of the Church. There is no doubt about the timeliness of such a task. The aim is to manifest guiding principles. The document places the permanent validity of the dogmatic formulas in the foreground and at the same time presents suggestions for a renewed way of interpretation. The criteria for judging doctrinal development proposed by J. H. Newman can be helpful. And, that much achieved, the document makes timely reference to the role of the Church's Magisterium, since the authentic interpretation of God's Word was confided to it. In effect, eternal life for mankind is what is at stake in every element contributing to legitimate interpretation.

Msgr. Philippe Delhaye
Secretary General Emeritus of the ITC

A. THE PROBLEM

I. *The Philosophical Problem*

1. The Fundamental Problem of Interpretation

The problem of interpretation is fundamental to mankind from the beginning. As men, we try to understand the world and ourselves. Now, when faced with the question of truth and reality, we never begin at an absolute beginning, a zero point. The real in question meets us in preexisting interpretations, in the system of symbols of a given culture, and, most of all, in language.

Human understanding then is always in symbiosis with human community. Therefore, interpretation must make its own of, and understand, the witness of tradition already existing.

This symbiosis puts paid to any simplistic realism. We never meet the real in the nudity of birth, but always in man's cultural contexts, where what man learns has already an inherited cargo of interpretation.

As a result, the fundamental problem of interpretation may be stated as follows: how can man take the hermeneutic circle between subject and object seriously without becoming victims of a relativism which recognizes nothing but interpretations of interpretations, which, in turn, give birth to further interpretations. Is there, not as something external, but at the very heart of the historical process of interpretation, a truth existing of itself? May man claim an absolute truth? Are there certain propositions which must be admitted or denied, no matter what the culture is, or the particular point in mankind's history?

2. Two Reasons for the Timeliness of the Problem

The problem of interpretation is more acute today. Because of cultural breakdown, the gap has widened between the witness of tradition and our present-day culture. Particularly in the West, this has changed attitudes towards the truths, values and outlook of tradition, and, even more, has given the present an unilateral preponderance over against the past, and, again, led to giving an unilateral edge to novelty as judge of thought and action. In philosophy today, thanks especially to Marx, Nietzsche and Freud, a "hermeneutics of suspicion" is dominant which rejects tradition as an interpreting link between past and present. It is rejected as a falsification of human nature, and a tyranny. But, if man rejects the memory of what tradition has created, nihilism overpowers him. The worldwide crisis of tradition has become one of the most profound spiritual challenges of this age.

The crisis of tradition is further accentuated today by the very diffused phenomenon of cultural encounters with all their differing traditions. The problem of interpretation is not alone that of mediation between past and present, but how to mediate between a plurality of cultural traditions. Today, such a transcultural hermeneutic has become a condition for the survival of mankind in peace and justice.

3. Different Types of Hermeneutics

An hermeneutic of a positivistic nature stresses primarily the role of objectivity. This approach has contributed much to a better knowledge of reality. But it considers human knowledge one-sidedly as a function of natural, biological, psychological, historical and socio-economic factors and, in doing this, misunderstands the meaning of human subjectivity in the process of knowing.

The hermeneutic of an anthropocentric nature remedies that. But this hermeneutic, with a one-sided stress, makes the subjective pole decisive. In that way it limits knowledge of the real to its meaning for the human subject. The truth about reality is its human meaning alone.

The cultural hermeneutic understands reality through its objective realization in culture, in human institutions such as manners and customs and, above all, language. Each culture and its value system is imprinted with man's conception of himself and of the world. While acknowledging the significance of such an approach, one must raise the question of values that transcend culture and of the truth of the "*humanum*" which unites men over and above all cultural difference.

Unlike the more or less reductionist positions mentioned so far, a metaphysical hermeneutic raises the question of the very truth of reality itself. This begins with the fact that the truth manifests itself in and by means of human intelligence in such a fashion that in the light of the intelligence the very truth of reality itself shines forth. Since reality is always more vast and more profound than all its representations and conceptualizations, as these are conditioned for us by history and culture as we elaborate them, it is imperative to seek a constantly renewed and deepening interpretation of such cultural traditions.

Our principal task then is as follows: in our encounters with, and our discussions concerning, contemporary hermeneutics, and also with contemporary human sciences, we must endeavour to recreate metaphysics, and the metaphysical questions concerning truth and reality. The nub of the question is the relationship between truth and history.

4. The Basic Question: Truth in History

As far as the relationship between truth and history is concerned, it has become evident that, in principle, there is no human knowledge without presuppositions: what is more, all human knowledge and all human language depend on an already built-in structure of understanding and judgment. And, so much so, that in all that man knows, says, or does, which is conditioned by the operation of history, there is, at times, an awareness of something which has preceded; a sense of an ultimate; unconditioned, and absolute. In all our quest and search for truth, we presuppose that truth exists always, even certain basic truths (for example, the principle of contradiction). Thus, the light of truth is always preceding us: in other words, it appears as objectively evident to our intelligence when this approaches reality. These basic gears given in advance, and these given presuppositions, were known by the Stoa in antiquity by the name of dogma. Tailored in that way, in a very general sense one could speak of man being cut fundamentally to a dogmatic measure.

Inasmuch as our knowledge, thought and will are always determined collectively by respective cultures, and by language above all, the basic dogmatic structure we speak of concerns not alone the individual but human society as a whole. In the long run no society can survive without fundamental convictions and values which are common to all, and which characterize and shore up its culture. Unity, mutual comprehension, peaceful coexistence, as also mutual recognition of a common human dignity, also presuppose that in spite of the profound differences between cultures, there does exist a common pool of human values and, as a consequence, a truth common to all men. This conviction is very clear today in the recognition that each human being has universal and inalienable human rights.

But these truths of a universal nature are recognized as such for that matter only in particular historical contingencies, most of all, when cultures meet. We must then distinguish between such occasional situations and the sheer need for absolute value which is at the very heart of the truth that man knows. Truth, in the name of its essence, can only be one, unique, and, so, universal. That which was once known as truth must be recognized again as valid and true.

The Church, by means of the unique Gospel she preaches, and which, in time, is revelation for all men and for all time, can meet all essential needs of the human intelligence which is in history and also open to the universal. The Church can purify this and give it perfection.

II. *The Theological Problem Today*

1. The Specific Problem of Evangelization and the Renewal of Evangelization

Catholic theology begins from the certitude of faith that the *Paradosis*[1] of the Church and the dogmas she transmits are authentic statements of the truth revealed by God in the Old and New Testaments. She also affirms that the revealed truth, transmitted by the *Paradosis* of the Church, is universally valid and unchangeable in substance.

In the matter of dogmas, this certitude was already called into question during the Reformation in the sixteenth century. In a vastly more acute fashion and in entirely different conditions, the situation is now of global proportions as a result of the ideology of the Enlightenment and the modern demands for liberty. In our time dogmatic theology has been, without benefit of critical analysis, simply defined as dogmatism, and so rejected. Unlike the integral Christian faith of the past in the West, our contemporary secularized culture seems to find the traditional dogmatic language very hard to understand, even when it has not been downrightly misunderstood. This applies also in the case of many Christians, some of whom regard it even as an obstacle to a living transmission of faith.

The problem becomes aggravated when the Church tries to enter the African and Asian worlds with dogmas which have been forged, speaking historically, in the context of Greco-Roman and Western culture. This demands more than a mere translation. To achieve inculturation, the dogma must be stripped down to the original kernel to make it intelligible in a new culture. It is a problem involving all evangelization today, and especially where new factors affect the process of evangelization.

2. The Inadequate Solutions of Hermeneutical Theology

At the beginning of this century, Modernism addressed itself to the question. It was a poor solution: revelation was improperly conceived and dogmas were given a pragmatic slant.

---

[1] This word, which means *Tradition*, is from the German text. It will be maintained.

Contemporary theology of the hermeneutical school tries to build a bridge between the dogmatic tradition and modern thought by asking what meaning and what importance dogmas have for man today. But in acting like that, one detaches the dogmatic formulation as such from the *Paradosis* and one isolates it from the living life of the Church. In that way one makes the dogma a substance by itself. What is more, in harping on the practical, existential or social meaning of dogma, the question of truth is lost to sight.

A similar objection holds when dogma is held to be a thing of convention, that is a function of ecclesiastical language, necessary as a mark of unity, but ultimately merely provisional and open to further corrections. In that way, dogma is no longer regarded as an inevitable and obligatory mediator of revealed truth.

3. The Legitimacy and the Limits of New Approaches from Both Theoretical and Practical Viewpoints

In the case of liberation theology, the problem of the hermeneutics of dogma is based on the question of poverty and of social and political oppression in many Third World countries. What is theory and what is practice? A very important biblical idea of truth is involved—one must "do the truth" (Jn 3:21). There is without any doubt a theology of liberation in full conformity with the Gospel and with full standing in the Church. It comes from the priority of the spiritual mission of the Church but the Church insists on certain presuppositions and certain social consequences (cf. ITC, "Human Development and Christian Salvation" [1976], *Documenta*, pp. 161–203).[2]

In radical liberation theology, on the other hand, everything is based on economic, political and social factors only: the relationship between theory and practice is governed solely by Marxist materialistic ideology. In consequence, the message of divine grace and the eschatological destiny of man and universe disappear. Faith and its dogmatic formulations are no longer regarded in terms of truth but of economic realities, as the sole value. They function only as an inspiring force in the process of revolutionary political liberation.

There are also other hermeneutical systems today: in spite of certain differences between them, they agree in shifting the emphasis away from

---

[2] Commissio Theologica Internationalis, *Documenta/Documenti (1969–1985)* (Libreria Editrice Vaticana, 1988) (also cf. Commission Théologique Internationale, *Textes et documents*). [Published in English as International Theological Commission, *Texts and Documents, 1969–1985* (San Francisco: Ignatius Press, 1989 and 2009). "Human Development and Christian Salvation" appears as chap. 7.]

the proper place of a hermeneutics of the truth of being, in other words, from revelation as a source of meaning, to other components, legitimate but less than general, and these they make the centre and criterion for their whole enterprise. This is the case with radical feminist theology. Revealed data are no longer accepted as base or norm to vindicate the dignity of woman; an important and legitimate procedure. On the contrary, a certain idea of emancipation becomes the one and only hermeneutical key for the interpretation of Scripture and Tradition.

The question, then, of the interpretation of dogma brings us face to face with the fundamental problems of theology. In the last analysis, it is a question of theological understanding of truth and reality. Also, from the theological viewpoint, the question spills over into that of the relationship between universal truth, always valid, on the one hand, and the historicity of dogmas, on the other. The concrete question is how the Church today can pass on her teaching of the faith and its obligation so that from her memory and tradition hope will arise for now and for the future. And bearing in mind the different socio-cultural situations in which the Church lives today, the question also arises of unity and pluriformity in dogmatic explanations of the truth and reality of revelation.

B. THE THEOLOGICAL FOUNDATIONS

I. *The Biblical Foundations*

1. Tradition and the Interpretation of Sacred Scripture

Revelation, as attested in Sacred Scripture, was effected by words and deeds in the history of the relationship between God and man. The Old Testament is a process of constant re-interpretation and re-reading. Only in Jesus Christ is it finally and definitively interpreted, since the revelation which was prepared in the Old Testament came to completion only in Jesus Christ. Then the fullness of time came (Heb 1:1–3, to be compared with Gal 4:4; Eph 1:10; Mk 1:15). As Word of God become man, Jesus is the interpreter of his Father (Jn 1:14–18). Truth in person (Jn 14:6). In his being and life, through his words and the signs he gave, and, above all, by his death, resurrection and exaltation, as well as by the sending of the Spirit of truth (Jn 14:17), Jesus is full of grace and truth (Jn 1:14) (cf. *DV* 4).

The truth revealed once and for all cannot be recognized and accepted except by the gift of faith from the Holy Spirit. According to the meaning given it in Sacred Scripture, faith is man abandoning himself to the

God who reveals himself (*DV* 5). It involves cleaving to the words and deeds of revelation, professing them, and in particular, cleaving to Christ and the new life with which he has endowed us. Faith, consequently, is man's act in believing ("*fides qua*") and the content of this belief ("*fides quae creditur*"). It is "the guarantee of the good we hope for, the proof of realities so far invisible" (Heb 11:1).

Given once for all through the apostles, the faith is faithfully treasured in the Church as the "*depositum fidei*" (1 Tim 6:20; 2 Tim 1:14). The Church is in fact Christ's Body animated by the Holy Spirit, and she has received from Christ the promise that the Holy Spirit will constantly guide her towards the fullness of truth (Jn 16:13). The "Gospel of Truth" (Eph 1:13) was confided to the Church as God's people journeying on. In her life, the confession of her faith and her liturgy, she must witness to the faith before the eyes of the whole earth. She may be defined as "the pillar and ground of truth" (1 Tim 3:15). It is true that we now see the truth as it were in a mirror, and only in part: It is only at the end of all things that we shall see God face to face, and as he is (1 Cor 13:12; 1 Jn 3:2). Our knowledge of truth is poised in the tension between "already" and "not yet".

2. Hermeneutical Perspectives in Scripture

The way to interpret the biblical message springs from the very nature of the message. Revealed truth, as taught in Scripture, is the truth of God as he shows his fidelity in history ("*emeth*"): in the last analysis, it is the communication of himself that God makes in Jesus Christ, to be prolonged endlessly in the Holy Spirit. The words, actions and entire life of the Church witness to this. And that is why, for the Christian, Jesus Christ is the unique Word that is present in the depths of all words. Every statement of Old and New Testaments must be seen in relation to him and as beamed on him. This is their unity. Accordingly, the Old Testament must be interpreted in the light of its fulfilment in the New, and the New Testament is to be understood in the light of the Old Testament promises.

Both Testaments must be explained and made alive in the Holy Spirit who dwells in the Church. Each individual, in virtue of the gift of grace received "according to the degree of faith God has given him", must contribute to the building up of the Body of Christ, the Church (Rom 12:4–8; 1 Cor 12:45). For that reason, the Second Epistle of Peter (1:20) is already warning against arbitrary interpretation of Sacred Scripture.

Revealed truth wants to make its imprint on the lives of those who have received it. According to Saint Paul, existence in Christ and the

Spirit carries an imperative to lead a new life. What matters is to live in truth, and not only in terms of increasing intellectual appreciation, but to make it fully active in life: "to do the truth" (Jn 3:21). In that way, truth appears as the absolutely certain, and as the foundation stone of human existence. More than anything else, liturgy and prayer are a very important avenue of meaning for approaching and mediating the truth.

3. The Confession of Faith as Formulated in the Bible

What has been said is equally "valid" for the "homologies", modes of confessing the faith which are found already in the earliest strata of the text of the New Testament. Faith is expressed in Jesus as the Christ (Mt 16:16 and par.), as *Kyrios* (Lord) (Rom 10:9; 1 Cor 12:3; Phil 2:11), as Son of God (Mt 14:33; 16:16; Jn 1:34–48; 1 Jn 4:15; 5:5; etc.). They witness to faith in the death and resurrection of Jesus (1 Cor 15:3–5; 1 Thess 4:14; Rom 8:34; 14:9; etc.). They proclaim his mission and birth (Gal 4:4), the sacrifice of his life (Rom 4:25; 8:32; Gal 2:20; etc.) as well as his second coming (1 Thess 1:10; Phil 3:20f.). There are hymns which praise the divinity of Jesus, his incarnation and exaltation (Phil 2:6–11; Col 1:15–20; 1 Tim 3:16; Jn 1:1–18). It follows from all this that the faith of the New Testament communities was not based on the private witness of occasional individuals, but on a confession of faith common to all, which was public and of obligation.

We meet this confession of faith in the New Testament without its having a single monotonous cast. Rather, this unique truth is clothed in a striking richness of expressions. There is evidence even in the New Testament that there were stages in the arrival at truth: these expressions of truth reinforce one another mutually, go from depth to depth, but never contradict one another. It is always the identical mystery of God's salvation in Jesus Christ which has found expression in many forms and from different aspects.

II. *Declarations and Practice of the Church's Magisterium*

1. Declarations of the Magisterium with Regard to the Interpretation of Dogma

The path of history through Nicea (325), Constantinople I (381), Ephesus (431), Chalcedon (451), Constantinople II (553), and through the later councils of the ancient Church, shows the history of dogma as an unbroken, living process of interpretation of Tradition. The Second Council of Nicea encapsulates the teaching of the Fathers which clarifies the fact of the transmission of the Gospel in the *Paradosis* of the Catholic Church under the guidance of the Holy Spirit (DS 600, 602f., 609).

The Council of Trent (1545–1563) defended that teaching and warns the faithful against the private interpretation of Sacred Scripture, and adds that the assessment of the true meaning of Scripture and its interpretation is the province of the Church (DS 1501, 1507), and the First Vatican Council (1869–1870) confirms Trent (DS 3007). It goes further in recognizing a development of dogma, which however does not depart from the original sense and meaning (*"eodem sensu eademque sententia"*). The Council in that way teaches that, as far as dogma is concerned, there can be no departure from the meaning once and for all defined by the Church.

For that reason, the Church condemns anyone who sets that meaning aside under the pretext and in the name of superior knowledge or because of advances in science, or because of some alleged more profound interpretation of the existing formula, or a refinement in the scientific approach to the matter (DS 3020, 3043). Such an irreversible stance and the denial of the possibility of fundamental change is implied in the doctrine of the infallibility of the Church as guided by the Holy Spirit, with particular reference to the role of the Pope in matters of faith and morals (DS 3074). This is based on the fact that the Church, through the Holy Spirit, shares in God's truthfulness, which cannot deceive us any more than it can be self-deceptive in God himself (*"qui nec falli nec fallere potest"*, DS 3008).

The Church's Magisterium has defended this doctrine against the purely symbolic and factitious understanding of dogma on the part of the Modernists (DS 3401–8, 3420–66, 3483). Pius XII in the Encyclical, *Humani generis*, gave a new warning on relativism in the field of dogma, which abandoned the language traditionally used by the Church to express the content of faith in favour of language which changes with the contingent changes of history (DS 3881–83). In much the same way, Paul VI in the Encyclical *Mysterium fidei* (1965) insisted that the precise language of the Church must be maintained.

2. The Doctrine of Vatican Council II

The Second Vatican Council presented the Church's traditional doctrine on a much greater canvas, and, in doing so, it has accepted that dogma has an historical dimension. It teaches that the People of God as a whole has a share in the prophetic office of the Church (*LG* 12), and that, with the assistance of the Holy Spirit, a growth in the understanding of the apostolic tradition does take place (*DV* 8). In the matter of overall missionary commission and responsibility the Council lays strong emphasis both on the doctrine of an authentic Magisterium confided to bishops alone (*DV* 8, 10), and on the doctrine of the Church's infallibility (*LG* 25). But the Council wants the bishops to be primarily the heralds of the Gospel, and subordinates their role as teachers to their evangelizing role (*LG* 25; cf. *CD* 12–15). This valorization of the pastoral character of the Magisterium underlines the distinction between the unchanging basis of faith, on the one hand, and the way this is expressed, on the other. The point is that the teaching of the Church, while always the same in meaning and content, should be passed on to mankind in a living way, and adapted to what the times demand (*GS* 62; cf. John XXIII, the Opening Discourse of Vatican II, 11 October 1962; *AAS* 54 [1962]: 792).

The declaration *Mysterium Ecclesiae* (1973) makes the same distinction and adds precision and depth to it against the false interpretations of relativism in matters of dogma. It is true that dogmas are historical creations in the sense that their meaning "depends in part on the power of expression the language used had at a particular point in history and in particular circumstances." Later definitions preserve and ratify the earlier ones, and also explain their meanings, mostly in the case of new questions or in the case of error, and so make them alive to the benefit of the Church. This does not mean that infallibility can be reduced to a frozen truth. Dogmatic formulations do not define truth in an undetermined, changing or approximative fashion, much less do they transform or maim it. Truth must be kept to a determined form.

Here, it is the historical meaning of dogmatic formulations that is paramount (n. 5). Recently in his Apostolic Letter *Ecclesia Dei* (1988) Pope John Paul II has strongly reaffirmed this sense of living tradition. But the relationship between the formulation and the content of dogmas needs a further clarification (cf. ad rem, infra III, 3).

3. Theological Qualifications

The fact that tradition is a really live reality explains why there are so many declarations by the Magisterium of varying importance and varying degrees of obligation. To gauge these exactly and to interpret them, theology has worked out the doctrine of theological qualifications or notes, which, to some extent, the Magisterium has adopted. In recent times, this approach has unfortunately been more or less forgotten. But it is useful in the interpretation of dogma and should therefore be repristinated and developed further.

According to the doctrine of the Church, "an act of divine and Catholic faith must be made in what is contained in God's word, either as it is written in Scripture or handed on by tradition and proposed by the Church, whether that be by way of a solemn decision or by the ordinary Magisterium, and the obligation to believe is demanded because it is divine revelation" (DS 3011). This "*credendum*" includes the truths of faith (in the strict sense) and also those truths, witnessed to by revelation, which have a bearing on the moral life (DS 1501, 3074: "*fides et mores*"; LG 25: "*fidem credendam et moribus applicandam*").

Natural truths and natural moral doctrines may belong indirectly to the binding doctrine of the Church whenever they have a necessary and intrinsic connection with the truths of faith (LG 25: "*tantum patet quantum divinae Revelationis patet depositum, sancte custodiendum et fideliter exponendum*"). Nonetheless Vatican II makes a clear distinction between the doctrine of the faith and the principles of the natural moral order, inasmuch as for the first, the Council speaks of [the Church's duty] "to give utterance to, and authoritatively to teach" while for the second the language is "to declare and confirm by her authority" (DH 14).

Since the Church's teaching is a living whole, the faithful may not limit their assent to the truths which are formally defined. Other statements of the Magisterium which, without being definitive definitions, come from the Pope, the Congregation for the Doctrine of the Faith or from the bishops, must equally be accepted, in varying degrees, with religious assent (*religiosum obsequium*). Of these, those belong to the authentic Magisterium where a declaration of intent as magisterial is present. This can be recognized, first of all, "from the character of the documents, from [the Pope's] frequent repetition of the same doctrine, or from his manner of speaking" (LG 25; cf. DS 3044f.). The precise meaning of that Conciliar statement needs a more advanced theological explanation. It is desirable before all else to avoid the Church's authority becoming pointlessly blunted, that the Magisterium itself should, on every occasion, indicate the type and degree of obligation of the statements issued.

4. The Magisterium in Action

The Magisterium in practice should tend towards realizing her own pastoral character. Her task of witnessing authentically to the truth of Jesus Christ is at the heart of the larger mission of the care of souls. With this pastoral character in mind, the Magisterium will meet with prudence and judgment new social, political and ecclesial problems.

In recent centuries, one can see, on the part of the Magisterium of the Church, the interpretation of certain prior stands, as new developments arose, and especially when a complex situation had been well analysed and clarified. Such is the case in regard to the attitude to social questions against the background of the accomplishments of the modern sciences of nature, in the matter of human rights, religious liberty in particular, the historico-critical method, ecumenism, the appreciation of the Oriental Churches, and many of the basic demands of the Reformers, etc.

In a world which is noticeably pluralistic and in a Church where differences are more pronounced, the Magisterium fulfills its mission in having more and more recourse to discussion. In such circumstances, the heritage of faith cannot be passed on except by a willingness on the part of the Magisterium and others with pastoral and theological responsibility to engage in a common dialogue. When account is taken of the scientific and technical research of our time, it seems advisable to avoid taking a particular stance too quickly, but to favour instead nuanced decisions which indicate the lines to be followed, and this with subsequent definitive decisions of the Magisterium in mind.

III. *Basic and Fundamental Theological Reflections*

1. Dogma at the Heart of the *Paradosis* of the Church

The basic statement of Christian faith is the confession that the Logos, which already and in a partial way was alight in all reality, and whose coming was promised specifically in the Old Testament, came on earth in all fullness in the actual historical figure of Jesus Christ (Jn 1:3–14). In the fullness of time (Gal 4:4), the fullness of the Divinity was bodily present in Jesus Christ (Col 2:9). In him are hidden all the wealth of wisdom and knowledge (Col 2:3). He is in person the way, the truth, the life (Jn 14:6).

The presence of the Eternal in a specific figure in history is therefore of the essence of the Christian mystery of Salvation. In him the vague opening in man's heart towards God finds a definite answer. This very concrete event, and no mistake about it, must be equally imperative in the matter of our confession of faith in Jesus Christ. In virtue of that very thing, Christianity is, so to speak, dogmatic in its intimate nature.

God's truth would not have come definitively and as the end of history in Jesus Christ, through the Holy Spirit who recalls us, time and time again, to Jesus Christ and leads us to the fullness of truth, if it had not been accepted and publicly proclaimed by the community of the faithful. In Mary and the *Yes* which she gave without reservation on behalf of the human race to God's salvific will, the Church sees the prototype of her own *Yes* in faith. In the Holy Spirit, the Church is the Body of Christ, in which and through which God's many-facetted wisdom is proclaimed to all mankind (Eph 3:10f.; cf. Rom 16:25f.; Col 1:26f.). In Tradition, the communication of himself which the Father makes through the Logos in the Holy Spirit remains present always in the Church in many forms: in the words and actions of the Church, in her liturgy and prayer, and in all aspects of her life (*DV* 8). The dogmatic definitions are only one element within a tradition which is very much larger.

It is the fact then that we do not "possess" the truth and reality of Christ except as it is mediated to us by the testimony of the Church animated, as it is, by the Holy Spirit. Without the Church, we "have" nothing of Christ, nor do we have Gospel or Sacred Scripture. An a-dogmatic Christianity which would subtract itself from such a mediation through the Church would be simply tinsel.

The Church's *Paradosis* makes her own the expressivity and universality of human language, and of language's images and concepts. It gives them their definitive meaning by a process of purification and transformation. A new language corresponds to the new creation through which all peoples acquire mutual understanding, and the definitive unity of a new humanity begins to prepare itself. This is made possible because the *Paradosis* incarnates itself in the symbols and languages of all mankind, purifies and transforms their inherent values and inserts them into the whole process of the unique mystery of salvation (Eph 3:9). In this process in history, the Church adds nothing new (*non nova*) to the Gospel, but she constantly renews (*noviter*) the newness of Christ. Everything new that she picks from her treasure dovetails with what was there from the outset (*DH* 1).

This interior continuity of the *Paradosis* is owing to the fact that the Church is the home of a faith that surpasses time and space. For that reason, the Church must at all times have the history of her faith in a *memoria* animated by the Holy Spirit; and she must present it vibrantly and vitally in a prophetic way for now and for the future.

2. The Teaching of the Church (Dogma in a Wider Sense)

At the centre of all that we mean by the *Paradosis* of the Church, the meaning of dogma in a wider sense is the Church's testimony, expressed as obligatory doctrine, to the saving truth of God as promised in the Old

Testament, and definitively revealed in all its fullness in the person of Jesus Christ; this truth lives on in the Church through the action of the Holy Spirit. There is no doubt that from the very origins of the New Testament this doctrinal ingredient belonged to the preaching of the faith. Jesus himself is presented as a teacher (Rabbi). For that matter, he was addressed by that very title. He was a teacher and gave his disciples a teaching role (Mt 28:20). In the primitive communities there were teachers properly so called (Rom 12:7; 1 Cor 12:28; Eph 4:11). It is noteworthy that a special form of teaching seems to have accompanied baptism in the *Paradosis* (Rom 6:17). The importance of doctrine comes much more clearly to the fore in the later apostolic writers (1 Tim 1:10; 2 Tim 4:2f.; Tit 1:9, etc.).

The presentation by the Magisterium of the revealed truth is a testimony to God's word in and by means of human language. It shares in the definitive and final character of the divine truth that appeared in Jesus Christ, as it also shares in the temporal and limited character of all human language. The doctrine of the Church cannot be grasped and interpreted without faith. It follows from this that:

— Dogmas are to be interpreted as a *verbum rememorativum*. They are to be interpreted as a return journey by memory, a memory-laden recall of the *mighty acts* of God, which the testimony of revelation presents. For that reason, they must be brought into focus beginning with Scripture and Tradition, and be explained within and by means of those parameters. They must be interpreted within the whole corpus of Old and New Testaments according to the analogy of faith (cf. *DV* 12);

— Dogmas are to be interpreted as a *verbum demonstrativum*. They are not confined to the works of salvation of past times, but are meant to express salvation effectively in the here and now. They are meant to be light and truth. That is why they should be given a salvific meaning and presented in a living, attractive and stimulating fashion to the people of each and every epoch;

— Dogmas are to be interpreted as a *verbum prognosticum*. As a testimony to the truth and reality of salvation and the last things, dogmas are anticipatory statements about the end of all. They must give birth to hope and be explained in terms of the last end, of man's final destiny and that of the universe (DS 3016), and as a hymn of praise to God.

3. Dogmas in the Strict Sense

The teaching of the Magisterium on revealed truth can take different forms, be more or less a full expression, and have a sliding scale in the matter of obligation (*LG* 25). In the strict sense (and this approach is a creation that belongs to the modern epoch only), a dogma is a teaching in which the Church proposes a revealed truth definitively, and in a way that is binding for the universal Church, so much so that denial is rejected as heresy and falls under an anathema. So in dogma understood in this sense there are twin components, one doctrinal, and the other, juridical or disciplinary. Doctrinal statements with sacred obligation have an undeniable foundation in Sacred Scripture, in particular in the power of binding and loosing which Jesus gave his Church, and which is binding also in heaven, that is in God's eyes (Mt 16:19; 18:18). Even the matter of anathema has New Testament foundations (1 Cor 16:22; Gal 1:8f.; cf. 1 Cor 5:2–5; 2 Jn 10; etc.).

This focusing, both doctrinal and juridical, on a single proposition corresponds to the concrete and determinative character of Christian faith. It carries with it, by the same token, a danger of a legal positivism and a diminution of dogmatic emphasis. To avoid both these hazards, a twofold integration is necessary in the dogmatic field:

— The integration of the ensemble of dogmas in the fullness of the doctrine and life of the Church. This is because "the Church, in her teaching, life and worship, perpetuates and hands on to all generations all that she herself is, all that she believes" (*DV* 8). As a result the dogmas must be interpreted in the overall context of the Church's life and teaching.

— The inclusion of each individual dogma in the ensemble of all dogmas. They are not intelligible unless we begin with their internal linkage (*nexus mysteriorum*, DS 3016) and within their integrated structure. In this respect particular attention must be given to their rank or to the "hierarchy of truths" in Catholic teaching. This arises from the different ways according to which the dogmas are tied in with the christological foundation of Christian faith (*UR* 11). Without doubt, all revealed truths must be held in virtue of an identical divine faith, but their meaning and weight differ in proportion to their relationship with the mystery of Christ.

4. The Theological Significance of Dogmas

In the last analysis, all revelation is the revelation and communication of himself that God gives through his Son in the Holy Spirit so that we may enter into communion with him (*DV* 2). For that reason, God is the one object, all-encompassing, of faith and theology (Saint Thomas Aquinas). As a result, it is quite correct to say that "*actus credentis non terminatur ad enuntiabile, sed ad rem*" (IIa IIae, q. 1, a. 2, ad 2). In line with that, the medieval theological tradition laid down regarding the article of faith: "*Articulus fidei est perceptio divinae veritatis tendens in ipsam*" (cited in the *sed contra* in the *Summa theologica*, IIa IIae, q. 1, a. 6). This means that the article of faith is really and truly a grasp of divine truth. It is a mediation, effected in doctrine, containing the truth to which it gives testimony. For the very reason that it is true, it recoils, beyond itself, into the mystery of divine truth. It follows from this that the interpretation of dogmas, like all interpretation, is a path which leads us from the word on the outside into the heart of its meaning and finally to the unique and eternal Word of God. And that is why the interpretation of dogmas does not go from a particular word or formula to more of the same. It goes from words, images and concepts to the truth of what they hold within. It also follows that all knowledge by faith is in the end an anticipation of the eternal vision of God's face. It ensues then from this theological meaning of dogmas that:

— Like all other human statements about God, dogmas must be understood analogically, which means that as between the Creator and the creature the dissimilarity is away greater than the similarity (DS 806). This analogy is also a bulwark against an understanding of faith which objectifies it too much, reducing it to a thing, as much as against the excesses of a negative theology, which sees dogmas as mere "cyphers", so transcendent as to be unreachable, and in that way misconceiving the historical and concrete nature of the Christian mystery of salvation.
— The analogical character of dogmas must not be incorrectly confused with a purely symbolic conception which would consider dogma as a subsequent objectivization, whether of an original existential religious experience or of certain social or ecclesiastical practices. Dogmas must rather be understood as an obligatory doctrinal form of the truth of salvation directed by God at us. They are a doctrinal form the content of which is God's own word and truth. They should be interpreted theologically before all else.
— According to the teaching of the Fathers, the theological interpretation of dogmas is not an intellectual process only. At a deeper level still, it is a spiritual enterprise, brought about by the Spirit of Truth and possible only when preceded by a purification of the "eyes of the heart". It presupposes God's gift to us of the light of faith, participation in divine things and also a spiritual experience of that which is believed. That is worked in us by the Holy Spirit. It is above all at this profound level that the interpretation of dogmas involves both theory and practice; it is indissolubly linked to a life of communion with Jesus Christ in the Church.

C. CRITERIA OF INTERPRETATION

I. *Dogma and Sacred Scriptures*

1. The Fundamental Meaning of Sacred Scripture

The writings of the Old and New Testaments were composed under the inspiration of the Holy Spirit, so as to be "useful for teaching the truth and refuting error, or for reformation of manners and for discipline in right living" (2 Tim 3:16). These writings are collected in a Canon. The Church through her Magisterium has recognized in the Canon the apostolic witness to the faith, the authentic and certain faith of the primitive Church, and on this she continues to insist (DS 1502–4, 3006, 3029). "The Church has always venerated the divine Scriptures just as she has also done always for the very Body of the Lord and she never ceases, especially in the holy liturgy, to take the bread of life from the table of the Word of God and from that of the Body of Christ to offer to the faithful." It is necessary therefore that all preaching in the Church "be nourished and governed by Sacred Scripture" (*DV* 21). The story of Sacred Scripture should be at the same time the soul of theology and of all preaching (*DV* 24; *OT* 16). The witness of Sacred Scripture then should be the starting point and the basis for the understanding of dogma.

2. Crisis and Positive Findings of Modern Exegesis

The conflict between exegesis and dogma is a modern phenomenon. Following on the "age of Enlightenment", the tools of historical criticism were developed with the aim in mind also of favouring emancipation where dogmatic and ecclesiastical authority were concerned. This critical method became more and more radical. Soon it was no longer a question alone of a conflict between Scripture and Dogma: the very text of Scripture itself came under critical scrutiny to discover the so-called "dogmatic second-coatings" in Scripture itself. This line has been continued in the socio-political and psychological critical methods and these have searched the text for socio-political conflicts or for suppressed psychic data. All these approaches are based on the common suspicion that the dogma of the Church and Scripture conceal a primitive reality which can only be uncovered by critical questioning.

Certainly, the positive side and the results of "Enlightenment" criticism of tradition should not be neglected. The historical criticism of Scripture has revealed that the Bible itself is a thing of the Church; it is rooted in the *Paradosis* of the primitive Church, and the fixing of the limits of the Canon was itself a process of decision by the Church. In that way exegesis leads us back to dogma and tradition.

But the historico-critical method has not come to the conclusion that Jesus himself was absolutely "a-dogmatic". In the most severe critical analysis a most incontestable historical core remains of the life of Jesus on earth. This core contains what is shown by the words and deeds of Jesus, to wit, his statements concerning his mission, his person, his relationship with God, his "Abba". These claims contain implicitly, and already present in the New Testament, the subsequent evolution of dogma and are the core of all dogmatic definitions.

The primitive form then of Christian dogma is the confession, central indeed to the New Testament, that Jesus Christ is the Son of God (Mt 16:16).

3. The Teaching of Vatican II on the Interpretation of Scripture

The Second Vatican Council has taken up the positive concerns of modern historical criticism. It has underlined the fact that in the interpretation of Sacred Scripture, the task is to investigate with care "what the sacred writers really wanted to say and what God wanted to say by means of their words". To discover this, it is necessary to know the historical background as well as the thought forms, and the ways of speaking and the nature of narrative in that epoch. The historico-critical interpretation is to be inserted as a contribution to the theological and ecclesial interpretation. "Since Holy Scripture must be read and interpreted in the sacred spirit in which it was written, no less serious attention must be given to the content and unity of the whole of Scripture" (*DV* 12).

The theological interpretation of Scripture must begin with its centre, Jesus Christ. He is the only interpreter (*exegesato*) of the Father (Jn 1:18). From the outset, he has given his disciples a share in this interpretation since he introduced them to his way of life, confided his message to them and the gifts of his power and Spirit to take them towards the fullness of truth (Jn 16:13). It is in the power of that Spirit that the apostles and their disciples received and transmitted the witness of Jesus. The interpretation of the witness of Jesus is then indissolubly linked to the action of his Spirit in continuing this witness (apostolic succession) and in maintaining the sense of faith of God's people.

Correct interpretation of Scripture is vital in the matter of the dogma of the Church. In this question of dogmatic interpretation of Scripture and the obligation involved, the Magisterium is not in an inferior position to God's Word, but rather at its service (cf. *DV* 10). The Magisterium does not judge the Word of God but the correctness of its own interpretation of it. No age can go back on what has been formulated dogmatically through the Holy Spirit as a key to the interpretation of Scripture. This does not exclude the fact of new points of view in the future or new formulations. Finally, the judgment of the Church in matters of faith is constantly being enriched thanks to to the advance work of the exegetes and their careful studies of what Sacred Scripture intended to say (*DV* 12).

4. The Christocentric Nature of Scripture as a Criterion

In spite of all modern progress and the radical spiritual upheavals following on the "age of Enlightenment", it is still the fact that Christ is the definitive revelation of God, and there is nothing to come, no new age of salvation, no new gospel, which will surpass the age of Christ. The time that remains until Christ returns remains bound essentially to the "once-for-all" (*ephapax*) that took place in the Christ of history. The same is true of the tradition of Scripture and the *Paradosis* of the Church which are his witnesses. The present Lordship of Jesus Christ, albeit hidden, is the measure and the touchstone from now on that separate truth and falsehood. It is in terms of Jesus Christ also that the distinction is made in the new methods of scriptural interpretation between what sets forth the real Christ and what is a misunderstanding, or even more so, a falsification.

Many of the perspectives made available by the historico-critical method and more recent methods (the history of comparative religions, structuralism, semiotics, social history, depth psychology) may help to put the figure of Christ in greater relief for men of our time.

Nevertheless, they will bear no fruit unless they are employed subject to faith, and without claims to autonomy. The communion of the Church remains the place where the interpretation of Scripture is sheltered from the danger of being swept away by the currents of opinion common to one age or the other.

II. *Dogma in the Tradition and in the Communion of the Church*

1. The Indissoluble Bond between Scripture, Tradition and the Communion of the Church

The one Gospel, which, as the fulfilment of Old Testament promises, was revealed once and for all in its fullness by Jesus Christ, remains unshaken as the source of all salvific truth and all moral teaching (DS 1501). Thanks to the assistance of the Holy Spirit, the apostles and their disciples have passed on the Gospel in their preaching, by their example, by the institutions they founded; under the inspiration of the same Spirit, they have committed it to written documents (*DV* 7). Thus, Scripture and tradition form together a single depository of faith (*depositum fidei*) which the Church must protect faithfully (1 Tim 6:20; 2 Tim 1:14). The Gospel was not given to the Church as a dead letter, a mere parchment: it is written by the Holy Spirit in the hearts of the faithful (2 Cor 3:3). In that way, thanks to the Holy Spirit, the Gospel is permanently present in the community of the Church, in her doctrine, her life and above all her liturgy (*DV* 8).

Scripture, tradition and the community of the Church do not then run on parallel paths; they form an intimate unity (*DV* 9f.; cf. supra B, I, 1; C, I, 2), which has its most profound basis in the Father's sending of his Word and his Spirit to us as gift. The Spirit produces the great works of salvation: he calls and inspires the prophets who explain these works; he raises up a people who acknowledge them in faith and witness to them. In the fullness of time, he brings about the incarnation of God's eternal Word (Mt 1:20; Lk 1:35); through baptism, he constructs the Church, the Body of Christ (1 Cor 12:13), and always brings to its mind the words, deeds and person of Jesus Christ, and guides her in the fullness of truth (Jn 14:26; 15:26; 16:13f.).

Through the action of the Holy Spirit, the spoken word becomes "spirit and life" in the hearts of the faithful. God himself anoints them with knowledge (1 Jn 2:20, 27; Jn 6:45). The Holy Spirit awakens and nourishes the *sensus fidelium*, which is that inner sense in virtue of which, and under the guidance of the Magisterium, the people of God recognize in preaching that the words are God's not man's and accept and guard them with unbreakable fidelity (*LG* 12; cf. *LG* 35).

2. The One Tradition and the Plurality of Traditions

Tradition (*Paradosis*) in the end is nothing else but the communication of himself which God, the Father, gives through Jesus Christ in the Holy Spirit, with a view to a presence forever new in the community of the Church. From the outset, this living Tradition in the Church took on a large number of different forms in particular traditions (*traditiones*). Its inexhaustible richness is expressed in a plurality of doctrines, chants, symbols, rites, regulations and institutions. Tradition also displays its fecundity by way of "inculturation" in different local Churches according to their local cultural situation. These multiple traditions are orthodox inasmuch as they testify to the one apostolic Tradition, and pass it on.

The discernment of spirits (1 Cor 12:10; 1 Thess 5:21; 1 Jn 4:1) is therefore an element in the entrance through the agency of the Holy Spirit into "the fullness of truth". The problem is to make a distinction between Tradition as received from the Lord (1 Cor 11:23) and the traditions of men (Mk 7:8; Col 2:8). The apostolic tradition in the Church cannot undergo any essential corruption because of the permanent assistance of the Holy Spirit which guarantees its indefectibility. The Church is holy, but at the same time a Church of sinners, and for that reason human traditions can slip in which diminish the one apostolic tradition in the case where the nucleus is violated by a certain exaggeration of certain aspects. And that is why the Church always feels the need for purification, penance and renewal with regard to the traditions in her (*LG* 8). The criteria for judging such a "discernment of spirits" flow from the very nature of Tradition.

Since it is the one Spirit who acts during the whole history of salvation, in Scripture, in Tradition, and also in the whole life of the Church along the centuries, the internal coherence of Tradition is a fundamental criterion. This coherence is made certain by the fact that Jesus Christ is the centre of revelation. Jesus Christ himself is then the focus of unity for the multiple forms of tradition: He is the criterion for discernment and interpretation. It is from this centre as origin that Scripture, Tradition and particular traditions as well, with their correspondences and connections, are to be examined and interpreted.

Since the faith has been transmitted once and for all (Jude 3), the Church is permanently bound to the heritage of the apostles. Consequently, apostolicity is an essential criterion. The Church must constantly renew itself through living the memory of its origin, and interpret dogma in the light of those origins.

The one apostolic faith which was given to the Church in its entirety takes form in the diversity of the traditions of local Churches. An essential criterion is catholicity, that is, agreement within the communion of the Church. Uncontested agreement on a point of faith over a long lapse of time is a sign of the apostolicity of that doctrine.

The connection of Tradition with the ecclesial *communio* is shown and made living before all else in the celebration of the liturgy. This is why the *lex orandi* is also the *lex credendi* (DS 246). The liturgy is the living and all-inclusive theological home of faith. This is not simply in the sense that liturgical and doctrinal expressions must correspond; the liturgy makes "the mystery of faith" actual. The reception of the eucharistic Body of Christ ministers to the building up and growth of the ecclesial Body of the Lord, the community we call the Church (1 Cor 10:17).

3. The Interpretation of Dogmas within the Communion of the Church

The Church is the sacrament, that is, all together, the place, sign and instrument of the *Paradosis*. She announces God's saving deeds (*martyria*); she passes on the confession of faith to those she baptizes (Rom 6:17); she confesses her faith at the time of the breaking of bread and at prayer (*leiturgia*, Acts 2:42); she serves Jesus Christ in the poor, the persecuted, the prisoners, the sick and dying (*diakonia*, Mt 25). The dogmas are an expression of that same tradition at doctrinal level. One may not then sever them from their context in the life of the Church and interpret them in a purely conceptual manner. The meaning and interpretation of dogmas is more a matter of redemptive value; they are to guard the family of the Church against error, heal its wounds, and serve the growth of living faith.

The service of the *Paradosis* and its interpretation has been confided to the Church as a whole. At the heart of the Church, it falls to the bishops, who are established as the apostolic succession, to give a faithful interpretation of the Tradition of the faith (*DV* 10). In union with the Bishop of Rome, to whom the ministry of unity has been entrusted in a special fashion, the bishops have the power to give the authentic definition and interpretation of dogmas. This may take place by the assembly of bishops in union with the Pope, or by the Pope alone, the head of the episcopal College (*LG* 25).

The task of interpreting the dogmas in the Church appertains as well to the "witnesses" and to the doctors in communion with the bishops. The unanimous agreement of the Church Fathers (*unanimis consensus Patrum*, DS 1507, 3007), the testimony of those who have undergone martyrdom for the faith and that of the other canonised saints of the Church, in particular Church doctors, have, in this matter, an altogether special function.

4. Assisting the *Consensus Fidelium*

An essential criterion for the discernment of spirits is the building up of the unity of the Body of Christ (1 Cor 12:4–11). This is the reason why the action of the Holy Spirit in the Church also appears in a process of "exchange". Scripture and Tradition set free their meaning above all when they are made real and actual in the liturgy. And they are fully accepted by the community of the Church when they are celebrated in the depths of the "mystery of faith". The interpretation of dogmas is a form of the service supplied by the *consensus fidelium*, through which the people of God, "from the bishops to the last believing layman" (Saint Augustine), expresses its general agreement in questions of faith and morals (*LG* 12). The dogmas and their interpretation should buttress this consensus of the faithful in confessing "that which we have known from the beginning" (1 Jn 2:7–24).

III. *Dogma and Contemporary Interpretation*[3]

1. The Need for Contemporary Interpretation

The living Tradition of God's people on pilgrimage through history does not come to a stop at a particular point in that history. It arrives at the present only to move on to the future. A dogmatic definition is not only the end of a development but equally a new start. If a truth of faith has become dogma it becomes part for good of the *Paradosis* which travels on. Following on definition comes acceptance, which is a living grasp of the dogma in the common life of the Church, and a deeper insight into the truth the dogma presents. For dogma should not simply be a relic of times past; it should bear fruit in the life of the Church. For that reason, attention should not be limited to the negative or restrictive side of it, but to its positive side since that is its doorway to truth.

Such a contemporary process of dogmatic interpretation should bear two principles in mind, which at first sight seem to contradict each other: the permanent value of truth, and its contemporary form. This means that one cannot deny or betray the tradition nor, in the guise of loyalty, pass on an ossified tradition. The tradition must release from its memory

---

[3] The word "contemporary" is used here, and in what follows, to translate the German *heutige*. It is not intended to give it any unique standing as against other epochs. Interpretation is a perennial task.

hope for the present and for the future. A definition, in fine, can have no significance here and now except to the extent that it is true. The permanence of truth and its contemporary form interact. Only the truth makes free (cf. Jn 8: 32).

2. The Guiding Principles of Contemporary Interpretation

Since the contemporary interpretation of dogma is a part of an ongoing history of Tradition and dogmas, it is directed specifically by the same principles as that history itself.

This means, first of all, that such a process of contemporary interpretation is not a purely intellectual enterprise, nor for that matter purely existential or sociological. Further, it does not consist exclusively in more precise definition of individual concepts, nor in the reshaping or invention of formulations. It is inspired, sustained and guided by the action of the Holy Spirit in the Church and in each believer's heart. It takes place in the light of faith; it gets its drive from the charisms and the witness of the saints which God's Spirit gives to his Church for an appointed epoch. In the same context it is the place for the prophetic witness of spiritual movements and the interior wisdom pouring forth from the spiritual experience of lay people filled with God's Spirit (cf. *DV* 8).

Just as in the case of the *Paradosis* of the Church as a whole, contemporary interpretation of dogmas takes place in and by means of the life of the Church in all its aspects. This happens in preaching and catechesis, in the celebration of the liturgy, in the life of prayer, in service, in the daily witness of Christians, and also in the juridical and disciplinary side of the Church. The prophetic witness of the single Christian, or of groups, must find its place as follows: is it, and to what extent, in communion with the life of the Church as a whole? In other words, can it be received and accepted by the Church in the course of a lengthy and sometimes painful process?

The faith and living understanding of faith are also genuinely human acts, and make use of all man's faculties: his intelligence, his will and his emotional nature (cf. Mk 12:30 par.). The faith should give an answer before all mankind (*apo-logia*) concerning the reasons for hope (*logos*) (cf. 1 Pet 3:15). And this is why the work of theology, the historical study of sources, the contribution of the human sciences, hermeneutics and linguistics, and philosophy as well, have great importance for the contemporary interpretation of dogma. All these disciplines can act as a spur to the witness of the Church and do a preparatory work in presenting that witness to the demands of reason. But in doing this, their basis and norm remain the preaching, teaching and life of the Church.

3. The Permanent Value of Dogmatic Formulas

The question of the contemporary interpretation of dogmas is centred on the problem of the permanent value of dogmatic formulas (cf. ITC, "Unité de la foi et pluralisme théologique" [1972], in *Documenta*, op. cit., p. 36[4]). Without doubt a distinction must be made between the permanently valid content of dogmas and the form in which this is expressed. The mystery of Christ transcends all possible elucidations, no matter what the epoch, and therefore can never lend itself to a finally exclusive system of interpretation (cf. Eph 3:8–10; ITC cited above, p. 32). In different cultural situations and as the successive signs of the times demand, the Holy Spirit continues without pause to make the mystery of Christ present in all its freshness.

At the same time, it is not possible to make a neat distinction between content and form of expression. The symbolic nature of language is not simply an item of apparel, but in some way truth itself incarnate. This applies in a very particular way, since the foundations are the incarnation of the eternal Word, to the profession of faith of the Church. This profession takes concrete form in a proper formula, which as a real-symbolic expression of the content of faith, contains and makes present what it indicates. For that reason the images and concepts used are not interchangeable at will.

The study of the history of dogma shows clearly that in these dogmas the Church has not simply taken up already existing conceptual schemes. She has rather subjected existing concepts, imprinted by the upper levels of the language of the milieu, to a process of purification and transformation, or reworking. In that way, she has created the language that fits her message. Take for example the distinction between "substance" (or nature) and "hypostasis", and the working out of the concept of person which was unknown, as such, to Greek philosophy. In fact, it came about as a result of reflection on the reality of the mystery of Salvation and on biblical language.

The language of the Church's dogma was then forged partly in debate with certain philosophical systems, but is not bound in any way to any definitive philosophical system. In the process of seeking language for the faith, the Church has created a language of her own in which she has given expression to realities hitherto unperceived and unknown, but which belong now, precisely by means of such linguistic expression, to the *Paradosis* of the Church and through it to the historical heritage of humanity.

As a community of faith the Church is a community in the language of the profession of faith. That is the reason unity in the basic expressions

---

[4] *Textes et documents*, p. 53. [Published in English as "Theological Pluralism", in *Texts and Documents*, chap. 3.]

of faith, both in the course of history and in the here and now (dia-chronically and synchronically), is also part of the Church's unity. The basic expressions of faith may not be revised, even when it is claimed that the reality they express will not be lost to sight. The effort must always be made to assimilate them more and more, and to push on with explain-ing them, thanks to a whole range of different forms of evangelization. In particular, the inculturation of Christianity in other cultures may give occasion for this task, or indeed make it obligatory. Revealed truth for all that remains unchanged "not alone in what constitutes substantial con-tent but also decisive expressions in language" (ITC, supra cit., p. 37).

4. The Criteria for Contemporary Interpretation

For this process of the Paradosis in our time the criteria presented in the preceding paragraphs are valuable. It is essential that the "christological axis" be preserved, in such a way that Jesus Christ remains the beginning, centre and measuring rod for all interpretation. To make certain of this, the criterion of origin, that is apostolicity, and that of communion (koi-nonia), that is catholicity, have pride of place (cf. C, II, 2).

In addition to the two criteria already considered, the "anthropological criterion" has also an important role today in the field of interpretation. In saying that, there is obviously no intention of suggesting that man in himself, certain of his needs or interests, or even the tendencies of fash-ion, can function as the measure of faith and the interpretation of dogma.

That is already out of court for the very fact that man himself is an unresolved question to which the only full response is God (GS 21). Only in Jesus Christ is the mystery of man made clear: in him, the New Man, God has fully revealed man to man and opened up to him his most sublime vocation (GS 22). Man then is not the measure, but the point of reference for faith and dogma. This is the road too the Church follows in the explanation of her dogmas (cf. John Paul II, Redemptor hominis, 14).

The First Vatican Council had already taught that a deeper knowledge of the mysteries of faith is made possible if they are viewed by analogy with ordinary human ways of knowing and if they are seen in relation-ship with man's last end (DS 3016). The Second Vatican Council speaks of the "signs of the times" which, on the one hand, are to be interpreted on the basis of the faith, but which, on the other hand, can stimulate a greater understanding of the faith as it has reached us (GS 3f., 10f., 22, 40, 42f., 44, 62, etc.). In this way, the Church wishes to illuminate the mystery of man by the light of Christ and to cooperate in the search for a solution to the most urgent problems of our times (GS 10).

5. The Seven Criteria of J. H. Newman

Newman worked out a criteriology for the development of dogma, which serves both as preparation and finishing touch to what is being argued. It can be applied in proper proportions to that further interpretation of dogmas aimed at giving them contemporary relevance. Newman lists seven principles, namely the following criteria:

1. The conservation of the type, which is to say the basic form, and of the proportions and relationships existing between the whole and the parts. When the structure as a totality remains, its type holds fast, even if some particular concepts change. But this total structure may become corrupt, even in the case where the concepts remain unchanged, if the latter are made part of a context or a system of coordinates which is altogether different.

2. The continuity of principle: the different doctrines represent principles existing at a deeper level, even when these are often not recognized until a later stage. The same doctrine, if detached from its founding principle, may be interpreted in more ways than one, and lead to contradictory conclusions. Continuity of principle then is a criterion which can distinguish proper and legitimate development from the erroneous.

3. Capacity for being assimilated: a living idea shows its edge by its ability to get at reality, attract other ideas to itself, stimulate reflection and develop itself further without loss of its internal unity. This capacity for being integrated is a criterion of legitimate development.

4. Logical coherence: the development of dogmas is a vital process which is too complex to be regarded simply a logical explanation and deduction from given premises. Nevertheless, there must be logical coherence between the conclusions and the initial data. Conversely, one can judge what a development is from its consequences or recognize it as legitimate or otherwise by its fruits.

5. Anticipation of the future: trends which come to realization and succeed only later may make themselves noticeable early on, even if as isolated phenomena where the outline is still dim. Such advance trends are signs of the agreement of subsequent development with the original idea.

6. The conservation of past values: development becomes corruption when it contradicts the original doctrine or earlier development. True development conserves and safeguards the development and formulations that went before.

7. Durability: corruption leads to disintegration. Whatever corrupts itself cannot last for long. Whatever is vital and durable on the contrary is a sign of authentic development.

6. The Importance of the Magisterium for Contemporary Interpretation

The criteria which we have enumerated will be incomplete if we omit to remind ourselves of the function of the Church's Magisterium, to which the authentic interpretation of God's word has been committed, both written and passed on by tradition, and as a mandate exercised in the name of Jesus Christ and assisted by the Holy Spirit (*DV* 10). Her mission does not consist in merely ratifying and making definitive, as if she were a supreme "notary", the process of interpretation in the Church. She must also stimulate it, follow it step by step, and direct it, and to the extent that the process comes to a positive conclusion, give it, by an act of official validation, objective standing, and make it a matter of universal obligation. In this way, the Magisterium will give a sense of direction and certainty to the faithful who find themselves faced with confusing opinions and endless theological disputes: this may take place in various ways and with varying degrees of obligation, beginning with the usual preaching, exhortations and encouragement and on to authentic statements of doctrine, even infallible ones.

"Faced with doctrinal statements that are gravely ambiguous, even perhaps incompatible with the Faith of the Church, the Church has the capacity to discern error and the duty to dispel it, even resorting to the formal rejection of heresy as the final remedy for safeguarding the Faith of the people of God" (ITC, "Unité de la foi et pluralisme théologique", op. cit., p. 34[5]). "A Christianity which can no longer say what it is and what it is not, or where its frontiers lie, will have nothing more to say." The apostolic function of excommunication belongs, even today to the rights of the Magisterium of the Church; and an obligation to exercise it may arise (ITC 1972, Commentary, in *Die Einheit des Glaubens und der theologische Pluralismus* [Einsiedeln, 1973], pp. 48, 50f.).

All dogmatic interpretation has one aim only, and that is that in the Church and in each believer "spirit and life" may be born from the words of the dogmas. In a present constantly made new, hope should spring from the memory of the Church's tradition; in the diversity of the human condition, cultural, political, economic, in the plurality of peoples, the unity and catholicity of the faith must be strengthened and promoted as a sign of and an agent of unity and peace on earth. What is at stake is that men should have eternal life in knowing the one true God and Jesus Christ, his Son (Jn 17:3).

---

[5] *Textes et documents*, p. 52. [2009 Eng. ed.: "Theological Pluralism", 1:90.]

17

SOME CURRENT QUESTIONS
IN ESCHATOLOGY

INTRODUCTION:
THE PERPLEXITY OF MANY TODAY IN THE FACE
OF DEATH AND EXISTENCE AFTER DEATH

1. Without the affirmation of Christ's resurrection Christian faith is in vain (cf. 1 Cor 15:14). Since there is indeed an intimate relationship between the fact of Christ's resurrection and our hope of our own future resurrection (cf. 1 Cor 15:12), the Risen Christ also constitutes the foundation of our hope, which opens itself up to horizons far beyond the limits of this earthly life. For "if our hopes in Christ are limited to this life only, we are the most pitiable of men" (1 Cor 15:19). Yet without this hope it would be impossible to lead a Christian life.

This intimate bond between the firm hope of future life and the possibility of responding to the demands of Christian life was clearly recognized in the Church from its inception. For then it was recalled that the Apostles obtained glory through their suffering;[1] moreover, those who were led to martyrdom discovered strength in the hope of reaching Christ through their own death and in the hope of their own future resurrection.[2]

Right down to our own days saints, motivated by this hope or supporting themselves by it, have either given up their lives in martyrdom or devoted their lives to the service of Christ and their brothers and sisters.

This document of the International Theological Commission, under the leadership of Rev. Candido Pozo, S.J., was prepared by a subcommission made up of Professors J. Ambaum, G. Gnilka, J. Ibanez Langlois, M. Ledwith, S. Nagy, C. Peter (+), as well as the Most Reverends B. Kloppenburg, J. Medina Estevez and C. Schönborn. After it was submitted to debate in the plenary session of December 1991 it was fully approved by written vote *in forma specifica*. According to the statutes of the International Theological Commission it is now published with the approval of His Eminence Joseph Cardinal Ratzinger, President of the Commission.

[1] Cf. St. Clement of Rome, *Ad Corinthios* 5; Funk, 1:104–6.
[2] Cf. St. Ignatius of Antioch, *Ad Romanos* 4; Funk, 1:256–8.

When other Christians look upon the witness that these saints offer, they too become stronger in their pilgrimage to Christ. This hope raises the hearts of Christians to heavenly things, without keeping them from fulfilling their duties in this age, because "the expectation of a new earth must not weaken but rather stimulate our concern for cultivating this one."[3]

Nevertheless, the contemporary world is in many ways an enemy of Christian hope. For the contemporary world is strongly influenced by secularism, "which consists in an autonomous vision of humanity and of the world, a vision that prescinds from the dimension of mystery, neglecting or even denying this dimension. This immanentism is a diminution of the total picture of man."[4] Secularism constitutes, as it were, the atmosphere in which very many Christians of our day live. It is with great difficulty that they shake this off. Because of this, it is not surprising that even among some Christians perplexities about eschatological hope arise. It is not rare that they look apprehensively toward their future death; [man is] tormented not only "by pain and by the advancing deterioration of his body, but even more so by a dread of perpetual extinction."[5] In every period of history Christians have been exposed to temptations of doubt. But in our days the anxieties of many Christians seem to indicate a weakening of hope.

Since "faith is the confident assurance concerning what we hope for, and conviction about things we do not see" (Heb 11:1), it will be fitting to have constantly before our eyes the truths of Catholic faith regarding our own future lot. We will try to make a kind of synthesis, emphasizing above all those aspects that may more directly respond to contemporary anxieties. Faith will support hope.

But before we embark on this task, the principal elements that cause the present perplexities ought to be described. It must first be noted that in our day the faith of Christians is not only shaken by influences which must be regarded as external to the Church. For today there can be detected the existence of a certain "theological darkness". For there are some novel interpretations of dogmas, interpretations which are perceived by the faithful as calling into doubt the very divinity of Christ or the reality of his resurrection. From these interpretations the faithful receive no support for their faith, but rather an occasion for doubting many other truths of faith. The image of Christ which they deduce from such reinterpretations cannot safeguard their hope. In the field of eschatology itself we

---

[3] GS 39, AAS 58 (1966): 1057.
[4] Synod 1985, Relatio finalis, II, A, 1 (E Civitate Vaticana, 1985), p. 6.
[5] GS 18, AAS 58: 1038.

ought to keep in mind "theological controversies everywhere publicly disputed, whose precise subject and significance the greater part of the faithful cannot understand. In fact, it is to be noted that the existence of the soul has been made the subject of debate, as well as the meaning of life after death; in the same way, questions have been raised about what happens between the death of the Christian and the universal resurrection. The faithful are perturbed by all these questions, since they are no longer able to recognize the idiom to which they are accustomed and the concepts already familiar to them." [6] Such theological doubts often exert a significant influence on catechesis and preaching; for they either come to the surface in the teaching of doctrine, or lead to a silence about the last things.

The phenomenon of secularism goes hand in hand with the widespread opinion, which the media foster, that people, like all other things existing in space and time, are no more than matter and are utterly dissolved in death. Moreover, contemporary culture, which unfolds in this historical context, seeks by every means to cast into oblivion death and those questions that are inevitably linked with it. From another side hope is shattered by a pessimism regarding the goodness of human nature itself, a pessimism arising from the increase in distress and affliction. After the immense cruelty shown by people of our century in the Second World War, it was everywhere hoped that humanity, taught by this terrible experience, would establish a better order of liberty and justice. But bitter deception soon followed: "for everywhere today there is an increase in famine, oppression, injustice and war, torture and terrorism, and other forms of violence of every kind." [7] In the rich nations many are attracted "to the idolatry of material commodities (the so-called 'consumerism')",[8] and neglect all their neighbours. It is easy to imagine that people today, enslaved to such a degree to the senses and to greed and the exclusive pursuit of worldly goods, are destined to no superior end.

Thus many are in doubt about whether death leads to annihilation or to a new life. Even among those who think that there is another life after death, not a few imagine it to be a new life on earth through reincarnation, so that the earthly course of our life is thought not to be only one. Religious indifferentism raises doubts about the foundation of hope in eternal life: namely, about whether it consists in the promise of God given through Jesus Christ or is to be based on some other saviour to be

---

[6] Congregation for the Doctrine of the Faith, Letter *Recentiores episcoporum Synodi*, Introduction, *AAS* 71 (1979): 940.

[7] Synod 1985, *Relatio finalis*, II, D, 1, p. 17.

[8] Ibid., I, 4, p. 4.

hoped for. "Theological obscurity" favours this indifferentism, since by raising doubts about the true image of Christ it makes it difficult for some Christians to hope in him.

2. There is silence about eschatology today for other reasons, of which we single out one: that is, the rebirth of the tendency to establish an innerworldly eschatology. This tendency is well known in the history of theology, and beginning with the Middle Ages it constituted what came to be called "the spiritual heritage of Joachim de Fiore".[9]

This tendency is found in some theologians of liberation, who so insist on the importance of establishing the kingdom of God as something within our own history on earth that the salvation which transcends history seems to become of rather secondary interest. Certainly, these theologians do not deny in any way the truth of realities beyond human life and history. But since the kingdom of God is located in a society without divisions, "the third age" in which "the eternal Gospel" (Rev 14:6–7) and the kingdom of the Spirit are to flourish is introduced in a new and secularized form.[10]

In this way a certain kind of "eschaton" is brought within historical time. This "eschaton" is not presented as the ultimate absolute, but as a relative absolute. Nonetheless, Christian praxis is directed so exclusively to the establishment of this eschaton that the Gospel is read reductively, so that whatever pertains to the eschatological realities absolutely considered is in great part passed over in silence. In this way, in a theological system of this sort, "one places oneself within the perspective of a temporal messianism, which is one of the most radical of the expressions of secularisation of the Kingdom of God and of its absorption into the immanence of human history."[11]

Theological hope loses its full strength when it is replaced by a political dynamism. This happens when a political dimension becomes the "principal and exclusive dimension, leading to a reductionist reading of Scripture".[12] It must be noted that a way of proposing eschatology that introduces a reductionist reading of the Gospel cannot be admitted, even if there are taken from the Marxist system none of those elements which could hardly be reconciled with Christianity.

It is well known that classical Marxism considered religion as the "opium" of the people: for religion, "by arousing man's hope for a deceptive future

---

[9] On this cf. H. de Lubac, *La postérité spirituelle de Joachim de Fiore*, 2 vols. (Paris, 1978 and 1981).

[10] For the relationship between Marx and Hegel cf. ibid., 2:256–360.

[11] Congregation for the Doctrine of the Faith, Instruction *Libertatis nuntius* (Instruction on Certain Aspects of the "Theology of Liberation"), 10, 6, *AAS* 76 (1984): 901; Vatican translation.

[12] Ibid., 10, 5, p. 900.

life, thereby [diverted] him from the constructing of the earthly city." [13]
This accusation is entirely without objective basis. It is rather materialism
that deprives people of true motives for building up the world. For why
would one struggle, if there is nothing for us to await after this earthly
life? "Let us eat and drink, for tomorrow we die" (Is 22:13). On the
contrary, it is certain that "a hope related to the end of time does not
diminish the importance of intervening duties but rather undergirds the
acquittal of them with fresh incentives." [14]

Nonetheless, we cannot deny that there have been Christians, and
not a few, choosing a pietistic way and giving themselves over too much
to thought about the future life, abandoning their social responsibilities.
This way of proceeding must be rejected. On the other hand, it is not
right to devise a merely "temporal" version of Christianity by forgetting about the future world, either in one's personal life or in the exercise of pastoral duties. The notion of an "overall" liberation proposed
by the Magisterium of the Church [15] preserves, at one and the same
time, the balance and the riches of the diverse elements of the gospel
message. [16] Therefore, this notion teaches us the true attitude of Christianity and the right mode of pastoral action, inasmuch as it indicates
the false and pointless oppositions between spiritual mission and service
(diaconia) for the world that must be put aside and superseded. [17] Finally,
this notion is the true expression of love for one's brothers and sisters
since it seeks to free them completely from every kind of slavery and,
first of all, from the slavery to one's own heart. If Christians are concerned with liberating others in all respects, they will in no way be
closed in on themselves.

3. The Christian response to the perplexities of people today, as indeed
people of every age, has the Risen Christ as its foundation and is contained in the hope of the glorious future resurrection of all who are
Christ's, [18] a resurrection which is made in the image of the resurrection
of Christ himself: "just as we have borne the likeness of the man from
earth, so shall we bear the likeness of the man from heaven" (1 Cor
15:49), that is, of the Risen Christ himself. Our own resurrection will be

---

[13] GS 20, AAS 58: 1040.

[14] GS 21, AAS 58: 1041.

[15] Cf. Paul VI, Apostolic Exhortation Evangelii nuntiandi, 31, AAS 68 (1976): 28.

[16] Cf. International Theological Commission, "Human Development and Christian Salvation" (1976), in International Theological Commission, Texts and Documents, 1969–
1985 (San Francisco: Ignatius Press, 1989), pp. 145–61.

[17] Synod 1985, Relatio finalis, II, D, 6, p. 19.

[18] It is not necessary now to explain that human beings can be Christ's without visibly
belonging to his Church: cf. LG 15f., AAS 57 (1965): 19f.

an ecclesial event in connection with the second coming of the Lord when the number of the brethren will be fully made up (cf. Rev 6:11). In the meanwhile there is, immediately after death, a communion of the blessed with the Risen Christ, which, if necessary, presupposes an eschatological purification. The communion with the Risen Christ prior to our final resurrection implies a definitive anthropological concept and a vision of death that are specifically Christian. The "communication of spiritual goods"[19] that exists among the members of the Church is made intelligible in and through the Risen Lord, who is the Head of all. Christ is the end and goal of our existence: to him we must direct ourselves with the help of his grace in this short life on earth. The serious nature of this journey can be gathered from the infinite greatness of him toward whom we go. We long for Christ—and there is no other earthly being like to him—as the supreme fulfilment of all our desires.

THE CHRISTIAN HOPE OF THE RESURRECTION

1. *The Resurrection of Christ and Our Resurrection*

1.1. The Apostle Paul wrote to the Corinthians: "I handed on to you first of all what I myself received: that Christ died for our sins in accordance with the Scriptures; that he was buried and, in accordance with the Scriptures, rose on the third day" (1 Cor 15:3–4). Indeed, not only did Christ really rise, but he is "the resurrection and the life" (Jn 11:25) and also the hope of our resurrection. For this reason Christians today, as in former times, when they recite the Nicene-Constantinople Creed, in the very formula "of the immortal tradition of the holy Church of God"[20] in which they profess their faith in Jesus Christ, who "rose on the third day according to the Scriptures", add the following: "We look forward to the resurrection of the dead."[21] In this profession of faith we hear the testimonies of the New Testament: "The dead who are in Christ will rise" (1 Thess 4:16).

"Christ is now raised from the dead, the first fruits of those who have fallen asleep" (1 Cor 15:20). This manner of speaking implies that the fact of Christ's resurrection is not an end in itself, but must be extended at some time to those who are Christ's. Since our future resurrection is

---

[19] *LG* 49, *AAS* 57: 55.
[20] Paul VI, *Credo of the People of God*, 3, *AAS* (1968): 434.
[21] DS 150.

"the extension of the very Resurrection of Christ to humankind",[22] it is well understood that the resurrection of the Lord is the model of our own resurrection. Christ's resurrection is also the cause of our future resurrection: for "death came through a man; hence the resurrection of the dead comes through a man also" (1 Cor 15:21). Through birth in baptism in the Church and in the Holy Spirit we rise sacramentally in the Risen Christ (cf. Col 2:12). The resurrection of those who are Christ's must be considered as the culmination of the mystery already begun in baptism. For this reason, the resurrection is presented as the supreme communion with Christ and with the brethren and also as the highest object of faith: "and thenceforth we shall be with the Lord unceasingly" (1 Thess 4:17; "we shall be" in the plural!). Therefore the final glorious resurrection will be the most perfect communion, even bodily, between those, now risen, who are Christ's, and the glorious Lord. From all this it is evident that the resurrection of the Lord is, as it were, the "space" of our future glorious resurrection and that our own future resurrection must be interpreted as a corporate and an ecclesial event.

Because of this article of faith, Christians of the present day, when they affirm this resurrection of the dead, are subject to ridicule, just as Paul was at the Areopagus (cf. Acts 17:32). The actual state of affairs with regard to this matter is no different from that which Origen described in his time: "Is not the mystery of the resurrection subjected to mockery in the mouth of the unbelievers, because they do not understand it?" [23]

This opposition and such ridicule did not succeed in making Christians of the first centuries desist from professing faith in the resurrection, nor did it succeed in making the earliest theologians desist from expounding it. All the Symbols of the faith, as the one already cited, reach their culminating point in this nodal point of the resurrection. The resurrection of the dead is "the most frequent single theme of pre-Constantinian theology; there is scarcely any early Christian writing that does not speak of the resurrection." [24] Nor ought contemporary opposition deter us today.

The profession of the resurrection was made in a realistic way even from Patristic times. The formula "the resurrection of the *flesh*" seems to have entered into the old Roman Creed, and after it into many others, so that a spiritualised interpretation of the resurrection might be avoided, an

[22] Congregation for the Doctrine of the Faith, *Recentiores episcoporum Synodi*, 2, p. 941.
[23] *Contra Celsum* 1, 7; GCS 2, 60.
[24] A. Stuiber, *Refrigerium interim: Die Vorstellungen vom Zwischenzustand und die frühchristliche Grabeskunst* (Bonn, 1957), p. 101.

interpretation which was attractive to some Christians under the influence of the Gnostics.[25] In the Eleventh Council of Toledo (675) the doctrine was set forth in a fully reflective way: the view is rejected that the resurrection takes place "in flesh without substance or any other kind of flesh"; faith refers to a resurrection in "the very same flesh in which we live, in which we subsist, and in which we move"; this confession is made on the analogy of "the example of our Head", that is, in the light of the resurrection of Christ.[26] This last allusion to the Risen Christ shows that realism must be maintained in such a way that it does not exclude the transformation of the bodies of those living on earth into glorified bodies. But an ethereal body, which would be a new kind of creation, would not correspond to the reality of the resurrection of Christ and consequently would pertain to the realm of fables. The Fathers of this Synod presupposed that concept of the resurrection of Christ which alone is coherent with the biblical affirmations of the empty tomb and of the appearances of the Risen Jesus (the uses of the verb *ôpthê* for expressing the appearances of the Risen Lord should be called to mind as well, and also the appearance narratives, the so-called "scenes of recognition"); moreover, that resurrection keeps in tension the real identity of the body (the body that had been fastened to the cross) and the glorious transformation of that same body. The Risen Jesus not only invited his disciples to touch him, because "a ghost does not have flesh and bones as I do", but also showed to them his hands and his feet, that they might have proof that "it is really I" (Lk 24:39; *'oti egô eimi autós*); in his resurrection, however, he did not return to the conditions of an earthly and mortal life. Holding fast in this way to a realism with regard to the future resurrection of the dead, we should in no way forget that our own true flesh will be conformed to the body of the glory of Christ (cf. Phil 3:21). This body which is now shaped by the soul (*psyche*) will be shaped in the glorious resurrection by the spirit (*pneuma*) (cf. 1 Cor 15:44).

1.2. It is a novelty in the history of this dogma (novel at least since the overcoming of the tendency which appeared in the second century under Gnostic influence) that this realistic presentation should be subjected to criticism by some theologians in our day. To them the traditional representation of the resurrection seems too crude. In particular (they believe) that the too physical descriptions of the resurrection event raise a difficulty. Because of this at times they seek refuge in a certain kind of spiritualised explanation. And for this they demand a new kind of interpretation of the traditional affirmations about the resurrection.

[25] Cf. J. N. D. Kelly, *Early Christian Creeds*, 2nd ed. (London, 1952), pp. 163–65.
[26] DS 540.

There should be a correct theological hermeneutic of eschatological affirmations.[27] These cannot be treated as assertions referring merely to the future (which as such have a different logical status than assertions about past and present realities which can for practical purposes be described as provable objects), because, although with respect to us they have *not yet* taken place, they have *already* been realized in Christ.

In order to avoid exaggerations, whether through excessively physical descriptions, or through a spiritualization of the events, certain fundamental guidelines can be indicated.

1.2.1. A theological hermeneutic involves a full acceptance of revealed truths. God has knowledge of the future, which he can reveal also to people as a truth worthy of faith.

1.2.2. This has been made evident in the resurrection of Christ, to which the entire Patristic literature refers when it speaks of the resurrection of the dead. That which is a growth in hope among the chosen people has been realized in the resurrection of Christ. The resurrection of Christ accepted through faith also says something definitive about the resurrection of the dead.

1.2.3. A conception based on Scripture and reason of people and of the world must be held, one that is appropriate for appreciating the superior vocation of people and of the world as God's creatures. But even more to be emphasized is the fact that "God is 'the last thing' for the creature. Gained, he is heaven; lost, hell; testing, judgment; purifying, purgatory. He himself is that in which the finite dies and through which it rises again in him and to him. He himself is such that he turns himself to the world, namely; in his Son *Jesus Christ* who is the manifestation of God and therefore also the sum of the 'last things'." [28] Due concern for maintaining realism in the doctrine on the risen body must not forget the primacy of the aspects of communion and society with God in Christ (our communion in the Risen Christ will be complete as such when we have risen bodily). This community and society with God in Christ is the last end of humanity, of the Church, and of the world.[29]

1.2.4. The rejection of an eschatological "docetism" also demands that the communion with God in this last stage will not be merely spiritual. God, who in his revelation invites us to this final communion, is at the same time the God of this world of creation. This "first creation" will

---

[27] On hermeneutics, cf. International Theological Commission, "The Interpretation of Dogma" (1988) in *Irish Theological Quarterly* 56 (1990): 251–77. [See chap. 16 of this volume.]

[28] H. U. von Balthasar, "Eschatologie", in *Fragen der Theologie Heute* (Zürich-Köln, 1957), pp. 407–8.

[29] Cf. *DV* 2, *AAS* 58 (1966): 818.

also be in the end assumed into the final glorification. It is in this sense that Vatican Council II declared: "Enduring with charity and its fruits, all that creation which God made on man's account will be unchained from the bondage of vanity."[30]

1.2.5. Finally, we must note that in the Creeds there are dogmatic formulas of a very realistic kind referring to the body of the resurrection. The resurrection will take place "in this flesh, in which now we live".[31] Therefore, the body that now lives and that will ultimately rise is one and the same. This faith shines forth clearly in early Christian theology. Thus Saint Irenaeus admits the "transfiguration" of the flesh, "because being mortal and corruptible it becomes immortal and incorruptible" in the final resurrection;[32] but this resurrection will take place "in the very same bodies in which they had died: for if (the resurrection were) not in these very same (scil. bodies), neither would those who had died be the same as those who would rise."[33] The Fathers therefore think that personal identity cannot be defended in the absence of bodily identity. The Church has never taught that the very same matter is required for the body to be said to be the same. But the cult of relics, whereby Christians profess that the bodies of the saints "who were living members of Christ and the temple of the Holy Spirit" must be "raised and glorified" by Christ,[34] shows that the resurrection cannot be explained independently of the body that once lived.

2. The Parousia of Christ, Our Resurrection

2.1. A fixed moment of time is attributed in the New Testament to the resurrection of the dead. Paul, after he announced that the resurrection of the dead will take place through Christ and in Christ, added: "but each in proper order: Christ the first fruits and then, at his coming (en te parousia autou), all those who belong to him" (1 Cor 15:23). A specific event is designated as the moment of the resurrection of the dead. For by the Greek word parousia is signified the future second coming of the Lord in glory, different from his first coming in humility;[35] the manifestation of his glory (cf. Tit 2:13) and the manifestation of the parousia (cf. 2 Thess 2:8) refer to the same coming. The same event is expressed in the

---

[30] GS 39, AAS 58: 1057.

[31] Fides Damasi, DS 72.

[32] Adversus haereses 5, 13, 3; SCh 153, 172. This fragment is preserved in Greek; for the word "transfiguration" the Greek term Metaschematismos is used.

[33] Ibid., 5, 13, 1; SCh 153, 162, and 164.

[34] Cf. Council of Trent, sess. 25, Decretum de ... reliquiis, DS 1822.

[35] Cf. Nicene-Constantinople Creed, DS 150: "and he will come again in glory".

Gospel according to John (6:54) by the words "on the last day" (cf. also Jn 6:39–40). The same connection of events is given vivid expression in the First Epistle to the Thessalonians, 4:16–17, and is affirmed by a great tradition of the Fathers: "at his coming all men will rise." [36]

A new theory of "the resurrection at the moment of death" is opposed to this affirmation. In the most widely diffused form of this theory, the explanation given appears to pose a grave threat to the realism of the resurrection, since the resurrection is affirmed without any relationship to the body that once lived and is now dead. Concerning "the resurrection in death", the theologians who propose it want to suppress the existence after death of a "separated soul", which they consider to be, as it were, a remnant of Platonism. The fear of Platonism that motivates the theologians espousing resurrection in death is quite understandable; Platonism would be a most serious deviation from Christian faith, since for Christian faith the body is not a prison from which the soul is to be liberated. But precisely for this reason, it is not at all clear that these theologians, in fleeing Platonism, affirm the final or resurrection bodiliness in a way which shows that bodiliness truly involves "this flesh in which now we live". [37] The older formulas of faith spoke with quite another force about the raising up of the very same body that is now alive.

The conceptual separation between a body and a corpse, or the introduction into the notion of body of two diverse concepts (a difference is expressed in German by the words "Leib" and "Körper", while in many other languages it cannot be expressed) are scarcely understood outside academic circles. Pastoral experience shows us that the Christian people are greatly perplexed when they hear sermons affirming that the dead person has already risen while his corpse is still buried. It is to be feared that such sermons have a negative influence on the Christian faithful, and foster today doctrinal confusion. In this secularized world in which the faithful are beguiled by the materialistic philosophy of absolute death, it would be a very serious matter to increase their perplexities.

Moreover, the parousia in the New Testament is a specific event concluding history. Violence is done to the texts of the New Testament if one seeks to explain the parousia as a permanent event that is nothing other than the encounter of an individual with the Lord in his own death.

2.2. "On the last day" (Jn 6:54), when people will rise gloriously, they will reach complete communion with the Risen Christ. This is evident, from the fact that then the communion of people with Christ will be in accord with the full existential reality of both. Moreover, with history at

[36] *Quicumque vult*, DS 76.
[37] *Fides Damasi*, DS 72.

an end, the resurrection of all his fellow servants and brothers and sisters will complete the mystical body of Christ (cf. Rev 6:11). Thus Origen said: "There is only one body that is said to rise in judgment." [38] Rightly, therefore, did the Eleventh Council of Toledo profess that the glorious resurrection of the dead would be not only on the model of Christ but also on "the model of *our Head*". [39]

This community aspect of the final resurrection seems to be dissolved in the theory of resurrection in death, since the latter kind of resurrection would be purely individual. For this reason, some theologians who favour the theory of resurrection in death seek a solution in a so-called *atemporalism*: they say that after death time can in no way exist, and hold that the deaths of people are successive (viewed from the perspective of this world); whereas the resurrection of those people in the life after death, in which there would be no temporal distinctions, is (they think) simultaneous. But this attempted atemporalism, according to which successive individual deaths would coincide with a simultaneous collective resurrection, implies recourse to a philosophy of time quite foreign to biblical thought. The New Testament's way of speaking about the souls of the martyrs does not seem to remove them either from all reality of succession or from all perception of succession (cf. Rev 6:9–11). Similarly, if time should have no meaning after death, not even in some way merely analogous with its terrestrial meaning, it would be difficult to understand why Paul used formulas referring to the future (*anastesontai*) in speaking about their resurrection, when responding to the Thessalonians who were asking about the fate of the dead (cf. 1 Thess 4:13–18). Moreover, a radical denial of any meaning for time in those resurrections, deemed both simultaneous and taking place in the moment of death, does not seem to take sufficiently into account the truly corporeal nature of the resurrection; for a true body cannot be said to exist devoid of all notion of temporality. Even the souls of the blessed, since they are in communion with the Christ who has been raised in a bodily way, cannot be thought of without any connection with time.

3. Communion with Christ Immediately after Death according to the New Testament

3.1. The early Christians, whether they thought that the parousia was imminent or considered it to be quite remote, soon learned through experience

---

[38] *In Leviticum homilia* 7, 2; GCS 29, 378.
[39] DS 540.

that some of them would be taken away by death before the parousia. Paul comforted those who were anxious about the fate of those who had died (cf. 1 Thess 4:13), reminding them of the teaching concerning the future resurrection of the dead: "those who have died in Christ will rise first" (1 Thess 4:16). This datum of faith left other questions open, which were bound to be soon raised. In what state, for example, will such departed be found in the meantime? It was not necessary to devise an altogether new response to this question, since elements for resolving it had long been present in the whole biblical tradition. The people of Israel from the very first stages of their history as it is known to us thought that something of mortal human beings subsisted after death. This thought was already evident in the most ancient representation of what was called *sheol*.

3.2. The ancient Jewish concept of *sheol* was quite imperfect in the first stage of its evolution. It was thought to exist under earth in contrast to heaven. Hence the expression, "to descend into the nether world [*sheol*]" (Gen 37:35; Ps 55:16; etc.). Those who dwell there are called the *refaim*. This Hebrew word lacks a singular, something which seems to indicate that those in *sheol* were not considered to have an individual life. They do not praise God and are separated from him. All, like an anonymous mass, have the same fate. Understood in this way, the survival after death which was attributed to them did not include the idea of retribution.

3.3. Simultaneously with this representation, there began to appear the Israelite belief that the omnipotence of God could bring someone back from *sheol* (1 Sam 2:6; Amos 9:2; etc.). Through this faith the idea of a resurrection of the dead was prepared, the idea expressed in Daniel 12:2 and Isaiah 26:19, and at the time of Jesus widely prevalent among the Jews, with the notable exception of the Sadducees (cf. Mk 12:18).

Faith in the resurrection introduced an evolution in the way of conceiving of *sheol*. *Sheol* was no longer conceived as the common domicile of the dead, but was divided as it were into two floors or levels, of which one was destined for the just and the other for the wicked. The dead remain there up to the last judgment, in which a definitive sentence will be pronounced; but already in these different "floors" they receive a due retribution. This way of conceiving matters appears in *Henoch aethiopicus* 22[40] and is presupposed in Lk 16:19–31.

3.4. A certain intermediate state of this kind is affirmed in the New Testament insofar as an immediate survival after death is taught as a theme quite different from that of the resurrection—a resurrection which in the New Testament is certainly never posited in connection with death. It

[40] GCS 5, 51–55.

must also be added that the affirmation of this survival underscores, as a cardinal idea, communion with Christ.

Thus the crucified Jesus promises to the good thief: "I assure you [*amen*], this day you will be with me in paradise" (Lk 23:43). Paradise is the Jewish technical term corresponding to the expression "Gan Eden". But it is affirmed, without being further described; the fundamental idea is that Jesus wishes to receive the good thief into communion with him immediately after death. The same hope is evidenced by Stephen in his stoning; in the words, "I see the heavens opened and the Son of Man standing at God's right hand" (Acts 7:56), along with his final prayer, "Lord Jesus, receive my spirit" (Acts 7:59), he affirms that he hopes to be immediately received by Jesus into communion with him.

In John 14:1–3, Jesus speaks to his disciples of the many mansions which are in his Father's house. "I am indeed going to prepare a place for you, and then I shall come back to take you with me, that where I am you also may be" (v. 3). It can hardly be doubted that these words refer to the time of the death of the disciples and not to the parousia, which in the Gospel according to John passes to a secondary level (although not in the First Epistle of John). Again, the idea of communion with Christ is central. He is not only "the way [but] the truth and the life" (Jn 14:6). The similarity between the words *monai* (mansions) and *menein* (to remain) is also to be noted. Jesus, referring to earthly life, exhorts us: "Abide in me, as I do in you" (Jn 15:4), "Abide in my love" (v. 9). Already on earth, "Anyone who loves me will be true to my word, and my Father will love him; we will come to him and make our dwelling place [our mansion; *monên*] with him" (Jn 14:23). This "mansion", which is communion, becomes more intense after death.

3.5. Paul merits special attention. The principal passage in Paul regarding this intermediate state is Philippians 1:21–24: "For, to me, 'life' means Christ; hence dying is so much gain. If, on the other hand, I am to go on living in the flesh, that means productive toil for me—and I do not know which to prefer. I am strongly attracted by both: I long to be freed from this life and to be with Christ, for that is the far better thing; yet it is more urgent that I remain alive for your sakes." In v. 21 "life" (*to zen*) is the subject and "Christ" is the predicate. Thus the idea of communion with Christ is always emphasized, a life which, begun on earth, is declared to be the unique object of hope in the state after death: "to be with Christ" (v. 23). The communion after death is more intense and for that reason the state after death is desirable.

Paul does not proceed from a perspective of contempt for earthly life; he finally decides to remain "in the flesh" (cf. v. 25). Paul naturally does not desire death (cf. 2 Cor 5:2–4). To lose one's body is painful. It is customary to contrast the attitudes of Socrates and of Jesus before death. Socrates considers death to be the liberation of the soul from the prison or tomb (*sema*) of the body (*soma*); Jesus, who hands himself over for the sins of the world (cf. Jn 10:15), in the garden of Gethsemani trembles at the prospect of his approaching death (cf. Mk 14:33). Nor is Paul's attitude unlike that of Jesus. The state after death is desirable only because in the New Testament (the exception is Luke 16:19–31, where another and totally different context is present) it always implies union with Christ.

It would be quite false to affirm that in Paul there is an evolution from a faith in the resurrection to a faith in immortality. Both coexisted in him from the beginning. In the same Epistle to the Philippians in which he explained the reason why an intermediate state can be hoped for, he speaks with great joy of the expectation of the parousia of the Lord, "who will give a new form to this lowly body of ours and remake it according to the pattern of his glorified body" (Phil 3:21). Therefore an intermediate state is conceived of as transitory, something acceptable because of the union with Christ that it implies, but in such a way that the resurrection of the body always remains as the supreme hope: "This corruptible body must be clothed with incorruptibility, this mortal body with immortality" (1 Cor 15:53).

4. *The Reality of the Resurrection in the Context of Theology Today*

4.1. One can easily grasp from this twofold doctrinal line of reasoning in the New Testament that the whole Christian tradition, without any important exceptions, has, up to our own day, conceived of the object of eschatological hope as embracing two phases. Between the death of people and the consummation of the world, it believes that a conscious element of people subsists which it calls by the name of "soul" (*psyche*), a term used also by Holy Scripture (cf. Wis 3:1; Mt 10:28); this element is already in that phase the subject of retribution. At the parousia of the Lord which will take place at the end of history, there is to be expected the blessed resurrection of those "who are Christ's" (1 Cor 15:23). From that moment, the eternal glorification of the whole person who has now been raised begins. The survival of a conscious soul prior to the resurrection safeguards the continuity and identity of subsistence between the person who lived and the person who will rise, inasmuch as in virtue of such a survival the concrete individual never totally ceases to exist.

4.2. As exceptions in the face of this tradition must be remembered certain Christians of the second century who, under the influence of the

Gnostics, were opposed to the "salvation of the flesh", calling the resurrection the mere survival of a soul endowed with a kind of corporeity.[41] Another exception is the *thnêtopsychism* of Tatian and some Arabian heretics, who thought that human beings died so totally that not even their souls survived. The final resurrection was conceived as a new creation of the dead person from nothing.[42]

After these there are, for all practical purposes, no exceptions on this theme almost up to our own days. Nor does Martin Luther constitute an exception, since he admitted the twofold eschatological phase. For him death is "the separation of the soul from the body";[43] he himself held that souls survive between death and the final resurrection, although he expressed doubts about the way of conceiving the state in which souls are found between death and the resurrection: for at times he admitted that perhaps the saints in heaven pray for us,[44] while elsewhere he rather thought that these souls were in a state of sleep.[45] He therefore never denied an intermediate state, although at times he interpreted it in a way divergent from Catholic faith.[46] Lutheran orthodoxy keeps this double phase, abandoning the idea of the sleep of the souls of the departed.

4.3. During the twentieth century for the first time the denial of the twofold phase began to be propagated. The new current of thought appeared among some evangelical theologians and, indeed, in the form of

---

[41] Tertullian attacked these Christians as new kinds of Sadducees (*De resurrectione mortuorum* 2, 2; CCL 2, 922). St. Irenaeus refuted them as persons who "were not willing to understand that, if things were as they say, the Lord himself, in whom they say they believe, would not have risen on the third day but rather, expiring upon the cross, would immediately have gone above, leaving his body on the earth" (*Adversus haereses* 5, 31, 1; SCh 153, 388–90). For Irenaeus the whole "economy" of God has its unity through *the flesh*: God made man of *flesh* and sent his Son in *the flesh* so that he might save the flesh of man (ibid., 5, 14, 1; SCh 153, 182). Here we should call to mind that the formula "the resurrection of the flesh" entered into the Creeds of the faith precisely to exclude this influence of the Gnostics (cf. above, note 25).

[42] According to Eusebius of Caesarea (*Historia ecclesiastica* 6, 37; GCS 9/2, 592), Origen persuaded these Arabian heretics of their error.

[43] *Vorlesungen über 1. Mose 22, 11*; WA 218.

[44] *Articuli Schmalkaldenses* 2, 2, in *Die Bekenntnisschriften der Evangelisch-lutherischen Kirche*, 3rd ed. (Göttingen, 1956), p. 425.

[45] *Brief am Amsdorf* (Wartburg, 13 January 1522); WA, *Briefwechsel*, 2, 422.

[46] Cf. Benedict XII, Const. *Benedictus Deus* (DS 1000), where it is affirmed that the souls of the saints, "immediately after death" and "before the resumption of their bodies and the general judgement" "have seen and do see the divine essence with an intuitive and even face-to-face vision, without the mediation of any creature by way of object of vision; rather the divine essence immediately manifests itself to them, plainly, clearly, and openly, and in this vision they enjoy the divine essence; moreover, by this vision and enjoyment the souls of those who have already died are truly blessed and have eternal life and rest."

total death (*Ganztod*, like the ancient *thnētopsychism*) and of a resurrection at the end of time explained as a creation from nothing. The reasons to which appeal was made were predominantly confessional: before God people can present nothing of their own, neither their works nor the natural immortality of their souls; the seriousness of death could only be maintained if it affected the entire person and not only his body; since death is the punishment of sin and the whole person is a sinner, the whole person must be affected by death lest it be understood that the soul, in which the root of sin is found, is liberated from death. Little by little, and as it were programmatically, a new eschatological schema was proposed: the resurrection *alone*, in place of immortality *and* the resurrection.

This first form of the current of thought presented many difficulties: if the whole person disappears in death, God could create a person entirely equivalent to him/her; but if there is no existential continuity between the two, then that second person cannot be the same as the first. Because of this, new theories were elaborated that affirmed the resurrection *in death*, lest some empty space arise between death and the parousia. But it must be acknowledged that in this a theme is introduced which is unknown to the New Testament, since the New Testament always speaks of the resurrection at the parousia of the Lord, never at the time of man's death.[47] When the new current of thought began to pass over to some Catholic theologians, the Holy See, in a letter sent to all the bishops,[48] considered it to be incompatible with a legitimate theological pluralism.

4.4. All these theories ought to be assessed in the light of a dispassionate consideration of the biblical testimony and of the history of tradition both as to eschatology itself and as to its anthropological presuppositions. But above all it may justly be asked whether a current of thought can be rescued from all the motives that have contributed to its origin. This is particularly important when de facto a definite theological line has sprung from non-Catholic confessional principles.

Moreover, we must note the disadvantages for ecumenical dialogue that are caused by this novel conception. Although the new tendency arose among some evangelical theologians, it does not correspond to the great tradition of Lutheran orthodoxy, which even now is prevalent among the faithful of that confession. The persuasion is even stronger among separated Eastern Christians regarding an eschatology of souls that is prior to

---

[47] In section 2 above allusion was made to the principal theories by which resurrection in death is proposed today. Also, in section 4.2 above a few predecessors of this tendency were mentioned who flourished in Patristic times.

[48] Congregation for the Doctrine of the Faith, *Recentiores episcoporum Synodi*, pp. 939–43.

the resurrection of the dead. All these Christians consider the eschatology of the soul necessary, because they understand the resurrection of the dead in connection with the parousia of Christ.[49] Indeed, if we look beyond the ambit of Christian confessions, we find that the eschatology of the soul is considered an almost universal good by non-Christian religions.

In traditional Christian thought the eschatology of the soul is a state in which, during the course of history, brothers and sisters in Christ are successively united with him and in him. The idea of a family union of souls through death is not foreign to many African religions and offers the opportunity for interreligious dialogue with them. It ought further to be added that in Christianity such a union reaches its culmination at the end of history when people will be led to their full, existential and therefore bodily reality, through the resurrection.

4.5. In the history of this question, another way of arguing for a single phase has more recently been proposed. The objection is raised that the schema of a twofold phase arose from a certain contamination produced by Hellenism. The idea which is the Bible's uniquely is that of resurrection; on the other hand, the immortality of the soul would stem from Greek philosophy. So, it is proposed that Christian eschatology be purged of every accretion of Hellenism.

It must be confessed that the idea of the resurrection is somewhat recent in Holy Scripture (Daniel 12:1–3 is the first undisputed text concerning it). The most ancient concept of the Jews affirmed rather the survival of the shades of people who had lived (*refaim*) in a sort of common house of the dead (*sheol*), which was different from their graves. This way of thinking is sufficiently similar to that whereby Homer spoke of the souls (*psychai*) in the lower world (*Hades*). This parallelism between Hebrew and Greek culture, which is found also in other periods, makes their supposed opposition doubtful. In antiquity the cultural similarities and mutual influences of one culture upon another through the whole of the Mediterranean world were much greater than is often thought, and they do not constitute a phenomenon later than Sacred Scripture and contaminating its message.

Looking at matters from another perspective it cannot be supposed that Hebrew categories alone were the instrument of divine revelation. God has spoken "in many and varied ways" (Heb 1:1). The books of Sacred Scripture in which inspiration is expressed in Greek words and cultural concepts must be considered as enjoying no less authority than those which were written in Hebrew or Aramaic.

---

[49] For evangelical Christians cf. *Confessio Augustana*, 17, in *Die Bekenntnisschriften der evangilisch-lutherischen Kirche*, p. 73.

Finally, it is not possible to speak of a Hebrew and a Greek mentality as if it were a matter of simple unities. The imperfect eschatological conceptions of the patriarchs were perfected by later revelation. Greek philosophy is not reducible to Platonism or Neoplatonism. It ought not to be forgotten that not a few of the Fathers were in touch not only with middle Platonism but also with Stoicism.[50] For this reason both the history of revelation and tradition and its relationships with Hebrew and Greek culture must be stated with care.

5. *People Called to Resurrection*

5.1. The Second Vatican Council teaches: "Though made of body and soul, man is one. Through his bodily composition he gathers to himself the elements of the material world; thus they reach their crown through him, and through him raise their voice in free praise of the Creator.... Now, man is not wrong when he regards himself as superior to bodily concerns, and as more than a speck of nature or a nameless constituent of the city of man. For by his interior qualities he outstrips the whole sum of mere things. He plunges into the depths of reality whenever he enters into his own heart; God, Who probes the heart, awaits him there; there he discerns his proper destiny beneath the eyes of God. Thus, when he recognizes in himself a spiritual and immortal soul, he is not being mocked by a fantasy born only of physical or social influences, but is rather laying hold of the proper truth of the matter."[51] By these words the Council acknowledged the value of the spontaneous and elemental experience through which people perceive themselves to be superior to all other earthly creatures and indeed capable by knowledge and love of possessing God. The basic difference between people and these other creatures appears in the innate desire for happiness which causes man to reject and abhor the idea of the total destruction of his person; "he rebels against death because he bears in himself an eternal seed which cannot be reduced to sheer matter."[52] Because this immortal soul is spiritual, the Church holds that God is its creator for every person.[53]

This anthropology makes possible the already noted eschatology of the twofold phase. Since this Christian anthropology includes a *duality* of

---

[50] Cf. M. Spanneut, *Le Stoïcisme des Pères de l'Église: De Clément de Roma à Clément d'Alexandrie* (Paris, 1957).

[51] GS 14, *AAS* 58: 1035–36.

[52] Ibid., *AAS* 58: 1038.

[53] Paul VI, *Credo of the People of God*, 8, p. 436. Cf. also Pius XII, Encyclical *Humani Generis*, DS 3896.

elements (the "body-soul" schema) which can be so separated that one of them ("the spiritual and immortal soul") subsists and endures separately, an accusation is sometimes made of a Platonic dualism. The word "dualism" can be understood in many ways. For this reason, when we speak of Christian anthropology, it is better to use the word "duality". From another perspective, since in the Christian tradition the state of the survival of the soul after death is neither definitive nor ontologically supreme, but "intermediate" and transitory and ultimately ordered to the resurrection, Christian anthropology has characteristics proper to itself and quite different from the anthropology of the Platonic philosophers.[54]

5.2. Moreover, Christian anthropology cannot be confused with Platonic dualism inasmuch as in the former, person is not a mere soul such that the body ought to be abhorred as a prison. Christians are not ashamed of their bodies, as Plotinus was.[55] The hope of a resurrection would have seemed absurd to Platonists, because one cannot put one's hope in a return to prison. But this hope of the resurrection is central to the New Testament. In consequence of this hope, early Christian theology considered the separated soul "half a person", and from this deduced that the resurrection ought to follow: "How unfitting it would be for God to raise half a person to salvation."[56] The common mind of the Fathers was well expressed by Saint Augustine, when he wrote concerning the separated soul: "There is in it a certain natural appetite for ruling a body: ... while there is no underlying body for that appetite to take rest."[57]

5.3. The anthropology of duality is found in Matthew 10:28: "Do not fear those who deprive the body of life but cannot destroy the soul. Rather, fear him who can destroy both body and soul in Gehenna." This "logion", understood in the light of the anthropology and eschatology of the period, teaches us that it has been willed by God that the soul survives after earthly death until it is united once more to the body in the resurrection. It is not surprising that these words of the Lord were spoken in the context of giving a teaching about martyrdom. Biblical history shows that martyrdom for the truth constitutes a privileged moment in which the creation accomplished by God, the future eschatological resurrection, and

---

[54] Among the Jews to this day, when they rise from sleep a *berekah* is recited in which a distinction is made between "souls" and the "mortal bodies", with a further allusion to the "resurrection". The text for this comes from the Babylonian Talmud: cf. *Seder R. Amram Gaon*, part 1, *Hebrew Text with Critical Apparatus, Translation with Notes and Introduction* by D. Hedegard (Lund, 1951), p. 13.

[55] Cf. Porphyry, *De Plotini vita* 1; *Plotins Schriften*, ed. R. Harder, vol. 5 (Hamburg, 1958), p. 2. Cf. also St. Augustine, *De civitate Dei* 22, 26 (CCL 48, 853) for the position of Porphyry.

[56] Tertullian, *De resurrectione mortuorum* 34, 3; CCL 2, 964.

[57] St. Augustine, *De Genesi ad litteram* 12, 35; CSEL 28/1, 432–33.

the promise of life eternal are all illuminated by the light of faith (cf. 2 Mac 7, 9, 11, 14, 22–23, 28 and 36).

In the book of Wisdom too the revelation of the eschatology of souls is placed in a context in which it is said of those who "suffered torment before men" (Wis 3:4), that although "in the view of the foolish they seemed to be dead, and their passing away was thought an affliction" (Wis 3:2), nonetheless "the souls of the just are in the hand of God" (Wis 3:1). This eschatology of souls is joined in the same book with the clear affirmation of the power of God to effect the resurrection of people (cf. Wis 16:13–14).

5.4. In faithfully accepting the words of our Lord in Matthew 10:28, "the Church affirms the continuity and subsistence after death of a spiritual element, endowed with consciousness and will, so that the 'human I' subsists, while lacking in the interim the complement of its body."[58] This affirmation is rooted in the characteristic duality of Christian anthropology.

Sometimes, however, certain words of Saint Thomas are opposed to this assertion, for he said: "My soul is not I."[59] But the words immediately preceding constitute the context for this statement, and in them he had emphasized that the soul is a part of people. This doctrine is constant in Saint Thomas in his *Summa Theologiae*: for when it is objected that "the separated soul is an individual substance of a rational nature, but it is not however a person", he replies: "The soul is a part of the human species: and therefore, although it is separated, nevertheless since it retains the nature of unibility, it cannot be called an individual substance, which is hypostasis, or first substance; nor likewise can the hand or any other part of a person. And thus there belongs to it neither the definition nor the name of person."[60] In this sense, that is, inasmuch as the human soul is not the entire person, it can be said that the soul is not the "I" or the person. Indeed, this ought to be held so that the traditional line of Christian anthropology can be maintained. Therefore, arguing from this, Saint Thomas deduced in the separated soul an appetite for the body or for the resurrection.[61] This position of Saint Thomas manifests the traditional

---

[58] Congregation for the Doctrine of the Faith, *Recentiores episcoporum Synodi*, 3, p. 941.

[59] *Super primam epistolam ad Corinthios* 15, 2, 924, in *Super epistolas Sancti Pauli lectura*, ed. R. Cai, vol. 1 (Taurini-Romae, 1953), p. 411.

[60] *STh* I, q. 29, a. 1, 5 and ad 5. When St. Thomas considers it erroneous "to say that Christ was a man during the three days of his death" (III, q. 50, a. 4, c.), he holds that the union of soul and flesh are of the very meaning of man.

[61] In the place cited in note 59 St. Thomas wrote: "It is evident that the soul is naturally united to the body, but is separated from it against its own nature and *per accidens*. Whence the soul, cut off from the body, while it is without the body is imperfect. But it is impossible

sense of Christian anthropology as that had been already expressed by Saint Augustine.[62]

However, in another sense it can and ought to be said that "the 'human I' itself" subsists in the separated soul.[63] Through it, since it is the conscious and subsistent element of people, we are able to hold a true continuity between the person who once lived on earth and the person who will rise; without such a continuity of a certain subsisting human element the person who once lived on earth and the one who is to rise would not be the same "I". Through the separated soul the acts of the intellect and will that were done on earth remain after death. Although separated, it performs personal acts of understanding and will. Moreover, the subsistence of the separated soul is clear from the practice of the Church, which directs its prayers to the souls of the blessed.

From these considerations it is evident that the separated soul is, on the one hand, an ontologically incomplete reality and, on the other hand, is conscious; indeed, according to the definition of Benedict XII, the souls of the saints fully purified "immediately after death" and indeed already as separated ("before the reassuming of their bodies") enjoy the full beatitude of the intuitive vision of God.[64] Such beatitude is perfect in itself and nothing specifically superior can be given. The glorious transformation of the body in the resurrection is itself an effect of this vision upon the body; in this sense, Paul speaks of a spiritual body or a body shaped under the influence of the "spirit" and not merely under the influence of the soul ("spiritual body") (cf. 1 Cor 15:44).

The final resurrection also involves an ecclesial aspect with respect to the beatitude of the individual soul, inasmuch as in the end all brothers and sisters who are Christ's will arrive at their fullness (cf. Rev. 6:11). Then the whole of creation will be subject to Christ (cf. 1 Cor 15:27–28) and thus it too "will be freed from its slavery to corruption" (Rom 8:21).

6. Christian Death

6.1. The characteristically Christian anthropological conception offers a specific understanding of the meaning of death. Since in Christian anthropology the body is not a prison from which a prisoner hopes to

---

that that which is natural and *per se* be finite and as it were nothing, that that which is contrary to nature and *per accidens* be infinite, if the soul were to endure forever without a body."

[62] Cf. the text of St. Augustine to which reference is made in note 57.

[63] Congregation for the Doctrine of the Faith, *Recentiores episcoporum Synodi*, 3, p. 941.

[64] *Benedictus Deus*, DS 1000.

escape, nor a kind of vestment that can easily be put aside, death, naturally considered, is not an object of human hope or an event that human beings can tranquilly embrace without overcoming their antecedent natural repugnance. No one ought to be ashamed of the natural feelings of repugnance which are experienced in the face of death, since our Lord himself willed to suffer these before his own death, and Paul testifies that he had experienced them: "We do not wish to be stripped naked but to be clothed again" (2 Cor 5:4). Death intrinsically tears people asunder. Indeed, since the person is not the soul alone, but the body and soul essentially united, death affects the person.

The absurdity of death appears even more radically if we consider that death, though natural, exists in the historical order against the will of God (cf. Wis 1:13–14; 2:23–24): for "man would have been immune" from bodily death "had he not sinned".[65] Death must be accepted by Christians with a certain sense of penance, for Christians have before their eyes the words of Paul: "The wages of sin is death" (Rom 6:23).

It is also natural that Christians suffer at the death of persons whom they love. "Jesus wept" over his dead friend Lazarus (Jn 11:35). We too can and ought to weep over our dead friends.

6.2. The repugnance that people experience in the face of death and the possibility of overcoming this repugnance constitute a characteristically human attitude utterly different from that of any other animal. In this way death is an occasion in which people can and ought to show themselves as people. Christians can, moreover, overcome the fear of death, relying on other motives.

Faith and hope teach us another face of death. Jesus faced the fear of death under the light of the will of his Father (cf. Mk 14:36). He died to "free those who through fear of death had been slaves their whole life long" (Heb 2:15). Consequently, Paul can already have the desire to be dissolved and be with Christ; that communion with Christ after death was considered by Paul to be "much better" than the state of his present life (cf. Phil 1:23). The advantage of this life consists in that "we are present in body" and thus have our full existential reality; but relative to our full communion after death "we are far away from the Lord" (cf. 2 Cor 5:6). Although through death we stray away from our body and are deprived of our full existential plenitude, we accept death in good heart; indeed, we can hope that with death's coming "we will be at home with the Lord" (2 Cor 5:8). This mystical hope of a communion after death with Christ, which can coexist with a natural fear of death, appears again and again in the spiritual tradition of the Church, especially among the saints,

---

[65] GS 18, AAS 58: 1038.

and must be understood in its true meaning. When this hope leads one to praise God for death, such praise is in no way rooted in a positive estimation of the state in which the soul lacks the body, but in the hope of possessing the Lord through death.[66] Then death is considered as a door leading to communion after death with Christ, and not as freeing the soul from a body that burdened it.

In the Eastern tradition there is frequently thought of the goodness of death inasmuch as it is the very condition of and way to a future glorious resurrection. "Therefore, if it cannot happen that nature be led to a better form and state without the resurrection, and if the resurrection cannot take place unless death precedes, then *death becomes a good thing*, inasmuch as it is for us the beginning and the way of changing for the better."[67] Christ has given this goodness to death through his death and resurrection: "As if extending his hand to what was lying in the grave, and looking therefore upon our corpse, he drew so close to death that to the degree that he touched mortality so with his body he gave to nature the beginning of the resurrection."[68] In this sense, Christ "changed sunset to sunrise".[69]

The pain and sickness that are the beginning of death ought also to be taken up by Christians in a new way. In themselves they are endured as vexatious, but even more so insofar as they are signs of the gradual dissolution of the body.[70] But now indeed through the acceptance of the pain and sickness permitted by the will of God, we become partakers in the passion of Christ, and through offering them up we are united to that act whereby the Lord offered his own life to his Father for the salvation of the world. Each one of us ought to affirm, as did Paul of old: "In my own flesh I fill up what is lacking in the sufferings of Christ for the sake of his body, the Church" (Col 1:24). We are led to attain to the glory of the Risen Christ through our association with his passion: "Continually we carry about in our bodies the dying of Christ, so that in our bodies the life of Christ may also be revealed" (2 Cor 4:10).[71]

---

[66] Cf. *Canticum fratris Solis*, 12–13, in *Opuscula Sancti Patris Francisci Assisiensis*, ed. C. Esser (Grottaferrata, 1978), pp. 85f.: "You are praised, my Lord, for our sister bodily death. . . . Blessed are those whom death finds in your most holy will, because a second death will not bring them evil."

[67] St. Gregory of Nyssa, *Oratio consolatoria in Pulcheriam*, in *Sermones*, ed. G. Heil, A. Van Heck, E. Gebhardt, and A. Spira, Gregorii Nysseni opera 9 (series eds. W. Jaeger and H. Langerbeck) (Leiden, 1967), p. 472.

[68] St. Gregory of Nyssa, *Oratio catechetica magna* 32, in *The Catechetical Oration of Gregory of Nyssa*, ed. J. H. Strawley (Cambridge, 1903), p. 116.

[69] St. Clement of Alexandria, *Protrepticus* 11; GCS 12, 80.

[70] GS 18, AAS 58: 1038.

[71] Cf. John Paul II, Apostolic Letter *Salvifici doloris*, AAS 76 (1984): 201–50.

In the same way it is not right for us to be saddened over the death of our friends "as are the others who do not have hope" (1 Thess 4:13). For them, with "tearful cries and groans it is often the custom to bewail the wretchedness of those who die, or even their complete extinction"; we, on the other hand, like Augustine thinking of his mother's death, are consoled by this thought: "she [Monica] died neither miserably nor completely." [72]

6.3. This positive aspect of death is only reached through that way of dying which the New Testament calls "death in the Lord": "Blessed are the dead who die in the Lord" (Rev 14:13). This "death in the Lord" is to be hoped for inasmuch as it leads to beatitude and is prepared for by a holy life: "Yes, the Spirit says, they shall find rest from their labours, for their good works accompany them" (Rev 14:13). Thus life on earth is ordered to communion with Christ after death, a communion which is already effective in the state of the separated soul, although ontologically imperfect and incomplete.[73] Because communion with Christ is of higher value than existential fullness, life on earth cannot be considered the greatest good. This justifies that mystic hope of death which, as we have said, is frequent among the saints.

Through a holy life, to which God calls us by his grace and helps us by his aid, the original bond between sin and death is as it were broken, not because death is physically overcome, but inasmuch as it begins to lead to life eternal. Such a way of dying is a participation in the paschal mystery of Christ. The sacraments prepare us for such a death. The baptism in which we die mystically to sin consecrates us for participating in the resurrection of the Lord (cf. Rom 6:3–7). Through the reception of the Eucharist, which is the "medicine of immortality",[74] we obtain a pledge of participating in the resurrection of Christ.

Death in the Lord implies the possibility of another way of dying, namely death outside the Lord, which leads to a second death (cf. Rev 20:14). For in this death, the power of sin through which death entered (cf. Rom 5:12) manifests to the fullest extent its capacity to separate us from God.

6.4. Christian customs relative to the burial of the corpses of the faithful were quickly formed, and indeed were formed under the influence of faith in the resurrection of the dead. Ways of speaking, in words such as "cemetery" (a Greek word that signifies a "sleeping place") or "deposit" (the Latin *depositio*, involving Christ's right to take back the body of the

---

[72] *Confessions* 9, 12, 29; CCL 27, 150.

[73] Cf. Benedict XII, *Benedictus Deus*, DS 1000.

[74] St. Ignatius of Antioch, *Ad Ephesios* 20, 2; Funk, 1:230.

Christian as opposed to considering it as a gift, *donatio*), presuppose this faith. It was considered a "duty of people" to exercise care for the body of the dead (the corpse); but "if those who do not believe in the resurrection of the flesh do these things", even more particularly are they to be carried out by those "who believe that this obligation is to be fulfilled for a body which is dead but will rise and live for all eternity; for then it is also in a way to witness to this very faith." [75]

For a long time the cremation of corpses was forbidden,[76] because historically this was seen to be connected with a Neoplatonic mentality which intended the destruction of the body as a way of freeing the soul more promptly from prison[77] (more recently, however, it implied a materialistic or agnostic attitude). The Church no longer prohibits this, "unless it is chosen for reasons contrary to Christian doctrine." [78] Care must be taken lest the contemporary spread of cremation even among Catholics should in any way render obscure their right understanding about the resurrection of the flesh.

7. The "Living Fellowship" of All Members of the Church in Christ [79]

7.1. The ecclesiology of communion, which is strongly characteristic of the Second Vatican Council, believes that death does not undo the communion of saints, that is that union in the bond of love of all the brethren in Christ: "on the contrary", it is enriched "according to the perpetual faith of the Church ... by communication of spiritual goods." [80] Faith gives to the wayfaring Christians on earth "the power to be united in Christ with [their] loved ones who have already been snatched away by death." [81] It is in particular through the various forms of prayer that this is effected.

The celestial liturgy is a large feature of Saint John's Apocalypse. The souls of the blessed take part in it. In the liturgy on earth it is [in] "celebrating the Eucharistic sacrifice [that] we are most closely united to the Church in heaven in communion with and venerating the memory first

---

[75] St. Augustine, *De cura pro mortuis gerenda* 18, 22; CSEL 41, 658–59.

[76] Cf. Holy Office, *Decretum*, 15 December 1886, DS 3195–96; *Instructio*, 19 June 1926, DS 3680.

[77] Cf. F. Cumont, *Lux perpetua* (Paris, 1949), p. 290.

[78] CIC 1176, 3.

[79] LG 51, *AAS* 57: 57.

[80] LG 49, *AAS* 57: 55.

[81] GS 18, *AAS* 58: 1038.

of all of the glorious ever-Virgin Mary, of Blessed Joseph and the blessed apostles and martyrs and of all the saints." [82] In fact, in the celebration of the earthly liturgy a desire to unite it with the heavenly liturgy is expressed. This is shown in the Roman anaphora, not alone in the *Communicantes* prayer (at least in its present form), but in the transition from preface to canon and in the prayer within the canon, *Supplices te rogamus*, where the petition is made that the earthly offering be taken aloft to the altar in Heaven.

This heavenly liturgy however is not simply a matter of praise. The Lamb who was slain is at the centre (cf. Rev 5:6), to wit, "Christ Jesus, who died, who was raised again moreover, who is at God's right hand, and who also intercedes for us" (Rom 8:34; cf. Heb 7:25). Since the souls of the blessed partake in this liturgy of intercession, they are able to care for us as we journey on our pilgrim way; "they are a great help to our weakness by their intercession and brotherly concern." [83] Because we are made conscious of this conjoined heavenly and earthly liturgy, "it is supremely fitting ... that we love these friends and coheirs of Jesus Christ, who are also our brothers and extraordinary benefactors, [and] that we render due thanks to God for them." [84]

In addition the Church earnestly exhorts us "to implore them for blessings from God through his Son, Jesus Christ, our Lord, our sole redeemer and saviour and to commit ourselves to their prayers and assistance." [85] An invocation of the saints of this nature is an act whereby the believer in Christ commits himself with confidence to their charity. Since God is the source of all love (cf. Rom 5:5), any invocation of the saints is an acknowledgement of God as the ultimate foundation of the charity of the saints, and tends in the last analysis towards Him.

7.2. This concept of invocation is completely different from the notion of evoking spirits. The Second Vatican Council, while commending us to invoke the souls of the blessed, calls on us to remember the principal documents of the Church's magisterium aimed "against any form whatsoever of the evocation of spirits". [86] This enduring interdiction has biblical roots already in the Old Testament (Deut 18:10–14; cf. also Ex 22:17; Lev 19:31; 20:6, 27). A most famous instance is the evocation of the spirit of Samuel (*'ôbôt*) on the part of King Saul (1 Sam 28:3–25) to which Scripture attributes both the rejection and the death of Saul: "Saul

---

[82] LG 50, *AAS* 57: 57.

[83] Paul VI, *Profession of Faith*, 29, *AAS* 60 (1968): 444.

[84] LG 50, *AAS* 57: 56.

[85] Council of Trent, Sess. 25, *Decretum de invocatione ... Sanctorum*, DS 1821; LG 15f., *AAS* 57.

[86] LG 49, note 148 [chapter 7, note 2], *AAS* 57: 19f.

died because he committed evil inasmuch as he transgressed the divine mandate, failing to observe it, and, what is more, consulted ghosts and not the Lord for guidance. And the Lord killed him and transferred his kingdom to David, the son of Jesse" (1 Chron 10:13–14). In the New Testament the Apostles sustain this prohibition and banish all magical practices (Acts 13:6–12; 16:16–18; 19:11–20).

The Doctrinal Commission at the Second Vatican Council explained the meaning of "evocation": it would involve any method whereby "the effort is made by human techniques to establish communication in the external order with spirits or disembodied souls in the hope of acquiring various kinds of information and forms of help." [87] This complex of techniques is commonly known as "spiritualism". As often as not—as the response referred to makes clear—the intention is to use the evocation of spirits to obtain hidden information. The faithful are directed in all that concerns such matters to God's own revelation. "They have Moses and the prophets; let them heed them" (Lk 16:29). Any further curiosity about postmortem affairs would be utterly foolish and should therefore be simply repressed.

There are sects today who reject the Catholic invocation of saints by claiming it falls under the biblical prohibition. In so doing they are failing to distinguish it from the evocation of spirits. On our side, as we urge the invocation of the saints to the faithful, we must teach them the nature of that invocation in such a way as to give the sects no handle for such misunderstanding.

7.3. As to the question of the need for purification of souls of the departed, "the pilgrim Church from the very first ages of the Christian religion ... [offered] suffrages for them." [88] The Church indeed believes that such a purification is benefitted "by the suffrages of the faithful on earth, that is, by the sacrifice of the Mass, prayer, alms-giving, and other pious works, which by custom and in accordance with what the Church lays down have been offered by the faithful for fellow faithful." [89] Since the postconciliar liturgical renewal *The General Instruction on the Roman Missal* gives an excellent interpretation of this multiple symbiosis of all the members of the Church, which reaches its peak in the liturgical celebration of the Eucharist: the intercessions signify "that the Eucharist is celebrated in communion with the whole Church, in heaven and on earth, and that an offering is made for the Church itself and all the members, living and dead, who are called to share in the

---

[87] Chapter VII *de Ecclesia*, response to *modus* 35; *Acta Synodalia* 3/8, p. 144.

[88] *LG* 50, *AAS* 57: 55.

[89] Council of Florence, *Decretum pro graecis*, DS 1304.

redemption and salvation that were won by the Body and Blood of Christ." [90]

8. *The Purification of the Soul Prior to Meeting Christ in His Glory*

8.1. When the magisterium of the Church asserts that the souls of the sanctified will enjoy the beatific vision of God and perfect union with Christ shortly after death, there is a presupposition: it is souls which are purified that are meant.[91] Therefore, the words of Psalm 15:1–2, albeit that they have the earthly sanctuary in mind, have a great bearing on the subject of life after death. "Lord, who will live in your tabernacle? Who will find rest on your holy mountain? He who enters without a blemish." [92] For nothing soiled can approach the divine presence.

These words express a consciousness of a reality which is so fundamental that, one way or another, a certain surmise of the necessity of postmortem purification exists in many of the great historical religions.

The Church also holds that any stain is an impediment when it comes to our intimate meeting with God and Christ. This principle is not concerned only with stains which break or destroy friendship with God and which, therefore, should they persist in death, make a meeting with God definitively impossible (grave sins), but also with those which darken such a friendship and require a prior purification, so as to make possible such a meeting with God and Christ. To this class belong the so-called "daily sins", which we call venial,[93] and also those remains of sin which may persist in the justified when guilt has been remitted and its attendant eternal punishment.[94] The sacrament of the Anointing of the Sick is aimed at wiping away before death these remains of sin.[95] Only if we are made like to Christ can we have communion with God (cf. Rom 8:29).

---

[90] *Missale Romanum* (editio typica 1970), *Institutio generalis Missalis Romani*, 55, g, p. 40.

[91] Cf. Benedict XII, *Benedictus Deus*, DS 1000.

[92] Origen, *In Exodum homilia* 9, 2 (SCh 321, 282–86), is of the opinion that the heavenly tabernacle is in question here. St. Augustine, *Enarrat. in Psalmos* 14, 1 (CCL 38, 88), doubts this.

[93] On the distinction of sins cf. the International Theological Commission, "De reconciliation et paenitentia" (C, III, in *Documenta, 1967–1985*, pp. 408–14). [See "Penance and Reconciliation" in *Texts and Documents, 1967–1985* (San Francisco: Ignatius Press, 1989 and 2009), chap. 11.]

[94] Cf. Council of Trent, Sess. 6, *Decretum de justificatione*, canon 30, DS 1580.

[95] Council of Trent, Sess. 14, *Doctrina de sacramento extremae unctionis*, c. 2, DS 1696.

For that reason, we are bidden to seek purification. Even those who are washed, must also free their feet of dust (cf. Jn 13:10). In the case of those who have not achieved this adequately by penance on earth, the Church teaches that there is a postmortem purificatory phase,[96] to wit, "a purification preceding the vision of God".[97] Since this postmortem purification is to take place before the final resurrection, it is a state that belongs to an intermediate eschatological stage; indeed the very existence of such a state shows that an intermediate eschatology exists.

The Church's faith in such a state was already implicitly expressed in the prayers for the dead, and the catacombs have most ancient testimonies of this,[98] all of which find their basic foundation in the witness of Second Maccabees 12:46.[99] In such prayers it is presupposed that the departed can be helped on the way of purification by the prayers of the faithful. The theology of that state began to develop in the third century in the case of those who had been restored to peace with the Church without having made the full penance before death.[100]

The practice of praying for the dead must be fully retained. It contains a profession of faith in the existence of such a purificatory state. This too is the meaning of the burial liturgy, a meaning we may not forget: the justified may still need further purification. There is a beautiful portrait of the deceased in the Byzantine liturgy, as it cries out to the Lord: "I still remain, no matter how much I am wounded, as an image of your surpassing glory." [101]

8.2. The Church believes that the definitive state of damnation awaits those who die burdened with grave sin.[102] It is categorically important to avoid any too close assimilation of the purificatory process which precedes our meeting with God with the process of damnation, as if all that lay between them was the opposition of eternal and temporal: the postmortem purification is "straightforwardly other than the pain of damnation".[103] In fact, a state whose centre is love, and another, whose centre is hate, cannot be compared. The justified are alive in the love of Christ. Death strengthens the consciousness of such a love. When there is a delay in reaching the possession of the beloved, there is sorrow, a sorrow that

---

[96] Council of Trent, *Decretum de justificatione*, canon 30, DS 1580; cf. also Council of Florence, *Decretum pro graecis*, DS 1304.

[97] Congregation for the Doctrine of the Faith, *Recentiores episcoporum Synodi*, 7, p. 942.

[98] Cf. also Tertullian, *De corona* 3, 3; CCL 2, 1043.

[99] Cf. *LG* 50, *AAS* 57: 55.

[100] Cf. St. Cyprian, *Epistula* 55, 20, 3 (ed. L. Bayard, 2nd ed., vol. 2 [Paris, 1961], p. 144).

[101] *Euloghitaria* in the exequies before the reading of the Gospel.

[102] Cf. *LG* 48, *AAS* 57: 54.

[103] Congregation for the Doctrine of the Faith, *Recentiores episcoporum Synodi* 7, p. 942.

purifies.[104] Saint John of the Cross explains how the Holy Spirit as "the flame of living love" purifies the soul to enable it to reach the perfect love of God, both on earth and, where necessary, after death. In this way, he established a certain parallelism between the purification associated with the so-called "dark nights" and the passive purification of purgatory.[105] In the history of this dogma, carelessness in distinguishing properly between the states of damnation and purification created great problems in conducting a dialogue with the Eastern Christians.[106]

9. The Irrepeatability and Singleness of Human Life: The Problem of Reincarnation

9.1. The word "reincarnation" (and equivalents such as the Greek *metempsychosis* or *metemsomatosis*) describes a doctrine which holds that the human soul assumes another body after death. It has, that is, a new incarnation or enfleshment. This is a child of paganism in direct opposition to Scripture and Church tradition, and has been always rejected by Christian faith and theology.[107]

In our time, "reincarnation" has a substantial vogue even in the West, and among many who define themselves as Christians. It has great currency in the media, and, increasingly, the influence of Eastern religions and philosophies which have a reincarnational character is spreading. The reason for this is the growth of a syncretistic mentality. The reason for its acceptance by many people is possibly due to an instinctive and spontaneous reaction to the rampant materialism of the present day. Many of our contemporaries view this life on earth as too brief to realise the full potential of the individual, or to correct and surpass life's failures.

---

[104] Cf. St. Catherine of Genoa, *Treatise on Purgatory*.

[105] Cf. *The Living Flame of Love*, 1, 24; *The Dark Night*, 2, 6, 6, and 2, 20, 5.

[106] When the Latins spoke of the fire of purgatory they were understood by the Eastern Christians as if they were presenting Origen's system, explaining matters as merely a question of "medicinal" punishments. As a result, the doctrine of postmortem purification was set forth with great balance in the Council of Florence (*Decretum pro graecis*, DS 1304). In the sixteenth century, the Reformers, on a different tack, found difficulties in this idea connected with their concept of extrinsic justification by faith alone: this connection is explicitly stated in the *Apologia Confessionis Augustanae*, 12, in *Die Bekentnisschriften der evangelisch-lutherischen Kirche*, p. 255). In character, the Council of Trent treats this matter of postmortem purification dogmatically in Session 6 in the decree on justification (canon 30, DS 1580); the decree on purgatory in Session 25 is of a disciplinary nature and is explicitly referred to in the above dogmatic declaration (DS 1820).

[107] Cf. L. Scheffczyk, *Der Reinkarnationsgedanke in der altchristlichen Literatur* (München, 1985).

The Catholic faith has a full response to this way of thinking. It is true that human life is too short to correct and surpass its failures and deficiencies. But the eschatological purification will be perfect. It is granted that a single earthly life is too short to realise all human potential in time. But the final, glorious resurrection will lead people to a state surpassing all their desires.

9.2. It is not possible to give in detail here all aspects of present reincarnational systems. The main thrust of reincarnationalism, however, in the West today may be summarised under four heads.[108]

9.2.1. There are many earthly existences. Our present existence is not our first bodily existence, nor our last. We lived before, and again and again we shall inhabit new bodies.

9.2.2. There is a law in nature which impels us to an enduring progress towards perfection. This same law leads souls to newer and newer lives. No regression is allowed, nor indeed any definitive standing still. A fortiori, any thought of a definitive state of eternal damnation is unthinkable. After many, or fewer, ages, they hold, a final perfection of pure spirit will be reached (a denial of hell).

9.2.3. The ultimate destination is achieved by one's own merits. In each and every new existence, the soul progresses in virtue of its own strivings. Whatever evil was done is atoned for by personal expiations which each spirit meets and suffers in new and difficult incarnations (a denial of redemption).

9.2.4. In proportion to the soul's progress towards final perfection the body in its new incarnations will grow less and less admixed with matter. This means that the soul has an innate tendency to definitive bodiless existence. Along this way, the soul will reach a definitive status, forever free of the body and independent of all matter (a denial of resurrection).

9.3. These four elements which constitute reincarnational anthropology are an outright negation of the central affirmations of Christian revelation. There is no need to insist further on how different it is from the characteristically Christian anthropology. Christianity defends *duality*, reincarnation defends *a dualism* in which the body is simply an instrument of the soul and is laid aside, existence by successive existence, as an altogether different body is assumed each time. As far as eschatology is concerned, the doctrine of reincarnation denies both the possibility of eternal damnation and the idea of the resurrection of the body.

---

[108] In many oriental cultures, reincarnation is presented with greater insistence on the purificatory aspect, and at times the punitive, than is the case in the current Western phase. For that reason, reincarnation is perceived as a painful thing one would wish to avoid. Some regard the escape from this cycle as personally won, others as a divine gift.

But the fundamental error is in the rejection of the Christian doctrine of salvation. For the reincarnationist the soul is its own saviour by its own efforts. Its soteriology is one of autoredemption, which is diametrically opposed to the heteroredemption of Christian soteriology. In fact, if such a heteroredemption is suppressed, any talk of Christ the Redeemer is null and void. The nub of New Testament soteriology is contained in the following words: "This was his will and pleasure in order that the glory of his gracious gift, so graciously conferred on us in his Beloved, might resound to his praise. In Christ our release is secured and our sins forgiven through the shedding of his blood. In the richness of his grace God has lavished on us all wisdom and insight" (Eph 1:6–8). The whole doctrine concerning Church, sacraments and grace stands or falls on this central point. The serious nature of the doctrines involved here is thus evident, and it can readily be understood why the Church's magisterium has rejected the system we have been discussing, categorizing it as a theosophism.[109]

As to the specific point asserted by reincarnationalists concerning the repeatability of human lives, the Epistle to the Hebrews is well known: "It is appointed to men to die once and after that the judgment" (9:27). The Second Vatican Council appealed to this text when teaching that we have only a single life on earth.[110]

In the phenomenon of reincarnation there may well be certain aspiration towards disavowing materialism. But this "spiritualistic" tendency does not in any way nullify the profound contradiction it contains over against the message of the gospel.

10. *The Greatness of the Divine Intentions and the Seriousness of Human Existence*

10.1. Since we have our human lives once only, it is clear how serious a matter our lives are. There is no second time around. Since our earthly life is the way to the reality of the last things, our behaviour in life has irrevocable consequences. Our life in the body has an eternal destiny.

The truth is that people begin to recognise the meaning of their final destiny only when they realise the divine origin of their own nature. God

---

[109] Holy Office, "Reply July 1919 on Theosophic Doctrines", DS 3648, refers to this complex of ideas.

[110] Cf. *LG* 48, *AAS* 57: 54. It is a well-known historical fact that the words "our singleness of earthly life having come to a close" were introduced into the final text in response to a *modus* proposed by 123 of the Fathers—"that the fact of the uniqueness of this earthly life be affirmed against reincarnationalists". *Ad caput VII de Ecclesia, modus* 30; *Acta Synodalia* 3/8, p. 143.

created humankind "to his own image and likeness" (Gen 1:26). What is implied here is that God has given people the capacity of knowing God and freely loving him, and of ruling over the other earthly creatures, of making them subject, and making use of them.[111] This capacity is rooted in the spiritual nature of the human soul. Since each human soul is a direct creation by God in each person,[112] each person is a product of a single concrete act of God's creative love.

10.2. God did not only make people, but placed them in Paradise (Gen 2:4), a biblical way of saying that the first person had the closest bonds of friendship with God.[113] It is easy to understand how Paradise was lost by a sin against a grave divine precept (Gen 3:23–34), since a sin of that sort destroys friendship with God.

A promise of salvation follows the sin of the first person (cf. Gen 3:15), which according to both Jewish and Christian exegesis will be brought by the Messiah (cf. in the context of the word *sperma* [the Septugint's *autos* and not *auto*]).

Indeed, in the fullness of time God "reconciled us to himself through Christ" (2 Cor 5:18). And that is to say that "he who was sinless was made sin by God for us, that we might be made one with the righteousness of God through him" (2 Cor 5:21). Moved by mercy, "God so loved the world that he gave his only begotten Son, so that whoever believes in him would not perish but have eternal life" (Jn 3:16). The redemption allows us "to uncover the depth of that love which does not recoil before the extraordinary sacrifice of the Son, in order to satisfy the fidelity of the Creator and Father towards human beings, created in His image and chosen from 'the beginning,' in this Son, for grace and glory."[114]

Jesus is the "true Lamb of God who takes away the sins of the world" (Jn 1:29). The forgiveness of sin won by the death and resurrection of Christ (cf. Rom 4:25) is not a legal thing merely but an inward renovation of the human being.[115] Moreover, it raises us higher than our natural condition. Christ was sent by the Father "that we might be adopted as sons" (Gal 4:5). If in his name we believe with a lively faith, he gives us "the power to be made sons of God" (cf. Jn 1:12). In that way we enter God's family. The Father's aim is that "we become like the image of his Son so that the Son is the firstborn of many brothers" (Rom 8:29). As a result, Jesus Christ's Father becomes our Father (cf. Jn 20:17).

---

[111] Cf. GS 12, AAS 58: 1034.

[112] Consult supra in note 53 some relevant texts from the magisterium.

[113] As to the reality of this state, cf. Council of Trent, Sess. 5, Decree on Original Sin, canon 1, DS 1511.

[114] John Paul II, Encyclical *Dives in misericordia*, 7, AAS 72 (1980): 1200.

[115] Council of Trent, *Decretum de justificatione*, canon 7, DS 1528.

As we are the Father's sons in the Son, we are "also heirs: heirs of God, and co-heirs with Christ" (Rom 8:17). The meaning then of the promise of eternal life to us is that we share in the inheritance of Christ: "We are citizens of heaven" (Phil 3:20), because, as far as heaven is concerned, already we are not "strangers or newcomers, but ... fellow citizens with the saints and intimates in God's household" (Eph 2:19).

10.3. In revealing the Father's secrets to us, Jesus wants to make us his friends (cf. Jn 15:15). But friendship cannot be forced on us. Friendship with God like adoption is an offer, to be freely accepted or rejected. The happiness of Heaven is the consummation of the gift of Christ's friendship freely offered and accepted freely. "To be with Christ" (Phil 1:23) in the way of friends, is the essence of the eternal blessedness of Heaven (cf. 2 Cor 5:6–8; 1 Thess 4:17). The theme of the vision of God "face to face" (1 Cor 13:12; cf. 1 Jn 3:2) is to be understood as an expression of intimate friendship (cf. already in Exodus 33:11: "God spoke to Moses *face to face* in the way a man speaks *to his friend*"). This consummated and freely accepted friendship implies a concrete possibility of rejection. What is freely accepted can be freely rejected. [No one who] thus chooses rejection, "has any inheritance in the kingdom of Christ and of God" (Eph 5:5). Eternal damnation has its origin in the free rejection to the very end of God's Love and Mercy.[116] The Church believes that this state consists of deprivation of the sight of God and that the whole "being" of the sinner suffers the repercussion of this loss eternally.[117]

This doctrine of faith shows equally the importance of the human capacity of freely rejecting God, and the gravity of such a freely willed rejection. The Christian while on earth is aware that he lives under Christ's future judgement: "For we must all have our lives laid open before the tribunal of Christ, where each must receive what is due to him for his conduct in the body, good or bad" (2 Cor 5:10). Only in the presence of Christ and by the light he conveys, can that mystery of iniquity which is resident in the sins we commit be understood. Through grave sin a human being comes, in his way of acting, to look on "*God as an enemy* of his own creature, and in the first place as an enemy of man, *as a source of danger and threat to man.*"[118]

Since we have only one lifetime (Heb 9:27),[119] in which the gift of divine friendship and adoption is offered gratuitously to our freedom,

---

[116] Paul VI, *Profession of Faith*, 12, p. 438.

[117] Congregation of the Doctrine of the Faith, *Recentiores episcoporum Synodi*, 7, pp. 941–42.

[118] John Paul II, Encyclical *Dominum et vivificantem*, 38, *AAS* 78 (1986): 851.

[119] LG 48, *AAS* 57: 54.

and since there is a danger of losing these, the serious nature of our life is obvious. Decisions we now make have eternal consequences. The Lord has set before us "the way of life and the way of death" (Jer 21:8). Although he invites us to the way of life by prevenient and cooperative (*adiuvians*) grace, we can choose the other way.[120] When we choose, God genuinely respects our liberty, without failing to continue to offer his saving grace even to those who are turned away from him. It must be stated that in fact God genuinely respects whatever we on our part freely will to do, whether we accept or reject grace. It follows that in a certain way salvation and damnation each begin on earth in that people by their moral actions open or close themselves to God. On the other hand, the greatness and the ensuing responsibility of human liberty is clear.

Every theologian is aware of the difficulties that people now, and in every former period, find in accepting the New Testament teaching on hell. For that reason there is much merit in keeping a mind open to the sober teaching of the gospel, whether in expounding it or in believing it. Such sobriety should content us, and we should avoid attempts to grasp in concrete detail how to reconcile God's infinite goodness and human liberty. The Church takes seriously both human liberty, and the divine Mercy which gives people the liberty which is a condition for obtaining salvation. Since the Church prays for the salvation of all people living, by that fact it is praying for the conversion of all. God wants "all men to be saved and to come to the knowledge of the truth" (1 Tim 2:4). The Church has always believed that such a universal salvific will on God's part has an ample efficacy. The Church has never once declared the damnation of a single person as a concrete fact. But, since hell is a genuine possibility for every person, it is not right—although today this is something which is forgotten in the preaching at exequies—to treat salvation as a kind of quasi-automatic consequence. For these reasons, we should, where this doctrine is concerned, make Paul's words our own. "How deep are the wealth and the wisdom and the knowledge of God! How inscrutable his judgements, how unsearchable his ways!" (Rom 11:33).

10.4. Reincarnationalists believe our earthly life too brief to constitute our only life. This is why they insist on repeatability. The Christian ought to be aware of the brevity of life since he knows we have one life only. As we "all sin . . . in many ways" (Jas 3:2), and since there often was sin in our past lives, we must "use the present opportunity to the full" (Eph 5:16) and "throwing off every encumbrance and the sin that all too readily restricts us, run with resolution the race that lies ahead of us, our eyes fixed on Jesus, the pioneer and perfecter of faith" (Heb 12:1–2). "We

---

[120] Cf. Council of Trent, *Decretum de justificatione*, canon 5, DS 1525.

have not here a lasting city, but seek one that is to come" (Heb 13:14). The Christian then as an alien and a pilgrim (cf. 1 Pet 2:11) hurries in holiness of life to his own country (cf. Heb 11:14), where he will be with the Lord (cf. 1 Thess 4:17).

11. *The Law of Prayer Is the Law of Belief*

11.1. It is a principle of theology that "the law of prayer establishes the law of belief." [121] We can and should find the faith of the Church in the liturgy. Since a full investigation of the doctrine of the Last Things in the liturgy is not possible here, we shall attempt a synthesis of the main ideas which are found in the renewed liturgy which followed the Second Vatican Council.

11.2. The first thing to observe is that in the liturgy for the dead [122] the resurrection of Christ is the ultimate reality which lights up all the other realities concerned with Last Things. As a result the resurrection of the body is our supreme hope. "Since then Christ arose as the firstborn among the dead and will give our frail body a shape similar to his own glorious body, we commend our brother to the Lord that he may take him into his peace and raise up his body on the last day." [123] It is clear from this text that the resurrection not only belongs to the future—that is, it is not yet in effect—but will take place at the end of the world.

11.3. Since the resurrection of the body will take place at the end of time, there is in the interim an eschatology of souls. For this reason, prayers are said for the blessing of the grave "that when the body (of the deceased) is swallowed in it, the soul may be stored up in paradise." [124] In biblical terms inspired by Luke 23:43 mention is made of the soul's retribution being "soon after death". There are other forms of prayer of the same tenor with regard to the soul. *The Burial Service*, for instance, has this prayer which is said as the body is placed on the bier: "Accept, O Lord, the *soul* of your servant, N., which you have called from this world to yourself, so that free from the fetters of every sin, it may be granted the blessedness of peace and eternal light and may merit

[121] *Indiculus*, 8, DS 246.

[122] The Latin word *defunctus* means someone who has completed a task. *Defunctus* now stands as a subject. Whoever has fulfilled his duties on earth is allowed into the kingdom either immediately after death or after a final purification, if necessary.

[123] *Ordo exsequiarum* (editio typica 1969) no. 55, p. 25, and the same words in no. 72, p. 32, and no. 184, p. 73.

[124] Ibid., no. 195, p. 77.

being raised to the glory of the resurrection among your saints and chosen ones."[125] A prayer for the "soul" of the deceased is repeated in other places.[126] The prayer spoken as the very moment of death approaches is thoroughly traditional and very ancient. "Go, Christian soul, from this world in the name of God, the Almighty, who created you, in the name of Jesus Christ, Son of the Living God, who suffered for you, in the name of the Holy Spirit, poured forth into your heart; today may you dwell in peace and live with God in holy Sion."[127]

The formulas used in prayers of this kind include a petition which would be unintelligible if there were no postmortem purification. "May his soul suffer no injury ... forgive him all his wrongs and sins."[128] The reference to wrongdoing and sins must be understood here in connection with daily faults and the remains of mortal sins since the Church offers no prayers for the damned.

In one prayer the ordination of the eschatology of souls towards the resurrection is beautifully expressed: "Most Merciful Father, we commend the soul of our brother into your hands, buoyed up by the certain hope that he like all who have died in Christ will rise with Christ on the last day."[129] Such a resurrection is envisaged in a thoroughly realistic way both because of the parallelism with Christ's own resurrection and because of the relationship with the dead body in the sepulchre: "Lord Jesus Christ, who, in the three days you lay in the tomb, so sanctified the graves of all who believe in you that while they serve to bury the body they also augment the hope of resurrection, please grant that your servant may sleep in peace until you, who are resurrection and life, awaken him and fill him with light."[130] The Third Eucharistic Prayer also brings out the realistic nature of the resurrection of the dead (together of course with the idea of a glorious transformation), its relationship with Christ's own resurrection, and the fact that it belongs to the future: "Grant that the person who [in baptism] died with Christ may also share his resurrection, when Christ will raise our mortal bodies and make them like his own in glory."[131] This text has great theological significance since it is contained within the anaphora.

---

[125] No. 30, p. 16.

[126] Cf. ibid., no. 33, p. 18; nos. 36–48, p. 22; no. 65, p. 29; no. 67, p. 30; no. 167, p. 67; no. 174, p. 70; nos. 192–93, p. 76; no. 195, p. 77; no. 200, p. 80; no. 230, p. 87.

[127] *Ordo unctionis infirmorum eorumque pastoralis cura* (editio typica 1972), no. 146, p. 60.

[128] *Ordo exsequiarum*, no. 167, p. 68.

[129] Ibid., no. 48, p. 22.

[130] Ibid., no. 53, p. 24.

[131] *Missale Romanum*, p. 456.

CONCLUSION

We wanted to conclude this exposition of ours on certain contemporary eschatological questions with the testimony of the liturgy. The Church's faith appears in the liturgy, which is a privileged locus when it comes to professing that faith. That testimony has made it clear that the liturgy serves to strike a balance between the individual and collective elements in eschatology and to bring forth the christological meaning of the ultimate realities, without which eschatology would be reduced to mere human speculation.

It is now in order, as we end this exposition, to introduce, by way of a final doctrinal synthesis, the paragraph with which the Introduction to the book of the *Order of Burial* begins, and in which moreover the spirit of the new Roman liturgy is crystal clear:

> In burying its children the Church celebrates with confidence the Paschal Mystery of Christ, so that they, having been made of one body with Christ's death and resurrection, may pass with him from death to life, to be purified indeed in their souls and to be assumed into heaven with the saints and chosen ones, while awaiting in their bodies for the blessed hope of Christ's advent and the resurrection of the dead. Wherefore the Church offers the eucharistic sacrifice of the Pasch of Christ for the dead and pours out prayers and commendations for them so that, in virtue of the mutual interaction of all Christ's members, what brings spiritual help to some affords to others the consolation of hope.[132]

---

[132] *Ordo exsequiarum Praenotanda*, no. 1, p. 7.

18

SELECT QUESTIONS ON THE THEOLOGY
OF GOD THE REDEEMER

PRELIMINARY NOTE

The study of the theology of redemption was proposed to the members of the International Theological Commission by His Holiness Pope John Paul II in 1992. A Sub-Commission was established to prepare this study composed of Prof. Jan Ambaum, Prof. Joseph Doré, Prof. Avery Dulles, Prof. Joachim Gnilka, Prof. Sebastian Karotemprel, Msgr. Miceál Ledwith (President), Prof. Francis Moloney, Msgr. Max Thurian, and Prof. Ladislaus Vanyo.

General discussions on this theme took place during several meetings of the Sub-Commission, and at the Plenary sessions of the International Theological Commission itself, held at Rome in 1992, 1993 and 1994. This text was approved in *forma specifica* by vote of the Commission on 29 November 1994, and was submitted to its President, His Eminence Joseph Cardinal Ratzinger, Prefect of the Congregation for the Doctrine of the Faith, who has approved it for publication.

The International Theological Commission does not propose to offer new theological elements, but rather, by providing here a synthesis of contemporary theological approaches, offers a sure point of reference for the continuing discussion and investigation of this question.

7 October 1995

PART I: THE HUMAN CONDITION AND
THE REALITY OF REDEMPTION

A. *The Actual Situation*

1. An adequate consideration of the theology of redemption today has to begin with an outline of the authentic Christian teaching on redemption

and its bearing on the human condition, as the Church has propounded this teaching in the course of her tradition.

2. The primary statement that needs to be made is that the doctrine of redemption concerns what God has accomplished for us in the life, death and resurrection of Jesus Christ, namely the removal of the obstacles lying between God and us, and the offer to us of participating in God's life. In other words, redemption is about God—as the author of our redemption—before it is about us, and it is only because this is so, that redemption can truly mean liberation for us and can be for all time and all times the Good News of Salvation. That is to say, it is only because redemption is primarily about the glorious goodness of God, rather than about our need, for all that redemption takes care of that need—that it is a liberating reality for us. If redemption, on the contrary, *were* to be judged or measured by the existential need of human beings, how could we avoid the suspicion of having simply created a Redeemer-God in the image of our own need?

3. There is a parallelism here with what we find in the doctrine of creation. God created all things, and human beings in his own image, and found his creation to be "very good" (Gen 1:31). This all precedes the beginning of our history in which human activity does not turn out to be as unambiguously "good" as God's creation. However despite that, the Church's teaching down through the centuries—based on Scripture—has always been that the image of God in the human person, although often concealed and twisted in history as a result of original sin and its effects, has never been completely eradicated or destroyed. The Church believes that sinful human beings have not been abandoned by God, but rather that God, in his redeeming love, intends a glorious destiny for the human race, and indeed for the whole created order, which is already seminally present in and through the Church. From the Christian perspective such considerations underlie and support the belief that life here and now is worth living. Yet any general call to "affirm life" or "to say 'yes' to life", while undoubtedly relevant in this regard and to be welcomed, does not exhaust the mystery of redemption, as the Church tries to live it.

4. Christian faith is therefore careful not, on the one hand, to divinize or to idolize human beings because of their greatness, their dignity and their achievements, nor, on the other hand, to condemn them or crush them because of their failures and misdeeds. Christian faith does not underestimate the human potential and desire for growth and fulfillment, and the achievements to which the actualization of this potential and desire can effectively lead. Not only are such achievements not considered a priori by faith as obstacles to be overcome or adversaries to be combated, but they are, on the contrary, positively evaluated from the outset. From

the first pages of the book of Genesis to the encyclicals of recent Popes, the invitation addressed to human beings—and, of course, in the first place to Christians—is always to organize the world and society in such a way as to improve at all levels the conditions of human life, and beyond that, to enhance the happiness of individuals, promote justice and peace among all and, as far as possible, foster a love, which, in being translated into words and actions, does not exclude anyone on the face of the earth.

5. As regards human evil and suffering, they are in no sense underestimated by faith: faith is not, under the pretext of proclaiming eternal happiness in a world to come, in any way inclined to ignore the many kinds of pain and suffering which afflict individuals, nor the obvious collective tragedy inherent in many situations. But for all that, neither does faith rejoice in evil and times of trial in themselves, as if it would not exist without them.

6. Here, as a first step at least, faith is content simply to take note and to record. It is therefore not permissible to accuse faith of closing its eyes; but it is just as impermissible to be resentful towards faith, accusing it of treating evil and suffering as fundamental facts without which faith would have no credible foundation, as if, in short, faith could only be based, as a sine qua non condition of its existence, on the wretchedness of the human condition, and on the effect and recognition of such despondency.

7. Evil and suffering are not, in fact, in the first place, a function of any particular *theological interpretation* of life, but are a universal *experience*. And the first movement of faith, in the face of evil and suffering, is not to exploit them for its own ends! If Christian faith takes account of them it is, *in the first place*, simply in order to make a coherent and honest assessment of the real, concrete historical situation of the human race. And faith's only concern is to know whether, how and under what conditions, its vision of this actual historical situation can still win people's attention and adherence today—while taking into consideration their own analyses of their condition, and the attitudes they adopt in the different situations they have to face.

8. Christian faith does however have a specific perspective on the human condition which in many respects illuminates what many non-Christian world views assert in their own way. Firstly, faith underlines that evil appears *as being always—already there in history and in humanity*: evil transcends and precedes all our individual responsibilities and appears to spring from "powers" and even a "spirit" that are present before we act, and to a certain extent are external to any personal consciousness and will acting in the here and now.

9. Secondly, faith points out that the evil and suffering that affect the historical condition of human beings have also, and even to a large extent,

their *source in the heart of human beings*, in their selfish reflexes, their appetites for pleasure and power, their silent complicity in evil, their cowardly capitulation to evil, their terrible hard-heartedness. Nevertheless, biblical revelation and Christian faith do not despair of the human person; on the contrary, they continue to appeal to free will, to the sense of responsibility, to the ability to take decisive action in order to change—and to those moments of lucid awareness in which these faculties can be effectively exercised. Faith believes indeed that all are fundamentally capable both of distancing themselves from everything that conditions them negatively, and of giving up their own selfishness and self-absorption, in order to commit themselves to the service of others, and in that way open themselves to a living hope that could even surpass all their desires.

10. For Christian faith, then, human beings are as a matter of historical fact alienated from the holiness of God because of sin, over and above the fact that we are distinct from God by virtue of being created and not intrinsically divine. This twofold difference between God and humanity is witnessed to in Scripture and is presupposed by all orthodox Christian writing in post-biblical times. But the divine initiative in moving in love towards sinful humanity is a continuous feature of God's dealings with us before and within history, and is the underlying presupposition of the doctrine of redemption. Thus, the dialectic of grace and sin presupposes that before any sin entered the world, God's grace had already been offered to human beings. The internal logic of the Christian view of the human condition demands also that God be the author of redemption, since what is in need of being healed and saved is nothing less than the very image of God himself in us.

11. The value of created human nature is, then, for Christian faith, guaranteed from the beginning by God himself and is indestructible, and similarly the reality of redemption has been won and is guaranteed by God in Christ also for ever. Both creation and redemption, the Church teaches, are rooted in God's gracious and unfathomable goodness and freedom, and from our point of view remain incomprehensible, inexplicable and wonderful. The search for an understanding of these realities springs from a prior, underivable and hence irreducible act or attitude of thanksgiving for them.[1]

12. While a full understanding of redemption is surely impossible for us, nevertheless some understanding of the doctrine is not only possible but demanded by the very nature of redemption which is concerned with the truth, value and ultimate destiny of all created reality. If no attempt to understand redemption were to be permitted, the reasonableness of faith

---

[1] Cf. *"fides quaerens intellectum"*.

would be undermined, the legitimate search for understanding would be denied to faith and the result would be fideism. Furthermore since the whole human person is redeemed by Christ, this must be capable of being shown to be true in the intellectual order.[2]

13. For Christian faith the truth of redemption has always illuminated in particular those aspects of the human condition which point most obviously to the human need for salvation. Human beings experience fragmentation, inadequacies and frustrations in their lives at many levels. To the extent that human beings often consider themselves responsible for the fragmented, unsatisfactory quality of their experience, they confess, in traditional language, their sinfulness. However, if the full picture of the human condition is to be painted, those aspects of life which disfigure and destroy human existence and for which no one is, apparently, directly responsible, must also be noted. For they too speak eloquently of the human need for redemption. Such realities as famine, pestilence, natural catastrophes, illness, physical and mental suffering, and death itself, reveal that evil—as the Christian tradition has of course always recognized—is by no means exhausted by what is termed "*malum culpae*" (moral evil), but covers also "*malum poenae*" (suffering), whether this be evil in itself or arise from the limitations of nature. Traditionally, however—as the biblical witness itself reveals—all suffering, and indeed death itself, has been understood as springing from sin, "the mystery of iniquity" in Saint Paul's phrase (2 Thess 2:7).

14. While the challenges just mentioned are the most basic existential difficulties faced by human beings, there are also a whole series of other more intimate problems that confront people. They have, in the first place, difficulties in achieving as individuals personal, inner equilibrium. Secondly, they have difficulties in living in harmony with their fellow human beings, as the history of warfare, with all its attendant cruelty and horror, reveals. Thirdly, their inability to live well with non-human nature is reflected dramatically in the contemporary world in the ecological question. Fourthly, when the pressures of living become too intense, there can easily arise the suspicion that human existence is doomed to failure and ultimate meaninglessness. Underlying the above critical areas there is, finally, the question of humanity's as yet unfinished search for that peace with God, which is frustrated by the powerful and all-pervasive reality of sin.

15. This preliminary sketch of how for Christian faith the truth of redemption illuminates the human condition must be complemented by an assessment of how today human beings themselves see their actual historical situation.

[2] Cf. 2 Cor 10:5.

16. We turn firstly, however, to review briefly the understanding of redemption propounded by the great World Religions. In doing so, here in this review section, we may leave aside Judaism, in which Christianity has its roots, and shares with it a view of redemption based on the sovereign goodwill of God the Creator towards the errant human race as expressed in the Covenant.

B. *Relationships with the World Religions*

17. *Hinduism* is not a monolithic religion. It is rather a mosaic of religious beliefs and practices that claims to offer the human race redemption and salvation. Although early Vedic Hinduism was polytheistic, later Vedic tradition came to speak of ultimate Reality, also referred to as "Atman" or "Brahman", as One, out of which all things emerged with a specific, triadic mode of manifestation. "Brahman" itself is incomprehensible and formless, but is also the Self-existent Conscious being who is the fullness of Bliss. At a more popular, personal level, divinities such as Shiva, destroyer of the imperfect, Vishnu and his "avatars" ("incarnations") like Ram, the Enlightened One, Krishna and the Mother Goddess Shakti—correspond to the attributes of the Supreme Reality. God's "incarnations" descend to earth to deal with evil when it becomes powerful on earth.

18. Making due allowances for over-simplification, one could say that for Hinduism the human person is a spark of the divine, a soul ("atman") embodied because of "avidya" (ignorance: either a kind of metaphysical ignorance of one's true nature or a kind of original ignorance). As a result, the human being is subject to the law of "karma" or rebirth, the cycle of birth and rebirth being known as "karma-samsara", or the law of retribution. Selfish desire, leading to spiritual ignorance, is the source of all evil, misery and suffering in the world.

19. Redemption for Hinduism—expressed by such terms as "moksha" and "mukti"—is thus liberation from the law of "karma". Although human beings can in three (not mutually exclusive) ways take some steps towards their salvation—through disinterested action, spiritual intuition and loving devotion to God—the final stage of salvific communion with God can only be attained with the help of grace.

20. As regards *Buddhism*, one can begin by saying that Buddha, in dealing with the suffering of the world, rejected the authority of the Vedas, the usefulness of sacrifices, and saw no use either in metaphysical speculations about the existence of God and the soul. He sought deliverance from suffering *from within man himself.* His central insight is that human desire is the root of all evil and misery—which in turn gives

rise to "ignorance" ("avidya")—and the ultimate cause of the cycle of birth and rebirth.

21. After Buddha there arose many schools of thought which elaborated his simple basic teachings into systems dealing with the doctrine of "karma" as the tendency, inherent in action, to be born again. Historical human life has no unifying, personal, substantive existential thread; it is made up merely of unconnected existential fragments of birth, growth, decay and death. The doctrine of "anicca", or the "non-permanence" of all reality, is central to Buddhism. The notion of existential impermanence precludes the possibility of the existence of an "atman" and hence Buddha's silence on the existence of God or the "atman". Everything is appearance ("maya"). Nothing can be said about reality, either positively or negatively.

22. Redemption for Buddhism consists therefore in a state of liberation ("Nirvana") from this world of appearance, a liberation from the fragmentary nature and the impermanence of existence, achieved through the suppression of all desire and all consciousness. Through such liberation a pure, indeterminate state of emptiness is attained. Being radically other than the transitory torment of this world of Maya, Nirvana—literally: "extinction" or "going out" (i.e. of all desires), as the light of a candle goes out when the wax has been burned away—eludes earthly definition, but it is not simply a state of *sheer* extinction or *total* annihilation. Nirvana is not an intellectual goal but an experience that is indefinable. It is the liberation from all desires and cravings, the release from the cycle of rebirth and sorrow ("dukha"). The most perfect way to liberation for Buddhists is the Eight-fold Way—right understanding, right intention, right speech, right conduct, right occupation, right endeavor, right contemplation, and right concentration ("Vinayana Pitaka")—which places all its emphasis on human efforts. From the perspective of Buddhism all other religious paths are imperfect and secondary.

23. Like Judaism and Christianity, *Islam* ("Submission") is a monotheistic, covenantal religion with a firm belief in God as the Creator of all things. As its name suggests, it sees the key to true religion and hence to salvation in Faith, Trust and total Submission to the will of the all-merciful God.

24. According to the faith of the Moslems the religion of Islam was revealed by God from the very beginning of humankind and confirmed through successive covenants with Noah, Abraham, Moses and Jesus. Islam sees itself as the completion and fulfillment of all the covenants that have existed from the beginning.

25. Islam has no concept of original sin and the Christian sense of redemption has no place in Islamic thought. All human beings are simply

seen as in need of salvation which they can obtain only by turning to God in total faith. The concept of salvation is expressed also by the term "success" or "prosperity". However, the idea of salvation is best expressed by terms like "safety" or "protection": in God the human race finds definitive safety. The fullness of salvation—conceived of in terms of corporeal and spiritual delights[3]—is achieved only on the Last Day with the Final Judgment and in life in the hereafter ("Akhira"). Islam believes in a kind of predestination in the matter of salvation, either to the bliss of paradise or to the suffering of hell fire ("Nar"), but the human being remains free to respond by faith and good works. The means of achieving salvation apart from the profession of faith are: ritual prayer, legal alms-giving, the fast of Ramadan and pilgrimage to the house of God in Mecca. A few traditions add to these means "jihad" or "struggle", as holy war to spread or defend Islam, or, more rarely, as personal spiritual struggle.

26. Apart from the great classical religions of the world, there are other religions, variously called Traditional, Primal, Tribal or Natural religions. The origins of these religions are lost in antiquity. Their beliefs, cults and ethical codes are transmitted by living oral tradition.

27. The followers of such religions believe in a Supreme Being, identified under different names and believed to be the creator of all things, but himself uncreated and eternal. The Supreme Being has delegated the supervision of the affairs of the world to lesser divinities known as the spirits. These spirits influence human well-being or woe. Propitiation of the spirits is very important for human well-being. In Traditional Religions the sense of a group's communion with the ancestors of the clan, the tribe and the wider human family is important. The departed ancestors are revered and venerated in various ways though not worshipped.

28. Most Traditional Religions have myths and epic stories that speak of a state of bliss with God, fall from an ideal situation, and expectation of some kind of redeemer-savior to reestablish the lost relationship, and bring about reconciliation and the state of bliss. Salvation is conceived of in terms of reconciliation and harmony with the departed ancestors, the spirits and God.

C. *The Christian Doctrine of Redemption and the Modern World*

29. Apart from considering the views of redemption propounded by the great world religions and the more localized traditional ancestral religions of many human cultures, one must, however, also pay some attention to

---

[3] Cf. the Garden ("Genna") of supreme bliss.

other *contemporary* alternative movements and lifestyles which promise salvation to their followers (e.g., modern cults, the many different "New Age" movements, and ideologies of autonomy, emancipation and revolution). Yet caution is called for in this area, and the risk of oversimplification must, if possible, be avoided.

30. It would be misleading to suggest, for example, that *contemporary* people fall into one of only two categories: either that of a self-confident "modernity" believing in the possibility of auto-redemption, or that of a disenchanted post-modernity despairing of any improvement in the human condition from, as it were, "within" and relying only on the possibility of salvation from "without". Instead, what one does find is a cultural and intellectual pluralism, a wide range of differing analyses of the human condition and a variety of ways of trying to cope with it. Alongside a kind of flight into pleasurable diversion or the absorbing, passing attractions of hedonism, one finds a retreat to various ideologies and new mythologies. Alongside a more or less resigned, lucid and courageous stoicism, one finds both a disillusionment claiming to be tough-minded and realistic, and resolute protest against the reduction of human beings and their environment to marketable resources that can be exploited, and against the corresponding relativization, underestimation and ultimately trivialization of the dark side of human existence.

31. One fact in the contemporary situation is therefore abundantly clear: *the concrete condition of human beings is full of ambiguities*. One could describe in many ways the two "poles" between which each particular individual human being, and humanity in its totality, are in fact torn. There is, for instance, in each individual, on the one hand, an ineradicable desire for life, happiness and fulfillment, and on the other hand, the inevitable experience of limitation, dissatisfaction, failure and suffering. If one passes from the individual to the general sphere one can see the same picture on a larger canvas. Here too, one can point, on the one hand, to the immense progress that has been made possible by science and technology, by the spread of the means of communication, and by the advances made, for example, in the domain of private, public and international law. But, on the other hand, one would also have to point to so many catastrophes in the world, and, among human beings, to so much depravity, the result of all of which is that a very great number of people suffer terrible oppression and exploitation and become helpless victims of what can only in fact appear to them to be a cruel fate. It is clear that, despite differences of emphasis, any unclouded optimism about general and universal progress through technology has been losing ground perceptibly in our day. And it is in the contemporary context of widespread injustice and lack of hope that the doctrine of redemption has to be presented today.

32. Yet it is important to note that Christian faith does not rush into judgment: either to reject *in toto*, or to endorse too uncritically. Proceeding with both goodwill and discernment, it does not fail to note, in the great diversity of analyses and attitudes which it encounters, several fundamental insights which appear to it to correspond in themselves to a profound truth about human existence.

33. Faith notes also, for example, that despite their limitations and within them, human beings nevertheless seek a possible "fulfillment" for their lives; that evil and suffering are experienced by them, in short, as something profoundly "abnormal"; that the different forms of protest raised from this perspective are in themselves alone the sign that human beings cannot but be seeking for "something else", "something more", "something better". And finally, as a consequence of this, Christian faith sees that contemporary human beings are not simply looking for an *explanation* of their condition but are waiting or hoping—whether they acknowledge it or not—for an *effective deliverance* from evil, and a *confirmation and fulfillment* of all that is positive in their lives: the desire for the good and the better, etc.

34. Yet while the Church recognizes the importance of trying to understand and assess the actual problems of human beings in the world, the differing attitudes provoked by them and the concrete proposals made to tackle them, she also recognizes the need never to lose sight of the fundamental question underlying these problems and necessarily underlying also any proposed way of resolving them, the question of truth: What *is* the truth of the human condition? What is the meaning of human existence, and what—from the perspective of the present itself—can human beings ultimately hope for? In presenting the doctrine of redemption to the world, the Church can perhaps address various differing perspectives on ultimate questions by concentrating on the aspect of the Christian faith in redemption which is perhaps the most crucial one for humanity: hope. For redemption is the only reality powerful enough to meet real human need, and the only reality deep enough to persuade people of what is really in them.[4] This redemptive message of hope is grounded in the two key Christian doctrines of Christology and the Trinity. In these doctrines one finds the ultimate rationale for the Christian understanding of human history, and of the human person, made in the image of the Triune God, a Unity in Community, and redeemed out of love by God's only Son, Jesus Christ, for the purpose of participation in the divine life, for which we were in the first place created. This participation is what is indicated by the doctrine of the resurrection of the body, when human beings in their total reality share in the fullness of divine life.

[4] Cf. Jn 2:25.

35. The Christian assessment of the human condition does not thus stand by itself but is an aspect of a much larger vision at whose center is the Christian understanding of God and of God's relationship to the human race and the whole of the created order. This larger vision is that of a *Covenant* which God willed and wills for the race. It is a Covenant by which God wills to associate human beings with his life, fulfilling—even beyond everything that they can themselves desire or conceive—all that is positive within them, and liberating them from all that is negative within them and that frustrates their life, happiness and development.

36. But it is essential to point out that if Christian faith speaks in this way about God and his will to institute a Covenant with human beings, it is not because we have been, as it were, only informed (by way of mere teaching) of God's intentions. It is because, in a much more radical way, God has literally *intervened in history*, and has acted at the very heart of history: by his "mighty deeds", throughout the whole Old Covenant in the first place, but supremely and definitively through and in Jesus Christ, his own, true and only Son, who entered, incarnate, *into* the human condition, in its totally concrete and historical form.

37. Strictly speaking, it follows from this that, in order to set out what they have to say about the human condition, believers do not begin by questioning themselves about it, and then go on to ask themselves what further enlightenment the God they profess can shed on it. Correlatively, and still strictly speaking, Christians do not begin by affirming God on the strength of a line of argument or, at least, not on the strength of purely abstract reflection, and then go on, only as a secondary move, to examine what enlightenment this prior acknowledgement of his existence could bring to bear on the historical destiny of humanity.

38. In reality, for biblical revelation, and thus for Christian faith, to know God, is to confess him on the basis of what he himself has done for human beings, *revealing them fully to themselves* in the very act of *revealing himself to them*, precisely by entering into relation with them: by setting up and offering a Covenant to them, and by going, for this purpose, to the point of coming into and becoming incarnate in their very human condition.

39. It is, finally, from this perspective that the vision of the human person and of the human condition, put forward by Christian faith, acquires its whole specificity and its whole richness.

40. Finally, some attention should be paid to what one might call the internal Christian debate on redemption, and especially to the question of how the suffering and death of Christ is related to the winning of the world's redemption. The importance of this question is heightened today

in many quarters because of the perceived inadequacy—or at least perceived openness to serious and dangerous misunderstanding—of certain traditional ways of understanding Christ's work of redemption in terms of compensation or punishment for our sins. Furthermore the acuteness of the problem of evil and suffering has not lessened with the passage of time, but rather intensified, and the ability of many to believe that it *can* be adequately dealt with at all, has in this century been undermined as a matter of factual record. In such circumstances it would seem to be important to think anew about how the redemption reveals the glory of God. The question can be posed whether an attempt to understand the doctrine of the redemption might be, at heart, an exercise in theodicy, an attempt to suggest a credible answer to the "mystery of iniquity", in Saint Paul's phrase, in the light of Christian faith. The mystery of Christ and the Church is the divine answer. In short, is redemption God's *justification*, that is to say, most profound *revelation* of himself to us, and thereby the gift to us of the peace "which passes all understanding" (Phil 4:7)?

41. The purpose of this document is not to be a comprehensive treatment of the whole area of redemption theology, but rather to face selected questions in redemption theology that pose themselves with a particular force in the Church today.

PART II: BIBLICAL REDEMPTION:
THE POSSIBILITY OF FREEDOM

1. The biblical record reflects a never-ending search for the ultimate significance of the human condition.[5] For Israel, God is made known through Torah, and for Christianity, God is made known through the person, the teaching, the death and resurrection of Jesus of Nazareth. Yet, both the Law and the incarnation still leave humanity in the ambiguity of a revelation given, matched by a human history which does not respond to the truths revealed. We still "groan inwardly, as we wait for adoption as sons, the redemption of our bodies" (Rom 8:23).

2. The human being faces a dramatic situation where all efforts to free itself from its self-imposed suffering and slavery are doomed to failure. Finite because of our origin as creatures, infinite because of our call to be one with our Creator, we are not capable, on the basis of our own efforts, of passing from the finite to the infinite. Thus, the Christian looks beyond

---

[5] Cf. for example, Gen 1–11; Mk 13:1–37; Rev 22:20.

human achievement. "Restless are our hearts, until they rest in you" (Augustine, *Confessions* 1, 1).

3. Already in its civil legislation, Israel had a consciousness of a "redeemer" (*go'el*). Families could pay the ransom for a relative, to preserve the solidarity of the family.[6] The importance of the solidarity of the family lies behind such legal institutions as levirate marriage,[7] blood vengeance[8] and the jubilee year.[9] Israelite law allows for a condemned person to be bought back.[10] The payment of the *kofer* frees the guilty person, his or her family, the injured family, and the whole community, as conflict is resolved. There are some Old Testament narratives where redeeming activities which have their roots in this legal background take place. Through the self-offering of Judah, who reverses his crime against Joseph,[11] the family is redeemed from vengeance. Similarly, Jacob, who had robbed Esau of his inheritance blessing, repays this with a large part of his property.[12] Vengeance is avoided.

4. Israelite religion developed a liturgy of expiation. It was the symbolic act of homage by which the guilty person covers and repays a debt to YHWH. The essential elements of this liturgy were:

a. The rites are of divine institution (holy places, holy priesthood and rites dictated by YHWH).

b. YHWH is the one who forgives.[13]

c. The rites are all sacrificial, and generally blood sacrifices, where the blood that represents life is poured out. YHWH gives human beings blood for the rite of forgiveness.[14] Sacrificial blood expresses the gratuity of forgiveness at the level of ritual expression.

5. Holy people, and especially Moses and the prophets who followed him, had great value before God. This counterbalanced the disvalue of the evil and sin of others. Thus, they attached great importance to intercession for the forgiveness of sin.[15] The figure of the Suffering Servant in Isaiah 53:4–12 would be repeatedly used in the New Testament as a type of Christ the Redeemer.

---

[6] Cf. Ex 21:2, 7; Deut 25:7–10.

[7] Cf. Deut 25.

[8] Cf. Lev 25; Num 35:9–34.

[9] Cf. Ex 21:2; Lev 25; Jer 34:8–22; Deut 15:9–10.

[10] Cf. Ex 21:29–30 (Hebrew: *kofer*; Greek: *lutron*).

[11] Cf. Gen 37:26–27; 44:33–34.

[12] Cf. Gen 32:21.

[13] Cf. Lev 17:10, 12.

[14] Cf. Lev 17:11.

[15] Cf. Ex 32:7–14, 30–34; 33:12–17; 34:8–9; Num 14:10–19; Deut 9:18–19; Amos 7; Jer 15:1; Is 53:12; 2 Mac 15:12–16.

6. The narratives of the action of God in the Exodus (Ex 1–15), and the redeeming love of Esther and Ruth[16] show how freedom comes from the unselfish gift of self for a nation or a family. These same sentiments are found in the prayer life of Israel, which celebrates God's redeeming love for his people in the Exodus[17] and his care and goodness which brings freedom and wholeness to the life of the people.[18]

7. These ancient themes of liberation and redemption are brought to a sharper focus in Jesus Christ. A product of this world, and a gift of God to the world, Jesus of Nazareth points the way to an authentic and lasting freedom. In his person, his words and his deeds, he showed that the reigning presence of God was at hand, and he called everyone to conversion so that they might be part of this kingdom.[19] Jesus of Nazareth told parables of the kingdom which shattered the deep structure of our accepted world view.[20] They remove our defenses and make us vulnerable to God. Here God touches us, and the kingdom of God arrives.

8. Jesus, the teller of the parables of the kingdom of God, was the Parable of God. His unswerving openness to God is found in his relationship to the traditional God of Israel, God as *Abba*.[21] It can be seen in his preparedness, as the Son of Man, to undergo all possible insult, suffering and death, in the conviction that—in the end God would have the last word.[22] He gathered followers,[23] and shared his table with sinners, reversing accepted values as he offered them salvation.[24] He persevered in his life-style and in his teaching, despite the tension that this created around him,[25] culminating in his symbolic "destruction" of the Temple (Mk 11:15–19; Mt 21:12–13; Lk 19:45–48; Jn 2:13–22), his final supper which promised to be the first of many such suppers,[26] and his death upon the Cross.[27] Jesus of Nazareth was the most free human being that ever lived. He had no desire to *control* his future, as his radical trust in his Abba-Father freed him from all such concerns.

---

[16] Cf. especially Esther 14:3–19; Ruth 1:15–18.
[17] Cf. e.g. Ps 74:2; 77:16.
[18] Cf. e.g. Ps 103:4; 106:10; 107; 111:9; 130:7.
[19] Cf. Mk 1:5.
[20] Cf. e.g. Lk 15.
[21] Cf. Mk 14:36.
[22] Cf. Mk 8:31; 9:31; 10:32–34.
[23] Cf. Mk 1:16–20.
[24] Cf. Mk 2:15–17; 14:17–31; Lk 5:29–38; 7:31–35, 36–50; 11:37–54; 14:1–24; 19:1–10.
[25] Cf. Mk 2:15–17; Lk 5:27–32; 15:2; 19:7.
[26] Cf. Mk 14:17–31; Mt 26:20–35; Lk 22:14–34.
[27] Cf. Jn 19:30, *Consummatum est!*

9. The Johannine story of the Cross tells of the revelation of a God who so loved the world that he gave his own Son.[28] The Cross is the place where Jesus is "lifted up",[29] to glorify God and thus come to his own glory.[30] "No one has greater love than this, to lay down one's life for one's friends" (15:13). Because the Cross makes God known, all subsequent believers must "look upon him whom they have pierced" (19:37).

10. So much of the search for liberation, freedom, or any other of the terms used today to speak of what might be called a "redemption" from the ambiguities of the human situation, are attempts to avoid and ignore suffering and death. The way of Jesus of Nazareth indicates that the free gift of oneself to the ways of God, cost what it may, brings glory to ourselves and also to God. The death of Jesus is not the act of a merciless God exacting the supreme sacrifice; it is not a "buying back" from some alienating power which has enslaved. It is the time and the place where a God who is love and who loves us is made visible. Jesus crucified tells how much God loves us, and affirms that in this gesture of love a human being has given unconditional assent to God's ways.

11. The Gospel of the crucified Jesus demonstrated the solidarity of the love of God with suffering. In the person of Jesus of Nazareth this saving love of God and his solidarity with us is given its historical and physical form. Crucifixion, a despicable form of death, became "Gospel". Although much of the Old Testament sees death as final and tragic,[31] this view is gradually overcome by the emerging idea of an after-life[32] and in Jesus' teaching that God is a God of the living, not of the dead.[33] But the bloody event of Calvary demanded that the early Church explain, both for itself and for its mission, the atoning efficacy of a sacrificial death of Jesus on the Cross.[34]

12. The New Testament uses sacrificial images to explain the death of Christ. Salvation cannot be obtained through mere moral perfection, and sacrifice cannot be regarded as the relic of an outmoded religiosity. Judaism already provided the model of the expiatory death of the model martyr,[35] but this is carried further in the New Testament because of the decisive significance given to "the blood of Christ". The Cross of Jesus, which occupied a central position in the early proclamation, involved the

---

[28] Cf. Jn 3:16.
[29] Cf. 3:14; 8:28; 12:32–33.
[30] Cf. 11:4; 12:23; 13:1; 17:1–4.
[31] For example, Job 2:4; Eccles 9:4; Is 38:18; Ps 6:5; 16:10–11; 73:27–28.
[32] Cf. Dan 12:5–13; Wis 3:1–13.
[33] Cf. Mt 22:31–32.
[34] Cf. 1 Cor 1:22–25.
[35] Cf. 4 Mac.

shedding of blood. The salvific significance of Jesus' death was explained in terms borrowed from the Old Testament sacrificial liturgy, where blood played an important role. Continuing but transforming the Old Testament understanding of blood as the essential mark of life, sacrificial language and theology emerged in the early Church:

i. By a typological argument, the blood of Christ was regarded as effective in establishing a new and perfect covenant between God and the New Israel.[36] But unlike the repeated actions of the priests of the former covenant, the blood of Jesus, the only means of obtaining remission and sanctification,[37] flows only once, in a sacrifice which is offered once for all.[38]

ii. The term "death" by itself would not signify a redemptive work. "Blood" implies more than death. It has the active connotation of life.[39] The sprinkling of blood upon the altar was regarded as the essential and decisive act of offering (Leviticus), but for Paul, the efficacy assigned to the blood of Christ (justification, redemption, reconciliation and atonement) goes far beyond the scope claimed for blood in Leviticus, where its effect is only negative, the covering or neutralizing of that which forbids safe or acceptable worship of God (Rom 3:24–25). Christ is regarded as the *kaporeth*: at the same time offering and propitiation.

iii. To be in covenant means to obey.[40] The idea of obedience and loyalty to Torah unto death was well known in first-century Judaism. Paul is able to explain the death of Jesus as obedience to the demands of God.[41] This obedience is not the placating of an angry God, but a free offering of self which enables the creation of the New Covenant. The Christian enters the New Covenant by imitating the patience and obedience of Jesus.[42]

iv. Like the whole of the earthly life of Jesus[43] his death on the Cross took place in the presence of, and with the assistance of, the Holy Spirit.[44] Here every analogy with the Old Testament falls short. It is Jesus Christ "who through the eternal Spirit offered himself" (Heb 9:14). Everything that happens on the Cross is a witness to the Father, and according to Paul, nobody can call God Father except in the Spirit, and the Spirit of

---

[36] Cf. Ex 24; Mt 26:27–28; 1 Cor 11:23–26; Heb 9:18–21.
[37] Cf. Heb 9:22.
[38] *Ephapax*: Rom 6:10; Heb 7:27; 9:12; 10:10.
[39] Cf. Rom 5:8–10.
[40] Cf. Ps 2:8.
[41] Cf. Rom 5:13–18; Phil 2:8. Cf. also Heb 10:5.
[42] Cf. also 1 Pet 1:18–20.
[43] Cf. Mt 1:21; 3:17; 4:1, 10; Lk 1:35; 4:14, 18; Jn 1:32.
[44] Cf. Lk 23:46.

God attests to him in believers.[45] For the Fourth Gospel the Spirit is given to the Church as Jesus cries out, "It is finished", and hands down the Spirit (Jn 19:30: *Paredoken to pneuma*).

v. Jesus' death was praise and exaltation of God. He remained faithful in death; he demonstrated the reign of God, and thus in the death of Jesus God was present. For this reason the earliest Church attributed to Jesus' death a redemptive power: "Although he was a Son, he learned obedience through what he suffered; and having been made perfect, he became the source of eternal salvation for all who obey him, having been designated by God a high priest according to the order of Melchizedek" (Heb 5:8–10). The sacrifice of Jesus on the Cross was not only *passio*, but also *actio*. The latter aspect, the voluntary self-offering to the Father, with its pneumatic content, is the most important aspect of his death. The drama is not a conflict between fate and the individual. On the contrary, the Cross is a liturgy of obedience manifesting the unity between the Father and the Son in the eternal Spirit.

13. Jesus risen affirms God's gracious response to such self-giving love. In the end, Christianity gazes upon an empty Cross. Jesus of Nazareth's unconditional acceptance of all that was asked of him by his Father has led to the Father's unconditional "yes" to all that Jesus has said and done. It is the resurrection which proclaims that the way of Jesus is the way that overcomes sin and death into a life which has no limits.

14. Christianity has the task of announcing in word and deed the inbreak of freedom from the many slaveries which de-humanize God's creation. The revelation of God in and through Jesus of Nazareth, crucified but risen, calls us to be all that we were created to be. The person who participates in the love of God revealed in and through Jesus Christ becomes what he or she was created to be: the image of God,[46] as Jesus is the icon of God.[47] The story of Jesus shows that it will cost no less than everything. But the response of God to Jesus' story is equally dramatic—death and sin have been conquered once and for all.[48]

15. The power of destruction remains in our hands; the story of Adam is still with us.[49] But the gift of Christ-like obedience offers the hope of transformation to the world,[50] free from the Law for a fruitful union with Christ (7:1–6). To live under the Law makes true freedom impossible (7:7–25), while life in the Spirit enables a freedom which comes

[45] Cf. Rom 8:15; Gal 4:6.
[46] Cf. Gen 1:26–27.
[47] Cf. Col 1:15.
[48] Cf. Rom 6:5–11; Heb 9:11–12; 10:10.
[49] Cf. Rom 5:12–21.
[50] Cf. Rom 6:1–21.

from the gracious gift of God (8:1–13). But such freedom is only possible through death to sin so that we may be "alive to God in Christ Jesus".[51]

16. The redeemed life of Christians has an obvious historical character, and an inevitable social dimension. Relationships between masters and slaves can never be the same again;[52] there is no longer slave and free person, no longer Greek or Jew, no longer male and female.[53] Christians are called to be authentically human in a divided world, the unique manifestation of love, joy, peace, patience, kindness, goodness, faithfulness, gentleness and self-control, living by the Spirit and walking by the Spirit.[54]

17. In the soteriology of the Letter to the Ephesians and the Letter to the Colossians, the themes of peace and reconciliation stand out: "He [Christ] is our peace" (Eph 2:14). Peace (*shalom*) and reconciliation here become the heart and best expression of redemption. But this aspect of redemption is not new. The word "peace" is to be understood in the light of its rich use across the biblical tradition. It has a threefold dimension:

i. It means peace with God: "Therefore, since we are justified by faith, we have peace with God through our Lord, Jesus Christ" (Rom 5:1).

ii. It means peace among human beings. It involves their being well-disposed to one another. The peace, which is Christ, destroys the walls of hatred, division and disagreement, and is built upon mutual trust.

iii. It means the all-important internal peace which the human being can find within himself or herself. This aspect of the peace of Christ has far-reaching consequences. Paul speaks in Romans 7:14–25 of the human person divided against itself, whose will and actions are in conflict with each other. This person, without the liberating power which comes from the gift of the grace and peace of Jesus Christ, can only cry out: "Wretched man that I am! Who will deliver me from this body of death?" (Rom 7:24). Paul immediately provides the answer: "Thanks be to God through Jesus Christ our Lord!" (v. 25a).

18. In the hymn to Christ which opens the Letter to the Colossians (Col 1:15–20) the redemption brought about by Christ is praised as a universal, cosmic redemption. The whole creation is to be liberated from its bondage to decay to obtain the glorious liberty of the children of God. This theme of the essentially God-oriented integrity of the whole of creation, already eloquently spelt out in Paul's earlier Letter to the Romans,[55] makes us conscious of our contemporary responsibilities towards creation.

---

[51] Cf. Rom 6:10–11.
[52] Cf. Philem, esp. vv. 15–17.
[53] Cf. Gal 3:28.
[54] Cf. 1 Cor 13; Gal 5:22–26.
[55] Cf. Rom 8:18–23.

19. In the Letter to the Hebrews we find the image of the wandering people of God, on their way to the promised land of God's rest (Heb 4:11). The model is that of Moses' generation, journeying through the wilderness for forty years in search of the promised land of Canaan. In Jesus Christ, however, we have the "pioneer of salvation" (2:10) who, because of his Sonship, far surpasses Moses.[56] He is the high priest according to the order of Melchizedek. His priesthood not only surpasses the priesthood of the Old Covenant, but has abolished it (7:1–28). Jesus Christ has freed us from our sins through his sacrifice. He has sanctified us and made us his brethren. He has redeemed those who, through fear of death, were subject to lifelong bondage (2:10–15). He appears now as our advocate before the face of God (9:24; 7:25).

20. Thus, the Christian journey through history is marked by an unshakeable trust. It is true that "hope that is seen is not hope. For who hopes for what he sees? But if we hope for what we do not see, we wait for it with patience" (Rom 8:24–25). We may not see it, but we have been given the promise of the New Jerusalem, the place where: "He will dwell with them, and they shall be his people, and God himself will be with them; he will wipe away every tear from their eyes, and death shall be no more, neither shall there be mourning nor crying nor pain any more, for the former things have passed away. . . . Behold, I make all things new" (Rev 21:3–5). Already gifted with the Spirit, the freedom and the guarantee[57] which flows from the death and resurrection of Jesus, we move confidently towards the end of time crying: "Come, Lord Jesus!" (Rev 22:20).

PART III: HISTORICAL PERSPECTIVES

A. *Patristic Interpretations of Redemption*

Introduction

1. The Fathers continued the New Testament teaching on redemption, developing and elaborating certain themes in the light of their own religious and cultural situation. Stressing liberation from paganism, idolatry, and demonic powers, and in accordance with the contemporary mentality, they interpreted redemption mainly as a liberation of the mind and

---

[56] Cf. Heb 3:5–6.
[57] Cf. 2 Cor 1:22; 5:5; Eph 1:13–14.

spirit. However, they did not ignore the importance of the body, in which the signs of deterioration and death, as consequences of sin,[58] appeared most obviously. Adhering to the axiom "*caro cardo salutis*", they repudiated the Gnostic conception of the redemption of the soul only.

2. The Fathers have a clear notion of the "objective" work of redemption and reconciliation which brings about the salvation of the whole world, and a "subjective" work which concerns individual human beings. The "objective" is intimately concerned with the incarnation and Christology, while the "subjective" is concerned with the sacraments and the doctrine of grace, which accompany and direct human history towards the *eschaton*.

The Apostolic Fathers and the Apologists

3. Ignatius of Antioch uses the soteriological title *Christos iatros* (*Christus medicus*). "There is one Physician who is both flesh and spirit, born and yet not born, who is God in man, true life in death, both of Mary and of God, first passible and then impassible, Jesus Christ our Lord." [59] Christ does not merely cure the illness, but he embraces death, in as much as it is life; indeed true life is found in death. His healing activity, which is part of his redemptive work in the Gospels, expresses first of all his divine goodness: he intended his healings and exorcisms to be good deeds for which people would praise the Father. His healings were founded on his divine power to forgive sins, for which he required faith as the sole condition. This stream of thought can be found in the First Letter of Clement,[60] the Letter to Diognetus,[61] and in Origen.[62]

4. Justin's thought is intimately tied to the creed. His understanding of the *Christos didaskalos* and the *Logos didaskalos* recalls Jesus' teaching under Pontius Pilate. The Apologists emphasize the figure of *Christus Magister* (*Christos didaskalos*), and their interest still centers on his teaching and exorcisms, but Justin relies mainly on the tradition of the sacramental practice of the Church and on the credal formulations for his explanation of the healing presence of Christ. The words of the Logos come with divine force; they have liberating power. Genesis 6:1–4 set in motion evil forces, and salvation history is marked by the encounters between Christ and the demons in a struggle against ever-growing depravity, as is taught in Justin's *Apologia* (5–6, 6) and in Athenagoras (*Supplic.* 25, 3, 3–4). The

---

[58] Cf. Rom 5:12.

[59] *Ephesians* 7, 2 (CL, trans. K. Lake, *Apostolic Fathers*, 1:181).

[60] Cf. 59, 4.

[61] Cf. 9, 6.

[62] Cf. *Contra Celsum* 2, 67 (PG 11, 902B–C).

article of the Apostles' Creed "*descendit ad inferos*" describes the culmination of this battle through Jesus' baptism, temptation, exorcisms and resurrection. In a similar fashion, Justin's use of *soter* to speak of the continuation of Christ's redeeming work comes from the formulas of the liturgy and the creed. The same can be said for his idea of Jesus as *Redemptor* and helper, Son of God, first born of all creation, born of a virgin, who suffered under Pontius Pilate, died and rose from the dead, and who ascended into heaven, expelling, defeating and subduing all the demons.[63] Justin, while continuing the thought of the Apostolic Fathers, depends also upon the baptismal creeds, the New Testament, and the *soteria* lived out in the sacraments of the Church.

Irenaeus

5. Irenaeus, at the beginning of *Adversus haereses* Book 5, explains: Christ the teacher (*Christus Magister*) is the Word made man who has established communion with us, so that we can see him, grasp his word, imitate his deeds, fulfill his commands, and put on incorruptibility. In this we are remade in the likeness of Christ. At the same time, Christ is mighty Word and true man (*Verbum potens et homo verus*), who intelligibly (*rationabiliter*) redeemed us by his blood, giving himself as a ransom (*redemptionem*) for us. For Irenaeus, redemption was realized in a way which the human being was capable of understanding (*rationabiliter*): the Word, who is absolute in power, is also perfect in justice. The Word can therefore oppose the enemy, not with force, but with persuasion and kindness, assuming all that rightfully belongs to him (*sua proprie et benigne assumens*). Irenaeus does not concede that Satan has any right to domination over humankind after the Fall. On the contrary, Satan rules unjustly (*injuste*) because we belong to God according to our nature (*natura essemus Dei omnipotentis*). In redeeming us by his blood Christ inaugurated a new stage in the history of salvation, sending forth the Spirit of the Father so that God and humanity can unite and be in harmony. Through his incarnation he truly and surely granted incorruptibility to humanity.[64] The Redeemer and the redemption are inseparable because redemption is nothing else than the unity of the redeemed with the Redeemer.[65] The very presence of the divine Logos in humanity has a healing and elevating impact on human nature in general.

6. Irenaeus' notion of "recapitulation" (*anakephalaiosis*) involves the restoration of God's image in man. Although the expression comes from

---

[63] Cf. Justin, *Dialogue with Trypho* 30, 3.

[64] *Adversus haereses* 5, 1, 1 (Harvey, 2:314–17).

[65] Ibid., 5, praef.: "*uti nos perficeret esse quod est ipse*" (Harvey, 2:314).

Ephesians 1:10, Irenaeus' thought has a broad biblical basis. The *terminus a quo* of redemption is deliverance from the dominion of Satan and the recapitulation of the previous history of humankind. The *terminus ad quem* is the positive aspect: the renewal of God's image and likeness. The first Adam carries in himself the seed of the whole human race; the second Adam, by means of the incarnation, recapitulates every individual who has lived until then, and addresses all people and languages. Redemption does not only look to the past; it is an openness to the future. For the recapitulation of God's image and likeness both the *Verbum* and the *Spiritus* must be present. The first Adam foreshadows the incarnate Word, in view of whom the *Verbum* and the *Spiritus* had formed the first man, but he came to a standstill in "childhood" because the Spirit who gives growth left him. The granting of the likeness of the Holy Spirit introduces the new and final period of the "*oeconomia*", which was completed at the resurrection when the whole human race received the form of the new Adam.[66] The pneumatic aspect of the *anakephalaiosis* is important because the enduring possession of life is possible only through the Spirit.[67] Although the incarnation summarizes the past, condensing it in the recapitulation, it in some sense brings the past to an end. The outpouring of the Holy Spirit, which was inaugurated at the resurrection, directs history towards the *eschaton*, and makes the *anakephalaiosis* truly universal.

Greek Traditions

7. Athanasius never overlooked the significance of sin, but he saw clearly that the redeemer had to heal, not only the reality of sin itself, but also its consequences: the loss of likeness to God, corruption and death.[68] Athanasius held that if God had only needed to consider sin, he could have effected the redemption in some other way than by the incarnation and crucifixion. He did not deny that Christ entered into immediate contact with sin, but affirmed that although sin did not affect Christ's divine nature, he experienced in his human nature the consequences of sin. He entered the world of sin and corruption, because corruption and death are themselves sin.[69]

8. Gregory of Nazianzus teaches that the incarnation took place because humankind needed greater help. Previous to the incarnation, God's pedagogy had been insufficient.[70] Christ took on the whole of the human

---

[66] Ibid., 1, 2, 1 (Harvey, 1:91); 3, 17, 6 (Harvey, 2:87).

[67] Ibid., 5, 7, 2 (Harvey, 2:338).

[68] *De Incarnatione Verbi* 7 (ed. and trans. R. W. Thomson [Oxford, 1971], 148–50).

[69] *Orationes contra Arianos* 2, 68–69 (PG 26, 292A and 296A).

[70] *Orationes* 38, 13 (PG 37, 325A–B); *Epistula* 101 (PG 37, 177C).

condition to free us from the domination of sin,[71] but the source of salvation, made possible by the incarnation, is the crucifixion and resurrection of Christ.[72] Gregory totally rejects the supposition that God entered into negotiation with Satan, and the suggestion that a ransom was paid to the Father. Whatever was touched by the divinity was sanctified.[73] This notion is developed by Gregory of Nyssa who combines Johannine imagery to claim that the Word, as a shepherd, united himself to the hundredth sheep. Drawing an analogy with "the Word became flesh", he states that "the shepherd became the sheep." [74] This idea returns in Augustine: "Ipse et pro omnibus pateretur, ovis est factus." [75]

Latin Traditions

9. In the Latin tradition, Ambrose and Augustine drew from the richness of the Church's "mysteries", the liturgical life, the prayer and especially the sacramental life, flourishing in the Latin Church by the fourth century. Ambrose, whose knowledge of Greek enabled him to bring much of the Eastern tradition to the West, based his teachings upon the sacraments of Baptism, Penance and Eucharist. This not only furnishes us with a priceless testimony to the sacramental life of the Latin Church, but to the way in which the *Ecclesia orans* understood the mystery of God's redeeming action in the event of Christ, past (objective redemption), present and future (subjective redemption).[76]

10. Augustine is not an innovator in Christian thought on redemption. However, with depth and insight, he elaborates and synthesizes the traditions, the practices and the prayers of the Church which he received. Only God can help humankind in its powerlessness.[77] Augustine reveals the deep gulf between our actual state and our divine vocation. There can be no dealing between God and Satan. Redemption can only be a work of grace.[78] In God's plan of salvation the mission of Christ is restricted to a certain time, but yet is a supra-terrestrial reality: the love of the angry God towards

---

[71] Ibid., 30, 21 (PG 36, 132B).

[72] Ibid., 12, 4 (PG 35, 148B); 30, 6 (PG 36, 109C).

[73] Ibid., 12, 4 (PG 35, 848A–C).

[74] *Adversus Apollinarem* 3, 1 (*Gregorii Nysseni Opera*, ed. Mueller, 151–52).

[75] *In Johannis Evangelium tractatus* 123, 5 (CCSL 36, 678).

[76] Cf., for example, *De incarnationis dominicae sacramento, De mysteriis, De sacramentis, De paenitentia, De sacramento regenerationis sive de philosophia*.

[77] *De gratia Christi et de peccato originali* 25 (PL 44, 399).

[78] *De natura et gratia* 23, 5; 30, 34 (PL 44, 259 and 263); *De Trinitate* 14, 15, 21 (PL 40, 246).

humanity. This everlasting love, through the crucifixion and death of Christ, brings about reconciliation and Sonship.[79] The work of redemption must be worthy of both God and man, and thus God forgives and forgets sin only if the human person repents and atones for it. When this happens, God abolishes sin and death. Thus reparation and reconciliation are based on righteousness, as only in this way can humanity be responsibly involved in the history of salvation. Humanity is lured towards reconciliation to such an extent that it actively accepts salvation and redemption.

11. Redemption is not an event which simply happens to the human being. We are actively involved in it, through our head, Jesus Christ. The redeeming sacrifice of Christ is the apex of the cultic and moral activity of humankind. It is the one and only meritorious sacrifice (*sacrificium singulare*). The death of Jesus Christ is a perfect sacrifice and an act of worship. The crucifixion is a summation of all the sacrifices previously offered to God. Accepted by the Father, it obtains salvation for Christ's brothers and sisters. Repeating an idea, which, as with Ambrose, was associated with his understanding of the redemptive effect of the sacramental life of the Church, especially Baptism, Augustine taught that all sacrifices, including that of the Church, can only be a "figure"[80] of the *sacrificium singulare*, the sacrifice of Christ.[81]

12. Although it is sheer grace, redemption involves the *satis-factio* made through the obedience of the Son of God, whose blood is the ransom by means of which he merited and obtained justification and liberation.[82] Jesus Christ fights his battle as a human being and in this way saves the honor of humanity in his perfect response to God (the "*factio*" called for from humankind) and also reveals the majesty of God (the "*satis*" from God which completes "*satisfactio*"). Thus Christ is not only a healer but also a hallower, who saves by sanctifying. Continuing a tradition of the earlier Fathers, Augustine insists that Christ is the head of humankind, but because he was already also Savior of humankind before all time and before his incarnation, Christ influences all individuals, as well as humanity in general.

Conclusion

13. Themes which come to us from the biblical tradition form the basis of the patristic reflection upon redemption. The gulf between the human condition, and the hope for freedom to be sons and daughters of the one

---

[79] *Enchiridion* 10, 33, (PL 40, 248–49).
[80] Latin: *figura*; Greek: *heterosis*.
[81] Cf. *Enchiridion* 10, 13; 13, 41 (PL 40, 248–49 and 253).
[82] Cf. *De Trinitate* 14, 18–15, 19.

true God, are clearly understood and presented. God's initiative bridges the gulf through the sacrifice of Jesus Christ and his resurrection. Within the different schools of thought, these elements form the basis of the patristic reflection. Equally important to the Fathers is the association of human history and of human individuals with the death and resurrection of Jesus Christ. A life of love and obedience mirrors, and, in some way, involves us in the perennial significance of his life and death. Although they spoke in different ways, reflecting their own world views and their own problems, the Fathers of the Church further elaborated, on the basis of the New Testament and the growing "mysteries" of the Church's life, prayer and practice, a solid body of tradition upon which later theological reflection could build.

B. *More Recent Theories of Redemption*

14. Holy Scripture and the Fathers of the Church provide a solid foundation for reflection on the redemption of the human race through the life, teaching, death, and resurrection of Christ as the incarnate Son of God. They provide also an abundance of metaphors and analogies with which to illustrate and contemplate Christ's redemptive work. Speaking of Christ as conqueror, teacher, and physician, the Fathers tended to emphasize the "descending" action of God, but they did not neglect the work of Christ as one who offers satisfaction, paying the "ransom" that is due, and offering the one acceptable sacrifice.

15. It would be beyond the scope of the present document to trace the history of the theology of redemption down through the centuries. It may suffice for our purposes to indicate a few highlights of that history for the sake of ferreting out the main issues that have to be dealt with in a contemporary treatment.

Middle Ages

16. The medieval contribution to the theology of redemption may be studied in Anselm, Abelard, and Thomas Aquinas. In his classic work *Cur Deus Homo*, Anselm, without forgetting the "descending" initiative of God in the incarnation, puts the accent on the "ascending" work of legal restitution. He begins with the idea of God as sovereign Lord, whose honor is offended by sin. The order of commutative justice demands adequate reparation, which can only be given by the God-man. "This debt was so great that, while none but man must solve the debt, none but God was able to do it; so that he who does it must be both God and

man."[83] By offering adequate satisfaction, Christ delivers humanity from the penalty due to sin. Emphasizing the satisfactory death of Christ, Anselm is silent regarding the redemptive efficacy of Christ's resurrection. Concerned with deliverance from guilt, he pays little attention to the aspect of divinization. Concentrating his attention on objective redemption, Anselm does not expatiate on the subjective appropriation of the effects of redemption by the redeemed. He does, however, recognize that Christ set an example of holiness for all to follow.[84]

17. Peter Abelard, while not denying the satisfactory value of Christ's death, prefers to speak of Christ as teaching by way of example. In his view, God could have satisfied his honor without the Cross of Christ, but God wanted sinners to recognize themselves as objects of the crucified love of Jesus and thereby be converted. Abelard sees in the passion of Christ a revelation of God's love, an example that stirs us to imitation. As his *locus classicus* he appeals to John 15:13: "No one has greater love than this, to lay down one's life for one's friends."[85]

18. Thomas Aquinas takes up Anselm's satisfaction concept but interprets it in ways reminiscent of Abelard. For Aquinas satisfaction is the concrete expression of sorrow for sin. He holds that Christ's passion compensated for sin by being preeminently an act of love, without which there could be no satisfaction.[86] In his sacrifice Christ offered God more than was demanded. Quoting 1 John 2:2, Aquinas declares that the passion of Christ satisfied superabundantly for the sins of the whole world.[87] The death of Christ was necessary only as a result of God's free decision to redeem humankind in a suitable manner, showing forth both the justice and the mercy of God.[88] For Aquinas Christ the Redeemer heals and divinizes sinful human beings not only by his Cross but also by his incarnation and by all his *acta et passa in carne*, including his glorious resurrection. In his suffering and death Christ is not a mere substitute for fallen sinners, but rather the representative head of a regenerated humanity. Aquinas maintains "that Christ is the head of the Church, and that the grace that he possesses as head is passed on to all the members of the Church because of the organic conjunction that obtains within the Mystical Body."[89]

---

[83] *Cur Deus Homo* 2, 18a (S. N. Deane, *Basic Writings of St. Anselm*, 279).

[84] Ibid., 2, 18b (Deane, 280).

[85] *Sermo* 9 (PL 178, 447).

[86] *STh* III, 14, 1 ad 1; cf. Suppl. 14, 2.

[87] *STh* III, 48, 2c.

[88] *STh* III, 46, 1c and ad 3.

[89] "Select Questions on Christology", in *International Theological Commission: Texts and Documents, 1969–1985* (San Francisco: Ignatius Press, 1989), 185–205, at 201.

Reformation and Counter-Reformation

19. The Protestant Reformers took over the Anselmian theory of satisfaction, but they did not distinguish, as he did, between the alternatives of satisfaction and punishment. For Luther, satisfaction takes place precisely through punishment. Christ stands under God's wrath, for, as Paul teaches in the Letter to the Galatians, 3:13, he took on not only the consequences of sin, but sin itself.[90] Christ, according to Luther, is the greatest robber, murderer, adulterer, and blasphemer that ever lived.[91] At some points Luther speaks paradoxically of Christ as altogether pure and yet the greatest sinner.[92] Because Christ has fully paid the debt due to God, we are dispensed from any performance. Sinners can complete the "happy exchange" if they cease to rely on any merits of their own and clothe themselves by faith with the merits of Christ, just as he clothed himself with humanity's sins.[93] Justification takes place through faith alone.

20. Calvin presents an imputative understanding of the sinfulness of Christ. Christ, he says, was covered by the filth of sin through "transferred imputation".[94] "The guilt that held us liable for punishment has been transferred to the head of the Son of God. We must above all remember this substitution"[95] in order to be delivered from anxiety. Not only did Jesus die as a malefactor; he also went to hell and suffered the pains of the damned.[96]

21. In the seventeenth century Hugo Grotius cast the soteriology of Calvin into a more juridical form, explaining at some length how the shedding of Christ's blood shows forth God's hatred for sin.[97]

22. The Council of Trent gives a brief discussion of redemption in its Decree on Justification. Basing itself on Augustine and Aquinas, the Council maintained that Christ through his great love merited our justification and satisfied for us on the tree of the Cross.[98] The doctrine of satisfaction is integrated by Trent into a broader framework that includes the divinization imparted to justified sinners through the Holy Spirit, who makes them living members of the Body of Christ.[99]

---

[90] *Commentary on Galatians* (1535) (WA 40/1, 434, 7–9).

[91] Ibid., 433, 26–29.

[92] Ibid., 435, 17–19.

[93] Ibid., 434, 7–9.

[94] *Institutes of the Christian Religion*, 11, 16, 6.

[95] Ibid., 16, 5.

[96] Ibid., 16, 10.

[97] *Defensio fidei catholicae de satisfactione Christi* (1617); cf. Sesboüé, *Jésus-Christ l'unique médiateur* (Paris: Desclée, 1988), 1, 71.

[98] Sess. 6, chap. 7.

[99] Ibid., also canon 11.

Liberal Protestantism

23. In some versions of Protestant, and even Catholic, pulpit oratory, the penal substitution theory depicted God almost as a vengeful sovereign exacting reparation for his offended honor. The idea that God would punish the innocent in place of the guilty seemed incompatible with the Christian conviction that God is eminently just and loving. It is understandable, therefore, that liberal Christians took a very different approach, in which the vindictive justice of God held no place. Going back in some respects to Abelard, some nineteenth-century theologians emphasized the exemplary love of Jesus, which evokes a response of gratitude, enabling others to imitate his loving actions and thereby attain justification. Under the influence of Kant the doctrine of redemption was purified of its supposed "sacerdotal corruptions", including the concepts of sacrifice and penal satisfaction. Albrecht Ritschl, with due credit to Kant, redefined redemption in terms of freedom to collaborate in an association of virtue with a view to the "kingdom of God".[100]

24. A variant of the liberal theory may be found in Schleiermacher, who maintained that Jesus draws us to perfection not so much by what he does as by what he is, as the supreme instance of human consciousness transformed by union with the divine. Rather than speaking simply of moral influence, Schleiermacher used organic, even physical, categories of causality. "By imparting to them a new vital principle the Redeemer assumes the believers into the fellowship of his unclouded blessedness, and this is his reconciling activity." [101]

Twentieth-Century Movements

25. Several new theories of redemption have surfaced in the twentieth century. In the kerygmatic theology of Rudolf Bultmann God redeems humanity by means of the proclamation of the Cross and the resurrection. The redemptive significance of the Cross, for Bultmann, lies not in any "ascending" theory of sacrifice or vicarious satisfaction (both of which savor of mythology), but in the "descending" judgment of the world and its deliverance from the power of evil. The paradoxical message of salva-

---

[100] Albrecht Ritschl, *The Christian Doctrine of Justification and Reconciliation* (Edinburgh: T. and T. Clark, 1902); German original, *Die christliche Lehre von der Rechtfertigung und Versöhnung*, vol. 3 (Bonn, 1874).

[101] *The Christian Faith*, 101; Harper Torchbooks ed., p. 431; German original, *Der christliche Glaube nach den Grundsätzen der evangelischen Kirche im Zusammenhang dargestellt* (1821–1822), 2nd rev. ed., vol. 2 (Berlin, 1960), 97.

tion through the Cross arouses in its hearers a response of loving submission, whereby they are moved from inauthentic to authentic existence. "To believe in the cross of Christ does not mean to concern ourselves with a mythical process wrought outside of us and our world, with an objective event turned by God to our advantage, but rather to make the cross of Christ our own, to undergo crucifixion with him."[102]

26. Paul Tillich has a similar existential theory, except that he ascribes the power to overcome human estrangement to the biblical image of Jesus as the Christ, and especially to the symbol of the Cross. "The Cross is not the cause but the effective manifestation of God's taking the consequences of human guilt upon himself."[103] As God participates in human suffering, so we are redeemed by freely participating in the divine participation and allowing it to transform us.[104]

27. In either form the existential theory attributes redemption to the power of God working through the words or symbols that transform human self-understanding. Only secondary attention is paid to Jesus himself, who is considered to be an obscure, myth-encumbered figure of history.

28. Reacting against the neglect of the historical Jesus in kerygmatic theology and against the Church-centered piety of recent centuries, some recent theologians have striven to reconstruct the actual history of Jesus and have emphasized the manner in which his death resulted from his struggle against oppressive and unjust structures, both political and religious. Jesus, it is held, championed the rights of the poor, the marginalized, the persecuted. His followers are required to enter into solidarity with the downtrodden. Jesus' life and death are seen as redemptive insofar as they inspire others to take up the struggle for a just society. This type of soteriology is characteristic of liberation theology and some versions of political theology.[105]

29. Liberation theology can seem to be one-sided in its emphasis on social reform. As some of its adherents acknowledge, holiness cannot be achieved, nor can sin be overcome, by a mere change of social and economic structures. Because evil has its source to a great extent in the human heart, hearts and minds must be transformed and imbued with life from

---

[102] R. Bultmann, "New Testament and Mythology", in H. W. Bartsch, ed., *Kerygma and Myth* (Harper Torchbooks, 1961), 36; German original, "Neues Testament und Mythologie", in H. W. Bartsch, ed., *Kerygma und Mythos: Ein theologisches Gespräch* (Hamburg-Berstedt, 1960), 15–48.

[103] *Systematic Theology*, 2:176.

[104] Ibid.

[105] The doctrine of redemption in liberation theology may be studied in works such as Gustavo Gutierrez, *Teologia de la liberacion* (1971), Leonardo Boff, *Jesus Cristo Libertador* (1972), and Jon Sobrino, *Cristologia desde america latina* (1976).

above. Liberation theologians differ among themselves in the emphasis that they give to eschatological hope. Some of them state explicitly that the kingdom of God cannot be fully established by human action within history but only by God's action at the *Parousia*.

30. Among modern theologians who wish to restore the sense of God's "descending" action on behalf of his needy creatures, Karl Rahner deserves special mention. He depicts Jesus as the unsurpassable symbol that manifests God's irreversible universal salvific will. As a symbolic reality, Christ effectively represents both God's irrevocable self-communication in grace and the acceptance of that self-communication by humanity.[106] Rahner is very reserved towards the idea of expiatory sacrifice, which he describes as an ancient notion that was presupposed as valid in New Testament times, but one that "offers little help today toward understanding what we are looking for", i.e. the causal significance of the death of Jesus.[107] In Rahner's theory of quasi-sacramental causality God's salvific will posits the sign, in this case the death of Jesus along with his resurrection, and in and through the sign it causes what is signified.[108]

31. It would seem that for Rahner the essential benefits of redemption may be obtained through the acceptance of the inner self-communication of God which is given to all, as a "supernatural existential", even before the good news of Jesus Christ is heard. The message of the gospel, when it becomes known, makes it possible to understand better what is already implied in God's inner word of grace. All who hear and believe the Christian message obtain assurance that God's final word toward human beings is not one of severity and judgment but one of love and mercy.

32. Rahner's theory is of unquestionable value in placing the emphasis on God's loving initiative and on the appropriate response of trust and gratitude. It gets away from the legalistic and moralistic limitations of some earlier theories. Some have questioned, however, whether the theory gives sufficient place to the causal efficacy of the Christ event and especially to the redemptive character of Jesus' death on the Cross. Does the Christ-symbol simply express and communicate what is antecedently given in God's universal salvific will? Is God's inner word (as "transcendental revelation") emphasized at the expense of the outer word given in the proclamation of the gospel as good news?

33. Going beyond Rahner, several contemporary theologians have introduced a more radical distinction between the transcendental and the

---

[106] Karl Rahner, *Foundations of Christian Faith* (New York: Crossroad, 1982), 194–95; German original, *Grundkurs des Glaubens*, 3rd ed. (Freiburg, 1976), 193–95.

[107] Ibid., 282; German original, 276f.

[108] Ibid., 284; German original, 278.

predicamental aspects of religion. For them revelation as a transcendental orientation is given to the human spirit always and everywhere. In the various religions, including Judaism and Christianity, they find historically and culturally conditioned symbolizations of a spiritual experience common to them all. All religions are regarded as redemptive to the extent that their "myths" arouse awareness of the inward working of grace and impel their adherents to liberative action. Notwithstanding their doctrinal divergences, it is contended, the various religions are united in their orientation to salvation. "The common thrust, however, remains *soteriological*, the concern of most religions being *liberation (vimukti, moksa, nirvana)*."[109] On the basis of reasoning such as this, one contemporary theologian calls for a transition from theocentrism or Christocentrism to what he calls "soteriocentrism".[110]

34. These interreligious approaches are praiseworthy attempts to achieve harmony between different religious conceptions and to reclaim the centrality of soteriology. But the distinct identities of the religions are placed in jeopardy. Christianity, in particular, is denatured if deprived of its doctrine that all redemption comes not simply through an interior working of divine grace or through human commitment to liberative action but through the saving work of the incarnate Word, whose life and death are actual historical events.

35. From the transcendental theology of religions there is but a short step to the New Age theories to which allusion has been made in Part I. On the assumption that the divine is an inherent constituent of human nature, some theologians urge a creation-centered religion of celebration in place of the traditional Christian emphasis on the Fall and the redemption. Salvation is held to consist in the discovery and actualization of the immanent divine presence through cosmic spirituality, joyous liturgy, and psychological techniques of consciousness-raising or self-mastery.[111]

36. The methods of spiritual awareness and discipline that have been developed in the great religious traditions and in some contemporary "human potential" movements should not be neglected, but they are not to be equated with redemption in the Christian sense of the word. There

[109] Aloysius Pieris, "The Place of Non-Christian Religions and Cultures in the Evolution of Third World Theology", in *Irruption of the Third World: Challenge to Theology*, Virginia Fabella and Sergio Torres, eds. (Maryknoll, N.Y.: Orbis Books, 1983), 133.

[110] Paul F. Knitter, "Toward a Liberation Theology of Religions", in *The Myth of Christian Uniqueness: Toward a Pluralistic Theology of Religions*, ed. John Hick and Paul F. Knitter, 178–200, at 187.

[111] Many of these themes are exemplified in the works of Matthew Fox, notably his *Original Blessing: A Primer in Creation Spirituality* (Santa Fe, N.M.: Bear and Co., 1983; expanded edition, 1990).

are no valid grounds for minimizing the pervasive effects of sin and the incapacity of humanity to redeem itself. Humanity is not redeemed, nor is God fittingly glorified, except through God's merciful action in Jesus Christ.

Retrieval of Earlier Tradition

37. A number of contemporary Catholic theologians are seeking to maintain in tension the "descending" and "ascending" themes of classical soteriology. Often leaning towards a narrative or dramatic theology of redemption, these authors have retrieved important themes in the biblical accounts, in Irenaeus, Augustine, and Thomas Aquinas. The following composite sketch is based on materials taken from a variety of recent authors.

38. As distinct from legalistic theories of restitution or penal substitution, these theories put the accent on what we may call representative headship. While not overlooking the opposition between the Redeemer and the redeemed, these theories emphasize the way in which Christ identifies himself with fallen humanity. He is the new Adam, the progenitor of a redeemed humanity, the Head or the Vine into whom individuals must be incorporated as members or branches. Sacramental participation is the normal manner whereby individuals become members of the Body of Christ and grow in their union with him.

39. The theory of representative headship understands redemption as God's gracious intervention into the human situation of sin and suffering. The incarnate Word becomes the gathering point for the constitution of a reconciled and restored humanity. The entire career of Jesus, including the mysteries of his hidden and public life, is redemptive, but it comes to a culmination in the paschal mystery whereby Jesus, through his loving submission to the Father's will, seals a new covenant relationship between God and humanity. The death of Jesus, which results inevitably from his courageous opposition to human sin, constitutes his supreme act of sacrificial self-giving, and is under that aspect pleasing to the Father, satisfying in an eminent way for the disorder of sin. Without being personally guilty or being punished by God for the sins of others, Jesus lovingly identifies with sinful humanity and experiences the pain of its alienation from God.[112] In his meekness Jesus allows his enemies to unload their resentment upon him. Returning love for hatred, and consenting to suffer as though he were guilty, Jesus makes God's merciful love present in

---

[112] Cf. *Catechisme de l'Église Catholique* (Paris: Mame, 1992), no. 603, pp. 132–33.

history and opens a channel through which redemptive grace can flow forth upon the world.

40. The work of redemption completes itself in the risen life of the Savior. In raising Jesus from the dead, God establishes him as the source of life for the many. The resurrection is the outpouring of God's creative love into the empty space created by Jesus' "kenotic" self-abnegation. Through the risen Christ, acting in the Holy Spirit, the process of redemption continues to the end of time, as new individuals are, so to speak, "grafted" into the Body of Christ. Sinners are redeemed when they open themselves to God's generous self-bestowal in Christ; when, with the help of his grace, they imitate his obedience, and when they place their hope of salvation in God's continued mercy in his Son. To be redeemed, in short, is to enter into communion with God through solidarity with Christ. In the Body of Christ the walls of division are progressively demolished; reconciliation and peace are achieved.

PART IV: SYSTEMATIC PERSPECTIVES

A. The Identity of the Redeemer: Who Is the Redeemer?

1. From the very ideas of sin or fallenness, on the one hand, and of grace or divinization on the other, it seems evident that fallen human nature was not by itself capable of restoring its broken relationship with God and entering into friendship with him. A true Redeemer, therefore, would have to be divine. It was highly fitting, however, that humankind should play a part in repairing for its own collective fault. In the words of Thomas Aquinas, "A mere man could not satisfy for the whole human race; but God did not have to make satisfaction; therefore it was needed [oportebat] for Jesus Christ to be both God and man." [113] According to Christian faith, God did not cancel out human guilt without the participation of humanity in the person of the new Adam, in whom the whole race was to be regenerated.

2. The redemption, therefore, is a process involving both the divinity and the humanity of Christ. If he were not divine he could not pronounce God's effective judgment of forgiveness nor could he bring a share in God's inner Trinitarian life. But if he were not man Jesus Christ could not make reparation in the name of humanity for the offenses committed by Adam and Adam's posterity. Only because he has both natures could

---

[113] STh III, 1, 2c.

he be the representative head who offers satisfaction for all sinners and who bestows grace upon them.

3. As a work of God *ad extra*, redemption is attributable to all three of the divine persons, but in different respects it is attributed to each of them. The initiative whereby the Son and the Spirit are sent into the world is attributed to the Father, the aboriginal source from whom all blessings flow. The Son, inasmuch as he becomes incarnate and dies on the Cross, effects the reversal whereby we are transformed from enmity into friendship with God. The Holy Spirit, sent into the minds and hearts of believers, enables them to partake personally in the benefits of God's redemptive action. After the Ascension of Christ, the Holy Spirit makes present the fruits of Christ's redemptive activity in and through the Church.[114]

4. Who is the Redeemer? This question can only be answered from within the Church and through the Church. To know the Redeemer is to belong to the Church. Augustine emphasized this in his teaching on the whole Christ, *Christus totus*, Head and Members together. As Gregory the Great put it, "Our Redeemer is seen to be one person with the holy Church that he has made his own."[115] The life of the Church as the Body of Christ is not to be amputated from the life of the Head. John Eudes provides an initial approach to a description of the Redeemer's uniqueness: "We must continue to accomplish in ourselves the stages of Jesus' life and his mysteries and often to beg him to perfect and realize them in us and in his whole Church.... For it is the plan of the Son of God to make us ... partake in his mysteries and to extend them to and continue them in us and in his whole Church."[116] *Gaudium et spes*, 22, expresses this all-embracing uniqueness of the Redeemer: "The truth is that only in the mystery of the incarnate Word does the mystery of man take on light. For Adam, the first man, was a figure of Him Who was to come, namely Christ the Lord. Christ, the final Adam, by the revelation of the mystery of the Father and His love, fully reveals man to man himself and makes his supreme calling clear.... Since human nature as He assumed it was not annulled, by that very fact it has been raised up to a divine dignity in our respect too. For by His incarnation the Son of God has united Himself in some fashion with every man. He worked with human hands, He thought with a human mind, acted

---

[114] The links between the missions of the Son and the Holy Spirit in the mystery of redemption are explored by John Paul II in his 1986 encyclical *Dominum et vivificantem*, especially nos. 11, 14, 24, 28, and 63.

[115] *Mor. praef.* 1, 6, 4; cf. *CCC* 795 for further references.

[116] Quoted in *CCC* 521; for this whole question cf. *CCC* 512–70.

by human choice and loved with a human heart." John Paul II echoes this in *Redemptor hominis*, 13, 3: "With each [man] Christ has united himself for ever through this mystery [of the redemption]."

5. Through the incarnation of the Word the Redeemer's uniqueness becomes discernible to us already in its redeeming force. In the paschal mystery the Redeemer has made salvation available to all: "And I, when I am lifted up from the earth, will draw all people to myself" (Jn 12:32). The gift of Pentecost enabled his apostles and disciples finally to recognize who and what Jesus was as in the fellowship of the Church—the teaching, the breaking of bread, the prayers (Acts 2:42)—they became aware of what Jesus had done for them, what he had taught and commanded. This is precisely the function of the Holy Spirit in Johannine theology (cf. Jn 16:13–15).

6. Hence we as human beings can come to know who the Redeemer is, but only within the community of the Church and through it. Christ cannot be isolated from the Church. Christ is precisely the one who nourishes his body as Church and so draws the community of believers into the work of bringing about the redemption. It would also be a mistake to burden the Church with an autonomy it could not bear on its own.

7. Christ's uniqueness is to be understood within this "Christological constellation" that takes concrete shape in the Church. The Easter mystery forms the context for the Church's liturgical year.[117] Christians are invited—through the objectivity of their faith (*fides quae*) and also in accordance with their own possibilities within the Church community—to confess and preach Christ as the one and only Redeemer of this world so that the Church is the sacrament of universal salvation. The Christ event will be made available through the Church in so far as the Church perceives, explains and preaches the uniqueness of the Redeemer.

8. The Church makes present the one and only Redeemer in that as a community (*koinonia*) living out the Easter mystery, the Church welcomes all who experience justification in Christ in Baptism or in the sacrament of Reconciliation and want to live out the redemption. Though here we must also take into account that communion in Christ's sacrifice ("*prosphora*") also involves a share in his sufferings;[118] this suffering with Christ which is expressed both sacramentally and effectively in the Christian life contributes to the building up of the Church and is hence redemptive.

9. The meaning of the redemption and the uniqueness of the Redeemer are revealed in the activities that are constitutive of the Church in this

---

[117] Cf. *SC* 102–4.
[118] Cf. Col 1:2.

world: *martyria, diakonia* and *leitourgia*. As the Lord's *koinonia* the Church summons humanity to a selfless *prosphora* lifestyle which has its basis principally in the Eucharist but also in the communion of saints—in which Mary has a special place. This knowledge, acquired from the lived faith of the Church, that an inter-subjectivity exists between the redeemed and the one and only Redeemer, can be objectified in genuine theological statements. Such statements, when they start from the objectivity of the Redeemer, can strengthen the individual's life of faith and give it a precise shape. Very ancient, for example, and inseparably linked to knowledge of the uniqueness of the Redeemer, is the celebration of Sunday as the Day of the Resurrection of the one who was crucified.

10. The association of the Church in the redemptive work of Christ is eminently verified in the person of Mary, Mother of the Church. By singular grace she was preserved from all sin, and her association with Christ's redemptive work would come to a climax at the crucifixion, when, "grieving exceedingly with her only begotten Son, [she united] herself with a maternal heart with His sacrifice, and lovingly consent[ed] to the immolation of this Victim which she herself had brought forth." [119] In the words of John Paul II, "With the redeeming death of her Son, the maternal mediation of the handmaid of the Lord took on a universal dimension.... Mary's cooperation shares, in its subordinate character, in the universality of the mediation of the Redeemer, the one Mediator." [120]

11. The Father has made us his children in that he redeemed us through the human will of Christ. In that Christ obeyed the Father's will and gave his life for many,[121] his person and his work of redemption in our world acquire a meaning and a dignity that are unique and beyond comparison. Christ's being-from-the-Father continues in his surrender-for-us. This unique relationship, of its very nature, cannot be theologically integrated into any other religion, even though the work of redemption is accessible to all. The fact that Christ's human will as Redeemer is historically conditioned does not of itself exclude the possibility that it is humanly *sui generis* which is perhaps what Hebrews refers to as "learning obedience", an obedience that Christ will radically fulfill in the Easter mystery. Because this human will of Christ as Redeemer is totally in agreement with the divine will ("Not my will, but thy will, be done") Christ is, as incarnate mediator, also our advocate in the heavenly sanctuary.[122]

---

[119] LG 58.
[120] *Redemptoris Mater* (1987), 40.
[121] Cf. Mk 14:24; 10:45; ITC 1985, thesis 2.
[122] Hebrews; Eucharistic Prayers.

12. The notion of the self-giving of the Redeemer for all is undoubt-edly dependent on the Easter mystery, but it is no less dependent on the mystery of the incarnation and the mysteries of the life of Christ which are for Christians invitation and example in living their lives as *"filii in Filio"*.[123] Here it becomes clear that the Christian life has a Trinitarian dimension. In the course of the justification that the believer can receive in the Church, Christian experience passes over with the Redeemer into a sanctification of the redeemed life which is guided and perfected—more intensively than in justification—by the Holy Spirit. This means that we are invited through Christ in the Holy Spirit to share, already now, in the divine life of the Trinity. The Father's gift, namely the person of his Son and the sharing in the Holy Spirit, thus forbids a Pelagianism that would attempt to justify human nature through its own resources—and likewise excludes a quietism that would involve the human person too little.

12. The Christian life is correctly seen in the tradition as a preparation for eternal fellowship with God. In this sense we are journeying "in the flesh" towards our one and only Lord, the Redeemer, in order, one day, to be more fully united with him. However, the uniqueness of the Redeemer is revealed in the life of believers here and now. In this world, marked as it is both by the goodness of creation and the sinfulness of the Fall, Christians try, by their imitation of Christ, to live out and to propagate the redemp-tion. Their virtuous living and the example of a Christian lifestyle make it possible for people in every epoch to come to know who the one and only Redeemer of this world is. Evangelization is precisely this.

B. *Humanity Fallen and Redeemed*

14. Christian faith in the redemption is first of all faith in God. In Jesus Christ, his own and only incarnate Son, "the one whom men call God" (Saint Thomas) reveals himself in revealing himself as the one and true Savior in whom all can trust. At the same time, however, we must note that this God-Savior also reveals *mankind* to itself: its own condition is therefore radically situated and constantly called to define itself, in rela-tion to the salvation which is offered.

15. How is the human condition enlightened by the salvation which God offers it in Jesus Christ? How does humanity appear in the face of redemption? The answer could enlighten the human historic situation, but as we have noted in Chapter I, it is also marked by important contrasts.

---

[123] Cf. Rom 8:15–17.

16. It could be said that in face of the redemption that Jesus Christ offers, humanity discovers that it is fundamentally oriented towards salvation (1) and profoundly marked by sin (2).

Humanity for Salvation

17. The first light that Christ's redemption throws on humanity is that he reveals it to itself as at one and the same time *destined* for salvation and *capable* of accepting it.

18. The entire biblical tradition is full of situations in which the people of Israel—or the groups of poor people who are called to become the people of Israel—were led to search for and to confess their God through interventions by which God rescues them from distress and perdition. From the Exodus adventures where Yahweh intervened with a strong hand and an outstretched arm, to the pardon given to the broken and repentant heart, it is clear that for God's people and for every believer, it is to the extent to which God appears to bring *salvation*, that God reveals himself.

19. But correlatively it is clear that God intervenes and thus reveals himself in relation to a *need* for salvation clearly manifested in its true dimensions to those who benefit from the salvation which God gives them. This general characteristic of biblical revelation will be highlighted in the New Testament.

20. God was so faithful to his "commitment" to humanity, to his plan for a covenant with humanity that "at the appointed time" he sent them his only Son. In other words, God was not simply satisfied to intervene "from outside", by means of intermediaries, that is to say, remaining at a distance from those whom he wished to save. In Jesus Christ, God came among them, God became one of them. The Father sent his only Son, in the Holy Spirit, to share the human condition (in all things except sin), so as to establish communication with mankind. This was done to allow them to return fully to God's favor and to enter fully into the divine life. The result is that the human condition sees itself in a completely new perspective.

21. The human condition appears first of all as *the object of love* which can go "to the extreme": the proof that God loves us is that Christ, while we were still sinners, "died for us" (Rom 5:8) and "if God is for us, who will be against us. He who did not spare his only Son, but delivered him up for us all, will not refuse us any favors" (Rom 8:31–32).

22. Then there is the fullness of destiny which awaits humanity in accordance with the salvific will which God manifested in its regard in

his Son who became incarnate, died and rose from the dead. There is also the radical nature of salvation which God destines for humanity in Jesus Christ: it is invited to enter in turn into the dynamism of the paschal mystery of Jesus, the Christ. On the one hand this salvation takes the form of a *sonship*, in the Spirit of Christ the Son. Drawn and supported by the Spirit (participants through the sacraments), they are called to live by faith and in hope their condition of sons of the Father who is in heaven, but with the duty of fulfilling his will on earth, by loving and serving their brethren in love.

23. On the other hand if they are not spared the experiences of hope and sadness, indeed the sufferings of this world, they know that the grace of God—the active presence in them of his love and mercy—will accompany them in all circumstances. And if they must also experience death, they know that it will not seal their destiny, for they have the promise of the resurrection of the body and life everlasting.

24. Although humanity may appear to be impoverished and unworthy, we must not conclude that it is totally worthless in the eyes of God. On the contrary, the Bible constantly reminds us that if God intervenes on behalf of humanity, it is precisely because God considers human beings worthy of his intervention. We should note for instance the assurance given to Israel in the depth of its suffering: "because you are precious in my eyes, because you are honored and I love you" (Is 43:4).

25. In other words, according to the biblical and Christian faith, despite all that is negative in humanity, there remains there something that is "*capable of being saved*", because it is *capable of being loved* by God himself and is consequently *loved by him*. How can this be and how does the human person become aware of it?

26. The biblical and Christian response is given in the doctrine of creation. According to this doctrine humanity and the world have no right to exist, and yet they are not the result of "chance or necessity". They exist because they have been and are called. They were called when they were not in existence but so that they might come into being. They are called from non-being to be given to themselves and thus to exist in themselves.

27. But if such is man's native condition in this world—this condition which defines him precisely as a preacher—there are important consequences which faith makes explicit.

28. God does not create humanity without having an intention. He creates it for the very reason that the divine interventions in history reveal: out of love for humanity and for its good. To put it more precisely, he creates the human person to make a covenant with it, with a view to making it a participant in God's own life. In other words if there is creation it is *for grace*, for the life of God, with God and for God.

29. If God calls us to a destiny which clearly surpasses our human powers, since it can only be pure grace, it is nevertheless true that this destiny should *correspond to what the human person is as such*. Otherwise it would be a person other than the one who is called to be saved who would receive the gift of God, and who would be the beneficiary of grace. In this sense, while respecting the gratuity of grace, human nature is orientated towards the supernatural, and fulfills itself in and through it in such a way that the nature of humanity is open to the supernatural (*capax Dei*).

30. However, as this is only meaningful in the context of a covenant, it must also be noticed that God does not impose his grace on humanity; he simply offers it. However, *this involves a risk*. Using the freedom which God has given, the human being may not always act in harmony with God's intentions but may misuse the talents which God has given for its own ends and its own glory.

31. God has given these gifts so that the desire which would lead mankind to seek and to find God as the only fulfillment should come from the human person itself. But the human person can always re-orientate the dynamism of his nature and the movement of his heart. It nevertheless remains true that the human being has been constituted and will remain so for the love of God: for the grace and salvation that God intends for it.

Humanity in Sin

32. Christ's redemption gives us a second viewpoint on humanity in its historical condition: the negative aspects which mark it (1) are also the result of human sin (2), but this does not cast in doubt God's faithfulness to his creative and saving love.

33. As in the case of any common experience, faith must take note of the negative aspects of the human condition. It cannot ignore that, in history, everything does not take place in accordance with the intentions of God the Creator. This however does not invalidate faith: the God in whom faith is professed can be trusted. Not only did God not renounce his first intention, but he took means of restoring, in a most admirable manner, what was compromised. Intervening in Jesus Christ, he showed himself to be faithful to himself, despite the infidelity of the human person, his partner.

34. In sending his own Son in human form, God the Creator of the world and Savior, removed every justification for doubting the divine plan for a saving covenant.

35. This manifestation of God's faithfulness to his covenant shows up the negative aspects of the human condition and consequently the extent and depth of the need for salvation among the human race.

36. If indeed God had to send his only Son to *restore* his plan of salvation founded in the very act of creation, it is because this plan had been radically compromised. His success has to do with this "rebeginning" which Irenaeus called "recapitulation". If the Son became incarnate to reestablish God's covenant, it is because the covenant was broken not by the will of God, but by the will of human beings. And if in order to reestablish it, the incarnate Son had to do the will of the Father, if he had to become *obedient unto death* even to death on the Cross, it is because the true source of human misfortune is in its disobedience, its sin, its refusal to walk in the ways of the covenant offered by God.

37. Thus the incarnation, life, death and resurrection of God's own Son, as well as revealing the love of God the Savior, at the same time reveal the human condition to itself.

38. If Jesus appears as the only way to salvation, it is because humanity needs him for its salvation, and because without him it will be lost. We must therefore acknowledge that all people, and the entire world, were "enclosed in sin" (Gal 3:22), and that this has been so "from the beginning". It can therefore be said that Jesus appeared to "restore" the human condition in a radical way, that is to say with a new beginning.

39. It could be said that Christ represents more of a "beginning" than Adam himself. "Originating" *Love* is more important than "Original" *Sin*, since the human race only took full cognizance of the extent and depth of sin which marks its condition at the time when in Jesus Christ the "length, breadth, height, and depth" (Eph 3:18) of God's love for the whole human race was revealed.

40. If God sent his only Son to re-open the gates of salvation to all, it is because he did not change his attitude in their regard; the change was on the part of the human race. The covenant which was willed from the beginning by the God of love was compromised by human sin. Consequently there was a conflict between God's plan on the one hand, and human desires and behavior on the other (Rom 5:12).

41. In refusing God's invitation from the beginning, humanity deviated from its true destiny and the events of history are marked by an alienation from God and from his plan of love; history is indeed marked by a rejection of God.

42. The coming of God's only Son into the heart of human history reveals the divine will to pursue the application of its plan despite opposition. As well as taking account of the gravity of sin and its consequence on humanity's part—the "mystery" of iniquity—the mystery of Christ, and

particularly his Cross, is the clear and definitive revelation of the gratuitous, radically pardoning, and eschatologically victorious nature of the love of God.

43. Here we may note the traditional patristic and Augustinian theme of the two "Adams". There is no effort to equate them, but their traditional *rapprochement* is nevertheless rich in meaning. The main Pauline passages which make the parallel (Rom 5:12–15 and 1 Cor 15:21–22, 45–47) use it to highlight the universal dimension of sin on the one hand and of salvation on the other. This parallel is in its application dominated by the idea of a "how much the more" which tips the balance in favor of Christ and of salvation: if the first Adam has a universal dimension in the order of the Fall, how much the more has the second acquired this universal dimension *in the order of salvation*: that is to say through the universal dimension of his offer and the eschatological efficacy of his communication.

44. This then is how the human condition appears: divided between two Adams, and this is how the Christian faith interprets this "contrasted" situation which anybody, even outside of the context of faith, can recognize as a characteristic of the historical condition of the human person. Immersed in a history of sin, disobedience and death, as a result of its origins in Adam, humanity is called to enter into the solidarity of the new Adam whom God has sent: his only Son who died for our sins, and who rose again for our justification. Christian faith makes it clear that with the first Adam there has been a proliferation of sin, and with the second Adam a superabundance of grace.[124]

45. The entire course of human history and the heart of each person constitute the stage on which the drama of the salvation and the life of all human beings, as well as the grace and glory of God, is being played out between these two Adams.

C. The World under Redeeming Grace; Humanity under the Sign of Redemption

46. It was primarily to rescue human beings that the Son of God made himself our brother (Heb 2:17), like us in all things except sin (Heb 4:15). In agreement with certain patristic writers (including Irenaeus and Athanasius, as mentioned in Part III above) it may be affirmed that even though there can be no question of a "collective incarnation", the incarnation of the Logos affects the whole of human nature. Inasmuch as one member of the human family is God's own Son, all others have been raised to the new dignity of being his brothers and sisters. Precisely because the human

---

[124] Cf. *CCC* 412, quoting Rom 5:20 and Aquinas, *STh* III, 1, 3 ad 3.

nature that Christ assumed retained its creaturely identity, human nature itself was raised to a higher status. As we read in the Pastoral Constitution on the Church in the Modern World, "By His incarnation the Son of God has united Himself in some fashion with every man."[125] As "second Adam" Christ recapitulates humanity before God, becomes the head of a renewed family, and restores the image of God to its pristine truth. By revealing the mystery of the Father's love, Christ fully reveals humanity to itself and discloses the supreme calling of every individual.[126]

47. In its relation to their final destiny Christ's redemptive work affects all human beings, since all are called to eternal life. By shedding his blood on the Cross, Christ established a new covenant, a regime of grace, that is directed to all humanity. Each of us can say with the apostle, "He loved me and gave himself up for me" (Gal 2:20). Everyone is called to share by adoption in Christ's own Sonship. God does not issue this call without providing the capacity to respond to it. Thus Vatican II can teach that no human being, even one who has never heard of the gospel, is untouched by the grace of Christ.[127] "We ought to believe that the Holy Spirit in a manner known only to God offers to every man the possibility of being associated with this paschal mystery."[128] While fully respecting the mysterious ways of divine Providence with regard to the unevangelized, attention is here focused on the revealed plan of salvation which shows forth God's merciful counsels and the manner in which God is fittingly glorified.

The Response of Faith

48. The first condition of entering the new covenant of grace is to have a faith modelled on that of Abraham (Rom 4:1–25). Faith is the fundamental response to the good news of the gospel. No one can be saved without faith, which is the foundation and root of all justification.[129]

49. For the life of faith it is not sufficient to assent with one's mind to the contents of the gospel or to place one's trust in the divine mercy. Redemption takes hold of us only when we acquire a new existence grounded in loving obedience.[130] Such an existence corresponds to the classical conception of faith enlivened by charity.[131]

---

[125] GS 22; cf. *Redemptor hominis*, 8, 13, and passim.

[126] GS, 22; *Veritatis splendor*, 2.

[127] LG 16.

[128] GS 22.

[129] Council of Trent, sess. 6, chap. 8 (DS 1532).

[130] Rom 16:26; cf. *Veritatis splendor*, 66, 88.

[131] Cf. Council of Trent, sess. 6, chaps. 7–9 (DS 1530–34).

50. By Baptism, the sacrament of faith, the believer is inserted into the body of Christ, freed from original sin, and assured of redemptive grace. The believer "puts on" Christ and walks in newness of life (Rom 4:6). A renewed consciousness of the mystery of Baptism, as death to sin and resurrection to true life in Christ, can enable Christians to experience the actuality of redemption and gain the joy and freedom of life in the Holy Spirit.

Liberation

51. Baptism is the sacrament of liberation from sin and rebirth in the freedom newly chosen. Freed from sin by the grace of God, which arouses the response of faith, the believer begins the journey of the Christian life. Through the faith aroused by grace, the believer is liberated from the domination of evil and is entrusted to Jesus Christ, the master who bestows interior freedom. This is not a mere liberty of indifference that authorizes every possible choice, but a freedom of conscience that invites people, enlightened by the grace of Christ, to obey the deepest law of their being and observe the rule of the gospel.

52. It is only with the light of the gospel that conscience can be formed to follow the will of God without any constraint upon its freedom. As Vatican II teaches, "All men are bound to seek the truth, especially in what concerns God and His Church, and to embrace the truth they come to know, and to hold fast to it. This Vatican Council likewise professes its belief that it is upon the human conscience that these obligations fall and exert their binding force. The truth cannot impose itself except by virtue of its own truth, as it makes its entrance into the mind at once quietly and with power." [132]

53. Living members of the Body of Christ are made friends of God and heirs in hope of eternal life. [133] They receive the first fruits of the Holy Spirit (Rom 8:23), whose charity is poured forth into their hearts. [134] Such charity, overflowing into obedience and good works, [135] renews believers from within, rendering them capable of freely adhering to the new law of the gospel. [136] The grace of the Holy Spirit gives interior peace and supplies joy and ease in believing and observing the commandments.

[132] DH 1; cf. 10.
[133] Council of Trent, sess. 6, chap. 7 (DS 1528–31).
[134] Rom 5:5; cf. GS 22.
[135] Council of Trent, sess. 6, chaps. 7–10 (DS 1530–35).
[136] Ibid., chap. 11 (DS 1536).

Reconciliation

54. Liberation from sin by redemption in Christ reconciles a person with God, with neighbor, and with all creation. Since original and actual sin are essentially rebellion against God and the divine will, redemption re-establishes peace and communication between the human being and the Creator: God is experienced as the Father who pardons and receives back his child. Saint Paul eloquently dwells on the aspect of reconciliation: "If anyone is in Christ, there is a new creation: everything old has passed away; see, everything has become new! All this is from God, who reconciled *us* to himself through Christ ... that is, in Christ God was reconciling the world to himself, not counting their trespasses against them, and entrusting the message of reconciliation to us [the ministers]. We entreat you on behalf of Christ, be reconciled to God" (2 Cor 5:17–20).

55. The word of the gospel reconciles those who have rebelled against the law of God and points out a new path of obedience to the depths of a conscience enlightened by Christ. Christians are to be reconciled with their neighbors before presenting themselves at the altar.[137]

56. The sacrament of Penance and Reconciliation permits a sanctifying return to the mystery of Baptism and constitutes the sacramental form of reconciliation with God and the actuality of his pardon thanks to the redemption given in Christ.

57. Within the Church Christians continually experience the mystery of reconciliation. Re-established in peace with God and obeying the commandments of the gospel, they carry on a reconciled life with others with whom they are called into community. Reconciled with the world, they no longer violate its beauties or fear its powers. Rather they seek to protect and contemplate its wonders.

Communion

58. Freedom from sin, fortified by reconciliation with God, neighbor, and creation, permits Christians to find true communion with their Creator who has become their Savior. In this communion they realize their latent potentialities. However great are the intellectual and creative powers of human nature, they cannot bring about the fulfillment that is made possible by communion with God. Communion with the person of the Redeemer becomes communion with the body of Christ, that is to say, the communion of all the baptized in Christ. Redemption therefore has a social character: it is in

---

[137] Cf. Mt 5:24.

and by the Church, the Body of Christ, that the individual is saved and finds communion with God.

59. United with baptized believers of all times and places, the Christian lives in the communion of the saints, which is a communion of sanctified persons (*sancti*) through the reception of holy things (*sancta*): the word of God and the sacraments of the presence and action of Christ and the Holy Spirit.

Striving and Suffering

60. All who live in Christ are summoned to become active participants in the continuing process of redemption. Incorporated into the Body of Christ, they carry his work forward and thereby enter into closer union with him. Just as he was a sign of contradiction, so the individual Christian and the whole Church become signs of contradiction as they struggle against the forces of sin and destruction, amidst suffering and temptation. The faithful are united with the Lord by their prayers (2 Cor 1:11; 1 Tim 2:1–4), their works (1 Cor 3:9–14), and their sufferings,[138] all of which have redemptive value when united with, and taken up into, the action of Christ himself. Since every meritorious human action is inspired and directed by divine grace, Augustine was able to declare that God wills that his gifts should become our merits.[139]

61. The communion of the saints involves an exchange of sufferings, honors and joys, prayers and intercession, among all the members of the Body of Christ, including those who have passed before us into glory. "If one member suffers, all suffer together with it; if one member is honored, all rejoice together with it. Now you are the body of Christ and individually members of it" (1 Cor 12:26–27).

62. In view of the mutual reconciliation of Christians in the Body of Christ, the suffering of each is a participation in the redemptive suffering of Christ. By suffering in the service of the gospel the Christian completes what is lacking in his flesh of Christ's afflictions "for the sake of the body of Christ, that is, the Church" (Col 1:24). The faithful do not flee from suffering but find in it an effective means of union with the Cross of Christ. It becomes for them an intercession through Christ and the Church. Redemption involves an acceptance of suffering with the Crucified. External trials are alleviated by the consolation of God's promises and by a foretaste of the eternal blessings.

---

[138] Cf. 2 Cor 4:10–11; Col 1:24.

[139] Augustine, *De gratia et libero arbitrio* 8, 20 (PL 44, 893); cf. Council of Trent, sess. 6, chap. 16 (DS 1548).

Ecclesial Solidarity

63. Redemption has an ecclesial aspect inasmuch as the Church was insti-tuted by Christ "to perpetuate the saving work of redemption".[140] Christ loved the Church as his bride and delivered himself up that he might sanctify it (Eph 5:25–26). Through the Holy Spirit Christ makes himself present in the Church, which is "on earth, the initial budding forth of that kingdom [of God]." [141] Although marred by the sinfulness and divi-sions of its members, who frequently fail to reflect the true countenance of Christ,[142] the Church remains, in its deeper reality, the holy temple of which the faithful are "living stones".[143] It continually seeks to purify itself so that it may manifestly appear as the "universal sacrament" of salvation,[144] the sign and instrument of the union of human beings with one another and with God.[145] The Church has the task of proclaiming the saving message and actualizing the saving event by sacramental celebration.

64. The different stages of redemption unfold within the Church in which the liberation, reconciliation, and communion already described are to be attained. Life in the Holy Church, the Body of the Redeemer, permits Christians to achieve progressive healing of their nature, wounded by sin. In solidarity with fellow believers in the Church the Christian experiences progressive liberation from all the alienating slaveries and finds a true community that overcomes isolation.

65. The life of faith fortifies Christians in the assurance that God has pardoned their sins and that they have found communion and peace with one another. The spiritual life of the individual is enriched by the exchange of faith and prayer in the communion of saints.

66. In the celebration of the Eucharist the Christian finds the fullness of ecclesial life and communion with the Redeemer. In this sacrament the faithful give thanks for God's gifts, unite themselves to the self-offering of Jesus, and participate in the salutary movement of his life and death. In the Eucharist the community is freed from the weight of sin and revivified at the very source of its existence. "As often as the sacrifice of the cross in which Christ our Passover was sacrificed (1 Cor 5:7), is celebrated on the altar, the work of our redemption is carried on".[146] By partaking of the Eucharist the individual Christian is nourished and

---

[140] *Pastor aeternus* (DS 3050).
[141] *LG* 5.
[142] *GS* 19.
[143] 1 Pet 2:5; cf. *LG* 6.
[144] *LG* 48.
[145] *LG* 1.
[146] *LG* 3.

transformed into the Body of Christ, being inserted more deeply into the liberating communion of the Church.

67. Eucharistic communion grants forgiveness of sins in the blood of Christ. As the medicine of immortality, this sacrament removes the effects of sin and imparts the grace of a higher life.[147]

68. The Eucharist as sacrifice and communion is an anticipation of the Kingdom of God and the happiness of eternal life. This joy is expressed in the Eucharistic liturgy, which enables the Christian to live, at the level of the sacramental memorial, the mysteries of the Redeemer who liberates, pardons, and unites the members of the Church.

Sanctification

69. Freed from sin, reconciled and living in communion with God and the Church, the faithful undergo a process of sanctification that begins with baptism into death from sin and into new life with the risen Christ. By hearing the word of God and participating in the sacraments and life of the Church, the Christian is gradually transformed according to the will of God and configured to the image of Christ to bring forth the fruits of the Spirit.

70. Sanctification is a sharing in the holiness of God who, through grace received in faith, progressively modifies human existence to shape it according to the pattern of Christ. This transfiguration can undergo heights and depths according to whether the individual obeys the promptings of the Spirit or submits again to the seductions of sin. Even after sin the Christian is raised up again by the grace of the sacraments and directed to go forward in sanctification.

71. The whole Christian life is comprised and summed up in charity, unselfish love for God and neighbor. Saint Paul calls charity the "fruit of the Holy Spirit" (Gal 5:22) and then indicates the many implications of this charity, both in his list of the fruits of the Holy Spirit (Gal 5:22–23) and in his hymn to charity (1 Cor 13:4–7).

Society and Cosmos

72. Redemption has effects that extend beyond the inner lives and mutual relations of Christians in the Church. It spreads its influence outward insofar as the grace of Christ tends to alleviate all that leads to conflict,

---

[147] Ignatius of Antioch *Ephesians* 20, 2.

injustice and oppression, thus contributing to what Pope Paul VI referred to as a "civilization of love". The "structures of sin" erected by the thirst for personal profit and power cannot be overcome except by "a commitment to the good of one's neighbor with the readiness, in the gospel sense, to 'lose oneself' for the sake of the other".[148] The selfless love of Christ, transforming the lives of believers, breaks the vicious circle of human violence. True friendship establishes a climate favorable to peace and justice, thus contributing to the redemption of society.

73. It remains true that, as several Popes have warned, redemption cannot be reduced to liberation of the socio-political order.[149] "Such cases of social sin are the result of the accumulation and concentration of many personal sins."[150] Changes in social structures, while ameliorating the lot of the poor, cannot of themselves overcome sin or instill holiness, which lies at the heart of God's redemptive design and is also, in a sense, its goal.[151] Conversely, people who suffer poverty and oppression, evils from which Christ himself was not spared, may receive abundantly of God's redemptive grace, and be numbered among the poor whom Christ called blessed (Mt 5:3).

74. Redemption has a cosmic aspect because God is pleased through Christ "to reconcile to himself all things, whether on earth or in heaven, making peace by the blood of his cross" (Col 1:20). Paul can speak of all creation being in travail and groaning inwardly as it waits for a redemption that will set it free to share in the glorious liberty of God's children (Rom 8:19–25). The book of Revelation, following Isaiah, speaks of "a new heaven and a new earth" as the final result of redemption.[152] The Church in its Good Friday liturgy sings of the skies and seas being purified by the blood of Christ (*"terra, pontus, astra, mundus, / quo lavantur flumine"*—*Pange lingua*).

Eschatological Perspectives

75. The reception of redemption in the present life is fragmentary and incomplete. We have the first fruits of the Spirit, but we still groan with all creation "as we wait for adoption as sons, the redemption of our bodies. For in this hope we were saved. Now hope that is seen is not hope. For who hopes for what he sees? But if we hope for what we do not see, we wait for it with patience" (Rom 8:23–25).

[148] John Paul II, *Sollicitudo rei socialis*, 38.
[149] Paul VI, *Evangelii nuntiandi*, 32–35.
[150] John Paul II, *Reconciliatio et paenitentia*, 16.
[151] Cf. 1 Thess 4:3; cf. Eph 1:4.
[152] Rev 21:1; cf. Is 65:17; 66:22.

76. Although faithful Christians receive the forgiveness of sin and the infusion of grace, so that sin no longer reigns in them,[153] their sinful tendencies are not fully overcome. The marks of sin, including suffering and death, will remain until the end of time. Those who conform their lives to Christ's in faith are assured that through their own death they will be given a definitive participation in the victory of the risen Savior.

77. Christians must constantly combat the presence of evil and suffering in so many forms in the world and in society, by the promotion of justice, peace and love, in an attempt to secure the happiness and well-being of all.

78. Redemption will attain its completeness only when Christ reappears to establish his final kingdom. Then he will present to the Father the abiding fruits of his struggle. The blessed in heaven will share in the glory of the new creation. The divine presence will permeate all created reality; all things will glow with the splendor of the Eternal, so that "God may be everything to everyone" (1 Cor 15:28).

---

[153] Rom 5:21; cf. 8:2.

19

CHRISTIANITY AND THE WORLD RELIGIONS

PRELIMINARY NOTE

The study of the theme "Christianity and the World Religions" was adopted for study by a large majority of the members of the International Theological Commission. To prepare this study a subcommission was established composed of Bishop Norbert Strotmann Hoppe, M.S.C.; Rev. Barthelemy Adoukonou; Rev. Jean Corbon; Rev. Mario de Franca Miranda, S.J.; Rev. Ivan Golub; Rev. Tadahiko Iwashima, S.J.; Rev. Luis F. Ladaria, S.J. (president); Rev. Hermann J. Pottmeyer; and Rev. Andrzej Szostek, M.I.C. General discussion on this theme took place during several meetings of the subcommission and in the plenary sessions of the International Theological Commission held at Rome in 1993, 1994 and 1995. The present text was approved "in forma specifica" by vote of the commission on 30 September 1996 and was submitted to its president, Joseph Cardinal Ratzinger, prefect of the Congregation for the Doctrine of the Faith, who has given his approval for its publication.

INTRODUCTION

1. The question of the relations among religions is becoming daily more important. Various factors contribute to the current interest in this problem. There is above all the increasing interdependence among the different parts of the world, which can be seen at various levels: For example, an ever greater number of people in most countries have access to information; migrations are far from being a thing of the past; and modern technology and industry have given rise to exchanges among many countries in a way that was formerly unknown. These factors, of course, affect the various continents and countries differently, but to some extent or other all parts of the world are touched by them.

2. These factors of communication and interdependence among the different peoples and cultures have brought about a greater consciousness of the plurality of religions on the planet, with the dangers and at the same time the opportunities this implies. Despite secularization, the religious sense of the people of our time has not disappeared. The different phenomena which reflect this religious sense are well known despite the crisis affecting the great religions, each in different measure.

The importance of the religious dimension in human life and the increasing encounters among people and cultures make interreligious dialogue necessary. In view of the problems and needs affecting humanity, there is a need to seek enlightenment about the meaning of life and to bring about common action for peace and justice in the world. Christianity does not in fact and cannot remain on the margins of this encounter and consequent dialogue among religions. If the latter have sometimes been and still can be factors of division and conflict among peoples, it is to be desired that in our world they should appear in the eyes of all as elements of peace and unity. Christianity has to contribute toward making this possible.

3. For this dialogue to be fruitful, Christianity, and specifically the Catholic Church, must try to clarify how religions are to be evaluated theologically. On this evaluation will depend to a great extent the relation between Christians and the different religions and their followers, and the subsequent dialogue which will be established with them in different forms. The principal object of the following reflections is to work out some theological principles which may help in this evaluation. In proposing these principles we are clearly aware that many questions are still open and require further investigation and discussion. Before setting out these principles, we believe it is necessary to trace the fundamental lines of the current theological debate. Against this background the proposals which will be subsequently formulated will be better understood.

I. THEOLOGY OF RELIGIONS
(*STATUS QUAESTIONIS*)

I.1. *Object, Method and Aim*

4. The theology of religions does not yet have a clearly defined epistemological status. This fact constitutes one of the reasons governing the current discussion. In Catholic theology prior to Vatican II one can find two lines of thought relating to the problem of the salvific value of religions.

One, represented by Jean Danielou, Henri de Lubac and others, considers that religions are based on the covenant with Noah, a cosmic covenant involving God's revelation in nature and conscience and which is different from the covenant with Abraham. Insofar as they uphold the contents of this covenant, religions have positive values but, as such, they do not have salvific value. They are "stepping-stones to hope" (*pierres d'attente*), but also "stumbling blocks" (*pierres d'achoppement*) because of sin. In themselves they go from man to God. Only in Christ and in his Church do they reach their final and definitive fulfillment.

The other line, represented by Karl Rahner, affirms that the offer of grace in the present order of things reaches all men and that they have a vague, even if not necessarily conscious awareness of its action and its light. Given that man is by nature a social being, religions, insofar as they are social expressions of the relation of man with God, help their followers to receive the grace of Christ (*fides implicita*) which is necessary for salvation, and to be open in this way to love of neighbor which Jesus identified with the love of God. In this sense they can have salvific value even though they contain elements of ignorance, sin and corruption.

5. At the present time the demand for a greater knowledge of each religion is gaining ground; this is necessary before a theology of it can be worked out. Very different elements are involved in the origin and scope of each religious tradition. Hence theological reflection must be limited to a consideration of concrete, well-defined phenomena if sweeping a priori judgments are to be avoided. Thus some advocate a theology of the history of religions; others take into consideration the historical evolution of religions, their respective characteristics which are at times mutually incompatible; others recognize the importance of the phenomenological and historical material that relates to each religion, without however discounting the value of the deductive method; still others refuse to give any blanket positive recognition to religions.

6. In an age which values dialogue, mutual comprehension and tolerance, it is natural that there should appear attempts to work out a theology of religions on the basis of criteria acceptable to all, that is to say, which are not exclusive to any one particular religious tradition. For that reason the conditions for interreligious dialogue and the fundamental presuppositions of a Christian theology of religions are not always clearly distinguished. To avoid dogmatism, external models are sought which are supposed to allow one to evaluate the truth of a religion. Efforts made in this direction are not finally convincing. If theology is *fides quaerens intellectum*, it is not clear how one can abandon the "dogmatic principle" or reflect theologically if one dispenses with one's own sources of truth.

7. In this situation, a Christian theology of religions is faced with different tasks. In the first place Christianity will have to try to understand and evaluate itself in the context of a plurality of religions; it will have to think specifically about the truth and the universality to which it lays claim. In the second place it will have to seek the meaning, function and specific value of religions in the overall history of salvation. Finally, Christian theology will have to study and examine religions themselves, with their very specific contents, and confront them with the contents of the Christian faith. For that reason it is necessary to establish criteria which will permit a critical discussion of this material and a hermeneutics for interpreting it.

I.2. *Discussion on the Salvific Value of Religions*

8. The fundamental question is this: Do religions mediate salvation to their members? There are those who give a negative reply to this question; even more, some do not even see any sense in raising it. Others give an affirmative response, which in turn gives rise to other questions: Are such mediations of salvation autonomous or do they convey the salvation of Jesus Christ? It is a question therefore of defining the status of Christianity and of religions as sociocultural realities in their relation to human salvation. This question should not be confused with that of the salvation of individuals, Christian or otherwise. Due account has not always been taken of this distinction.

9. Many attempts have been made to classify the different theological positions adopted toward this problem. Let us see some of these classifications: Christ against religions, in religions, above religions, beside religions. An ecclesiocentric universe or exclusive Christology; a Christocentric universe or inclusive Christology; a theocentric universe with a normative Christology; a theocentric universe with a non-normative Christology. Some theologians adopt the tripartite division *exclusivism, inclusivism, pluralism*, which is seen as parallel to another: *ecclesiocentrism, Christocentrism, theocentrism*. Given that we have to choose one of these classifications in order to continue our reflection, we will follow the latter, even though we might complement it with the others if necessary.

10. Exclusivist ecclesiocentrism—the fruit of a specific theological system or of a mistaken understanding of the phrase *extra ecclesiam nulla salus*—is no longer defended by Catholic theologians after the clear statements of Pius XII and Vatican Council II on the possibility of salvation for those who do not belong visibly to the Church (cf., e.g., *LG* 16; *GS* 22).

11. Christocentrism accepts that salvation may occur in religions, but it denies them any autonomy in salvation on account of the uniqueness and universality of the salvation that comes from Jesus Christ. This position is undoubtedly the one most commonly held by Catholic theologians, even though there are differences among them. It attempts to reconcile the universal salvific will of God with the fact that all find their fulfillment as human beings within a cultural tradition that has in the corresponding religion its highest expression and its ultimate foundation.

12. Theocentrism claims to be a way of going beyond Christocentrism, a paradigm shift, a Copernican revolution. This position springs, among other reasons, from a certain bad conscience over the way missionary activity in the past was linked with the politics of colonialism, even though sometimes the heroism that accompanied the work of evangelization is forgotten. It tries to acknowledge the riches of religions and the moral witness of their members, and, as a final concern, it aims at facilitating the unity of all religions in order to encourage joint work for peace and justice in the world.

We can distinguish a theocentrism in which Jesus Christ, without being constitutive of, is considered normative for salvation, and another theocentrism in which not even this normative value is recognized in Jesus Christ. In the first case, without denying that others may also mediate salvation, Jesus Christ is acknowledged as the mediator who best expresses it; the love of God is revealed most clearly in his person and in his actions, and thus he is the paradigm for the other mediators. But without him we would not remain without salvation, only without its most perfect manifestation.

In the second case Jesus Christ is not considered either as constitutive of nor as normative for human salvation. God is transcendent and incomprehensible, so that we cannot judge his intentions with our human modes of understanding. Thus we can neither evaluate nor compare the different religious systems. *Soteriocentrism* radicalizes even further the theocentric position, since it is less interested in the question of Jesus Christ (orthodoxy) than in the actual commitment each religion makes to aid suffering humanity (orthopraxis). In this way the value of religions lies in promoting the kingdom, salvation and the well-being of humanity. This position can thus be characterized as pragmatic and immanentist.

I.3. *The Question of Truth*

13. The problem of the truth of religions underlies this whole discussion. Today one can see a tendency to relegate it to a secondary level, separating it from reflection on the salvific value of religions. The question of

truth gives rise to serious problems of a theoretical and practical order, since in the past it had negative consequences in interreligious encounters. Hence the tendency to ease or privatize this problem with the assertion that criteria of truth are only valid for each individual religion.

Some introduce a more existential notion of truth, taking only the correct moral conduct of the person into consideration and discounting the fact that his or her beliefs may be condemned. A certain confusion is produced between *being in salvation* and *being in the truth*. One should take more account of the Christian perspective of *salvation as truth* and of *being in the truth as salvation*. The omission of discourse about truth leads to the superficial identification of all religions, emptying them basically of their salvific potential. To assert that all are true is equivalent to declaring that all are false. To sacrifice the question of truth is incompatible with the Christian vision.

14. The epistemological conception underlying the pluralist position uses the Kantian distinction between *noumenon* and *phenomenon*. Since God, or ultimate Reality, is transcendent and inaccessible to man, he will only be able to be experienced as a phenomenon expressed by culturally conditioned images and notions; this explains why different representations of the same reality are not a priori necessarily mutually exclusive. The question of truth is relativized still further with the introduction of the concept of *mythological truth*, which does not imply any correspondence with a reality but simply awakens in the subject a disposition corresponding to what has been enunciated. Nevertheless it must be noted that such contrasting expressions of the *noumenon* in fact end up dissolving it, obliterating the meaning of the mythological truth. Underlying this whole problematic is also a conception which separates the Transcendent, the Mystery, the Absolute radically from its representations; since the latter are all relative because they are imperfect and inadequate, they cannot make any exclusive claims in the question of truth.

15. A criterion for the truth of a religion which is to be accepted by the other religions must be located outside the religion itself. The search for this criterion is a serious task for theological reflection. Certain theologians avoid Christian terms in speaking of God (*Eternal One, Ultimate Reality, the Real*) or in designating correct behavior (*Reality-centeredness* and not *self-centeredness*). But one can see that such expressions either manifest a dependence on a specific tradition (Christian) or they become so abstract that they cease to be useful.

Recourse to the *humanum* is not convincing because with it one is dealing with a merely phenomenological criterion, which would make the theology of religions dependent on the anthropology dominant in any particular age. It is also said that one must consider as the true religion that which best succeeds either in reconciling finitude, the provisional and changeable nature of its own self-understanding, with the infinitude to which it points, or in reducing to unity (power of integration) the plurality of experiences of reality and of religious conceptions.

I.4. *The Question of God*

16. The pluralist position aims at eliminating from Christianity any claim to exclusivity or superiority in relation to other religions. For this reason it must assert that the ultimate reality of the different religions is identical, and at the same time relativize the Christian conception of God in its dogmatic and binding form. In this way it distinguishes between God as he is in himself, inaccessible to man, and God as he is revealed in human experience. Images of God are constituted by the experience of transcendence and by the particular sociocultural context. These images are not God, but they point accurately toward him; this can be also said of the nonpersonal representations of the divinity. In consequence, none of them can be considered as exclusively valid.

Hence it follows that all religions are relative not in that they merely point toward the Absolute, but in their positive expressions and in their omissions. Since there is only one God and one plan of salvation, which is the same for all humanity, the expressions of religion are interconnected and mutually complementary. As the Mystery is universally active and present, none of its manifestations can claim to be the ultimate and definitive one. In this way the question of God is intimately bound up with the question of revelation.

17. The phenomenon of prayer which is found in the various religions is also related to the same question. Is it, in short, the same addressee who is invoked in the prayers of the faithful under different names? Divinities and religious powers, personified forces of nature, life and society, psychic or mythical projections—do they all represent the same reality? Is one not taking here an unwarranted step from a subjective attitude to an objective judgment? A polytheistic prayer may be directed to the true God, since a salvific act may occur through an erroneous mediation. But this does not mean that this religious mediation is objectively recognized as a salvific mediation, although it does mean that this authentic prayer was enkindled by the Holy Spirit (Pontifical Council for Interreligious Dialogue and Congregation for the Evangelization of Peoples, "Dialogue and Proclamation: Reflections and Orientations on Interreligious Dialogue and the Proclamation of the Gospel of Jesus Christ" [1991], 27).

I.5. *The Christological Debate*

18. Behind the theological problematic which we have just looked at, the Christological question which we shall now tackle has always been present. They are intimately interrelated. We treat them separately because of the complexity of the problem. Christianity's major difficulty has always been focused on the "incarnation of God", which confers on the person and action of Jesus Christ the characteristics of uniqueness and universality with respect to the salvation of humanity. How can a particular historical event lay claim to universal relevance? How can one enter into an inter-religious dialogue, respecting all religions and not considering them in advance as imperfect and inferior, if we recognize in Jesus Christ and only in him the unique and universal savior of mankind? Could one not conceive of the person and salvific action of God starting from other mediators as well as Jesus Christ?

19. The Christological problem is essentially bound up with that of the salvific value of religions to which we have already referred. We shall focus here a little more on the study of the Christological consequences of the theocentric positions. One consequence of the latter is *salvific theocentrism* so-called, which accepts a pluralism of legitimate and true salvific mediations. Within this position, as we already observed, a group of theologians attributes a normative value to Jesus Christ, since his person and life reveal God's love for men in the clearest and most decisive way. The major difficulty with this conception is that it does not offer, either from within or from outside Christianity, any foundation for this normative role which is attributed to Jesus.

20. Another group of theologians defends a salvific theocentrism with a non-normative Christology. To break the link between Christ and God deprives Christianity of any universalist claim about salvation (and thus authentic dialogue with other religions would be made possible), but by implication one would then have to confront the Church's faith and specifically the dogma of Chalcedon. These theologians consider that the latter, as an expression of the Church's faith historically conditioned by Greek philosophy, must be updated because it is hindering interreligious dialogue. The meaning of the incarnation in this view is not objective, but metaphorical, poetic and mythological. It aims only to express the love of God which is incarnate in men and women whose lives reflect the action of God. Assertions of the exclusive salvific meaning of Jesus Christ can be explained in terms of the historico-cultural context: classical culture (only one certain and immutable truth), eschatologico-apocalyptic mentality (final prophet, definitive revelation) and the attitude of a minority (language of survival, only one savior).

21. The most important consequence of this conception is that Jesus Christ cannot be considered to be the unique, exclusive mediator. Only for Christians is he the human form of God, who makes possible in an adequate way man's encounter with God, although without any claim to exclusivity. He is *totus Deus* because he is the active love of God on this earth, but he is not *totum Dei* since he does not exhaust in himself the love of God. We could also say: *Totum Verbum, sed non totum Verbi.* The Logos, being greater than Jesus, can be incarnate also in the founders of other religions.

22. This same problematic crops up again when one asserts that Jesus is Christ, but Christ is more than Jesus. This greatly facilitates an understanding of the universal active presence of the Logos in other religions. But the New Testament texts do not conceive of the Logos of God in isolation from Jesus. Another way of arguing along these lines consists in attributing to the Holy Spirit the universal salvific action of God, which would not necessarily lead to faith in Jesus Christ.

I.6. *Mission and Interreligious Dialogue*

23. The different positions adopted toward religions give rise to diverse ways of understanding the Church's missionary activity and interreligious dialogue. If religions are simply roads to salvation (pluralist position), then conversion ceases to be the primary object of mission, since the important thing is that each one, encouraged by the witness of others, should live profoundly his or her faith.

24. The inclusivist position no longer considers mission as a task undertaken to prevent the damnation of those who have not been evangelized (exclusivist position). Even while acknowledging the universal action of the Holy Spirit, it observes that the latter, in the economy of salvation willed by God, possesses an incarnational dynamic that leads it to express and objectify itself. In this way the proclamation of the word brings this very dynamic to its full realization. In placing man before a radical decision, it is not simply providing a way of interpreting transcendence, but it is its greatest realization. The announcement and explicit acceptance of faith increases the possibilities of salvation and also personal responsibility. Moreover, mission is today considered as a task directed not only to individuals, but above all to peoples and cultures.

25. Interreligious dialogue is based theologically either on the common origin of all human beings created in God's image, or on their common destiny which is the fullness of life in God, or on the single divine

plan of salvation through Jesus Christ, or on the active presence of the divine Spirit among the followers of other religious traditions ("Dialogue and Proclamation", 28). The presence of the Spirit does not occur in the same way in the biblical tradition and in the other religions because Jesus Christ is the fullness of revelation. But different experiences and perceptions, expressions and understandings, coming perhaps from the same "transcendental event", increase greatly the value of interreligious dialogue. Precisely through it the very process of interpretation and understanding of God's salvific action can unfold.

26. "A faith which has not become inculturated is a faith which has not been fully received, which has not been completely thought through, which has not been faithfully lived." These words of John Paul II in a letter to the papal secretary of state (20 May 1982) show clearly the importance of the inculturation of faith. It is recognized that religion is the heart of all culture as the last court of appeal on the question of meaning and as the fundamental structuring force. Hence the inculturation of faith cannot ignore the encounter with religions, which should take place above all through interreligious dialogue.[1]

II. FUNDAMENTAL THEOLOGICAL PRESUPPOSITIONS

27. The preceding *status quaestionis* has shown how the different approaches to the theology of religions and to their salvific value depend to a great extent on the view which is taken of the universal salvific will of God the Father, to whom the New Testament attributes the initiative for salvation, the unique mediation of Christ, the universality of the action of the Holy Spirit and his relation to Jesus, the function of the Church as the universal sacrament of salvation. The reply to the questions posed requires some brief reflection on these fundamental theological issues.

II.1. *The Father's Initiative in Salvation*

28. Only in the light of the divine plan of salvation for mankind, which knows no frontiers of peoples or races, does it make sense to approach the problem of the theology of religions. The God who wishes to save all is the Father of our Lord Jesus Christ. The plan of salvation in Christ precedes the creation of the world (cf. Eph 1:3–10) and is realized with

---

[1] Cf. International Theological Commission, "Faith and Inculturation", 3, 10; cf. *Gregorianum* 70 (1989): 640. [See chap. 15, pp. 1–21 above.]

the sending of Jesus into the world, proof of the infinite love and tenderness which the Father has for humanity (cf. Jn 3:16–17; 1 Jn 4:9–10; etc.). This love of God goes as far as "handing over" Christ to death for the salvation of mankind and the reconciliation of the world (cf. Rom 5:8–11; 8:3; 32; 2 Cor 5:18–19; etc.). The fatherhood of God, which in general in the New Testament is bound up with faith in Jesus, is seen in more comprehensive perspectives in some passages (cf. Eph 3:14–15; 4:6). God is God of Jews and gentiles (cf. Rom 3:29). God's salvation, which is Jesus, is offered to all nations (cf. Lk 2:30; 3:6; Acts 28:28).

29. The Father's initiative in salvation is affirmed in First John 4:14: "The Father has sent his Son as the savior of the world." God, "the Father, from whom are all things" (1 Cor 8:6), is the origin of the work of salvation realized by Christ. The title *savior*, with which Christ is frequently named (cf. Lk 2:11; Jn 4:42; Acts 5:31; etc.) is applied first to God in some New Testament writings (cf. 1 Tim 1:1; 2:3; 4:10; Tit 1:3; 2:10; 3:4; Jude 25), without its being on that account denied to Christ (cf. Tit 1:4; 2:13; 3:6). According to First Timothy 2:3–4, "God our savior ... desires all men to be saved and to come to the knowledge of the truth." The salvific will knows no restrictions, but is always united to the desire that men should recognize the truth, that is to say, should adhere to the faith (cf. 1 Tim 4:10, God is "the savior of all men, especially of those who believe"). This salvific will, therefore, should in consequence be proclaimed. It is bound up, on the other hand, with Christ's unique mediation (cf. 1 Tim 2:5–6), to which we will refer in a moment.

30. God the Father is at the same time the goal toward which everything is heading. The ultimate end of God's creative and saving action will be realized when all things have been made subject to the Son; "then the Son himself will also be subjected to him who put all things under him, that God may be everything to everyone" (1 Cor 15:28).

31. The Old Testament already has some prefiguration of this universality which will be fully revealed only in Christ. All men, without exception, have been created in the image and likeness of God (cf. Gen 1:26f.; 9:6); given that in the New Testament the image of God is Christ (2 Cor 4:4; Col 1:15), it is possible to think of all men as being determined toward conformity with Christ. God's covenant with Noah embraces all the living beings of the earth (cf. Gen 9:9, 12, 17f.). In Abraham "all the families of the earth shall bless themselves" (Gen 12:3; cf. 18:18); this blessing for all comes also through the descendants of Abraham, because of the latter's obedience (cf. Gen 22:17–18; 26:4–5; 28:14). The God of Israel was recognized as such by some foreigners (cf. Josh 2; 1 Kings 10:1–13; 17:17–24; 2 Kings 5:1–27).

In second and third Isaiah one also finds texts which make reference to the salvation of the nations in the context of the salvation of the people of Israel (cf. Is 42:1–4; 49:6–8; 66:18–21; etc., the offerings of the nations will be accepted by God just like the offerings of the Israelites; also Ps 86; 47:10, "the princes of the nations are united to the people of the God of Abraham"). It is a question of a universality which has Israel as its center. Wisdom also is directed to all without distinction of peoples or races (cf. Prv 1:20–23; 8:2–11; Wis 6:1–10, 21; etc.).

II.2. *The Unique Mediation of Jesus*

A. Some New Testament Themes

32. We have already pointed out that God the Father's salvific will is linked to faith in Jesus. He is the only one in whom the saving plan is realized: "There is no other name under heaven given among men by which we must be saved" (Acts 4:12). That salvation is attained only through faith in Jesus is a constant affirmation in the New Testament. Precisely those who believe in Christ are the true descendants of Abraham (cf. Rom 9:6–7; Gal 3:29; Jn 8:31–58; Lk 1:55). The blessing of all in Abraham finds its meaning in the blessing of all in Christ.

33. According to the Gospel of Matthew, Jesus felt that he had been sent especially to the people of Israel (Mt 15:24; cf. Mt 10:5–6). These assertions correspond to Matthew's characteristic presentation of the history of salvation: The history of Israel is directed toward its fulfillment in Christ (cf. Mt 1:22–23; 2:5–6, 15, 17–18, 23), and the perfection of the divine promises will be achieved when heaven and earth have passed away and all has been fulfilled (cf. Mt 5:18).

This fulfillment has already begun in the eschatological events of Christ's death (cf. Mt 27:51–53) and resurrection (cf. Mt 28:2–4). But Jesus does not exclude the gentiles from salvation: He praises the faith of some of them, which is not found in Israel (cf. Mt 8:10; Lk 7:9, the centurion; Mt 15:21–28; Mk 7:24–30, the Syrophoenician woman); they will come from the East and the West to sit at table in the kingdom while the children of the kingdom will be thrown outside (Mt 8:11–12; Lk 13:18–29; cf. 11:20–24).

Jesus, raised from the dead, gives the eleven disciples a universal mission (cf. Mt 28:16–20; Mk 16:15–18; Acts 1:8). The early Church soon begins the mission to the gentiles, by divine inspiration (Acts 10:34). In Christ there is no difference between Jews and gentiles (Gal 4:24; Col 3:11).

34. In the first instance, the universality of the saving work of Jesus is based on the fact that his message and his offer of salvation are directed to all human beings, and all can welcome it and receive it in faith. But in the New Testament we find other texts which appear to show that the significance of Jesus goes further, that in some way it is prior to the reception of his message on the part of the faithful.

35. We should note above all that all that exists has been made through Christ (cf. 1 Cor 8:6; 1:3–10; Heb 1:2). According to Colossians 1:15–20, everything has been created in him and through him, and everything is moving toward him. This same text shows that this causal role of Christ in creation is related to his saving mediation, toward which creation is directed. Jesus is the firstborn of creation and the firstborn from among the dead; in being the firstborn from among the dead, the fact that Jesus is the firstborn of creation seems to attain its full meaning. The recapitulation of everything in Christ is the ultimate intention of God the Father (cf. Eph 1:10). In this universal recapitulation the special role of Christ in the Church stands out: "He has put all things under his feet and has made him the head over all things for the church, which is his body, the fullness of him who fills all in all" (Eph 1:22–23; cf. Col 1:17). The Pauline parallelism between Adam and Christ (cf. 1 Cor 15:20–22, 44–49; Rom 5:12–21) seems to point in an identical direction. If the first Adam has a universal relevance as the first man and the first sinner, Christ also must have a salvific significance for all, even though the terms of this significance are not clearly spelled out. The vocation of every human being, who now bears the image of the earthly Adam, is to become an image of the heavenly Adam.

36. "[The Word] was the true light which, in coming into the world, enlightens all men" (Jn 1:9).[2] It is Jesus, as the Logos incarnate, who enlightens all men. The Logos has already carried out the role of mediator in creation, not without reference to the future incarnation and salvation, and therefore Jesus comes to his own, who do not receive him (cf. Jn 1:3–4, 10, 11). Jesus announces that God is to be worshipped in spirit and in truth. This worship goes beyond Jerusalem and Mount Gerizim (cf. Jn 4:21–24) and is recognized by the confession of the Samaritans: "This is indeed the savior of the world" (Jn 4:42).

37. The unique mediation of Jesus Christ is connected with the universal salvific will of God in First Timothy 2:5–6: "There is one God, and there is one mediator between God and men, the *man* Christ Jesus, who gave himself as a ransom for all." The uniqueness of the mediator (cf. also Heb 8:6; 9:15; 12:24) corresponds to the uniqueness of the God, who desires the

---

[2] It appears that this reading is preferable to that of the Vulgate: *omnem hominem venientem in mundum*. The New Vulgate translates *veniens in mundum*.

salvation of all. The only mediator is the man Christ Jesus; what is at stake here is also the universal significance of Jesus as the Son of God incarnate. He is the mediator between God and men because he is the Son, become man, who has given himself up to death as a ransom for all.

38. In Paul's discourse on the Areopagus (Acts 17:22–31) it comes across clearly that conversion to Christ implies a break with the past. Religions have in fact led men to idolatry. But at the same time the authenticity of a philosophical search is acknowledged, which even if it has not attained knowledge of the true God was nevertheless not on a completely wrong track. The groping search for God corresponds to the designs of providence; it too, apparently, must have positive aspects. Is there also a relation to the God of Jesus Christ before conversion (cf. Acts 10:34)? The New Testament does not have a closed attitude toward everything that does not come from faith in Christ; this openness can extend also to religious values (cf. Phil 4:8).

39. The New Testament shows us at once the universality of the salvific will of God and the link between salvation and the redemptive work of Christ Jesus, the only mediator. Human beings attain salvation in recognizing and accepting in faith Jesus the Son of God. This message is directed to all without exception. But some passages seem to suggest that Jesus has a salvific significance for each human being which may apply even to those who do not know him. The New Testament message is not compatible with any limiting of the salvific will of God, or with admitting mediations parallel to that of Jesus or with attributing this universal mediation to the eternal Logos in isolation from Jesus.

B. Motifs from the Tradition Cited in Recent Statements of the Church's Magisterium

40. The universal significance of Christ has been expressed in different ways in the Church's tradition from the earliest times. We have selected some themes that have found an echo in the recent documents of the magisterium, especially in Vatican Council II.

41. The *semina verbi*, "seeds of the word", can be found outside the limits of the visible Church and specifically in the different religions; this motif is frequently combined with that of the light which enlightens all men and with that of the preparation for the Gospel (*AG* 11, 15; *LG* 16, 17; *NA* 2; *Redemptoris missio* [*RM*], 56).

42. The theology of the seeds of the word stems from Saint Justin Martyr. Faced with the polytheism of the Greek world, Justin sees in philosophy an ally of Christianity since it has followed reason; now this reason is

found in its totality only in Jesus Christ, the Logos in person. Only Christians know the Logos in its entirety.[3] But the whole human race has participated in this Logos. Hence from the beginning there have been those who have lived in accordance with the Logos, and in this sense there have been "Christians" even though the knowledge they have had of the seminal Logos has only been partial.[4] There is a great difference between the seed of something and the thing itself. But in any case the partial and seminal presence of the Logos is a gift and a divine grace. The Logos is the sower of these "seeds of truth".[5]

43. For Clement of Alexandria, man is rational to the extent that he participates in the Logos, the true reason that governs the universe. He has full access to this reason if he is converted and follows Jesus, the Logos incarnate.[6] With the incarnation, the world has been filled with seeds of salvation.[7] But God has been sowing since the beginning of time, so that different parts of the truth are to be found among the Greeks and among the barbarians, especially in philosophy considered in its totality,[8] even though alongside the truth there has been darnel as well.[9] Philosophy has had for the Greeks a function similar to that of the law for the Hebrews; it has been a preparation for the fullness of Christ.[10] But there is a clear difference between the action of God in these philosophers and in the Old Testament. On the other hand, only in Jesus, the light which enlightens every man, can one contemplate the perfect Logos, the whole truth. The fragments of truth belong to the whole.[11]

44. Justin and Clement are at one in pointing out that these fragments of the total truth known to the Greeks come, in part at least, from Moses and the prophets. The latter are older than the philosophers.[12] According to the plans of providence, the Greeks "stole" from them, for they were incapable of thanking for what they had received.[13] This knowledge of

---

[3] Cf. *Apologia* 1, 5, 4; 2, 6, 7; 2, 7, 2–3 (Biblioteca de autores cristianos [BAC] 116, 186f.; 268; 269).

[4] Cf. *Apologia* 1, 46, 2–4; 2, 7, 1–3 (ibid., 232f.; 269).

[5] Cf. *Apologia* 1, 44, 10; 2, 10, 2; 2, 13, 2–6 (ibid., 230; 272; 276f.).

[6] Cf. *Protrepticus* 1, 6, 4; 10, 98, 4 (Sources chretiennes [SCh] 2 bis, 60; 166); *Paedagogus* 1, 96, 1 (SCh 70, 280).

[7] Cf. *Protrepticus* 10, 110, 1–3 (SCh 2 bis, 178).

[8] Cf. *Stromata* 1, 37, 1–7 (SCh 30, 73–74).

[9] Cf. *Stromata* 6, 67, 2 (Die griechische christliche Schriftsteller der ersten drei Jahrhunderte [GCS] 15, 465).

[10] Cf. *Stromata* 1, 28, 1–3; 1, 32, 4 (SCh 30, 65; 69); 6, 153–54 (GCS 15, 510f.).

[11] Cf. *Stromata* 1, 56–57 (SCh 30, 89–92).

[12] Justin, *Apologia* 1, 44, 8–9; 1, 59–60 (BAC 116, 230; 247–49).

[13] Clement of Alexandria, *Protrepticus* 6, 70 (SCh 2 bis, 135); *Stromata* 1, 59–60; 1, 87, 2 (SCh 30, 93f.; 113); 2, 1, 1 (SCh 38, 32f.).

the truth is therefore not unrelated to the historical revelation which will find its fullness in the incarnation of Jesus.

45. Irenaeus makes no direct use of the idea of the seeds of the word. But he stresses very much that at all moments in history the Logos has been close to human beings, has accompanied them, in view of the incarnation;[14] with the incarnation, Jesus, in bringing himself, has brought all newness. Salvation is tied therefore to the appearance of Jesus, even though this appearance had already been announced and its effects in a certain sense anticipated.[15]

46. The Son of God has united himself to every man (cf. GS 22; Redemptoris missio, 6, among many other places). The idea is repeated frequently in the fathers, who take their inspiration from some passages in the New Testament.

One of the passages which gave rise to this interpretation is the parable of the lost sheep (cf. Mt 18:12–24; Lk 15:1–7): The latter is identified with the erring human race, which Jesus has come to seek out. In assuming human nature, the Son has placed all of humanity on his shoulders to present it to the Father. Gregory of Nyssa expresses himself thus:

"We human beings are this sheep.... The Savior takes the whole sheep on his shoulders, for ... since it had been entirely lost, it had to be led back in its entirety. The shepherd carries it on his shoulders, that is to say, on his divinity.... Having taken this sheep upon himself, he makes it one with himself."[16]

John 1:14, "the Word became flesh and dwelt among us", has also been interpreted on not a few occasions in the sense of dwelling "within us", that is to say, within each person; from the idea of his being in us one can go easily to that of our being in him.[17] Containing us all in himself, he can reconcile us all with God the Father.[18] In his glorified humanity we can all find resurrection and rest.[19]

---

[14] Cf. Adversus haereses 3, 16, 6; 3, 18, 1 (SCh 211, 312; 342); 4, 6, 7; 4, 20, 4; 4, 28, 2 (SCh 100, 454; 634f.; 758); 5, 16, 1 (SCh 153, 214); Demonstratio Apostolica 12 (SCh 406, 100).

[15] Cf. Adversus haereses 4, 34, 1 (SCh 100, 846f.).

[16] Contra Apollinaristas 16 (Patrologia graeca [PG] 45, 1153). Cf. also Irenaeus of Lyons, Adversus haereses 3, 19, 3 (SCh 211, 380); 5, 12, 3 (SCh 153, 150); Demonstratio Apostolica 33 (SCh 406, 130); Hilary of Poitiers, In Evangelium Matthaei 18, 6 (SCh 258, 80f.).

[17] Cf. Hilary of Poitiers, De Trinitate 2, 24–25 (Corpus Christianorum: Series Latina [CCL] 62, 605); Athanasius, Contra Arianos 3, 25, 33, 34 (PG 26, 376; 393–97); Cyril of Alexandria, Commentarius in Johannem 1, 9; 5, 2 (PG 73, 161; 753). The idea of "exchange" could also be introduced here; cf. Irenaeus, Adversus haereses 5 Prol. (SCh 153, 14), etc.

[18] Cyril of Alexandria, Commentarius in Johannem 1, 9 (PG 73, 164).

[19] Cf. Hilary of Poitiers, Tractatus super Psalmos 13, 14; 14, 5 and 17; 51, 3 (Corpus scriptorum ecclesiasticorum latinorum [CSEL] 22, 81; 87f.; 96; 98).

47. The fathers do not forget that this union of human beings in the body of Christ is brought about above all in baptism and the eucharist. But the union of all in Christ through his assuming our nature constitutes an objective presupposition on the basis of which the believer grows in personal union with Jesus. The universal significance of Christ is also revealed for the early Christians in the fact that he liberates man from the princes of this world, who keep him imprisoned in his own particular and national interests.[20]

48. The Christological dimension of the image [of God]. According to Vatican Council II, Jesus is the "perfect man"; in following him man becomes more human (GS 41; cf. ibid., 22, 38, 45). Moreover the council indicates that only "*in mysterio Verbi incarnati mysterium hominis vere clarescit*" (ibid., 22). Among other bases for this affirmation, a passage in Tertullian is mentioned according to which, in molding Adam from the clay of the earth, God was already thinking of Christ, who was to become incarnate.[21] Irenaeus had already pointed out that the Word, the universal architect, had prefigured in Adam the future economy of salvation for humanity, which humanity he himself was to take on.[22] Even though the patristic interpretations of the "image of God" are very varied, one cannot dismiss this current of thought, which sees in the Son who is to become incarnate (and is to die and rise from the dead) the model according to which God made the first man. If man's destiny is to bear the image of the heavenly man (1 Cor 15:49) it does not appear mistaken to think that in every man there must be a certain internal disposition toward this end.

C. Conclusions

49. a. Only in Jesus can human beings be saved, and therefore Christianity has an evident claim to universality. The Christian message is directed consequently to all human beings and has to be announced to all.

b. Some texts from the New Testament and from the oldest Christian tradition hint that Christ has a universal significance which is not reducible to

---

[20] Cf. Origen, *Homilies on Luke* 35 (CGS Orig. W. 9, 200f.); *De principiis* 4, 11–12 (Or. W. 5, 339s); Augustine, *De civitate Dei* 5, 13, 19 (CCL 47, 146–48; 154–56).

[21] *De carnis resurrectione* (*De res. mort.*) 6 (CCL 2, 928; cited in GS 22, note 20): "Quodcumque limus exprimebatur, Christus cogitabatur, homo futurus"; almost immediately is added: "Id utique quod finxit, ad imaginem Dei fecit illum, scilicet Christi.... Ita limus ille, iam tunc imaginem induens Christi futuri in carne, non tantum Dei opus erat, sed et pignus"; the same in *Adversus Praxean* 12, 4 (CCL 2, 1173).

[22] *Adversus haereses* 3, 22, 3 (SCh 211, 438).

that which we have just mentioned. With his coming into the world, Jesus enlightens every human being; he is the final and definitive Adam to whom all are called to be conformed, etc. The idea of the universal presence of Jesus is found, worked out in somewhat more detail, in the ancient doctrine of the *logos spermatikos*. But even there a clear distinction is drawn between the full appearance of the Logos in Jesus and the presence of the seeds of the Logos in those who do not know him. This presence, which is real, excludes neither error nor contradiction.[23] Because of Jesus' coming into the world, and above all because of his death and resurrection, the ultimate meaning of the closeness of the Word to all human beings can be understood. Jesus leads all of history toward its fulfillment (cf. GS 10, 45).

c. If salvation is bound up with the historical appearance of Jesus, personal adherence to him in faith cannot be a matter of indifference for anyone. Only in the Church, which is in historical continuity with Jesus, can his mystery be fully lived out. Hence the inescapable necessity for the Church of announcing Christ.

d. Other possibilities of salvific "mediation" cannot be seen in isolation from the man Jesus, the only mediator. It will be more difficult to determine how human beings who do not know Jesus and other religions are related to Jesus. Mention should be made of the mysterious ways of the Spirit, who gives to all the possibility of being associated with the paschal mystery (*GS* 22) and whose work cannot be without reference to Christ (*Redemptoris missio*, 29). The question of the salvific value of religions as such must be situated in the context of the universal active presence of the Spirit of Christ.

e. Since Jesus is the only mediator, who carries out the saving plan of the one God the Father, salvation is one and the same for all human beings: full conformity to Jesus and communion with him in participation in his divine sonship. Consequently one must rule out the existence of different economies of salvation for those who believe in Jesus and those who do not believe in him. There can be no roads leading to God that do not converge in the only road which is Christ (cf. Jn 14:6).

II.3. *The Universality of the Holy Spirit*

50. The universality of the salvific action of Christ cannot be understood without the universal action of the Holy Spirit. An initial element of this

---

[23] In addition to the texts already quoted cf. Augustine, *Epistolae* 137, 12 (Patrologia latina [PL] 33, 520f.); *Retractationes* 1, 13, 3 (PL 32, 603).

universality of the work of the Holy Spirit is already found in creation. The Old Testament shows us the Spirit of God hovering over the waters (Gen 1:2). And the book of Wisdom (1:7) points out that "the spirit of the Lord fills the world, is all-embracing and knows what man says."

51. If this can be said of the whole universe, it is especially true of man, created in the image and likeness of God, according to Genesis 1:26–27. God makes man so that he, God, may be present in him, may dwell in him, to look on him with good will, to be joined to him, to be his friend. Thus we can speak of an original friendship, an *amicitia originalis*, of man with God and of God with man (Council of Trent, Session 6, Ch. 7, Denzinger-Schönmetzer [DS] 1528) as a fruit of the action of the Spirit. Life in general—and man's in particular—is placed in a more or less explicit relationship with the Spirit of God in various places in the Old Testament (cf. Ps 104:29–30; Job 34:4–15; Eccl 12:7). John Paul II links the creation of man in the image of God and in divine friendship to the communication of the Spirit (cf. *Dominum et vivificantem*, 12, 34).

52. The tragedy of sin is this: Instead of closeness between God and man, there is a distance. The spirit of darkness presents God as man's enemy, as a threat (cf. Gen 3:4–5; *Dominum et vivificantem*, 38). But God has drawn close to man through the different covenants of which the Old Testament speaks. From the beginning, the "image and likeness" signifies a capacity for personal relationship with God and therefore the capacity for a covenant. Thus God gradually drew close to men through the different covenants with Noah (cf. Gen 7:1ff.), with Abraham and with Moses, with whom God made himself a friend (Jas 2:23; Ex 33:11).

53. In the new covenant God drew so close to man that he sent his own Son into the world, becoming incarnate through the action of the Holy Spirit in the womb of the Virgin Mary. The new covenant, in contrast to the old, is not of the letter but of the Spirit (2 Cor 3:6). It is the new and universal covenant, the covenant of the universality of the Spirit. *Universality* means *versus unum*, toward one. The word *spirit* means movement, and this movement includes the "toward", the direction. The Spirit is called *dynamis* (power) (Acts 1:8) and *dynamis* includes the possibility of a direction. From the words of Jesus about the Spirit, the Paraclete, one can conclude that the "to be toward" is a reference to Jesus.

54. The tight bond between the Spirit and Christ is shown in the anointing of Jesus. Jesus Christ means precisely: Jesus is the anointed of God with the ointment of the Spirit: "The Spirit of the Lord is upon me; therefore he has anointed me" (Lk 4:18; Is 61:1–2). God has anointed Jesus "with the Holy Spirit and with power", and thus he "went about

doing good works and healing all who were in the grip of the devil" (Acts 10:38). As Irenaeus said:

"In the name of Christ one can understand him who anoints, him who is anointed and the very anointing with which he is anointed. He who anoints is the Father, the anointed is the Son, and the Spirit is the unction or the anointing. As the Word says through Isaiah: 'The Spirit of the Lord is upon me because he has anointed me' (Is 61:1–2), signifying the Father who anoints, the Son who is anointed, and the unction which is the Spirit." [24]

55. The universality of the covenant of the Spirit is therefore that of the covenant in Jesus. He has offered himself to the Father through the eternal Spirit (Heb 9:14), in whom he has been anointed. This anointing is extended to the whole Christ, to the Christians anointed by the Spirit and to the Church. Ignatius of Antioch already indicated that Jesus received the anointing "in order to breathe incorruption into his Church".[25] Jesus has been anointed in the Jordan, according to Irenaeus, "so that we might be saved upon receiving the abundance of his anointing." [26] Gregory of Nyssa expressed this with a profound and beautiful image:

"The concept of the anointing suggests ... that there is no distance between the Son and the Spirit. In fact, just as between the surface of the body and the anointing of oil neither reason nor sense knows any intermediaries, so the contact of Son with the Spirit is equally immediate; therefore, he who is about to enter into contact with the Son through faith must of necessity enter beforehand into contact with the oil. Neither part lacks the Holy Spirit." [27]

The whole Christ includes all men in a certain way, because Christ has united himself to all men (GS 22). Jesus himself says: "As often as you did it for one of my least brothers, you did it for me" (Mt 25:40).

56. The Church is the privileged place for the action of the Spirit. In her, the body of Christ, the Spirit stirs up different gifts for the common good (cf. 1 Cor 12:4–11). The formula of Irenaeus is well known: "Where the Spirit of the Lord is, there is the Church, and where the Church is, there is the Spirit of the Lord and all grace." [28] And Saint John Chrysostom: "If the Holy Spirit were not present, then the Church

---

[24] *Adversus haereses* 3, 18, 3 (SCh 211, 350–52). Basil of Cesarea, *De Spiritu Sancto* 12, 28 (SCh 17 bis, 344) and Ambrose of Milan, *De Spiritu Sancto* 1, 3, 44 (CSEL 79, 33) repeat this idea almost literally.

[25] *Ad Ephesios* 17, 1 (SCh 10, 86).

[26] *Adversus haereses* 3, 9, 3 (SCh 211, 112). For the same Irenaeus the Spirit descends on Jesus in order to "habituate himself" for dwelling in the human race. Ibid., 17, 1 (330).

[27] *De Spiritu Sancto contra Macedonianos* 16 (PG 45, 1321A–B).

[28] Irenaeus, *Adversus haereses* 3, 24, 1 (SCh 211, 474).

would not exist; if the Church exists, this is a clear sign of the presence of the Spirit."[29]

57. Some passages of the New Testament seem to insinuate the universal scope of the Spirit's action, always in relationship with the evangelizing mission of the Church, which must reach out to all men. The Holy Spirit precedes and guides the preaching; he is at the origin of the mission to the pagans (Acts 10:19, 44–47).

The overcoming of the sin of Babel will take place in the Spirit. There is a great contrast between the work of those who built the tower of Babel and the work of the Holy Spirit. Those who built the tower of Babel wanted to storm heaven, God's dwelling place, by their own powers. The Holy Spirit, who has descended from heaven as a gift, makes it possible to speak all languages and to hear, each in his own tongue, the wonderful works of God (cf. Acts 2:1–11).

The tower of Babel was an effort to achieve unity without universality: "Let us make a name for ourselves [a sign of unity]; otherwise we shall be scattered all over the earth" (Gen 11:4). Pentecost was the gift of universality in unity: "All were filled with the Holy Spirit. They began to express themselves in foreign tongues and make bold proclamation as the Spirit prompted them" (Acts 2:4). In the gift of the Spirit of Pentecost can be seen also the perfection of the covenant of Sinai (cf. Ex 19:1ff.), which thus turns out to be universal.

58. The gift of the Spirit is the gift of Jesus, who has been raised and ascended into heaven at the right hand of the Father (Acts 2:32; cf. Jn 14:15, 26; 15:26; 16:7; 20:22); this is a constant teaching in the New Testament. The resurrection of Jesus itself is realized through the intervention of the Spirit (cf. Rom 1:4; 8:11). The Holy Spirit is given to us as the Spirit of Christ, the Spirit of the Son (cf. Rom 8:9; Gal 4:6; Phil 1:19; Acts 16:7). Therefore one cannot think about a universal action of the Spirit which is not related to a universal action of Jesus. The fathers did not hesitate to put this into relief.[30]

Only through the action of the Spirit can we men be conformed to the image of the risen Jesus, the new Adam, in whom man definitively acquires the dignity to which he has been called from the beginning:

---

[29] *Hom. Pent.* 1, 4 (PG 49, 459).

[30] For example see Irenaeus of Lyon, *Adversus haereses* 3, 17, 2 (SCh 211, 334): "Dominus accipiens munus a Patre ipse quoque his donavit qui ex ipso participantur, in universam terram mittens Spiritum Sanctum"; Hilary of Poitiers, *Tractatus super Psalmos* 56, 6 (CSEL 22, 172): "Et quia exaltatus super caelos impleturus esset in terris omnia sancti spiritus gloria, subiecit: et super omnem terram gloria tua (Ps 57:6, 12). Cum effusum super omnem carnem spiritus donum gloriam exaltati super coelos domini protestaretur."

"All of us, gazing on the Lord's glory with unveiled faces, are being transformed from glory to glory into his very image by the Lord who is the Spirit" (2 Cor 3:18). Man, who has been created in the image of God through the presence of the Spirit, is re-created in the image of God (or of Christ) because of the action of the Spirit. The Father is the painter; the Son is the model after whom man is painted; the Holy Spirit is the artist's brush used to paint man in creation and in redemption.

59. Thus the Holy Spirit leads to Christ. The Holy Spirit directs all men to Christ, the Anointed One. Christ, in his turn, directs all to the Father. No one comes to the Father save through Jesus, because he is the way (Jn 14:6), but it is the Holy Spirit who guides the disciples to the whole truth (Jn 16:12–13). The word *he will guide* (Greek: *hodegesei*) includes the way (Greek: *hodos*). The Holy Spirit guides therefore along the way that Jesus is, the way that leads to the Father. Consequently, no one can say "Jesus is Lord" save under the action of the Holy Spirit (1 Cor 12:3). And the name *Paraclete*, used by John, shows us that the Spirit is the advocate in the judgment which begins in Jerusalem and continues in history. The Spirit, the Paraclete, will defend Jesus from the accusations made against him in the person of his disciples (cf. Jn 16:8–11). The Holy Spirit is thus the witness to Christ, and through him they are able to be disciples: "He will bear witness on my behalf. You must bear witness as well, for you have been with me from the beginning" (Jn 15:26–27).

60. The Spirit, therefore, is the gift of Jesus and leads to him, although the specific way that leads men is known only by God. Vatican II has clearly formulated this matter: "For since Christ died for all men, and since the ultimate vocation of man is in fact one, and divine, we ought to believe that the Holy Spirit in a manner known only to God offers to every man the possibility of being associated with this paschal mystery" (*GS* 22). There is no sense in affirming a universality of the action of the Spirit which is not encountered in relationship with the meaning of Jesus, the incarnate Son, dead and risen. All men by virtue of the work of the Spirit can enter into relationship with Jesus, who lived, died and rose in a specific place and at a specific time. On the other hand, the action of the Spirit is not limited to the intimate and personal aspects of man but embraces also the social dimensions.

As John Paul II says, "This is the same Spirit who was at work in the Incarnation and in the life, death and resurrection of Jesus, and who is at work in the Church. He is therefore not an alternative to Christ, nor does he fill a sort of void which is sometimes suggested as existing between Christ and the Logos. Whatever the Spirit brings about in human hearts and in the history of peoples, in cultures and religions serves as a preparation for the Gospel and can only be understood in reference to Christ" (*Redemptoris missio*, 29).

61. The privileged sphere of the Spirit's action is the Church, the body of Christ. But all peoples are called, in different ways, to the unity of the people of God that the Spirit promotes: "This characteristic of universality which adorns the people of God is a gift from the Lord Himself. By reason of it, the Catholic Church strives constantly and with due effect to bring all humanity and all its possessions back to its source in Christ, with Him as its head and united in His Spirit.... All men are called to be part of this catholic unity of the people of God which in promoting universal peace presages it. And there belong to or are related to it in various ways, the Catholic faithful, all who believe in Christ, and indeed the whole of mankind, for all men are called by the grace of God to salvation" (*LG* 13). It is the very universality of the salvific action of Christ and of the Spirit that leads us to ask about the function of the Church as the universal sacrament of salvation.

II.4. *"The Church, the Universal Sacrament of Salvation"*

62. It is not possible to develop a theology of the religions without taking into account the universal salvific mission of the Church, attested to by Holy Scripture and by the tradition of faith of the Church. A theological evaluation of the religions was impeded over a long time because of the principle *extra ecclesiam nulla salus*, understood in an exclusivist sense. With the doctrine about the Church as *the universal sacrament of salvation* or *the sacrament of the kingdom of God*, theology seeks to respond to the new way of posing the problem. This teaching, which was also welcomed by Vatican Council II, is linked to the sacramental vision of the Church in the New Testament.

63. The primary question today is not whether men can attain salvation even if they do not belong to the visible Catholic Church; this possibility is considered theologically certain. The plurality of religions, something increasingly evident to Christians, better knowledge of these religions and the necessary dialogue with them, without leaving until the end the clearer awareness of the spatial and temporal frontiers of the Church—all these considerations make us ask whether one can nonetheless speak about the necessity of the Church for salvation and about the compatibility of this principle with the universal salvific will of God.

A. "Extra Ecclesiam Nulla Salus"

64. Jesus linked the proclamation of the kingdom of God with his Church. After Jesus' death and resurrection, the reunion of the people of God, now in the name of Jesus Christ, took place. The Church of Jews and gentiles was understood as a work of God and as the community in which one experienced the action of the Lord exalted in the heavens and his Spirit. With faith in Jesus Christ, the universal mediator of salvation, was joined baptism in his name; this mediated participation in his redemptive death, pardon of sins and entrance into the community of salvation (cf. Mk 16:16; Jn 3:5). For this reason baptism is compared with the ark of salvation (1 Pet 3:20ff.). According to the New Testament, the necessity of the Church for salvation is based on the unique salvific mediation of Jesus.

65. One speaks of the necessity of the Church for salvation in two senses: the necessity of belonging to the Church for those who believe in Jesus and the necessity for salvation of the ministry of the Church which, on mission from God, must be at the service of the coming of the kingdom of God.

66. In his encyclical *Mystici Corporis*, Pius XII addresses the question, How are those who attain salvation outside visible communion with the Church related to her? He says that they are oriented to the mystical body of Christ by a yearning and desire of which they are not aware (DS 3821). The opposition of the American Jesuit Leonard Feeney, who insisted on the exclusivist interpretation of the expression *extra ecclesiam nulla salus*, afforded the occasion for the letter of the Holy Office, dated 8 August 1949, to the archbishop of Boston, which rejected Feeney's interpretation and clarified the teaching of Pius XII. The letter distinguishes between the necessity of belonging to the Church for salvation (*necessitas praecepti*) and the necessity of the indispensable means of salvation (*intrinseca necessitas*); in relationship to the latter, the Church is a general help for salvation (DS 3867–69). In the case of invincible ignorance the implicit desire of belonging to the Church suffices; this desire will always be present when a man aspires to conform his will to that of God (DS 3870). But faith, in the sense of Hebrews 11:6, and love are always necessary with intrinsic necessity (DS 3872).

67. Vatican Council II makes its own the expression *extra ecclesiam nulla salus*. But in using it the council explicitly directs itself to Catholics and limits its validity to those who know the necessity of the Church for salvation. The council holds that the affirmation is based on the necessity of faith and of baptism affirmed by Christ (*LG* 14). In this way the council aligned itself in continuity with the teaching of Pius XII,

but emphasized more clearly the original parenthentical character of this expression.

68. In contrast to Pius XII, the council refused to speak of a votum implicitum (implicit desire) and applied the concept of the votum only to the explicit desire of catechumens to belong to the Church (LG 14). With regard to non-Christians, it said that they are ordered in diverse ways to the people of God. In accord with the different ways with which the salvific will of God embraces non-Christians, the council distinguished four groups: first, Jews; second, Muslims; third, those who without fault are ignorant of the Gospel of Christ and do not know the Church but who search for God with a sincere heart and try to fulfill his will as known through conscience; fourth, those who without fault have not yet reached an express knowledge of God but who nonetheless try to lead a good life (LG 16).

69. The gifts which God offers all men for directing themselves to salvation are rooted, according to the council, in his universal salvific will (LG 2, 3, 26; AG 7). The fact that even non-Christians are ordered to the people of God is rooted in the fact that the universal call to salvation includes the vocation of all men to the catholic unity of the people of God (LG 13). The council holds that the close relationship of both vocations is rooted in the unique mediation of Christ, who in his body that is the Church makes himself present in our midst (LG 14).

70. Thus the original meaning is restored to the expression *extra ecclesiam nulla salus*, namely, that of exhorting the members of the Church to be faithful.[31] Once this expression is integrated into the more universal *extra Christum nulla salus*, it is no longer in contradiction to the universal call of all men to salvation.

B. *Paschali Mysterio Consociati*

71. The Dogmatic Constitution on the Church (*Lumen gentium*) speaks of a gradual ordering to the Church from the perspective of the universal call to salvation, which includes the call to the Church. But on the other hand the pastoral constitution *Gaudium et spes* opens up a wider Christological, pneumatological and soteriological perspective. What it says about Christians is also valid for all men of good will, in whose hearts grace works in an invisible way. They also can be associated with the paschal mystery through the Holy Spirit, and they can consequently

[31] Cf. Origen, *In Jesu Nave* 3, 5 (SCh 71, 142ff.); Cyprian, *De ecclesiae catholicae unitate* 6 (CSEL 3/1, 214ff.); *Epistulae* 73, 21 (CSEL 3/2, 795).

be conformed to the death of Christ and be on the road to the encounter of the resurrection (GS 22).

72. When non-Christians, justified by means of the grace of God, are associated with the paschal mystery of Jesus Christ, they are also associated with the mystery of his body, which is the Church. The mystery of the Church in Christ is a dynamic reality in the Holy Spirit. Although the visible expression of belonging to the Church is lacking to this spiritual union, justified non-Christians are included in the Church, "the Mystical Body of Christ" and "a spiritual community" (LG 8). In this sense the fathers of the Church were able to say that justified non-Christians belong to the *ecclesia ab Abel*. While these are reunited in the universal Church joined to the Father (LG 2), those who certainly belong "to the body" but not "to the heart" of the Church because they do not persevere in love will not be saved (LG 14).

73. Therefore, one can speak not only in general of an ordering of justified non-Christians to the Church, but also of a bond with the mystery of Christ and his body, the Church. But one ought not to speak of belonging or membership, not even of a gradual belonging, to the Church or of an imperfect communion with the Church, something reserved for non-Catholic Christians (UR 3; LG 15); for the Church in her essence is a complex reality constituted by a visible union and a spiritual communion. Of course, those non-Christians who are not culpable of not belonging to the Church enter into the communion of those called to the kingdom of God; they do so by putting into practice love of God and neighbor; this communion will be revealed as the *ecclesia universalis* at the consummation of the kingdom of God and of Christ.

C. *Universale Salutis Sacramentum*

74. When it was presupposed that all would enter into contact with the Church, the necessity of the Church for salvation was understood above all as the necessity of belonging to it. Since the Church has been made aware of her condition as a minority, both diachronically and synchronically, the necessity of the universal salvific function of the Church has become a matter of prime importance. This universal mission and this sacramental efficacy in the order of salvation have found their theological expression in calling the Church the universal sacrament of salvation. As such, the Church is at the service of the coming of the kingdom of God, in the union of all men with God and in the unity of men among themselves (LG 1).

75. God in fact has revealed himself as love, not only because he gives us already a part in the kingdom of God and its fruits, but also because he

calls us and frees us to collaborate in the coming of his kingdom. Thus the Church is not only a sign, but also an instrument of the kingdom of God, which breaks out with force. The Church carries out her mission as the universal sacrament of salvation in *martyria*, *leitourgia* and *diakonia*.

76. Through the *martyria* of the Gospel of universal redemption carried out by Jesus Christ, the Church announces to all men the paschal mystery of salvation, which is offered to them or which they already live without knowing it. As the universal sacrament of salvation, the Church is essentially a missionary Church. For God in his love has not only called men to attain their final salvation in communion with him. Rather, it belongs to the full vocation of man that he realize his salvation, not in the service of "the shadow of things to come" (Col 2:17), but in full knowledge of the truth, in the communion of the people of God and in their active collaboration on behalf of the coming of his kingdom, strengthened by the sure hope in God's faithfulness (*AG* 1–2).

77. In the *leitourgia*, the celebration of the paschal mystery, the Church fulfills her mission of priestly service in representing all humankind. In a way that, in accord with God's will, it is efficacious for all men, it makes present the representation of Christ who "was made sin" for us (2 Cor 5:21) and who in our place "was hanged on the tree" (Gal 3:13) in order to free us from sin (*LG* 10). Finally, in the *diakonia* the Church bears witness to the loving gift of God to men and of the eruption of the kingdom of justice, of love and of peace.

78. Also belonging to the mission of the Church as universal sacrament of salvation is the fact that "whatever good is in the minds and hearts of men ... is not only saved from destruction but is also cleansed, raised up and perfected" (*LG* 17). For the action of the Spirit at times even visibly precedes the apostolic activity of the Church (*AG* 4) and his action can be shown also in the religious search and restlessness of men. The paschal mystery into which, in the way God knows, all men can be incorporated is the salvific reality which embraces all mankind, which unites beforehand the Church with those non-Christians to whom she directs herself and to whose service her revelation must always be directed. To the extent to which the Church recognizes, discerns and makes her own the truth and the good that the Holy Spirit has worked in the words and deeds of non-Christians, she makes herself to be more and more the true Catholic Church, "which speaks all tongues, understands and accepts all tongues in her love, and so supersedes the divisiveness of Babel" (*AG* 4).

79. "So it is that that messianic people, although it does not actually include all men, and at times may look like a small flock, is nonetheless a lasting and sure seed of unity, hope and salvation for the whole human race. Established by Christ as a communion of life, charity and truth, it is

also used by Him as an instrument for the redemption of all, and is sent forth into the whole world as the light of the world and the salt of the earth (cf. Mt 5:13–16)" (*LG* 9).

III. SOME CONSEQUENCES FOR A CHRISTIAN THEOLOGY OF THE RELIGIONS

80. Now that the salvific initiative of the Father, the universal mediation of Christ, the universal gift of the Spirit, the function of the Church in the salvation of all have been examined, we have the elements for providing a sketch of a theology of religions. In the face of the new situation created by religious pluralism, the question arises again about the universal significance of Jesus Christ in relationship to other religions and the function which these may play in God's plan, which is nothing other than bringing all things into one in Christ (Eph 1:10). There is nothing surprising that old themes from the tradition are used to illuminate new situations. Positively, we must keep in mind the universal significance of Jesus, of his Spirit and also of the Church. The Church in truth proclaims the Gospel, is at the service of human communion and represents all of humanity through her priestly service in the liturgical celebration of the paschal mystery. Negatively, this universality is exclusive. There is not a Logos which is not Jesus Christ nor is there a Spirit that is not the Spirit of Christ. On these coordinates are inscribed the specific problems that are dealt with in the following. We will study some of the points already highlighted in the *status quaestionis*.

III.1. *The Salvific Value of the Religions*

81. The object of discussion today is not the possibility of salvation outside the Church of those who live according to their conscience. This salvation, as was seen before, is not produced independently of Christ and his Church. It is based on the universal presence of the Spirit, which cannot be separated from the paschal mystery of Jesus (*GS* 22; *Redemptoris missio*, 10, etc.). Some texts of Vatican Council II deal specifically with non–Christian religions: Those which have not yet received or heard the Gospel are oriented in different ways to the people of God, and belonging to these different religions does not seem to be indifferent to the effects of this "orientation" (*LG* 16). It is recognized that in the different religions are rays of truth which illuminate all men (*NA* 2) and seeds of

the word (*AG* 11); because of God's disposing, there are in these religions elements of truth and goodness (*OT* 16); one finds elements of truth, of grace and goodness not only in the hearts of men but also in the rites and customs of peoples, although all must be "healed, elevated and completed" (*AG* 9; *LG* 17). Whether the religions as such can have salvific value is a point that remains open.

82. The encyclical *Redemptoris missio*, following and developing the way traced by Vatican Council II, has emphasized more clearly the presence of the Holy Spirit not only in men of good will taken individually, but also in society and history, in peoples, in cultures, in religions, always with reference to Christ (nos. 28, 29). A universal action of the Spirit exists which cannot be separated from or confused with the specific, peculiar action that develops in the body of Christ which is the Church (ibid.). From the formulation of the third chapter of the encyclical, titled "The Holy Spirit, Principal Agent of Mission", it appears that it can be deduced that these two forms of presence and action of the Spirit are derived from the paschal mystery. In fact, after developing the idea of the mission set into motion by the Holy Spirit in nos. 21–27, nos. 28–29 talk about the universal presence of the Spirit. At the end of no. 28 it is clearly affirmed that it is the risen Jesus who works in the hearts of men through the Holy Spirit and that it is the same Spirit who distributes the seeds of the word present in the rites and religions. The distinction between the two ways of the Holy Spirit's acting cannot lead us to separate them as if only the first were related to the salvific mystery of Christ.

83. Again there is talk of the presence of the Spirit and the action of God in the religions in nos. 55–56 of *Redemptoris missio* in the context of the dialogue with the brethren of other religions. The religions are a challenge to the Church, because they stimulate her to recognize the signs of the presence of Christ and the action of the Spirit. "In Christ, God calls all peoples to himself and he wishes to share with them the fullness of his revelation and love. He does not fail to make himself present in many ways, not only to individuals but also to entire peoples through their spiritual riches, of which their religions are the main and essential expression, even when they contain 'gaps, insufficiencies and errors' (Paul VI)" (*Redemptoris missio*, 55). Also in this context, the different way that Christ makes God present with his Gospel is singled out.

84. Given this explicit recognition of the presence of the Spirit of Christ in the religions, one cannot exclude the possibility that they exercise as such a certain salvific function; that is, despite their ambiguity, they help men achieve their ultimate end. In the religions is explicitly thematized the relationship of man with the Absolute, his transcendental dimension. It would be difficult to think that what the Holy Spirit works in the

hearts of men taken as individuals would have salvific value and not think that what the Holy Spirit works in the religions and cultures would not have such value. The recent magisterium does not seem to authorize such a drastic distinction. On the other hand, it is necessary to note that many of the texts to which we have referred not only speak of the religions, but also in conjunction with them speak of cultures, the history of peoples, etc. All these can also be "touched" by elements of grace.

85. In the religions the same Spirit who guides the Church is at work. But the universal presence of the Spirit cannot be compared to his special presence in the Church of Christ. Although one cannot exclude the salvific value of the religions, this does not mean that everything in them is salvific. One cannot forget the presence of the spirit of evil, the inheritance of sin, the imperfection of human response to God's action, etc. (cf. "Dialogue and Proclamation", 30–31). Only the Church is the body of Christ, and only in it is given in its full intensity the presence of the Spirit. Therefore, to no one can belonging to the Church of Christ and participation in the fullness of the saving gifts which alone are found in it be a matter of indifference (*Redemptoris missio*, 55). The religions can exercise the function of a *praeparatio evangelica*; they can prepare different peoples and cultures for welcoming the saving event, which has already taken place. In this sense, however, their function cannot be compared to that of the Old Testament, which was the preparation of the very event of Christ.

86. Salvation is obtained through the gift of God in Christ, but not without human response and acceptance. The religions can also help the human response, insofar as they impel man to seek God, to act in accord with his conscience, to live a good life (cf. *LG* 16; also *Veritatis splendor*, 94; the moral sense of peoples and religious traditions put the action of the Spirit of God into relief). The search for the good is in its ultimate sense a religious attitude (cf. *Veritatis splendor*, 9, 12). It is the human response to the divine invitation, which is always received in and through Christ.[32] It seems that these dimensions—objective and subjective, descending and ascending—must be taken as a unit, as they are given in the mystery of Christ. The religions can therefore be, in the terms indicated, means helping the salvation of their followers, but they cannot be compared to the function that the Church realizes for the salvation of Christians and those who are not.

---

[32] "Dialogue and Proclamation", 29: "It will be in the sincere practice of what is good in their own religious traditions and by following the dictates of their conscience that the members of other religions respond positively to God's invitation and receive salvation in Jesus Christ, even while they do not recognize or acknowledge him as their savior."

87. The affirmation of the possibility of the existence of salvific elements in the religions does not imply in itself a judgment about the presence of these elements in each one of the specific religions. On the other hand, the love of God and of one's neighbor, made possible in the final analysis by Jesus the sole mediator, is the only way to reach God himself. The religions can be carriers of saving truth only insofar as they raise men to true love. If it is true that this can be found in those who do not practice any religion, it nonetheless seems that true love for God must lead to adoration and religious practice in union with other men.

III.2. *The Question of Revelation*

88. The specificity and unrepeatability of divine revelation in Jesus Christ is based on the fact that only in his person does the triune God communicate himself. Therefore, from this it follows that in the strict sense one cannot speak of the revelation of God save insofar as God gives himself of himself. Christ is thus at the same time the mediator and the fullness of all revelation (*DV* 2). The theological concept of revelation cannot be confused with that of religious phenomenology (religions of revelation, those which consider themselves based on divine revelation). Only in Christ and in his Spirit has God given himself completely to men; consequently, only when this self-communication gives itself to be known is there given the revelation of God in the full sense. The gift which God makes of himself and his revelation are two inseparable aspects of the Jesus event.

89. Before the coming of Christ, God revealed himself in a special way to the people of Israel as the only living and true God. Insofar as they bear witness to this revelation, the books of the Old Testament are the word of God and have a perennial value (cf. *DV* 14). Only in the New Testament do the books of the Old Testament receive and manifest their complete meaning (cf. *DV* 16). But in Judaism the true divine revelation of the Old Testament perdures. Certain elements of biblical revelation have been recognized by Islam, which has interpreted them in a definite context.

90. God has given himself to be known and continues to give himself to be known by men in many ways: through the works of creation (cf. Wis 13:5; Rom 1:19–20), through the judgments of conscience (cf. Rom 2:14–15), etc. God can enlighten men in different ways. Fidelity to God can give rise to a kind of knowledge through connaturality. The religious traditions have been characterized by "sincere individuals marked by the Spirit of God" ("Dialogue and Proclamation", 30). The action of the Spirit does not allow

itself to go unperceived in some way by human beings. If, according to the teaching of the Church, "the seeds of the word" and "rays of the truth" are found in the religions, one cannot exclude from them elements of a true knowledge of God, albeit with imperfections (cf. *Redemptoris missio*, 55). The gnoseological dimension cannot be totally absent where we recognize elements of grace and of salvation.

91. But although God has been able to enlighten men in different ways, we are never guaranteed that these lights will be properly welcomed and interpreted by those to whom they are given. Only in Jesus do we have the guarantee of the full welcoming of the will of God the Father. The Spirit assisted the apostles in a special way in bearing witness to Jesus and in transmitting his message; from the apostolic preaching the New Testament emerged and thanks to it also the Church received the Old Testament. The divine inspiration which the Church recognizes in the writings of the Old and New Testaments assures us that she has recognized in them all and only what God wanted written about himself.

92. Not all religions have sacred books. Although one cannot explicitly exclude any divine illumination in the composition of those books (in the religions which have them), it is much more fitting to reserve the qualification of *inspired* to the books of the canon (cf. *DV* 11). The expression *the word of God* has been reserved in the tradition for the writings of the two testaments. The distinction is clearly included in the ancient ecclesiastical writers, who have recognized seeds of the Word in philosophical and religious writings. The sacred books of the different religions, even when they can form part of an evangelic preparation, cannot be considered equivalent to the Old Testament, which is the immediate preparation for the coming of Christ to the world.

III.3. *Truth as a Problem in the Theology of the Religions and the Pluralist Position*

93. The interreligious dialogue is not only a desire stemming from Vatican Council II and fostered by the present pope [John Paul II]. It is also a necessity in the present situation of the world. We know that this dialogue is the major preoccupation of the pluralist theology of the religions during recent times. In order to make this dialogue possible, the representatives of these theologies think that it is necessary for Christians to get rid of any claim of superiority and absoluteness. It is necessary [they think] to consider all the religions as having equal value. They think that one claim of superiority is to consider Jesus to be the sole savior and mediator for all men.

94. Abandoning this claim is therefore considered essential in order for the dialogue to take place. This is undoubtedly the most important issue we must confront. Faced with this way of setting the stage, we must show that Catholic theology in no way undervalues or does not appreciate the other religions when it affirms that everything true and worthy of value in the other religions comes from Christ and the Holy Spirit. This is the best way that the Christian has of expressing his appreciation for these religions.

95. If we compare some of the theological opinions expressed in Chapter 1 with present magisterial concepts and their basis in Scripture and the tradition that was the object of Chapter 2, it can be seen that common to both is the fundamental intention to recognize with respect and gratitude the truths and values encountered in the different religions. Both seek dialogue with them, without prejudices and without wearisome polemics.

96. But the basic difference between the two starting points [the plurality-of-religions school and Catholic theology and the magisterium] is found in the position taken regarding the theological problem of truth and at the same time regarding the Christian faith. The teaching of the Church on the theology of the religions presents its argument from the center of the truth of Christian faith. It takes into account, on the one hand, the Pauline teaching of the natural knowledge of God and at the same time expresses its confidence in the universal action of the Spirit. It sees both lines anchored in the theological tradition. It values the truth, the good and the beauty of the religions from the inmost depths of the truth of faith itself, but it does not attribute in general the same validity to the truth claim of other religions. To do so would lead to indifference, that is to say, to not taking seriously either one's own truth claim or the truth claim of another.

97. The theology of the religions which we find in official documents argues from the very center of faith. With regard to the way of proceeding taken by pluralist theologies and weighing the different opinions and constant changes which take place in them, it can be affirmed that at bottom they hold an "ecumenical" strategy of dialogue; that is, they are preoccupied with restoring unity among the different religions. But this unity [according to the pluralist view] can be achieved only by eliminating aspects of one's own self-understanding. It—the pluralist view—seeks to gain unity by denying any value to [religious] differences, which are regarded as something threatening; it believes that at least these must be eliminated as particularities or reductions proper to a specific culture.

98. There are many aspects of the change in the way one understands one's own faith in the pluralist theology of the religions. We note the

most important: (a) on the historical level a schema of three phases—exclusivism, inclusivism and pluralism—is suggested, a schema which reaches its culmination in pluralism; it is supposed, erroneously, that only the last position—pluralism—is helpful in giving true attention to other religions and achieving religious peace; (b) on the level of the theory of knowledge, the truth capacity of theological affirmations (forms of expression specific to a culture) is reduced or suppressed (theological affirmations are made the equivalent of mythologies); and (c) on the level of theology a platform of unity is sought; [but] the possibility of recognizing the equal dignity [of religions] is purchased by a methodical partialization and reduction (of ecclesiocentrism to Christocentrism and of Christocentrism to theocentrism, while an undefined concept of God is suggested), and by the modification and reduction of the specific contents of faith, especially in Christology.

99. In an epoch characterized by a pluralism of the marketplace, this theology acquires a high degree of plausibility, but only when it is not applied to the position of the interlocutor in the dialogue. The religious dialogue comes to an end the moment one of the following possibilities is presented: (a) that the interlocutor recognizes the thesis of "equal dignity" as historically plural; (b) that he accepts for his own religion the thesis of the limitation or suppression of the truth capacity of all theological affirmations; or (c) he modifies his own theological method and the content of his own affirmations of faith in such a way that they are valid only in relationship to the canons of his own religiosity. In truth, there is nothing to be done except to take account of this indistinct plurality. Therefore, the pluralist theology, as a strategy of dialogue among the religions, not only is not justified in consideration of the truth claim of one's own religion, but simultaneously destroys the truth claim of the other side.

100. Faced with the historical, epistemological or theological oversimplification of the relationship between Christianity and the other religions in the pluralist theology, it is necessary to take as our point of departure the different vision of the religions in the declaration *Nostra aetate* of Vatican Council II. It describes what the religions of the world have in common, to wit, the attempt "to counter the restlessness of the human heart, each [religion] in its own manner, by proposing 'ways', comprising teachings, rules of life, and sacred rites" (no. 2), but without denying differences that are equally fundamental: The different forms of Buddhism show man ways through which he perceives the meaning of being by recognizing the radical insufficiency of this contingent world; in the richness of the myths of Hinduism, in its ascetical practices and deep meditations is expressed the trusting search of a refuge in God. With

Islam, the Church has more in common, since it recognizes that its followers "adore the one God ... the Creator of heaven and earth" (*NA* 3).

Recognizing in total clarity what separates us, we cannot, nonetheless, ignore common elements in history and in doctrine. Christianity is united with Judaism in its origin and in their rich common heritage. The history of the covenant with Israel, the confession of the one and only God who reveals himself in that history, the hope in God who comes and in his future kingdom—all this is common to Jews and Christians (cf. *NA* 4). A Christian theology of the religions must be able to express theologically the common elements and the differences between its own faith and the convictions of different religious groups.

The council situates the task in a tension between two aspects: On the one hand, it contemplates the unity of the human race based on a common origin (*NA* 1). For this reason, anchored in the theology of creation, "the Catholic Church rejects nothing that is true and holy in these religions" (*NA* 2). But on the other hand, the same Church insists on the necessity to announce the truth which is Christ himself: "Indeed, she [the Church] proclaims, and ever must proclaim Christ 'the way, the truth, and the life' (Jn 14:6), in whom men may find the fullness of religious life, in whom God has reconciled all things to Himself (2 Cor 5:18–19)" (*NA* 2).

101. Every dialogue lives on the truth claim of those who participate in it. But the dialogue between the religions is further characterized by applying the deep structure of each one's original culture to the truth claim of a quite different culture. It is clear that this dialogue is demanding and requires a special sensibility in facing the other culture. In the most recent decades especially this sensibility to the cultural context both of the different religions and of Christianity and its theologies has developed. It suffices to recall the "theologies in context" and the growing significance of the theme of inculturation both in the magisterium and in theology.

The International Theological Commission has already spoken about these themes[33] (here it seems necessary to mention only two indications):

1. A differentiated theology of the religions, which is grounded in one's own truth claim, is the basis of any serious dialogue and the necessary presupposition for understanding the diversity of positions and their cultural means of expression.

---

[33] "Select Themes of Ecclesiology: On the Occasion of the 20th Anniversary of Vatican Council II" (1985), esp. Chapter 4; cf. text in *International Theological Commission: Texts and Documents, 1969–1985* (San Francisco: Ignatius Press, 1985); see also "Faith and Inculturation", *Gregorianum* 70 (1989): 625–46. [Chapter 15 of the present volume].

2. The context—literary, sociological, etc.—is an important means of understanding, at times the only one, texts and situations; such contexts are a possible place for truth, but they are not identified with truth itself.

This indicates the meaning and the limits of the cultural contextuality. The interreligious dialogue treats "coincidences and convergences" with other religions with caution and respect. For the treatment of the "differences" one must take into account that this treatment must not annul coincidences and elements of convergence, and moreover that dialogue about these differences has been inspired by one's own doctrine and corresponding ethics: In other words, the form of the dialogue cannot invalidate the content of one's own faith and ethics.

102. The growing interrelationship of cultures in the present world society and its constant interpenetration into the means of communication bring about the situation in which the question of the truth of the religions has passed to the center of the daily conscience of the person of today. Our present reflections consider some presuppositions of this new situation, but the discussion of the contents of the different religions does not enter into these reflections. This ought to be taken up in the theology of the different places, that is to say, in the different centers of study which are in cultural contact with the other religions.

Faced with the situation of a change of the conscience of man and the situation of believers, it is clear that the discussion about the truth claim of the religions cannot be a marginal or partial aspect of theology. The respectful confrontation with this truth claim must play a role in the center of the daily work of theology; it must be an integral part of it. Today's Christian, respecting the diversity of religions, must learn to live a form of communion which has its foundation in the love of God for men and which is based on God's respect of man's freedom. This respect before the "otherness" of the different religions is at the same time conditioned by one's own truth claim.

103. Along with love, interest in the truth claim of the other shares the presupposition, structural in character, of appreciation of oneself. The basis of every communication, and hence also of the dialogue among religions, is the recognition of the exigent character of truth. But the Christian faith has its own proper structure of truth: The religions talk "of" the holy, "of" God, "about" him, "in his place" or "in his name". Only in the Christian religion is God himself the one who speaks to man in his Word. Only this way of speaking makes his personal being in a true sense possible for man and at the time communion with God and with all men. The tripersonal God is the heart of this faith. Only the Christian faith takes its life from the God one and three. From the background of

Christianity's culture arose the social differentiation which characterizes modernity.

104. To the unique salvific mediation of Christ for all is attributed, on the part of the pluralist position, a claim of superiority; therefore it asks that a more acceptable theocentrism take the place of that theological Christocentrism from which this claim is necessarily deduced. In view of this demand, it is necessary to affirm that the truth of faith is not at our disposal. In facing a strategy of dialogue which asks for a reduction of Christological dogma in order to exclude this claim of Christianity's superiority, we opt instead—with the aim of excluding a "false" claim of superiority—for a radical application of the Christological faith to the form of proclamation proper to it.

Every form of evangelization that does not correspond to the message, to the life, to the death and to the resurrection of Jesus Christ compromises this message and, in final analysis, Jesus Christ himself. The truth as truth is always "superior"; but the truth of Jesus Christ, as made clear by our need for him, is always service to man; it is the truth of the one who gives his life for men in order to make them enter definitively into the love of God. Every form of proclamation which seeks above all and over all to impose itself on its hearers or to dispose them by means of a strategic or instrumental rationality is opposed to Christ, to the Gospel of the Father and to the dignity of the man of whom he has himself spoken.

III.4. *Interreligious Dialogue and the Mystery of Salvation*

105. Since Vatican Council II, the Catholic Church has definitively committed herself to interreligious dialogue;[34] the present document has been developed with a view to this dialogue, although this is not its fundamental theme. The state of the question about Christianity and its relationship with the religions, theological presuppositions and the consequences which are deduced from them about the saving value of the religions, divine revelation—all these are reflections intended to enlighten Christians in their dialogues with the faithful of other religions.

106. To the extent that these dialogues take place among specialists and are effected in everyday life in words and actions, they not only engage the persons who carry on the dialogue but also and in first place the God

---

[34] Among the documents of John Paul II see *Redemptoris missio*, 55–57; *Tertio millennio adveniente*, 52–53; cf. also the document of the Pontifical Council for Interreligious Dialogue and the Congregation for the Evangelization of Peoples, "Dialogue and Proclamation", cited already many times.

whom they profess. The interreligious dialogue as such implies three participants. Therefore in it the Christian is faced with two fundamental questions on which the meaning of the dialogue depends: the understanding of God and the understanding of man.

A. The Understanding of God

107. In the interreligious dialogue, each participant in fact expresses himself according to a definite understanding of God; implicitly he poses to the other the question, Who is your God? The Christian cannot hear and understand the other without posing this question to himself. Christian theology is more than a discourse about God: It is concerned with speaking of God in human language as he is made known through the incarnate Word (cf. Jn 1:18; 17:3). Hence the need of some discernment in the dialogue:

108. a. If the discussion concerns the divinity as a transcendent and absolute value, are we treating an impersonal reality or a personal being?

b. Does the transcendence of God mean that he is a nontemporal myth or is this transcendence compatible with divine action in the history of men?

c. Is God known only through reason or is he also known through faith because he reveals himself to men?

d. Given that a "religion" is a certain relationship between God and man, does it express a God in the image of man or rather does it imply that man is in the image of God?

e. If it is granted that God is one as required by reason, what does it mean to profess that he is one? A monopersonal God is acceptable to reason, but only in his self-revelation in Christ can the mystery of God be welcomed through faith as consubstantial and indivisible one-in-three. This is a major discernment because of the consequences flowing from this for the anthropology and sociology inherent in each religion.

f. The religions recognize essential attributes of the divinity as omnipotence, omniscience, goodness, justice. But to understand the doctrinal coherence of each religion and to overcome ambiguities of an apparently common language, it is necessary to understand the axis on which these divine names turn. This discernment especially concerns the biblical vocabulary, whose axis is the covenant between God and man as this has been fulfilled in Christ.

g. Another discernment is made necessary concerning the specifically theological vocabulary to the extent that it is a tributary of the culture of each participant in the dialogue and of his implicit philosophy. Therefore, it is most important to pay attention to the cultural peculiarity of the two parties, even if both share the same original culture.

h. The contemporary world seems to be preoccupied, at least in theory, with the rights of man. Some integrists, even among Christians, oppose to these the rights of God. But in this opposition what is the God one is dealing with, and in the final analysis, what is the man with whom one is concerned?

B. The Understanding of Man

109. An implicit anthropology is also involved in the interreligious dialogue, and this for two major reasons. On the one hand, the dialogue puts two persons into communication, each one of whom is the subject of his own word and behavior. On the other hand, when believers of different religions dialogue, there takes place an event much more profound than verbal communication: an encounter between human beings with respect to the end toward which each one tends, bearing the weight of his own human condition.

110. In an interreligious dialogue, do the parties have the same concept of the person? The question is not theoretical, but it raises a question for both the one and the other. The Christian party knows without doubt that the human person has been created "in the image of God", that is to say, in a constant call of an essentially relational God and capable of opening "to the other". But are all the participants aware of the mystery of the human person and of the mystery of the God "beyond all"?[35] Also the Christian is forced to ask himself the question, From whence does he talk when he dialogues? Whence the scene of his social or religious personage? Whence the depth of his "superego" or of his ideal image? Given that he must bear witness to his Lord and Savior, in what "dwelling" of his soul is this one encountered? In the interreligious dialogue, more than in any other interpersonal relationship, the relationship of each person with the living God is at stake.

111. Here is shown the importance of prayer in the interreligious dialogue: "Man is in search of God.... All religions bear witness to men's essential search for God."[36] Now then, prayer, as a living and personal relationship with God, is the act of the virtue of religion and finds expression in all the religions. The Christian knows that God "tirelessly calls each person to that mysterious encounter known as prayer."[37] If God

---

[35] Gregory Nanzianzen, *Carmimum* 1, 1, 29 (PG 37, 507).
[36] *Catechism of the Catholic Church*, 2566.
[37] Ibid., 2567.

can be known better only if he himself takes the initiative of revealing himself, prayer shows itself as absolutely necessary because it disposes man to receive the grace of revelation. Thus, in the common search for truth which must motivate the interreligious dialogue: "There is a close relationship between prayer and dialogue.... If on the one hand, dialogue depends on prayer, so, in another sense, prayer also becomes the ever more mature fruit of dialogue."[38]

To the extent that the Christian lives the dialogue in a state of prayer, he is docile to the movement of the Spirit who works in the heart of the two interlocutors. Then the dialogue makes itself more than an interchange: It becomes an encounter.

112. More profoundly, at the level of what is not said, the interreligious dialogue is in truth an encounter between beings created "in the image of God", although this image is found in them somewhat obscured by sin and death. Put differently, Christians and those who are not are all hoping to be saved. For this reason each one of the religions presents itself as a search for salvation and proposes ways to reach it.

This encounter in the common human condition puts the parties on an equal plane much more real than their merely human religious discourse. Such a discourse is already an interpretation of experience and passes through the filter of confessional mentalities. The problems of personal maturity, the experience of human community (husband and wife, family, education, etc.) and all the questions which gravitate around work in order to "earn one's way in life", far from being themes that would distract from the interreligious dialogue, constitute the ground "to be explored" in this dialogue. Then in this encounter one finds that the "place" of God is man.

113. Now then, the constant factor which underlies all the other problems of the common human condition is nothing other than death. Suffering, sin, failure, deception, failure to communicate, conflicts, injustices ... death is present in all parts and in every moment as the opaque problem of the human condition. Surely man, unable to exorcise death, does everything possible not to think about it. But nonetheless it is in death that the call of the living God resounds with greatest intensity. It is the permanent sign of the divine otherness, for only he who calls nothingness to being can give life to the dead. No one can go to God without passing through death, that fiery place in which the Transcendent reaches the abyss of the human condition.

The only serious question, because it is existential and unavoidable, without which religious discussions are "alibis", is this: Does or does not

[38] John Paul II, *Ut unum sint*, 33.

the living God assume the death of man? Theoretical answers to this question are not lacking, but they cannot evade the scandal which remains: How can God remain hidden and silent before the wounded innocent and the oppressed just man? It is the cry of Job and of all humankind. The answer is "crucial", but beyond all words: On the cross the Word is silence. Relying on his Father, he entrusts to him his last breath. And there (on the cross) is the encounter of all men: Man is in his death, and God unites himself with him in it.

Only the God of love is the victor over death, and only through faith in him is man liberated from the slavery of death. The fiery wood of the cross is thus the hidden place of the encounter. The Christian contemplates on it "him whom they have pierced" and from it receives "a spirit of grace and petition" (Jn 19:37; Zech 12:10). The testimony of his new experience will be that of the risen Christ, the conqueror of death through death.

Interreligious dialogue receives then its meaning in the economy of salvation: It means more than to follow the message of the prophets and the mission of the Precursor; it is grounded in the event of salvation accomplished through Christ and is oriented toward the second coming of the Lord. The interreligious dialogue takes place in the Church in an eschatological situation.

IV. CONCLUSION: DIALOGUE AND THE MISSION OF THE CHURCH

114. At this end of the second millennium, the Church is called to give witness to the crucified and risen Christ "to the ends of the earth" (Acts 1:8), in different cultures and religions throughout the world. The religious dialogue is connnatural to the Christian vocation. It is inscribed in the dynamism of the living tradition of the mystery of salvation, whose universal sacrament is the Church; it is an act of this tradition.

115. As a dialogue of the Church, it has its source, its model and its end in the Holy Trinity. It manifests and actualizes the mission of the eternal Word and of the Holy Spirit in the economy of salvation. Through his Word, the Father calls all human beings from nothing into existence, and it is his breath which gives them life. Through his Son, who assumes our flesh and is anointed by his Spirit, he directs himself to them as to his friends, "he speaks with them on the earth" and reveals to them "all the ways of understanding" (cf. Bar 3:36–38). His living Spirit makes the Church the body of Christ sent to the nations to proclaim to them the good news of the resurrection.

116. The Word can enable us to know the Father, for he has learned all from him, and he has accepted to learn all of man. Thus this must take place in the Church for those who want to encounter their brothers and sisters of other religions and to dialogue with them. It is not Christians who are sent, but the Church; it is not their ideas that they present but Christ's; it will not be their rhetoric that will touch hearts but the Spirit, the Paraclete. To be faithful to the "sense of the Church", the interreligious dialogue begs for the humility of Christ and the transparency of the Holy Spirit.

117. The divine pedagogy of the dialogue does not consist only in words but also in deeds; the words manifest the "Christian newness", that of the love of the Father, to which deeds give testimony. Working in this way, the Church shows herself as the sacrament of the mystery of salvation. In this sense the interreligious dialogue forms a part, according to the times and moments fixed by the Father, of the *praeparatio evangelica*. In truth, the mutual witness is something inherent in the dialogue between persons of different religions.

The Christian witness here is not, however, the proclaiming of the Gospel, but is already an integral part of the mission of the Church as an irradiation of the love poured out from her through the Holy Spirit. Those who in the different ways of interreligious dialogue give witness to the love of Christ the Savior realize, at the level of the *praeparatio evangelica*, the burning desire of the apostle "to be a minister of Christ Jesus among the gentiles, with the priestly duty of preaching the Gospel of God so that the gentiles may be offered up as a pleasing sacrifice, consecrated by the Holy Spirit" (Rom 15:16).

20

MEMORY AND RECONCILIATION: THE CHURCH AND THE FAULTS OF THE PAST

PRELIMINARY NOTE

The study of the topic "The Church and the Faults of the Past" was proposed to the International Theological Commission by its President, Joseph Cardinal Ratzinger, in view of the celebration of the Jubilee Year 2000. A sub-commission was established to prepare this study; it was composed of Rev. Christopher Begg; Msgr. Bruno Forte (President); Rev. Sebastian Karotemprel, S.D.B.; Msgr. Roland Minnerath; Rev. Thomas Norris; Rev. Rafael Salazar Cardenas, M.Sp.S.; and Msgr. Anton Strukelj. The general discussion of this theme took place in numerous meetings of the sub-commission and during the plenary sessions of the International Theological Commission held in Rome from 1998 to 1999. The present text was approved *in forma specifica* by the International Theological Commission, by written vote, and was then submitted to the President, Cardinal Ratzinger, Prefect of the Congregation for the Doctrine of the Faith, who gave his approval for its publication.

INTRODUCTION

The Bull of Indiction of the Great Jubilee of the Year 2000, *Incarnationis mysterium* (November 29, 1998), includes the purification of memory among the signs "which may help people to live the exceptional grace of the Jubilee with greater fervor". This purification aims at liberating personal and communal conscience from all forms of resentment and violence that are the legacy of past faults, through a renewed historical and theological evaluation of such events. This should lead—if done correctly—to a corresponding recognition of guilt and contribute to the path of reconciliation. Such a process can have a significant effect on the present, precisely because the consequences of past faults still make themselves felt and can persist as tensions in the present.

The purification of memory is thus "an act of courage and humility in recognizing the wrongs done by those who have borne or bear the name of Christian." It is based on the conviction that because of "the bond which unites us to one another in the Mystical Body, all of us, though not personally responsible and without encroaching on the judgement of God who alone knows every heart, bear the burden of the errors and faults of those who have gone before us." John Paul II adds: "As the Successor of Peter, I ask that in this year of mercy the Church, strong in the holiness which she receives from her Lord, should kneel before God and implore forgiveness for the past and present sins of her sons and daughters." [1] In reiterating that "Christians are invited to acknowledge, before God and before those offended by their actions, the faults which they have committed", the Pope concludes, "Let them do so without seeking anything in return, but strengthened only by 'the love of God which has been poured into our hearts' (Rom 5:5)." [2]

The requests for forgiveness made by the Bishop of Rome in this spirit of authenticity and gratuitousness have given rise to various reactions. The unconditional trust in the power of Truth which the Pope has shown has met with a generally favorable reception both inside and outside the Church. Many have noted the increased credibility of ecclesial pronouncements that has resulted from this way of acting. Some reservations, however, have also been voiced, mainly expressions of unease connected with particular historical and cultural contexts in which the simple admission of faults committed by the sons and daughters of the Church may look like acquiescence in the face of accusations made by those who are prejudicially hostile to the Church. Between agreement and unease, the need arises for a reflection which clarifies the reasons, the conditions, and the exact form of the requests for forgiveness for the faults of the past.

The International Theological Commission, in which a diversity of cultures and sensitivities within the one Catholic faith are represented, decided to address this need with the present text. The text offers a theological reflection on the conditions which make acts of "purification of memory" possible in connection with the recognition of the faults of the past. The questions it seeks to address are as follows: Why should it be

---

[1] *Incarnationis mysterium*, 11.

[2] Ibid. In numerous prior statements, in particular, number 33 of the Apostolic Letter *Tertio millennio adveniente* (*TMA*), the Pope has indicated to the Church the path forward for purifying her memory regarding the faults of the past and for giving an example of repentance to individuals and civil societies.

done? Who should do it? What is the goal and how should this be determined, by correctly combining historical and theological judgement? Who
will be addressed? What are the moral implications? And what are the
possible effects on the life of the Church and on society? The purpose of
the text is, therefore, not to examine particular historical cases but rather
to clarify the presuppositions that ground repentance for past faults.

Having noted the kind of reflection which will be presented here, it is
important also to make clear what is referred to when the text speaks of
the Church: it is not a question of the historical institution alone or solely
the spiritual communion of those whose hearts are illumined by faith.
The Church is understood as the community of the baptized, inseparably
visible and operating in history under the direction of her Pastors, united
as a profound mystery by the action of the life-giving Spirit. According
to the Second Vatican Council, the Church "by no weak analogy ... is
compared to the mystery of the incarnate Word. As the assumed nature
inseparably united to Him, serves the divine Word as a living organ of
salvation, so, in a similar way, does the visible social structure of the Church
serve the Spirit of Christ, who vivifies it, in the building up of the body
(cf. Eph 4:16)."[3] This Church, which embraces her sons and daughters
of the past and of the present, in a real and profound communion, is the
sole Mother of Grace who takes upon herself also the weight of past
faults in order to purify memory and to live the renewal of heart and life
according to the will of the Lord. She is able to do this insofar as Christ
Jesus, whose mystical body extended through history she is, has taken
upon himself once and for all the sins of the world.

The structure of the text mirrors the questions posed. It moves from a
brief historical revisiting of the theme (Chapter 1), in order to be able to
investigate the biblical foundation (Chapter 2) and explore more deeply
the theological conditions of the requests for forgiveness (Chapter 3).
The precise correlation of historical and theological judgement is a decisive element for reaching correct and efficacious statements that take proper
account of the times, places, and contexts in which the actions under
consideration were situated (Chapter 4). The final considerations, that
have a specific value for the Catholic Church, are dedicated to the moral
(Chapter 5), pastoral and missionary (Chapter 6) implications of these
acts of repentance for the faults of the past. Nevertheless, in the knowledge that the necessity of recognizing one's own faults has reason to be
practiced by all peoples and religions, one hopes that the proposed reflections may help everyone to advance on the path of truth, fraternal dialogue, and reconciliation.

[3] LG 8.

At the conclusion of this introduction, it may be useful to recall the purpose of every act of "purification of memory" undertaken by believers, because this is what has inspired the work of the Commission: it is the glorification of God, because living in obedience to Divine Truth and its demands leads to confessing, together with our faults, the eternal mercy and justice of the Lord. The *"confessio peccati"*, sustained and illuminated by faith in the Truth which frees and saves (*"confessio fidei"*), becomes a *"confessio laudis"* addressed to God, before whom alone it becomes possible to recognize the faults both of the past and of the present, so that we might be reconciled by and to him in Christ Jesus, the only Savior of the world, and become able to forgive those who have offended us. This offer of forgiveness appears particularly meaningful when one thinks of the many persecutions suffered by Christians in the course of history. In this perspective, the actions undertaken by the Holy Father, and those requested by him, regarding the faults of the past have an exemplary and prophetic value, for religions as much as for governments and nations, beyond being of value for the Catholic Church, which is thus helped to live in a more efficacious way the Great Jubilee of the Incarnation as an event of grace and reconciliation for everyone.

1. THE PROBLEM: YESTERDAY AND TODAY

1.1 *Before Vatican II*

The Jubilee has always been lived in the Church as a time of joy for the salvation given in Christ and as a privileged occasion for penance and reconciliation for the sins present in the lives of the People of God. From its first celebration under Boniface VIII in 1300, the penitential pilgrimage to the tombs of the Apostles Peter and Paul was associated with the granting of an exceptional indulgence for procuring, with sacramental pardon, total or partial remission of the temporal punishment due to sin.[4] In this context, both sacramental forgiveness and the remission of temporal punishment have a personal character. In the course of the "year of pardon and grace",[5] the Church dispenses in a particular way the treasury of grace that

---

[4] Cf. *Extravagantes communes* 5, 9, 1 (A. Friedberg, *Corpus iuris canonici*, t. 2, c. 1304).

[5] Cf. Clement XIV, Letter *Salutis nostrae*, 30 April 1774, no. 2. Leo XII in the Letter *Quod hoc ineunte*, 24 May 1824, no. 2, speaks of the "year of expiation, forgiveness and redemption, of grace, remission and of indulgence".

Christ has constituted for her benefit.[6] In none of the Jubilees celebrated till now has there been, however, an awareness in conscience of any faults in the Church's past, nor of the need to ask God's pardon for conduct in the recent or remote past.

Indeed, in the entire history of the Church there are no precedents for requests for forgiveness by the Magisterium for past wrongs. Councils and papal decrees applied sanctions, to be sure, to abuses of which clerics and laymen were found guilty, and many pastors sincerely strove to correct them. However, the occasions when ecclesiastical authorities— Pope, Bishops, or Councils—have openly acknowledged the faults or abuses which they themselves were guilty of, have been quite rare. One famous example is furnished by the reforming Pope Adrian VI who acknowledged publicly in a message to the Diet of Nuremberg of November 25, 1522, "the abominations, the abuses ... and the lies" of which the "Roman court" of his time was guilty, "deep-rooted and extensive ... sickness", extending "from the top to the members".[7] Adrian VI deplored the faults of his times, precisely those of his immediate predecessor Leo X and his curia, without, however, adding a request for pardon. It will be necessary to wait until Paul VI to find a Pope express a request for pardon addressed as much to God as to a group of contemporaries. In his address at the opening of the second session of the Second Vatican Council, the Pope asked "pardon of God ... and of the separated brethren" of the East who may have felt offended "by us" (the Catholic Church), and declared himself ready for his part to pardon offences received. In the view of Paul VI, both the request for and offer of pardon concerned solely the sin of the division between Christians and presupposed reciprocity.

1.2 The Teaching of the Council

Vatican II takes the same approach as Paul VI. For the faults committed against unity, the Council Fathers state, "We humbly beg pardon of God and of our separated brethren, just as we forgive them that trespass against

---

[6] This is the sense of the definition of *indulgence* given by Clement VI when in 1343 he instituted the practice of having a Jubilee every fifty years. Clement VI sees in the Church's Jubilee "the spiritual accomplishment" of the "Jubilee of remission and of joy" in the Old Testament (Lev 25).

[7] "Each of us must examine [his conscience] with respect to what he has fallen into and examine himself even more rigorously than God will on the day of his wrath." In *Deutsche Reichstagsakten*, n.s., 3:390–99 (Gotha, 1893).

us."[8] In addition to faults against unity, it noted other negative episodes from the past for which Christians bore some responsibility. Thus, it "deplore[s] certain habits of mind, which are sometimes found too among Christians" and which led people to think that faith and science are mutually opposed.[9] Likewise, it considers the fact that in "the birth of atheism", Christians may have had "some responsibility" insofar as through their negligence they "conceal rather than reveal the authentic face of God and religion."[10] In addition, the Council "decries" the persecutions and manifestations of anti-Semitism "at any time and by anyone".[11] The Council, nevertheless, does not add a request for pardon for the things cited.

From a theological point of view, Vatican II distinguishes between the indefectible fidelity of the Church and the weaknesses of her members, clergy or laity, yesterday and today,[12] and therefore, between the Bride of Christ "with neither blemish nor wrinkle . . . holy and immaculate" (cf. Eph 5:27), and her children, pardoned sinners, called to permanent *metanoia*, to renewal in the Holy Spirit. "The Church, embracing in its bosom sinners, at the same time holy and always in need of being purified, always follows the way of penance and renewal."[13]

The Council also elaborated some criteria of discernment regarding the guilt or responsibility of persons now living for faults of the past. In effect, the Council recalled in two different contexts the nonimputability to those now living of past faults committed by members of their religious communities:

— "What happened in [Christ's] passion cannot be charged against all the Jews, without distinction, then alive, nor against the Jews of today."[14]

— "Large communities came to be separated from full communion with the Catholic Church—for which, often enough, men of both sides were to blame. The children who are born into these Communities and who grow up believing in Christ cannot be accused of the sin involved in the separation, and the Catholic Church embraces upon them as brothers, with respect and affection."[15]

[8] *UR* 7.

[9] *GS* 36.

[10] *GS* 19.

[11] *NA* 4.

[12] *GS* 43, par. 6.

[13] *LG* 8; cf. *UR* 6: "Christ summons the Church to continual reformation as she sojourns here on earth. The Church is always in need of this, in so far as she is an institution of men here on earth."

[14] *NA* 4.

[15] *UR* 3.

When the first Holy Year was celebrated after the Council, in 1975, Paul VI gave it the theme of "renewal and reconciliation",[16] making clear in the Apostolic Exhortation *Paterna cum benevolentia* that reconciliation should take place first of all among the faithful of the Catholic Church.[17] As in its origin, the Holy Year remained an occasion for conversion and reconciliation of sinners to God by means of the sacramental economy of the Church.

1.3. John Paul II's Requests for Forgiveness

Not only did John Paul II renew expressions of regret for the "painful memories" that mark the history of the divisions among Christians, as Paul VI and the Second Vatican Council had done,[18] but he also extended a request for forgiveness to a multitude of historical events in which the Church, or individual groups of Christians, were implicated in different respects.[19] In the Apostolic Letter *Tertio millennio adveniente*,[20] the Pope expresses the hope that the Jubilee of 2000 might be the occasion for a purification of the memory of the Church from all forms of "counter-witness and scandal" which have occurred in the course of the past millennium.[21]

The Church is invited to "become more fully conscious of the sinfulness of her children". She "acknowledges as her own her sinful sons and daughters" and encourages them "to purify themselves, through repentance, of past errors and instances of infidelity, inconsistency, and slowness to act." [22] The responsibility of Christians for the evils of our time is

[16] Cf. Paul VI, Apostolic Letter *Apostolorum limina*, 23 May 1974 (*Enchiridion Vaticanum* 5, 305).

[17] Paul VI, Exhortation *Paterna cum benevolentia*, 8 December 1974 (*Enchiridion Vaticanum* 5, 526553).

[18] Cf. Encyclical Letter *Ut unum sint*, 25 May 1995, 88: "To the extent that we are responsible for these, I join my Predecessor Paul VI in asking forgiveness."

[19] For example, the Pope, addressing himself to the Moravians, asked "forgiveness, on behalf of all Catholics, for the wrongs caused to non-Catholics in the course of history" (cf. Canonization of Jan Sarkander in the Czech Republic, 21 May 1995). The Holy Father also wanted to undertake "an act of expiation" and ask forgiveness of the Indians of Latin America and from the Africans deported as slaves ("Message to the Indians of America", Santo Domingo, 13 October 1992, and General Audience Discourse of 21 October 1992). Ten years earlier he had already asked forgiveness from the Africans for the way in which they had been treated (Discourse at Yaoundé, 13 August 1985).

[20] Cf. TMA 33–36.

[21] Cf. TMA 33.

[22] Ibid.

likewise noted,[23] although the accent falls particularly on the solidarity of the Church of today with past faults. Some of these are explicitly mentioned, like the separation of Christians,[24] or the "intolerance and even the use of violence" used in the past to evangelize.[25]

John Paul II also promoted the deeper theological exploration of the idea of taking responsibility for the wrongs of the past and of possibly asking forgiveness from one's contemporaries,[26] when in the Exhortation *Reconciliatio et paenitentia*, he states that in the sacrament of Penance "the sinner stands alone before God with his sin, repentance and trust. No one can repent in his place or ask forgiveness in his name." Sin is therefore always personal, even though it wounds the entire Church, which, represented by the priest as minister of Penance, is the sacramental mediatrix of the grace which reconciles with God.[27] Also the situations of "social sin"—which are evident in the human community when justice, freedom, and peace are damaged— are always "the result of the accumulation and concentration of many personal sins." While moral responsibility may become diluted in anonymous causes, one can only speak of social sin by way of analogy.[28] It emerges from this that the imputability of a fault cannot properly be extended beyond the group of persons who had consented to it voluntarily, by means of acts or omissions, or through negligence.

1.4. *The Questions Raised*

The Church is a living society spanning the centuries. Her memory is not constituted only by the tradition which goes back to the Apostles and is normative for her faith and life, but she is also rich in the variety of historical experiences, positive and negative, which she has lived. In large part, the Church's past structures her present. The doctrinal, liturgical, canonical, and ascetical tradition nourishes the life of the believing community, offering it an incomparable sampling of models to imitate. Along the entire earthly pilgrimage, however, the good grain always remains inextricably mixed with the chaff; holiness stands side by side with infidelity and sin.[29] And it

---

[23] Cf. *TMA* 36.

[24] Cf. *TMA* 34.

[25] Cf. *TMA* 35.

[26] This final aspect appears in *TMA* only in number 33, where it is said that the Church "before God and man" acknowledges as her own her sinful sons and daughters.

[27] John Paul II, Exhortation *Reconciliatio et paenitentia*, 2 December 1984, 31.

[28] Ibid., 16.

[29] Cf. Mt 13:24–30, 36–43; St. Augustine, *De civitate Dei* 1, 35 (CCL 47, 33); 11, 1 (CCL 48, 321); 19, 26 (CCL 48, 696).

is thus that the remembrance of scandals of the past can become an obstacle to the Church's witness today, and the recognition of the past faults of the Church's sons and daughters of yesterday can foster renewal and reconciliation in the present.

The difficulty that emerges is that of defining past faults, above all, because of the historical judgement which this requires. In events of the past, one must always distinguish the responsibility or fault that can be attributed to members of the Church as believers from that which should be referred to society during the centuries of "Christendom" or to power structures in which the temporal and spiritual were closely intertwined. An historical hermeneutic is therefore more necessary than ever in order to distinguish correctly between the action of the Church as community of faith and that of society in the times when an osmosis existed between them.

The steps taken by John Paul II to ask pardon for faults of the past have been understood in many circles as signs of the Church's vitality and authenticity, such that they strengthen her credibility. It is right, moreover, that the Church contribute to changing false and unacceptable images of herself, especially in those areas in which, whether through ignorance or bad faith, some sectors of opinion like to identify her with obscurantism and intolerance. The requests for pardon formulated by the Pope have also given rise to positive emulation both inside and outside the Church. Heads of state or government, private and public associations, religious communities are today asking forgiveness for episodes or historical periods marked by injustices. This practice is far from just an exercise in rhetoric, and for this reason, some hesitate to do so, calculating the attendant costs—among which are those on the legal plane—of an acknowledgement of past wrongs. Also from this point of view, a rigorous discernment is necessary.

Nevertheless, some of the faithful are disconcerted and their loyalty to the Church seems shaken. Some wonder how they can hand on a love for the Church to younger generations if this same Church is imputed with crimes and faults. Others observe that the recognition of faults is for the most part one-sided and is exploited by the Church's detractors, who are satisfied to see the Church confirm the prejudices they had of her. Still others warn against arbitrarily making current generations of believers feel guilty for shortcomings they did not consent to in any way, even though they declare themselves ready to take responsibility to the extent that some groups of people still feel themselves affected today by the consequences of injustices suffered by their forebears in previous times. Others hold that the Church could purify her memory with respect to ambiguous actions in which she was involved in the past simply by taking part in the critical work on memory developed in our society. Thus she could affirm that she joins with her contemporaries in rejecting what the moral conscience of our time reproaches, though without putting herself forward as the only guilty party responsible for the evils of the past, by seeking at the same time a dialogue in mutual understanding with those who may feel themselves still wounded by past acts imputable to the children of the Church. Finally, it is to be expected that certain groups might demand that forgiveness be sought in their regard, either by analogy with other groups, or because they believe that they have suffered wrongs. In any case, the purification of memory can never mean that the Church ceases to proclaim the revealed truth that has been entrusted to her whether in the area of faith or of morals.

Thus, a number of questions can be identified: Can today's conscience be assigned "guilt" for isolated historical phenomena like the Crusades or the Inquisition? Isn't it a bit too easy to judge people of the past by the conscience of today (as the Scribes and Pharisees do according to Matthew 23:29–32), almost as if moral conscience were not situated in time? And, on the other hand, can it be denied that ethical judgement is always possible, given the simple fact that the truth of God and its moral requirements always have value? Whatever attitude is adopted must come to terms with these questions and seek answers that are based in revelation and in its living transmission in the faith of the Church. The first question is therefore that of clarifying the extent to which requests for forgiveness for past wrongs, especially if addressed to groups of people today, are within the biblical and theological horizon of reconciliation with God and neighbor.

2. BIBLICAL APPROACH

The investigation of Israel's acknowledgement of faults in the Old Testament and the topic of the confession of faults as found in the traditions of the New Testament can be developed in various ways.[30] The theological nature of the reflection undertaken here leads us to favor a largely thematic approach, centering on the following question: What background does the testimony of Sacred Scripture furnish for John Paul II's invitation to the Church to confess the faults of the past?

2.1. *The Old Testament*

Confessions of sins and corresponding requests for forgiveness can be found throughout the Bible—in the narratives of the Old Testament, in the

---

[30] On different methods of reading Sacred Scripture, see *The Interpretation of the Bible in the Church*, Pontifical Biblical Commission (1993).

Psalms, and in the Prophets, as well as in the Gospels of the New Testament. There are also sporadic references in the Wisdom Literature and in the Letters of the New Testament. Given the abundance and diffusion of these testimonies, the question of how to select and catalogue the mass of significant texts arises. One may inquire here about the biblical texts related to the confession of sins: Who is confessing what (and what kind of fault) to whom? Put in this way, the question helps distinguish two principal categories of "confession texts", each of which embraces different subcategories, viz., (a) confession texts of individual sins, and (b) confession texts of sins of the entire people (and of those of their forebears). In relation to the recent ecclesial practice that motivates this study, we will restrict our analysis to the second category.

In this second category, different expressions can be found, depending on who is making the confession of the sins of the people and on who is, or is not, associated with the shared guilt, prescinding from the presence or absence of an awareness of personal responsibility (which has only matured progressively: cf. Ezek 14:12–23; 18:1–32; 33:10–20). On the basis of these criteria, the following rather fluid cases can be distinguished:

— A first series of texts represents the entire people (sometimes personified as a single "I") who, in a particular moment of its history, confesses or alludes to its sins against God without any (explicit) reference to the faults of the preceding generations.[31]

— Another group of texts places the confession—directed to God—of the current sins of the people on the lips of one or more leaders (religious), who may or may not include themselves explicitly among the sinful people for whom they are praying.[32]

---

[31] In this series, for example, are: Deut 1:41 (the generation of the desert recognizes that it had sinned by refusing to go forward into the promised land); Judg 10:10, 12 (in the time of the Judges the people twice say "we have sinned" against the Lord, referring to their service of the Baals); 1 Sam 7:6 (the people of Samuel's time say "we have sinned against the Lord!"); Num 21:7 (this text is distinctive in that here the people of the generation of Moses admit that, in complaining about the food, they had become guilty of "sin" because they had spoken against the Lord and against their human guide, Moses); 1 Sam 12:19 (the Israelites of the time of Samuel recognize that—by having asked for a king—they have added this to "all their sins"); Ezra 10:13 (the people acknowledge in front of Ezra that they had greatly "transgressed in this matter" [marrying foreign women]); Ps 65:2–3; 90:8; 103:10; (107:10–11, 17); Is 59:9–15; 64:5–9; Jer 8:14; 14:7; Lam 1:14, 18a, 22 (in which Jerusalem speaks in the first person); 3:42 (4:13); Bar 4:12–13 (Zion speaks of the sins of her children which led to her destruction); Ezek 33:10; Mic 7:9 ("I"), 18–19.

[32] For example: Ex 9:27 (Pharaoh says to Moses and Aaron: "This time I have sinned; the Lord is in the right; I and my people are guilty"); 34:9 (Moses prays "forgive our iniquity and our sin"); Lev 16:21 (the high priest confesses the sins of the people on the head of the "scapegoat" on the day of atonement); Ex 32:11–13 (cf. Deut 9:26–29: Moses;

— A third group of texts presents the people or one of their leaders in the act of mentioning the sins of their forebears without, however, making mention of those of the present generation.[33]

— More frequent are the confessions that mention the faults of the forebears, linking them expressly to the errors of the present generation.[34]

We can conclude from the testimonies gathered that in all cases where the "sins of the fathers" are mentioned, the confession is addressed solely to God, and the sins confessed by the people and for the people are those committed directly against him rather than those committed (also) against other human beings (only in Numbers 21:7 is mention made of a human party harmed, Moses).[35] The question arises as to why the

---

32:31 (Moses); 1 Kings 8:33ff. (cf. 2 Chron 6:22ff.: Solomon prays that God will forgive the future sins of the people); 2 Chron 28:13 (the leaders of the Israelites acknowledge "our guilt is already great"); Ezra 10:2 (Shecaniah says to Ezra, "We have broken faith with our God, by marrying foreign women"); Neh 1:5–11 (Nehemiah confesses the sins committed by the people of Israel, by himself, and by the house of his father); Esther 4:17(n) (Esther confesses: "We have sinned against you and you have delivered us into the hands of our enemies, because we have given glory to their gods"); 2 Mac 7:18–32 (the Jewish martyrs say that they are suffering because of "our sins" against God).

[33] Among the examples of this type of national confession are: 2 Kings 22:13 (cf. 2 Chron 34:21: Josiah fears the anger of the Lord "because our fathers did not heed the words of this book"); 2 Chron 29:6–7 (Hezekiah says, "Our fathers have been unfaithful"); Ps 78:8ff. (the psalmist recounts the sins of past generations from the time of the Exodus from Egypt). Cf. also the popular saying cited in Jer 31:29 and Ezek 18:2: "The fathers have eaten sour grapes and the children's teeth are set on edge."

[34] As in the following texts: Lev 26:40 (the exiles are called to "confess their iniquity and the iniquity of their fathers"); Ezra 9:5b–15 (the penitential prayer of Ezra, v. 7: "From the days of our fathers to this day we have been deeply guilty"; cf. Neh 9:6–37); Tob 3:1–5 (in his prayer Tobit prays: "Do not punish me for my sins and for my errors and those of my fathers" [v. 3] and continues with the statement: "We have not kept your commandments" [v. 5]; Ps 79:8–9 (this collective lament implores God: "Do not impute to us the offenses of our fathers ... deliver us and forgive us our sins"); 106:6 ("Both we and our fathers have sinned"); Jer 3:25 ("We have sinned against the Lord our God ... we and our fathers"); Jer 14:19–22 ("We acknowledge our iniquity and the iniquity of our fathers", v. 20); Lam 5 ("Our fathers sinned and they are no more, and we bear the penalty for their iniquities" [v. 7]—"Woe to us for we have sinned" [v. 16b]; Bar 1:15— 3:18 ("We have sinned against the Lord" [1:17, cf. 1:19, 21; 2:5, 24]—"Remember not the iniquities of our fathers" [3:5, cf. 2:33; 3:4, 7]); Dan 3:26–45 (the prayer of Azariah: "With truth and justice you have inflicted all this because of our sins": v. 28); Dan 9:4–19 ("On account of our sins and the iniquity of our fathers, Jerusalem [has] become the reproach", v. 16).

[35] These include failing to trust God (for example, Deut 1:41; Num 14:10), idolatry (as in Judg 10:10–15), requesting a human king (1 Sam 12:9), marrying foreign women contrary to the law of God (Ezra 9–10). In Is 59:13b the people say of themselves that they are guilty of "talking oppression and revolt, conceiving lying words and uttering them from the heart".

biblical writers did not feel the need to address requests for forgiveness to present interlocutors for the sins committed by their fathers, given their strong sense of solidarity in good and evil among the generations (one thinks of the notion of "corporate personality"). We can propose various hypotheses in response to this question. First, there is the prevalent theocentrism of the Bible, which gives precedence to the acknowledgement, whether individual or national, of the faults committed against God. What is more, acts of violence perpetrated by Israel against other peoples, which would seem to require a request for forgiveness from those peoples or from their descendants, are understood to be the execution of divine directives, as for example Genesis 2–11 and Deuteronomy 7:2 (the extermination of the Canaanites), or First Samuel 15 and Deuteronomy 25:19 (the destruction of the Amalekites). In such cases, the involvement of a divine command would seem to exclude any possible request for forgiveness.[36] The experiences of maltreatment suffered by Israel at the hands of other peoples and the animosity thus aroused could also have militated against the idea of asking pardon of these peoples for the evil done to them.[37]

In any case the sense of intergenerational solidarity in sin (and in grace) remains relevant in the biblical testimony and is expressed in the confession before God of the "sins of the fathers", such that John Paul II could state, citing the splendid prayer of Azaria: "'Blessed are you, O Lord, the God of our fathers.... For we have sinned and transgressed by departing from you, and we have done every kind of evil. Your commandments we have not heeded or observed' (Dan 3:26, 29–30). This is how the Jews prayed after the exile (cf. also Bar 2:11–13), accepting the responsibility for the sins committed by their fathers. The Church imitates their example and also asks forgiveness for the historical sins of her children."[38]

---

[36] Cf. the analogous case of the repudiation of foreign wives described in Ezra 9–10, with all the negative consequences which this would have had for these women. The question of a request for forgiveness addressed to them (and/or to their descendents) is not treated, since their repudiation is presented as a requirement of God's law (cf. Deut 7:3) in all these chapters.

[37] In this context, the case of the permanently strained relationship between Israel and Edom comes to mind. The Edomites as a people—despite the fact that they were Israel's "brother"—participated and rejoiced in the conquest of Jerusalem by the Babylonians (cf., for example, Obad 10–14). Israel, as a sign of outrage for this betrayal, felt no need to ask forgiveness for the killing of defenseless Edomite prisoners of war by King Amaziah as recounted in 2 Chron 25:12.

[38] John Paul II, General Audience Discourse of 1 September 1999, in *L'Osservatore Romano*, Eng. ed., 8 September 1999, 7.

2.2. *The New Testament*

A fundamental theme connected with the idea of guilt, and amply present in the New Testament, is that of the absolute holiness of God. The God of Jesus is the God of Israel (cf. Jn 4:22), invoked as "Holy Father" (Jn 17:11), and called "the Holy One" in First John 2:20 (cf. Acts 6:10). The triple proclamation of God as "holy" in Isaiah 6:3 returns in Acts 4:8, while First Peter 1:16 insists on the fact that Christians must be holy "for it is written: 'You shall be holy, for I am holy'" (cf. Lev 11:44–45; 19:2). All this reflects the Old Testament notion of the absolute holiness of God; however, for Christian faith the divine holiness has entered history in the person of Jesus of Nazareth. The Old Testament notion has not been abandoned but developed, in the sense that the holiness of God becomes present in the holiness of the incarnate Son (cf. Mk 1:24; Lk 1:35; 4:34; Jn 6:69; Acts 3:14; 4:27, 30; Rev 3:7), and the holiness of the Son is shared by "his own" (cf. Jn 17:16–19), who are made sons in the Son (cf. Gal 4:4–6; Rom 8:14–17). There can be no aspiration to divine sonship in Jesus unless there is love for one's neighbor (cf. Mk 12:29–31; Mt 22:37–38; Lk 10:27–28).

Love of neighbor, absolutely central in the teaching of Jesus, becomes the "new commandment" in the Gospel of John; the disciples should love as he has loved (cf. Jn 13:34–35; 15:12, 17), that is, perfectly, "to the end" (Jn 13:1). The Christian is called to love and to forgive to a degree that transcends every human standard of justice and produces a reciprocity between human beings, reflective of the reciprocity between Christ and the Father (cf. Jn 13:34f.; 15:1–11; 17:21–26). In this perspective, great emphasis is given to the theme of reconciliation and forgiveness of faults. Jesus asks his disciples to be always ready to forgive all those who have offended them, just as God himself always offers his forgiveness: "Forgive us our trespasses as we forgive those who trespass against us" (Mt 6:12; 6:12–15). He who is able to forgive his neighbor shows that he has understood his own need for forgiveness by God. The disciple is invited to forgive the one who offends him "seventy times seven" [times], even if the person may not ask for forgiveness (cf. Mt 18:21–22).

With regard to someone who has been injured by another, Jesus insists that the injured person should take the first step, canceling the offense through forgiveness offered "from the heart" (cf. Mt 18:35; Mk 11:25), aware that he too is a sinner before God, who never refuses forgiveness sincerely entreated. In Matthew 5:23–24, Jesus asks the offender to "go and reconcile himself with his brother who has something against him" before presenting his offering at the altar. An act of worship on the part of one who has no desire beforehand to repair the damage to his neighbor is not pleasing to God. What matters is changing one's own heart and showing in an appropriate way that one really wants reconciliation. The sinner, however, aware that his sins wound his relationship with God and with his neighbor (cf. Lk 15:21), can expect pardon only from God, because only God is always merciful and ready to cancel our sins. This is also the significance of the sacrifice of Christ who, once and for all, has purified us of our sins (cf. Heb 9:22; 10:18). Thus, the offender and the offended are reconciled by God who receives and forgives everyone in his mercy.

In this context, which could be expanded through an analysis of the Letters of Paul and the Catholic Epistles, there is no indication that the early Church turned her attention to sins of the past in order to ask for forgiveness. This might be explained by the powerful sense of the radical newness of Christianity, which tended to orient the community toward the future rather than the past. There is, however, a more broad and subtle insistence pervading the New Testament: in the Gospels and in the Letters, the ambivalence of the Christian experience is fully recognized. For Paul, for example, the Christian community is an eschatological people that already lives the "new creation" (cf. 2 Cor 5:17; Gal 6:15), but this experience, made possible by the death and resurrection of Jesus (cf. Rom 3:21–26; 5:6–11; 8:1–11; 1 Cor 15:54–57), does not free us from the inclination to sin present in the world because of Adam's fall. From the divine intervention in and through the death and resurrection of Jesus, it follows that there are now two scenarios possible: the history of Adam and the history of Christ. These proceed side by side and the believer must count on the death and resurrection of the Lord Jesus (cf., for example, Rom 6:1–11; Gal 3:27–28; Col 3:10; 2 Cor 5:14–15) to be part of the history in which "grace overflows" (cf. Rom 5:12–21).

A similar theological re-reading of the paschal event of Christ shows how the early Church had an acute awareness of the possible deficiencies of the baptized. One could say that the entire "*corpus paulinum*" recalls believers to a full recognition of their dignity, albeit in the living awareness of the fragility of their human condition. "For freedom Christ set us free; so stand firm and do not submit again to the yoke of slavery" (Gal 5:1). An analogous reason can be found in the Gospel narratives. It arises decisively in Mark where the frailties of Jesus' disciples are one of the dominant themes of the account (cf. Mk 4:40–41; 6:36–37, 51–52; 8:14–21, 31–33; 9:5–6, 32–41; 10:32–45; 14:10–11, 17–21, 27–31, 50; 16:8). Even if understandably nuanced, the same motif recurs in all of the Evangelists. Judas and Peter are respectively the traitor and the one who denies the Master, though Judas ends up in desperation for his act (cf. Acts 1:15–20), while Peter repents (cf. Lk 22:61) and arrives at a triple profession of

love (cf. in Jn 21:15–19). In Matthew, even during the final appearance
of the risen Lord, while the disciples adore him, "some still doubted"
(Mt 28:17). The Fourth Gospel presents the disciples as those to whom
an incommensurable love was given even though their response was one
of ignorance, deficiencies, denial, and betrayal (cf. Jn 13:1–38).

This constant presentation of Jesus' disciples, who vacillate when it
comes to yielding to sin, is not simply a critical re-reading of the early
history. The accounts are framed in such a way that they are addressed to
every other disciple of Christ in difficulty who looks to the Gospel for
guidance and inspiration. Moreover, the New Testament is full of exhortations to behave well, to live at a higher level of dedication, to avoid evil
(cf., for example, Jas 1:5–8, 19–21; 2:1–7; 4:1–10; 1 Pet 1:13–25; 2 Pet
2:1–22; Jude 3:13; 1 Jn 1:5–10; 2:1–11, 18–27; 4:1–6; 2 Jn 7–11; 3 Jn
9–10). There is, however, no explicit call addressed to the first Christians
to confess the faults of the past, although the recognition of the reality of
sin and evil within the Christian people—those called to the eschatological life proper to the Christian condition—is highly significant (it is enough
to note the reproaches in the letters to the seven Churches in the Book
of Revelation). According to the petition found in the Lord's Prayer, this
people prays: "Forgive us our trespasses, as we forgive those who trespass
against us" (Lk 11:4; cf. Mt 6:12). Thus, the first Christians show that
they are well aware that they could act in a way that does not correspond
to their vocation, by not living their Baptism into the death and resurrection of Jesus.

2.3. The Biblical Jubilee

An important biblical precedent for reconciliation and overcoming of past
situations is represented by the celebration of the Jubilee, as it is regulated
in the Book of Leviticus (Ch. 25). In a social structure made up of tribes,
clans, and families, situations of disorder were inevitably created when
struggling individuals or families had to "redeem" themselves from their
difficulties by consigning their land, house, servants, or children to those
who had more means than they had. Such a system resulted in some
Israelites coming to suffer intolerable situations of debt, poverty, and servitude in the same land that had been given to them by God, to the
advantage of other children of Israel. All this could result in a territory or
a clan falling into the hands of a few rich people for greater or lesser
periods of time, while the rest of the families of the clan came to find
themselves in a condition of debt or servitude, compelling them to live in
total dependence upon a few well-off persons.

The legislation of Leviticus 25 constitutes an attempt to overturn this state of affairs (such that one could doubt whether it was ever put into practice fully!). It convened the celebration of the Jubilee every fifty years in order to preserve the social fabric of the People of God and restore independence even to the smallest families of the country. Decisive for Leviticus 25 is the regular repetition of Israel's profession of faith in God who had liberated his people in the Exodus. "I, the Lord, am your God, who brought you out of the land of Egypt to give you the land of Canaan and to be your God" (Lev 25:38; cf. vv. 42, 45). The celebration of the Jubilee was an implicit admission of fault and an attempt to re-establish a just order. Any system which would alienate an Israelite—once a slave but now freed by the powerful arm of God—was in fact a denial of God's saving action in and through the Exodus.

The liberation of the victims and sufferers becomes part of the much broader program of the prophets. Deutero-Isaiah, in the Suffering Servant songs (Is 42:1–9; 49:1–6; 50:4–11; 52:13—53:12) develops these allusions to the practice of the Jubilee with the themes of ransom and of freedom, of return and redemption. Isaiah 58 is an attack on ritual observance that has no regard for social justice; it is a call for liberation of the oppressed (Is 58:6), centered specifically on the obligations of kinship (v. 7). More clearly, Isaiah 61 uses the images of the Jubilee to depict the Anointed One as God's herald sent to "evangelize" the poor, to proclaim liberty to captives, and to announce the year of grace of the Lord. Significantly, it is precisely this text, with an allusion to Isaiah 58:6, that Jesus uses to present the task of his life and ministry in Luke 4:17–21.

2.4. Conclusion

From what has been said, it can be concluded that John Paul II's appeal to the Church to mark the Jubilee Year by an admission of guilt for the sufferings and wrongs committed by her sons and daughters in the past, as well as the ways in which this might be put into practice, do not find an exact parallel in the Bible. Nevertheless, they are based on what Sacred Scripture says about the holiness of God, the intergenerational solidarity of God's people, and the sinfulness of the people. The Pope's appeal correctly captures the spirit of the biblical Jubilee, which calls for actions aimed at re-establishing the order of God's original plan for creation. This requires that the proclamation of the "today" of the Jubilee, begun by Jesus (cf. Lk 4:21), be continued in the Jubilee celebration of his Church. In addition, this singular experience of grace prompts the People of God as a whole, as well as each of the baptized, to take still greater cognizance of the mandate received from the Lord to be ever ready to forgive offenses received.[39]

3. THEOLOGICAL FOUNDATIONS

"Hence it is appropriate that, as the Second Millennium of Christianity draws to a close, the Church should become more fully conscious of the sinfulness of her children, recalling all those times in history when they departed from the spirit of Christ and his Gospel and, instead of offering to the world the witness of a life inspired by the values of faith, indulged in ways of thinking and acting which were truly *forms of counter-witness and scandal*. Although she is holy because of her incorporation into Christ, the Church does not tire of doing penance: before God and man *she always acknowledges as her own her sinful sons and daughters.*"[40] These words of John Paul II emphasize how the Church is touched by the sin of her children. She is holy in being made so by the Father through the sacrifice of the Son and the gift of the Spirit. She is also in a certain sense sinner, in really taking upon herself the sin of those whom she has generated in Baptism. This is analogous to the way Christ Jesus took on the sin of the world (cf. Rom 8:3; 2 Cor 5:21; Gal 3:13; 1 Pet 2:24).[41] Furthermore, in her most profound self-awareness in time, the Church knows that she is not only a community of the elect, but one which in her very bosom includes both righteous and sinners, of the present as well as the past, in the unity of the mystery which constitutes her. Indeed, in grace and in the woundedness of sin, the baptized of today are close to, and in solidarity with, those of yesterday. For this reason one can say that the Church—one in time and space in Christ and in the Spirit—is truly "at the same time holy and always in need of being purified".[42] It is from this paradox, which is characteristic of the mystery of the Church, that the question arises as to how one can reconcile the two aspects: on the one hand, the Church's affirmation in faith of her holiness, and on the other hand, her unceasing need for penance and purification.

---

[39] Cf. *TMA* 33–36.

[40] *TMA* 33.

[41] One thinks of the reason why Christian authors of various historical periods reproached the Church for her faults. Among these, one of the most representative examples is the *Liber asceticus* by Maximus the Confessor (PL 90, 912–56).

[42] *LG* 8.

3.1. *The Mystery of the Church*

"The Church is in history, but at the same time she transcends it. It is only 'with the eyes of faith' that one can see her in her visible reality and at the same time in her spiritual reality as bearer of divine life." [43] The ensemble of her visible and historical aspects stands in relation to the divine gift in a way that is analogous to how, in the incarnate Word of God, the assumed humanity is sign and instrument of the action of the divine Person of the Son. The two dimensions of ecclesial being form "one complex reality which coalesces from a divine and a human element",[44] in a communion that participates in the Trinitarian life and brings about baptized persons' sense of being united among themselves despite historical differences of time and place. By the power of this communion, the Church presents herself as a subject that is absolutely unique in human affairs, able to take on the gifts, the merits, and the faults of her children of yesterday and today.

The telling analogy to the mystery of the incarnate Word implies too, nevertheless, a fundamental difference. "While Christ, holy, innocent and undefiled (Heb 7:26) knew nothing of sin (cf. 2 Cor 5:21), but came to expiate only the sins of the people (cf. Heb 2:17), the Church, embracing in its bosom sinners, at the same time holy and always in need of being purified, always follows the way of penance and renewal." [45] The absence of sin in the incarnate Word cannot be attributed to his ecclesial Body, within which, on the contrary, each person—participating in the grace bestowed by God—needs nevertheless to be vigilant and to be continually purified. Each member also shares in the weakness of others: "All members of the Church, including her ministers, must acknowledge that they are sinners (cf. 1 Jn 1:8–10). In everyone, the weeds of sin will still be mixed with the good wheat of the Gospel until the end of time (cf. Mt 13:24–30). Hence the Church gathers sinners already caught up in Christ's salvation but still on the way to holiness." [46]

Already Paul VI had solemnly affirmed that the Church is "holy, though she has sinners in her bosom, because she herself has no other life but that of grace.... This is why she suffers and does penance for these offenses, of which she has the power to heal her children through the blood of Christ and the gift of the Holy Spirit." [47] The Church in her "mystery"

---

[43] *Catechism of the Catholic Church* (*CCC*), 770.

[44] *LG* 8.

[45] Ibid. Cf. also *UR* 3 and 6.

[46] *CCC* 827.

[47] Paul VI, *Credo of the People of God*, 30 June 1968, no. 19 (*Enchiridion Vaticanum* 3, 264f.).

is thus the encounter of sanctity and of weakness, continually redeemed, and yet always in need of the power of redemption. As the liturgy—the true "*lex credendi*"—teaches, the individual Christian and the community of the saints implore God to look upon the faith of his Church and not on the sins of individuals, which are the negation of this living faith: "*Ne respicias peccata nostra, sed fidem Ecclesiae Tuae*"! In the unity of the mystery of the Church through time and space, it is possible to consider the aspect of holiness, the need for repentance and reform, and their articulation in the actions of Mother Church.

3.2. *The Holiness of the Church*

The Church is holy because, sanctified by Christ who has acquired her by giving himself up to death for her, she is maintained in holiness by the Holy Spirit who pervades her unceasingly: "The Church . . . is believed to be indefectibly holy. Indeed Christ, the Son of God, who with the Father and the Spirit is praised as 'uniquely holy', loved the Church as His bride, delivering Himself up for her. He did this that He might sanctify her (cf. Eph 5:25–26). He united her to Himself as His own body and brought it to perfection by the gift of the Holy Spirit for God's glory. Therefore in the Church, everyone . . . is called to holiness." [48] In this sense, from the beginning, the members of the Church are called the "saints" (cf. Acts 9:13; 1 Cor 6:1; 16:1). One can distinguish, however, the *holiness of the Church* from *holiness in the Church*. The former—founded on the missions of the Son and Spirit—guarantees the continuity of the mission of the People of God until the end of time and stimulates and aids the believers in pursuing subjective personal holiness. The form which holiness takes is rooted in the vocation that each one receives; it is given and required of him as the full completion of his own vocation and mission. Personal holiness is always directed toward God and others, and thus has an essentially social character: it is holiness "in the Church" oriented towards the good of all.

Holiness *in* the Church must therefore correspond to the holiness *of* the Church. "The followers of Christ are called by God, not because of their works, but according to His own purpose and grace. They are justified in the Lord Jesus, because in the baptism of faith they truly become sons of God and sharers in the divine nature. In this way they are really made holy. Then too, by God's gift, they must hold on to and complete in their lives this holiness they have received." [49] The baptized person is

[48] LG 39.
[49] LG 40.

called to become with his entire existence that which he has already become by virtue of his baptismal consecration. And this does not happen without the consent of his freedom and the assistance of the grace that comes from God. No one becomes himself so fully as does the saint, who welcomes the divine plan and, with the help of grace, conforms his entire being to it! The saints are in this sense like lights kindled by the Lord in the midst of his Church in order to illuminate her; they are a prophecy for the whole world.

3.3 The Necessity of Continual Renewal

Without obscuring this holiness, we must acknowledge that due to the presence of sin there is a need for continual renewal and for constant conversion in the People of God. The Church on earth is "marked with a true holiness", which is, however, "imperfect".[50] Augustine observes against the Pelagians: "The Church as a whole says: Forgive us our trespasses! Therefore she has blemishes and wrinkles. But by means of confession the wrinkles are smoothed away and the blemishes washed clean. The Church stands in prayer in order to be purified by confession and, as long as men live on earth it will be so."[51] And Thomas Aquinas makes clear that the fullness of holiness belongs to eschatological time; in the meantime, the Church still on pilgrimage should not deceive herself by saying that she is without sin: "To be a glorious Church, with neither spot nor wrinkle, is the ultimate end to which we are brought by the Passion of Christ. Hence, this will be the case only in the heavenly homeland, not here on the way of pilgrimage, where 'if we say we have no sin we deceive ourselves.'"[52] In reality, "though we are clothed with the baptismal garment, we do not cease to sin, to turn away from God. Now, in this new petition ['forgive us our trespasses'], we return to him like the prodigal son (cf. Lk 15:11–32) and, like the tax collector, recognize that we are sinners before him (cf. Lk 18:13). Our petition begins with a 'confession' of our wretchedness and his mercy."[53]

Hence it is the entire Church that confesses her faith in God through the confession of her children's sins and celebrates his infinite goodness and capacity for forgiveness. Thanks to the bond established by the Holy

---

[50] LG 48.
[51] St. Augustine, Sermo 181, 5, 7 (PL 38, 982).
[52] St. Thomas Aquinas, STh III, q. 8, art. 3 ad 2.
[53] CCC 2839.

Spirit, the communion that exists among all the baptized in time and space is such that in this communion each person is himself, but at the same time is conditioned by others and exercises an influence on them in the living exchange of spiritual goods. In this way, the holiness of each one influences the growth in goodness of others; however, sin also does not have an exclusively individual relevance, because it burdens and poses resistance along the way of salvation of all and, in this sense, truly touches the Church in her entirety, across the various times and places. This distinction prompts the Fathers to make sharp statements like this one of Ambrose: "Let us beware then that our fall not become a wound of the Church." [54] The Church therefore, "although she is holy because of her incorporation into Christ, ... does not tire of doing penance: before God and man, *she always acknowledges as her own her sinful sons and daughters*" [55] of both yesterday and today.

3.4. The Motherhood of the Church

The conviction that the Church can make herself responsible for the sin of her children by virtue of the solidarity that exists among them through time and space because of their incorporation into Christ and the work of the Holy Spirit, is expressed in a particularly effective way in the idea of "Mother Church" ("*Mater Ecclesia*"), which "in the conception of the early Fathers of the Church sums up the entire Christian aspiration." [56] The Church, Vatican II affirms, "by means of the Word of God faithfully received, becomes a mother, since through preaching and baptism she brings forth children to a new and immortal life, who have been conceived by the Holy Spirit and born of God." [57] Augustine, for example, gives voice to the vast tradition, of which these ideas are an echo: "This holy and honored mother is like Mary. She gives birth and she is a virgin, from her you were born—she generates Christ so that you will be members of Christ." [58] Cyprian of Carthage states succinctly: "One cannot

---

[54] St. Ambrose, De virginitate 8, 48 (PL 16, 278D): "*Caveamus igitur, ne lapsus noster vulnus Ecclesiae fiat.*" LG 11 also speaks of the wound inflicted on the Church by the sins of her children.

[55] TMA 33.

[56] Karl Delahaye, Ecclesia Mater chez les Pères des trois premiers siècles (Paris, 1964), 128; cf. also Hugo Rahner, S.J., Mater Ecclesia: Lobpreis der Kirche aus dem ersten Jahrtausend christlicher Literatur (Einsiedeln, 1944).

[57] LG 64.

[58] St. Augustine, Sermo 25, 8 (PL 46, 938): "*Mater ista sancta, honorata, Mariae similis, et parit et Virgo est. Ex illa nati estis et Christum parit: nam membra Christi estis.*"

have God as a father who doesn't have the Church as a mother." [59] And Paulinus of Nola sings of the motherhood of the Church like this: "As a mother she receives the seed of the eternal Word, carries the peoples in her womb and gives birth to them." [60]

According to this vision, the Church is continually realized in the exchange and communication of the Spirit from one believer to another, as the generative environment of faith and holiness, in fraternal communion, unanimity in prayer, solidarity with the cross, and common witness. By virtue of this living communication, each baptized person can be considered to be at the same time a child of the Church, in that he is generated in her to divine life, and Mother Church, in that, by his faith and love he cooperates in giving birth to new children for God. He is ever more Mother Church, the greater is his holiness and the more ardent is his effort to communicate to others the gift he has received. On the other hand, the baptized person does not cease to be a child of the Church when, because of sin, he separates himself from her in his heart. He may always come back to the springs of grace and remove the burden that his sin imposes on the entire community of Mother Church. The Church, in turn, as a true Mother, cannot but be wounded by the sin of her children of yesterday and today, continuing to love them always, to the point of making herself responsible in all times for the burden created by their sins. Thus, she is seen by the Fathers of the Church to be the Mother of sorrows, not only because of persecutions coming from outside, but above all because of the betrayals, failures, delays, and sinfulness of her children.

Holiness and sin *in* the Church are reflected therefore in their effects on the entire Church, although it is a conviction of faith that holiness is stronger than sin, since it is the fruit of divine grace. The saints are shining proof of this, and are recognized as models and help for all! There is no parallelism between grace and sin, nor even a kind of symmetry or dialectical relationship. The influence of evil will never be able to conquer the force of grace and the radiance of good, even the most hidden good! In this sense the Church recognizes herself to be holy in her saints. While she rejoices over this holiness and knows its benefit, she nonetheless confesses herself a sinner, not as a subject who sins, but rather in assuming the weight of her children's faults in maternal

---

[59] St. Cyprian, *De ecclesiae catholicae unitate* 6 (CCL 3, 253): "*Habere iam non potest Deum patrem qui ecclesiam non habet matrem.*" St. Cyprian also states: "*Ut habere quis possit Deum Patrem, habeat ante ecclesiam matrem*" (*Epist.* 74, 7; CCL 3C, 572). St. Augustine: "*Tenete ergo, carissimi, tenete omnes unanimiter Deum patrem, et matrem Ecclesiam*" (*In Ps 88, Sermo* 2, 14; CCL 39, 1244).

[60] St. Paulinus of Nola, *Carmen* 25, 171–72 (CSEL 30, 243): "*Inde manet mater aeterni semine verbi / concipiens populos et pariter pariens.*"

solidarity, so as to cooperate in overcoming them through penance and newness of life. For this reason, the holy Church recognizes the duty "to express profound regret for the weaknesses of so many of her sons and daughters who sullied her face, preventing her from fully mirroring the image of her crucified Lord, the supreme witness of patient love and humble meekness." [61]

This expression of regret can be done in a particular way by those who by charism and ministry express the communion of the People of God in its weightiest form: on behalf of the local Churches, Bishops may be able to make confessions for wrongs and requests for forgiveness. For the entire Church, one in time and space, the person capable of speaking is he who exercises the universal ministry of unity, the Bishop of the Church "which presides in love",[62] the Pope. This is why it is particularly significant that the invitation came from him that "the Church should become more fully conscious of the sinfulness of her children" and recognize the necessity "to make amends for . . . [the sins of the past], and earnestly to beseech Christ's forgiveness." [63]

4. HISTORICAL JUDGEMENT AND THEOLOGICAL JUDGEMENT

The determination of the wrongs of the past, for which amends are to be made, implies, first of all, a correct historical judgement, which is also the foundation of the theological evaluation. One must ask: What precisely occurred? What exactly was said and done? Only when these questions are adequately answered through rigorous historical analysis can one then ask whether what happened, what was said or done, can be understood as consistent with the Gospel, and, if it cannot, whether the Church's sons and daughters who acted in such a way could have recognized this, given the context in which they acted. Only when there is moral certainty that what was done in contradiction to the Gospel in the name of the Church by certain of her sons and daughters could have been understood by them as such and avoided, can it have significance for the Church of today to make amends for faults of the past.

The relationship between "historical judgement" and "theological judgement" is therefore as complex as it is necessary and determinative. For this

---

[61] *TMA* 35.

[62] St. Ignatius of Antioch, *Ad Romanos, Prooem.* (SCh 10, 124) (ed. Th. Camelot, 2nd ed., Paris, 1958).

[63] *TMA* 33, 34.

reason, it is necessary to undertake it without falsehoods on one side or the other. Both an apologetics that seeks to justify everything and an unwarranted laying of blame, based on historically untenable attributions of responsibility, must be avoided. John Paul II, referring to the historical-theological evaluation of the work of the Inquisition, stated: "The Church's Magisterium certainly cannot perform an ethical act, such as asking for forgiveness, without first being accurately informed about the situation at the time. Nor can it be based on the images of the past spread by public opinion, since they are often charged with an intense emotionalism that prevents calm, objective analysis. If the Magisterium does not bear this in mind, it would fail in its fundamental duty of respecting the truth. That is why the first step is to question historians, who are not asked to make an ethical judgement, which would exceed their sphere of competence, but to help in the most precise reconstruction possible of the events, customs and mentality of the time, in the light of the era's historical context." [64]

4.1. *The Interpretation of History*

What are the conditions for a correct interpretation of the past from the point of view of historical knowledge? To determine these, we must take account of the complexity of the relationship between the subject who interprets and the object from the past which is interpreted.[65] First, their mutual extraneousness must be emphasized. Events or words of the past are, above all, "past". As such they are not completely reducible to the framework of the present, but possess an objective density and complexity that prevent them from being ordered in a solely functional way for present interests. It is necessary, therefore, to approach them by means of an historical-critical investigation that aims at using all of the information available, with a view to a reconstruction of the environment, of the ways of thinking, of the conditions and the living dynamic in which those events and those words are placed, in order, in such a way, to ascertain the contents and the challenges that—precisely in their diversity—they propose to our present time.

Second, a certain *common belonging* of interpreter and interpreted must be recognized without which no bond and no communication could

[64] Discourse to the participants in an international symposium of study on the Inquisition, sponsored by the Historical-Theological Commission of the Central Committee of the Jubilee, 31 October 1998, 4.

[65] Cf. for what follows, Hans-Georg Gadamer, *Wahrheit und Methode*, 2nd ed. (Tübingen, 1965); Eng. trans., *Truth and Method* (London: Sheed and Ward, 1975).

exist between past and present. This communicative bond is based on the fact that every human being, whether of yesterday or of today, is situated in a complex of historical relationships, and in order to live these relationships, the mediation of language is necessary, a mediation which itself is always historically determined. Everybody belongs to history! Bringing to light this communality between interpreter and the object of interpretation—which is reached through the multiple forms by which the past leaves evidence of itself (texts, monuments, traditions, etc.)—means judging both the accuracy of possible correspondences and possible difficulties of communication between past and present, as indicated by one's own understanding of the past words and events. This requires taking into account the questions which motivate the research and their effect on the answers which are found, the living context in which the work is undertaken, and the interpreting community whose language is spoken and to whom one intends to speak. For this purpose, it is necessary that the pre-understanding—which is part of every act of interpretation—be as reflective and conscious as possible, in order to measure and moderate its real effect on the interpretative process.

Finally, through the effort to know and to evaluate, an *osmosis* (a "fusion of horizons") is accomplished between the interpreter and the object of the past that is interpreted, in which the act of comprehension properly consists. This is the expression of what is judged to be the correct understanding of the events or words of the past; it is equivalent to grasping the meaning which the events can have for the interpreter and his world. Thanks to this encounter of living worlds, understanding of the past is translated into its application to the present. The past is grasped in the potentialities which it discloses, in the stimulus it offers to modify the present. Memory becomes capable of giving rise to a new future.

This fruitful *osmosis* with the past is reached through the interwovenness of certain basic hermeneutic operations, which correspond to the stages of extraneousness, communality, and understanding true and proper. In relation to a "text" of the past (understood in a general sense as evidence which may be written, oral, monumental, or figurative), these operations can be expressed as follows: "(1) understanding the text; (2) judging how correct one's understanding of the text is; and (3) stating what one judges to be the correct understanding of the text." [66] Understanding the evidence of the past means reaching it as far as possible in its objectivity through all the sources that are available. Judging the correctness of one's own interpretation means verifying honestly and rigorously to what extent it could have been oriented or conditioned in any way by one's prior

---

[66] Bernard Lonergan, S.J., *Method in Theology* (London, 1972), 155.

understanding or by possible prejudices. Stating the interpretation reached means bringing others into the dialogue created with the past, in order both to verify its importance and to discover other possible interpretations.

4.2. *Historical Investigation and Theological Evaluation*

If these operations are present in every hermeneutic act, they must also be part of the interpretative process within which historical judgement and theological judgement come to be integrated. This requires, in the first place, that in this type of interpretation, maximum attention be given to the elements of differentiation and extraneousness between past and present. In particular, when one intends to judge the possible wrongs of the past, it must be kept in mind that the historical periods are different, that the sociological and cultural times within which the Church acts are different, and so, the paradigms and judgements proper to one society and to one era might be applied erroneously in the evaluation of other periods of history, producing many misunderstandings. Persons, institutions, and their respective competencies are different; ways of thinking and conditioning are different. Therefore, responsibility for what was said and done has to be precisely identified, taking into account the fact that the Church's request for forgiveness commits the single theological subject of the Church in the variety of ways and levels in which she is represented by individual persons and in the enormous diversity of historical and geographical situations. Generalization must be avoided. Any possible statement today must be situated in the contemporary context and undertaken by the appropriate subject (universal Church, Bishops of a country, particular Churches, etc.).

Second, the correlation of historical judgement and theological judgement must take into account the fact that, for the interpretation of the faith, the bond between past and present is not motivated only by the current interest and by the common belonging of every human being to history and its expressive mediations, but is based also on the unifying action of the Spirit of God and on the permanent identity of the constitutive principle of the communion of the faithful, which is revelation. The Church—by virtue of the communion produced in her by the Spirit of Christ in time and space—cannot fail to recognize herself in her supernatural aspect, present and operative in all times, as a subject in a certain way unique, called to correspond to the gift of God in different forms and situations through the choices of her children, despite all of the deficiencies that may have characterized them. Communion in the one Holy Spirit also establishes a communion of "saints" in a diachronic sense, by virtue of which the baptized of today feel connected to the baptized of yesterday and—as they benefit from their merits and are nourished by their witness of holiness—so likewise they feel the obligation to assume any current burden from their faults, after having discerned these by attentive historical and theological study.

Thanks to this objective and transcendent foundation of the communion of the People of God in its various historical situations, interpretation done by believers recognizes in the Church's past a very particular significance for the present day. The encounter with the past, produced in the act of interpretation, can have particular value for the present, and be rich in a "performative" efficaciousness that cannot always be calculated beforehand. Of course, the powerful unity between the hermeneutic horizon and the Church as interpreting agent exposes the theological vision to the risk of yielding to apologetic or tendentious readings. It is here that the hermeneutic exercise aimed at understanding past events and statements and at evaluating the correctness of their interpretation for today is more necessary than ever. For this reason, the reading undertaken by believers will avail itself of all possible contributions by the historical sciences and interpretative methods. The exercise of historical hermeneutics should not, however, prevent the evaluation of faith from questioning the texts according to its own distinctive vision, thus making past and present interact in the conscience of the one fundamental subject involved in these texts, the Church. This guards against all historicism that would relativize the weight of past wrongs and make history justify everything. As John Paul II observes, "An accurate historical judgment cannot prescind from careful study of the cultural conditioning of the times.... Yet the consideration of mitigating factors does not exonerate the Church from the obligation to express profound regret for the weaknesses of so many of her sons and daughters."[67] The Church is "not afraid of the truth that emerges from history and is ready to acknowledge mistakes wherever they have been identified, especially when they involve the respect that is owed to individuals and communities. She is inclined to mistrust generalizations that excuse or condemn various historical periods. She entrusts the investigation of the past to patient, honest, scholarly reconstruction, free from confessional or ideological prejudices, regarding both the accusations brought against her and the wrongs she has suffered."[68] The examples offered in the following chapter [section] may furnish a concrete demonstration.

[67] *TMA* 35.
[68] John Paul II, General Audience Discourse of 1 September 1999, 7.

5. ETHICAL DISCERNMENT

In order for the Church to carry out an appropriate historical examination of conscience before God with a view to her own interior renewal and growth in grace and holiness, it is necessary that she recognize the "forms of counter-witness and of scandal" that have taken place in her history, especially in the past millennium. It is not possible to undertake such a task without being aware of its moral and spiritual significance. This entails defining some key terms, as well as making some necessary ethical clarifications.

5.1. *Some Ethical Criteria*

On the level of morality, the request for forgiveness always presupposes an admission of *responsibility*, precisely the responsibility for a wrong committed against others. Usually, *moral responsibility* refers to the relationship between the action and the person who does it. It establishes who is responsible for an act, its attribution to a certain person or persons. The responsibility may be *objective* or *subjective*. Objective responsibility refers to the moral value of the act in itself, insofar as it is good or evil, and thus refers to the imputability of the action. Subjective responsibility concerns the effective perception by individual conscience of the goodness or evil of the act performed. Subjective responsibility ceases with the death of the one who performed the act; it is not transmitted through generation; the descendants do not inherit (subjective) responsibility for the acts of their ancestors. In this sense, asking for forgiveness presupposes a contemporaneity between those who are hurt by an action and those who committed it. The only responsibility capable of continuing in history can be the objective kind, to which one may freely adhere subjectively or not. Thus, the evil done often outlives the one who did it through the consequences of behaviors that can become a heavy burden on the consciences and memories of the descendants.

In such a context, one can speak of a *solidarity* that unites the past and the present in a relationship of reciprocity. In certain situations, the burden that weighs on conscience can be so heavy as to constitute a kind of moral and religious memory of the evil done, which is by its nature a *common memory*. This common memory gives eloquent testimony to the solidarity objectively existing between those who committed the evil in the past and their heirs in the present. It is then that it becomes possible to speak of an *objective common responsibility*. Liberation from the weight of this responsibility comes above all through imploring God's forgiveness for the wrongs of the past, and then, where appropriate, through the "purification of memory" culminating in a mutual pardoning of sins and offenses in the present.

Purifying the memory means eliminating from personal and collective conscience all forms of resentment or violence left by the inheritance of the past, on the basis of a new and rigorous historical-theological judgement, which becomes the foundation for a renewed moral way of acting. This occurs whenever it becomes possible to attribute to past historical deeds a different quality, having a new and different effect on the present, in view of progress in reconciliation in truth, justice, and charity among human beings and, in particular, between the Church and the different religious, cultural, and civil communities with whom she is related. Emblematic models of such an effect, which a later authoritative interpretative judgement may have for the entire life of the Church, are the reception of the Councils or acts like the abolition of mutual anathemas. These express a new assessment of past history, which is capable of producing a different characterization of the relationships lived in the present. The memory of division and opposition is purified and substituted by a reconciled memory, to which everyone in the Church is invited to be open and to become educated.

The combination of historical judgement and theological judgement in the process of interpreting the past is connected to the ethical repercussions that it may have in the present and entails some principles corresponding, on the moral plane, to the hermeneutic foundation of the relationship between historical judgement and theological judgement. These are:

a. *The principle of conscience*. Conscience, as "moral judgement" and as "moral imperative", constitutes the final evaluation of an act as good or evil before God. In effect, only God knows the moral value of each human act, even if the Church, like Jesus, can and must classify, judge, and sometimes condemn some kinds of action (cf. Mt 18:15–18).

b. *The principle of historicity*. Precisely inasmuch as every human act belongs to the subject who acts, every individual conscience and every society chooses and acts within a determined horizon of time and space. To truly understand human acts or their related dynamics, we need therefore to enter into the world of those who did them. Only in such a way can we come to know their motivations and their moral principles. This must be said without prejudice to the solidarity that binds the members of a specific community through the passage of time.

c. *The principle of "paradigm change"*. While before the Enlightenment there existed a sort of osmosis between Church and State, between faith and culture, morality and law, from the eighteenth century onward this relationship was modified significantly. The result was a transition from a sacral society to a pluralist society, or, as occurred in a few cases, to a secular society. The models of thought and action, the so-called "paradigms" of actions and evaluation, change. Such a transition has a direct impact on moral judgements, although this influence does not justify in any way a relativistic idea of moral principles or of the nature of morality itself.

The entire process of purification of memory, however, insofar as it requires the correct combination of historical evaluation and theological perception, needs to be lived by the Church's sons and daughters not only with the rigor that takes account of the criteria and principles indicated above, but is also accompanied by a continual calling upon the help of the Holy Spirit. This is necessary in order not to fall into resentment or unwarranted self-recrimination, but to arrive instead at the confession of the God whose "mercy is from age to age" (Lk 1:50), who wants life and not death, forgiveness and not condemnation, love and not fear. The quality of *exemplarity* which the honest admission of past faults can exert on attitudes within the Church and civil society should also be noted, for it gives rise to a renewed obedience to the Truth and to respect for the dignity and the rights of others, most especially, of the very weak. In this sense, the numerous requests for forgiveness formulated by John Paul II constitute an example that draws attention to something good and stimulates the imitation of it, recalling individuals and groups of people to an honest and fruitful examination of conscience with a view to reconciliation.

In the light of these ethical clarifications, we can now explore some examples—among which are those mentioned in *Tertio millennio adveniente*[69]—of situations in which the behavior of the sons and daughters of the Church seems to have contradicted the Gospel of Jesus Christ in a significant way.

5.2. *The Division of Christians*

Unity is the law of the life of the Trinitarian God revealed to the world by the Son (cf. Jn 17:21), who, in the power of the Holy Spirit, loving until the end (cf. Jn 13:1), communicates this life to his own. This unity should be the source and the form of the communion of mankind's life with the Triune God. If Christians live this law of mutual love, so as to be one "as the Father and the Son are one", the result will be that "the world will believe that the Son was sent by the Father" (Jn 17:21) and "everyone will know that these are his disciples" (Jn 13:35).

---

[69] Cf. *TMA* 34–36.

Unfortunately, it has not happened this way, particularly in the millennium which has just ended and in which great divisions appeared among Christians, in open contradiction to the explicit will of Christ, as if he himself were divided (cf. 1 Cor 1:13). Vatican Council II judges this fact in this way: "Such division openly contradicts the will of Christ, scandalizes the world, and damages the holy cause of preaching the Gospel to every creature." [70]

The principal divisions during the past millennium which "affect the seamless robe of Christ" [71] are the schism between the Eastern and Western Churches at the beginning of this millennium, and in the West—four centuries later—the laceration caused by those events "which are usually referred to as 'The Reformation'." [72] It is true that "these various divisions differ greatly from one another not only by reason of their origin, place and time, but especially in the nature and seriousness of questions bearing on faith and the structure of the Church." [73] In the schism of the eleventh century, cultural and historical factors played an important role, while the doctrinal dimension concerned the authority of the Church and the Bishop of Rome, a topic which at that time had not reached the clarity it has today, thanks to the doctrinal development of this millennium. In the case of the Reformation, however, other areas of revelation and doctrine were objects of controversy.

The way that has opened to overcome these differences is that of doctrinal development animated by mutual love. The lack of supernatural love, of *agape*, seems to have been common to both the breaches. Given that this charity is the supreme commandment of the Gospel, without which all the rest is but "a noisy gong or a clanging cymbal" (1 Cor 13:1), such a deficiency needs to be seen in all its seriousness before the Risen One, the Lord of the Church and of history. It is by virtue of the recognition of this lack that Pope Paul VI asked pardon of God and of the "separated brethren", who may have felt offended "by us" (the Catholic Church). [74]

In 1965, in the climate produced by the Second Vatican Council, Patriarch Athenagoras, in his dialogue with Paul VI, emphasized the theme of the restoration (*apokatastasis*) of mutual love, so essential after a history

---

[70] *UR* 1.

[71] Ibid., 13. *TMA* 34 states, "In the course of the thousand years now drawing to a close, even more than in the first millenium, ecclesial communion has been painfully wounded."

[72] *UR* 13.

[73] Ibid.

[74] Cf. Opening Speech of the Second Session of the Second Vatican Council, 29 September 1964 (*Enchiridion Vaticanum* 1, [106], n. 176).

laden with opposition, mutual mistrust, and antagonism.[75] It was a question of a past that, through memory, was still exerting its influence. The events of 1965 (culminating on December 7, 1965, with the abolition of the anathemas of 1054 between East and West) represent a confession of the fault contained in the earlier mutual exclusion, so as to purify the memory of the past and generate a new one. The basis of this *new memory* cannot be other than mutual love or, better, the renewed commitment to live it. This is the commandment *ante omnia* (1 Pet 4:8) for the Church in the East and in the West. In such a way, memory frees us from the prison of the past and calls Catholics and Orthodox, as well as Catholics and Protestants, to be the architects of a future more in conformity with the new commandment. Pope Paul VI's and Patriarch Athenagoras' testimony to this new memory is in this sense exemplary.

Particularly problematic for the path toward the unity of Christians is the temptation to be guided—or even determined—by cultural factors, historical conditioning, and those prejudices which feed the separation and mutual distrust among Christians, even though they do not have anything to do with matters of faith. The Church's sons and daughters should sincerely examine their consciences to see whether they are actively committed to obeying the imperative of unity and are living an "interior conversion", because "it is from renewal of the inner life of our minds (cf. Eph 4:23), from self-denial and an unstinted love that desires of unity take their rise and develop in a mature way."[76] In the period from the close of the Council until today, resistance to its message has certainly saddened the Spirit of God (cf. Eph 4:30). To the extent that some Catholics are pleased to remain bound to the separations of the past, doing nothing to remove the obstacles that impede unity, one could justly speak of solidarity in the sin of division (cf. 1 Cor 1:10–16). In this context the words of the Decree on Ecumenism could be recalled: "We humbly beg pardon of God and of our separated brethren, just as we forgive them that trespass against us."[77]

5.3. *The Use of Force in the Service of Truth*

To the counter-witness of the division between Christians should be added that of the various occasions in the past millennium when doubtful means were employed in the pursuit of good ends, such as the

---

[75] Cf. the documentation from the dialogue of charity between the Holy See and the Ecumenical Patriarch of Constantinople in *Tomos agapēs: Vatican—Phanar (1958–1970)* (Rome and Istanbul, 1971).

[76] *UR* 7.

[77] Ibid.

proclamation of the Gospel or the defense of the unity of the faith. "Another painful chapter of history to which the sons and daughters of the Church must return with a spirit of repentance is that of the acquiescence given, especially in certain centuries, to *intolerance and even the use of violence* in the service of truth."[78] This refers to forms of evangelization that employed improper means to announce the revealed truth or did not include an evangelical discernment suited to the cultural values of peoples or did not respect the consciences of the persons to whom the faith was presented, as well as all forms of force used in the repression and correction of errors.

Analogous attention should be paid to all the failures, for which the sons and daughters of the Church may have been responsible, to denounce injustice and violence in the great variety of historical situations: "Then there is the lack of discernment by many Christians in situations where basic human rights were violated. The request for forgiveness applies to whatever should have been done or was passed over in silence because of weakness or bad judgement, to what was done or said hesitantly or inappropriately."[79]

As always, establishing the historical truth by means of historical-critical research is decisive. Once the facts have been established, it will be necessary to evaluate their spiritual and moral value, as well as their objective significance. Only thus will it be possible to avoid every form of mythical memory and reach a fair critical memory capable—in the light of faith—of producing fruits of conversion and renewal. "From these painful moments of the past a lesson can be drawn for the future, leading all Christians to adhere fully to the sublime principle stated by the Council: 'The truth cannot impose itself except by virtue of its own truth, as it wins over the mind with both gentleness and power.'"[80]

5.4. *Christians and Jews*

The relationship between Christians and Jews is one of the areas requiring a special examination of conscience.[81] "The Church's relationship to the Jewish people is unlike the one she shares with any other religion."[82] Nevertheless, "the history of relations between Jews and Christians is a tor-

---

[78] *TMA* 35.

[79] John Paul II, General Audience Discourse of 1 September 1999, 7.

[80] *TMA* 35. The citation from the Second Vatican Council is from *DH* 1.

[81] The argument is rigorously treated in the Declaration of the Second Vatican Council, *Nostra aetate*.

[82] Commission for Religious Relations with the Jews, "We Remember: A Reflection on the Shoah", Rome, 16 March 1998, I, in *Information Service* (Pontifical Council for Pro-

mented one. . . . In effect, the balance of these relations over two thousand years has been quite negative."[83] The hostility or diffidence of numerous Christians toward Jews in the course of time is a sad historical fact and is the cause of profound remorse for Christians aware of the fact that "Jesus was a descendent of David; that the Virgin Mary and the Apostles belonged to the Jewish people; that the Church draws sustenance from the root of that good olive tree onto which have been grafted the wild olive branches of the Gentiles (cf. Rom 11:17–24); that the Jews are our dearly beloved brothers, indeed in a certain sense they are 'our elder brothers'."[84]

The Shoah was certainly the result of the pagan ideology that was Nazism, animated by a merciless anti-Semitism that not only despised the faith of the Jewish people, but also denied their very human dignity. Nevertheless, "it may be asked whether the Nazi persecution of the Jews was not made easier by the anti-Jewish prejudices imbedded in some Christian minds and hearts. . . . Did Christians give every possible assistance to those being persecuted, and in particular to the persecuted Jews?"[85] There is no doubt that there were many Christians who risked their lives to save and to help their Jewish neighbors. It seems, however, also true that "alongside such courageous men and women, the spiritual resistance and concrete action of other Christians was not that which might have been expected from Christ's followers."[86] This fact constitutes a call to the consciences of all Christians today, so as to require "an act of repentance (*teshuva*)",[87] and to be a stimulus to increase efforts to be "transformed by renewal of your mind" (Rom 12:2), as well as to keep a "moral and religious memory" of the injury inflicted on the Jews. In this area, much has already been done, but this should be confirmed and deepened.

5.5 *Our Responsibility for the Evils of Today*

"The present age in fact, together with much light, also presents not a few shadows."[88] First among the latter, we might mention the phenomenon of the denial of God in its many forms. What is particularly

---

moting Christian Unity), n. 97, 19. Cf. John Paul II, Discourse at the Synagogue of Rome, 13 April 1986 (*AAS* 78 [1986]: 1120).

[83] This is the judgement of the recent document of the Commission for Religious Relations with the Jews, "We Remember", op. cit., III, in *Information Service*, n. 97, 19.

[84] Ibid., V, 22.

[85] Ibid., IV, 20, 21.

[86] Ibid., IV, 21.

[87] Ibid., V, 22.

[88] *TMA* 36.

apparent is that this denial, especially in its more theoretical aspects, is a process that emerged in the Western world. Connected to the eclipse of God, one encounters then a series of negative phenomena, like religious indifference, the widespread lack of a transcendent sense of human life, a climate of secularism and ethical relativism, the denial of the right to life of the unborn child sanctioned in pro-abortion legislation, and a great indifference to the cry of the poor in entire sectors of the human family.

The uncomfortable question to consider is in what measure believers are themselves responsible for these forms of atheism, whether theoretical or practical. *Gaudium et spes* responds with well-chosen words: "Believers themselves frequently bear some responsibility for this situation. For, taken as a whole, atheism is not a spontaneous development, but stems from a variety of causes, including a critical reaction against religious beliefs, and in some places against the Christian religion in particular. Hence believers can have more than a little to do with the birth of atheism." [89]

The true face of God has been revealed in Jesus Christ, and thus, Christians are offered the incommensurable grace to know this face. At the same time, however, Christians have the *responsibility* to live in such a way as to show others the true face of the living God. They are called to radiate to the world the truth that "God is love [*agape*]" (1 Jn 4:8, 16). Since God is love, he is also a Trinity of Persons, whose life consists in their infinite mutual communication in love. It follows from this that the best way Christians can radiate the truth that God is love is by their own mutual love. "By this all will know that you are my disciples, if you love one another" (Jn 13:35). For this reason, it can be said of Christians that often "to the extent that they neglect their own training in the faith, or teach erroneous doctrine, or are deficient in their religious, moral or social life, they must be said to conceal rather than reveal the authentic face of God and religion." [90]

Finally, it must be emphasized that the mentioning of these faults of Christians of the past is not only to confess them to Christ the Savior, but also to praise the Lord of history for his merciful love. Christians, in fact, do not believe only in the existence of sin, but also, and above all, in the *forgiveness of sins*. In addition, recalling these faults means accepting our solidarity with those who, in good and bad, have gone before us on the way of truth. It offers to those of the present a powerful reason to convert to the requirements of the Gospel, and it provides a necessary prelude to the request for God's forgiveness that opens the way for mutual reconciliation.

[89] GS 19.
[90] Ibid.

6. PASTORAL AND MISSIONARY PERSPECTIVES

In the light of these considerations, it is now possible to ask the question: What are the pastoral aims of the Church's taking responsibility for past faults committed in her name by her sons and daughters, and for which she makes amends? What are its implications for the life of the People of God? And what are the consequences in relation to the Church's missionary effort and her dialogue with various cultures and religions?

6.1 *The Pastoral Aims*

The following are some of the pastoral reasons for acknowledging the faults of the past.

First, these acts tend towards the *purification of memory*, which—as noted above—is a process aimed at a new evaluation of the past, capable of having a considerable effect on the present, because past sins frequently make their weight felt and remain temptations in the present as well. Above all, if the causes of possible resentment for evils suffered and the negative influences stemming from what was done in the past can be removed as a result of dialogue and the patient search for mutual understanding with those who feel injured by words and deeds of the past, such a removal may help the community of the Church grow in holiness through reconciliation and peace in obedience to the Truth. "Acknowledging the weaknesses of the past", the Pope emphasizes, "is an act of honesty and courage which helps us to strengthen our faith, which alerts us to face today's temptations and challenges and prepares us to meet them."[91] To that end, it is good that the remembering of faults also includes all possible omissions, even if only some of these are mentioned frequently today. One should not forget the price paid by many Christians for their fidelity to the Gospel and for their service to their neighbor in charity.[92]

A second pastoral aim, closely connected to the first, is the promotion of the continual *reform of the People of God*. "Thus if, in various times and circumstances, there have been deficiencies in moral conduct or in Church discipline, or even in the way that Church teaching has been formulated—to be carefully distinguished from the deposit of faith itself—these can and should

---

[91] *TMA* 33.
[92] One need only think of the sign of martyrdom: cf. *TMA* 37.

be set right at the opportune moment."[93] All of the baptized are called to "examine their own faithfulness to Christ's will for the Church and accordingly to undertake with vigor the task of renewal and reform."[94] The criterion of true reform and of authentic renewal must be fidelity to the will of God regarding his people[95] that presupposes a sincere effort to free oneself from all that leads away from his will, whether we are dealing with present faults or the inheritance from the past.

A further aim can be seen to be the *witness* that the Church gives to the God of mercy and to his liberating and saving Truth, from the experience which she has had and continues to have of him in history. There is also the *service* which the Church in this way gives to humanity to help overcome current evils. John Paul II states that "many Cardinals and Bishops expressed the desire for a serious examination of conscience above all on the part of *the Church of today*. On the threshold of the new Millennium Christians need to place themselves humbly before the Lord and examine themselves on *the responsibility which they too have for the evils of our day*"[96] in order to help overcome them in obedience to the splendor of saving Truth.

6.2 *Ecclesial Implications*

What are the implications for the life of the Church of an ecclesial request for forgiveness? A number of aspects can be mentioned.

It is necessary above all to take into account the different processes of *reception* of acts of ecclesial repentance, because these will vary according to religious, cultural, political, social, and personal contexts. In this light, one needs to consider that events or words linked to a contextualized history do not necessarily have a universal significance, and vice versa, that acts conditioned by a determined theological and pastoral perspective have had powerful consequences for the spread of the Gospel (one thinks, for example, of the various historical models of the theology of mission). Furthermore, there needs to be an evaluation of the relationship between the spiritual benefits and the possible costs of such acts, taking into account also the undue accentuation which the media may give to certain aspects

---

[93] UR 6. It is the same text which states that "Christ summons the Church to continual reformation [*ad hanc perennem reformationem*] as she sojourns here on earth. The Church is always in need of this, in so far as she is an institution of men here on earth."

[94] "*opus renovationis nec non reformationis*", UR 4.

[95] UR 6: "Every renewal of the Church is essentially grounded in an increase of fidelity to her own calling."

[96] TMA 36.

of the Church's statements. One should always remember the Apostle Paul's admonition to welcome, consider, and support the "weak in faith" with prudence and love (cf. Rom 14:1). In particular, attention must be given to the history, the identity, and the current situation of the Eastern Churches and those Churches which exist in continents or countries where the Christian presence is a minority.

It is necessary to specify the *appropriate subject* called to speak about the faults of the past, whether it be local Bishops, considered personally or collegially, or the universal Pastor, the Bishop of Rome. In this perspective, it is opportune to take into account—in recognizing past wrongs and the present day subjects who could best assume responsibility for these—the distinction between Magisterium and authority in the Church. Not every act of authority has magisterial value, and so behavior contrary to the Gospel by one or more persons vested with authority does not involve per se the magisterial charism, which is assured by the Lord to the Church's Bishops, and consequently does not require any magisterial act of reparation.

It is necessary to underscore that *the one addressed* by any request for forgiveness is God and that any human recipients—above all, if these are groups of persons either inside or outside the community of the Church—must be identified with appropriate historical and theological discernment, in order to undertake acts of reparation which are indeed suitable, and also in order to give witness to them of the good will and the love for the truth of the Church's sons and daughters. This will be accomplished to the extent that there is dialogue and reciprocity between the parties, oriented toward a possible reconciliation connected with the recognition of faults and repentance for them. However, one should not forget that reciprocity—at times impossible because of the religious convictions of the dialogue partner—cannot be considered an indispensable condition, and that the gratuity of love often expresses itself in unilateral initiatives.

Possible gestures of *reparation* must be connected to the recognition of a responsibility which has endured through time, and may therefore assume a symbolic-prophetic character, as well as having value for effective reconciliation (for example, among separated Christians). It is also desirable that in the definition of these acts there be joint research with those who will be addressed, by listening to the legitimate requests which they may present.

On the *pedagogical* level, it is important to avoid perpetuating negative images of the other, as well as causing unwarranted self-recrimination, by emphasizing that, for believers, taking responsibility for past wrongs is a kind of sharing in the mystery of Christ, crucified and risen, who took upon himself the sins of all. Such an interpretation, rooted in Christ's

Paschal Mystery, is able in a particular way to produce fruits of liberation, reconciliation, and joy for all those who, with living faith, are involved in the request for forgiveness—both the subjects and those addressed.

6.3 *The Implications for Dialogue and Mission*

On the level of dialogue and mission, the foreseeable implications of the Church's acknowledgement of past faults are varied.

On the level of *the Church's missionary effort*, it is important that these acts do not contribute to a lessening of zeal for evangelization by exacerbating negative aspects. At the same time, it should be noted that such acts can increase the credibility of the Christian message, since they stem from obedience to the truth and tend to produce fruits of reconciliation. In particular, with regard to the precise topics of such acts, those involved in the Church's mission *ad gentes* should take careful account of the local context in proposing these, in light of the capacity of people to receive such acts (thus, for example, aspects of the history of the Church in Europe may well turn out to have little significance for many non-European peoples).

With respect to *ecumenism*, the purpose of ecclesial acts of repentance can be none other than the unity desired by the Lord. Therefore, it is hoped that they will be carried out reciprocally, though at times prophetic gestures may call for a unilateral and absolutely gratuitous initiative.

On the *inter-religious* level, it is appropriate to point out that, for believers in Christ, the Church's recognition of past wrongs is consistent with the requirements of fidelity to the Gospel, and therefore constitutes a shining witness of faith in the truth and mercy of God as revealed by Jesus. What must be avoided is that these acts be mistaken as confirmation of possible prejudices against Christianity. It would also be desirable if these acts of repentance would stimulate the members of other religions to acknowledge the faults of their own past. Just as the history of humanity is full of violence, genocide, violations of human rights and the rights of peoples, exploitation of the weak and glorification of the powerful, so too the history of the various religions is marked by intolerance, superstition, complicity with unjust powers, and the denial of the dignity and freedom of conscience. Christians have been no exception and are aware that all are sinners before God!

In the dialogue with *cultures*, one must, above all, keep in mind the complexity and plurality of the notions of repentance and forgiveness in the minds of those with whom we dialogue. In every case, the Church's taking responsibility for past faults should be explained in the light of the Gospel and of the presentation of the crucified Lord, who is the revelation of mercy and the source of forgiveness, in addition to explaining the nature of ecclesial communion as a unity through time and space. In the case of a culture that is completely alien to the idea of seeking forgiveness, the theological and spiritual reasons which motivate such an act should be presented in appropriate fashion, beginning with the Christian message and taking into account its critical-prophetic character. Where one may be dealing with a prejudicial indifference to the language of faith, one should take into account the possible double effect of an act of repentance by the Church: on the one hand, negative prejudices or disdainful and hostile attitudes might be confirmed; on the other hand, these acts share in the mysterious attraction exercised by the "crucified God".[97] One should also take into account the fact that in the current cultural context, above all of the West, the invitation to a purification of memory involves believers and non-believers alike in a common commitment. This common effort is itself already a positive witness of docility to the truth.

Lastly, in relation to *civil society*, consideration must be given to the difference between the Church as a mystery of grace and every human society in time. Emphasis must also be given, however, to the character of exemplarity of the Church's requests for forgiveness, as well as to the consequent stimulus this may offer for undertaking similar steps for purification of memory and reconciliation in other situations where it might be urgent. John Paul II states: "The request for forgiveness ... primarily concerns the life of the Church, her mission of proclaiming salvation, her witness to Christ, her commitment to unity, in a word, the consistency which should distinguish Christian life. But the light and strength of the Gospel, by which the Church lives, can illumine and support more than abundantly the decisions and actions of civil society, with full respect for their autonomy.... On the threshold of the third millennium, we may rightly hope that political leaders and peoples, especially those involved in tragic conflicts fueled by hatred and the memory of often ancient wounds, will be guided by the spirit of forgiveness and reconciliation exemplified by the Church and will make every effort to resolve their differences through open and honest dialogue."[98]

[97] This particular strong formulation comes from St. Augustine, *De Trinitate* 1, 13, 28 (CCL 50, 69, 13); *Epist.* 169, 2 (CSEL 44, 617); *Sermo* 341A, 1 (*Misc. Agost.* 314, 22).

[98] John Paul II, Discourse to the participants in an international symposium of study on the Inquisition, 5.

CONCLUSION

At the conclusion of this reflection, it is appropriate to stress yet again that in every form of repentance for the wrongs of the past, and in each specific gesture connected with it, the Church addresses herself in the first place to God and seeks to give glory to him and to his mercy. Precisely in this way she is able to celebrate the dignity of the human person called to the fullness of life in faithful covenant with the living God: "The glory of God is man fully alive; but the life of man is the vision of God." [99] By such actions, the Church also gives witness to her trust in the power of the truth that makes us free (cf. Jn 8:32). Her "request for pardon must not be understood as an expression of false humility or as a denial of her 2,000-year history, which is certainly rich in merit in the areas of charity, culture, and holiness. Instead she responds to a necessary requirement of the truth, which, in addition to the positive aspects, recognizes the human limitations and weaknesses of the various generations of Christ's disciples." [100] Recognition of the Truth is a source of reconciliation and peace because, as the Holy Father also states, "Love of the truth, sought with humility, is one of the great values capable of reuniting the men of today through the various cultures." [101] Because of her responsibility to Truth, the Church "cannot cross the threshold of the new millennium without encouraging her children to purify themselves, through repentance, of past errors and instances of infidelity, inconsistency, and slowness to act. Acknowledging the weaknesses of the past is an act of honesty and courage." [102] It opens a new tomorrow for everyone.

---

[99] *"Gloria Dei vivens homo: vita autem hominis visio Dei"*. St. Ireneus of Lyon, *Adversus haereses* 4, 20, 7 (SC 100/2, 648).

[100] John Paul II, General Audience Discourse of 1 September 1999, 7.

[101] Discourse at the Centre de l'Organisation Europeénne pour la Recherche Nucléaire (CERN), Geneva, 15 June 1982, in *Insegnamenti di Giovanni Paolo II*, 5, 2 (Vatican, 1982), 2321.

[102] *TMA* 33.

21

FROM THE DIAKONIA OF CHRIST TO THE DIAKONIA OF THE APOSTLES

CHAPTER I

FROM THE DIAKONIA OF CHRIST TO THE DIAKONIA
OF THE APOSTLES

I. *Diakonia of Christ and Christian Existence*

Through the incarnation of the Word who is God and by whom all was made (cf. Jn 1:1–18) the strangest revolution imaginable has come about. The *Kyrios*, Lord, becomes the *diakonos*, servant, of all. The Lord God comes out to meet us in his Servant Jesus Christ, the only Son of God (Rom 1:3), who, being in the "form of God", "did not see in the form of God a prize to be coveted, but emptied himself, taking the form of a slave. Having become like men ... he abased himself and became obedient to death, even death on a cross" (Phil 2:6–8).

The essence of being a Christian can thus be grasped in a Christological perspective. Christian existence is a sharing in the *diakonia* or service which God himself fulfilled in favour of mankind; it likewise leads to an understanding of the fulfilment of mankind. Being a Christian means following Christ's example in putting oneself at the service of others to the point of self-renunciation and self-giving, for love.

Baptism confers this *diakonein*, power of service, on every Christian. Through it, by virtue of their participation in the *diakonia*, *leiturgia* and *martyria*, the service, worship and witness of the Church, Christians cooperate in Christ's own diakonia for the salvation of mankind. As members of the Body of Christ, all should become servants of one another, using the charisms which they have received for the building up of the Church and their brethren in faith and love: "If anyone claims to serve, let it be as by a command received from God" (1 Pet 4:11–12; cf. Rom 12:8; 1 Cor 12:5).

This diakonia done to others by Christians can take the form of different expressions of fraternal charity, service to the physically or spiritually sick, to the needy, to prisoners (Mt 25); the help given to the Churches (Rom 15:25; 1 Tim 5:3–16); or different kinds of assistance given to Apostles, as can be seen in the case of the men and women collaborators of Saint Paul, who sends them his greetings (Rom 16:3–5; Phil 4:3).

II. *Diakonia of the Apostles*

Because he was the *doulos*, or slave, carrying out the Father's saving will in total obedience, Jesus Christ was made Lord of all creation. He made himself the instrument through which God's sovereignty was achieved, by giving his life: "The Son of Man has not come to be served but to serve, and to give his life as a ransom for many" (Mk 10:45). In the same way, Jesus instituted the Twelve "to be his companions, and sent them out to preach, giving them the power to cast out demons" (Mk 3:14–15). In a way that was radically opposed to the lords and rulers of this world who abuse their power to oppress and exploit others, the disciple must be ready to become *diakonos* and *doulos* of all (Mk 10:42–43).

Diakonein, to serve, is the essential characteristic of the Apostle's ministry. Apostles are collaborators and servants of God (cf. 1 Thess 3:2; 1 Cor 3:9; 2 Cor 6:1), "servants of Christ and witnesses of God's mysteries" (1 Cor 4:1). They are "ministers of a new covenant" (2 Cor 3:6) and ministers of the Gospel (cf. Col 1:23; Eph 3:6ff.), "servants of the word" (Acts 6:4). They are, in their function as Apostles, "ministers of the Church" in order to bring about the coming of the word of Christ in its fullness to believers (cf. Col 1:25), and to organise the building up of the Church, the Body of Christ, in love (cf. Eph 4:12). The Apostles become the servants of believers because of Christ, since it is not themselves whom they are proclaiming, but Christ Jesus the Lord (2 Cor 4:5). They are sent in the name of Christ, the word having been passed on to them so that they may proclaim it in the service of reconciliation. Through them, God himself *exhorts* and *acts* in the Holy Spirit and in Christ Jesus, who has reconciled the world with him (cf. 2 Cor 5:20).

III. *Diakonia of the Apostles' Collaborators*

Within the pauline communities, with, as well as, or after Saint Paul, Saint Peter and the other eleven Apostles (cf. 1 Cor 15:3–5; Gal 2), are to be found direct collaborators with Saint Paul in the apostolic ministry (for example, Sylvanus, Timothy, Titus, Apollos) as well as many others allied to him in apostolic activities and service to local Churches (2 Cor 8:23). These include Epaphroditus (Phil 2:25), Epaphras (Col 4:12) and Archippus (Col 4:17), who are named as servants of Christ. In the opening words of the Epistle to the Philippians (around A.D. 50) Saint Paul sends a special greeting to "their bishops and their deacons" (Phil 1:1). This necessarily calls to mind the ministries that were then taking shape in the Church.

It is of course recognised that the terminology of these ministries was not yet fixed. Reference is made to the *proistamenoi* (Rom 12:8) "who are at your head in the Lord and who reprimand you", and whom the Thessalonians are to hold "in extreme charity, by reason of their work" (1 Thess 5:12); reference is also made to leaders (*hegoumenoi*), "who have made you hear the word of God"; the Epistle to the Hebrews adds, "Obey your leaders and be docile to them" (13:7, 17; cf. 13:24; cf. 1 Clem 1:3; 21:6); and reference is made to the "men who were sent" who guide the communities (cf. Acts 15:22), to apostles, prophets, and teachers (cf. 1 Cor 12:28; Gal 6:6; Acts 13:1; 4:14), and to "evangelists, or rather shepherds and teachers" (Eph 4:11). Saint Paul says of Stephanas, Fortunatus and Achaicus, "the first-fruits of Achaia", "that they spontaneously put themselves at the service of the saints" (1 Cor 16:15); and he exhorts the Corinthians: "Place yourselves under such men, and under whoever works and labours with them" (1 Cor 16:16).

The activity expressed in these terms points to the official titles which were to take shape soon afterwards. It is clear from these documents that the early Church attributed the formation of the various ministries to the action of the Holy Spirit (1 Cor 12:28; Eph 4:11; Acts 20:28) and to the personal initiative of the Apostles, who owed their sending forth on their mission to the Most High and Lord of this world, and who anchored their role of upholding the Church in the power they had received from him (Mk 3:13–19; 6:6–13; Mt 28:16–20; Acts 1:15–26; Gal 1:10–24).

Diakonein is shown to be a radical determination of *Christian life*, expressing itself in the sacramental basis of Christian existence, of the charismatic building up of the Church, and also of the sending out of the Apostles on their mission and of the *ministry* which flows from the apostolate, of the proclamation of the Gospel, and of the sanctification and governance of Churches.

CHAPTER II

THE DIACONATE IN THE NEW TESTAMENT AND IN THE WRITINGS OF THE FATHERS

I. *The Diaconate in the New Testament*

1. Difficulties in Terminology

The word *diakonos* is almost absent from the Old Testament, by contrast with *presbyteros* which is abundantly used. In the Septuagint, in the rare places where the word *diakonos* is attested, it means messenger or servant.[1] The Latin Bible (Vulgate) renders it in a general sense by *minister* or, in a specific sense, by transliterating the Greek word to give *diaconus*. But the terms *minister*, *ministerium*, and *ministrare* are also used to render other Greek terms, such as *hyperetes* and *leitourgos*. In the Vulgate the use of *diaconus* is found three times,[2] and in the remaining cases the word is translated by *minister*.[3]

Apart from the words *diakoneo*, *diakonia*, and *diakonos*, Greek could choose between the following words: *douleuo* (to serve as a servant), *therapeuo* (someone who volunteers to serve), *latreuo* (to serve for wages), *leitourgeo* (someone who holds public office), and *hypereteo* (governor).[4] In any case, it is characteristic that the verbal form *diakonein* is unknown in the Septuagint, the functions of service being translated by the verbs *leitourgein* or *latreuein*. Philo only used it in the sense of "to serve".[5] Josephus knew it in the sense of "to serve", "to obey" and "priestly service".[6] In the New Testament, the word *douleuo* meant service of a very personal kind: the service of charity. In the language of the Gospels[7] and at Acts 6:2, *diakoneo* means "ministering at table". Making a collection whose proceeds

---

[1] Neh 1:10: "They are your servants and your people, whom you redeemed by your great power and your strong hand"; 3:6: "I sent messengers to them, saying"; 6:5: "Sanballat sent his servant to me"; Prov 10:4a (Septuagint); 1 Mac 11:58; 4 Mac 9:17; Esther (Greek) 6:13.

[2] Phil 1:1; 1 Tim 3:8, 12.

[3] Cf. E. Cattaneo, *I ministeri nella chiesa antica, testi patristici dei primi tre secoli* (Milan, 1997), 33ff.; J. Lecuyer, *Le sacrement de l'ordination*, ThH 65 (Paris, 1983), 131.

[4] H. W. Beyer, *diakoneo, diakonia, diakonos*, in *ThWNT* 2:81–93.

[5] *De vita contemplativa* 70 and 75.

[6] *Antiquitates* 7, 365; 10, 72.

[7] Lk 17:8; 12:37; 22:26; Jn 12:2.

Paul would take to Jerusalem was a service of this kind.[8] The Apostle goes to Jerusalem for "a ministry to the saints".[9] As for the use of the words *cheirotonia*, *cheirotesia*, *ordinatio*, there is a degree of uncertainty with regard to these terms.[10]

2. Data from the New Testament

The first fundamental fact of relevance from the New Testament is that the verb *diakonein* designates Christ's actual mission as servant (Mk 10:45 and parallels; cf. Mt 12:18; Acts 4:30; Phil 2:6–11). This word or its derivatives also designate the exercise of service or ministry by his disciples (Mk 10:43ff.; Mt 20:26ff.; 23:11; Lk 8:3; Rom 15:25), the ministries of different kinds in the Church, especially the apostolic ministry of preaching the Gospel, and other charismatic gifts.[11]

The words *diakonein* and *diakonos* are widely used, with a wide range of meanings, in the language of the New Testament.[12]

---

[8] 2 Cor 8:19.

[9] Rom 15:25.

[10] "The meaning of the laying on of the hands in Acts 6:6 and 13:3 has been much disputed, but the stress laid on this gesture in both texts makes it difficult to see it as a mere act of blessing and not as an ordination rite. . . . The usual verb to denote the election of a minister by the community is *eklegein*, Latin *eligere*. The verb *cheirotonein* may have the same meaning, 'to choose by stretching out the hand' (Did. 15, 1), but it becomes a technical term for the appointment, i.e., the ordination of a minister, in Latin *ordinare*. In this meaning it is synonymous with *kathistanai*, Latin *instituere*. Another synonym is *procheirizein*. It is less usual and sometimes denotes the aspect of election and appointment by God. All these verbs are synonymous with *cheira(s) epitheinai*, but whereas the former group denotes the juridical aspect, the latter lays emphasis on the liturgical act. Moreover all the terms of the former group can be used for an appointment/ordination which does not include an imposition of hands, but there is apparently a preference for *cheirotonein/cheirotonia*, as they are composed with *cheir-*, when the imposition of the hand (or of both hands) is included. A first attempt for such a distinction is made by Hippolytus, *Trad. A* 10." J. Ysebaert, "The Deaconesses in the Western Church of Late Antiquity and Their Origin", in *Eulogia: Mélanges offerts à Antoon A. R. Bastiaensen*, IP 24 (Steenbrugis, 1991), 423.

[11] Rom 11:13; 12:6ff.; 1 Cor 12:5; 2 Cor 4:1; Eph 4:11ff.; Heb 1:14: "leitourgika pneumata"; Acts 21:19; Col 4:17.

[12] "Amt im Sinne Jesu muss immer 'diakonia' sein; nicht zufällig, nicht nebenbei, sondern sehr bewusst und ausdrücklich wählt die Heilige Schrift dieses Wort zu seiner Wesensbestimmung. Die griechische Sprache bot eine ganze Reihe von Möglichkeiten, das Amt in einer menschlichen Gemeinschaft—auch im religiös-kultischen Bereich—zu charakterisieren (archai, exousiai, archontes). Das Neue Testament wählte keine davon, sondern entschied sich für eine Bezeichnung, die weder in der jüdischen, noch in der hellenistischen Umwelt üblich war." E. Dassmann, *Ämter und Dienste in der frühchristlichen Gemeinden*, Hereditas 8 (Bonn, 1994), 37.

The *diakonos* may mean the servant who waits at table (e.g. Jn 2:5 and 9), the servant of the Lord (Mt 22:13; Jn 12:26; Mk 9:35; 10:43; Mt 20:26; 23:11), the servant of a spiritual power (2 Cor 11:14; Eph 3:6; Col 1:23; Gal 2:17; Rom 15:8; 2 Cor 3:6), the servant of the Gospel, of Christ or of God (2 Cor 11:23). Pagan authorities are also in the service of God (Rom 13:4); the deacons are the servants of the Church (Col 1:25; 1 Cor 3:5). In the case where the deacon belongs to one of the Churches, the Vulgate does not use the word *minister*, but retains the Greek word *diaconus*.[13] This fact shows clearly that in Acts 6:1–6 it is not the institution of the diaconate which is being referred to.[14]

"Diaconate" and "apostolate" are sometimes synonymous, as in Acts 1:17–25, where, on the occasion of the addition of Matthias to the eleven Apostles, Peter calls the apostolate "a share in our service" (v. 17: *ton kleron tes diakonias tautes*) and speaks of service and apostolate (v. 25: *ton topon tes diakonias kai apostoles*, which is sometimes translated as "the service of the apostolate". This text from Acts also quotes Psalm 109:8: "Let another take over his position [*ten episkopen*]". The question therefore arises as to whether *diakonia*, *apostole*, and *episkope* are equivalent to each other or not. In the opinion of M. J. Schmitt and J. Colson, "apostolate" is "an editorial term correcting 'diakonias'."[15]

---

[13] Phil 1:1: "cum episcopis et diaconis"; 1 Tim 3:8, 12: "diaconos similiter ... [sicut episcopi] diaconi sint."

[14] "Dieser Tatbestand zeigt, dass der Ursprung des Diakonenamtes nicht in Ag 6 zu finden ist.... Der Diakonos ist nicht nur Diener seiner Gemeinde, sondern auch seines Bischofes." Beyer, *diakoneo, diakonia, diakonos*, 90. Cf. M. Dibelius, "Bischöfe und Diakonen in Philippi" (1937), in *Das kirchliche Amt im Neuen Testament*, WdF 439 (Darmstadt, 1977), 413ff.; E. Schweizer, "Das Amt: Zum Amtsbegriff im Neuen Testament", in *Gemeinde und Gemeindeordnung im Neuen Testament*, AThANT 35 (Zürich, 1955), 154–64: "Als allgemeine Bezeichnung dessen, was wir 'Amt' nennen, also des Dienstes Einzelner innerhalb der Gemeinde, gibt es mit wenigen Ausnahmen nur ein einziges Wort: 'diakonia', Diakonie. Das NT wählt also durchwegs und einheitlich ein Wort, das völlig unbiblisch und unreligiös ist und nirgends eine Assoziation mit einer besonderen Würde oder Stellung einschliesst. Im griechischen AT kommt das Wort nur einmal rein profan vor.... In der griechischen Sprachentwicklung ist die Grundbedeutung 'zu Tischen dienen' auch zum umfassenden Begriff 'dienen' ausgeweitet worden. Es bezeichnet fast durchwegs etwas Minderwertiges, kann aber im Hellenismus auch die Haltung des Weisen gegen Gott (nicht gegen den Mitmenschen) umschreiben"; K. H. Schelke, "Dienste und Diener in den Kirchen der Neutestamentlichen Zeit", *Concilium* 5 (1969): 158–64; J. Brosch, *Charismen und Ämter in der Urkirche* (Bonn, 1951). Cf. B. Kötting, "Ämt und Verfassung in der Alten Kirche", in *Ecclesia peregrinans: Das Gottesvolk unterwegs*, METh 54, 1 (Münster, 1988), 429; G. Schöllgen, *Die Anfänge der Professionalisierung des Klerus und das kirchliche Amt in der Syrischen Didaskalie*, JAC, Ergbd 26 (Münster, 1998), 93.

[15] Cf. J. Colson, *Ministre de Jésus-Christ ou le Sacerdoce de l'Évangile*, ThH 4 (Paris, 1966), 191.

Acts 6:1–6 describes the institution of the "Seven"[16] "to serve at tables". The reason for this is given by Luke as stemming from internal tensions within the community: "The Hellenists complained [*egeneto goggysmos*] against the Hebrews because their widows were being neglected in the daily distribution of food" (Acts 6:1). It has not yet been ascertained whether the widows of the "Hellenists" belonged to the community or not, according to strict respect for ritual purity. Were the Apostles hoping to send to the provinces the rebellious "Hellenists" of Jerusalem who, in their preaching in the synagogue, were responsible for much provocation? Is this why the Apostles chose "Seven", which was the number of provincial community magistrates attached to a synagogue? But at the same time, through the imposition of hands, they wished to preserve the unity of the Spirit and avoid a schism.[17] Commentators on Acts do not explain the significance of this laying on of the Apostles' hands.

It is possible that the Apostles appointed the Seven to be at the head of the "Hellenists" (baptised Greek-speaking Jews) to fulfil the same task as the presbyters among the "Hebrew" Christians.[18]

The reason given for the designation of the chosen Seven (complaints by the Hellenists) is in contradiction with their actual activity as later described by Luke. We hear nothing about serving at tables. Out of the Seven, Luke only speaks of the activities of Stephen and Philip; or more precisely, Stephen's discourse in the synagogue at Jerusalem, and his martyrdom, and the apostolate carried out in Samaria by Philip, who also baptised people.[19] There is no word of the others.[20]

---

[16] It was Irenaeus of Lyons (*Adv. haer.* 3, 12, 10) who first referred to the "Seven" as "deacons".

[17] "Die Siebenzahl wohl nach Analogie der sieben Mitglieder, aus denen in den jüdischen Gemeinden meist der Ortsvorstand sich zusammensetzte. Dieser hiess deshalb geradezu 'die Sieben einer Stadt' oder 'die Sieben Besten einer Stadt', während seine einzelnen Mitglieder ... 'Hirten' oder 'Vorsteher' genannt wurden." H. L. Strack and P. Billerbeck, *Kommentar zum Neuen Testament aus Talmud und Midrasch*, vol. 2 (Munich, 1969), 641.

[18] E. Haenchen, *Die Apostelgeschichte*, Neu übersetzt und erklärt, 12. neubearb. Auflage, Kritisch-exegetischer Kommentar (Göttingen, 1959), 228–22; Dassmann, *Ämter und Dienste*, 232: "Uber die Entstehung des Diakonenamtes sind keine genauere Angaben bekannt, seitdem feststeht, dass Apg 6 nicht die Bestellung von Diakonen, sondern von Beauftragten für die griechisch sprechende Gruppe der Urgemeinde beschreibt."

[19] Cf. Acts 8:12, 26–40 and 21:8, where Philip is called "the evangelist". "The next day we left and came to Caesarea; and went into the house of Philip the evangelist, one of the seven [*Philippou tou euaggelistou, ontos ek ton epta*], and stayed with him."

[20] "Nicolaitae autem magistrum quidem habent Nicolaum, unum ex VII qui primi ad diaconium ab apostolis ordinati sunt: qui indiscrete vivunt." *Adv. haer.* 1, 26, 3; Harvey, 1:214. Hippolytus, *Philosophomena* 7, 36; Tertullian, *De praescriptione* 33. For the opposing view, Clement of Alexandria, *Strom.* 2, 118, 3 and 3, 25, 5—26, 2.

In the Churches entrusted to Saint Paul's apostolic care, deacons appear beside the *episkopoi* as exercising a ministry subordinate to or coordinated with theirs (Phil 1:1; 1 Tim 3:1–13). In the apostolic writings mention is often made of deacons with the bishop, or else of the bishop with priests. However, historical sources which cite all three together, bishop, priest and deacon, are very rare.

II. *The Apostolic Fathers*

The first epistle of Saint Clement of Rome to the Corinthians (first century) mentions that the bishops and deacons have a spiritual function in the community: "The Apostles received for us the good news through the Lord Jesus Christ; Jesus, the Christ, was sent by God. Therefore the Christ comes from God, the Apostles come from Christ; both proceeded in due order from the will of God [*egenonto oun amphotera eutaktos ek thelematos Theou*]. They therefore received instructions and, filled with conviction by the resurrection of our Lord Jesus Christ, strengthened by the word of God, with the full conviction of the Holy Spirit, they set out to announce the good news of the coming of God's kingdom. They preached in the countryside and in the towns and they established [*kathistanon*] its first-fruits, they tested them by the Spirit, so as to make them bishops and deacons [*eis episkopous kai diakonous*] of those who were to believe. And there was nothing new [*ou kainos*] in this; for long ago Scripture spoke of bishops and deacons [*egegrapto peri episkopon kai diakonon*]; for it is written somewhere, 'I shall establish their bishops in justice and their deacons in faith'."[21]

When the author of the Epistle of Clement speaks of liturgical functions he refers to the Old Testament;[22] when he explains the institution of the *episkopoi kai diakonoi*, he refers to the will of God, and to the Apostles.[23] The order of bishops and deacons was not an innovation, but was founded on the will of God, and therefore was a "due order"; their sending originated in God himself. The successors chosen by the Apostles were the first-fruits offered to God. The Apostles had tested the chosen ones by the Spirit; those who succeeded them would be established by the choice of the whole assembly.[24] Here we find the tradition of the

---

[21] Cf. Is 60:17, where the Septuagint does not mention "deacons", which must be an addition by St. Clement; cf. 1 Clem 42:1–5; SCh 167, 173, 168–71.

[22] Cf. 40:1 and 41:2–4.

[23] Colson, *Ministre de Jésus-Christ*, 228ff.

[24] 1 Clem 44:3; SCh 167, 172–73.

pastoral letters in reverse order: (1) the testing in the Spirit (cf. 1 Tim 3:1–7 and 8:10ff.); (2) the use side by side of the terms *episkopos kai diakonos* (cf. Phil 1:1), where *episkopos* does not yet correspond to the present definition of bishop.[25] It is worth noting the way Saint Polycarp linked the ministry of deacons with the service of Christ the Saviour: "Let them walk in the truth of the Lord who became the servant [*diakonos*] of all" (Letter of Saint Polycarp to the Philippians 5:2).

The text of the *Didache* (written before A.D. 130) at 15, 1 only mentions bishops and deacons as the successors of the prophets and the *didaskaloi*, and says nothing of priests: "Choose yourselves therefore bishops and deacons worthy of the Lord, mild men, fair-minded, truthful and reliable, for they too fulfil towards you the offices of prophets and teachers."[26] J.-P. Audet comments, "The two words admittedly sound different to us. But in Greek, at the time of the Didache, an *episkopos* was a supervisor, foreman, guardian, moderator, warden or steward ... whereas a *diakonos* was simply a servant able to fulfil different functions according to the particular conditions of his service. The two terms are widely used with a variety of meanings.... The specific way they were appointed (*cheirotonesate*) remains unclear. They were chosen and appointed, perhaps by election; that is all that can be said."[27] The *Didache* does not say anything about ordination. According to K. Niederwimmer, the term *cheirotonein* means election.[28]

It is certain that at that period the deacons were responsible for the life of the Church with regard to works of charity towards widows and orphans, as was the case in the first community at Jerusalem. Their activities were doubtless linked to catechesis and also probably to the liturgy. However information on this subject is so brief[29] that it is difficult to learn from it the precise range of their functions.

The letters of Saint Ignatius of Antioch point to a new stage. His statements about the ecclesiastical hierarchy with its three grades are similar to those of Clement of Rome: "Let everyone revere the deacons as Jesus Christ, the bishop as the image of the Father, and the presbyters as the

---

[25] "Von den zwei erwähnten Ämtern, *episkopoi* und *diakonoi*, wurde das erste mit 'Episkopen' wiedergegeben, um das sehr missverständliche 'Bischöfe' zu vermeiden. Denn auf keinen Fall handelt es sich dabei um die Institution des Monepiskopats." H. E. Lona, *Der erste Clemensbrief*, Kommentar zu den Apostolischen Vätern 2 (Göttingen, 1998), 446. Cf. Dassmann, *Ämter und Dienste*, 40.

[26] J.-P. Audet, *La Didachè: Instructions des Apôtres* (Paris, 1958), 241.

[27] Ibid., 465.

[28] "'*Cheirotonein*' heisst hier (natürlich) 'wählen' und nicht 'ernennen'." *Die Didache*, Kommentar zu den Apostolischen Vätern 1 (Göttingen, 1989), 241.

[29] *Did.* 14, 1–3; 15, 1.

senate of God and the assembly of the Apostles. For without them one cannot speak of the Church."[30] And again, "All of you, follow the bishop, as Jesus Christ [follows] his Father, and the presbyterium as the Apostles; as for the deacons, respect them as the law of God."[31] Saint Ignatius speaks of the bishop in the singular and of priests and deacons in the plural, but says nothing on the character of the diaconate, simply exhorting the faithful to venerate the deacons as appointed by God.

Saint Justin (†165) gives information especially about the liturgical activity of deacons. He describes the role of deacons in the Eucharist during the *oblatio* and the *communio*: "Then there is brought to him who presides over the assembly of the brethren, some bread and a cup of water and wine mixed.... Once the prayers and giving of thanks are over, all the people present express their assent by replying Amen.... When the president of the assembly has finished the prayer of thanksgiving [eucharist] and all the people have made their response, those who among us are called deacons [*oi kaloumenoi par 'emin diakonoi*] give to each of those present to share in the bread and in the wine mixed with water over which has been said the prayer of thanksgiving [eucharist], and they carry it to those who are absent."[32]

III. *Consolidation and Development of the Diaconate in the Third and Fourth Centuries*

According to Clement of Alexandria there are in the Church, as in the life of civil society, positions which are intended to benefit either the body or the soul (*therapeia beltiotike, hyperetike*). There are also people who in themselves are ordered to the service of people of a higher grade. Priests are of the first kind, and deacons of the second.[33] In Origen, the *diakonia* of the bishop is always the service of the whole Church (*ekklesiastike diakonia*). The bishop is called "prince" and, at the same time, also called "servant of all".[34] Deacons are often criticised by Origen because they are particularly infected by the spirit of covetousness. Because of their responsibility for charitable works, they were more in contact with money. In a passage on the expulsion of the traders from the Temple,

---

[30] *Letter to the Trallians* 3, 1; SCh 10, 113.

[31] *Letter to the Smyrnaeans* 8, 1; SCh 10, 163.

[32] *Apol.* 1, 65, 3–5. St. Justin, *Apologies*, introduction, texte critique, traduction, commentaire et index par A. Wartelle (Paris, 1987), 188–91.

[33] *Strom.* 7, 1, 3; GCS 17, 6.

[34] *Comm. in Mat.* 16:8; GCS 40, 496.

Origen speaks of those "deacons who do not administer rightly the tables of the money of the Church [*sc.* of the poor], but always act fraudulently towards them." [35] "They amass riches for themselves, misappropriating money meant for the poor." [36]

The *Didascalia* (third century) evidences a degree of supremacy of deacons over priests, since deacons are compared to Christ, while priests are only compared to the Apostles. [37] But in the first place, priests are presented as the senate of the Church and the bishop's assessors; they are placed around the altar and the episcopal throne. The deacons are called the "third ones", which probably suggests that they come after the bishop and the priests. However, the status and activity of deacons undoubtedly seem to have surpassed those of priests. The laity ought to have great confidence in the deacons and not importune the head, but make their wishes known to him through the *hyperetai*, that is through the deacons, for no one can approach the almighty Lord and God either except through Christ. [38] In the *Didascalia* the increase in the status of the diaconate in the Church is remarkable, resulting in a growing crisis in the reciprocal relations of priests and deacons. To the deacons' social and charitable responsibilities was added that of providing various services during liturgical assemblies: ushering in newcomers and pilgrims; taking care of the offerings; supervising orderliness and silence; and ensuring that people were suitably dressed.

The *Traditio Apostolica* of Hippolytus of Rome (†235) presents the theological and juridical status of the deacon in the Church for the first time. It includes them among the group of the *ordinati* by the imposition of hands (*cheirotonein*), contrasting them with those in the hierarchy who are called *instituti*. The "ordination" of deacons is done only by the bishop (Chapter 8). This connection defines the scope of the tasks of the deacon, who is at the disposition of the bishop, to fulfil his orders, but is excluded from taking part in the council of priests.

A comparison should be made between the two texts for the ordination of deacons, that of the *Veronense* (L, Latin version) and that of the Sahidic Ethiopian (S[AE]), because there are some differences between them. L says: "Diaconus vero cum ordinatur, eligatur secundum ea, quae praedicta sunt, similiter imponens manus episcopus solus sicuti praecipimus." S[AE] is clearer: "Episcopus autem instituet [*kathistasthai*] diaconum qui electus est, secundum quod praedictum est." There is still, however, a difference between *ordinatio* and *institutio*. The tenth chapter,

---

[35] Ibid., 16:22; GCS 40, 552.

[36] Ibid., 16:22; GCS 40, 553.

[37] *Didascalia apostolorum*, ed. R. H. Connolly (Oxford, 1969), 89.

[38] Cf. A. Vilela, *La condition collégiale des prêtres au IIIe siècle*, ThH 14 (Paris, 1971).

speaking of the widows of the *Traditio Apostolica* contributes some significant elements. "Non autem imponetur manus super eam, quia non offert
oblationem neque habet liturgiam. Ordinatio [*cheirotonia*] autem fit cum
clero [*kleros*] propter liturgiam. Vidua [*xera*] autem instituitur [*kathistasthai*] propter orationem: haec autem est omnium." [39] According to this
text, if the imposition of hands is absent from the rite, then it is only an
institution (*katastasis, institutio*) and not an *ordinatio*. Thus, in the course
of the third century, the imposition of hands already constituted the distinctive sign of the rite of ordination to major orders. In the fourth century it was extended to minor orders as well.

In what concerns the liturgy, the task of the deacon was to bring the
offerings and distribute them. In the administration of baptism, his role
was to accompany the priest and serve him "the oil of the catechumens
and the chrism and also to go down into the water with the person who
was to receive baptism" (Chapter 21). Another field of work for the deacons was teaching: "Let them come together and instruct those with whom
they are in the Church" (Chapter 39). Their social activity is emphasized, specifically in close union with the bishop.

According to Saint Cyprian, "The deacons should not forget that the
Lord himself chose the Apostles, that is, the bishops and the heads of the
Church, while in the case of deacons, it was the Apostles who instituted
them after the Lord's Ascension, to be ministers of their episcopate and of
the Church. Hence, just as we cannot undertake anything in defiance of
God who makes us bishops, neither can they too undertake anything
in defiance of us, who make them deacons." [40] It seems that, from time
to time, even at Carthage, the deacons wished to take the place of the
priests. They had to be warned that deacons came in third place in the
order of the hierarchy. While the see was vacant they also had an important role in the governance of the Church. In exile, Cyprian normally
addressed his letters "to the priests and deacons" to discuss disciplinary
problems. In Cyprian's writings priests and deacons were sometimes designated by the word *clerus*, and less frequently were called *praepositi*.[41]
The priest Gaius Didensis and his deacons were both charged to offer the
Eucharist, but the fifth letter indicates that in reality it was the priests
who offered it, attended by the deacons.[42] To deacons, on the other hand,

---

[39] SCh 11(2), 66.

[40] *Ep.* 3, 3: "Meminisse autem diaconi debent quoniam apostolos id est episcopos et
praepositos Dominus elegit, diaconos autem post ascensum Domini in caelos apostoli sibi
constituerunt episcopatus sui et ecclesiae ministros. Quod si nos aliquid audere contra Deum
possumus qui episcopos facit, possunt et contra nos audere diaconi a quibus fiunt."

[41] *Ep.* 15, 2; 16, 3.

[42] *Ep.* 34, 1; *Ep.* 5, 2.

falls the practice of charity by prison-visiting. They are described as "boni viri et ecclesiasticae administrationis per omnia devoti".[43] The word *administratio* is found in the expression *sancta administratio* applied to the deacon Nicostratus in regard to the Church money that he looked after. Thus deacons would be charged not only with the practice of charity towards the poor, but also with the administration of the finances belonging to the community.[44]

To sum up, as well as the fact of the existence of the diaconate in all the Churches from the beginning of the second century, and the fact of the ecclesiastical nature of the diaconate as such, it can be said that the role fulfilled by deacons was basically the same everywhere, although the emphasis placed on the various elements of their commitment may have differed in different regions. The diaconate was stabilised in the course of the fourth century. In the synodal and conciliar directives of this period the diaconate was regarded as an essential element of the hierarchy of the local Church. At the synod of Elvira (c. 306–309) the diaconate's preeminent role in the administrative sector of the Church was primarily underlined. Paradoxically, at the same time as it imposed a certain limitation on the involvement of deacons in the liturgical sector, this synod attributed to them the possibility of giving absolution of sins in urgent cases. This tendency to invade the field of competences of priests, which was also manifested in the claim to preside at the Eucharist (albeit as an exception) was put a stop to by the synod of Aries (314) and particularly by the Council of Nicaea (325, can. 18).

The *Constitutiones Apostolorum* (*CA*), which forms the most impressive of the juridical collections drawn up in the fourth century, cites the different parts of the *Didache* and the *Didascalia* which refer to deacons, and comments on them in ways which reflect the point of view of the period. Also included are the statements of Saint Ignatius in his letters, thus providing a considerable amount of information. The text is characterised by a tendency to historicism, the more so since the author-editor looks for prefigurations in parallel passages of the Old Testament. He introduces his discourse with a solemn formula (cf. Deut 5:31 and 27:9): "Hear, O sacred and catholic Church. . . . For these are your pontiffs; your priests are the presbyters, and your Levites are now the deacons, these are your lectors, cantors and door-keepers, these are your deaconesses, your widows, your virgins and your orphans. . . . The deacon will attend him as Christ attends the Father."[45] He describes the relation of the bishop with the deacon

---

[43] *Ep.* 15, 1; 43, 1.
[44] *Ep.* 52, 1.
[45] *CA* 2, 26, 4.5.6; SCh 320, 239–41.

through the prefigurations of the Old Covenant and the heavenly models: "For you now, Aaron is the deacon and Moses the bishop; if therefore Moses was called a god by the Lord, among you the bishop shall be likewise honoured as a god and the deacon as his prophet ... and as the Son is the angel and prophet of the Father, in the same way the deacon is the angel and prophet of the bishop." [46] The deacon represents the eye, the ear, and the mouth of the bishop "so that the bishop does not have to concern himself with a multitude of matters, but only with the most important ones, as Jethro established for Moses, and his counsel was well received." [47] The prayer of ordination of a deacon by the bishop attests that the diaconate was envisaged as a transitory grade towards the presbyterate: "Grant that he may satisfactorily accomplish the service which has been entrusted to him, in a seemly manner, without deviation or blame or reproach, to be judged worthy of a higher rank [*meizonos axiothenai bathmou*], through the mediation of your Christ, your only-begotten Son." [48]

In the *Euchologion* of Serapion (towards the end of the fourth century) there appears a prayer of ordination of a deacon whose terminology is similar to that of the Sahidic version of the *Traditio Apostolica*. The text of the prayer alludes to the canons of the Church, to the three hierarchical grades, and refers to the Seven in Acts chapter 6; to designate the ordination of the deacon it employs the verb *katisthanai*: "Pater unigeniti, qui *filium misisti* tuum et ordinasti res super terra atque ecclesiae canones et ordines dedisti in utilitatem et salutem gregum, qui elegisti episcopos et presbyteros et diaconos in ministerium catholicae tuae ecclesiae, qui elegisti per unigenitum tuum septem diaconos eisque largitus es spiritum sanctum: constitue [*katasteson*] et hunc diaconum ecclesiae tuae catholicae et da in eo *spiritum cognitionis ac discretionis*, ut possit inter populum sanctum pure et immaculate ministrare in hoc ministerio per unigenitum tuum Iesum Christum, per quem tibi gloriam et imperium in sancto spiritu et nunc et in omnia saecula saeculorum, amen." [49]

The prayer of consecration of a deacon in the *Sacramentarium Veronense* speaks of the service of the holy altar, and, like the text in the *Constitutiones Apostolorum*, considers the diaconate to be a transitory grade. "Oremus ... quos consecrationis indultae propitius dona conservet ... quos ad

---

[46] Ibid., 30, 1–2; SCh 320, 249–51.

[47] Ibid., 44, 4; SCh 285.

[48] *CA* 8, 18, 3; SCh 336, 221.

[49] *Sacramentarium Serapionis*, in *Didascalia et Constitutiones Apostolorum*, ed. F. X. Funk, vol. 2, *Testimonia et Scripturae propinquae* (Paderbornae, 1905), 188. The quotation is given here in the Latin translation of the editor. The same use of the word (*constituat*) is found in can. 3 (33) of *Constitutiones Ecclesiae Aegypciacae*, De diaconis, ibid., 103–4.

officium levitarum vocare dignaris, altaris sancti ministerium tribuas sufficienter implere ... trinis gradibus ministrorum nomini tuo militare constituens ... dignisque successibus de inferiori gradu per gratiam tuam capere potiora mereantur."[50] The *Sacramentarium Gregorianum* is similar at every point to the texts already cited. It also recalls the three grades, and uses the word "*constituere*" to designate the ordination of the deacon.[51]

Behind their apparent unanimity, the declarations of the Fathers of the Church in the fourth century give a glimpse of certain dissensions which had been well known since the third century, as for example the deacons' claim to appropriate the places, rank and tasks of the priests.[52]

There is also evidence of the idea that the three grades (bishop, priest and deacon) were like elements of one and the same order. Pseudo-Athanasios speaks of this in his work *De Trinitate* as a "consubstantiality".[53] In addition, Christianity was beginning to spread in provincial areas, with bishops or priests leaving the town against their will, and deacons doing so very willingly, but abusing the situation in that they used to appropriate certain of priests' rights. The historical context also contributed to this development. What had happened was that the Arians had compromised the standing of the episcopate. Contrasting with bishops and priests avid for power and money, the popularity of deacons grew strongly because of their close links with monks and laypeople. The widespread opinion in the fourth century was that deacons had been instituted by the Apostles and the bishop ordained them in the same way as priests. Deacons belonged to the clergy, but only assisted at the liturgy.[54]

The sources show us that even Chrysostom did not manage to place the three grades of the ecclesial order in a clear historical continuity. There were Jewish models for the priesthood, but the episcopate and diaconate were instituted by the Apostles. It is not clear what should be understood

---

[50] *Sacramentarium Veronense*, ed. L. C. Mohlberg (Rome, 1966), 120–21.

[51] *Le Sacramentaire Grégorien*, ed. J. Deshusses, vol. 1 (Fribourg [Switzerland], 1992), 96–97.

[52] Jerome, *Ep.* 146, 1; PL 22, 1192–95: "Audio quemdam in tantam erupisse vecordiam, ut diaconos, presbyteris, id est episcopis anteferret. Nam cum Apostolus perspicue doceat eosdem esse presbyteros, quos episcopos, quid patitur mensarum et viduarum minister, ut super eos se tumidus efferat, ad quorum preces Christi corpus sanguinisque conficitur?" Jerome, *Comm. in Ez.* 6, 17, 5–6; PL 25, 183B: "Quod multos facere conspicimus, clientes et pauperes, et agricolas, ut taceam de militantium et iudicum violentia, qui opprimunt per potentiam, vel furta committunt, ut de multis parva pauperibus tribuant, et in suis sceleribus glorientur, publiceque diaconus, in Ecclesiis recitet offerentium nomina. Tantum offert illa, tantum ille pollicitus est, placentque sibi ad plausum populi, torquente eis conscientia."

[53] *De Trinitate* 1, 27; PG 28, 1157B: "episkopos, presbyteros, diakonoi homoousioi eisin".

[54] Origen, *Hom. in Jer.* 11, 3; *Concilium Ancyranum*, can. 14.

by these notions.[55] Chrysostom stated that the diaconate had been instituted by the Holy Spirit.[56] In the course of this century the Latins also
took up the use of the Greek word "diaconus", as Saint Augustine attests.[57]

The fourth century marked the end of the process which led to the
recognition of the diaconate as a grade or degree in the ecclesial hierarchy, placed after the bishop and the priests, with a well-defined role.
Linked to the bishop himself and his mission, this role encompassed three
tasks: the service of the liturgy, the service of preaching the Gospel and
teaching catechesis, and a vast social activity concerning the works of
charity and administrative action in accordance with the bishop's directives.

IV. The Ministry of Deaconesses

In the apostolic era different forms of diaconal assistance offered to the
Apostles and communities by women seem to have been institutional. Thus
Paul recommends to the community at Rome "our sister Phoebe, servant
[he diakonos] of the Church at Cenchreae" (cf. Rom 16:1–4). Although the
masculine form of diakonos is used here, it cannot therefore be concluded
that the word is being used to designate the specific function of a "deacon"; firstly because in this context diakonos still signifies servant in a very
general sense, and secondly because the word "servant" is not given a
feminine suffix but preceded by a feminine article. What seems clear is that
Phoebe exercised a recognised service in the community of Cenchreae, subordinate to the ministry of the Apostle. Elsewhere in Paul's writings the
authorities of the world are themselves called diakonos (Rom 13:4), and in
Second Corinthians 11:14–15 he refers to diakonoi of the devil.

Exegetes are divided on the subject of First Timothy 3:11. The mention of "women" following the reference to deacons may suggest women

---

[55] Hom. 14, 3 in Act.; PG 60:116: "Quam ergo dignitatem habuerunt illi [sc. the deacons and the bishops]. . . . Atqui haec in Ecclesiis non erat; sed presbyterorum erat oeconomia. Atqui nullus adhuc episcopus erat, praeterquam apostoli tantum. Unde puto nec
diaconorum nec presbyterorum tunc fuisse nomen admissum nec manifestum."

[56] "And rightly so; for it is not a man, nor an angel, nor an archangel, nor any other
created power, but the Paraclete himself who instituted this order, persuading men who
are still in the flesh to imitate the service of the angels", De sacerdotio 3, 4, 1–8; SCh 272,
142.

[57] "Graecum codicem legite, et diaconum invenietis. Quod enim interpretatus est lati-
nus, Minister; graecus habet, Diaconus; quia vere diaconus graece, minister latine; quomodo martyr graece, testis latine; apostolus graece, missus latine. Sed iam consuevimus
nominibus graecis uti pro latinis. Nam multi codices Evangeliorum sic habent: 'Ubi sum
ego, illic et diaconus meus'." Sermo 329, De Stephana martyre 6, 3, PL 38, 1441.

deacons (by parallel reference), or the deacons' wives who had been mentioned earlier. In this epistle, the functions of the deacon are not described, but only the conditions for admitting them. It is said that women must not teach or rule over men (1 Tim 2:8–15). But the functions of governance and teaching were in any case reserved to the bishop (1 Tim 3:5) and to priests (1 Tim 5:17), and not to deacons. Widows constituted a recognised group in the community, from whom they received assistance in exchange for their commitment to continence and prayer. First Timothy 5:3–16 stresses the conditions under which they may be inscribed on the list of widows receiving relief from the community, and says nothing more about any functions they might have. Later on they were officially "instituted" but "not ordained";[58] they constituted an "order" in the Church,[59] and would never have any other mission apart from good example and prayer.

At the beginning of the second century a letter from Pliny the Younger, governor of Bithynia, mentioned two women who were described by the Christians as *ministrae*, the probable equivalent of the Greek *diakonoi* (10, 96–97). It was not until the third century that the specific Christian terms *diaconissa* or *diacona* appeared.

From the end of the third century onwards, in certain regions of the Church[60] (and not all of them), a specific ecclesial ministry is attested to on the part of women called deaconesses.[61] This was in Eastern Syria and Constantinople. Towards 240 there appeared a singular canonico-liturgical compilation, the *Didascalia Apostolorum* (*DA*), which was not official in character. It attributed to the bishop the features of an omnipotent biblical patriarch (cf. *DA* 2, 33—35, 3). He was at the head of a little community which he governed mainly with the help of deacons and deaconesses. This was the first time that deaconesses appeared in an ecclesiastical document. In a typology borrowed from Ignatius of Antioch, the bishop held the place of God the Father, the deacon the place of Christ, and the deaconess that of the Holy Spirit (the word for "Spirit" is feminine in Semitic languages), while the priests (who are seldom

---

[58] *Traditio Apostolica* 10; SCh 11(2), 67.

[59] Cf. Tertullian, *To his wife* 1, 7, 4; SCh 273; *Exhortation to chastity* 13, 4; SCh 319.

[60] "It is at the Eastern limits of the Roman Empire that deaconesses finally make their appearance. The first document to refer to them, which is in some sort their birth certificate, is the *Didascalia Apostolorum* ... known since the publication in 1854 ... of its Syriac text." A. G. Martimort, *Les diaconesses: Essai historique* (Rome, 1982), 31.

[61] The most ample collection of all the testimony about this ecclesiastical ministry, accompanied by a theological interpretation, is that of John Pinius, *De diaconissarum ordinatione*, in *Acta Sanctorum*, 1 September (Antwerp, 1746), 1–27. Most of the Greek and Latin documents referred to by Pinius are reproduced by J. Mayer, *Monumenta de viduis diaconissis virginibusque tractantia* (Bonn, 1938). Cf. R. Gryson, *Le ministère des femmes dans l'Église ancienne*, Recherches et synthèses: Section d'histoire 4 (Gembloux, 1972).

mentioned) represented the Apostles, and the widows, the altar (*DA* 2, 26, 4–7). There is no reference to the ordination of these ministers.

The *Didascalia* laid stress on the charitable role of the deacon and the deaconess. The ministry of the diaconate should appear as "one single soul in two bodies". Its model is the diakonia of Christ, who washed the feet of his disciples (*DA* 3, 13, 1–7). However, there was no strict parallelism between the two branches of the diaconate with regard to the functions they exercised. The deacons were chosen by the bishop to "concern themselves about many necessary things", and the deaconesses only "for the service of women" (*DA* 3, 12, 1). The hope was expressed that "the number of deacons may be proportionate to that of the assembly of the people of the Church" (*DA* 3, 13, 1).[62] The deacons administered the property of the community in the bishop's name. Like the bishop, they were maintained at its expense. Deacons are called the ear and mouth of the bishop (*DA* 2, 44, 3–4). Men from among the faithful should go through the deacons to have access to the bishop, as women should go through the deaconesses (*DA* 3, 12, 1–4). One deacon supervised the entries into the meeting place, while another attended the bishop for the Eucharistic offering (*DA* 2, 57, 6).

Deaconesses should carry out the anointing of women in the rite of baptism, instruct women neophytes, and visit the women faithful, especially the sick, in their homes. They were forbidden to confer baptism themselves, or to play a part in the Eucharistic offering (*DA* 3, 12, 1–4). The deaconesses had supplanted the widows. The bishop may still institute widows, but they should not either teach or administer baptism (to women), but only pray (*DA* 3, 5, 1—3, 6, 2).

The *Constitutiones Apostolorum*, which appeared in Syria towards 380, used and interpolated the *Didascalia*, the *Didache* and the *Traditio Apostolica*. The *Constitutiones* were to have a lasting influence on the discipline governing ordinations in the East, even though they were never considered to be an official canonical collection. The compiler envisaged the imposition of hands with the epiklesis of the Holy Spirit not only for bishops, priests and deacons, but also for the deaconesses, sub-deacons and lectors (cf. *CA* 8, 16–23).[63] The concept of *klèros* was broadened to

---

[62] This norm is repeated in the *Constitutiones Apostolorum* 3, 19, 1. On the origins of the professionalisation of the clergy, cf. Schöllgen, *Die Anfänge der Professionalisierung*.

[63] The compiler was attentive to the nuances of vocabulary. At *CA* 2, 11, 3 he says, "We do not allow the priests to ordain [*cheirotonein*] deacons, deaconesses, lectors, servants, cantors or door-keepers: that belongs to the bishops alone." However, he reserves the term *cheirotonia* to the ordination of bishops, priests, deacons and sub-deacons (8, 4–5; 8, 16–17; 8, 21). He employs the expression *epitithenai tèn (tas) cheira(s)* for deaconesses and lectors

all those who exercised a liturgical ministry, who were maintained by the Church, and who benefited from the privileges in civil law allowed by the Empire to clerics, so that the deaconesses were counted as belonging to the clergy, while the widows were excluded. Bishop and priests were paralleled with the high priest and the priests respectively of the Old Covenant, while to the Levites corresponded all the other ministries and states of life: "deacons, lectors, cantors, door-keepers, deaconesses, widows, virgins and orphans" (*CA* 2, 26, 3; *CA* 8, 1, 21). The deacon was placed "at the service of the bishop and the priests" and should not impinge on the functions of the latter.[64] The deacon could proclaim the Gospel and conduct the prayer of the assembly (*CA* 2, 57, 18), but only the bishop and the priests exhorted (*CA* 2, 57, 7). Deaconesses took up their functions through an *epithesis cheirôn* or imposition of hands that conferred the Holy Spirit,[65] as did the lectors (*CA* 8, 20, 22). The bishop pronounced the following prayer: "Eternal God, Father of our Lord Jesus Christ, creator of man and woman, who filled Myriam, Deborah, Anne and Hulda with your spirit; who did not deem it unworthy for your Son, the Only-Begotten, to be born of a woman; who in the tent of witness and in the temple did institute women as guardians of your sacred doors, look now upon your servant before you, proposed for the diaconate: grant her the Holy Spirit and purify her of all defilement of flesh and spirit so that she may acquit herself worthily of the office which has been entrusted to her, for your glory and to the praise of your Christ, through whom be glory and adoration to you, in the Holy Spirit, world without end. Amen."[66]

The deaconesses were named before the sub-deacon who, in his turn, received a *cheirotonia* like the deacon (*CA* 8, 21), while the virgins and

---

(8, 16, 2; 8, 17, 2). He does not seem to wish to give these expressions a different meaning, since all these impositions of hands are accompanied by an epiklesis of the Holy Spirit. For confessors, virgins, widows, and exorcists, he specifies that there is no *cheirotonia* (8, 23–26). The compiler additionally distinguishes between *cheirotonia* and *cheirothesia*, which is simply a gesture of blessing (cf. 8, 16, 3 and 8, 28, 2–3). *Cheirothesia* may be practiced by priests in the baptismal rite, the re-integration of penitents, or the blessing of catechumens (cf. 2, 32, 3; 2, 18, 7; 7, 39, 4).

[64] Cf. *CA* 3, 20, 2; 8, 16, 5; 8, 28, 4; 8, 46, 10–11.

[65] Can. 19 of the Council of Nicaea (325) could be interpreted not as refusing the imposition of hands to all deaconesses in general, but as the simple statement that the deaconesses from the party of Paul of Samosata did not receive the imposition of hands, and "were anyway counted among the laity", and that it was also necessary to re-ordain them, after having re-baptised them, like the other ministers of this dissident group who returned to the Catholic Church. Cf. G. Alberigo, *Les conciles oecuméniques*, vol. 2 *Les décrets*, bk. 1 (Paris, 1994), 54.

[66] *CA*, 8, 20, 1–2; SCh 336; Metzger, 221–23.

widows could not be "ordained" (8, 24–25). The *Constitutiones* insist that the deaconesses should have no liturgical function (3, 9, 1–2), but should devote themselves to their function in the community which was "service to the women" (*CA* 3, 16, 1) and as intermediaries between women and the bishop. It is still stated that they represent the Holy Spirit, but they "do nothing without the deacon" (*CA* 2, 26, 6). They should stand at the women's entrances in the assemblies (2, 57, 10). Their functions are summed up as follows: "The deaconess does not bless, and she does not fulfil any of the things that priests and deacons do, but she looks after the doors and attends the priests during the baptism of women, for the sake of decency" (*CA* 8, 28, 6).

This is echoed by the almost contemporary observation of Epiphanius of Salamis in his *Panarion*, in around 375: "There is certainly in the Church the order of deaconesses, but this does not exist to exercise the functions of a priest, nor are they to have any undertaking committed to them, but for the decency of the feminine sex at the time of baptism."[67] A law of Theodosius of 21 June 390, revoked on 23 August of the same year, fixed the age for admission to the ministry of deaconesses at 60. The Council of Chalcedon (can. 15) reduced the age to 40, forbidding them subsequent marriage.[68]

Even in the fourth century the way of life of deaconesses was very similar to that of nuns. At that time the woman in charge of a monastic community of women was called a deaconess, as is testified by Gregory of Nyssa among others.[69] Ordained abbesses of the monasteries of women, the deaconesses wore the *maforion*, or veil of perfection. Until the sixth century they still attended women in the baptismal pool and for the anointing. Although they did not serve at the altar, they could distribute communion to sick women. When the practice of anointing the whole body at baptism was abandoned, deaconesses were simply consecrated virgins who had taken the vow of chastity. They lived either in monasteries or at home. The condition for admission was virginity or widowhood and their activity consisted of charitable and health-related assistance to women.

At Constantinople the best-known of the fourth-century deaconesses was Olympias, the superior of a monastery of women, who was a protégée of Saint John Chrysostom and had put her property at the service of the Church. She was "ordained" (*cheirotonein*) deaconess with three of her companions by the patriarch. Canon 15 of the Council of Chalcedon (451) seems to confirm the fact that deaconesses really were "ordained"

---

[67] Epiphanius of Salamis, *Panarion haer.* 79, 3, 6, ed. K. Holl, GCS 37 (1933), p. 478.

[68] Cf. Alberigo, *Décrets*, bk. 1, 214.

[69] Gregory of Nyssa, *Life of St. Macrina* 29, 1; SCh 178; Maraval, 236–37.

by the imposition of hands (*cheirotonia*). Their ministry was called *lei-tourgia* and after ordination they were not allowed to marry.

In eighth-century Byzantium, the bishop still imposed his hands on a deaconess, and conferred on her the orarion or stole (both ends of which were worn at the front, one over the other); he gave her the chalice, which she placed on the altar without giving communion to anyone. Deaconesses were ordained in the course of the Eucharistic liturgy, in the sanctuary, like deacons.[70] Despite the similarities between the rites of ordination, deaconesses did not have access to the altar or to any liturgical ministry. These ordinations were intended mainly for the superiors of monasteries of women.

It should be pointed out that in the West there is no trace of any deaconesses for the first five centuries. The *Statuta Ecclesiae antiqua* laid down that the instruction of women catechumens and their preparation for baptism was to be entrusted to the widows and women religious "chosen *ad ministerium baptizandarum mulierum*".[71] Certain councils of the fourth and fifth centuries reject every *ministerium feminae*[72] and forbid any ordination of deaconesses.[73] According to the *Ambrosiaster* (composed at Rome at the end of the fourth century), the female diaconate was an adjunct of Montanist ("Cataphrygian") heretics.[74] In the sixth century women admitted into the group of widows were sometimes referred to as deaconesses. To prevent any confusion the Council of Epaone forbade "the consecrations of widows who call themselves deaconesses".[75] The Second Council of Orleans (533) decided to exclude from communion women who had "received the blessing for the diaconate despite the canons forbidding this and who had remarried".[76] Abbesses, or the wives of deacons, were also called *diaconissae*, by analogy with *presbyterissae* or even *episcopissae*.[77]

---

[70] Byzantine Ritual of ordination of deaconesses: *Euchologe du manuscrit grec Barberini 336*, in Vatican Library, ff. 169R–17/v. Quoted by J.-M. Aubert, *Des femmes diacres*, Le Point Théologique 47 (Paris, 1987), 118–19.

[71] Cf. can. 100 (Munier, 99). In addition, it is expressly forbidden to women, "even well-instructed and holy" ones, to teach men and to baptize (cf. can. 37, 41; Munier, 86).

[72] Council of Nîmes (394–396), can. 2. Cf. J. Gaudemet, *Conciles gaulois du IVe siècle*, SCh 241 (Paris, 1977), 127–29.

[73] First Council of Orange (441), can. 26.

[74] Cf. ed. H. I. Vogels, CSEL 81/3 (Vienna, 1969), 268.

[75] Council of Epaone (517), can. 21 (C. de Clercq, *Concilia Galliae 511–695*, 250: 148A [1963], 29). Blessings of women as deaconesses had become widespread because the ritual did not provide a blessing for widows, as was noted in the Second Council of Tours (567), can. 21 (ibid., 187).

[76] Ibid., 101.

[77] Cf. Second Council of Tours, can. 20 (ibid., 184).

The present historical overview shows that a ministry of deaconesses did indeed exist, and that this developed unevenly in the different parts of the Church. It seems clear that this ministry was not perceived as simply the feminine equivalent of the masculine diaconate. At the very least it was an ecclesial function, exercised by women, sometimes mentioned together with that of sub-deacon in the lists of Church ministries.[78] Was this ministry conferred by an imposition of hands comparable to that by which the episcopate, the priesthood and the masculine diaconate were conferred? The text of the *Constitutiones Apostolorum* would seem to suggest this, but it is practically the only witness to this, and its proper interpretation is the subject of much debate.[79] Should the imposition of hands on deaconesses be considered the same as that on deacons, or is it rather on the same level as the imposition of hands on sub-deacons and lectors? It is difficult to tackle the question on the basis of historical data alone. In the following chapters some elements will be clarified, and some questions will remain open. In particular, one chapter will be devoted to examining more closely how the Church through her theology and Magisterium has become more conscious of the sacramental reality of Holy Orders and its three grades. But first it is appropriate to examine the causes which led to the disappearance of the permanent diaconate in the life of the Church.

---

[78] Many commentators have followed the model of *Ambrosiaster* in his Commentary on 1 Tim 3:11 (CSEL 81, 3; G. L. Muller, ed., *Der Empfänger des Weihesakraments: Quellen zur Lehre und Praxis der Kirche, nur Männern das Weihesakrament zu spenden* (Würzburg, 1999), 89): "But the Cataphrygians, seizing this opportunity of falling into error, uphold in their foolish rashness, under the pretext that Paul addressed women after deacons, that it is also necessary to ordain deaconesses. They know however that the Apostles chose seven deacons (cf. Acts 6:1–6); is it to be supposed that no woman was found suitable at that point, when we read that there were holy women grouped around the eleven Apostles (cf. Acts 1:14)? ... And Paul orders women to keep silence in church (cf. 1 Cor 14:34–35)." See also John Chrysostom, *In 1 Tim hom.* 11; PG 62, 555; Epiphanius, *Haer.* 79, 3 (Müller, *Quellen*, 88); Council of Orange (Müller, *Quellen*, 98); Council of Dovin (Armenia, 527): "Feminis non licet ministeria diaconissae praestare nisi ministerium baptismi" (Müller, *Quellen*, 105); Isidore of Seville, *De Eccl. Off.* 2, 18, 11 (Müller, *Quellen*, 109); *Decretum Gratiani*, can. 15 (Müller, *Quellen*, 115); Magister Ruftnus, *Summa Decretorum*, can. 27, q. 1 (Müller, *Quellen*, 320); Robert of Yorkshire, *Liber poenitentialis*, q. 6, 42 (Müller, *Quellen*, 322); Thomas Aquinas, *In 1 Tim* 3, 11 (Müller, *Quellen*, 333); etc.

[79] Cf. Vanzan, "Le diaconat permanent féminin: Ombres et lumières", in *Documentation Catholique* 2203 (1999): 440–46. The author refers to the discussions which have taken place between R. Gryson, A. G. Martimort, C. Vagaggini and C. Marucci. Cf. L. Scheffczyk, ed., *Diakonat und Diakonissen* (St. Ottilien, 2002), especially M. Hauke, "Die Geschichte der Diakonissen: Nachwort und Literaturnachtrag zur Neuauflage des Standardwerkes von Martimort über die Diakonissen", 321–76.

CHAPTER III

THE DISAPPEARANCE OF THE PERMANENT DIACONATE

I. *The Changes in the Diaconal Ministry*

At Rome, from the third century onwards, each deacon was at the head of one of the seven pastoral regions, while the priests had a smaller *titulus* (the future parish). Deacons were charged with administering funds and organising charitable works. The Council of Neo-Caesarea, at the beginning of the fourth century, had asked that each Church, however big it was, should have no more than seven deacons, in memory of Acts 6:1–6.[80] This provision, still remembered by Isidore of Seville[81] but infrequently observed, particularly in the East,[82] heightened the prestige of the diaconal order and encouraged deacons still more to leave their original functions to other members of the clergy. They were to define themselves more and more explicitly by reference to their liturgical attributes, and come into conflict with the priests.

The functions of deacons were progressively being taken over by other ministers. As early as the *Traditio Apostolica* (13), "sub-deacons" were appointed "to follow the deacon". Those who "followed the deacon" soon became his "acolytes".[83] The acolytes had the job of taking the *fermentum*, the portion of the bishop's Eucharist, to the priests of the *tituli* in the town. It was also the acolytes who took it to those who were absent. The "door-keepers" also fulfilled a function which had originally been the task of the deacons. It may be considered that the minor ministries resulted from a sharing-out of diaconal functions.

The state of sub-deacon approached that of deacon more closely. Towards 400, in the East, the Council of Laodicea tried to prevent sub-deacons from encroaching on the liturgical functions of deacons, stating that they should content themselves with looking after the doors.[84] Sub-deacons adopted the rule of life of deacons. The African councils of the last part of the fourth century demanded continence on the part of clergy "who

---

[80] Council of Neo-Caesarea (314 or 319), can. 15, in Mansi, *Sacrorum conciliorum nova et amplissima collectio*, vol. 2, new ed. (Paris-Leipzig, 1901), 539.

[81] Isidore of Seville, *De Eccl. Off.* 2, 8.

[82] There were one hundred deacons at Constantinople in the time of Justinian. Cf. Justinian, *Novellae* 3, 1 (*Corpus juris civilis*, ed. Kriegel, vol. 3 [Leipzig, 1887], 20).

[83] Cf. *CA* 2, 28, 6.

[84] Cf. cann. 21, 22, 43, in P.-P. Joannou, *Discipline générale antique IIe–IXe siècle*, 1/2 (Rome, 1962), 139–48.

serve at the altar".[85] The *Canones in causa Apiarii* (419–425) extended this requirement to sub-deacons, "who touch the sacred mysteries".[86] Leo the Great (440–461) confirmed this requirement for sub-deacons.[87] Leo made a ready distinction between *sacerdotes* (the bishop and priests), *levitae* (the deacons and sub-deacons), and *clerici* (the other ministers).[88]

Cyprian had already found it necessary to remind people that deacons had been instituted by the Apostles and not by the Lord himself.[89] In certain places deacons must have been tempted to take the place of priests. The Council of Arles (314) reminded them that they could not offer the Eucharist (can. 15) and that they should show due honour to priests (can. 18). Nicaea forbade them to give communion to priests, or to receive it before the bishops: they were to receive communion from the bishop or from a priest, and after them. They were not to sit among the priests. "Let the deacons remain within the limits of their competence, knowing that they are the servants of the bishop and are inferior to priests in rank" (can. 19).[90]

Towards 378 the anonymous *Ambrosiaster*, composed at Rome, witnessed to the persistent tension between the presbyterate and the diaconate.[91] Jerome went further, exclaiming that deacons were not superior to priests![92] Priests came to exercise more and more of the functions reserved to deacons, at the same time as they received progressively more autonomy in their responsibilities within the urban *tituli* and the rural parishes. Deacons, who had wanted to exercise the liturgical and teaching functions reserved to priests, now suffered from a backlash against such an attitude: they became subordinate to the priests, their direct link with the bishop faded away, and they ended up having no specific function. The clergy of the Church in the Empire progressively forgot about their function of service and maintained the concept of the sacredness of the priesthood, towards which all the other degrees of the clerical career tended. The deacons were the first to suffer the consequences of this.

Towards the end of the fifth century the thinking of Pseudo-Dionysius began to have a lasting influence both in the East and in the West. In

---

[85] Council of Carthage sub Genethlio (390), can. 2, in C. Munier, *Concilia Africae*, CCSL 259 (Turnhout, 1974), 13.

[86] Cf. can. 25 (ibid., 108–9).

[87] Leo the Great, *Ep.* 14, 4 to Anastasius of Thessalonica; PL 54, 672–73.

[88] Ibid.

[89] Cf. chapter II supra, note 40.

[90] Cf. Alberigo, *Décrets*, 54.

[91] The short treatise *De jactantia Romanorum diaconum* (CSEL 50, 193–98) reproves deacons for wanting to work their way up into the ranks of the priests, for refusing tasks of service, and for concerning themselves with liturgical singing alone.

[92] Jerome, *Letter 146 to Evangelus*; PL 22, 1192–95.

Dionysius' hierarchically structured view of heaven and the Church, every being received its specific determination and function from the order to which it belonged. The ecclesiastical hierarchy was composed of two groups of three. The first group contained the order of the hierarchs or bishops, the order of priests, and the order of "liturges" or ministers. This latter order included the ecclesiastical orders from deacon to door-keeper. The diaconate no longer had any specific mark to distinguish it from the other orders beneath the priests.[93]

Still towards the end of the fifth century, the career path of the clergy was defined in function of their liturgical attributes as well as the demand of continence for those who served in the sanctuary, or related positions. Leo the Great considered that the ideal path, before proceeding to the priesthood and the episcopate, was to go through all the degrees of the clergy with an appropriate interval between each.[94] The number and names of the different degrees (*gradus*) of the clergy fluctuated. There were eight at Rome in the time of Pope Cornelius.[95] In the fifth century, the door-keeper and the exorcist were no longer included among them.[96] The author of *De septem ordinibus* at the beginning of the fifth century speaks of grave-diggers, door-keepers, lectors, sub-deacons, deacons, priests and bishops.[97] The *Statuta Ecclesiae antiqua*, also composed in the south of Gaul towards 480, re-proposed a list of eight *officiales ecclesiae* who received an *ordinatio*: bishop, priest and deacon received an imposition of hands, [while] the candidates for orders inferior to these (sub-deacon, acolyte, exorcist, lector and door-keeper) were installed by a rite of handing over of the instruments of their office.[98] Thus the functions which had in the past been autonomous and practical, became stages in the career path towards the priesthood. The sacramentary of Verona (around 560–580) contained a prayer of "consecration" for the bishop and the priest, and a prayer of "blessing" for the deacon. It said that the deacon was essentially ordained in view of liturgical ministry; he should be an example of chastity.[99]

---

[93] Pseudo-Dionysius, *Ecclesiastical Hierarchy* 5, 7; 5, 6; PG 3, 506–8.

[94] Leo the Great, *Ep*. 6, 6 to Anastasius of Thessalonica; PL 54, 620. Leo himself was a deacon when he was elected to the episcopate. See also L. Duchesne, *Liber Pontificalis*, vol. 1 (Paris: de Boccard, 1981), 238–39.

[95] Cf. Eusebius of Caesarea, *Hist. Eccl.* 6, 43.

[96] Cf. *The Decretals of Siricius*, PL 13, 1142–43; *The Decretals of Innocent I*, PL 20, 604–5.

[97] Pseudo-Jerome, *Ep. XII de septem ordinibus ecclesiae*, PL 30, 150–62.

[98] Cf. C. Munier, *Les Statuta Ecclesiae antiqua*, editions-études critiques (Paris, 1960), 95–99. The author adds the psalmist to this list. Isidore of Seville, *Etymologies* 7, 12 (PL 82, 290) spoke of nine degrees, including the psalmist. In his terminology, all nine *ordines* were also called *sacramenta*; cf. *De Eccl. Off.* 2, 21.

[99] Cf. L. C. Mohlberg, *Sacramentarium Veronense*, RED.F 1 (Rome, 1956), 120–21.

Progress through the clerical career path was still often made *per saltum*. At Rome in the ninth century the sub-diaconate was the only obligatory degree before major orders. All the popes between 687 and 891 had been sub-deacons. Five had then become deacons before being raised to the episcopate, and nine passed directly from the sub-diaconate to the priesthood and then to the episcopate.

One of the former competencies of deacons, the management of the funds of the community, was also lost to them. The Council of Chalcedon (451) sanctioned this development, laying down that each bishop should entrust this responsibility to an officer chosen from "among his own clergy" (can. 26), not necessarily from among the deacons. Aid to the poor was often looked after by monasteries. Under Gregory the Great, the huge "Patrimony of Saint Peter" was managed by *defensores* or *notarii*, who were added to the clergy, in other words at least given the tonsure.

In the East, the Byzantine Council in Trullo in 692 analysed the contents of Acts 6:1–6. The Seven, it observed, were neither deacons nor priests nor bishops. They were people who were "charged with administering the common property of the community of that time. . . . They are an example of charity" (can. 7).[100] At the end of the ninth century in the East, the deacons still formed a permanent order of clergy, but for liturgical needs alone. The Byzantine rite had two preparatory stages for the sacred ministry: those of lector (or cantor) and sub-deacon, conferred by *cheirothesia*, and obligatory before the diaconate.[101] But the sub-diaconate was often conferred at the same time as the lectorate, or just before the diaconate. According to the ritual of the *Constitutiones Apostolorum*, which was still applied in the East, admission to the minor orders of sub-diaconate and lectorate was accomplished by the imposition of hands and the handing over of the instruments of office. In the West too, the activity of deacons was reduced, in practice, to their liturgical functions.[102] When rural parishes were created the Coun-

---

[100] P.-Joannou, *Discipline générale antique IIe–IXe siècle*, vol. 1, pt. 1, *Les canons des conciles oecuméniques* (Rome, 1962), 132–34.

[101] Cf. F. Mercenier and F. Paris, *La prière des Eglises de rite byzantin*, 2 vols. (Prieuré d'Ainay sur Meuse, 1937). From the eighth century onwards, usage became fixed. The term *cheirotonia* was now reserved to the ordinations of bishops, priests and deacons, while *cheirothesia* was the term used for orders below those. Thus can. 15 of the Second Council of Nicaea (ed. G. Alberigo, vol. 2/1, 149). Cf. C. Vogel, "Chirotonie et chirothésie", in *Irénikon* 37 (1972): 7–21; 207–38.

[102] Pseudo-Jerome, *De septem ordinibus*, says that deacons "do not leave the temple of the Lord. . . . They are the altar of Christ. . . . Without the deacon, the priest has no name nor origin nor function" (PL 30, 153).

cils insisted that they should be endowed with a priest. It did not occur to them to call for deacons.[103]

From the tenth century onwards, at least in the Holy Roman Empire, the rule was ordination *per gradum*. The reference document was the *Pontifical Romano-Germanique*,[104] composed at Mainz in around 950. It was in direct continuity with the tradition of the *Ordines Romani* of the preceding centuries,[105] to which it added plentiful elements from the Germanic ritual. The ordination of deacons included the handing over of the book of the Gospels, signifying their function of proclaiming the Gospel in the liturgy. The deacon here appears closer to the sub-deacon than to the priest. The priest was the man of the Eucharist; the deacon attended him at the altar. This ritual was introduced at Rome through the Germanic emperors' zeal for reform at the end of the tenth century. Rome fell into line with the *per gradum* career path for clergy which was the rule in the Empire. From that time on the history of the ordination rites attests perfect continuity.[106] The First Lateran Council (1123) can. 7, and the Second Lateran Council (1139) can. 6, deprived of their office any clergy who contracted marriage, from the sub-diaconate inclusive. Can. 7 of the Second Lateran Council declared that such a marriage would be null and void.[107] From that time on the Latin Church normally ordained only celibate men.

The patristic and liturgical texts of the first millennium all mentioned the ordination of bishops, priests and deacons, but they did not yet explicitly raise the question of the sacramentality of each of these ordinations.

The history of the ministries shows that the priesthood has had a tendency to take over the functions of the lesser orders. When the progression through the various orders became stabilised, each grade possessed the competencies of the previous grade, plus some additional ones—what a deacon can do, a priest can also do. The bishop, being at the summit of

---

[103] Cf. Council of Aix-la-Chapelle (817), can. 11 (C.J. Hefele and H. Leclercq, *Histoire des conciles*, vol. 4 [Paris, 1910], 27).

[104] C. Vogel, *Le Pontifical romano-germanique du dixième siècle*, 3 vols., Studi e testi 226, 227, 269 (Vatican, 1963–1972).

[105] See M. Andrieu, *Les Ordines Romani du haut moyen âge*, SSL 24 (Louvain, 1951).

[106] The various Roman Pontificals of the twelfth century had as their common foundation the tenth-century *Pontifical Romano-Germanique*. Cf. M. Andrieu, *Le Pontifical romain au moyen âge*, vol. 1 *Le Pontifical du XIIe siècle*, Studi e testi 86 (Vatican, 1938). This was widely used in the Latin Church and was brought up to date by Innocent III. See M. Andrieu, ibid., vol. 2, *Le Pontifical de la Curie romaine du XIIIe siècle*, Studi e testi 87 (Vatican, 1940). This in its turn was included in the Pontifical composed by Guillaume Durand, bishop of Mende at the end of the thirteenth century. Cf. M. Andrieu, ibid., vol. 3, *Le Pontifical de Guillaume Durand*, Studi e testi 88 (Vatican, 1940). It was to serve as a model for the edition printed by Burchard of Strasbourg in 1485.

[107] Cf. Alberigo, *Décrets*, bk. 1, 419 and 435.

the hierarchy, can exercise all the ecclesiastical functions. The fact that the different competencies fitted together in this way and that lesser functions were taken over by higher ones; the fragmentation of the original role of deacons into many different functions to be performed by subordinate clergy; and the progression to the higher functions *per gradum*, all go to explain how the diaconate as a permanent ministry lost its reason for existing. All that was left were liturgical tasks exercised for a given time by candidates for the priesthood.

II. *Towards the Disappearance of Deaconesses*

After the tenth century deaconesses were only named in connection with charitable institutions. A Jacobite author of that time notes: "In ancient times, deaconesses were ordained. Their function was to look after women so that they should not have to uncover themselves before the bishop. But when religion spread more widely and it was decided to administer baptism to infants, this function was abolished." [108] We find the same statement in the Pontifical of Patriarch Michael of Antioch (1166–1199).[109] When commenting on can. 15 of the Council of Chalcedon, Theodore Balsamon, at the end of the twelfth century, observed that "the topic of this canon has altogether fallen into disuse. For today deaconesses are no longer ordained, although the name of deaconesses is wrongly given to those who belong to communities of ascetics." [110] Deaconesses had become nuns. They lived in monasteries which no longer practised works of *diakonia* except in the field of education, medical care, or parish service.

The presence of deaconesses is still attested in Rome at the end of the eighth century. While the Roman rituals had previously not mentioned deaconesses, the sacramentary *Hadrianum*, sent by the pope to Charlemagne and spread by him throughout the Frankish world, includes an *Oratio ad diaconam faciendam*. It was in fact a blessing, placed as an appendix among other rites of first institution. The Carolingian texts often combined deaconesses and abbesses. The Council of Paris of 829 contained a general prohibition on women performing any liturgical

---

[108] Cf. G. Khouri-Sarkis, "Le livre du guide de Yahya ibn Jarîr", *Orient syrien* 12 (1967): 303–18.

[109] "Long ago the *cheirotonia* or ordination was also done for deaconesses: and for that reason the rite concerning them was given in ancient manuscripts. In those times deaconesses were needed mainly for the baptism of women" (quoted by Martimort, *Les diaconesses*, 167).

[110] *Scholia in concilium Chalcedonense*; PG 137, 441 (quoted by Martimort, *Les diaconesses*, 171).

function.[111] The Decretals of Pseudo-Isidore contain no mention of deaconesses; and neither does a Bavarian Pontifical from the first half of the ninth century.[112] A century later, in the Pontifical Romano-Germanique of Mainz, the prayer *Ad diaconam faciendam* is to be found after the *ordinatio abbatissae*, between the *consecratio virginum* and the *consecratio viduarum*. Once again, this was merely a blessing accompanied by the handing over of the stole and veil by the bishop, as well as the nuptial ring and the crown. Like widows, the deaconess promised continence. This is the last mention of "deaconesses" found in the Latin rituals. In fact the Pontifical of Guillaume Durand at the end of the thirteenth century speaks of deaconesses only with reference to the past.[113]

In the Middle Ages, the nursing and teaching religious orders of nuns fulfilled in practise the functions of *diakonia* without, however, being ordained for this ministry. The title, with no corresponding ministry, was given to women who were instituted as widows or abbesses. Right up until the thirteenth century, abbesses were sometimes called deaconesses.

CHAPTER IV

THE SACRAMENTALITY OF THE DIACONATE FROM THE TWELFTH TO THE TWENTIETH CENTURIES

The sacramentally of the diaconate is a question which remains *implicit* in biblical, patristic and liturgical texts which have just been discussed. We now need to see how the Church first became *explicitly* conscious of it in a period in which, apart from certain rare exceptions, the diaconate was simply a stage on the way to the priesthood.

I. *In the First Scholastic Teaching*

Although "sacramentality" can have a broad, generic meaning, in the strict sense it refers to the seven sacraments (outward and effective signs of grace), among which is the sacrament of "Holy Orders". Within this

---

[111] Cap. 45 (ed. A. Werminghoff, *Concilia aevi Karolini*, 1:639).

[112] Cf. F. Unterkircher, *Das Kollectar-Pontifikale des Bischofs Baturich von Regensburg (817–848)*, Spicilegium Friburgense 8 (Freiburg, 1962).

[113] Between *De ordinatione abbatissae* and *De benedictione et consecratione virginum*, the passage *De ordinatione diaconissae* occupies a few lines phrased as follows: "Diaconissa olim, non tamen ante annum quadragesimum, ordinabatur hoc modo." See Andrieu, *Pontifical de Guillaume Durand*, vol. 3 (1, 21–23), 411.

sacrament were different "orders" or "grades", between seven and nine in number. The diaconate and the priesthood were always listed among the *ordines sacri* of the sacrament, and the sub-diaconate began to be included among them because of its requirement of celibacy; the episcopate was excluded from them in most cases.[114]

According to Peter Lombard (†1160),[115] the diaconate was an *ordo* or *gradus officiorum* (the sixth). Although he held that all the *ordines* were *spirituales et sacri*, he underlined the excellence of the diaconate and the priesthood, the only ones which existed in the primitive Church by the will of the Apostles, while the others had been instituted by the Church in the course of time. He did not consider the episcopate to share in this excellence, saying that it did not belong to the sacramental *ordines* but rather to the domain of dignities and offices.[116]

II. *From St. Thomas Aquinas (†1273) to Trent (1563)*

1. Affirmation of Sacramentality

Saint Thomas' teaching on the diaconate[117] included the fact that it was a sacrament insofar as it belonged to Holy Orders, one of the seven sacraments of the new law. He considered that each of the different orders constituted in some way a sacramental reality; however, only three (priest, deacon and sub-deacon) could strictly be said to be *ordines sacri* by reason of their special relation to the Eucharist.[118] But it should not be concluded that their sacramentality meant that the priesthood and the diaconate were different sacraments; the distinction between the orders did not indicate that each was a universal or integral whole, but indicated a potestative wholeness.[119]

The way that the unity and oneness of the sacrament of Holy Orders was bound together in its different grades had to do with their reference

---

[114] For these variations, see L. Ott, *Das Weihesakrament*, HbDG 4/5 (Freiburg am Breisgau, 1964).

[115] Peter Lombard introduced in *IV Sent.*, d. 24 the treatise *De ordinibus ecclesiasticis* which, with the exception of certain lines, was copied from Hugh of St. Victor (†1141), Yves of Chartres (†1040–1115) and the *Decretum Gratiani*; all these authors depend in their turn on *De septem ordinibus ecclesiae* (fifth to seventh centuries), one of the first treatises of the Western Church (cf. St. Isidore of Seville) devoted to an exposition of the competencies of the different grades of the hierarchy.

[116] *IV Sent.*, d. 24, c. 14.

[117] Cf. *In IV Sent.*, d. 24–25; *Suppl.*, qq. 34–40; *SCG* 4, 74–77, *De art. fidei et Eccl. sacramentis.*

[118] *In IV Sent.*, d. 24, q. 2, a. 1 ad 3.

[119] Ibid., d. 24, q. 2, a. 1, sol. 1.

to the Eucharist, *Sacramentum sacramentorum*.[120] Because of that, the different orders needed a sacramental consecration depending on their type of power with respect to the Eucharist. Through ordination priests received the power to consecrate, while deacons received the power to serve the priests in the administration of the sacraments.[121]

The relationship of each order to the Eucharist became the deciding factor in avoiding the idea that each order gave the power to administer a specific sacrament. The same criterion also served to exclude the orders of psalmist and cantor from the sacramental orders. But this criterion was also used to exclude the episcopate from sacramentality.[122] In spite of everything, although Saint Thomas refuses to recognise in the episcopate any sort of power superior to that of the priest in relation to the *verum corpus Christi*, he considers the episcopate to be also an *ordo* in a certain way, by reason of the powers which the bishop holds over the *corpus mysticum*.[123]

Because the diaconate is a sacrament, it is an *ordo* which imprints a character on the soul. Saint Thomas applies this doctrine to baptism, confirmation and Holy Orders. His thinking on this developed with time. Starting from the priesthood of Christ he defined Holy Orders alone as imprinting a character (*In IV Sent.*), but finally defined the complete doctrine of character (*STh*).[124]

On the subject of the diaconate, he explained all its *potestates*, in relation to the *dispensatio* of the sacraments, as something that seemed to belong rather within the domain of what was "licit" and not within the domain of a new radical enablement with regard to the "validity" of the functions in question.[125] In his turn, in *Summa theologiae*, III, q. 67, a. 1, he asks whether evangelizing and baptizing are part of the deacon's office, and he answers that no direct administration of the sacraments belongs to the diaconate *quasi ex proprio officio*, any more than any task in relation with *docere*, but only with *cathechizare*.[126]

2. Sacramentality Called into Question

Durandus of Saint-Pourçain (†1334) represented a doctrinal line which was to reappear intermittently up until the present day. According to this

---

[120] Ibid., d. 24, q. 2, a. 1, sol. 2.
[121] Ibid.
[122] Ibid., d. 24, q. 3, a. 2, sol. 2.
[123] Ibid., d. 24, q. 3, a. 2, sol. 2.
[124] Cf. *In IV Sent.*, d. 7, q. 2 ad 1; *STh* III, q. 63, a. 3.
[125] *In IV Sent.*, d. 24, q. 1, a. 2, sol. 2.
[126] *STh* III, q. 67, a. 1.

line, only ordination to the priesthood is a "sacrament"; the other orders, including the diaconate, were only "sacramentals".[127] The reasons for his position were as follows:

a. with regard to the Eucharist, the distinction between the power of consecrating, which belonged exclusively to the order of the priesthood (which should be considered a sacrament) and the preparatory actions, which belonged to the other orders (merely considered as sacramentals);

b. in the same way as with baptism, there was a "potestas ad suscipiendum sacramenta"; but it was only the priesthood that was granted a "postestas ordinis ad conficiendum vel conferendum ea", which was not granted to any of the orders inferior to the priesthood, not even to the diaconate;

c. ordination to the priesthood grants a power *ad posse* and not *ad licere*, so that the ordained priest can really do something which he could not do before his ordination. The diaconate, on the other hand, grants the capacity to do *licite* something that he could in fact do before, although illicitly, and this is why the diaconate can be considered as an institution or ecclesial deputation to exercise certain functions;

d. it is also demanded by the unity of the sacrament of Orders and the evaluation of the priesthood as the fullness of this sacrament, since otherwise it would be hard to preserve the meaning of what Saint Thomas said on the unity and oneness of the sacrament of Holy Orders;[128]

e. the distinction between *sacramentum* and *sacramentalia* did not, however, prevent Durandus from saying that each of the orders imprints a "character". He distinguished in his turn between a *deputatio* which had its origin in God himself, and made the order in question a *sacramentum*, and an ecclesiastical *deputatio* instituted by the Church, which only made the orders in question (all the other orders) *sacramentalia*. In this sense it could be said that the diaconate imprints a character; the doubt or debate concerned exactly when the character was imprinted, since some maintained that it would come "in traditione libri evangeliorum" (an opinion which Durandus rejected) while others held that it came "in impositione manuum" (an opinion which he appeared to adopt).[129]

---

[127] As for the episcopate, he tended to state that it was "ordo et sacramentum, non quidem praecise distinctum a sacerdotio simplici, sed est unum sacramentum cum ipso, sicut perfectum et imperfectum". Durandus of Saint-Pourçain, *Super Sententias Comm. libri quatuor* (Parisii, 1550), 4, d. 24, q. 6.

[128] Ibid., q. 2 for what is said under a, b, c and d.

[129] Ibid., q. 3.

3. The Teaching of Trent (1563)

The Council of Trent chose to make a dogmatic definition of Holy Orders as a sacrament; the direction of its doctrinal statements leaves no doubt on the subject. However, it is not clear to what extent the sacramentality of the diaconate should be considered as being included in this definition. The question has remained a controversial one to the present day, although very few people indeed now debate the subject. This makes it necessary to interpret the statements of the Council of Trent.

As against the denials of the Reformers, Trent declared the existence of a *hierarchia in Ecclesia ordinatione divina* (which led to a rejection of the statement "omnes christianos promiscue Novi Testamenti sacerdotes esse") and also a *hierarchia ecclesiastica* (which led to the distinction between the different grades within the sacrament of Holy Orders).[130]

The references by Trent to the diaconate (which it also refers to explicitly) need to be set within the general theology of the sacrament of Holy Orders. However, it is not entirely certain that the dogmatic declarations of Trent on the sacramentality and the sacramental character of the priesthood, to which Trent refers explicitly, include an intention on the part of the Council to define the sacramentality of the diaconate as well.

According to Trent deacons are mentioned directly in the New Testament, although it is not stated that they were instituted directly by Christ the Saviour. In accordance with the way the other orders are envisaged, the diaconate is also conceived of as a help to exercising "dignius et maiore cum veneratione ministerium tam Sancti sacerdotii" and to serve the priesthood "ex officio" (it is not said to be "ad ministerium episcopi"). Furthermore, the diaconate appears to be a stage on the way to the priesthood—there is no explicit mention of a permanent diaconate.[131]

When Trent defined dogmatically that *ordo* or *sacra ordinatio* was "vere sacramentum",[132] there was no explicit mention of the diaconate, which was included among the *ordines ministrorum*.[133] Thus, if the dogmatic statement of sacramentality is to be applied to the diaconate, it should perhaps be applied equally to the other *ordines ministrorum*, which seems excessive and unjustified.

Something similar can be said on the subject of the doctrine of "sacramental character".[134] In view of the expressions used by the Council, there can be no doubt that Trent referred explicitly and directly to the

---

[130] Cf. DS 1767, 1776.
[131] Cf. DS 1765, 1772.
[132] Cf. DS 1766, 1773.
[133] Cf. DS 1765.
[134] Cf. DS 1767, 1774.

"priests of the New Testament", to distinguish them clearly from the "laypeople". There is no mention made of "deacons", either direct or indirect; therefore it would be difficult to see in the text of Trent any intention to establish the dogma of character for the diaconate.

Can. 6 merits particular attention ("si quis dixerit in Ecclesia catholica non esse hierarchiam, divina ordinatione institutam, quae constat ex episcopis, presbyteris et ministris, a.s." [135]) because of different interpretations of the word *ministris*: deacons, or deacons and other ministers, or all the other orders? Right up until the day before its approval (14 July 1563), the text of can. 6 said "et aliis ministris". That day, in view of petitions made by a Spanish group, the expression *aliis ministris* was altered to exclude the word *aliis*. But the reasons and scope of this change are not very clear.[136]

How should the term *ministris*, and their inclusion in the *hierarchia*, be interpreted? The exclusion of the word *aliis* means, according to some, that the dividing line within the ecclesiastical hierarchy should be drawn between *sacerdotes* (bishops and priests) on the one hand, and *ministri* on the other; the suppression of the word *aliis* was intended to stress once again that the bishops and priests are not "nudi ministri" but "sacerdotes Novi Testamenti". The history of the text in question, in the light of its previous formulations, would seem to suggest a broad understanding of *ministri*, to include "diaconos caeterosque ministros", corresponding to a triple division of the hierarchy ("praecipue episcopi, deinde praesbyteri, diaconi et alii ministri"). But it must not be forgotten that according to other authors the suppression of the term *aliis* meant that the subdiaconate and other minor orders were excluded from the hierarchy "divina ordinatione instituta"—an expression whose interpretation is in its turn polemical.[137]

To sum up, whether one interprets it exclusively or inclusively, it cannot be doubted that deacons are included in the term *ministri*. But the dogmatic consequences concerning their sacramentality and their inclusion in the hierarchy will differ, depending on whether the word *ministri* refers to deacons alone, or includes the other orders too.

III. *Theological Nuances after Trent*

After the Council of Trent, in the theology of the sixteenth and seventeenth centuries, a majority of opinions maintained the sacramentality

---

[135] Cf. DS 1776.

[136] Cf. Council of Trent, 3, 682f., 686, 690; 7/2, 603, 643.

[137] Cf. K. J. Becker, *Wesen und Vollmachten des Priestertums nach dem Lehramt*, QD 47 (Freiburg, 1970), 19–156; J. Freitag, *Sacramentum ordinis aus dem Konzil von Trient: Ausgeblendeter Dissens und erreichter Konsens* (Innsbruck, 1991), 218ff.

of the diaconate, with only a minority questioning or denying it. However, the form in which this sacramentality was defended had many differing nuances, and it was generally considered to be a point which had not been dogmatically defined by Trent, and which was reasserted doctrinally in the *Roman Catechism* where it describes the functions of deacons.[138]

Thus for example, F. de Vitoria (†1546) considers as *probabilissima* the opinion that "solum sacramentum est sacerdotium" and that all the other orders are sacramentals. D. de Soto (†1560), for his part, although in favour of the sacramentality of both the diaconate and the subdiaconate, considered that anyone who followed Durandus was not to be reprehended.[139]

Robert Bellarmine (†1621) well described the *status quaestionis* at that point. He established the sacramentality of Holy Orders ("vere ac proprie sacramentum novae legis") as a fundamental principle admitted by all Catholic theologians and denied by (Protestant) heretics. But as regarded the sacramentality of the individual orders he felt it necessary to make a distinction, because although there was unanimous agreement on the sacramentality of the priesthood, this was not the case for the other orders.[140]

Bellarmine declared himself clearly in favour of the sacramentality of the episcopate ("ordinatio episcopalis sacramentum est vere ac proprie dictum"), as against the scholastics of old who denied it; and he considered this an *assertio certissima*, based on Scripture and Tradition. Moreover, he spoke of an episcopal character which was distinct from and superior to the character of the presbyterate.

As regards the doctrine of the sacramentality of the diaconate, Bellarmine adopted it, considering it very probable; however, he did not take it as a certainty *ex fide*, since it could not be deduced from the evidence of Scripture nor Tradition nor any explicit pronouncement on the part of the Church.[141]

Bellarmine was also in favour of the sacramentality of the subdiaconate, basing his opinion on the doctrine of character, on celibacy, and on the common opinion of theologians, although he recognised that this doctrine was not as certain as that of the diaconate.[142] Still less certain, in his view, was the sacramentality of the other minor orders.

---

[138] Cf. *Catechismus Romanus*, p. 2, can. 7, q. 20.

[139] Cf. F. de Vitoria, *Summa sacramentorum*, no. 226 (Venice, 1579), f. 136v; D. de Soto, *In Sent.* 4, d. 24, q. 1, a. 4, concl. 5 (633ab).

[140] Cf. R. Bellarminus, *Controversiarum de sacramento ordinis liber unicus*, in *Opera omnia*, vol. 5 (Paris, 1873), 26.

[141] Ibid., 27–28.

[142] Ibid., 30.

IV. *The Sacramentality of the Diaconate in Vatican II*

Concerning deacons or the diaconate in the texts of Vatican II (*SC* 86; *LG* 20, 28, 29, 41; *OE* 17; *CD* 15; *DV* 25; *AG* 15, 16) the sacramentality of both modes (permanent and transitory) was taken for granted. Sometimes it was stated simply in passing, or indirectly, or faintly. Taken all together, the texts of Vatican II repeated what had been the majority opinion in theology up to that time, but went no further. Neither did the Council clarify a number of uncertainties which were expressed in the course of the debates.

1. In the Conciliar Debates

The sacramentality of the diaconate was a theme tackled in several interventions in the second period of the Council (1963). The result was a majority in favour, particularly among those who upheld the institution of the permanent diaconate; among who opposed such an institution, there was no majority in favour of the sacramentality of the diaconate.[143]

In the *relatio* of the doctrinal Commission, some explanatory notes on the text are presented which are of interest in interpreting it. The notes give the exegetical reason for not directly mentioning Acts 6:1–6,[144] and also explain the moderate way in which the sacramentality of the diaconate is mentioned, as caused by unwillingness to give the impression of condemning those who questioned it.[145] The conciliar debate did not in fact reach unanimity on the sacramental nature of the diaconate.

Also of interest for interpretation of the texts are the nuances introduced into the summary of the discussion. Among the arguments in favour of restoration, mention was first made of the sacramental nature of the diaconate, of which the Church ought not to be deprived. Among the arguments against restoration the main one was undoubtedly that of cel-

---

[143] Cf., in favor: *Acta Synodalia Sacrosancti Concilii Oecumenici Vaticani II* (*AS*) 2/2, 227f., 314f., 317f., 359, 431, 580; raising doubts about or calling into question the sacramentality of the diaconate: *AS* 2/2, 378, 406, 447f.

[144] "Quod attinet ad Act. 6, 1–6, inter exegetas non absolute constat viros de quibus ibi agitur diaconis nostris correspondere" (*AS* 3/1, 260).

[145] "De indole sacramentali diaconatus, statutum est, postulantibus pluribus ... eam in schemate caute indicare, quia in Traditione et Magisterio fundatur. Cf. praeter canonem citatum Tridentini: Pius XII, Const. Apost. *Sacramentum Ordinis*, DS 3858f.... Ex altera tamen parte cavetur ne Concilium paucos illos recentes auctores, qui de hac re dubia moverunt, condemnare videatur", ibid.

ibacy. But others were added, such as whether or not the diaconate was needed for tasks which could be carried out by laypeople. The following questions were asked under this heading: whether all tasks were to be considered, or only some of them; whether those tasks were of a regular nature or were exceptional; whether or not there was a privation of the special graces linked to the sacramentality of the diaconate; whether negative or positive influences on the apostolate of the laity could be considered; whether it was appropriate to recognise ecclesially, by ordination, the diaconal tasks which were in fact already being carried out; and whether deacons' (and especially married deacons') possible situation as a "bridge" between the higher clergy and the laity could be considered.[146]

2. In the Texts of Vatican II

In *Lumen gentium* 29, the proposition according to which there was an imposition of hands on deacons "*non ad sacerdotium, sed ad ministerium*" was to become a key reference for the theological understanding of the diaconate. However, many questions have been left open up until the present day for the following reasons: the suppression of the reference to the bishop in the formula which was settled upon;[147] the dissatisfaction felt by certain people about the ambiguity in that formula;[148] the interpretation given by the Commission;[149] and the scope of the actual distinction between *sacerdotium* and *ministerium*.

In *Lumen gentium* 28a, the term *ministerium* is used in a double sense in turn: (a) to refer to the ministry of the bishops, who as successors of the Apostles partake of the "consecration" and "mission" received by Christ from his Father, which they hand on in various degrees to different individuals, without explicit mention being made of deacons;[150] [and] (b) to refer to the "ecclesiastical ministry" as a whole, divinely established on different levels, embracing those who from antiquity have been called

---

[146] Cf. *AS* 3/1, 260–64; *AS* 3/2, 214–18.

[147] The original text said: "in ministerio episcopi". On the origin of and variations on this formula, cf. A. Kerkvoorde, "Esquisse d'une théologie du diaconat", in P. Winninger and Y. Congar, eds., *Le Diacre dans l'Eglise et le monde d'aujourd'hui*, UnSa 59 (Paris, 1966), 163–71, which, for its part, includes the warning that "it would be a mistake ... to make it [*sc.* this formula] the basis for a future theology of the diaconate."

[148] The expression is ambiguous: "nam sacerdotium est ministerium" (*AS* 3/8, 101).

[149] The words of the *Statuta* are interpreted as follows: "significant diaconos non ad corpus et sanguinem Domini offerendum sed ad *servitium caritatis* in Ecclesia", ibid.

[150] "Christus ... consecrationis missionisque suae per Apostolos suos, eorum successores, videlicet Episcopos participes effecit, qui *munus ministerii sui*, vario gradu, variis subiectis in Ecclesia legitime tradiderunt", *LG* 28a.

bishops, priests and deacons.[151] In the relevant note, Vatican II gives a reference to Trent, session 23, cap. 2 and can. 6.[152] The same sort of caution can be observed in both sources in the expressions which relate to the diversity of grades: "ordinatione divina" (Trent), "divinitus institutum" (Vatican II); "ab ipso Ecclesiae initio" (Trent), "ab antiquo" or else "inde ab Apostolis" according to *Ad gentes* 16 (Vatican II).[153]

The statement which relates most directly to the sacramentality of the diaconate is found in *Lumen gentium* 29a: "*gratia enim sacramentali roborati, in diaconia liturgiae, verbi et caritatis populo Dei, in communione cum Episcopo eiusque presbyterio, inserviunt*"; and also in *Ad gentes* 16: "ut ministerium suum per *gratiam sacramentalem* diaconatus efficacius expleant". The expression *gratia sacramentalis* is prudent, appropriate for an interjection, and much more nuanced than the formula "sacramental ordination" employed in the previous project of *Lumen gentium* in 1963. Why was this caution apparent in the expressions finally used? The doctrinal Commission referred to the basis in tradition of what is affirmed, and to the concern to avoid giving the impression that those who had doubts on the subject were being condemned.[154]

3. The Sacramentality of the Diaconate in Post-Conciliar Developments

1. Mention must first be made of the document which puts the Council's decisions into effect, i.e. the Motu Proprio of Pope Paul VI, *Sacrum diaconatus ordinem* (1967). In what concerns the theological nature of the diaconate, it takes up what Vatican II said about the *gratia* of the diaconate, while adding a reference to the indelible "character" (absent from the Council texts), and it is understood as a "stable" service.[155]

As a grade of the sacrament of Holy Orders, it bestows the capacity to exercise tasks which mostly belong to the domain of the liturgy (eight out of the eleven mentioned). In some expressions these appear as tasks

---

[151] "Sic *ministerium ecclesiasticum* divinitus institutum diversis ordinibus exercetur ab illis qui iam ab antiquo Episcopi, Presbyteri, Diaconi vocantur", ibid.

[152] DS 1765, 1776.

[153] Cf. the different references to Trent in the conciliar debates. Some identified *ministri* with *diaconi*, although their semantic equivalence does not justify making an instant theological identification between the two; others considered it to have been *dogmatically* defined at Trent that the diaconate constitutes the third grade of the hierarchy, but this evaluation seems to go beyond what was intended at Trent. Cf. notes 136 and 143 supra.

[154] Cf. *AS* 3/1, 260.

[155] Cf. *AAS* 59 (1967): 698.

which are deputized or delegated.[156] Thus it is not clear up to what point the diaconal "character" confers the capacity for some competencies or powers which could only be exercised by reason of previous sacramental ordination; since there is another way of accessing them (by delegation or deputizing, and not by reason of the sacrament of Holy Orders).

2. The most recent step taken in the Motu Proprio of Pope Paul VI, *Ad pascendum* (1972) refers to the instituting of the permanent diaconate (not excluding it as a transitory stage) as a "middle order" between the upper hierarchy and the rest of the People of God. In what concerns sacramentality, as well as considering this *medius ordo* as "signum vel sacramentum ipsius Christi Domini, qui non venit ministrari, sed ministrare", the document presupposes the sacramentality of the diaconate and limits itself to repeating the aforementioned expressions such as *sacra ordinatio* or *sacrum ordinem*.[157]

3. Following some positions which had already been taken up before Vatican II, certain authors expressed their doubts with regard to the sacramentality of the diaconate more explicitly and with detailed arguments, after the Council too. Their motives were varied. J. Beyer (1980) primarily presented his analysis of the conciliar texts, whose silence on the distinction between the power of "order" and of "jurisdiction" seemed to him to avoid rather than provide a solution to the questions which were still unresolved.[158] The same would apply to the fluctuation in meaning which could be accorded to the term *ministerium*, and the contrast between it and *sacerdotium*. He further evaluated the caution shown in the Council texts not only as the result of concern to avoid condemning anyone, but also as a result of doctrinal hesitations.[159] This was why further clarification was needed of the question: "Estne diaconatus pars sacerdotii sicut et episcopatus atque presbyteratus unum sacerdotium efficiunt?" This need was not satisfied by referring to the "common priesthood" of the faithful and excluding deacons from the "sacrificing" priesthood (cf. Philips). According to Tradition, the ministerial priesthood was "unum" and "unum sacramentum". If it was this sacramental

---

[156] Cf. ibid., 702.

[157] Cf. *AAS* 64 (1972): 536, 534, 537.

[158] Cf. J. Beyer, "Nature et position du sacerdoce", *NRTh* 76 (1954): 356–73, 469–80; J. Beyer, "De diaconatu animadversiones", *Periodica* 69 (1980): 441–60.

[159] Beyer especially disagreed with G. Philips' evaluation of this caution. Given that the Council wished to act *non dogmatice, sed pastorale*, even a much more explicit statement would not *ipso facto* imply condemnation of the contrary opinion. Hence in Beyer's view the reason for this caution was due to the fact that in what concerned the sacramentality of the diaconate the *haesitatio* was indeed "manifesta et doctrinalis quidem".

priesthood alone which rendered someone capable of acting *in persona Christi* with effect *ex opere operato*, then it would be hard to call the diaconate a "sacrament" because it was not instituted to accomplish any act *in persona Christi* with effect *ex opere operato*.

Additionally, further careful investigation was needed into the statements of Trent and also into the normative value of its references to the diaconate.[160] The acts of Vatican II, the development of the schemas, the various interventions and the *relatio* of the relevant Commission, also needed a careful re-reading. It could be concluded from this *relatio* that a solution had not altogether been found of the difficulties with regard to the following points: (a) the exegetical foundation of the institution of the diaconate (Acts 6:1–6 was excluded because it was open to debate, and consideration was limited to the simple mentions of deacons in Philippians 1:1 and First Timothy 3:8–12); [and] (b) the theological justification of the sacramental nature of the diaconate, in connection with the intention of re-establishing its permanent mode.

In conclusion: if Vatican II spoke cautiously and *ex obliquo* of the sacramental nature of the diaconate, it was not only from a concern not to condemn anyone, but rather because of the "incertitudo doctrinae".[161] Therefore, to confirm its sacramental nature, neither the majority opinion of theologians (which had also existed concerning the sub-diaconate), nor the mere description of the rite of ordination (which needed to be clarified from other sources) nor the mere imposition of hands (which could be non-sacramental in character) was sufficient.

4. In the new *Codex Iuris Canonici* of 1983, the diaconate is spoken of from the standpoint of its sacramentality, introducing certain developments which deserve comment.

This is true of cann. 1008–1009. The diaconate is one of the three orders, and the CIC seems to apply to it the general theology of the sacrament of Holy Orders in its integrity.[162] If this application is valid, then it follows from it that the diaconate is a sacramental reality, of divine

---

[160] According to Beyer, the term *ministri* had a generic sense; it had not been intended to give a dogmatic statement only of what the Protestant reform refused. The sense in which Trent was now invoked often went "ultra eius in Concilio Tridentino pondus et sensum".

[161] The biggest reason for this uncertainty lay in the fact of affirming "diaconum non ad sacerdotium sed ad ministerium ordinari, atque nihil in hoc ministerio agere diaconum quin et laicus idem facere non possit".

[162] "Sacramento ordinis ex divina institutione inter christifideles quidam, charactere indelebili suo signantur, constituuntur sacri ministri, qui nempe consecrantur et deputantur ut, pro suo quisque gradu, in persona Christi Capitis munera docendi, sanctificandi et regendi adimplentes, Dei populum pascant", CIC, can 1008.

institution, which makes deacons *sacri ministri* (in the CIC, those who are baptized and ordained), imprints on them an "indelible character" (taking for granted what was said by Paul VI) and by reason of their consecration and deputation ("consecrantur et deputantur") renders them capable of exercising *in persona Christi Capitis* and in the grade which corresponds to them ("pro suo quisque gradu") the tasks of teaching, sanctifying and ruling, in other words the functions proper to those who are called to guide the People of God.

Integrating the diaconate within the general theology of the sacrament of Holy Orders in this way raises certain questions. Can it be theologically maintained that deacons, even *pro suo gradu*, really exercise the "munera docendi, sanctificandi et regendi" *in persona Christi Capitis* as do bishops and priests? Is that not something particular and exclusive to those who have received sacramental ordination and the consequent power to "conficere corpus et sanguinem Christi", i.e. to consecrate the Eucharist, which does not belong to deacons in any way? Should the CIC's expression *in persona Christi Capitis* be understood in a broader sense so that it can also be applied to the functions of deacons? How, then, should the Council's statement be interpreted, which says that deacons are "non ad sacerdotium, sed ad ministerium"? Can the task of "pascere populum Dei" be considered an effect of the sacramentality of the diaconate? Would not arguing over its "powers" lead to an impasse?

It is very natural that the CIC should concern itself specially and at length with the faculties proper to deacons, and it does so in several canons.[163] In cann. 517, 2 and 519 deacons are mentioned with reference to cooperation with the parish priest as "pastor proprius", and to the possibility of granting them a share in the exercise of the *cura pastoralis* (can. 517, 2). This possibility of sharing in the exercise of the *cura pastoralis paroeciae* (which refers in the first place to deacons, although it can also be granted to laypeople) raises the question of the capacity of the deacon to assume the pastoral guidance of the community, and takes up again, with different nuances, what had already been established by *Ad gentes* 16 and *Sacrum diaconatus* 5/22. Although these points referred directly to *regere*, can. 517, 2 speaks in a more nuanced way of "participatio in exercitio curae pastoralis". In any case, with reference to the possibility opened by can. 517, which is presented as a last

---

[163] In cann. 757, 764, 766, 767 (the homily is reserved "sacerdoti aut diacono", while laypeople may also be admitted "ad praedicandum"), 835, 861, 910, 911, 1003 (deacons are not ministers of the anointing of the sick, for "unctionem infirmorum valide administrat omnis et solus sacerdos": is this an application of the principle which speaks of deacons as "non ad sacerdotium, sed ad ministerium"?), 1079, 1081, 1108, 1168, 1421, 1425, 1428, 1435 (they can be "judges", something which forms part of the power of governance or jurisdiction).

solution, more precise thought needs to be given to the real participation of deacons, by reason of their diaconal ordination, in the "cura animarum" and the task of "pascere populum Dei".[164]

5. The recent *Catechismus Catholicae Ecclesiae* (*CCE*), in its definitive 1997 edition, seems to speak more decidedly in favour of the sacramentality of the diaconate.

It states that the *potestas sacra* to act *in persona Christi* only corresponds to the bishops and priests, whereas deacons hold "vim populo Dei serviendi" in their various diaconal functions (no. 875). It also mentions deacons when, concerning the sacrament of Holy Orders, it considers "ordination" as a "sacramental act" enabling recipients to exercise a "sacred power" which proceeds ultimately from Jesus Christ alone (no. 1538).

On the one hand it seems that according to the *CCE* deacons could also be included in a certain way in a general understanding of the sacrament of Holy Orders under some categories of the priesthood, since it mentions them from this point of view at the same time as bishops and priests in nos. 1539–43. On the other hand in the definitive version of no. 1554 it justifies the restriction of the term *sacerdos* to bishops and priests, excluding deacons, while maintaining that deacons also belong to the sacrament of Holy Orders (no. 1554).

Finally, the idea of sacramentality is strengthened by the explicit attribution of the doctrine of "character" to deacons as a special configuration with Christ, deacon and servant of all (no. 1570).

6. The recent *Ratio fundamentalis* (1998), which recognises the difficulties that exist in reaching an understanding of the "germana natura" of the diaconate, nevertheless firmly upholds the clarity of the doctrinal elements ("clarissime definita", nos. 3 and 10) on the basis of original diaconal practise and conciliar indications.

There is no doubt that we have here a way of speaking of the specific identity of the deacon which offers certain novelties in comparison with what has usually been the case up till now. The deacon has a specific configuration with Christ, Lord and Servant.[165] To this configuration there

---

[164] Such reflection is necessary, because the principle is maintained that the *pastor proprius* and the final moderator of the *plena cura animarum* can only be one who has received ordination to the priesthood (the *sacerdos*). This raises the possibility of an extreme case of a *sacerdos* (who is not in fact a *parochus*, although he has all the attributes of one) and a *diaconus* (who is a *quasi-parochus*, since he has in fact the responsibility for the *cura pastoralis*, though not in its totality because he lacks the sacramental powers relating to the Eucharist and Reconciliation).

[165] "Specificam configurationem cum Christo, Domino et Servo omnium ... specificam diaconi identitatem ... is enim, prout unici ministerii ecclesiastici particeps, est in Ecclesia specificum signum sacramentale Christi Servi", *Ratio*, 5.

corresponds a spirituality whose distinguishing mark is "serviceability", which by ordination makes the deacon into a living "icon" of Christ the Servant in the Church (no. 11). This is offered in justification of restricting the configuration with Christ the Head and Shepherd to priests. But configuration with Christ the "Servant", and "service" as a characteristic of the ordained minister, are also valid for priests; so that it is not very clear what is "specifically diaconal" in this service, what it is that might express itself in functions or "munera" (cf. no. 9) which were the exclusive competence of deacons by reason of their sacramental capacity.

All in all, the *Ratio* clearly affirms the sacramentality of the diaconate as well as its sacramental character, in the perspective of a common theology of the sacrament of Holy Orders and the respective character which it confers.[166] Here the language is decisive and explicit, although it is not altogether clear to what extent it is the expression of more consistent theological developments or a new or better-justified base.

V. *Conclusion*

The doctrinal position in favour of the sacramentality of the diaconate is broadly speaking the majority opinion of theologians from the twelfth century to the present day and it is taken for granted in the practise of the Church and in most documents of the Magisterium; it is upheld by those who defend the permanent diaconate (for celibate or married people) and constitutes an element which includes a large number of the propositions in favour of the diaconate for women.

Despite everything, this doctrinal position faces questions which need to be clarified more fully, either through the development of a more convincing theology of the sacramentality of the diaconate, or through a more direct and explicit intervention by the Magisterium, or by a more successful attempt to connect and harmonize the various elements. The path which was followed concerning the sacramentality of the episcopate could be taken as a decisive and instructive reference point. Among the questions requiring deeper or more fully developed theology are the following: (a) the normative status of the sacramentality of the diaconate as it was fixed by the doctrinal interventions of the Magisterium, especially in Trent and in Vatican II; (b) the "unity" and "oneness" of the sacrament of Holy Orders in

---

[166] "Prout gradus ordinis sacri, diaconatus characterem imprimit et specificam gratiam sacramentalem communicat ... signum configurativum-distinctivum animae modo indelebili impressum, quod ... configurat Christo, qui diaconus, ideoque servus omnium, factus est", *Ratio*, 7.

its diverse grades; (c) the exact scope of the distinction "non ad sacerdo-tium, sed ad ministerium (episcopi)"; (d) the doctrine of the character of the diaconate and its specificity as a configuration with Christ; [and] (e) the "powers" conferred by the diaconate as a sacrament.

To reduce sacramentality to the question of *potestates* would undoubt-edly be an overly narrow approach; ecclesiology offers broader and richer perspectives. But in the case of the sacrament of Holy Orders, this ques-tion cannot be passed over with the excuse that it is too narrow. The other two grades of Holy Orders, the episcopate and the priesthood, give a capacity, by reason of sacramental ordination, for tasks which an unor-dained person cannot perform validly. Why should it be otherwise for the diaconate? Does the difference lie in the *way* in which the *munera* are exercised or in the personal quality of the person performing them? But how could this be rendered theologically credible? If in fact these func-tions can be exercised by a layperson, what justification is there for the argument that they have their source in a new and distinct sacramental ordination?

The discussion of diaconal powers gives rise once again to general ques-tions on: the nature or condition of the *potestas sacra* in the Church, the connection of the sacrament of Holy Orders with the "potestas confi-ciendi eucharistiam", and the need to widen ecclesiological perspectives beyond a narrow view of this connection.

CHAPTER V

THE RESTORATION OF THE PERMANENT DIACONATE AT VATICAN II

In three places, Vatican II uses different terms to describe what it intends to do when it speaks of the diaconate as a stable rank of the hierarchy of the Church. *Lumen gentium* 29b uses the notion of *restitutio*,[167] *Ad gentes* 16f uses that of *restauratio*,[168] while *Orientalium Ecclesiarum* 17 employs the word *instauratio*.[169] All three connote the idea of restoring, renewing, re-establishing, and re-activating. In the present chapter two points will

---

[167] "Diaconatus in futurum tamquam proprius ac permanens gradus hierarchiae restitui poterit", *LG* 29b.

[168] "Ordo diaconatus ut status vitae permanens restauretur ad normam constitutionis de ecclesia", *AG* 16f.

[169] "Exoptat haec sancta synodus, ut institutum diaconatus permanentis, ubi in desue-tudinem venerit, instauretur", *OE* 17.

be dealt with. First, it is important to know the reasons why the Council restored the permanent diaconate, and secondly, to examine the figure it wished to bestow upon it.

I. *The Intentions of the Council*

The idea of re-establishing the diaconate as a permanent grade of the hierarchy did not originate with Vatican II. It was already current before the Second World War, but was developed as a definite possibility after 1945, especially in German-speaking countries.[170] The challenge of responding to the pastoral needs of communities at a time when priests were facing imprisonment, deportation or death led to serious consideration being given to this idea. Various specialists soon produced studies on the theological and historical aspects of the diaconate.[171] Some men who were thinking about a vocation to the diaconate even established a group called the "Community of the Diaconate".[172] A renewed theology of the Church issuing from biblical, liturgical and ecumenical movements opened up the way to the possibility of restoring the diaconate as a stable order of the hierarchy.[173]

Thus on the eve of the Council the idea of a permanent diaconate was very much alive in certain significant sectors of the Church, and influenced a certain number of bishops and experts during the Council.

The motivations which led Vatican II to open the possibility of restoring the permanent diaconate are mainly given in the Dogmatic Constitution on the Church *Lumen gentium* and the Decree on the missionary activity of the Church *Ad gentes*. Because of the doctrinal nature of *Lumen gentium*, the origin of its formulations concerning the permanent diaconate will be considered first.

During the first stage of the Council (1962)[174] the question of the diaconate did not attract much attention as a particular topic: this led

---

[170] Cf. J. Hornef and P. Winninger, "Chronique de la restauration du diaconat (1945–1965)", in Winninger and Congar, *Le Diacre dans l'Eglise*, 205–22.

[171] A huge dossier of theological and historical studies, edited by K. Rahner and H. Vorgrimler, was published in Germany, entitled *Diaconia in Christo: Uber die Erneuerung des Diakonates*, QD 15/16 (Freiburg am Breisgau, 1962).

[172] Cf. Hornef and Winninger, "Chronique", 207–8.

[173] For example, Yves Congar explored the impact of the theology of the People of God and the ontology of grace on a renewed understanding of the ministries which could open the possibility of restoring the diaconate. Cf. "Le diaconat dans la théologie des ministères", in Winninger and Congar, *Le Diacre dans l'Eglise*, especially pp. 126f.

[174] The Council discussed the first draft of *De Ecclesia* from the 31st General Congregation, 1 December 1962, to the 36th General Congregation, 7 December 1962.

certain Council Fathers to point to the absence of all mention of the diaconate in the chapter dealing with the episcopate and the priesthood.[175] But during the first intersession (1962–1963), a certain number of Council Fathers began to evoke the possibility of a restoration of the permanent diaconate, some pointing out its advantages in the missionary or ecumenical field, others recommending caution. However, most of them addressed practical questions rather than theoretical matters: they discussed in particular the question of the admission of married men and its consequences for the celibacy of the clergy.[176]

In comparison with the level of discussion of the first period, that of the second period (1963) covered more ground and proved essential for an understanding of the Council's intentions.[177] Three interventions on the permanent diaconate could be considered "foundational" in the sense that they established in some measure the directions and the parameters, both doctrinal and practical, which were taken in the course of the debate. These interventions were those of Julius Cardinals Döpfner,[178] Joannes Landazuri Ricketts[179] and Leo Joseph Suenens.[180] The other interventions took up themes which had been raised by these three.

Beginning with the Council Fathers who favoured the re-establishment of a permanent diaconate, it should be said that they stressed the fact that the Council was only examining the *possibility* of re-establishing the permanent diaconate at the time and in the places that the competent ecclesiastical authority should judge opportune. There was no indication to the effect that the establishment of a permanent diaconate might be something *obligatory* on all local Churches. The same contributors considered how the Church would benefit from such a decision from a practical and pastoral viewpoint. The presence of permanent deacons could help to resolve some of the pastoral problems caused by the shortage of priests in mission countries and in areas subject to persecution.[181] The

---

[175] Joseph Cardinal Bueno y Monreal (31 GC, 1 December 1962), *AS* 1/4, 131. Mgr. Raphael Rabban, for his part, asked why the schema made mention "de duobus gradibus ordinis, de episcopatu scilicet et de sacerdotio" and not of the diaconate "qui ad ordinem pertinet", ibid., 236.

[176] Cf. G. Caprile, *Il Concilio Vaticano II: Il primo periodo 1962–1963* (Rome, 1968), 337, 410, 413, 494, 498, 501, 536.

[177] The Council discussed the chapter on the hierarchical structure of the Church from 4 to 30 October 1963.

[178] Julius Cardinal Döpfner (43 GC, 7 October 1963), *AS* 2/2, 227–30.

[179] Joannes Cardinal Landazuri Ricketts (43 GC, 8 October 1963), ibid., 314–17.

[180] Leo Joseph Cardinal Suenens (43 GC, 8 October 1963), ibid., 317–20.

[181] Cf. Mgr. Franciscus Seper (44 GC, 9 October 1963), ibid., 359; Mgr. Bernardus Yago (45 GC, 10 October 1963), ibid., 406; Mgr. Joseph Clemens Maurer (45 GC, written intervention), ibid., 412; and Mgr. Paul Yü Pin (45 GC), ibid., 431.

encouragement of vocations to the diaconate could thus give greater prominence to the priesthood.[182] It could also help to improve the ecumenical relations of the Latin Church with the other Churches which have preserved the permanent diaconate.[183] Additionally, men who wanted to commit themselves more deeply to the apostolate, or those who were already engaged in a certain form of ministry could belong to the hierarchy.[184] Finally, the admission of married men to the diaconate could mean that the celibacy of priests shone out more clearly as a charism embraced in a spirit of freedom.[185]

The interventions also pointed to the theological basis for a re-establishing of the permanent diaconate. Some Council Fathers highlighted the fact that the question of the permanent diaconate was not merely a disciplinary matter, but was properly speaking a theological one.[186] As a rank within the sacred hierarchy of the Church, the diaconate had been part of the constitution of the Church from its beginnings.[187] Cardinal Döpfner stated vigorously: "Schema nostrum, agens de hierarchica constitutione Ecclesiae, ordinem diaconatus nullo modo silere potest, quia tripartitio hierarchiae ratione ordinis habita in episcopatum, presbyteratum et diaconatum est juris divini et constitutioni Ecclesiae essentialiter propria."[188] If the Council revived the permanent diaconate, it would not be altering the constitutive elements of the Church, but would only be reintroducing something that had been left aside. The teaching of the Council of Trent (session 23, can. 17) was often invoked. Moreover, the Fathers maintained that the diaconate was a sacrament conferring grace and a character.[189] A deacon should not be considered as the same as a layman who was in the service of the Church, because the diaconate confers the grace to exercise a particular office.[190] Thus a deacon is not a layman who has been raised to a higher degree of the lay apostolate, but

---

[182] Cf. Paul Cardinal Richaud (44 GC, 9 October 1963), ibid., 346–47; Mgr. Bernardus Yago, ibid., 406.

[183] Mgr. F. Seper, ibid., 359.

[184] Card. Landazuri Ricketts, ibid., 315; Card. J. Döpfner, ibid., 229.

[185] Cf. Mgr. J. Maurer, ibid., 411; Mgr. Emmanuel Talamàs Camandari (46 GC, 11 October 1963), ibid., 450; and Mgr. George Kémére (47 GC, 14 October 1963), ibid., 534.

[186] Cf. Card. J. Döpfner, ibid., 227; Card. J. Landazuri Ricketts, ibid., 314.

[187] Cf. Card. L. Suenens, ibid., 317; Mgr. Joseph Slipyj (46 GC, 10 October 1963), ibid., 445.

[188] Card. J. Döpfner, ibid., 227.

[189] Cf. Mgr. Armandus Fares (47 GC, 14 October 1963), ibid., 530–31; Mgr. Narcissus Jubany Arnau (48 GC, 15 October 1963), ibid., 580; Mgr. J. Maurer, ibid., 411.

[190] Card. J. Landazuri Ricketts, ibid., 314–15; Card. L. Suenens, ibid., 318; Mgr. Seper, ibid., 319.

a member of the hierarchy by reason of sacramental grace and the character received at the moment of ordination. But as it was assumed that permanent deacons would live and work in the middle of the lay population and the secular world, they could exercise the role of "bridge or mediation between the hierarchy and the faithful".[191] Thus there was the intention on the part of the Fathers to restore the diaconate as a permanent rank of the hierarchy destined to penetrate secular society in the same way as laypeople. The permanent diaconate was not perceived as a call to the priesthood, but as a distinct ministry in the service of the Church.[192] It could thus be a sign of the Church's vocation to be the servant of Christ and of God.[193] The presence of the deacon, consequently, could renew the Church in the evangelical spirit of humility and service.

These opinions in favour of the restoration of the diaconate met with objections. Certain Fathers underlined the fact that the permanent diaconate would not be useful in resolving the shortage of priests because deacons cannot replace priests completely.[194] A number expressed the fear that the fact of accepting married men as deacons might endanger the celibacy of priests.[195] It would create a group of clergy inferior to the members of secular institutes, who took a vow of chastity.[196] The Fathers suggested solutions which seemed less prejudicial, such as giving a share of pastoral work to a larger number of men and women, committed laypeople and members of secular institutes.[197]

The definitive text of *Lumen gentium*, promulgated on 21 November 1964, expresses some objectives which the Council set in re-establishing the diaconate as a proper and permanent rank of the hierarchy in the Latin Church.[198]

---

[191] Mgr. Yü Pin, ibid., 431.

[192] Mgr. B. Yago, ibid., 407.

[193] Mgr. J. Maurer, ibid., 410.

[194] Anicetus Fernandez, O.P. (45 GC, 10 October 1963), ibid., 424; Mgr. Joseph Drzazga (49 GC, 16 October 1963), ibid., 624.

[195] Mgr. Franciscus Franic (44 GC, 10 October 1963), ibid., 378; Mgr. Dinus Romoli (48 GC, 15 October 1963), ibid., 598; Mgr. Petrus Cule (47 GC, 14 October 1963), ibid., 518.

[196] Mgr. Joseph Carraro, ibid., 525–26.

[197] Card. F. Spellman, ibid., 83; A. Fernandez, ibid., 424; Mgr. Victorius Costantini, ibid., 447.

[198] On 15 September 1964, Mgr. Aloysius Eduardo Henriquez Jimenez read the *relatio* explaining the text of the Doctrinal Commission on the priesthood and the diaconate, before the Fathers proceeded to vote on the chapter of *Lumen gentium* dealing with the hierarchy. Explaining the position of the text, he stated that in the Church bishops, priests and deacons shared in power in different ways and to different degrees. As at Trent, the

In the first place, according to no. 28a of *Lumen gentium*, Vatican II re-established the diaconate as a proper and permanent rank of the hierarchy in recognition of the divinely established ecclesiastical ministry, just as it had evolved in the course of history. Hence a motive of faith, namely the recognition of the gift of the Holy Spirit in the complex reality of Holy Orders, furnished the ultimate justification for the Council's decision to re-establish the diaconate.

Lumen gentium 29, however, presented what might be termed the "circumstantial reason" for the restoration of the permanent diaconate.[199] Vatican II foresaw deacons as engaging in tasks (*munera*) which were very necessary to the life of the Church (*ad vitam ecclesiae summopere necessaria*), but which in many regions could be fulfilled only with difficulty because of the discipline of the Latin Church as it existed at the time. The present difficulties caused by the shortage of priests demanded some response. Care for the faithful (*pro cura animarum*) was the determining factor in re-establishing the permanent diaconate in a local Church. The re-establishment of the permanent diaconate was therefore intended to respond to pastoral needs which were grave, not merely peripheral ones. This explains in part why it was the responsibility of the territorial episcopal conferences, and not the pope, to determine if it was opportune to ordain such deacons, because they would have a more immediate grasp of the needs of the local Churches.

Indirectly, Vatican II was also to initiate a clarification of the identity of the priest, who did not have to fulfil all the tasks necessary to the life of the Church. In consequence, the Church would be able to experience the riches of different degrees of Holy Orders. At the same time Vatican II enabled the Church to go beyond a narrowly sacerdotal understanding of the ordained minister.[200] Since deacons were ordained "non ad sacerdotium, sed ad ministerium", it was possible to conceive of clerical life, the sacred hierarchy and ministry in the Church beyond the category of the priesthood.

It is also worth noting that the permanent diaconate could be conferred upon men of more mature age (*viris maturioris aetatis*), even upon

---

text taught that the diaconate belongs to the sacred hierarchy, of which it is the lowest degree. Ordained for ministry and not for the priesthood, deacons have received sacramental grace and have been charged with a triple service of the liturgy, of the word and of charity. The diaconate could be conferred on married men. Cf. *AS* 3/2, 211–18. Mgr. Franciscus Franic presented the opposing views, ibid., 193–201.

[199] K. Rahner, "L'Enseignement de Vatican II sur le diaconat et sa restauration", in Winninger and Congar, *Le Diacre dans l'Eglise*, 227.

[200] Cf. A. Borras and B. Pottier, *La grâce du diaconat* (Brussels, 1998), 22–40.

those living in the married state, but that the law of celibacy remained intact for younger candidates. *Lumen gentium* does not give the reasons for this decision. But the conciliar debates indicate that the Fathers wished to make of the permanent diaconate an order which would unite the sacred hierarchy and the secular life of laypeople more closely together.

Further motivations emerge from *Ad gentes* 16. Here it can be seen that the Council was not re-establishing the permanent diaconate merely because of a shortage of priests. There were already men who were in fact exercising the diaconal ministry. By the imposition of hands these were "to be strengthened and more closely associated with the altar" (*corroborari et altari arctius conjungi*). The sacramental grace of the diaconate would render them capable of exercising their ministry more effectively. Here Vatican II was not motivated only by current pastoral difficulties, but by the need to recognise the existence of the diaconal ministry in certain communities. It desired to confirm by sacramental grace those who were already exercising the diaconal ministry, or showing forth its charism.

From *Lumen gentium* to *Ad gentes*, there was a shift in the Council's intentions. These intentions can be of great importance in understanding not only the diaconate but the true nature of the sacrament. Three main reasons can be discerned in favour of the restoration of the permanent diaconate. In the first place, the restoration of the diaconate as a proper degree of Holy Orders enabled the constitutive elements of the sacred hierarchy willed by God to be recognised. Secondly, it was a response to the need to guarantee indispensable pastoral care to communities which had been deprived of this because of a shortage of priests. Finally, it was a confirmation, a reinforcement and a more complete incorporation into the ministry of the Church of those who were already de facto exercising the ministry of deacons.

II. *The Form of the Permanent Diaconate Restored by Vatican II*

Six of the documents promulgated by Vatican II contain some teachings concerning the diaconate: *Lumen gentium, Ad gentes, Dei Verbum, Sacrosanctum concilium, Orientalium Ecclesiarum* and *Christus Dominus*. The following paragraphs will cover the key elements of the teaching of Vatican II in order to identify more precisely the form or "figure" of the permanent diaconate which has been restored.

1. Vatican II recognised the diaconate as one of the sacred Orders. *Lumen gentium* 29a established that deacons belong to the lowest degree of the hierarchy (*in gradu inferiori hierarchiae sistunt diaconi*). They are "sustained by sacramental grace" (*gratia sacramentali roborati*) and receive the

imposition of hands "non ad sacerdotium, sed ad ministerium". But this important expression, drawn from the *Statuta Ecclesiae antiqua*, and a variation on a still more ancient expression from the *Traditio Apostolica* of Hippolytus, is not explained anywhere in the conciliar documents.[201]

Vatican II taught that Christ instituted the sacred ministries for the nurturing and constant growth of the People of God. Those ministers are endowed with a sacred power to serve the Body of Christ, so that all may arrive at salvation (*LG* 18a). Like the other sacred ministers, deacons should therefore consecrate themselves to the growth of the Church and the pursuit of its plan of salvation.

Within the body of ministers, bishops, who possess the fullness of the priesthood, have taken up the service of the community, presiding in place of God over the flock as teachers, priests and shepherds. Deacons, with the priests, help the bishops in their ministry (*LG* 20c). Belonging to the lowest order of the ministry, deacons grow in holiness through the faithful fulfilment of their ministry as a share in the mission of Christ the Supreme Priest. "Missionis autem et gratiae supremi Sacerdotis peculiari modo participes sunt inferioris quoque ordinis ministri, imprimis Diaconi, qui mysteriis Christi et ecclesiae servientes" (*LG* 41d). Although they occupy different ranks within the hierarchy, all three orders deserve to be called ministers of salvation (*AG* 16a), exercising one single ecclesiastical ministry in the hierarchical communion. Strictly speaking deacons belong to the mission of Christ, but not to that of the bishop or to that of the priest. However, the specific ways of exercising this participation are determined by the demands of the communion within the hierarchy. Far from degrading the orders of priest and deacon within the hierarchy, hierarchical communion situates them within the single mission of Christ, shared in by the different orders in different degrees.

2. The functions assigned to deacons by the Council also provide indications concerning the way it envisaged the diaconal order. It is good to remember that the basic function of all the sacred ministers, according to Vatican II, is to nurture the People of God and lead them to salvation. Thus *Lumen gentium* 29b declared that the permanent diaconate can be re-established if the competent authorities decide that it is opportune to choose deacons, even from among married men, *pro cura animarum*. All the tasks which deacons are authorised to fulfil are at the service of the basic duty of building up the Church and taking care of the faithful.

As for their specific tasks, *Lumen gentium* 29a presented the service which the deacon renders to the People of God in terms of the triple ministry

---

[201] Cf. Kerkvoorde, "Esquisse d'une théologie du diaconat", in Winninger and Congar, *Le Diacre dans l'Eglise*, 157–71.

of the liturgy, the word and charity. The particular tasks of the deacon are seen as falling within the framework of one or other of these ministries. The ministry of the liturgy, or sanctification, is developed at length in *Lumen gentium*. It includes the faculty of administering baptism solemnly (cf. *SC* 68), of being custodian and dispenser of the Eucharist, assisting at and blessing weddings in the name of the Church, bringing Viaticum to the dying, presiding over the worship and prayer of the faithful, administering sacramentals, and finally officiating at funeral and burial services. The function of teaching includes reading the Sacred Scripture to the faithful, and instructing and exhorting the people. *Dei Verbum* 25a and *Sacrosanctum concilium* 35 include deacons among those who are officially engaged in the ministry of the word. The ministry of "government" is not mentioned as such, but rather termed the ministry of charity. Administration is at least mentioned.

It is clear that the function of the deacon as described by *Lumen gentium* is above all liturgical and sacramental. Questions inevitably arise about the specific notion of diaconal ordination "non ad sacerdotium sed ad ministerium". The form of the diaconal ministry based on *Lumen gentium* invites a deeper exploration of the meaning of *sacerdotium* and *ministerium*.

Ad gentes gave a different configuration to the permanent diaconate, as can be seen by looking at the functions it assigned to it, probably because it sprang from the experience of mission territories. In the first place, *Ad gentes* contained little about the liturgical ministry of the deacon. Preaching the word of God was mentioned in connection with catechism teaching. What is called the ministry of "government" received broader treatment in *Ad gentes* 16f. Deacons preside over scattered Christian communities in the name of the parish priest and the bishop. They also practice charity in social or relief work.

Vatican II showed some hesitation in its description of the permanent diaconate which it was restoring. In the more doctrinal perspective of *Lumen gentium*, it tended to place the emphasis on the liturgical image of the deacon and his ministry of sanctification. In the missionary perspective of *Ad gentes*, the focus shifted towards the administrative, charitable aspect of the figure of the deacon, and his ministry of government. It is however interesting to note that nowhere did the Council claim that the form of the permanent diaconate which it was proposing was a restoration of a previous form. This explains why certain theologians avoid the term "restoration", because it might easily suggest something being brought back to its original state. But Vatican II never aimed to do that. What it re-established was *the principle of the permanent exercise of the diaconate*, and not one particular form which the diaconate had taken in the past.[202] Having established the possibility of re-establishing the permanent diaconate, the Council seemed open to the kind of form it might take in the future, in function of pastoral needs and ecclesial practise, but always in fidelity to Tradition. Vatican II could not be expected to provide a clearly defined picture of the permanent diaconate, because of the gap that existed in the pastoral life of those times, unlike the case of the episcopate or the priesthood. The most it could do was to open the possibility of reinstalling the diaconate as a proper, permanent degree in the hierarchy and as a stable way of life, give some general theological principles even though they might appear timid, and establish some general norms of practise. Beyond that it could do no more than wait for the contemporary form of the permanent diaconate to develop. Finally, the apparent indecision and hesitancy of the Council might serve as an invitation to the Church to continue working to discern the type of ministry appropriate to the diaconate through ecclesial practise, canonical legislation, and theological reflection.[203]

CHAPTER VI

THE REALITY OF THE PERMANENT DIACONATE TODAY

More than 35 years after Vatican II, what is the reality of the permanent diaconate?

To examine the available statistics is to realize the huge disparity which exists in the distribution of deacons around the world. Out of a total of 25,122 deacons in 1998,[204] North America alone accounts for 12,801, i.e. just over half (50.9%), while Europe has 7,864 (31.3%): this means a total of 20,665 deacons (82.2%) in the industrialized countries of the northern hemisphere. The remaining 17.8% are distributed as follows: South America 2,370 (9.4%); Central America and the Caribbean 1,387 (5.5%); Africa 307 (1.22%); Asia 219 (0.87%). Finally comes Australasia and the Pacific, with 174 deacons or 0.69% of the total.[205]

---

[202] Borras and Pottier, *La grâce du diaconat*, 20.

[203] Cf. Kerkvoorde, *"Esquisse d'une théologie du diaconat"*, 155–56.

[204] These figures and the analysis of them were kindly supplied to us in the course of the fall 1999 session of the Commission, by Prof. Enrico Nenna, Ufficio centrale statistica della Chiesa, Segretaria di Stato.

[205] If a comparison is made between the numbers of priests and deacons in the different continents, the same differences are observable as before. While in America as a whole there are 7.4 priests per deacon (mainly because of the high number of deacons in North

One very striking point is that it is in the advanced industrialized countries of the North[206] that the diaconate has developed particularly. Now that was not at all what the Council Fathers envisaged when they asked for a "reactivation" of the permanent diaconate. They expected, rather, that there would be a rapid increase among the young Churches of Africa and Asia, where pastoral work relied on a large number of lay catechists.[207] But they had laid down that it would pertain "to the competent territorial bodies of bishops, of one kind or another, with the approval of the Supreme Pontiff, to decide whether and where it [was] opportune for such deacons to be established for the care of souls" (LG 29b). It is therefore unsurprising that the diaconate did not develop uniformly throughout the Church, since the evaluation of the needs of the People of God made by the different episcopates could vary according to the specific circumstances of the Churches and their modes of organization.

What these statistics enable us to see is that there were two very different situations to be dealt with. On the one hand, after the Council most of the Churches in Western Europe and North America were faced with a steep reduction in the numbers of priests, and had to undertake a major reorganization of ministries. On the other hand, the Churches which were mainly in former mission territories had long since adopted a structure which relied on the commitment of large numbers of laypeople, the catechists.

These two typical situations need to be studied separately, without losing sight of the fact that many variations exist; and also that in both cases, a certain number of bishops may have wanted to institute the permanent diaconate in their dioceses not so much for pastoral reasons as from a theological motive which had also been invoked by Vatican II: to enable the ordained ministry to be expressed better, through the three degrees traditionally recognised.

First Typical Situation: Churches with a Low Number of Deacons

Many Churches, then, did not feel the need to develop the permanent diaconate. These were mainly Churches which had long since been

---

America), in Asia there are 336 priests to one deacon. In Africa there are 87 priests per permanent deacon, in Europe 27, and in Australasia and the Pacific, 31. The relative weight of the deacons within the ordained ministry therefore varies greatly from one place to another.

[206] Another source of information gives a list of countries where there are the greatest numbers of permanent deacons: United States (11,589), Germany (1,918), Italy (1,845), France (1,222), Canada (824), Brazil (826).

[207] Cf. H. Legrand, "Le diaconat dans sa relation à la théologie de l'Eglise et aux ministères: Réception et devenir du diaconate depuis Vatican II", in A. Haquin and P. Weber, eds., Diaconate, 21e siècle (Brussels, Paris, and Montreal, 1997), 13 and 14.

accustomed to function with a restricted number of priests, and to rely on the commitment of a very large number of laypeople, mainly as catechists. The case of Africa is an example in this regard.[208] It is undoubtedly matched by the experience of other young Churches.

It will be remembered that in the 1950s many missionaries and bishops in Africa had asked for the reactivation of the diaconate while thinking particularly of the catechists in mission countries. They saw it as a way of responding to the liturgical demands of the missions and the shortage of priests. These new deacons would thus be able to take care of the liturgy in the branch Churches, lead the Sunday gatherings in the absence of the missionary, officiate at funerals, assist at weddings, look after catechesis and the proclamation of the Word of God, take charge of *caritas* and the Church administration, confer certain sacraments, and so on.[209] This perspective was what many Council Fathers had in mind at Vatican II when, in *Ad gentes*, the Council referred to "the ranks of men and women catechists, well deserving of missionary work to the nations".[210]

But in the years that followed the Council, the African bishops displayed considerable reservations and did not undertake the road to the reactivation of the diaconate. A participant at the eighth Kinshasa theological week held in 1973 noted that the proposal for a restoration of the permanent diaconate in Africa raised much more opposition than enthusiasm. The objections raised would be widely repeated elsewhere. They had to do with deacons' state in life, the financial situation of the young Churches, the consequences on vocations to the actual priesthood, confusion and uncertainty about the nature of the diaconal vocation, the clericization of laypeople who were committed to me apostolate, the conservatism and lack of critical spirit of certain candidates, the marriage of clergy and the depreciation of celibacy, and the reaction of faithful who would content themselves with the diaconate as a sort of half-measure.[211]

The Congolese bishops therefore adopted an attitude of caution. Why should catechists be ordained as deacons if no new power was being given to them? They decided that it would be preferable to embark on a revaluation of the lay state, and work to renew the role of catechists. Other

---

[208] For the following points, cf. J. Kabasu Bamba, "Diacres permanents ou catéchistes au Congo-Kinshasa?" (Ph.D. thesis, University of Ottawa, 1999), 304 pages.

[209] The author is here quoting Mgr. W. Van Bekkum, Mgr. Eugène D'Souza (India), Mgr. J. F. Cornelis (Elizabethville) and, at the time of the preparation of the Council, the (mostly European) Ordinaries of Congo and Rwanda, Bamba, op. cit., 190.

[210] Decree on the Missionary Activity of the Church, 17a. This calls to mind the interventions of Mgr. B. Yago and Mgr. Paul Yü Pin referred to in the previous chapter.

[211] Cf. Bamba, op. cit., 195, which has a reference to M. Singleton, "Les nouvelles formes de ministère en Afrique", *Pro Mundi Vita* 50 (1974): 33.

countries would appeal for a greater participation of laypeople as "servants of the Word" or activity leaders of small communities. That could be done all the better now that the Council had so strongly highlighted the vocation of all the baptized to share in the Church's mission.

An often-heard objection, therefore, was "What can a deacon do that a layman can't?" It has to be recognised that the sacramental link which joins deacons to their bishop creates special, lifelong obligations for the bishop which can be difficult to manage, especially in the case of married deacons.[212] Furthermore, it is normally a question of Churches in which the place of the ordained ministry is well-defined and retains its full meaning, even though priests may be few in number.

That said, it is nevertheless worth mentioning initiatives such as that of the bishop of the Indian diocese of San Cristobal (Mexico), Monsignor Ruiz. Faced with the fact that his diocese had never succeeded in producing vocations to the priesthood among the indigenous Indians, he decided to undertake an intensive promotion of the permanent diaconate. Accordingly he put in place a long process of formation designed to lead married Amerindian men to the diaconate. These would thus be sacramentally associated to his episcopal ministry and form the beginnings of an indigenous Church.[213]

Second Typical Situation: Churches Where the Diaconate Is More Developed

The second typical situation is that of the Churches where the diaconate has undergone its greatest expansion. These are the Churches which have had to face a considerable drop in the number of priests: the United States, Canada, Germany, Italy, France, etc. The need to set about a reorganization of pastoral duties to respond to the needs of Christian communities which were accustomed to a wide range of services, and the obligation of finding new collaborators, all helped to stimulate the emergence of new ministries and an increase in the number of laypeople working full-time on parish or diocesan pastoral

---

[212] The archbishop of Santiago de Chile reported the objections of certain priests as follows: "They say for example that the diaconate is an unnecessary commitment, since its functions can be fulfilled by laymen and laywomen for given periods of time; if it works, their mandate is prolonged, and if not, it is not renewed." Mgr. C. Oviedo Cavada, "La promoción del diaconado permanente", *Iglesia de Santiago* (Chile), no. 24 (September 1992): 25.

[213] See a long text published by the Diocese of San Cristobal de las Casas, *Directorio diocesano para el diaconado indígena permanente* (1999), 172 pages.

work.[214] This also favoured the expansion of the diaconate. But at the same time it exercised a very strong pressure on the kind of tasks which were entrusted to deacons. Tasks which for a long time had been undertaken by priests without any problem because of their large numbers, now had to be given to other collaborators, some ordained (the deacons), others not ordained (lay pastoral officials). Because of this background the diaconate often came to be seen as a *supply ministry for the priesthood*.

This dynamic is reflected in the results of a broad study undertaken in the United States,[215] which is clearly representative of the situation existing in many countries. The study shows that deacons are mainly doing what priests used to do unaided before the restoration of the diaconate. They exercise their ministry in the parish where they live, and there they fulfil mainly liturgical and sacramental functions. Their parish priests find them particularly useful in sacramental activities such as baptisms, weddings and liturgical acts. The same applies to the care of the sick and homilies. The field in which they take least part is in the ministry to prisoners and the promotion of civil rights and human rights. Lay leaders, for their part, consider that deacons are most successful in more familiar and traditional roles such as the liturgy and the administration of the sacraments. And it is predicted that their numbers will increase because of the reduction in the numbers of priests. Thus, as they accomplish tasks traditionally fulfilled by priests, there may be a danger of deacons being seen as "incomplete priests" or else as "more advanced laymen". The danger is the greater since the first generations of deacons have received much less detailed theological training than that of priests or that of pastoral officials.

A similar development is also to be found in other areas which likewise suffer from a marked reduction in the numbers of priests.[216] It is the result of an effort to respond to the real needs of the People of God. It enables these Churches to guarantee a wider presence of the ordained ministry within Christian communities which are in danger of losing sight of the real meaning of that ministry. Together with the bishop and the priest, the deacon will remind them that it is Christ

---

[214] Depending on the country, these collaborators received different names: "pastoral officials", "pastoral workers or leaders", "pastoral auxiliaries", "pastoral lay agents", "parish auxiliaries", "parish assistants", "pastoral assistants" (*Pastoralassistenten und Pastoralassistentinnen), etc. Cf. A. Borras, Des laïcs en responsabilité pastorale?* (Paris, 1998).

[215] NCCB, "National Study of the Diaconate, Summary Report", *Origins* 25, no. 30 (18 January 1996).

[216] See for example Maskens, "Un enquête sur les diacres francophones de Belgique", in Haquin and Weber, *Diaconat, 21e siècle*, 217–32.

who is the foundation of the Church in every place and that through the Spirit he is still acting in the Church today.

In this context, however, the identity of the deacon tends to take the figure of the priest as a reference point; the deacon is perceived as the person who helps or replaces the priest in activities which previously he carried out in person. Many consider this development to be problematical, because it makes it more difficult for the diaconal ministry to evolve an identity of its own.[217] For this reason, here and there efforts are made to modify this development by identifying charisms which might be those proper to the diaconate, and tasks which might suitably belong primarily to the diaconate.

Lines of Development

For their part, the most recent texts from the Roman Congregations list the tasks which can be entrusted to deacons, and group them under the three recognised diakonias, namely those of the liturgy, the word and charity.[218] Even when it is considered that one or other of these diakonias could take up the greater part of a deacon's activity, it is insisted on that the three diakonias taken together "represent a unity in the service of the divine plan of Redemption: the ministry of the word leads to ministry at the altar, which in turn prompts the transformation of life by the liturgy, resulting in charity".[219] But it is recognised that in these tasks taken all together, "the service of charity"[220] is to be seen as particularly characteristic of the deacons' ministry.

In many regions, then, efforts have been made to identify a certain number of tasks for deacons which can be connected in one way or another

---

[217] Thus, B. Sesboüé, "Quelle est l'identité ministérielle du diacre?" in *L'Eglise à venir* (Paris, 1999), 255–57.

[218] See for example the text of the Congregation for the Clergy, *Directorium pro ministerio et vita diaconarum permanentium*, 22 February 1998, published as *Directory for the Ministry and Life of Permanent Deacons*, in *The Permanent Diaconate* (London, 1998), 88.

[219] Ibid., 39, 103. The text adds in the next paragraph: "It is important that deacons fully exercise their ministry, in preaching, in the liturgy and in charity, to the extent that circumstances permit. They should not be relegated to marginal duties, be made merely to act as substitutes, nor discharge duties normally entrusted to non-ordained members of the faithful."

[220] See Congregation for Catholic Education, *Basic Norms for the Formation of Permanent Deacons*, 9: "Finally the *munus regendi* is exercised in devotion to works of charity and assistance and in motivating communities or sectors of the ecclesial life, especially in what has to do with charity. *This is the ministry which is most characteristic of the deacon*" (emphasis added). In *Permanent Diaconate*, 27.

to the "service of charity". Particular advantage may be taken of the fact that most of them are married men, earning their own living, immersed in the world of work, and, together with their wives, contributing their own life experience.[221]

For example, a text by the bishops of France published in 1970 expressed their preference "for deacons who, in daily contact with others through their family and work situation, can witness with their whole lives to the service that the People of God should render to men, following Christ's example.... Permanent deacons will thus share in their own special way in the efforts of the hierarchical Church to go out to meet unbelief and poverty, and to be more fully present in the world. They will keep all previous commitments which are compatible with the diaconal ministry." [222] The mission entrusted to them, therefore, may often be situated "in the sphere of work and association or trade-union life (or even political life, particularly at the level of local government). Their mission is directed towards the care of the poor and marginalized in such places, but also in their own district and their parish, starting with home and family life." [223]

Hence in various places particular efforts have been made to make the diaconate a "threshold ministry", which aims to look after "the frontier Church": work in surroundings where the priest is not present, and also with one-parent families, couples, prisoners, young people, drug addicts, AIDS victims, the elderly, disadvantaged groups, etc. The tasks of deacons may be oriented towards activities in the social, charitable or administrative spheres, without however neglecting the necessary link with liturgical and teaching duties. In Latin America, the focus is placed upon families who proclaim the Gospel in the midst of zones of conflict; a presence in extreme situations such as drugs, prostitution and urban violence; an active presence in the sector of education, the world of work and the professional sphere; a greater presence in densely populated zones

[221] "It is not the wife who is ordained and nevertheless the mission entrusted to the deacon obliges the couple to redefine themselves in some way, in function of this ministry", M. Cacouet and B. Viole, *Les diacres*, quoted in a study document on the role of the deacon's wife (Quebec, 1993). For this reason, in many countries the wife joins her husband for the initial training period, and takes part in continued training activities with him.

[222] Note of the Episcopal Commission for the Clergy, cited by F. Deniau, "Mille diacres en France", *Etudes* 383, no. 5 (1995): 526.

[223] Ibid., 527. This direction taken by the bishops was confirmed in 1996 during their gathering at Lourdes, where they expressed their desire that "the image given by deacons should not be that of supplying for priests, but of communion with them in the exercise of the sacrament of Holy Orders." "Points d'attention", *Documentation Catholique*, no. 2149 (1996): 1012–13.

and likewise in the countryside; and finally, leadership given in small communities.[224] Very often, efforts are directed towards ensuring that these deacons receive progressively more thorough theological and spiritual formation.

The outcome of all this very diverse experience makes it clear that it is not possible to characterize the totality of the diaconal ministry by delineating tasks which belong exclusively to deacons because of ecclesial tradition—which is far from clear—or through a rigid distribution of tasks among the different ministers.[225] A text of Vatican II seems to have intuited this, since one of the reasons it invoked for re-establishing the diaconate "as a permanent state of life" was to strengthen, "by the imposition of hands which has come down from the Apostles" and to unite more closely to the altar, "men who *accomplish a truly diaconal ministry*, either by preaching the word of God, or by governing far-off Christian communities in the name of the parish priest and bishop, or by exercising charity in social or charitable works" (*AG* 16f.).[226] All of this leads certain people to propose that in order to define the character of the diaconate it is necessary to look rather at the *being* of the deacon. "It is in the aspect of *being* that the specificity of the permanent diaconate is to be sought, and not in the aspect of *doing*. It is what they *are* that gives its true meaning to what they do." [227]

It is in this perspective of configuration to Christ the Servant that theological and pastoral studies on the lines of development of the permanent diaconate are currently being made. This theological given is seen as providing the opportunity for an in-depth spiritual reflection which is particularly appropriate for the present era. It can also provide guidance to pastors in their choice of the tasks to entrust to deacons. In that case, the tasks selected for them will preferably be such as to highlight this particular characteristic of the diaconate. These will naturally include service to the poor and oppressed; a service which is not limited to mere assistance but which, following Christ's own example, will be a sharing of life with the poor in order to journey with them towards their total liberation.[228] Their tasks will include service to those who are on the threshold of the Church and who need to be led to the Eucharist. In many

---

[224] J. G. Mesa Angulo, O.P., "Aportes para visualizar un horizonte pastoral para el diaconado permanente en América Latina, hacia el tercer milenio", in CELAM, "I Congreso de diaconado permanente", Lima, August 1998, working document.

[225] A certain number of tasks, of course, are reserved to deacons by canon law, but they do not account for the whole of the deacon's activity.

[226] Emphasis added.

[227] R. Page, *Diaconat permanent et diversité des ministères: Perspectives du droit canonique* (Montreal, 1988), 61.

[228] V. Gerardi, "El diaconado en la Iglesia", in CELAM, "I Congreso", p. 8, referring to the First International Congress held in Turin in 1977.

countries this perspective is prominent in the minds of those responsible for deacons' formation, and a spirituality and a pastoral practise of the "service of charity" can be seen to develop in the deacons themselves. The true figure of the deacon should thus emerge little by little in the performance of various ministries, and be manifest through a definite way of doing—in the spirit of service—what all are called to do, but also through a pronounced dedication to particular tasks or functions which make Christ the Servant ever more visible. However, it seems to be an established fact that the development of the diaconal ministry must always be thought of in relation to the real needs of the Christian community. Certain Churches will not feel the need to develop it very widely. Other Churches will, on occasions, require the deacons to perform tasks other than those listed above; here one could think of those tasks which contribute to pastoral leadership in parishes and small Christian communities. The essential objective for pastors, inspired by Saint Paul, must always be that of seeing that the faithful are equipped "for the work of ministry, for building up the body of Christ, until all of us come to the unity of the faith and of the knowledge of the Son of God, to maturity, to the measure of the full stature of Christ" (Eph 4:12–13). At the service of the bishop and his presbyterium, the deacon should, in the way which is proper to him, go wherever pastoral care requires him to be.

CHAPTER VII

THEOLOGICAL APPROACH TO THE DIACONATE
IN THE WAKE OF VATICAN II

A theological approach to the diaconate in the wake of Vatican II should start from the Council texts, examine how they were received and how they were later enlarged upon in the documents of the Magisterium, take account of the fact that the restoration of the diaconate was accomplished very unevenly in the post-Conciliar period, and above all pay special attention to the doctrinal fluctuations which have closely shadowed the various pastoral suggestions. Today there are numerous very different aspects which require an effort at doctrinal clarification. This chapter will attempt to contribute to these efforts at clarification as follows. First it will pinpoint the roots and reasons which make the theological and ecclesial identity of the diaconate (both permanent and transitory) into a real "quaestio disputata" in certain respects. Then it will outline a theology of the diaconal ministry which may serve as a firm common basis to inspire the fruitful re-creation of the diaconate in Christian communities.

I. *The Texts of Vatican II and the Post-Conciliar Magisterium*

In the Council texts which mention the diaconate specifically (cf. *SC* 35, *LG* 20, *LG* 28, *LG* 29, *LG* 41, *OE* 17, *CD* 15, *DV* 25, *AG* 15, *AG* 16), Vatican II did not aim to offer a dogmatic decision on any of the questions debated in the course of the Council, nor to lay down a strict doctrinal system. Its true interest was in opening a path to the restoration of the permanent diaconate which could be put into effect in a plurality of ways. This is perhaps why, in the texts taken as a whole, certain fluctuations can be seen in the theology, depending on the place or context in which the diaconate is mentioned. Both with reference to pastoral priorities and in what concerns objective doctrinal difficulties, the Council texts show a diversity of theological nuances which it is quite hard to harmonize.

After the Council the theme of the diaconate was developed or referred to in other documents of the post-Conciliar Magisterium: Paul VI's Motu Proprio *Sacrum diaconatus ordinem* (1967); the Apostolic Constitution *Pontificalis romani recognitio* (1968); Paul VI's Motu Proprio *Ad pascendum* (1972); the new *Codex Iuris Canonici* (1983); and the *Catechismus Catholicae Ecclesiae* (1992, 1997).[229] These new documents develop the basic elements of Vatican II and sometimes add important theological, ecclesial or pastoral clarifications; but they do not all speak from the same perspective, nor at the same doctrinal level.[230] For this reason, in order to attempt a theological approach in the wake of Vatican II, it is appropriate to bear in mind the possible relation between the doctrinal fluctuations (in Vatican II texts) and the diversity of theological approaches perceptible in post-Conciliar proposals about the diaconate.

II. *Implications of the Sacramentality of the Diaconate*

As stated above (cf. Chapter IV), the most reliable doctrine and that most in accord with ecclesial practise is that which holds that the diaconate is

---

[229] Cf. *AAS* 59 (1967): 697–704; *AAS* 60 (1968): 369–73; *AAS* 64 (1973): 534–40; *Codex Iuris Canonici* (Città del Vaticano, 1983); *Catechismus Catholicae Ecclesiae* (Città del Vaticano, 1997). [English ed.: *Catechism of the Catholic Church.*]

[230] This is the case of two recent guidance documents: Congregatio de Institutione Catholica/Congregatio pro Clericis, *Ratio fundamentalis institutionis diaconorum permanentium* and *Directorium pro ministerio et vita diaconorum permanentium* (Città del Vaticano, 1998). According to Pio Cardinal Laghi, the *Ratio fundamentalis* is a document "di ordine eminentemente pedagogico e non dottrinale" and, according to Darìo Cardinal Castrillón, the *Directorium* "intende presentare linee pratiche." *L'Osservatore Romano*, March 11, 1998, pp. 6–7.

a sacrament. If its sacramentality were denied the diaconate would simply represent a form of ministry rooted in baptism; it would take on a purely functional character, and the Church would possess a wide faculty of decision-making with regard to restoring or suppressing it, and to its specific configuration. Whatever the context, the Church would have a much greater freedom of action than is granted to her over the sacraments instituted by Christ.[231] A denial of the sacramentality of the diaconate would dissipate the main reasons why the diaconate is a theologically disputed question. But to make such a denial would be to diverge from the path marked out by Vatican II. Hence it is with the sacramentality of the diaconate as a starting point that the other questions concerning the theology of the diaconate should be dealt with.

1. The Diaconate as Rooted in Christ

As a sacrament, the diaconate must ultimately be rooted in Christ. The Church, herself rooted in the free gift of the Blessed Trinity, has no capacity to create sacraments or to confer on them their salvific effectiveness.[232] In order to affirm that the diaconate is a sacrament, it is theologically necessary to state that it is rooted in Christ. Moreover, this fact enables us to understand the various theological attempts to link the diaconate directly to Christ himself (whether in regard to the mission of the Apostles,[233] or to the washing of the feet at the Last Supper[234]). But that does not

[231] "Christus, 'sedens ad dexteram Patris' et Spiritum Sanctum in Suum effundens corpus, quod est Ecclesia, iam operatur per sacramenta a Se instituta ad Suam gratiam communicandam.... Efficaciter gratiam efficiunt quam significant propter Christi actionem et per Spiritus Sancti virtutem", CCE 1084.

[232] "Sunt efficacia quia in eis Ipse Christus operatur: Ipse est qui baptizat, Ipse est qui in Suis agit sacramentis ut gratiam communicet quam sacramentum significat.... Hic est sensus affirmationis Ecclesiae: sacramenta agunt ex opere operato ... , i.e., virtute salvifici operis Christi, semel pro semper adimpleti", CCE 1127f.

[233] Cf. CCE 1536: "Ordo est sacramentum per quod missio a Christo Ipsius Apostolis concredita exerceri pergit in Ecclesia usque ad finem temporum: est igitur ministerii apostolici sacramentum. Tres implicat gradus: Episcopatum, presbyteratum et diaconatum."

[234] For the application of the passage about the washing of the feet to deacons, cf. Didascalia 16, 13 (trans. F. Nau [Paris, 1912], 135f.) and H. Wasserschleben, Die irische Canonensammlung (Leipzig, 1885), 26: "Diaconus [fuit] Christus, quando lavit pedes discipulorum": cf. K. Rahner and H. Vorgrimmler, Diaconia in Christo (Freiburg, 1962), 104. Recently, W. Kasper proposed seeing in the washing of the feet and in the words of Jesus at John 13:15 "die Stiftung des Diakonats", "Der Diakon in ekklesiologischer Sicht angesichts der gegenwärtigen Herausforderungen in Kirche und Gesellschaft", in Diakonia 32/3–4 (1997): 22. In reality it is the whole of the passage at Mark 10:43–45 that Didascalia 3, 13 cites in relation to deacons. For his part, St. Ignatius of Antioch considers that

imply that it is necessary to maintain that Christ himself "instituted" the diaconate directly as a degree of the sacrament. The Church played a decisive role in its specific historical establishment. That fact was implicitly recognised in the opinion (a minority one today) which identified the institution of the Seven (cf. Acts 6:1–6) with the first deacons.[235] This has emerged clearly from the exegetical and theological studies on the complex of historical developments and the progressive differentiation of ministries and charisms, finally arriving at the tripartite structure of bishop, priest and deacon.[236] The cautious language used by Trent ("divina ordinatione") and Vatican II ("divinitus institutum ... iam ab antiquo")[237] reflects the impossibility of totally identifying Christ's and the Church's activity with relation to the sacraments, and also reflects the complexity of the historical facts.

2. The Sacramental "Character" of the Diaconate and Its "Configuration" with Christ

Vatican II makes no explicit statement about the sacramental character of the diaconate; however, the post-Conciliar documents do. These speak of the "indelible character" linked to the stable condition of service (*Sacrum diaconatus*, 1967) or of an imprint which cannot be removed and which configures the deacon to Christ, who made himself the "deacon" or

---

deacons were entrusted with "the service of Jesus Christ" (*Magn.* 6, 1) and St. Polycarp exhorts them to walk in the truth of the Lord, who became the "diakonos" of all (*Phil.* 5, 2).

[235] Current exegetical debate on the consideration of Acts 6:1–6 as the origin of the diaconate goes back to the patristic texts: St. Irenaeus (second century), *Adv. haer.* 1, 26, 3; 3, 12, 10 sees the ordination of the "Seven" as the beginning of the diaconate; St. John Chrysostom (circa 400), *In Acta Apost.* 14, 3 (PG 60, 115f.) does not consider the "Seven" to be deacons, although he does interpret their post as an ordination and a share in the apostolic mission. This second opinion was adopted by the synod in Trullo (692), a synod which has the status of an ecumenical council for the Orthodox Church; cf. Concilium Quinisextum, can. 16 (Mansi, 11:949; ed. Joannou, 1/1, 132–34).

[236] The differentiation into three grades or degrees appears clearly in the post-Apostolic period, first perhaps with St. Ignatius of Antioch's *Ad Trall.* 3, 1. On this question, cf. E. Dassmann, *Ämter und Dienste in der frühchristlichen Gemeinden* (Bonn, 1994); E. Cattaneo, *I ministeri della Chiesa antica: Testi patristici dei primi tre secoli* (Milan, 1997).

[237] "Sic ministerium ecclesiasticum divinitus institutum diversis ordinibus exercetur ab illis qui iam ab antiquo Episcopi, Presbyteri, Diaconi vocantur", *LG* 28a, with references to Trent, DS 1765 ("in Ecclesiae ordinatissima dispositione plures et diversi essent ministrorum ordines ... ab ipso Ecclesiae initio") and DS 1776 ("hierarchiam, divina ordinatione institutam, quae constat ex episcopis, presbyteris et ministris").

servant of all (*CCE*, 1997).[238] The doctrine of the diaconal "character" is consistent with the sacramentality of the diaconate and is a specific application to it of what Trent (1563) said of the sacrament of Holy Orders as a whole.[239] It rests on the witness of theological tradition.[240] It corroborates God's fidelity to his gifts, and implies the unrepeatable nature of the sacrament and lasting stability in ecclesial service.[241] Finally, it confers upon the diaconate a theological solidity which cannot be dissolved into something purely functional. However, this doctrine does raise certain questions which demand further theological clarifications. For instance, *Lumen gentium* 10 lays down that the distinction between the common priesthood of the faithful and the ministerial priesthood is "essentia, non gradu tantum": in what sense should this be applied to the diaconate?[242] While maintaining the unity of the sacrament of Holy Orders, how should the particularity of the diaconal character be further clarified in its distinctive relation to the priestly character and the episcopal character? What resources should be used to differentiate symbolically the specific configuration with Christ of each of the three grades?

[238] "Non tamquam merus ad sacerdotium gradus est existimandus, sed indelebile suo charactere ac praecipua sua gratia insignis ita locupletatur, ut qui ad ipsum vocentur, ii mysteriis Christi et Ecclesiae stabiliter inservire possint", Paul VI, *Sacrum diaconatus*, *AAS* 59 (1967): 698. "Diaconi missionem et gratiam Christi, modo speciali, participant. Ordinis sacramentum eos signat *sigillo* ('charactere') quod nemo delere potest et quod eos configurat Christo qui factus est 'diaconus', id est, omnium minister", *CCE* 1570. "Prout gradus Ordinis sacri, diaconatus characterem imprimit et specificam gratiam sacramentalem communicat. Character diaconalis est signum configurativum-distinctivum animae modo indelebili impressum", *Ratio fundamentalis*, 7. In the measure in which can. 1008 of the CIC also refers to the diaconate, its indelible character may also be considered to be stated there.

[239] "Quoniam vero in sacramento ordinis, sicut et in baptismo et confirmatione, character imprimitur, qui nec deleri nec auferri potest: merito sancta Synodus damnat eorum sententiam, qui asserunt, Novi Testamenti sacerdotes temporariam tantummodo potestatem habere, et semel rite ordinatos iterum laicos effici posse, si verbi Dei ministerium non exerceant." Council of Trent, DS 1767.

[240] Cf. St. Thomas, *In IV Sent.*, d. 7, q. 2 ad 1; *STh* III, q. 63, a. 3.

[241] Although it does not specifically mention the doctrine of "character", as regards the diaconate the *Directorium* states (no. 21): "Sacra Ordinatio, semel valide recepta, numquam evanescit. Amissio tamen status clericalis fit iuxta normas iure canonico statutas."

[242] The *Directorium* (no. 28) speaks of the "essential difference" which exists between the ministry of the deacon at the altar and that of every other liturgical minister; however, it gives a reference not to *LG* 10, but to *LG* 29: "Constat eius diaconiam apud altare, quatenus a sacramento Ordinis effectam, essentialiter differre a quolibet ministerio liturgico, quod pastores committere possint christifidelibus non ordinatis. Ministerium liturgicum diaconi pariter differt ab ipso ministerio sacerdotali."

Vatican II does not use the vocabulary of configuration but instead employs sober expressions which include sacramentality.[243] It also speaks of a special share in the mission and grace of the Supreme Priest.[244] In the Motu Proprio *Ad pascendum* (1972) the permanent deacon is considered a sign or sacrament of Christ himself.[245] The *Catechismus Catholicae Ecclesiâe* (1997) does make use of the vocabulary of configuration, and links it to the doctrine of character.[246] All these texts therefore give evidence of a further development of the Conciliar texts, starting from the deacon's immediate relation with Christ by virtue of the sacrament of Holy Orders. It only remains to describe its precise scope.

3. Diaconal Action, "in Persona Christi (Capitis)"?

The technical expression *"in persona Christi (Capitis)"* is used in different ways in the texts of Vatican II. It is employed in reference to the episcopal ministry, considered either as a whole or in one of the functions proper to it;[247] particularly noticeable is its application to the Eucharistic ministry of the ministerial priesthood (presbyterate) as the maximum expression of this ministry,[248] because to preside at and to consecrate

---

[243] "Gratia sacramentali roborati", *LG* 29a; "gratiam sacramentalem diaconatus", *AG* 16f.

[244] "Missionis autem et gratiae supremi Sacerdotis peculiari modo participes sunt inferioris quoque ordinis ministri, imprimis Diaconi, qui mysteriis Christi et Ecclesiae servientes", *LG* 41d.

[245] "Diaconatus permanens . . . signum vel sacramentum ipsius Christi Domini, qui non venit ministrari, sed ministrare", Paul VI, *Ad pascendum*, *AAS* 54 (1972): 536.

[246] In reference to *LG* 41 and *AG* 16, the *CCE* says (no. 1570): "Diaconi missionem et gratiam Christi, modo speciali, participant. Ordinis sacramentum eos signat *sigillo* ('charactere') quod nemo delere potest et quod eos configurat Christo qui factus est 'diaconus', id est, omnium minister." Meanwhile the *Ratio* (nos. 5, 7) links this configuration to the outpouring of the Spirit and identifies it specifically by its assimilation to Christ as Servant of all: "Diaconatus confertur per peculiarem effusionem Spiritus (*ordinatio*), quae in recipientis persona specificam efficit configurationem cum Christo, Domino et Servo omnium . . . is (diaconus) enim, prout unici ministerii ecclesiastici particeps, est in Ecclesia specificum signum sacramentale Christi servi. . . . Character diaconalis est signum configurativum-distinctivum animae modo indelebili impressum, quod sacro ordine auctos configurat Christo."

[247] The sacramentality of the episcopate implies that "Episcopi, eminenti ac adspectabili modo, ipsius Christi Magistri, Pastoris et Pontificis partes sustineant et in Eius persona agant", *LG* 21b; at other points analogous formulas are used such as: "Episcopi sententiam de fide et moribus nomine Christi prolatam", *LG* 25; "potestas qua, nomine Christi personaliter funguntur", *LG* 27; "munus in ipsius nomine et potestate docendi, sanctificandi et regendi", *AA* 2b; "oves suas in nomine Domini pascunt", *CD* 11b.

[248] In *LG* 10b, on the subject of the essential difference between the common priesthood of the faithful and the ministerial priesthood, it is said of the ministerial priesthood

the Eucharist belongs to its exclusive competence.[249] The perspective is much wider in other texts, where the expression may embrace the whole ministerial activity of the priest as a personification of Christ the Head, or allude to other distinct specific functions.[250] However, in the Conciliar texts there is no question of applying this expression explicitly to the functions of the diaconal ministry. Nevertheless, such a mode of expression does emerge in the post-Conciliar documents.[251] That is

that "potestate sacra qua gaudet, populum sacerdotalem efformat ac regit, sacrificium eucharisticum in persona Christi conficit illudque nomine totius populi Deo offert"; in turn, *LG* 28a states of priests that "suum vero munus sacrum maxime exercent in eucharistico cultu vel synaxi, qua in persona Christi agentes ... unicum sacrificium ... repraesentant"; likewise *PO* 13b states that "praesertim in Sacrificio Missae, Presbyteri personam specialiter gerunt Christi."

[249] The connection of "in persona Christi" with the exclusive competence of the priest to consecrate the Eucharist was underlined in the post-Conciliar documents: the synod of 1971 stated that "solus sacerdos in persona Christi agere valet ad praesidendum et perficiendum sacrificale convivium", *Ench. Vat.* 4, 1166; the letter of the Congregation for the Doctrine of the Faith, *Sacerdotium ministeriale*, 1983, stresses that "munus tam grave conficiendi mysterium eucharisticum adimplere valeant [episcopi et presbyteri] ... ut ipsi ... non communitatis mandato, sed agant in persona Christi", *AAS* 75 (1983): 1006; this is recalled in the 1983 CIC: "Minister, qui in persona Christi sacramentum Eucharistiae conficere valet, est solus sacerdos valide ordinatus", can. 900, 1.

[250] "Presbyteri, unctione Spiritus Sancti, speciali charactere signantur et sic Christo Sacerdoti configurantur, ita ut in persona Christi Capitis agere valeant", *PO* 2c; the equivalent expression in *PO* 12a goes in the same direction : "omnis sacerdos, suo modo, ipsius Christi personam gerat". The priestly ministry as a whole is included in the references of *AG* 39a ("Presbyteri personam Christi gerunt ... in triplici sacro munere") and *LG* 37a ("illos, qui ratione sacri sui muneris personam Christi gerunt"); in *SC* 33a it is made more specific as a presiding at the celebration of the Eucharist: "Immo, preces a sacerdote, qui coetui in persona Christi praeest, ... dicuntur". Post-Conciliar documents: in *Evangelii nuntiandi*, Paul VI applies the formula to the ministry of evangelization: "Cum Episcopis in ministerium evangelizationis consociantur ... ii qui per sacerdotalem ordinationem personam Christi gerunt", *EN* 68, *Ench. Vat.* 5, 1683; John Paul II employs it when referring to the specific ministry of reconciliation in the sacrament of penance: "Sacerdos, Paenitentiae minister ... agit 'in persona Christi'", *Reconciliatio et Paenitentia* (1984), 29; according to *Pastores dabo vobis* (1992), the priest represents Christ the Head, Shepherd and Spouse of the Church: "connectuntur cum 'consecratione', quae eorum propria est eosque ad Christum, Ecclesiae Caput et Pastorem configurat; vel cum 'missione' vel ministerio presbyterorum proprio, quod eos habiles efficit et instruit ut fiant 'Christi Sacerdotis aeterni viva instrumenta' et ad agendum provehit 'Ipsius Christi nomine et persona'", 20; "Presbyter, per sacramentalem hanc consecrationem, configuratur Christo Iesu quatenus Capiti et Pastori Ecclesiae", 21; "Sacerdos ergo advocatur ut sit imago vivens Iesu Christi, Ecclesiae sponsi: remanet ipse quidem semper communitatis pars ... , sed vi eiusdem configurationis ad Christum Caput et Pastorem, ipse presbyter positus est in eiusmodi relatione sponsali erga propriam communitatem", 22.

[251] The 1983 CIC applies the formula to the whole of the sacrament of Holy Orders, and consequently to the diaconate as well: "Sacramento ordinis ... consecrantur et deputantur

currently a source of differences of opinion on the part of theologians (especially in what concerns the representation of Christ the "Head"), because of the diverse meaning which the expression has in the documents of the Magisterium and in theological propositions.

If it is applied to the sacrament of Holy Orders as a whole, as being a specific participation in the threefold "munus" of Christ, then it can be said that the deacon also acts "in persona Christi (Capitis)" (or other equivalent expressions of a specific "representing" of Christ in the diaconal ministry), since the diaconate constitutes one of the grades of this sacrament. Today, many theologians follow this line, which is consistent with the sacramentality of the diaconate, and is supported by some documents of the Magisterium and certain theological trends. By contrast, those who reserve the expression to the functions of the priest alone, especially those of presiding at and consecrating the Eucharist, do not apply it to the diaconate and find corroboration of this opinion in the latest edition of the *CCE* (1997).

In the final edition of no. 875 of the *CCE* the expression "*in persona Christi Capitis*" is not applied to the diaconal functions of service.[252] In this case the capacity to act "*in persona Christi Capitis*" seems to be reserved to bishops and priests. Theological opinions are not unanimous on the question of whether this signifies a definitive exclusion or not. In a way, no. 875 of the *CCE* is a return to the language of *Lumen gentium* 28a, *Presbyterorum ordinis* 2c (priestly ministry) and *Lumen gentium* 29a (triple diakonia). Furthermore, other texts from the *CCE* itself do seem to apply the expression to the whole of the sacrament of Holy Orders,[253] while

---

ut, pro suo quisque gradu, in persona Christi Capitis munera docendi, sanctificandi et regendi adimplendi, Dei populum pascant. Ordines sunt episcopatus, presbyteratus et diaconatus", can. 1008/9. An intervention by John Paul II includes the idea of personification, but applied to Christ the servant, cf. note 255 infra. The 1998 *Directorium* prefers the formula "in the name of Christ" to refer to the Eucharistic ministry of the deacon ("nomine ipsius Christi, inservit ad Ecclesiam participem reddendam fructuum sacrificii sui", 28) and in relation with the diakonia of charity ("Vi sacramenti Ordinis diaconus ... munera pastoralia participat ... quae participatio, utpote per sacramentum peracta, efficit ut diaconi Populum Dei inserviant nomine Christi", 37).

[252] "Ab Eo [Christo] Episcopi et presbyteri missionem et facultatem ('sacram potestatem') agendi *in persona Christi Capitis* accipiunt, diaconi vero vim populo Dei serviendi in 'diaconia' liturgiae, verbi et caritatis", *CCE* 875.

[253] "Per ordinationem recipitur capacitas agendi tamquam Christi legatus, Capitis Ecclesiae", *CCE* 1581; "sacramento ordinis, cuius munus est, nomine et in persona Christi Capitis, in communitate servire", *CCE* 1591; "In ecclesiali ministri ordinati servitio, Ipse Christus, Ecclesiae suae est praesens, quatenus Caput Sui corporis", *CCE* 1548.

recognising a primordial role on the part of bishops and priests.[254] Thus there is a diversity of tendencies which are difficult to bring into harmony, and which are clearly reflected in the various theological understandings of the diaconate. And even if it is considered theologically sound to understand the diaconal ministry as an action *"in persona Christi (Capitis)"*, it still has to be clarified what characterizes the diaconate's specific way (the "specificum") of rendering Christ present as distinct from that of the episcopal ministry and the priestly ministry.

4. "In Persona Christi Servi" as the Specificity of the Diaconate?

One way of doing this is to underline the aspect of "service" and see the specific characteristic, or a particularly distinctive element, of the diaconate, in the representation of the Christ the "Servant". This course appears in the most recent documents[255] and in some theological essays. However, difficulties arise, not because of the central importance of the notion of service for every ordained minister, but because this is made the specific criterion of the diaconal ministry. Could "headship" and "service" in the representating of Christ be separated so as to make each of the two a principle of specific differentiation? Christ the Lord is at the same time the supreme Servant and the servant of all.[256] The ministries of the bishop[257] and the priest, precisely in their function of presiding and of representing Christ the Head, Shepherd and Spouse of his Church, also render Christ the Servant visible,[258] and require to be exercised as services. This

[254] "Per ministerium ordinatum, prasertim Episcoporum et presbyterorum, praesentia Christi, tamquam Capitis Ecclesiae, in communitate credentium, visibilis fit", *CCE* 1549.

[255] For example, the *Ratio fundamentalis* stresses the simultaneous configuration of the deacon "cum Christo, Domino et Servo omnium" and considers it to be "specificum signum sacramentale Christi Servi", 5. John Paul II, for his part, stated (16 March 1985): "Il diacono nel suo grado personifica Cristo servo del Padre, partecipando alla triplice funzione del sacramento dell' Ordine", *Insegnamenti* 8/1, 649.

[256] The same text of St. Polycarp, *Ad Phil.* 5, 2 (ed. Funk, 1:300), which *LG* 29a and the *Ratio* no. 5 apply to deacons, considers Christ as Lord and Servant (minister): "Misericordes, seduli, incedentes iuxta veritatem Domini, qui omnium minister factus est."

[257] On the subject of bishops, *LG* 24a declares: "Munus autem illud quod Dominus pastoribus populi sui commisit, verum est servitium quod in sacris Litteris 'diakonia' seu ministerium significanter nuncupatur (cf. Acts 1:17 and 25; 21:19; Rom 11:13; 1 Tim 1:12)."

[258] Cf. *Pastores dabo vobis*, 21: "Christus est Ecclesiae Caput, sui scilicet Corporis. 'Caput' est eo quidem novo et sibi proprio modo, 'servum' scilicet significandi, prout ab Ipsius verbis evincitur (Mk 10:45). . . . Quod servitium seu 'ministerium' plenitudinem sui attigit per mortem in cruce acceptam, id est per totale sui donum, in humilitate at amore (Phil 2:7–8). . . . Auctoritas autem Christi Iesu Capitis eadem est ac Ipsius servitium, donum,

is why it would seem problematic to aim to distinguish the diaconate through its exclusive representation of Christ as Servant. Given that service should be considered a characteristic common to every ordained minister,[259] the point in any case would be to see how in the diaconate it takes on predominant importance and particular solidity. To avoid disproportionate theological exchanges on this matter, it is appropriate to bear in mind simultaneously the unity of the person of Christ, the unity of the sacrament of order, and the symbolic character of the terms used to represent Christ ("head", "servant", "shepherd", "spouse").

5. Specific Diaconal "Functions"?

In Vatican II and the post-Conciliar documents, the functions attributed to deacons are many and diverse in varied fields, or, as *Lumen gentium* 29a puts it, "in diaconia liturgiae, verbi et caritatis". These documents do not discuss the fact that all those tasks and functions can be carried out (as happens today in many communities) by Christians who have not received diaconal ordination. Now, according to *Ad gentes* 16f there do seem to exist "actual functions of the deacon's office" previous to ordination; and in this case ordination would merely strengthen, bind more closely to the altar, and make more effective because of the sacramental grace of the diaconate.[260] This statement confirms the doubts felt by some in regard to the sacramentality of the diaconate. How can this sacramentality be said to exist if it does not confer any specific "potestas" like that conferred by the priesthood and the episcopate? This same statement is taken by certain local Churches as justifying mistrust and a negative attitude towards the institution of the permanent diaconate: why, they ask, proceed to this ordination if the same functions can be fulfilled by laypeople and lay ministers, who may be more effective and more adaptable? This theological matter thus has practical

---

totalis deditio, humilis atque dilectionis plena, erga Ecclesiam. Idque in perfecta erga Patrem oboedientia. Ille enim, unicus verusque est afflictus et dolens Domini Servus, idemque Sacerdos et Hostia seu Victima."

[259] The *CCE* states (876): "Intrinsece coniuncta naturae sacramentali ministerii ecclesialis est *eius indoles servitii*. Ministri etenim, prorsus dependentes a Christo qui missionem praebet et auctoritatem, vere sunt 'servi Christi' ad imaginem Christi qui libere propter nos 'formam servi' (Phil 2:7) accepit. Quia verbum et gratia quorum sunt ministri, eorum non sunt, sed Christi qui illa eis pro aliis concredidit, ipsi libere omnium fient servi."

[260] "Iuvat enim viros, qui ministerio vere diaconali fungantur ... per impositionem manuum inde ab Apostolis traditam corroborari et altari arctius coniungi, ut ministerium suum per gratiam sacramentalem diaconatus efficacius expleant", *AG* 16f.

and pastoral repercussions which Vatican II did not deal with explicitly and which need to be tackled in the perspective of an ecclesiology of communion (cf. section IV infra). The desire of the Council was to make it clear how each "potestas sacra" in the Church was rooted in the sacraments, and that was why the Council did not consider it indispensable to have recourse to the traditional distinction between "power of order" and "power of jurisdiction".[261] In any case that did not prevent it from reappearing in the post-Conciliar documents.[262]

III. The Diaconate in the Perspective of the Episcopate as "Plenitudo Sacramenti Ordinis"

Vatican II gave a clear and authentic statement of the sacramentality of the episcopate, considering it as the "fullness of the sacrament of Orders" (LG 21b).[263] The reversal of views implied in this statement does not make the episcopal "fullness" any reason for depriving the priesthood and the diaconate of their proper consistency, as though their only meaning lay in being preparatory stages for the episcopate. In their participation in the one priesthood of Christ and the mission of salvation, priests cooperate with bishops and depend on them in the pastoral exercise of

---

[261] Vatican II does not use the expression "potestas iurisdictionis" and only in PO 2b does it speak of "sacra ordinis potestas". However, in the Explanatory Note, 2, of LG, it affirms with reference to episcopal consecration: "In consecratione datur ontologica participatio sacrorum munerum, ut indubie constat ex Traditione, etiam liturgica. Consulto adhibetur vocabulum munerum, non vero potestatum, quia haec ultima vox de potestate ad actum expedita intelligi posset. Ut vero talis expedita potestas habeatur, accedere debet canonica seu iuridica determinatio per auctoritatem hierarchicam. Quae determinatio potestatis consistere potest in concessione particularis officii vel in assignatione subditorum, et datur iuxta normas a suprema auctoritate adprobatas. Huiusmodi ulterior norma ex natura rei requiritur, quia agitur de muneribus quae a pluribus subiectis, hierarchice ex voluntate Christi cooperantibus, exerceri debent." On the different interpretations of the "potestas sacra", cf. Krämer, Dienst und Vollmacht in der Kirche: Eine rechtstheologische Untersuchung zur Sacra Potestas-Lehre des II. Vatikanischen Konzils (Trier, 1973), 38f.; A. Celeghin, Origine e natura della potestà sacra: Posizioni postconciliari (Brescia, 1987).

[262] CIC, can. 966, distinguishes between "potestate ordinis" and "facultate eandem exercendi".

[263] "Docet autem Sancta Synodus episcopali consecratione plenitudinem conferri sacramenti Ordinis, quae nimirum et liturgica Ecclesiae consuetudine et voce Sanctorum Patrum summum sacerdotium, sacri ministerii summa nuncupatur", LG 21b. The doctrinal relatio understands the expression finally used (plenitudo sacramenti) as "totalitas omnis partes includens", AS 3/1, 238. LG 41b considers bishops to be "ad imaginem summi et aeterni Sacerdotis, Pastoris et Episcopi ... ad plenitudinem sacerdotii electi".

the ministry.[264] It now remains to see how the diaconate should be understood theologically from the same point of view.

1. The Unity of the Sacrament of Holy Orders

The statement of the unity of the sacrament of Holy Orders can be considered to form part of the common theological patrimony, and to have done so from the time (in the twelfth and following centuries) when the question was raised as to the sacramentality of the different degrees of Holy Orders.[265] This unity is maintained by Vatican II in speaking of the different orders, including the diaconate, in which the ecclesiastical ministry is exercised.[266] The post-Conciliar documents take the same line. The difficulties arise not from the assertion of this unity, but from the theological path taken in order to justify it. Traditionally, this unity was justified by the relation of this sacrament to the Eucharist, while respecting the different modalities proper to each degree.[267] Vatican II modified the viewpoints and the formulations. Hence the need to seek another path to justify it. Such a path might well take as its starting point some consideration of the episcopate as the "fullness" of the sacrament of Holy Orders and the foundation of its unity.

2. "Profile" and "Consistency" of the Diaconate

There is a theological understanding of the ordained ministry perceived as "hierarchy", which has been preserved by Vatican II and in subsequent

[264] "Presbyteri, quamvis pontificatus apicem non habeant et in exercenda sua potestate ab Episcopis pendeant, cum eis tamen sacerdotali honore coniuncti sunt et vi sacramenti Ordinis, ad imaginem Christi, summi atque aeterni Sacerdotis ... consecrantur, ut veri sacerdotes Novi Testamenti. Muneris unici Mediatoris Christi (cf. 1 Tim 2:5) participes in suo gradu ministerii.... Presbyteri, ordinis Episcopalis providi cooperatores eiusque adiutorium", LG 28.

[265] Cf. several references in L. Ott, *Das Weihesakrament*, HbDG 4/5 (Freiburg, 1969). Trent, cf. DS 1763–78, takes its unity for granted as a starting point when speaking of the "sacrament of Order", as in the case of baptism and confirmation (cf. DS 1767).

[266] "Sic ministerium ecclesiasticum divinitus institutum diversis ordinibus exercetur ab illis qui iam ab antiquo Episcopi, Presbyteri, Diaconi vocantur", LG 28a.

[267] Cf. St. Thomas, STh III, Suppl., q. 37, a. 2, resp.: "Distinctio ordinis est accipienda secundum relationem ad Eucharistiam. Quia potestas ordinis aut est ad consecrationem Eucharistiae ipsius, aut ad aliquod ministerium ordinandum ad hoc. Si primo modo, sic est ordo sacerdotum."

documents. This understanding[268] leads to the doctrine of the different "degrees" of Holy Orders. Here deacons represent the "lowest" degree in the hierarchical scale, in relation to bishops and priests.[269] The internal unity of the sacrament of Holy Orders means that each degree participates "suo modo" in the triple ministerial "munus", on a descending scale on which the higher degree includes and surpasses the whole reality and functions of the lower. This hierarchized and graded "participation" in one and the same sacrament means that the deacon is a minister who depends on the bishop and the priest.

The difficulty in giving the (permanent) diaconate its own profile and consistency in this hierarchized scheme of things has led to the proposal of other models of interpretation. It is obviously not compatible with the Conciliar texts to consider the episcopate, the priesthood and the diaconate as three totally autonomous sacraments, juxtaposed and equal. The unity of the sacrament of Holy Orders would be seriously damaged, and such a view would prevent the episcopate from being seen as the "fullness" of the sacrament. For this reason certain contemporary theological approaches highlight the tradition of ancient sources and rites of ordination in which the diaconate appears "ad ministerium *episcopi*". The diaconate's direct and immediate relation to the episcopal ministry[270] would make deacons the natural collaborators of the bishop: that would imply for them the possibility of performing (preferentially) tasks in the super-parochial and diocesan field.

In that case what still remains to be explained more fully is the relation of the (permanent) diaconate with the priesthood. According to certain people, priests and deacons are on the same level with regard to the "fullness" of the sacrament represented by the episcopal ministry. Such people see this reflected in the ancient practise of ordinations (a deacon could be ordained bishop without necessarily passing through the priesthood, and a layman could be ordained a priest without passing through the diaconate[271]). These are historical facts

---

[268] Cf. *LG* 10b: "sacerdotium ministeriale seu hierarchicum"; the *CCE* gives the heading "Hierarchica Ecclesiae constitutio" to the doctrine on the ecclesial ministry which it sets out in nos. 874–96.

[269] "In gradu inferiori hierarchiae sistunt Diaconi", *LG* 29a. With the suppression of the other degrees in *Ministeria quaedam* (1972), the diaconate became in fact the last degree.

[270] The *Directorium* (8) speaks explicitly of "participation" in the episcopal ministry: "Fundamentum obligationis consistit in ipsa participatione ministerii episcopalis, quae per sacramentum Ordinis et missionem canonicam confertur." Further on, no. 11 warns against what would prejudice the "relatio directa et inmediata, quam quilibet diaconus cum proprio episcopo habere debet".

[271] Cf. M. Andrieu, "La carrière ecclésiastique des papes et les documents liturgiques du Moyen-Âge", *RevScRel* 21 (1947): 90–120.

which need to be borne in mind when delineating the ecclesiological profile of the diaconate today. However, it does not seem theologically justifiable to exclude deacons from every form of help and cooperation with priests,[272] and especially not with the "presbyterium" as a whole.[273] The hypothesis of a "diaconal college" around the bishop, as a manifestation of the "ordo diaconorum" similar to the "presbyterium"[274] and in communion with it, would require further theological study. The Conciliar and post-Conciliar texts say practically nothing about this possibility.[275] On the other hand, some contemporary theologico-pastoral essays maintain that the idea of a diaconal college would contribute solidity to the ecclesial profile required by a ministry which entails the demand of stability (the permanent diaconate).[276]

---

[272] In regard to their relation with bishops, the *Ratio fundamentalis* (1998), 8, says that deacons "depend" on bishops in the exercise of their power; and speaks of a "special relationship" of deacons with priests: "Diaconi, cum ecclesiasticum ministerium in inferiore gradu participent, in sua potestate exercenda necessario ex Episcopis pendent prout plenitudinem sacramenti habentibus. Praeterea, necessitudinem peculiarem cum presbyteris ineunt, quippe in communione quorum ad populum Dei serviendum sunt vocati."

[273] "[Diaconi] Populo Dei, in communione cum Episcopo eiusque *presbyterio*, inserviunt", *LG* 29a. The Motu Proprio *Sacrum diaconatus,* 23, which applies the Conciliar decisions, underlines submission to the authority of the bishop and the priest: "Quae omnia munera in perfecta cum episcopo eiusque presbyterio communione exsequenda sunt, videlicet sub auctoritate episcopi et presbyteri, qui eo loci fidelium curae praesunt." The *Caeremoniale Episcoporum* . . . , Typ. Pol. Vat. 1985, no. 24, says with regard to deacons: "Spiritus Sancti dono roborati, Episcopo eiusque *presbyterio* adiumentum praestant in ministerio verbi, altaris et caritatis."

[274] Deacons cannot be members of the council of priests; cf. *LG* 28; *CD* 27; *PO* 7; and CIC, can. 495, 1. This is confirmed by the *Directorium*, 42: "Nequeunt tamen esse membra consilii presbyteralis, quia ipsum exclusive presbyterium repraesentat."

[275] The 1998 *Directorium* (6) recalls the "sacramental fraternity" which unites deacons, the importance of the bonds of charity, prayer, unity and cooperation, and that it is opportune for them to meet together; but it says nothing about the possibility of a collegial "ordo diaconorum", and it warns against the risks of "corporatism" which was a factor in the disappearance of the permanent diaconate in earlier centuries: "Diaconi, vi ordinis accepti, fraternitate sacramentali inter se uniti sunt.... Praestat ut diaconi, consentiente Episcopo et ipso Episcopo praesente aut eius delegato, statutis temporibus congregentur.... Ad Episcopum loci spectat inter diaconos in dioecesi operantes spiritum communionis alere, evitando ne ille 'corporativismus' efformetur, qui praeteritis saeculis tantopere ad diaconatum permanentem evanescendum influxit."

[276] "Specifica vocatio diaconi permanentis stabilitatem in hoc ordine supponit. Fortuitus igitur transitus ad presbyteratum diaconorum permanentium, non uxoratorum vel viduorum, rarissima exceptio semper erit, quae admitti non poterit, nisi graves et speciales rationes id suadeant", *Directorium*, 5.

3. The Imposition of Hands "non ad sacerdotium ..."

According to *Lumen gentium* 29a, deacons receive the imposition of hands "non ad sacerdotium, sed ad ministerium". On this point Vatican II refers to text such as the *Statuta Ecclesiae antiqua*,[277] whose formula has remained the same until our own times in the Roman Pontifical.[278] However, the formula goes back to the *Traditio Apostolica* (second and third centuries), which specifies something which is absent from the Council texts: "in ministerio episcopi".[279] Moreover, the interpretation of the precise meaning of this divergence is disputed in the current theology of the diaconate.[280] What seems excluded in this formulation ("sacerdotium") will be looked at first; after that, what seems to be stated in it (the relationship to "ministerium").

The diaconate is not "ad sacerdotium". How should this exclusion be interpreted? In a stricter sense the ministerial "sacerdotium" has been traditionally linked with the power "conficiendi eucharistiam",[281] "offerendi sacrificium in Ecclesia",[282] or "consecrandi verum corpus et sanguinem Domini".[283] Down the centuries, the basis for the sacramental equality of

---

[277] *LG* 29a gives a reference to *Constitutiones Ecclesiae Aegypciacae* 3, 2 (ed. Funk, *Didascalia* 2, 103); *Statuta Eccl. ant.* 37–41 (Mansi, 3:954) (but in fact it is taken from *Statuta Eccl. ant.* 4 [Mansi, 3:951]). The text of the *Statuta* 92 (4), CChr SL 148, 181, says: "Diaconus cum ordinatur, solus episcopus, qui eum benedicit, manum super caput illius ponat, quia non ad sacerdotium sed ad ministerium consecratur."

[278] Cf. *Pontifical Romano-Germanique* (950), vol. 1 (Città del Vaticano, 1963), 24. In the present *Pontificale Romanum* (ed. typ. 1968, 1989), the following expressions are found: "The mission of the deacon is a help for the bishop and his priests [episcopo eiusque presbyterio adiumentum] in the service of the word, of the altar and of charity" (opening address by the bishop); the deacon is ordained "in the service of the Church [ad ministerium Ecclesiae]" and "to provide help to the order of priests [in adiutorium ordinis sacerdotalis]" (bishop's questions to the ordinands). In the consecratory prayer it is recalled that the Apostles "chose seven men to help them in daily service". It will be noted that in the case of a priest, the question asked is whether he "wishes to become a priest, collaborator with the bishops in the priesthood, to serve and guide the people of God under the guidance of the Holy Spirit".

[279] The Latin version (L) says: "In diacono ordinando solus episcopus imponat manus, propterea quia non in sacerdotio ordinatur, sed in ministerio episcopi, ut faciat ea quae ab ipso iubentur." *Trad. Apost.* (ed. B. Botte), SCh 11(2) (Paris, 1968), 58.

[280] The interpretation given by the Council Commission is also controversial: "Verba desumuntur ex Statutis Eccl. Ant. ... et significant diaconos non ad corpus et sanguinem Domini offerendum, sed ad servitium caritatis in Ecclesia ordinari", *AS* 3/8, 101.

[281] "Et utique sacramentum nemo potest conficere, nisi sacerdos, qui rite fuerit ordinatus", Fourth Lateran Council (1215), DS 802; cf. *Trad. Apost.* 4.

[282] "Forma sacerdotii talis est: 'Accipe potestatem offerendi sacrificium in Ecclesia pro vivis et mortuis' ", Council of Florence (1439), DS 1326.

[283] Council of Trent (1563), DS 1771; cf. likewise DS 1764: "Apostolis eorumque successoribus in sacerdotio potestatem traditam consecrandi, offerendi et ministrandi corpus et sanguinem eius, nec non et peccata dimittendi et retinendi."

bishops and priests as "priests", i.e. those who offer sacrifice,[284] and the attribution of a solely jurisdictional origin to the distinction between the two,[285] has been based on this close connection between priesthood and Eucharist. This same reason, then, is why deacons are not ordained "ad sacerdotium", given the impossibility for them of presiding at and validly consecrating the Eucharist, which is a power reserved exclusively to "priests". Does this restriction also imply that the diaconate is excluded from "sacerdotium" understood in a less strict sense? Vatican II did indeed place the relationship between the ministerial priesthood and the Eucharist in a wider context: that of an ecclesiology centred on the Eucharist seen as *"totius vitae christianae fons et culmen"* [286] and that of a ministerial priesthood whose constitutive relationship with the Eucharist is rooted in a broader *"potestas sacra"*, also relating to the other ministerial *"munera"*. [287] If the diaconate is totally excluded from the "priesthood" in all senses of the term, then it will be necessary to re-think the unity of the sacrament of Holy Orders as "ministerial or hierarchical priesthood" (cf. *LG* 10b), as well as the use of "sacerdotal" categories to make a global definition or description of the sacrament. Different tendencies are to be observed on this point in the Conciliar texts, in later developments, and in theological studies of the diaconate.

On one hand the texts of Vatican II which explicitly mention the diaconate do not apply terms or categories of priesthood to it, but ministerial ones.[288] The same is true of the modifications introduced for

[284] "Distinctio ordinis est accipienda secundum relationem ad Eucharistiam. Quia potestas ordinis aut est ad consecrationem Eucharistiae ipsius, aut ad aliquod ministerium ordinandum ad hoc. Si primo modo, sic est ordo sacerdotum. Et ideo, cum ordinantur, accipiunt calicem cum vino et patenam cum pane, potestatem accipientes consecrandi corpus et sanguinem Christi." St. Thomas, *STh* III, *Suppl.*, q. 37, a. 2, resp.

[285] "Episcopatus non est ordo, secundum quod ordo est quoddam sacramentum ... ordinatur omnis ordo ad eucharistiae sacramentum; unde, cum Episcopus non habeat potestatem superiorem sacerdote quantum ad hoc, non erit episcopatus ordo." St. Thomas, *In IV Sent.*, d. 24, q. 3, a. 2, sol. 2.

[286] *LG* 11a. The statement of the central value of the Eucharist is repeated several times. Cf. *PO* 5b ("in Sanctissima ... Eucharistia totum bonum spirituale Ecclesiae continetur"), *UR* 15a ("celebrationem eucharisticam, fontem vitae ecclesiae et pignus futurae gloriae"), *CD* 30f ("ut celebratio Eucharistici Sacrificii centrum sit et culmen totius vitae communitatis christianae").

[287] "Sacerdos quidem ministerialis, potestate sacra qua gaudet, populum sacerdotalem efformat ac regit, sacrificium eucharisticum in persona Christi conficit illudque nomine totius populi Dei offert", *LG* 10b.

[288] Cf. *SC* 35d ("authorized person", which also includes deacons), *LG* 20c ("adiutoribus ... diaconis"), *LG* 28a ("ministerium ecclesiasticum ... Diaconi"), *LG* 29a ("ad ministerium"), *LG* 41d ("ministri, imprimis Diaconi"), *OE* 17 ("institutum diaconatus"), *CD* 15a ("diaconi, qui ad ministerium ordinati"), *DV* 25a ("clericos omnes ... qui ut diaconi"), *AG* 15i ("munera ... diaconorum"), *AG* 16a, f ("salutis ministros in ordine ... Diaconorum ... ordo diaconatus").

the sake of greater precision into the latest edition of the *CCE*, which distinguishes clearly, within the single sacrament of Holy Orders, between a degree of sacerdotal participation (episcopate and priesthood) and a degree of service (deacons), and which excludes the application of the term "sacerdos" to deacons.[289] On the other hand, when Vatican II speaks from the perspective of the single sacrament of Holy Orders, it seems to consider the "priestly" categories as all-inclusive and extends them beyond the distinction between "sacerdotium" and "ministerium". This is the case in *Lumen gentium* 10b, which states that there is a difference of essence and not merely of degree between the common priesthood of the faithful and the ministerial or hierarchical priesthood.[290] In the same way, when it speaks of the spirituality of different states of life in *Lumen gentium* 41d, the Council seems to attribute an intermediate role to deacons in the collection of different ministries (it should be noted that at that point the minor orders had not yet been suppressed), by attributing to deacons a special share in the mission and grace of the High Priest.[291] For its part, the 1983 CIC, in cann. 1008–9, includes deacons within the "sacri ministri", who by their consecration are enabled to pasture the People of God and to execute "pro suo quisque gradu" the functions of teaching, sanctifying and ruling "in persona Christi Capitis".[292]

---

[289] "Doctrina catholica, in liturgia, Magisterio et constanti Ecclesiae explicita praxi, agnoscit duos gradus paiticipationis ministerialis exsistere sacerdotii Christi: Episcopatum et presbyteratum. Diaconatus ad illos adiuvandos atque ad illis serviendum destinatur. Propterea verbum *sacerdos* designat, in usu hodierno, Episcopos et presbyteros, sed non diaconos. Tamen doctrina catholica docet gradus paiticipationis sacerdotalis (Episcopatum et presbyteratum) et gradum servitii (diaconatum) conferri, hos omnes tres, actu sacramentali qui 'ordinatio' appellatur, id est, sacramento Ordinis", *CCE* 1554. The *Ratio fundamentalis*, 4 and 5, also avoids applying terms of "priesthood" etc. to deacons: "Ad eius [cuiusque ministri ordinati] plenam veritatem pertinet esse participatio specifica et repraesentatio ministerii Christi ... manuum impositio diaconum non est 'ad sacerdotium sed ad ministerium', id est non ad celebrationem eucharisticam sed ad servitium ... is [diaconus] enim, prout unici ministerii ecclesiastici particeps, est in Ecclesia specificum signum sacramentale Christi servi."

[290] "Sacerdotium autem commune fidelium et sacerdotium ministeriale seu hierarchicum, licet essentia et non gradu tantum differant, ad invicem tamen ordinantur; unum enim et alterum suo peculiari modo de uno Christi sacerdotio participant", *LG* 10b.

[291] "Missionis autem et gratiae supremi Sacerdotis peculiari modo participes sunt inferioris quoque ordinis ministri, imprimis Diaconi", *LG* 41d. Referring to this text, *CCE* 1570 replaces the expression "supremi Sacerdotis" by that of "Christi": "Diaconi missionem et gratiam Christi, modo speciali participant."

[292] "Sacramento ordinis ex divina institutione inter christifideles quidam charactere indelebili quo signantur, constituuntur sacri ministri, qui nempe consecrantur et deputantur ut, pro suo quisque gradu, in persona Christi Capitis munera docendi, sanctificandi et regendi adimplentes, Dei populum pascant", can. 1008. "Ordines sunt episcopatus, presbyteratus et diaconatus", can. 1009. The 1983 CIC uses the expression "sacri ministri" to designate

Since this was the state of affairs it is not surprising to find that the post-Conciliar efforts to arrive at a theological understanding of the diaconate were marked by tensions born of whether the diaconate was excluded from or included in the priestly categories. As long as the diaconate was merely a step on the way to the priesthood, these tensions were manageable. From the moment when the diaconate was instituted as a permanent state, and took shape and started to grow in many Churches,[293] the theological tensions became more pronounced and developed in two different directions.

On the basis of the unity of the sacrament of Holy Orders, and in the conviction that they were being faithful to the Conciliar and post-Conciliar texts, some people stressed the unity of the sacrament and applied to the diaconate theological principles which were valid in proportionate ways for the three degrees of the sacrament. They maintained, with some differences of emphasis, that it should be generally understood and described as "sacerdotium ministeriale seu hierarchicum" (cf. LG 10b), which, they held, was borne out by the language used in the ancient tradition of the Church.[294] In this line of argument the diaconate is a sacramental reality which implies a difference "essentia, non gradu tantum" (cf. LG 10b) in comparison with the common priesthood of the faithful. Hence the statement that the diaconate is "non ad sacerdotium" would then exclude only what related to the consecration of the Eucharist (and the sacrament of Reconciliation).[295] But both because of its integration within the single sacrament of Holy Orders, and because of its special relationship with the Eucharistic ministry, both by reason of the broadly "priestly" significance of the "munera" of teaching and government and by its specific participation in the mission and grace of the High Priest, the diaconate should still be included within the "ministerial or hierarchical priesthood", as distinct from the "common priesthood" of the faithful.

---

the baptized faithful who have received sacramental ordination. On one hand its expressions are briefer than those of Vatican II, and do not quote LG 29; on the other, despite the qualification "pro suo gradu", it goes further than the explicit texts of Vatican II in applying the notion of "in persona Christi Capitis" to the diaconate.

[293] Cf. the data given in Chapter VI.

[294] Cf., e.g., Tertullian, De exh. cast. 7, 5 (CCh SL 319, 94), in which bishops, priests and deacons constitute the "ordo sacerdotalis" or "sacerdotium"; Leo I, Ep. 12, 5; 14, 3f. (PL 54, 652, 672f.), who also adds sub-deacons as members of the "ordo sacerdotalis"; Optatus of Milevis, Contra Parmen. 1, 13 (SCh 412, 200), for whom deacons formed part of the "third priesthood" ("Quid diaconos in tertio, quid presbyteros in secundo sacerdotio constitutos?"); also St. Jerome, Ep. 48, 21 (CSEL 54, 387): "Episcopi, presbyteri, diaconi aut virgines eliguntur aut vidui aut certe post sacerdotium in aeternum pudici."

[295] Cf. Council of Trent, DS 1764.

Other opposing tendencies insist strongly on the distinction expressed by the formula "non ad sacerdotium, sed ad ministerium". In a line of argument contrary to that just outlined, these writers tend to exclude all "priestly" conceptualization or terminology from the correct understanding of the diaconate. At the same time they highlight this distinction as a decisive step towards overcoming the "sacerdotalization" of the sacrament of Holy Orders. They hold that this sacrament comprises three degrees, of which two (the episcopate and the priesthood) belong to the "sacerdotium" and one (the diaconate) is only "ad ministerium". In this way they avoid a theological understanding of the deacon in the image of a priest whose competencies are (still) limited. It would likewise enable a greater consistency and identity to be recognised in the deacon as a minister of the Church. However, the identity of the deacon is still to be defined in the light of *Lumen gentium* 10b, because, as a sacramental reality, the diaconate is not to be identified with the functions, services and ministries rooted in baptism.

4. "... Sed ad Ministerium (Episcopi)"

Certain theologico-pastoral studies of the (permanent) diaconate see the specific mention "in ministerio *episcopi*"[296] as a basis for asserting that the diaconate has a direct link with the episcopal ministry.[297] While maintaining that this link does exist,[298] Vatican II softened the force it had in the *Traditio Apostolica* by stating that the diaconate was only "ad ministerium", in other words a service for the people exercised in the domain of the liturgy, the word and charity, in communion with the bishop and his presbyterium.[299] John Paul II stressed this dimension of service to the People of God.[300] However, when it comes to specifying the theological

---

[296] Cf. note 279 supra.

[297] *CCE* 1569 itself, citing the formula of the *Traditio* and *LG* 29, underlines the fact that the bishop alone imposes his hands on the deacon at ordination, as a sign of a special connection with him: "Pro diacono ordinando, solus Episcopus manus imponit, ita significans diaconum in muneribus suae 'diaconiae' Episcopo speciatim annecti."

[298] "Episcopos ... qui munus ministerii sui, vario gradu, variis subiectis in Ecclesia legitime tradiderunt", *LG* 28.

[299] "Gratia etenim sacramentali roborati, in diaconia liturgiae, verbi et caritatis Populo Dei, in communione cum Episcopo eiusque presbyterio, inserviunt", *LG* 29. The *Directorium* (22) speaks of assistance given to "bishops" and "priests": "Sic diaconus auxiliatur et inservit episcopis et presbyteris, qui semper praesunt liturgiae, praevigilant super doctrinam et moderantur Populum Dei."

[300] "In this ancient text the 'ministry' is described as 'service of the bishop'; the Council lays the stress on service to the People of God", *Insegnamenti* 16/2, 1000.

scope of the expression "ad ministerium (episcopi)" and the possible integration of the diaconate into the ministry of apostolic succession, they
return in a way to the divergences outlined above. Here too, the Conciliar and post-Conciliar texts are ambivalent.

In the light of *Lumen gentium* 20 and 24a, it has been stated that the bishops are the successors of the Apostles so as to prolong the first apostolic mission until the end of time.[301] As for *Lumen gentium* 28a, it also seems to include
deacons in the line of succession which prolongs the mission of Christ in
that of the Apostles, that of the bishops and that of the ecclesiastical ministry.[302] The *CCE* defines the sacrament of Holy Orders in its three degrees
as "the sacrament of apostolic ministry".[303] With these texts as a basis, despite
the variations in their terminology ("ecclesiastical" and "apostolic" ministry),[304] the diaconate could be considered as an integral part of the ministry of apostolic succession. This would fit in with the unity of the sacrament
of Holy Orders, as rooted ultimately in Christ and with the deacons participating in their own way in the mission which the Apostles and their successors received from Christ.[305]

However, this conclusion is not shared by those who retain the distinction between "sacerdotium" and "ministerium" as a difference of quality,
and give decisive importance to the latest modifications to *CCE* no. 1154
(where the term "sacerdos" is reserved to bishops and priests). They see
these modifications as going beyond what had been said up until that
point, and as a key reference point for future developments. The apostolic ministry is understood as the continuation of the "diakonia" of Christ,
which cannot be dissociated from his "priesthood": the priestly offering
which he makes of his life actually constitutes his diaconal service for the

---

[301] "Inter varia illa ministeria quae inde a primis temporibus in Ecclesia exercentur,
teste traditione, praecipuum locum tenet munus illorum qui, in episcopatum constituti,
per successionem ab initio decurrentem, apostolici seminis traduces habent.... Proinde
docet Sacra Synodus Episcopos ex divina institutione in locum Apostolorum successisse,
tamquam Ecclesiae pastores", *LG* 20; "Episcopi, utpote apostolorum successores, a Domino ... missionem accipiunt", *LG* 24a. In the same sense, cf. DS 1768, 3061, *CCE*
1555.

[302] "Christus, quem Pater sanctificavit et misit in mundum (Jn 10:36), consecrationis
missionisque suae per Apostolos suos, eorum successores, videlicet Episcopos participes
effecit, qui munus ministerii sui, vario gradu, variis subiectis in Ecclesia legitime tradiderunt. Sic ministerium ecclesiasticum divinitus institutum diversis ordinibus exercetur
ab illis qui iam ab antiquo Episcopi, Presbyteri, Diaconi vocantur", *LG* 28a.

[303] "Ordo est sacramentum per quod missio a Christo Ipsius Apostolis concredita exerceri pergit in Ecclesia usque ad finem temporum: est igitur ministerii apostolici sacramentum. Tres implicat gradus: Episcopatum, presbyteratum et diaconatum." *CCE* 1536.

[304] See, even, the expression "ministerial or hierarchical priesthood" in *LG* 10b.

[305] "Apostolis eorumque successoribus a Christo collatum est munus in ipsius nomine
et potestate docendi, sanctificandi et regendi", *AA* 2b; cf. *LG* 19a.

salvation of the world. In this sense the "diakonia" or service characterizes the "munus" of the pastors (bishops) of the People of God[306] and it
would not be sufficient to represent deacons as the specific heirs of the
diaconal dimension of the ministry. The diaconate should be recognised
as apostolic in its foundation, and not in its theological nature. That is to
say, therefore, that the ministry of apostolic succession should be restricted
to "priests"[307] (bishops and priests), while deacons would form part of
the "ecclesiastical" ministry[308] and should be considered, consequently,
as auxiliary collaborators towards the ministry of apostolic succession, and
not, strictly speaking, an integral part of it.

5. The Diaconate as Mediating Function or "Medius Ordo"?

The interventions made at the Council, and the notes of the relevant
Conciliar Commission, already attributed to the permanent diaconate a
mediating or bridging function between the hierarchy and the people.[309]
Although this idea was not retained in the definitive Council texts, it was
in a way reflected in the order adopted in *Lumen gentium* 29: the text
speaks of deacons at the end of Chapter III as the last degree of the
hierarchy, just before dealing with the subject of laypeople in Chapter IV.
The same order is found in *Ad gentes* 16. The actual expression "medius
ordo" applied explicitly to the (permanent) diaconate is found only in
the Motu Proprio *Ad pascendum* (1972) and is presented as one way of
putting into effect the hopes and intentions which had led Vatican II to
restore it.[310] The idea spread widely in contemporary theology, and gave

---

[306] "Munus autem illud quod Dominus pastoribus populi sui commisit, verum est servitium quod in sacris Litteris 'diakonia' seu ministerium significanter nuncupatur", *LG* 24a.

[307] Cf. Council of Trent, DS 1764 ("Apostolis eorumque successoribus in sacerdotio
potestatem traditam consecrandi"), DS 1771 ("sacerdotium visibile et externum"), DS 1765
("tam sancti sacerdotii ministerium ... ministrorum ordines, qui sacerdotio ex officio
deservirent"), DS 1772 ("alios ordines, et maiores et minores, per quos velut per gradus
quosdam in sacerdotium tendatur").

[308] Cf. *LG* 29a.

[309] E.g., Mgr. Yü Pin thought that permanent deacons could exercise a function "pon-
tis seu mediationis inter hierarchiam et christifideles", *AS* 2/2, 431; likewise the Conciliar
Commission retained the idea that married deacons could constitute "quasi pontem" between
the clergy and the people, *AS* 3/1, 267.

[310] "Concilium denique Vaticanum II optatis et precibus suffragatum est, ut Diaconatus permanens, ubi id animarum bono conduceret, instauretur veluti medius ordo inter
superiores ecclesiasticae hierarchiae gradus et reliquum populum Dei, quasi interpres neces-
sitatum ac votorum christianorum communitatum, instimulator famulatus seu *diaconiae*
Ecclesiae apud locales christianas communitates, signum vel sacramentum ipsius Christi
Domini, qui non venit ministrari, sed ministrare." Paul VI, *Ad pascendum*, p. 536.

rise to different ways of conceiving this mediating function: between clergy and laity, between the Church and the world, between worship and ordinary life, between charity work and the Eucharist, between the centre and the periphery of the Christian community. Whatever the context, the notion merits some theological clarifications.

It would be a theological error to identify the diaconate as "medius ordo" with a kind of intermediate (sacramental?) reality between the baptized and the ordained faithful. The fact that the diaconate belongs to the sacrament of Holy Orders is sure doctrine. Theologically the deacon is not a "layperson". Vatican II considers that the deacon is a member of the hierarchy and the CIC refers to him as "sacer minister" or "clericus".[311] It is true that it belongs to the deacon to accomplish some sort of task of mediation, but it would not be theologically correct to make that task into the expression of the diaconate's theological nature or its specifying note. Additionally, there is a certain risk that the fixing of the diaconate in ecclesiological terms, and institutionalizing it in pastoral terms as "medius ordo" might end up by sanctioning and deepening, through that very function, the gap which it was supposed to fill.

These theological clarifications do not imply a total rejection of all mediating function on the part of the deacon. The notion is based on the witnesses of ecclesial tradition.[312] In a certain way it is reflected in the ecclesiological position which current canon law (CIC 1983) attributes to deacons between the mission of laypeople and that of priests. On the one hand, (permanent) deacons live in the middle of the world with a lay style of life (although there is the possibility of a religious permanent diaconate) and with certain "concessions" which are not (or not always) accorded to all clergy and priests.[313] On the other hand there are certain functions in which deacons and priests share alike, and in which both

---

[311] "Per receptum diaconatum aliquis fit clericus et incardinatur Ecclesiae particulari vel Praelaturae personali pro cuius servitio promotus est", CIC can. 266; cf. also cann. 1008–9, which are echoed in the 1998 *Directorium*, no. 1: "Per impositionem manuum et consecrationis precem ipse minister sacer et hierarchiae membrum constituitur. Haec conditio ipsius statum theologicum et iuridicum in Ecclesia determinat."

[312] Cf. *Trad. Apost.* 4, 8, 21, 24 (bridging function between the bishop and the Christian people); *STh* III, q. 82, a. 3 ad 1 ("diaconi sunt inter sacerdotes et populum").

[313] Thus they can be married (can. 281, 3), they are not obliged to wear ecclesiastical dress (can. 284), or to abstain from holding public office in the civil sphere (can. 285, 3) or from administering property; they can devote themselves to business and commerce (can. 286) and take an active part in party politics and trades unions (can. 287, 2; cf. can. 288). In this regard, see the further clarifications made in the *Directorium*, 7–14.

alike take precedence over the laity.[314] That does not mean that deacons can exercise completely all the functions which belong to priests (Eucharist, Reconciliation, Anointing of the Sick). However, except in certain exceptional cases, what the CIC lays down for "clergy" in general is, in principle, applied to deacons (cf. cann. 273ff.).

IV. The Diaconate in an "Ecclesiology of Communion"

Although it is based on the texts of Vatican II, what can be called the "ecclesiology of communion" was developed in greater depth in and after the synod of 1985.[315] This ecclesiology grants a clearer understanding of the Church as a "universal sacrament of salvation" (cf. LG 1, 9) which finds in the communion of the Trinitarian God the source and ecclesial model for all the dynamism of salvation. "Diakonia" is the realization of this model in history. It now remains to be seen how the specific sacramental configuration of the diaconal ministry is integrated within this "diakonia" as a whole.

1. The "Munera" of the Diaconate: Plurality of Functions, and Varying Priorities

Lumen gentium 29a lists and explains the diaconal functions in the field of the liturgy (which includes tasks where the deacon presides), of the word and of charity, to which administrative tasks are connected.[316] Ad gentes

---

[314] E.g.: the capacity to exercise power of government or jurisdiction by reason of one's order (can. 129); to obtain posts whose exercise requires the power of order or government (can. 274, 1) although they cannot be vicars-general or bishops (can. 475); deacons can be appointed diocesan judges (can. 1421, 1) and even the only judge (can. 1425, 4); they can also confer certain dispensations (can. 89; can. 1079, 2), or, as a general faculty, assist at weddings (cann. 1111f.); they are ordinary ministers of baptism (can. 861, 1), of communion (can. 910, 1) and of the exposition of the Eucharist (can. 943); they can preach everywhere (can. 764) and the homily is reserved to them as it is to the priests (can. 767, 1).

[315] Cf. Zukunft aus der Kraft des Konzils: Die ausserordentliche Bischofssynode 1985; Die Dokumente mit einem Kommentar von W. Kasper (Freiburg, 1986); W. Kasper, Kirche als Communio, in Theologie und Kirche (Mainz, 1987), 272–89.

[316] "In diaconia liturgiae, verbi et caritatis Populo Dei ... inserviunt ... fidelium cultui et orationi praesidere ... caritatis et administrationis officiis dediti", LG 29a. The Conciliar Commission clarified it in these terms: "Indicantur officia diaconorum in primis modo generali, brevi sed gravi sententia, in triplici campo, scilicet 'in diaconia liturgiae, verbi et caritatis': quod deinde magis specificatur per 'caritatis et administrationis officia'", AS 3/1, 260. The stress laid on the charitable dimension is also evident in the explanation given by the same Commission with regard to the formula "non ad sacerdotium, sed ad

16f follows another order: ministry of the word, of the government of communities, and of charity.[317] For its part, *Sacrum diaconatus* singles out eleven tasks, eight of which belong to the liturgical sphere (which is given first rank in this way) although sometimes they have the character of "supply" tasks. The charitable and social work is done in the name of the hierarchy, and also includes the duty of stimulating the lay apostolate.[318] The CIC goes into details on the faculties and tasks which properly belong to deacons; the possibility is there mentioned of conferring on deacons a share in the exercise of the "cura pastoralis" of the parish.[319] With reference to the Conciliar texts of *Lumen gentium* 29, *Sacrosanctum concilium* 35 and *Ad gentes* 16, the *CCE* takes up the familiar list of relationships to liturgical life (with an explicit mention of assistance to bishops and priests), to pastoral life, and to charitable and social works.[320] The *Ratio fundamentalis* presents the diaconal ministry as an exercise of the three "munera" in the specific light of "diakonia", enumerated as the "munus docendi", the "munus sanctificandi" (with the Eucharist as its point of departure and its destination) and the "munus regendi" (where charitable activities are given as the most characteristic ministry of the deacon).[321] And the

---

ministerium": "significant diaconos non ad corpus et sanguinem Domini offerentes, sed ad servitium caritatis in Ecclesia ordinari", *AS* 3/8, 101.

[317] "Iuvat enim viros, qui ministerio vere diaconali fungantur, vel verbum divinum tamquam catechistae praedicantes, vel nomine parochi et episcopi dissitas communitates christianas moderantes, vel caritatem exercentes in operibus socialibus seu caritativis, per impositionem manuum inde ab Apostolis traditam corroborari et altari arctius coniungi, ut ministerium suum per gratiam sacramentalem diaconatus efficacius expleant." *AG* 16f.

[318] "Ubi sacerdos deest, Ecclesiae nomine matrimoniis celebrandis assistere et benedicere ex delegatione episcopi vel parochi ... funeris ac sepulturae ritibus praeesse ... praesidere, ubi sacerdos non adest ... caritatis et administrationis officiis atque socialis subsidii operibus, Hierarchiae nomine, perfungi ... apostolica laicorum opera fovere et adiuvare", *Sacrum diaconatus*, 22, pp. 701f.

[319] On the tasks appointed to them and the questions raised by can. 517, 2, cf. supra Chapter IV, notes 162–63.

[320] When it speaks of deacons, it says quite simply: "Ad diaconos pertinet, inter alia, Episcopo et presbyteris in mysteriorum divinorum celebratione assistere, maxime Eucharistiae, eamque distribuere, Matrimonio assistere idque benedicere, Evangelium proclamare et praedicare, exsequiis praesidere atque se diversis caritatis consecrare servitiis", *CCE* 1570. When it makes an explicit reference to the permanent diaconate, citing *AG* 16, it reaffirms that it is appropriate and useful to give sacramental ordination to "viros qui in Ecclesia ministerium vere diaconale explent sive in vita liturgica et pastorali sive in operibus socialibus et caritativis", *CCE* 1571.

[321] "Ad munus docendi ... quidem elucet ex libri Evangelii traditione, in ipso ordinationis ritu praescripta. Diaconi munus sanctificandi impletur ... quo pacto apparet quomodo ministerium diaconale ex Eucharistia procedat ad eandemque redeat, nec in mero servitio sociali exhauriri possit. Munus regendi denique exercetur per deditionem operibus

Directorium takes up again the triple diakonia of *Lumen gentium* 29, though changing the order (word, liturgy, charity). In this way it retains the diakonia of the word as the main function of the deacon; it underlines the diakonia of the liturgy as an intrinsic and organic assistance to the priestly ministry, and it considers the diakonia of charity as a different way of participating in the pastoral tasks of the bishops and priests.[322]

The different functions attributed to the (permanent) diaconate in the Conciliar and post-Conciliar texts general come down to us from ancient liturgical tradition, from the rites of ordination and theological studies of them. These functions are also open to contemporary pastoral situations and needs, although in that case a certain reserve is noticeable in the documents. In general a sort of triple "diakonia" or a sort of triple "munus" is recognised and serves as the basis for the diaconal functions taken together. In the documents and in numerous theological studies, charitable works are given a certain pre-eminence;[323] however, it would be problematic to consider these as being specific to the diaconate, because they are also properly the responsibility of the bishops and the priests, whose auxiliaries the deacons are. Moreover, the witness of ecclesial tradition suggests that the three functions ought to be integrated into a single whole. From that point of view it is possible to point out different characteristic features in the figure of the diaconal ministry. This ministry may be more strongly focused either on charity, or on the liturgy, or on evangelization; it may be exercised in a service directly linked to the bishop, or else in the sphere of the parish; and the permanent diaconate and the transitory diaconate may be preserved alike, or a clear option for one single figure may be determined. How plausible, and how viable, would such diversity prove to be in the long term? That would depend not only on the way the diaconate is understood theologically, but also on the real situation of different local Churches.

---

caritatis ... peculiari habito ad caritatem, quae praeeminentem diaconalis ministerii notam constituit." *Ratio*, 9.

[322] "Diaconi proprium officium est Evangelium proclamare et Verbum Dei praedicare ... quae facultas oritur e sacramento.... Ministerio Episcopi et, subordinate, ministerio presbyterorum, diaconus praestat auxilium sacramentale, ac proinde intrinsecum, organicum, a confusione alienum.... Opera caritatis, dioecesana vel paroecialia, quae sunt inter primaria officia Episcopi et presbyterorum, ab his transmittuntur, secundum testimonium Traditionis Ecclesiae, servis ministerii ecclesiastici, hoc est diaconis." *Directorium*, 24, 28, 37.

[323] E.g.: "Itaque Diaconatus in Ecclesia mirabiliter effloruit simulque insigne praebuit testimonium amoris erga Christum ac fratres in caritatis operibus exsequendis, in ritibus sacris celebrandis atque in pastoralibus perfungendis muneribus." Paul VI, *Ad pascendum*, p. 535.

2. Communion in a Plurality of Ministries

The specific way the diaconate is exercised in different surroundings will also help to define its ministerial identity, modifying if necessary an ecclesial framework in which its proper connection with the ministry of the bishop hardly appears and in which the figure of the priest is identified with the totality of the ministerial functions. The living consciousness that the Church is "communion" will contribute to this development. However, it would be hard to arrive at a solution to the theological queries about the specific "powers" of the diaconate through practical experience alone. Not everyone considers this question to be an insoluble difficulty. Thus different propositions of contemporary theology may be observed which aim to give the diaconate theological substance, ecclesial acceptance and pastoral credibility.

There are some people who consider this question of the "powers" of the deacon to have only relative importance. For them, to make it into a central question would be a kind of reductionism, and would disfigure the true meaning of the ordained minister. Moreover, the observation, which was true in ancient times as well, that a layman can exercise the tasks of the deacon did not in practise prevent this ministry from being considered sacramental from every point of view. Additionally, neither would it be possible to reserve the exclusive exercise of certain functions to bishops and priests in great detail, save in the case of the "potestas conficiendi eucharistiam",[324] of the sacrament of Reconciliation[325] and the ordination of bishops.[326] Other people distinguish between what is or should be the normal and ordinary exercise of the whole collection of functions attributed to deacons, and what could be considered as an extraordinary exercise of them on the part of Christians,[327] determined by pastoral needs or emergencies, even on a long-term basis. A certain analogy could be drawn between this and the normal or ordinary competencies of the bishop in regard to confirmation (which the priest can also administer)[328] and in regard to the ordination of priests (which according to

---

[324] Cf. notes 249, 281, 282 supra.

[325] Cf. note 283 supra.

[326] LG 21b notes succinctly: "Episcoporum est per Sacramentum Ordinis novos electos in corpus episcopale assumere."

[327] E.g.: "Minister ordinarius sacrae communionis est Episcopus, presbyter et diaconus. Extraordinarius sacrae communionis minister est acolythus necnon alius christifidelis ad normam can. 230, 3 deputatus." CIC, can. 910.

[328] "Confirmationis minister ordinarius est Episcopus; valide hoc sacramentum confert presbyter quoque hac facultate vi iuris communis aut peculiaris concessionis competentis auctoritatis instructus." CIC, can. 882.

certain papal bulls seems to have been performed by priests too in exceptional cases).[329]

Finally, there are some who also throw doubt on whether in fact a non-ordained member of the faithful does perform exactly the same "munera" in the same way and with the same salvific effect as an ordained deacon.[330] Even if they seem to be the same functions as are exercised by a non-ordained member of the faithful, the deciding factor would be what the deacon *was* rather than what he *did*: the action of the deacon would bring about a special presence of Christ the Head and Servant that was proper to sacramental grace, configuration with Him, and the community and public dimension of the tasks which are carried out in the name of the Church. The viewpoint of faith and the sacramental reality of the diaconate would enable its particular distinctiveness to be discovered and affirmed, not in relation to its functions but in relation to its theological nature and its representative symbolism.

V. *Conclusion*

From the point of view of its theological meaning and its ecclesial role the ministry of the diaconate presents a challenge to the Church's awareness and practise, particularly through the questions that it still raises today. With reference to deacons, plenty of witnesses from Tradition recall that the Lord chose acts of humble service to express and render present the reality of the *morphe doulou* (Phil 2:7) which he assumed for the sake of his saving mission. Specifically, the diaconate was born as a help to the Apostles and their successors, who were themselves perceived as servants of Christ. If the diaconate has been restored as a permanent ministry by Vatican II it is especially to respond to specific needs (cf. *LG* 29b) or to grant sacramental grace to those who were already carrying out the functions of the deacon's office (*AG* 16f). But the task of identifying these needs and these functions more clearly in Christian communities is still to be done, although the rich experience of the particular Churches which, after the Council, gave the permanent diaconate a place in their pastoral practice, is already available.

---

[329] *LG* 26c considers bishops to be "dispensatores sacrorum ordinum", while CIC can. 1012 states that "sacrae ordinationis minister est Episcopus consecratus"; cf. likewise DS 1326 and 1777. Nevertheless, the problem raised by some papal documents which seemed to grant a priest the faculty of conferring the diaconate (cf. DS 1435) and even the priesthood (cf. DS 1145, 1146, 1290) does not appear to have been settled doctrinally.

[330] The *Ratio fundamentalis* itself (9) says this: "Ministerium diaconale distinctum est exercitio trium munerum, ministerio ordinato propriorum, in specifica luce diaconiae."

In the current consciousness of the Church there is only one single sacrament of Holy Orders. Vatican II, taking up the teaching of Pius XII,[331] affirmed this unity and saw the episcopate, the priesthood and the diaconate as included within it. According to the decision of Paul VI it is only these three ordained ministries which constitute the clerical state.[332] However, concerning the diaconate the Council cautiously speaks only of "sacramental grace". After Vatican II, Paul VI[333] and the *CCE* (no. 1570) teach that the deacon, through ordination, receives the character of the sacrament of Holy Orders. Can. 1008 of the CIC states that the three ordained ministries are exercised *in persona Christi Capitis*.[334] Following *Lumen gentium* 29, which attributed to the deacon the solemn administration of baptism (cf. *SC* 68), can. 861, 1 spoke of each of the three ordained ministers as ordinary ministers of this sacrament; can. 129 recognized that the *potestas regiminis* belonged to all those who have received the sacrament of Holy Orders.[335]

On the other hand, the difference between the sacerdotal ministries and the diaconal ministry is also underlined. The Council statement that the deacon is not ordained for priesthood but for ministry was taken up by various documents of the post-Conciliar Magisterium. Most clearly of all, the *CCE* (no. 154) distinguishes within one and the same *ordinatio*, the *gradus participationis sacerdotalis* of the episcopate and the priesthood, and the *gradus servitii* of the diaconate. The diaconate, by the very nature of its *way of participating* in the one mission of Christ, carries out this mission in the manner of an auxiliary service. It is "*icona vivens Christi servi in Ecclesia*", but, precisely as such, it maintains a constitutive link with the priestly ministry to which it lends its aid (cf. *LG* 41). It is not just any service which is attributed to the deacon in the Church: his service belongs to the sacrament of Holy Orders, as a close collaboration with the bishop and the priests, in the unity of the same ministerial actualization of the mission of Christ. The *CCE* (no. 1554) quotes Saint Ignatius of Antioch: "Let everyone revere the deacons as Jesus Christ, the bishop as the image of the Father, and the presbyters as the senate of God

---

[331] Constitutio apostolica *Sacramentum ordinis*, art. 4–5 (DS 3857–3861). On the imposition of hands and the prayer of consecration, cf. also Gregory IX, *Ep. Presbyter et diaconus ad episc. Olaf de Lund* (DS 826; cf. 1326).

[332] *Ministeria quaedam*, *AAS* 64 (1972): 531.

[333] *Sacrum diaconatus*, p. 698.

[334] The International Theological Commission has been notified that a revised version of this canon is in preparation, aiming to distinguish the priestly ("sacerdotal") ministries from the diaconal ministry.

[335] Cf. Erdö, "Der ständige Diakon: Theologisch-systematische und rechtliche Erwägungen", *AKathKR* 166 (1997): 79–80.

and the assembly of the Apostles. For without them one cannot speak of the Church." [336]

With regard to the ordination of women to the diaconate, it should be noted that two important indications emerge from what has been said up to this point:

1. The deaconesses mentioned in the tradition of the ancient Church—as evidenced by the rite of institution and the functions they exercised—were not purely and simply equivalent to the deacons;

2. The unity of the sacrament of Holy Orders, in the clear distinction between the ministries of the bishop and the priests on the one hand and the diaconal ministry on the other, is strongly underlined by ecclesial tradition, especially in the teaching of the Magisterium.

In the light of these elements which have been set out in the present historico-theological research document, it pertains to the ministry of discernment which the Lord established in his Church to pronounce authoritatively on this question.

Over and above all the questions raised by the diaconate, it is good to recall that ever since Vatican II the active presence of this ministry in the life of the Church has aroused, in memory of the example of Christ, a more vivid awareness of the value of service for Christian life.

---

[336] *Ad Trall.* 3, 1; SCh 10(2), 96.

22

COMMUNION AND STEWARDSHIP:
HUMAN PERSONS CREATED IN
THE IMAGE OF GOD

PRELIMINARY NOTE

The theme of "man created in the image of God" was submitted for study to the International Theological Commission. The preparation of this study was entrusted to a subcommission whose members included: Very Rev. J. Augustine Di Noia, O.P.; Most Reverend Jean-Louis Bruguès; Msgr. Anton Strukelj; Rev. Tanios Bou Mansour, O.L.M.; Rev. Adolpe Gesché; Most Reverend Willem Jacobus Eijk; Rev. Fadel Sidarouss, S.J.; and Rev. Shunichi Takayanagi, S.J.

As the text developed, it was discussed at numerous meetings of the subcommission and several plenary sessions of the International Theological Commission held at Rome during the period 2000–2002. The present text was approved *in forma specifica*, by the written ballots of the International Theological Commission. It was then submitted to Joseph Cardinal Ratzinger, the President of the Commission, who has given his permission for its publication.

INTRODUCTION

1. The explosion of scientific understanding and technological capability in modern times has brought many advantages to the human race, but it also poses serious challenges. Our knowledge of the immensity and age of the universe has made human beings seem smaller and less secure in their position and significance within it. Technological advances have greatly increased our ability to control and direct the forces of nature, but they have also turned out to have an unexpected and possibly uncontrollable impact on our environment and even on ourselves.

2. The International Theological Commission offers the following theological meditation on the doctrine of the *imago Dei* to orient our reflection on the meaning of human existence in the face of these challenges. At the same time, we want to present the positive vision of the human person within the universe which is afforded by this newly retrieved doctrinal theme.

3. Especially since Vatican Council II, the doctrine of the *imago Dei* has begun to enjoy a greater prominence in magisterial teaching and theological research. Previously, various factors had led to the neglect of the theology of the *imago Dei* among some modern western philosophers and theologians. In philosophy, the very notion of the "image" was subjected to a powerful critique by theories of knowledge which either privileged the role of the "idea" at the expense of the image (rationalism) or made experience the ultimate criterion of truth without reference to the role of the image (empiricism). In addition, cultural factors, such as the influence of secular humanism and, more recently, the very profusion of images by the mass media, have made it difficult to affirm the human orientation to the divine, on the one hand, and, on the other, the ontological reference of the image which are essential to any theology of the *imago Dei*. Contributing to the neglect of the theme within western theology itself were biblical interpretations that stressed the permanent validity of the injunction against images (cf. Ex 20:3–4) or posited a Hellenistic influence on the emergence of the theme in the Bible.

4. It was not until the eve of Vatican Council II that theologians began to rediscover the fertility of this theme for understanding and articulating the mysteries of the Christian faith. Indeed, the documents of this council both express and confirm this significant development in twentieth-century theology. In continuity with the deepening recovery of the theme of the *imago Dei* since Vatican Council II, the International Theological Commission seeks in the following pages to reaffirm the truth that human persons are created in the image of God in order to enjoy personal communion with the Father, Son and Holy Spirit and with one another in them, and in order to exercise, in God's name, responsible stewardship of the created world. In the light of this truth, the world appears not as something merely vast and possibly meaningless, but as a place created for the sake of personal communion.

5. As we seek to demonstrate in the following chapters, these profound truths have lost neither their relevance nor their power. After a summary review of the scriptural and traditional basis of the *imago Dei* in Chapter One, we move on to an exploration of the two great themes of the theology of the *imago Dei*: in Chapter Two, the *imago Dei* as the basis of communion with the triune God and among human persons and then, in

Chapter Three, the *imago Dei* as the basis of a share in God's governance of visible creation. These reflections gather together the main elements of Christian anthropology and certain elements of moral theology and ethics as they are illumined by the theology of the *imago Dei*. We are well aware of the breadth of the issues we have sought to address here, but we offer these reflections to recall for ourselves and for our readers the immense explanatory power of the theology of the *imago Dei* precisely in order to reaffirm the divine truth about the universe and about the meaning of human life.

CHAPTER I

HUMAN PERSONS CREATED IN THE IMAGE OF GOD

6. As the witness of Scripture, Tradition and the Magisterium makes clear, the truth that human beings are created in the image of God is at the heart of Christian revelation. This truth was recognized and its broad implications expounded by the Fathers of the Church and by the great scholastic theologians. Although, as we shall note below, this truth was challenged by some influential modern thinkers, today biblical scholars and theologians join with the Magisterium in reclaiming and reaffirming the doctrine of the *imago Dei*.

1. *The* Imago Dei *in Scripture and Tradition*

7. With few exceptions, most exegetes today acknowledge that the theme of the *imago Dei* is central to biblical revelation (cf. Gen 1:26f.; 5:1–3; 9:6). The theme is seen as the key to the biblical understanding of human nature and to all the affirmations of biblical anthropology in both the Old and New Testaments. For the Bible, the *imago Dei* constitutes almost a definition of man: the mystery of man cannot be grasped apart from the mystery of God.

8. The Old Testament understanding of man as created in the *imago Dei* in part reflects the ancient Near Eastern idea that the king is the image of God on earth. The biblical understanding, however, is distinctive in extending the notion of the image of God to include all men. An additional contrast with ancient Near Eastern thought is that the Bible sees man as directed, not first of all to the worship of the gods, but rather to the cultivation of the earth (cf. Gen 2:15). Connecting cult more directly

with cultivation, as it were, the Bible understands that human activity in the six days of the week is ordered to the Sabbath, a day of blessing and sanctification.

9. Two themes converge to shape the biblical perspective. In the first place, the whole of man is seen as created in the image of God. This perspective excludes interpretations which locate the *imago Dei* in one or another aspect of human nature (for example, his upright stature or his intellect) or in one of his qualities or functions (for example, his sexual nature or his domination of the earth). Avoiding both monism and dualism, the Bible presents a vision of the human being in which the spiritual is understood to be a dimension together with the physical, social and historical dimensions of man.

10. Secondly, the creation accounts in Genesis make it clear that man is not created as an isolated individual: "God created mankind in his image, in the image of God he created them, male and female he created them" (Gen 1:27). God placed the first human beings in relation to one another, each with a partner of the other sex. The Bible affirms that man exists in relation with other persons, with God, with the world, and with himself. According to this conception, man is not an isolated individual but a person—an essentially relational being. Far from entailing a pure actualism that would deny its permanent ontological status, the fundamentally relational character of the *imago Dei* itself constitutes its ontological structure and the basis for its exercise of freedom and responsibility.

11. The created image affirmed by the Old Testament is, according to the New Testament, to be completed in the *imago Christi*. In the New Testament development of this theme, two distinctive elements emerge: the christological and Trinitarian character of the *imago Dei*, and the role of sacramental mediation in the formation of the *imago Christi*.

12. Since it is Christ himself who is the perfect image of God (2 Cor 4:4; Col 1:15; Heb 1:3), man must be conformed to him (Rom 8:29) in order to become the son of the Father through the power of the Holy Spirit (Rom 8:23). Indeed, to "become" the image of God requires an active participation on man's part in his transformation according to the pattern of the image of the Son (Col 3:10) who manifests his identity by the historical movement from his incarnation to his glory. According to the pattern first traced out by the Son, the image of God in each man is constituted by his own historical passage from creation, through conversion from sin, to salvation and consummation. Just as Christ manifested his lordship over sin and death through his passion and resurrection, so each man attains his lordship through Christ in the Holy Spirit—not only over the earth and the animal kingdom (as the Old Testament affirms)— but principally over sin and death.

13. According to the New Testament, this transformation into the image of Christ is accomplished through the sacraments, in the first place as an effect of the illumination of the message of Christ (2 Cor 3:18—4:6) and of Baptism (1 Cor 12:13). Communion with Christ is a result of faith in him, and Baptism through which one dies to the old man through Christ (Gal 3:26–28) and puts on the new man (Gal 3:27; Rom 13:14). Penance, the Eucharist, and the other sacraments confirm and strengthen us in this radical transformation according to the pattern of Christ's passion, death and resurrection. Created in the image of God and perfected in the image of Christ by the power of the Holy Spirit in the sacraments, we are embraced in love by the Father.

14. The biblical vision of the image of God continued to occupy a prominent place in Christian anthropology in the Fathers of the Church and in later theology, right up to the beginning of modern times. An indication of the centrality of this theme can be found in the endeavor of early Christians to interpret the biblical prohibition against artistic representations of God (cf. Ex 20:2f.; Deut 27:15) in the light of the incarnation. For the mystery of the incarnation demonstrated the possibility of representing the God-made-man in his human and historical reality. Defense of artistic representation of the Incarnate Word and of the events of salvation during the iconoclastic controversies of the seventh and eighth centuries rested on a profound understanding of the hypostatic union which refused to separate the divine and the human in the "image".

15. Patristic and medieval theology diverged at certain points from biblical anthropology, and developed it at other points. The majority of the representatives of the tradition, for example, did not fully embrace the biblical vision which identified the image with the totality of man. A significant development of the biblical account was the distinction between image and likeness, introduced by Saint Irenaeus, according to which "image" denotes an ontological participation (*methexis*) and "likeness" (*mimêsis*) a moral transformation (*Adv. Haer.* 5, 6, 1; 5, 8, 1; 5, 16, 2). According to Tertullian, God created man in his image and gave him the breath of life as his likeness. While the image can never be destroyed, the likeness can be lost by sin (*Bapt.* 5, 6, 7). Saint Augustine did not take up this distinction, but presented a more personalistic, psychological and existential account of the *imago Dei*. For him, the image of God in man has a Trinitarian structure, reflecting either the tripartite structure of the human soul (spirit, self-consciousness, and love) or the threefold aspects of the psyche (memory, intelligence, and will). According to Augustine, the image of God in man orients him to God in invocation, knowledge and love (*Confessions* 1, 1, 1).

16. In Thomas Aquinas, the *imago Dei* possesses an historical character, since it passes through three stages: the *imago creationis* (*naturae*), the *imago recreationis* (*gratiae*), and the *similitudinis* (*gloriae*) (*STh* I, q. 93, a. 4). For Aquinas, the *imago Dei* is the basis for participation in the divine life. The image of God is realized principally in an act of contemplation in the intellect (*STh* I, q. 93, a. 4 and 7). This conception can be distinguished from that of Bonaventure, for whom the image is realized chiefly through the will in the religious act of man (*Sent.* II, d. 16, a. 2, q. 3). Within a similar mystical vision, but with a greater boldness, Meister Eckhart tends to spiritualize the *imago Dei* by placing it at the summit of the soul and detaching it from the body (*Quint.* 1, 5, 5–7; 5, 6, 9s).

17. Reformation controversies demonstrated that the theology of the *imago Dei* remained important for both Protestant and Catholic theologians. The Reformers accused the Catholics of reducing the image of God to an "*imago naturae*" which presented a static conception of human nature and encouraged the sinner to constitute himself before God. On the other side, the Catholics accused the Reformers of denying the ontological reality of the image of God and reducing it to a pure relation. In addition, the Reformers insisted that the image of God was corrupted by sin, whereas Catholic theologians viewed sin as a wounding of the image of God in man.

2. *The Modern Critique of the Theology of the* Imago Dei

18. Until the dawn of the modern period, the theology of the *imago Dei* retained its central position in theological anthropology. Throughout the history of Christian thought, such was the power and fascination of this theme that it could withstand those isolated critiques (as, for example, in iconoclasm) which charged that its anthropomorphism fostered idolatry. But, in the modern period, the theology of the *imago Dei* came under a more sustained and systematic critique.

19. The view of the universe advanced by modern science displaced the classical notion of a cosmos made in the divine image and thus dislodged an important part of the conceptual framework supporting the theology of the *imago Dei*. The theme was regarded as ill-adapted to experience by empiricists, and as ambiguous by rationalists. But more significant among the factors undermining the theology of the *imago Dei* was the conception of man as a self-constituting autonomous subject, apart from any relationship to God. With this development, the notion of the *imago Dei* could not be sustained. It was but a short step from these ideas to the reversal of biblical anthropology which took various forms in the

thought of Ludwig Feuerbach, Karl Marx and Sigmund Freud: it is not man who is made in the image of God, but God who is nothing else than an image projected by man. In the end, atheism appeared to be required if man was to be self-constituting.

20. At first, the climate of twentieth-century western theology was unfavorable to the theme of the *imago Dei*. Given the nineteenth-century developments just mentioned, it was perhaps inevitable that some forms of dialectical theology regarded the theme as an expression of human arrogance by which man compares or equates himself to God. Existential theology, with its stress on the event of the encounter with God, undermined the notion of a stable or permanent relationship with God which is entailed by the doctrine of the *imago Dei*. Secularization theology rejected the notion of an objective reference in the world locating man with respect to God. The "God without properties"—in effect, an impersonal God—espoused by some versions of negative theology could not serve as the model for man made in his image. In political theology, with its overriding concern for orthopraxis, the theme of the *imago Dei* receded from view. Finally, secular and theological critics alike blamed the theology of the *imago Dei* for promoting a disregard of the natural environment and animal welfare.

3. *The* Imago Dei *at Vatican Council II and in Current Theology*

21. Despite these unfavorable trends, interest in the recovery of the theology of the *imago Dei* rose steadily throughout the mid-twentieth century. Intense study of the Scriptures, of the Fathers of the Church, and of the great scholastic theologians produced a renewed awareness of the ubiquity and importance of the theme of the *imago Dei*. This recovery was well underway among Catholic theologians before the Second Vatican Council. The council gave new impetus to the theology of the *imago Dei*, most especially in the Constitution on the Church in the Modern World *Gaudium et spes*.

22. Invoking the theme of the image of God, the Council affirmed in *Gaudium et spes* the dignity of man as it is taught in Genesis 1:26 and Psalm 8:6 (*GS* 12). Within the conciliar vision, the *imago Dei* consists in man's fundamental orientation to God, which is the basis of human dignity and of the inalienable rights of the human person. Because every human being is an image of God, he cannot be made subservient to any this-worldly system or finality. His sovereignty within the cosmos, his capacity for social existence, and his knowledge and love of the

Creator—all are rooted in man's being made in the image of God. Basic to the conciliar teaching is the christological determination of the image: it is Christ who is the image of the invisible God (Col 1:15) (GS 10). The Son is the perfect Man who restores the divine likeness to the sons and daughters of Adam which was wounded by the sin of the first parents (GS 22). Revealed by God who created man in his image, it is the Son who gives to man the answers to his questions about the meaning of life and death (GS 41). The Council also underscores the Trinitarian structure of the image: by conformity to Christ (Rom 8:29) and through the gifts of the Holy Spirit (Rom 8:23), a new man is created, capable of fulfilling the new commandment (GS 22). It is the saints who are fully transformed in the image of Christ (cf. 2 Cor 3:18); in them, God manifests his presence and grace as a sign of his kingdom (GS 24). On the basis of the doctrine of the image of God, the Council teaches that human activity reflects the divine creativity which is its model (GS 34) and must be directed to justice and human fellowship in order to foster the establishment of one family in which all are brothers and sisters (GS 24).

24. The renewed interest in the theology of the *imago Dei* which emerged at the Second Vatican Council is reflected in contemporary theology, where it is possible to note developments in several areas. In the first place, theologians are working to show how the theology of the *imago Dei* illumines the connections between anthropology and Christology. Without denying the unique grace which comes to the human race through the incarnation, theologians want to recognize the intrinsic value of the creation of man in God's image. The possibilities that Christ opens up for man do not involve the suppression of the human reality in its creatureliness but its transformation and realization according to the perfect image of the Son. In addition, with this renewed understanding of the link between Christology and anthropology comes a deeper understanding of the dynamic character of the *imago Dei*. Without denying the gift of man's original creation in the image of God, theologians want to acknowledge the truth that, in the light of human history and the evolution of human culture, the *imago Dei* can in a real sense be said to be still in the process of becoming. What is more, the theology of the *imago Dei* also links anthropology with moral theology by showing that, in his very being, man possesses a participation in the divine law. This natural law orients human persons to the pursuit of the good in their actions. It follows, finally, that the *imago Dei* has a teleological and eschatological dimension which defines man as *homo viator*, oriented to the *parousia* and to the consummation of the divine plan for the universe as it is realized in the history of grace in the life of each individual human being and in the history of the whole human race.

CHAPTER II

IN THE IMAGE OF GOD: PERSONS IN COMMUNION

25. Communion and stewardship are the two great strands out of which the fabric of the doctrine of the *imago Dei* is woven. The first strand, which we take up in this chapter, can be summarized in the following way: The triune God has revealed his plan to share the communion of Trinitarian life with persons created in his image. Indeed, it is for the sake of this Trinitarian communion that human persons are created in the divine image. It is precisely this radical likeness to the triune God that is the basis for the possibility of the communion of creaturely beings with the uncreated Persons of the Blessed Trinity. Created in the image of God, human beings are by nature bodily and spiritual, men and women made for one another, persons oriented towards communion with God and with one another, wounded by sin and in need of salvation, and destined to be conformed to Christ, the perfect image of the Father, in the power of the Holy Spirit.

1. *Body and Soul*

26. Human beings, created in the image of God, are persons called to enjoy communion and to exercise stewardship in a physical universe. The activities entailed by interpersonal communion and responsible stewardship engage the spiritual—intellectual and affective—capacities of human persons, but they do not leave the body behind. Human beings are physical beings sharing a world with other physical beings. Implicit in the Catholic theology of the *imago Dei* is the profound truth that the material world creates the conditions for the engagement of human persons with one another.

27. This truth has not always received the attention it deserves. Present-day theology is striving to overcome the influence of dualistic anthropologies that locate the *imago Dei* exclusively with reference to the spiritual aspect of human nature. Partly under the influence first of Platonic and later of Cartesian dualistic anthropologies, Christian theology itself tended to identify the *imago Dei* in human beings with what is the most specific characteristic of human nature, viz., mind or spirit. The recovery both of elements of biblical anthropology and of aspects of the Thomistic synthesis has contributed to the effort in important ways.

28. The view that bodiliness is essential to personal identity is fundamental, even if not explicitly thematized, in the witness of Christian revelation. Biblical anthropology excludes mind-body dualism. It speaks of

man as a whole. Among the basic Hebrew terms for man used in the Old Testament, *nèfèš* means the life of a concrete person who is alive (Gen 9:4; Lev 24:17–18, Prov 8:35). But man does not have a *nèfèš*; he is a *nèfèš* (Gen 2:7; Lev 17:10). *Basar* refers to the flesh of animals and of men, and sometimes the body as a whole (Lev 4:11; 26:29). Again, one does not have a *basar*, but is a *basar*. The New Testament term *sarx* (flesh) can denote the material corporality of man (2 Cor 12:7), but on the other hand also the whole person (Rom 8:6). Another Greek term, *soma* (body) refers to the whole man with emphasis on his outward manifestation. Here too man does not *have* his body, but *is* his body. Biblical anthropology clearly presupposes the unity of man, and understands bodiliness to be essential to personal identity.

29. The central dogmas of the Christian faith imply that the body is an intrinsic part of the human person and thus participates in his being created in the image of God. The Christian doctrine of creation utterly excludes a metaphysical or cosmic dualism since it teaches that everything in the universe, spiritual and material, was created by God and thus stems from the perfect Good. Within the framework of the doctrine of the incarnation, the body also appears as an intrinsic part of the person. The Gospel of John affirms that "the Word became flesh [*sarx*]", in order to stress, against Docetism, that Jesus had a real physical body and not a phantom-body. Furthermore, Jesus redeems us through every act he performs in his body. His Body which is given up for us and His Blood which is poured out for us mean the gift of his Person for our salvation. Christ's work of redemption is carried on in the Church, his mystical body, and is made visible and tangible through the sacraments. The effects of the sacraments, though in themselves primarily spiritual, are accomplished by means of perceptible material signs, which can only be received in and through the body. This shows that not only man's mind but also his body is redeemed. The body becomes a temple of the Holy Spirit. Finally, that the body belongs essentially to the human person is inherent to the doctrine of the resurrection of the body at the end of time, which implies that man exists in eternity as a complete physical and spiritual person.

30. In order to maintain the unity of body and soul clearly taught in revelation, the Magisterium adopted the definition of the human soul as *forma substantialis* (cf. Council of Vienne and the Fifth Lateran Council). Here the Magisterium relied on Thomistic anthropology which, drawing upon the philosophy of Aristotle, understands body and soul as the material and spiritual principles of a single human being. It may be noted that this account is not incompatible with present-day scientific insights. Modern physics has demonstrated that matter in its most elementary particles

is purely potential and possesses no tendency toward organization. But the level of organization in the universe, which contains highly organized forms of living and non-living entities, implies the presence of some "information". This line of reasoning suggests a partial analogy between the Aristotelian concept of substantial form and the modern scientific notion of "information". Thus, for example, the DNA of the chromosomes contains the information necessary for matter to be organized according to what is typical of a certain species or individual. Analogically, the substantial form provides to prime matter the information it needs to be organized in a particular way. This analogy should be taken with due caution because metaphysical and spiritual concepts cannot be simply compared with material, biological data.

31. These biblical, doctrinal and philosophical indications converge in the affirmation that human bodiliness participates in the *imago Dei*. If the soul, created in God's image, forms matter to constitute the human body, then the human person as a whole is the bearer of the divine image in a spiritual as well as a bodily dimension. This conclusion is strengthened when the christological implications of the image of God are taken fully into account. "The truth is that only in the mystery of the incarnate Word does the mystery of man take on light.... Christ ... fully reveals man to man himself and makes his supreme calling clear" (GS 22). Spiritually and physically united to the incarnate and glorified Word, especially in the sacrament of the Eucharist, man arrives at his destination: the resurrection of his own body and the eternal glory in which he participates as a complete human person, body and soul, in the Trinitarian communion shared by all the blessed in the company of heaven.

2. Man and Woman

32. In *Familiaris consortio*, Pope John Paul II affirmed: "As an incarnate spirit, that is a soul which expresses itself in a body and a body informed by an immortal spirit, man is called to love in his unified totality. Love includes the human body, and the body is made a sharer in spiritual love" (11). Created in the image of God, human beings are called to love and communion. Because this vocation is realized in a distinctive way in the procreative union of husband and wife, the difference between man and woman is an essential element in the constitution of human beings made in the image of God.

33. "God created man in his image; in the image of God he created him; male and female, he created them" (Gen 1:27; cf. Gen 5:1–2). According

to the Scripture, therefore, the *imago Dei* manifests itself, at the outset, in the difference between the sexes. It could be said that human beings exist only as masculine or feminine, since the reality of the human condition appears in the difference and plurality of the sexes. Hence, far from being an accidental or secondary aspect of personality, it is constitutive of person identity. Each of us possesses a way of being in the world, to see, to think, to feel, to engage in mutual exchange with other persons who are also defined by their sexual identity. According to the *Catechism of the Catholic Church*: "*Sexuality* affects all aspects of the human person in the unity of his body and soul. It especially concerns affectivity, the capacity to love and to procreate, and in a more general way the aptitude for forming bonds of communion with others" (2332). The roles attributed to one or the other sex may vary across time and space, but the sexual identity of the person is not a cultural or social construction. It belongs to the specific manner in which the *imago Dei* exists.

34. The incarnation of the Word reinforces this specificity. He assumed the human condition in its totality, taking up one sex, but he became man in both senses of the term: as a member of the human community, and as a male. The relation of each one to Christ is determined in two ways: it depends on one's own proper sexual identity and that of Christ.

35. In addition, the incarnation and resurrection extend the original sexual identity of the *imago Dei* into eternity. The risen Lord remains a man when he sits now at the right hand of the Father. We may also note that the sanctified and glorified person of the Mother of God, now assumed bodily into heaven, continues to be a woman. When in Galatians 3:28, Saint Paul announces that in Christ all differences—including that between man and woman—would be erased, he is affirming that no human differences can impede our participation in the mystery of Christ. The Church has not followed Saint Gregory of Nyssa and some other Fathers of the Church who held that sexual differences as such would be annulled by the resurrection. The sexual differences between man and woman, while certainly manifesting physical attributes, in fact transcend the purely physical and touch the very mystery of the person.

36. The Bible lends no support to the notion of a natural superiority of the masculine over the feminine sex. Their differences notwithstanding, the two sexes enjoy an inherent equality. As Pope John Paul II wrote in *Familiaris consortio*: "Above all it is important to underline the equal dignity and responsibility of women with men. This equality is realized in a unique manner in that reciprocal self-giving by each one to the other and by both to the children which is proper to marriage and the family. . . . In creating the human race 'male and female', God gives man and woman an equal personal dignity, endowing them with the inalienable

rights and responsibilities proper to the human person" (22). Man and woman are equally created in God's image. Both are persons, endowed with intelligence and will, capable of orienting their lives through the exercise of freedom. But each does so in a manner proper and distinctive to their sexual identity, in such wise that the Christian tradition can speak of a reciprocity and complementarity. These terms, which have lately become somewhat controversial, are nonetheless useful in affirming that man and woman each needs the other in order to achieve fullness of life.

37. To be sure, the original friendship between man and woman was deeply impaired by sin. Through his miracle at the wedding feast of Cana (Jn 2:1ff.), our Lord shows that he has come to restore the harmony that God intended in the creation of man and woman.

38. The image of God, which is to be found in the nature of the human person as such, can be realized in a special way in the union between human beings. Since this union is directed to the perfection of divine love, Christian tradition has always affirmed the value of virginity and celibacy which foster chaste friendship among human persons at the same time that they point to the eschatological fulfillment of all created love in the uncreated love of the Blessed Trinity. In this very connection, the Second Vatican Council drew an analogy between the communion of the divine Persons among themselves, and that which human beings are invited to establish on earth (cf. *GS*, 24).

39. While it is certainly true that union between human beings can be realized in a variety of ways, Catholic theology today affirms that marriage constitutes an elevated form of the communion between human persons and one of the best analogies of the Trinitarian life. When a man and a woman unite their bodies and spirits in an attitude of total openness and self-giving, they form a new image of God. Their union as one flesh does not correspond simply to a biological necessity, but to the intention of the Creator in leading them to share the happiness of being made in his image. The Christian tradition speaks of marriage as an eminent way of sanctity. "God is love and in himself he lives a mystery of personal loving communion. Creating the human race in his own image ... God inscribed in the humanity of man and woman the vocation, and thus the capacity and responsibility, of love and communion" (*Catechism of the Catholic Church*, 2331). The Second Vatican Council also underlined the profound significance of marriage: "Christian spouses, in virtue of the sacrament of Matrimony, whereby they signify and partake of the mystery of that unity and fruitful love which exists between Christ and His Church (cf. Eph 5:32), help each other to attain to holiness in their married life and in the rearing and education of their children" (*LG* 11; cf. *GS* 48).

3. *Person and Community*

40. Persons created in the image of God are bodily beings whose identity as male or female orders them to a special kind of communion with one another. As Pope John Paul II has taught, the nuptial meaning of the body finds its realization in the human intimacy and love that mirror the communion of the Blessed Trinity whose mutual love is poured out in creation and redemption. This truth is at the center of Christian anthropology. Human beings are created in the *imago Dei* precisely as persons capable of a knowledge and love that are personal and interpersonal. It is of the essence of the *imago Dei* in them that these personal beings are relational and social beings, embraced in a human family whose unity is at once realized and prefigured in the Church.

41. When one speaks of the person, one refers both to the irreducible identity and interiority that constitutes the particular individual being, and to the fundamental relationship to other persons that is the basis for human community. In the Christian perspective, this personal identity that is at once an orientation to the other is founded essentially on the Trinity of divine Persons. God is not a solitary being, but a communion of three Persons. Constituted by the one divine nature, the identity of the Father is his paternity, his relation to the Son and the Spirit; the identity of the Son is his relation to the Father and the Spirit; the identity of the Spirit is his relation to the Father and the Son. Christian revelation led to the articulation of the concept of person, and gave it a divine, christological, and Trinitarian meaning. In effect, no person is as such alone in the universe, but is always constituted with others and is summoned to form a community with them.

42. It follows that personal beings are social beings as well. The human being is truly human to the extent that he actualizes the essentially social element in his constitution as a person within familial, religious, civil, professional, and other groups that together form the surrounding society to which he belongs. While affirming the fundamentally social character of human existence, Christian civilization has nonetheless recognized the absolute value of the human person as well as the importance of individual rights and cultural diversity. In the created order, there will always be a certain tension between the individual person and the demands of social existence. In the Blessed Trinity there is a perfect harmony between the Persons who share the communion of a single divine life.

43. Every individual human being as well as the whole human community are created in the image of God. In its original unity—of which Adam is the symbol—the human race is made in the image of the divine Trinity. Willed by God, it makes its way through the vicissitudes of human

history towards a perfect communion, also willed by God, but yet to be fully realized. In this sense, human beings share the solidarity of a unity that both already exists and is still to be attained. Sharing in a created human nature and confessing the triune God who dwells among us, we are nonetheless divided by sin and await the victorious coming of Christ who will restore and recreate the unity God wills in a final redemption of creation (cf. Rom 8:18–19). This unity of the human family is yet to be realized eschatologically. The Church is the sacrament of salvation and of the kingdom of God: catholic, in bringing together men of every race and culture; one, in being the vanguard of the unity of the human community willed by God; holy, sanctified herself by the power of the Holy Spirit, and sanctifying all men through the sacraments; and apostolic, in continuing the mission of the men chosen by Christ to accomplish progressively the divinely willed unity of the human race and the consummation of creation and redemption.

4. Sin and Salvation

44. Created in the image of God to share in the communion of Trinitarian life, human beings are persons who are so constituted as to be able freely to embrace this communion. Freedom is the divine gift that enables human persons to choose the communion which the triune God offers to them as their ultimate good. But with freedom comes the possibility of the failure of freedom. Instead of embracing the ultimate good of participation in the divine life, human persons can and do turn away from it in order to enjoy transitory or even only imaginary goods. Sin is precisely this failure of freedom, this turning away from the divine invitation to communion.

45. Within the perspective of the *imago Dei*, which is essentially dialogical or relational in its ontological structure, sin, as a rupture of the relationship with God, causes a disfigurement of the *imago Dei*. The dimensions of sin can be grasped in the light of those dimensions of the *imago Dei* which are affected by sin. This fundamental alienation from God also upsets man's relationship with others (cf. 1 Jn 3:17) and, in a real sense, produces a division within himself between body and spirit, knowing and willing, reason and emotions (Rom 7:14f.). It also affects his physical existence, bringing suffering, illness and death. In addition, just as the *imago Dei* has an historical dimension, so too does sin. The witness of Scripture (cf. Rom 5:12ff.) presents us with a vision of the history of sin, caused by a rejection of the divine invitation to communion which occurred at the beginning of the history of the human race. Finally, sin affects the social dimension of the *imago Dei*; it is possible to discern ideologies and

structures which are the objective manifestation of sin and which obstruct the realization of the image of God on the part of human beings.

46. Catholic and Protestant exegetes today agree that the *imago Dei* cannot be totally destroyed by sin since it defines the whole structure of human nature. For its part, Catholic tradition has always insisted that, while the *imago Dei* is impaired or disfigured, it cannot be destroyed by sin. The dialogical or relational structure of the image of God cannot be lost but, under the reign of sin, it is disrupted in its orientation towards its christological realization. Furthermore, the ontological structure of the image, while affected in its historicity by sin, remains despite the reality of sinful actions. In this connection—as many Fathers of the Church argued in their response to Gnosticism and Manicheanism—the freedom which as such defines what it is to be human and is fundamental to the ontological structure of the *imago Dei*, cannot be suppressed, even if the situation in which freedom is exercised is in part determined by the consequences of sinfulness. Finally, against the notion of the total corruption of the *imago Dei* by sin, the Catholic tradition has insisted that grace and salvation would be illusory if they did not in fact transform the existing, albeit sinful, reality of human nature.

47. Understood in the perspective of the theology of the *imago Dei*, salvation entails the restoration of the image of God by Christ who is the perfect image of the Father. Winning our salvation through his passion, death and resurrection, Christ conforms us to himself through our participation in the paschal mystery and thus reconfigures the *imago Dei* in its proper orientation to the blessed communion of Trinitarian life. In this perspective, salvation is nothing less than a transformation and fulfillment of the personal life of the human being, created in the image of God and now newly directed to a real participation in the life of the divine Persons, through the grace of the incarnation and the indwelling of the Holy Spirit. The Catholic tradition rightly speaks here of a realization of the person. Suffering from a deficiency of charity because of sin, the person cannot achieve self-realization apart from the absolute and gracious love of God in Christ Jesus. Through this saving transformation of the person through Christ and the Holy Spirit, everything in the universe is also transformed and comes to share in the glory of God (Rom 8:21).

48. For the theological tradition, man affected by sin is always in need of salvation, yet having a natural desire to see God—a *capax Dei*—which, as an image of the divine, constitutes a dynamic orientation to the divine. While this orientation is not destroyed by sin, neither can it be realized apart from God's saving grace. God the savior addresses an image of himself, disturbed in its orientation to him, but nonetheless capable of receiving the saving divine activity. These traditional formulations affirm both

the indestructibility of man's orientation to God and the necessity of salvation. The human person, created in the image of God, is ordered by nature to the enjoyment of divine love, but only divine grace makes the free embrace of this love possible and effective. In this perspective, grace is not merely a remedy for sin, but a qualitative transformation of human liberty, made possible by Christ, as a freedom freed for the Good.

49. The reality of personal sin shows that the image of God is not unambiguously open to God but can close in upon itself. Salvation entails a liberation from this self-glorification through the cross. The paschal mystery, which is originally constituted by the passion, death and resurrection of Christ, makes it possible for each person to participate in the death to sin that leads to life in Christ. The cross entails, not the destruction of the human, but the passage that leads to new life.

50. The effects of salvation for man created in the image of God are obtained through the grace of Christ who, as the second Adam, is the head of a new humanity and who creates for man a new salvific situation through his death for sinners and through his resurrection (cf. 1 Cor 15:47–49; 2 Cor 5:2; Rom 5:6ff.). In this way, man becomes a new creature (2 Cor 5:17) who is capable of a new life of freedom, a life "freed from" and "freed for".

51. Man is freed from sin, from the law, and from suffering and death. In the first place, salvation is a liberation from sin which reconciles man with God, even in the midst of a continuing struggle against sin conducted in the power of the Holy Spirit (cf. Eph 6:10–20). In addition, salvation is not a liberation from the law as such but from any legalism that is opposed to the Holy Spirit (2 Cor 3:6) and to the realization of love (Rom 13:10). Salvation brings a liberation from suffering and death which acquire new meaning as a saving participation through the suffering, death and resurrection of the Son. In addition, according to the Christian faith, "freed from" means "freed for": freedom from sin signifies a freedom for God in Christ and the Holy Spirit; freedom from the law means a freedom for authentic love; freedom from death means a freedom for new life in God. This "freedom for" is made possible by Jesus Christ, the perfect icon of the Father, who restores the image of God in man.

5. Imago Dei *and* Imago Christi

52. "The truth is that only in the mystery of the incarnate Word does the mystery of man take on light. For Adam, the first man, was a figure of Him Who was to come, namely Christ the Lord. Christ, the final Adam, by the revelation of the mystery of the Father and His love, fully reveals

man to man himself and makes his supreme calling clear. It is not surprising, then, that in Him all the aforementioned truths find their root
and attain their crown" (*GS* 22). This famous passage from the Second
Vatican Council's Constitution on the Church in the Modern World serves
well to conclude this summary of the main elements of the theology of
the *imago Dei*. For it is Jesus Christ who reveals to man the fullness of his
being, in its original nature, in its final consummation, and in its present
reality.

53. The origins of man are to be found in Christ: for he is created
"through him and in him" (Col 1:16), "the Word [who is] the life ...
and the light of every man who is coming into the world" (Jn 1:3–4, 9).
While it is true that man is created *ex nihilo*, it can also be said that he is
created from the fullness (*ex plenitudine*) of Christ himself who is at once
the creator, the mediator and the end of man. The Father destined us to
be his sons and daughters, and "to be conformed to the image of his Son,
who is the firstborn of many brothers" (Rom 8:29). Thus, what it means
to be created in the *imago Dei* is only fully revealed to us in the *imago
Christi*. In him, we find the total receptivity to the Father which should
characterize our own existence, the openness to the other in an attitude
of service which should characterize our relations with our brothers and
sisters in Christ, and the mercy and love for others which Christ, as the
image of the Father, displays for us.

54. Just as man's beginnings are to be found in Christ, so is his finality.
Human beings are oriented to the kingdom of Christ as to an absolute future,
the consummation of human existence. Since "all things have been created
through him and for him" (Col 1:16), they find their direction and destiny
in him. The will of God that Christ should be the fullness of man is to find
an eschatological realization. While the Holy Spirit will accomplish the ultimate configuration of human persons to Christ in the resurrection of the
dead, human beings already participate in this eschatological likeness to Christ
here below, in the midst of time and history. Through the incarnation, resurrection and Pentecost, the eschaton is already here; they inaugurate it and
introduce it into the world of men, and anticipate its final realization. The
Holy Spirit works mysteriously in all human beings of good will, in societies and in the cosmos to transfigure and divinize human beings. Moreover, the Holy Spirit works through all the sacraments, particularly the
Eucharist which is the anticipation of the heavenly banquet, the fullness of
communion in the Father, Son and Holy Spirit.

55. Between the origins of man and his absolute future lies the present
existential situation of the human race whose full meaning is likewise to
be found only in Christ. We have seen that it is Christ—in his incarnation, death and resurrection—who restores the image of God in man to

its proper form. "Through him, God was pleased to reconcile to himself all things, whether on earth or in heaven, by making peace through the blood of his cross" (Col 1:20). At the core of his sinful existence, man is pardoned and, through the grace of the Holy Spirit, he knows that he is saved and justified through Christ. Human beings grow in their resemblance to Christ and collaborate with the Holy Spirit who, especially through the sacraments, fashions them in the image of Christ. In this way, man's everyday existence is defined as an endeavor to be conformed ever more fully to the image of Christ and to dedicate his life to the struggle to bring about the final victory of Christ in the world.

CHAPTER III

IN THE IMAGE OF GOD: STEWARDS OF VISIBLE CREATION

56. The first great theme within the theology of the *imago Dei* concerns participation in the life of divine communion. Created in the image of God, as we have seen, human beings are beings who share the world with other bodily beings but who are distinguished by their intellect, love and freedom and are thus ordered by their very nature to interpersonal communion. The prime instance of this communion is the procreative union of man and woman which mirrors the creative communion of Trinitarian love. The disfigurement of the *imago Dei* by sin, with its inevitably disruptive consequences for personal and interpersonal life, is overcome by the passion, death and resurrection of Christ. The saving grace of participation in the paschal mystery reconfigures the *imago Dei* according to the pattern of the *imago Christi*.

57. In the present chapter, we consider the second of the main themes of the theology of the *imago Dei*. Created in the image of God to share in the communion of Trinitarian love, human beings occupy a unique place in the universe according to the divine plan: they enjoy the privilege of sharing in the divine governance of visible creation. This privilege is granted to them by the Creator who allows the creature made in his image to participate in his work, in his project of love and salvation, indeed in his own lordship over the universe. Since man's place as ruler is in fact a participation in the divine governance of creation, we speak of it here as a form of stewardship.

58. According to *Gaudium et spes*: "Man, created to God's image, received a mandate to subject to himself the earth and all it contains, and to govern the world with justice and holiness; a mandate to relate himself and

the totality of things to Him Who was to be acknowledged as the Lord and Creator of all. Thus, by the subjection of all things to man, the name of God would be wonderful in all the earth" (34). This concept of man's rule or sovereignty plays an important role in Christian theology. God appoints man as his steward in the manner of the master in the Gospel parables (cf. Lk 19:12). The only creature willed expressly by God for his own sake occupies a unique place at the summit of visible creation (Gen 1:26; 2:20; Ps 8:6–7; Wisdom 9:2–3).

59. Christian theology uses both domestic and royal imagery to describe this special role. Employing royal imagery, it is said that human beings are called to rule in the sense of holding an ascendancy over the whole of visible creation, in the manner of a king. But the inner meaning of this kingship is, as Jesus reminds his disciples, one of service: only by willingly suffering as a sacrificial victim does Christ become the king of the universe, with the Cross as his throne. Employing domestic imagery, Christian theology speaks of man as the master of a household to whom God has confided care of all his goods (cf. Mt 24:45). Man can deploy all the resources of visible creation according to his ingenuity, and exercises this participated sovereignty over visible creation through science, technology and art.

60. Above himself and yet in the intimacy of his own conscience, man discovers the existence of a law which the tradition calls the "natural law". This law is of divine origin, and man's awareness of it is itself a participation in the divine law. It refers man to the true origins of the universe as well as to his own (*Veritatis splendor*, 20). This natural law drives the rational creature to search for the truth and the good in his sovereignty of the universe. Created in the image of God, man exercises this sovereignty over visible creation only in virtue of the privilege conferred upon him by God. He imitates the divine rule, but he cannot displace it. The Bible warns against the sin of this usurpation of the divine role. It is a grave moral failure for human beings to act as rulers of visible creation [while separating] themselves from the higher, divine law. They act in place of the master as stewards (cf. Mt 25:14ff.) who have the freedom they need to develop the gifts which have been confided to them and to do so with a certain bold inventiveness.

61. The steward must render an account of his stewardship, and the divine Master will judge his actions. The moral legitimacy and efficacy of the means employed by the steward provide the criteria for this judgment. Neither science nor technology are ends in themselves; what is technically possible is not necessarily also reasonable or ethical. Science and technology must be put in the service of the divine design

for the whole of creation and for all creatures. This design gives meaning to the universe and to human enterprise as well. Human stewardship of the created world is precisely a stewardship exercised by way of participation in the divine rule and is always subject to it. Human beings exercise this stewardship by gaining scientific understanding of the universe, by caring responsibly for the natural world (including animals and the environment), and by guarding their own biological integrity.

1. *Science and the Stewardship of Knowledge*

62. The endeavor to understand the universe has marked human culture in every period and in nearly every society. In the perspective of the Christian faith, this endeavor is precisely an instance of the stewardship which human beings exercise in accordance with God's plan. Without embracing a discredited concordism, Christians have the responsibility to locate the modern scientific understanding of the universe within the context of the theology of creation. The place of human beings in the history of this evolving universe, as it has been charted by modern sciences, can only be seen in its complete reality in the light of faith, as a personal history of the engagement of the triune God with creaturely persons.

63. According to the widely accepted scientific account, the universe erupted 15 billion years ago in an explosion called the "Big Bang" and has been expanding and cooling ever since. Later there gradually emerged the conditions necessary for the formation of atoms, still later the condensation of galaxies and stars, and about 10 billion years later the formation of planets. In our own solar system and on earth (formed about 4.5 billion years ago), the conditions have been favorable to the emergence of life. While there is little consensus among scientists about how the origin of this first microscopic life is to be explained, there is general agreement among them that the first organism dwelt on this planet about 3.5–4 billion years ago. Since it has been demonstrated that all living organisms on earth are genetically related, it is virtually certain that all living organisms have descended from this first organism. Converging evidence from many studies in the physical and biological sciences furnishes mounting support for some theory of evolution to account for the development and diversification of life on earth, while controversy continues over the pace and mechanisms of evolution. While the story of human origins is complex and subject to revision, physical anthropology and molecular biology combine to make a convincing case for the origin of the

human species in Africa about 150,000 years ago in a humanoid population of common genetic lineage. However it is to be explained, the decisive factor in human origins was a continually increasing brain size, culminating in that of *homo sapiens*. With the development of the human brain, the nature and rate of evolution were permanently altered: with the introduction of the uniquely human factors of consciousness, intentionality, freedom and creativity, biological evolution was recast as social and cultural evolution.

64. Pope John Paul II stated some years ago that "new knowledge leads to the recognition of the theory of evolution as more than a hypothesis. It is indeed remarkable that this theory has been progressively accepted by researchers following a series of discoveries in various fields of knowledge" ("Message to the Pontifical Academy of Sciences on Evolution" [1996]). In continuity with previous twentieth-century papal teaching on evolution (especially Pope Pius XII's encyclical *Humani generis*), the Holy Father's message acknowledges that there are "several theories of evolution" that are "materialist, reductionist and spiritualist" and thus incompatible with the Catholic faith. It follows that the message of Pope John Paul II cannot be read as a blanket approbation of all theories of evolution, including those of a neo-Darwinian provenance which explicitly deny to divine providence any truly causal role in the development of life in the universe. Mainly concerned with evolution as it "involves the question of man", however, Pope John Paul's message is specifically critical of materialistic theories of human origins and insists on the relevance of philosophy and theology for an adequate understanding of the "ontological leap" to the human which cannot be explained in purely scientific terms. The Church's interest in evolution thus focuses particularly on "the conception of man" who, as created in the image of God, "cannot be subordinated as a pure means or instrument either to the species or to society." As a person created in the image of God, he is capable of forming relationships of communion with other persons and with the triune God, as well as of exercising sovereignty and stewardship in the created universe. The implication of these remarks is that theories of evolution and of the origin of the universe possess particular theological interest when they touch on the doctrines of the creation *ex nihilo* and the creation of man in the image of God.

65. We have seen human persons are created in the image of God in order to become partakers of the divine nature (cf. 2 Pet 1:3–4) and thus to share in the communion of Trinitarian life and in the divine dominion over visible creation. At the heart of the divine act of creation is the divine desire to make room for created persons in the communion of the uncreated Persons of the Blessed Trinity through adoptive participation

in Christ. What is more, the common ancestry and natural unity of the human race are the basis for a unity in grace of redeemed human persons under the headship of the New Adam in the ecclesial communion of human persons united with one another and with the uncreated Father, Son, and Holy Spirit. The gift of natural life is the basis for the gift of the life of grace. It follows that, where the central truth concerns a person acting freely, it is impossible to speak of a necessity or an imperative to create, and it is, in the end, inappropriate to speak of the Creator as a force, or energy, or ground. Creation *ex nihilo* is the action of a transcendent *personal* agent, acting freely and intentionally, with a view toward the all-encompassing purposes of personal engagement. In Catholic tradition, the doctrine of the origin of human beings articulates the revealed truth of this fundamentally relational or personalist understanding of God and of human nature. The exclusion of pantheism and emanationism in the doctrine of creation can be interpreted at root as a way of protecting this revealed truth. The doctrine of the immediate or special creation of each human soul not only addresses the ontological discontinuity between matter and spirit, but also establishes the basis for a divine intimacy which embraces every single human person from the first moment of his or her existence.

66. The doctrine of *creatio ex nihilo* is thus a singular affirmation of the truly personal character of creation and its order toward a personal creature who is fashioned as the *imago Dei* and who responds not to a ground, force or energy, but to a personal creator. The doctrines of the *imago Dei* and the *creatio ex nihilo* teach us that the existing universe is the setting for a *radically personal* drama, in which the triune Creator calls out of nothingness those to whom he then calls out in love. Here lies the profound meaning of the words of *Gaudium et spes*: "Man . . . is the only creature on earth which God willed for itself" (24). Created in God's image, human beings assume a place of responsible stewardship in the physical universe. Under the guidance of divine providence and acknowledging the sacred character of visible creation, the human race reshapes the natural order, and becomes an agent in the evolution of the universe itself. In exercising their stewardship of knowledge, theologians have the responsibility to locate modern scientific understandings within a Christian vision of the created universe.

67. With respect to the *creatio ex nihilo*, theologians can note that the Big Bang theory does not contradict this doctrine insofar as it can be said that the supposition of an absolute beginning is not scientifically inadmissible. Since the Big Bang theory does not in fact exclude the possibility of an antecedent stage of matter, it can be noted that the theory appears to provide merely *indirect* support for the doctrine of *creatio ex nihilo* which as such can only be known by faith.

68. With respect to the evolution of conditions favorable to the emergence of life, Catholic tradition affirms that, as universal transcendent cause, God is the cause not only of *existence* but also the cause of *causes*. God's action does not displace or supplant the activity of creaturely causes, but enables them to act according to their natures and, nonetheless, to bring about the ends he intends. In freely willing to create and conserve the universe, God wills to activate and to sustain in act all those secondary causes whose activity contributes to the unfolding of the natural order which he intends to produce. Through the activity of natural causes, God causes to arise those conditions required for the emergence and support of living organisms, and, furthermore, for their reproduction and differentiation. Although there is scientific debate about the degree of purposiveness or design operative and empirically observable in these developments, they have de facto favored the emergence and flourishing of life. Catholic theologians can see in such reasoning support for the affirmation entailed by faith in divine creation and divine providence. In the providential design of creation, the triune God intended not only to make a place for human beings in the universe but also, and ultimately, to make room for them in his own Trinitarian life. Furthermore, operating as real, though secondary causes, human beings contribute to the reshaping and transformation of the universe.

69. The current scientific debate about the mechanisms at work in evolution requires theological comment insofar as it sometimes implies a misunderstanding of the nature of divine causality. Many neo-Darwinian scientists, as well as some of their critics, have concluded that, if evolution is a radically contingent materialistic process driven by natural selection and random genetic variation, then there can be no place in it for divine providential causality. A growing body of scientific critics of neo-Darwinism point to evidence of design (e.g., biological structures that exhibit specified complexity) that, in their view, cannot be explained in terms of a purely contingent process and that neo-Darwinians have ignored or misinterpreted. The nub of this currently lively disagreement involves scientific observation and generalization concerning whether the available data support inferences of design or chance, and cannot be settled by theology. But it is important to note that, according to the Catholic understanding of divine causality, true contingency in the created order is not incompatible with a purposeful divine providence. Divine causality and created causality radically differ in kind and not only in degree. Thus, even the outcome of a truly contingent natural process can nonetheless fall within God's providential plan for creation. According to Saint Thomas Aquinas: "The effect of divine providence is not only that things should happen somehow, but that they should happen either by necessity or by contingency. Therefore,

whatsoever divine providence ordains to happen infallibly and of necessity happens infallibly and of necessity; and that happens from contingency, which the divine providence conceives to happen from contingency" (*STh* I, 22, 4 ad 1). In the Catholic perspective, neo-Darwinians who adduce random genetic variation and natural selection as evidence that the process of evolution is absolutely unguided are straying beyond what can be demonstrated by science. Divine causality can be active in a process that is *both* contingent and guided. Any evolutionary mechanism that is contingent can only be contingent because God made it so. An unguided evolutionary process—one that falls outside the bounds of divine providence—simply cannot exist because "the causality of God, Who is the first agent, extends to all being, not only as to constituent principles of species, but also as to the individualizing principles. . . . It necessarily follows that all things, inasmuch as they participate in existence, must likewise be subject to divine providence" (*STh* I, 22, 2).

70. With respect to the immediate creation of the human soul, Catholic theology affirms that particular actions of God bring about effects that transcend the capacity of created causes acting according to their natures. The appeal to divine causality to account for genuinely *causal* as distinct from merely *explanatory* gaps does not insert divine agency to fill in the "gaps" in human scientific understanding (thus giving rise to the so-called "God of the gaps"). The structures of the world can be seen as open to non-disruptive divine action in directly causing events in the world. Catholic theology affirms that the emergence of the first members of the human species (whether as individuals or in populations) represents an event that is not susceptible of a purely natural explanation and which can appropriately be attributed to divine intervention. Acting indirectly through causal chains operating from the beginning of cosmic history, God prepared the way for what Pope John Paul II has called "an ontological leap ... the moment of transition to the spiritual". While science can study these causal chains, it falls to theology to locate this account of the special creation of the human soul within the overarching plan of the triune God to share the communion of Trinitarian life with human persons who are created out of nothing in the image and likeness of God, and who, in his name and according to his plan, exercise a creative stewardship and sovereignty over the physical universe.

2. Responsibility for the Created World

71. Accelerated scientific and technological advances over the past 150 years have produced a radically new situation for all living things on our planet.

Along with the material abundance, higher living standards, better health and longer life spans have come air and water pollution, toxic industrial wastage, exploitation and sometimes destruction of delicate habitats. In this situation, human beings have developed a heightened awareness that they are organically linked with other living beings. Nature has come to be seen as a biosphere in which all living things form a complex yet carefully organized network of life. Moreover, it has now been recognized that there are limits both to nature's resourcefulness and to its capacity to recover from the harms produced by relentless exploitation of its resources.

72. An unfortunate aspect of this new ecological awareness is that Christianity has been accused by some as in part responsible for the environmental crisis, for the very reason that it has maximized the place of human beings created in the image of God to rule visible creation. Some critics go so far as to claim that the Christian tradition lacks the resources to field a sound ecological ethics because it regards man as essentially superior to the rest of the natural world, and that it will be necessary to turn to Asian and traditional religions to develop the needed ecological ethics.

73. But this criticism arises from a profound misunderstanding of the Christian theology of creation and of the *imago Dei*. Speaking of the need for an "ecological conversion", Pope John Paul II remarked: "Man's lordship ... is not absolute, but ministerial, ... not the mission of an absolute and unquestionable master, but of a steward of God's kingdom" (Discourse, 17 January 2001). A misunderstanding of this teaching may have led some to act in reckless disregard of the natural environment, but it is no part of the Christian teaching about creation and the *imago Dei* to encourage unrestrained development and possible depletion of the earth's resources. Pope John Paul II's remarks reflect a growing concern with the ecological crisis on the part of the Magisterium which is rooted in a long history of teaching found in the social encyclicals of the modern papacy. In the perspective of this teaching, the ecological crisis is a human and a social problem, connected with the infringement of human rights and unequal access to the earth's resources. Pope John Paul II summarized this tradition of social teaching when he wrote in *Centesimus annus*: "Equally worrying is *the ecological question* which accompanies the problem of consumerism and which is closely connected to it. In his desire to have and to enjoy rather than to be and grow, man consumes the resources of the earth and his own life in an excessive and disordered way. At the root of the senseless destruction of the natural environment lies an anthropological error, which unfortunately is widespread in our day. Man, who discovers his capacity to transform and in a certain sense create the world through his own work, forgets that this is always based on God's prior and original gift of the things that are" (37).

74. The Christian theology of creation contributes directly to the resolution of the ecological crisis by affirming the fundamental truth that visible creation is itself a divine gift, the "original gift", that establishes a "space" of personal communion. Indeed, we could say that a properly Christian theology of ecology is an application of the theology of creation. Noting that the term "ecology" combines the two Greek words *oikos* (house) and *logos* (word), the physical environment of human existence can be conceived as a kind of "house" for human life. Given that the inner life of the Blessed Trinity is one of communion, the divine act of creation is the gratuitous production of partners to share in this communion. In this sense, one can say that the divine communion now finds itself "housed" in the created cosmos. For this reason, we can speak of the cosmos as a place of personal communion.

75. Christology and eschatology together serve to make this truth even more profoundly clear. In the hypostatic union of the Person of the Son with a human nature, God comes into the world and assumes the bodiliness which he himself created. In the incarnation, through the only begotten Son who was born of a Virgin by the power of the Holy Spirit, the triune God establishes the possibility of an intimate personal communion with human beings. Since God graciously intends to elevate creaturely persons to dialogical participation in his life, he has, so to speak, come down to the creaturely level. Some theologians speak of this divine condescension as a kind of "hominization" by which God freely makes possible our divinization. God not only manifests his glory in the cosmos through theophanic acts, but also by assuming its bodiliness. In this christological perspective, God's "hominization" is his act of solidarity, not only with creaturely persons, but with the entire created universe and its historical destiny. What is more, in the perspective of eschatology, the second coming of Christ may be seen as the event of God's physical indwelling in the perfected universe which consummates the original plan of creation.

76. Far from encouraging a recklessly homocentric disregard of the natural environment, the theology of the *imago Dei* affirms man's crucial role in sharing in the realization of this eternal divine indwelling in the perfect universe. Human beings, by God's design, are the stewards of this transformation for which all creation longs. Not only human beings, but the whole of visible creation, are called to participate in the divine life. "We know that all creation is groaning in labor pains even until now; and not only that, but we ourselves, who have the first fruits of the Spirit, we also groan with ourselves as we wait for adoption, the redemption of our bodies" (Rom 8:23). In the Christian perspective, our ethical responsibility for the natural environment—our "housed existence"—is thus rooted in a profound theological understanding of visible creation and our place within it.

77. Referring to this responsibility in an important passage in *Evangelium vitae*, Pope John Paul II wrote: "As one called to till and look after the garden of the world (cf. Gen 2:15), man has a specific responsibility towards the environment in which he lives, towards the creation which God has put at the service of his personal dignity. . . . It is the ecological question—ranging from the preservation of the natural habitats of the different species of animals and other forms of life to 'human ecology' properly speaking—which finds in the Bible clear and strong ethical direction, leading to a solution which respects the great good of life, of every life. . . . When it comes to the natural world, we are subject not only to biological laws but also to moral ones, which cannot be violated with impunity" (42).

78. In the end, we must note that theology will not be able to provide us with a technical recipe for the resolution of the ecological crisis, but, as we have seen, it can help us to see our natural environment as God sees it, as the space of personal communion in which human beings, created in the image of God, must seek communion with one another and the final perfection of the visible universe.

79. This responsibility extends to the animal world. Animals are the creatures of God, and, according to the Scriptures, he surrounds them with his providential care (Mt 6:26). Human beings should accept them with gratitude and, even adopting a eucharistic attitude with regard to every element of creation, give thanks to God for them. By their very existence the animals bless God and give him glory: "Bless the Lord, all you birds of the air. All you beasts, wild and tame, bless the Lord" (Dan 3:80–81). In addition, the harmony which man must establish, or restore, in the whole of creation includes his relationship to the animals. When Christ comes in his glory, he will "recapitulate" the whole of creation in an eschatological and definitive moment of harmony.

80. Nonetheless, there is an ontological difference between human beings and animals because only man is created in the image of God and God has given him sovereignty over the animal world (Gen 1:26, 28; Gen 2:19–20). Reflecting the Christian tradition about a just use of the animals, the *Catechism of the Catholic Church* affirms: "God entrusted animals to the stewardship of those whom he created in his own image. Hence it is legitimate to use animals for food and clothing. They may be domesticated to help man in his work and leisure" (2417). This passage also recalls the legitimate use of animals for medical and scientific experimentation, but always recognizing that it is "contrary to human dignity to cause animals to suffer or die needlessly" (2418). Thus, any use of animals must always be guided by the principles already articulated: human sovereignty over the animal world is essentially a stewardship for which human beings must give an account to God who is the Lord of creation in the truest sense.

3. *Responsibility for the Biological Integrity of Human Beings*

81. Modern technology, along with the latest developments in biochemistry and molecular biology, continues to provide contemporary medicine with new diagnostic and therapeutic possibilities. These techniques not only offer new and more effective treatments for disease, however, but also the potential to alter man himself. The availability and feasibility of these technologies lend new urgency to the question, how far is man allowed to remake himself? The exercise of a responsible stewardship in the area of bioethics requires profound moral reflection on a range of technologies that can affect the biological integrity of human beings. Here, we can offer only some brief indications of the specific moral challenges posed by the new technologies and some of the principles which must be applied if we are to exercise a responsible stewardship over the biological integrity of human beings created in the image of God.

82. The right fully to dispose of the body would imply that the person may use the body as a means to an end he himself has chosen: i.e., that he may replace its parts, modify or terminate it. In other words, a person could determine the finality or teleological value of the body. A right to dispose of something extends only to objects with a merely instrumental value, but not to objects which are good in themselves, i.e., ends in themselves. The human person, being created in the image of God, is himself such a good. The question, especially as it arises in bioethics, is whether this also applies to the various levels that can be distinguished in the human person: the biological-somatic, the emotional and the spiritual levels.

83. Everyday clinical practice generally accepts a limited form of disposing of the body and certain mental functions in order to preserve life, as for example in the case of the amputation of limbs or the removal of organs. Such practice is permitted by the principle of totality and integrity (also known as the therapeutic principle). The meaning of this principle is that the human person develops, cares for, and preserves all his physical and mental functions in such a way that (1) lower functions are never sacrificed except for the better functioning of the total person, and even then with an effort to compensate for what is being sacrificed; and (2) the fundamental faculties which essentially belong to being human are never sacrificed, except when necessary to save life.

84. The various organs and limbs together constituting a physical unity are, as integral parts, completely absorbed in the body and subordinate to it. But lower values cannot simply be sacrificed for the sake of higher ones: these values together constitute an organic unity and are mutually dependent. Because the body, as an intrinsic part of the human person, is good in itself, fundamental human faculties can only be sacrificed to

preserve life. After all, life is a fundamental good that involves the whole of the human person. Without the fundamental good of life, the values—like freedom—that are in themselves higher than life itself also expire. Given that man was also created in God's image in his bodiliness, he has no right of full disposal of his own biological nature. God himself and the being created in his image cannot be the object of arbitrary human action.

85. For the application of the principle of totality and integrity, the following conditions must be met: (1) there must be a question of an intervention in the part of the body that is either affected or is the direct cause of the life-threatening situation; (2) there can be no other alternatives for preserving life; (3) there is a proportionate chance of success in comparison with drawbacks; and (4) the patient must give assent to the intervention. The unintended drawbacks and side effects of the intervention can be justified on the basis of the principle of double effect.

86. Some have attempted to interpret this hierarchy of values to permit the sacrifice of lower functions, like the procreative capacity, for the sake of higher values, like preserving mental health and improving relationships with others. However, the reproductive faculty is here sacrificed in order to preserve elements that may be essential to the person as a *functioning* totality but are not essential to the person as a *living* totality. In fact, the person as a functioning totality is actually violated by the loss of the reproductive faculty, and at a moment when the threat to his mental health is not imminent and could be averted in another way. Furthermore, this interpretation of the principle of totality suggests the possibility of sacrificing a part of the body for the sake of social interests. On the basis of the same reasoning, sterilization for eugenic reasons could be justified on the basis of the interest of the state.

87. Human life is the fruit of conjugal love—the mutual, total, definitive, and exclusive gift of man and woman to one another—reflecting the mutual gift in love between the three divine Persons which becomes fruitful in creation, and the gift of Christ to his Church which becomes fruitful in the rebirth of man. The fact that a total gift of man concerns both his spirit and his body is the basis for the inseparability of the two meanings of the conjugal act which (1) is the authentic expression of conjugal love on the physical level and (2) comes to completion through procreation during the woman's fertile phase (*Humanae vitae*, 12; *Familiaris consortio*, 32).

88. The mutual gift of man and woman to one another on the level of sexual intimacy is rendered incomplete through contraception or sterilization. Furthermore, if a technique is used that does not assist the conjugal act in attaining its goal, but replaces it, and the conception is then effected through the intervention of a third party, then the child does not

originate from the conjugal act which is the authentic expression of the mutual gift of the parents.

89. In the case of cloning—the production of genetically identical individuals by means of cleaving of embryos or nuclear transplantation—the child is produced asexually and is in no way to be regarded as the fruit of a mutual gift of love. Cloning, certainly if it involves the production of a large number of people from one person, entails an infringement of the identity of the person. Human community, which as we have seen is also to be conceived as an image of the triune God, expresses in its variety something of the relations of the three divine Persons in their uniqueness which, through being of the same nature, marks their mutual differences.

90. Germ line genetic engineering with a therapeutic goal in man would in itself be acceptable were it not for the fact that is it is hard to imagine how this could be achieved without disproportionate risks especially in the first experimental stage, such as the huge loss of embryos and the incidence of mishaps, and without the use of reproductive techniques. A possible alternative would be the use of gene therapy in the stem cells that produce a man's sperm, whereby he can beget healthy offspring with his own seed by means of the conjugal act.

91. Enhancement genetic engineering aims at improving certain specific characteristics. The idea of man as "co-creator" with God could be used to try to justify the management of human evolution by means of such genetic engineering. But this would imply that man has full right of disposal over his own biological nature. Changing the genetic identity of man as a human person through the production of an infrahuman being is radically immoral. The use of genetic modification to yield a superhuman or being with essentially new spiritual faculties is unthinkable, given that the spiritual life principle of man—forming the matter into the body of the human person—is not a product of human hands and is not subject to genetic engineering. The uniqueness of each human person, in part constituted by his bio-genetic characteristics and developed through nurture and growth, belongs intrinsically to him and cannot be instrumentalized in order to improve some of these characteristics. A man can truly improve only by realizing more fully the image of God in him, by uniting himself to Christ and in imitation of him. Such modifications would in any case violate the freedom of future persons who had no part in decisions that determine their bodily structures and characteristics in a significant and possibly irreversible way. Gene therapy, directed to the alleviation of congenital conditions like Down's syndrome, would certainly affect the identity of the person involved with regard to his appearance and mental gifts, but this modification would help the individual to give full expression to his real identity which is blocked by a defective gene.

92. Therapeutic interventions serve to restore the physical, mental and spiritual functions, placing the person at the center and fully respecting the finality of the various levels in man in relation to those of the person. Possessing a therapeutic character, medicine that serves man and his body as ends in themselves respects the image of God in both. According to the principle of proportionality, extraordinary life-prolonging therapies must be used when there is a just proportion between the positive results that attend these therapies and possible damage to the patient himself. Therapy may be abandoned, even if death is thereby hastened, when this proportion is absent. A hastening of death in palliative therapy by the administration of analgesics is an indirect effect which, like all side effects in medicine, can come under the principle of double effect, provided that the dosage is geared to the suppression of painful symptoms and not to the active termination of life.

93. Disposing of death is in reality the most radical way of disposing of life. In assisted suicide, direct euthanasia, and direct abortion—however tragic and complex personal situations may be—physical life is sacrificed for a self-selected finality. In the same category is the instrumentalization of the embryo through non-therapeutic experimentation on embryos, as well as by pre-implantation diagnostics.

94. Our ontological status as creatures made in the image of God imposes certain limits on our ability to dispose of ourselves. The sovereignty we enjoy is not an unlimited one: we exercise a certain participated sovereignty over the created world and, in the end, we must render an account of our stewardship to the Lord of the Universe. Man is created in the image of God, but he is not God himself.

CONCLUSION

95. Throughout these reflections, the theme of the *imago Dei* has demonstrated its systematic power in clarifying many truths of the Christian faith. It helps us to present a relational—and indeed personal—conception of human beings. It is precisely this relationship with God which defines human beings and founds their relationships with other creatures. Nonetheless, as we have seen, the mystery of the human is made fully clear only in the light of Christ who is the perfect image of the Father and who introduces us, through the Holy Spirit, to a participation in the mystery of the triune God. It is within this communion of love that the mystery of all being, as embraced by God, finds its fullest meaning. At one and the same time grand and humble, this conception of human being as the image of God constitutes a charter for human relations with

the created world and a basis upon which to assess the legitimacy of scientific and technical progress that has a direct impact on human life and the environment. In these areas, just as human persons are called to give witness to their participation in the divine creativity, they are also required to acknowledge their position as creatures to whom God has confided a precious responsibility for the stewardship of the physical universe.

23

THE HOPE OF SALVATION FOR INFANTS WHO DIE WITHOUT BEING BAPTISED

The International Theological Commission has studied the question of the fate of unbaptised infants, bearing in mind the principle of the "hierarchy of truths" and the other theological principles of the universal salvific will of God, the unicity and insuperability of the mediation of Christ, the sacramentality of the Church in the order of salvation, and the reality of original sin. In the contemporary context of cultural relativism and religious pluralism the number of non-baptised infants has grown considerably, and therefore the reflection on the possibility of salvation for these infants has become urgent. The Church is conscious that this salvation is attainable only in Christ through the Spirit. But the Church, as mother and teacher, cannot fail to reflect upon the fate of all men, created in the image of God, and in a more particular way on the fate of the weakest members of the human family and those who are not yet able to use their reason and freedom.

It is clear that the traditional teaching on this topic has concentrated on the theory of *Limbo*, understood as a state which includes the souls of infants who die subject to original sin and without Baptism, and who, therefore, neither merit the beatific vision, nor yet are subjected to any punishment, because they are not guilty of any personal sin. This theory, elaborated by theologians beginning in the Middle Ages, never entered into the dogmatic definitions of the magisterium, even if that same magisterium did at times mention the theory in its ordinary teaching up until the Second Vatican Council. It remains therefore a possible theological hypothesis. However, in the *Catechism of the Catholic Church* (1992), the theory of Limbo is not mentioned. Rather, the Catechism teaches that infants who die without Baptism are entrusted by the Church to the mercy of God, as is shown in the specific funeral rite for such children. The principle that God desires the salvation of all people gives rise to the hope that there is a path to salvation for infants who die without Baptism (cf. *CCC* 1261), and therefore also to the theological desire to find a coherent and logical connection between the diverse affirmations of the

Catholic faith: the universal salvific will of God; the unicity of the mediation of Christ; the necessity of Baptism for salvation; the universal action of grace in relation to the sacraments; the link between original sin and the deprivation of the beatific vision; the creation of man "in Christ".

The conclusion of this study is that there are theological and liturgical reasons to hope that infants who die without Baptism may be saved and brought into eternal happiness, even if there is not an explicit teaching on this question found in revelation. However, none of the considerations proposed in this text to motivate a new approach to the question may be used to negate the necessity of Baptism, nor to delay the conferral of the sacrament. Rather, there are reasons to hope that God will save these infants precisely because it was not possible to do for them that which would have been most desirable—to baptise them in the faith of the Church and incorporate them visibly into the body of Christ.

Finally, an observation on the methodology of the text is necessary. The treatment of this theme must be placed within the historical development of the faith. According to *Dei Verbum* 8, the factors that contribute to this development are the reflection and the study of the faithful, the experience of spiritual things, and the teaching of the magisterium. When the question of infants who die without Baptism was first taken up in the history of Christian thought, it is possible that the doctrinal nature of the question or its implications were not fully understood. Only when seen in light of the historical development of theology over the course of time until Vatican II does this specific question find its proper context within Catholic doctrine. Only in this way—and observing the principle of the hierarchy of truths mentioned in the Decree of the Second Vatican Council *Unitatis redintegratio* (no. 11)—the topic can be reconsidered explicitly under the global horizon of the faith of the Church. This document, from the point of view of speculative theology as well as from the practical and pastoral perspective, constitutes a useful and timely means for deepening our understanding of this problem, which is not only a matter of doctrine, but also of pastoral priority in the modern era.

PRELIMINARY NOTE

The theme "The Hope of Salvation for Infants Who Die without Being Baptised" was placed under the study of the International Theological Commission. In order to prepare for this study, a Committee was formed comprised by Most Rev. Ignazio Sanna; Most Rev. Basil Kyu-Man Cho; Rev. Peter Damien Akpunonu; Rev. Adelbert Denaux; Rev. Gilles Emery, O.P.;

Msgr. Ricardo Ferrara; Msgr. István Ivancsó; Msgr. Paul McPartlan; Rev. Dominic Veliath, S.D.B. (President of the Committee); and Sr. Sarah Butler, M.S.T.B. The Committee also received the collaboration of Rev. Luis Ladaria, S.J., the Secretary General of the International Theological Commission, and Msgr. Guido Pozzo, the Assistant to the ITC, as well as other members of the Commission. The general discussion on the theme took place during the plenary sessions of the ITC, held in Rome in October 2005 and October 2006. This present text was approved *in forma specifica* by the members of the Commission, and was subsequently submitted to its President, William Cardinal Levada who, upon receiving the approval of the Holy Father in an audience granted on 19 January 2007, approved the text for publication.

INTRODUCTION

1. Saint Peter encourages Christians to be always ready to give an account of the hope that is in them (cf. 1 Pet 3:15–16).[1] This document deals with the hope that Christians can have for the salvation of unbaptised infants who die. It indicates how such a hope has developed in recent decades and what its grounds are, so as to enable an account of that hope to be given. Though at first sight this topic may seem to be peripheral to theological concerns, questions of great depth and complexity are involved in its proper explication, and such an explication is called for today by pressing pastoral needs.

2. In these times, the number of infants who die unbaptised is growing greatly. This is partly because of parents, influenced by cultural relativism and religious pluralism, who are non-practising, but it is also partly a consequence of in vitro fertilisation and abortion. Given these developments, the question of the destiny of such infants is raised with new urgency. In such a situation, the ways by which salvation may be achieved appear ever more complex and problematic. The Church, faithful guardian of the way of salvation, knows that salvation can be achieved only in Christ, by the Holy Spirit. Yet, as mother and teacher, she cannot fail to reflect on the destiny of all human beings, created in the image of God,[2] and especially of the weakest. Being endowed with reason, conscience and freedom, adults are responsible for their own destiny in so far as they

---

[1] All scriptural references in this document are to the Revised Standard Version of the Bible (Catholic Edition).

[2] Cf. International Theological Commission, "Communion and Stewardship: Human Persons Created in the Image of God" (Vatican City, 2005). [See chap. 22 of this volume.]

accept or reject God's grace. Infants, however, who do not yet have the use of reason, conscience and freedom, cannot decide for themselves. Parents experience great grief and feelings of guilt when they do not have the moral assurance of the salvation of their children, and people find it increasingly difficult to accept that God is just and merciful if he excludes infants, who have no personal sins, from eternal happiness, whether they are Christian or non-Christian. From a theological point of view, the development of a theology of hope and an ecclesiology of communion, together with a recognition of the greatness of divine mercy, challenge an unduly restrictive view of salvation. In fact, the universal salvific will of God and the correspondingly universal mediation of Christ mean that all theological notions that ultimately call into question the very omnipotence of God, and his mercy in particular, are inadequate.

3. The idea of Limbo, which the Church has used for many centuries to designate the destiny of infants who die without Baptism, has no clear foundation in revelation, even though it has long been used in traditional theological teaching. Moreover, the notion that infants who die without Baptism are deprived of the beatific vision, which has for so long been regarded as the common doctrine of the Church, gives rise to numerous pastoral problems, so much so that many pastors of souls have asked for a deeper reflection on the ways of salvation. The necessary reconsideration of the theological issues cannot ignore the tragic consequences of original sin. Original sin implies a state of separation from Christ, and that excludes the possibility of the vision of God for those who die in that state.

4. Reflecting on the question of the destiny of infants who die without Baptism, the ecclesial community must keep in mind the fact that God is more properly the subject than the object of theology. The first task of theology is therefore to listen to the Word of God. Theology listens to the Word of God expressed in the Scriptures in order to communicate it lovingly to all people. However, with regard to the salvation of those who die without Baptism, the Word of God says little or nothing. It is therefore necessary to interpret the reticence of Scripture on this issue in the light of texts concerning the universal plan of salvation and the ways of salvation. In short, the problem both for theology and for pastoral care is how to safeguard and reconcile two sets of biblical affirmations: those concerning God's universal salvific will (cf. 1 Tim 2:4) and those regarding the necessity of Baptism as the way of being freed from sin and conformed to Christ (cf. Mk 16:16; Mt 28:18–19).

5. Secondly, taking account of the principle *lex orandi lex credendi*, the Christian community notes that there is no mention of Limbo in the

liturgy. In fact, the liturgy contains a feast of the Holy Innocents, who are venerated as martyrs, even though they were not baptised, because they were killed "on account of Christ".[3] There has even been an important liturgical development through the introduction of funerals for infants who died without Baptism. We do not pray for those who are damned. The *Roman Missal* of 1970 introduced a Funeral Mass for unbaptised infants whose parents intended to present them for Baptism. The Church entrusts to God's mercy those infants who die unbaptised. In its 1980 Instruction on Children's Baptism, the Congregation for the Doctrine of the Faith reaffirmed that: "with regard to children who die without having received Baptism, the Church can only entrust them to the mercy of God, as indeed she does in the funeral rite established for them".[4] The *Catechism of the Catholic Church* (1992) adds that: "the great mercy of God who desires that all men should be saved [1 Tim 2:4], and Jesus' tenderness toward children which caused him to say: 'Let the children come to me, do not hinder them' (Mk 10:14), allow us to hope that there is a way of salvation for children who have died without Baptism."[5]

6. Thirdly, the Church cannot fail to encourage the hope of salvation for infants who die without Baptism by the very fact that she "prays that no one should be lost",[6] and prays in hope for "all men to be saved".[7] On the basis of an anthropology of solidarity,[8] strengthened by an ecclesial understanding of corporate personality, the Church knows the help that can be given by the faith of believers. The Gospel of Mark actually describes an occasion when the faith of some was effective for the salvation of another (cf. Mk 2:5). So, while knowing that the normal way to achieve salvation in Christ is by Baptism *in re*, the Church hopes that there may be other ways to achieve the same end. Because, by his Incarnation, the Son of God "in a certain way united himself" with every human being, and because Christ died for all and all are in fact "called to one and the same destiny, which is divine", the Church believes that "the

---

[3] "Bethlehem, do not be sad, but be of good heart at the killing of the holy infants, because they were offered as perfect victims to Christ the King: having been sacrificed on account of him, they will reign with him", *Exapostilarion* of Matins in the Byzantine Liturgy, *Anthologion di tutto l'anno*, vol. 1 (Rome: Edizione Lipa, 1999), 1199.

[4] Congregation for the Doctrine of the Faith, *Pastoralis actio*, 13, *AAS* 72 (1980): 1144.

[5] *Catechism of the Catholic Church* (hereafter referred to as *CCC*), 1261.

[6] *CCC* 1058.

[7] *CCC* 1821.

[8] Cf. Gen 22:18; Wis 8:1; Acts 14:17; Rom 2:6–7; 1 Tim 2:4; Synod of Quiercy, in Henricus Denzinger and Adolfus Schönmetzer, eds., *Enchiridion symbolorum, definitionum et declarationum de rebus fidei et morum* (hereafter referred to as *DS*) (Rome: Herder, 1976), 623; also *NA* 1.

Holy Spirit offers to all the possibility of being made partners, in a way known to God, in the paschal mystery" (*GS* 22).[9]

7. Finally, when reflecting theologically on the salvation of infants who die without Baptism, the Church respects the hierarchy of truths and therefore begins by clearly reaffirming the primacy of Christ and his grace, which has priority over Adam and sin. Jesus Christ, in his existence for us and in the redemptive power of his sacrifice, died and rose again for all. By his whole life and teaching, he revealed the fatherhood of God and his universal love. While the necessity of Baptism is *de fide*, the tradition and the documents of the magisterium which have reaffirmed this necessity need to be interpreted. While it is true that the universal salvific will of God is not opposed to the necessity of Baptism, it is also true that infants, for their part, do not place any personal obstacle in the way of redemptive grace. On the other hand, Baptism is administered to infants, who are free from personal sins, not only in order to free them from original sin, but also to insert them into the communion of salvation which is the Church, by means of communion in the death and resurrection of Christ (cf. Rom 6:1–7). Grace is totally free, because it is always a pure gift of God. Damnation, however, is deserved, because it is the consequence of free human choice.[10] The infant who dies with Baptism is saved by the grace of Christ and through the intercession of the Church, even without his or her cooperation. It can be asked whether the infant who dies without Baptism, but for whom the Church in its prayer expresses the desire for salvation, can be deprived of the vision of God even without his or her cooperation.

1. *HISTORIA QUAESTIONIS*:
HISTORY AND HERMENEUTICS OF CATHOLIC TEACHING

1.1 *Biblical Foundations*

8. A sound theological enquiry should start with a study of the biblical foundations of any ecclesial doctrine or practice. Hence, as regards the issue under discussion, the question should be asked whether the Holy Scriptures deal in one way or another with the question of the destiny of

---

[9] All references in English to the documents of Vatican II have been taken from Austin Flannery, general ed., *Vatican II: The Conciliar and Post Conciliar Documents* (Dublin: Costello Publishing Company, 1975).

[10] Cf. Synod of Quiercy, DS 623.

unbaptised children. Even a quick look through the New Testament, however, makes it clear that the early Christian communities were not yet confronted with the question whether infants or children who had died without Baptism would receive God's salvation. When the New Testament mentions the practice of Baptism, it generally points to the Baptism of adults. But the New Testament evidence does not preclude the possibility of infants being baptised. In households (*oikos*) where Baptism is mentioned in the Book of Acts 16:15 and 33 (cf. 18:8) and First Corinthians 1:16, children may have been baptised along with adults. The absence of positive evidence may be explained by the fact that the New Testament writings are concerned mainly with the initial spread of Christianity in the world.

9. The lack of any positive teaching within the New Testament with respect to the destiny of unbaptised children does not mean that the theological discussion of this question is not informed by a number of fundamental biblical doctrines. These include:

i. God wills to save all people (cf. Gen 3:15; 22:18; 1 Tim 2:3–6), through Jesus Christ's victory over sin and death (cf. Eph 1:20–22; Phil 2:7–11; Rom 14:9; 1 Cor 15:20–28);

ii. the universal sinfulness of human beings (cf. Gen 6:5–6; 8:21; 1 Kings 8:46; Ps 130:3), and their being born in sin (cf. Ps 51:7; Sir 25:24) since Adam, and therefore their being destined to death (cf. Rom 5:12; 1 Cor 15:22);

iii. the necessity, for salvation, of the faith of the believer (cf. Rom 1:16), on the one hand, and of Baptism (cf. Mk 16:16; Mt 28:19; Acts 2:40–41; 16:30–33) and the Eucharist (cf. Jn 6:53) administered by the Church, on the other hand;

iv. Christian hope goes utterly beyond human hope (cf. Rom 4:18–21); Christian hope is that the living God, the Saviour of all humanity (cf. 1 Tim 4:10) will share his glory with all people and that all will live with Christ (cf. 1 Thess 5:9–11; Rom 8:2–5, 23–25), and Christians must be ready to give an account of the hope they have (cf. 1 Pet 3:15);

v. the Church must make "supplications, prayers and intercessions . . . for all" (1 Tim 2:1–8), based on faith that for God's creative power "nothing is impossible" (Job 42:2; Mk 10:27; 12:24, 27; Lk 1:37), and on the hope that the whole creation will finally share in the glory of God (cf. Rom 8:22–27).

10. There seems to be a tension between two of the biblical doctrines just mentioned: the universal salvific will of God on the one side, and the necessity of sacramental Baptism on the other. The latter seems to limit the extension of God's universal salvific will. Hence a hermeneutical reflection is needed about how the witnesses of tradition (Church Fathers, the

magisterium, theologians) read and used biblical texts and doctrines with respect to the problem being dealt with. More specifically, one has to clarify what kind of "necessity" is claimed with respect to the sacrament of Baptism in order to avoid a mistaken understanding. The necessity of sacramental Baptism is a necessity of the second order compared to the absolute necessity of God's saving act through Jesus Christ for the final salvation of every human being. Sacramental Baptism is necessary because it is the ordinary means through which a person shares the beneficial effects of Jesus' death and resurrection. In what follows, we will be attentive to the way scriptural witnesses have been used in the tradition. Moreover, in dealing with theological principles (Chapter 2) and with our reasons for hope (Chapter 3), we will discuss in greater detail the biblical doctrines and texts involved.

1.2. The Greek Fathers

11. Very few Greek Fathers dealt with the destiny of infants who die without Baptism because there was no controversy about this issue in the East. Furthermore, they had a different view of the present condition of humanity. For the Greek Fathers, as the consequence of Adam's sin, human beings inherited corruption, volatility, and mortality, from which they could be restored by a process of deification made possible through the redemptive work of Christ. The idea of an inheritance of sin or guilt— common in Western tradition—was foreign to this perspective, since in their view sin could only be a free, personal act.[11] Hence, not many Greek Fathers explicitly deal with the problem of the salvation of unbaptised children. They do, however, discuss the status or situation—but not the place—of these infants after their death. In this regard, the main problem they face is the tension between God's universal salvific will and the teaching of the Gospel about the necessity of Baptism. Pseudo-Athanasios says clearly that an unbaptised person cannot enter the Kingdom of God. He also asserts that unbaptised children will not enter the Kingdom, but neither will they be lost, for they have not sinned.[12] Anastasius of Sinai expresses this even more clearly: for him, unbaptised children do not go to Gehenna. But he is not able to say more; he does not express an

---

[11] Cf. D. Weaver, "The Exegesis of Romans 5:12 among the Greek Fathers and Its Implication for the Doctrine of Original Sin: The 5th–12th Centuries", *St. Vladimir's Theological Quarterly* 29 (1985): 133–59, 231–57.

[12] (Pseudo-) Athanasios, *Quaestiones ad Antiochum ducem*, q. 101 (*Patrologia cursus completus: Series graeca* [PG], ed. J.-P. Migne, 28, 660C). Likewise q. 115 (PG 28, 672A).

opinion about where they do go, but leaves their destiny to God's judgment.[13]

12. Alone among the Greek Fathers, Gregory of Nyssa wrote a work specifically on the destiny of infants who die, *De infantibus praemature abreptis libellum*.[14] The anguish of the Church appears in the questions he puts to himself: the destiny of these infants is a mystery, "something much greater than the human mind can grasp".[15] He expresses his opinion in relation to virtue and its reward; in his view, there is no reason for God to grant what is hoped for as a reward. Virtue is not worth anything if those who depart this life prematurely without having practised virtue are immediately welcomed into blessedness. Continuing along this line, Gregory asks: "What will happen to the one who finishes his life at a tender age, who has done nothing, bad or good? Is he worthy of a reward?"[16] He answers: "The hoped-for blessedness belongs to human beings by nature, and it is called a reward only in a certain sense."[17] Enjoyment of true life (*zoe* and not *bios*) corresponds to human nature, and is possessed in the degree that virtue is practised. Since the innocent infant does not need purification from personal sins, he shares in this life corresponding to his nature in a sort of regular progress, according to his capacity. Gregory of Nyssa distinguishes between the destiny of infants and that of adults who lived a virtuous life. "The premature death of newborn infants does not provide a basis for the presupposition that they will suffer torments or that they will be in the same state as those who have been purified in this life by all the virtues."[18] Finally, he offers this perspective for the reflection of the Church: "Apostolic contemplation fortifies our inquiry, for the One who has done everything well, with wisdom (Psalm 104:24), is able to bring good out of evil."[19]

13. Gregory of Nazianzus does not write about the place and status after death of infants who die without sacramental Baptism, but he enlarges the subject with another consideration. He writes, namely, that these children receive neither praise nor punishment from the Just Judge, because

---

[13] Anastasius of Sinai, *Quaestiones et responsiones*, q. 81 (PG 89, 709C).

[14] *De infantibus praemature abreptis libellum*, by H. Polack, prepared for the Leiden Colloquium and edited by Hadwiga Hörner, in J. K. Downing, J. A. McDonough, and H. Hörner (ed.), *Gregorii Nysseni opera dogmatica minora, Pars II*; W. Jaeger – H. Langerbeck, and H. Hörner (eds.), *Gregorii Nysseni opera, Volumen III, Pars II* (Leiden and New York, 1987), 65–97.

[15] Ibid., 70.

[16] Ibid., 81–82.

[17] Ibid., 83.

[18] Ibid., 96.

[19] Ibid., 97.

they have suffered injury rather than provoked it. "The one who does not deserve punishment is not thereby worthy of praise, and the one who does not deserve praise is not thereby deserving of punishment." [20] The profound teaching of the Greek Fathers can be summarized in the opinion of Anastasius of Sinai: "It would not be fitting to probe God's judgments with one's hands." [21]

14. On the one hand, these Greek Fathers teach that children who die without Baptism do not suffer eternal damnation, though they do not attain the same state as those who have been baptised. On the other hand, they do not explain what their state is like or where they go. In this matter, the Greek Fathers display their characteristic apophatic sensitivity.

1.3. The Latin Fathers

15. The fate of unbaptised infants first became the subject of sustained theological reflection in the West during the anti-Pelagian controversies of the early fifth century. Saint Augustine addressed the question because Pelagius was teaching that infants could be saved without Baptism. Pelagius questioned whether Saint Paul's letter to the Romans really taught that all human beings sinned "in Adam" (Rom 5:12) and that concupiscence, suffering, and death were a consequence of the Fall. [22] Since he denied that Adam's sin was transmitted to his descendants, he regarded newborn infants as innocent. Pelagius promised infants who died unbaptised entry into "eternal life" (not, however, into the "Kingdom of God" [Jn 3:5]), reasoning that God would not condemn to hell those who were not personally guilty of sin. [23]

16. In countering Pelagius, Augustine was led to state that infants who die without Baptism are consigned to hell. [24] He appealed to the Lord's precept, John 3:5, and to the Church's liturgical practice. Why are little children brought to the baptismal font, especially infants in danger of death, if not to assure them entrance into the Kingdom of God? Why are they

---

[20] Gregory of Nazianzus, *Oratio XL—In sanctum baptisma*, 23 (PG 36, 389B–C).

[21] Anastasius of Sinai, *Quaestiones et responsiones*, q. 81 (PG 89, 709C).

[22] Cf. Pelagius, *Expositio in epistolam ad Romanos*, in *Expositiones XIII epistolarum Pauli*, ed. A. Souter (Cambridge, 1926).

[23] Cf. Augustine, *Epistula* 156 (*Corpus scriptorum ecclesiasticorum latinorum* [hereafter CSEL], 44, 448f.); 175, 6 (CSEL 44, 660–62); 176, 3 (CSEL 44, 666f.); *De peccatorum meritis et remissione et de baptismo parvulorum* 1, 20, 26; 3, 5, 11—6, 12 (CSEL 60, 25f. and 137–39); *De gestis Pelagii* 11, 23–24 (CSEL 42, 76–78).

[24] Cf. *De pecc. mer.* 1, 16, 21 (CSEL 60, 20f.); *Sermo* 294, 3 (*Patrologia cursus completus: Series latina* [PL], ed. J.-P. Migne, 38, 1337; *Contra Iulianum* 5, 11, 44 (PL 44, 809).

subjected to exorcisms and exsufflations if they do not have to be delivered from the devil?[25] Why are they born again if they do not need to be made new? Liturgical practice confirms the Church's belief that all inherit Adam's sin and must be transferred from the power of darkness into the kingdom of light (Col 1:13).[26] There is only one Baptism, the same for infants and adults, and it is for the forgiveness of sins.[27] If little children are baptised, then, it is because they are sinners. Although they clearly are not guilty of personal sin, according to Romans 5:12 (in the Latin translation available to Augustine), they have sinned "in Adam".[28] "Why did Christ die for them if they are not guilty?"[29] All need Christ as their Saviour.

17. In Augustine's judgement, Pelagius undermined belief in Jesus Christ, the one Mediator (1 Tim 2:5), and in the need for the saving grace he won for us on the Cross. Christ came to save sinners. He is the "Great Physician" who offers even infants the medicine of Baptism to save them from the inherited sin of Adam.[30] The sole remedy for the sin of Adam, passed on to everyone through human generation, is Baptism. Those who are not baptised cannot enter the Kingdom of God. At the judgement, those who do not enter the Kingdom (Mt 25:34) will be condemned to hell (Mt 25:41). There is no "middle ground" between heaven and hell. "There is no middle place left, where you can put babies."[31] Anyone "who is not with Christ must be with the devil."[32]

18. God is just. If he condemns unbaptised children to hell, it is because they are sinners. Although these infants are punished in hell, they will suffer only the "mildest condemnation" ("*mitissima poena*"),[33] "the light-est punishment of all",[34] for there are diverse punishments in proportion to the guilt of the sinner.[35] These infants were unable to help themselves, but there is no injustice in their condemnation because all belong to "the same mass", the mass destined for perdition. God does no injustice to those who are not elected, for all deserve hell.[36] Why is it that some are

---

[25] Cf. *De pecc. mer.* 1, 34, 63 (CSEL 60, 63f.).

[26] Cf. *De gratia Christi et de peccato originali* 2, 40, 45 (CSEL 42, 202f.); *De nuptiis et concupiscentia* 2, 18, 33 (CSEL 42, 286f.).

[27] Cf. *Sermo* 293, 11 (PL 38, 1334).

[28] Cf. *De pecc. mer.* 1, 9–15, 20 (CSEL 60, 10–20).

[29] "Cur ergo pro illis Christus mortuus est si non sunt rei?" in *De nupt. et conc.* 2, 33, 56 (CSEL 42, 513).

[30] Cf. *Sermo* 293, 8–11 (PL 38, 1333f.).

[31] *Sermo* 294, 3 (PL 38, 1337).

[32] *De pecc. mer.* 1, 28, 55 (CSEL 60, 54).

[33] *Enchiridion ad Laurentium* 93 (PL 40, 275); cf. *De pecc. mer.* 1, 16, 21 (CSEL 60, 20f.).

[34] *C. Iul.* 5, 11, 44 (PL 44, 809).

[35] Cf. *Contra Iulianum opus imperfectum* 4, 122 (CSEL 85, 141–42).

[36] *Contra duas epistulas Pelagianorum* 2, 7, 13 (CSEL 60, 474).

vessels of wrath and others vessels of mercy? Augustine admits that he "cannot find a satisfactory and worthy explanation". He can only exclaim with Saint Paul: "How inscrutable [God's] judgments, and untraceable his ways!" [37] Rather than condemn divine authority, he gives a restrictive interpretation of God's universal salvific will.[38] The Church believes that if anyone is redeemed, it is only by God's unmerited mercy; but if anyone is condemned, it is by his well-merited judgment. We shall discover the justice of God's will in the next world.[39]

19. The Council of Carthage of 418 rejected the teaching of Pelagius. It condemned the opinion that infants "do not contract from Adam any trace of original sin, which must be expiated by the bath of regeneration that leads to eternal life." Positively, this council taught that "even children who of themselves cannot have yet committed any sin are truly baptised for the remission of sins, so that by regeneration they may be cleansed from what they contracted through generation." [40] It was also added that there is no "intermediate or other happy dwelling place for children who have left this life without Baptism, without which they cannot enter the kingdom of heaven, that is, eternal life." [41] This council did not, however, explicitly endorse all aspects of Augustine's stern view about the destiny of infants who die without Baptism.

[37] *Sermo* 294, 7, 7 (PL 38, 1339).

[38] Having taught the universal salvific will of God up to the start of the Pelagian controversy (*De Spiritu et littera* 33, 57–58 [CSEL 60, 215f.]), Augustine subsequently reduced the universality of the "everyone" in 1 Tim 2:4 in various ways: all those (and only those) who *in fact* will be saved; all *classes* (Jews and gentiles), not all individuals; *many*, i.e., not all (*Enchir.* 103 [PL 40, 280]; *C. Iul* 4, 8, 44 [PL 44, 760]). Unlike Jansenism, however, Augustine always taught that Christ died for all, including infants ("Numquid [parvuli] aut homines non sunt ut non pertineant ad id quod dictum est, *omnes homines* [1 Tim 2:4]?" *C. Iul.* 4, 8, 42 [PL 44, 759]; cf. *C. Iul.* 3, 25, 58 [PL 44, 732]; *Sermo* 293, 8 [PL 38, 1333]) and that God does not command the impossible (*De civitate Dei* 22, 2 [CSEL 40, 583–85]; *De natura et gratia* 43, 50 [CSEL 60, 270]; *Retractationes* 1, 10, 2 [PL 32, 599]). For more on this question, see F. Moriones, ed., *Enchiridion theologicum Sancti Augustini* (Madrid: La Editorial Católica, 1961), 327f. and 474–81.

[39] Cf. *Enchir.* 94–95 (PL 40, 275f.); *De nat. et grat.* 3, 3—5, 5 (PL 44, 249f.).

[40] DS 223. This teaching was adopted by the Council of Trent. Council of Trent, 5th Session, Decree on Original Sin, DS 1514; J. Neuner and J. Dupuis, eds., *The Christian Faith in the Doctrinal Documents of the Catholic Church* (Bangalore: Theological Publications in India, 2004) (hereafter referred to as ND), 511.

[41] DS 224: "Item placuit, ut si quis dicit, ideo dixisse Dominum: 'In domo Patris mei mansiones multae sunt (Io 14,2), ut intelligatur, quia in regno caelorum erit aliquis medius aut ullus alicubi locus, ubi beati vivant parvuli, qui sine baptismo ex hac vita migrarunt, sine quo in regno caelorum, quod est vita aeterna, intrare non possunt, anathema sit." Cf. *Concilia Africae a. 345–a. 525*, ed. C. Munier (Turnhout: Brepols, 1974), 70. This canon is found in some manuscripts, but it is missing from others. The *Indiculus* did not take it up. Cf. DS 238–49; ND 1907–14.

20. So great was Augustine's authority in the West, however, that the Latin Fathers (e.g., Jerome, Fulgentius, Avitus of Vienne, and Gregory the Great) did adopt his opinion. Gregory the Great asserts that God condemns even those with only original sin on their souls; even infants who have never sinned by their own will must go to "everlasting torments". He cites Job 14:4–5 (LXX), John 3:5, and Ephesians 2:3 on our condition at birth as "children of wrath".[42]

1.4. The Medieval Scholastics

21. Augustine was the point of reference for Latin theologians throughout the Middle Ages on this matter. Anselm of Canterbury is a good example: he believes that little children who die without Baptism are damned on account of original sin and in keeping with God's justice.[43] The common doctrine was summarized by Hugh of St. Victor: infants who die unbaptised cannot be saved because (1) they have not received the sacrament, and (2) they cannot make a personal act of faith that would supply for the sacrament.[44] This doctrine implies that one needs to be justified during one's earthly life in order to enter eternal life after death. Death puts an end to the possibility of choosing to accept or reject grace, that is, to adhere to God or turn away from him; after death, a person's fundamental dispositions before God receive no further modification.

22. But most of the later medieval authors, from Peter Abelard on, underline the goodness of God and interpret Augustine's "mildest punishment" as the privation of the beatific vision (*carentia visionis Dei*), without hope of obtaining it, but with no additional penalties.[45] This teaching, which modified the strict opinion of Saint Augustine, was disseminated by Peter Lombard: little children suffer no penalty except the privation of the vision of God.[46] This position led the theological reflection of the thirteenth century to assign unbaptised infants a destiny essentially different from that of the saints in heaven, but also partly different from that of the reprobate, with whom they are nonetheless associated. This did not prevent the medieval theologians from holding the existence of two (and not three) possible outcomes for human existence: the happiness of

---

[42] Gregory the Great, *Moralia* 9, 21, commenting on Job 9:17 (PL 75, 877). See also *Moralia* 12, 9 (PL 75, 992–93) and 13, 44 (PL 75, 1038).

[43] Cf. *De conceptu virginali et de originali peccato* (F. S. Schmitt, vol. 2, chap. 28, 170–71).

[44] Cf. *Summa sententiarum* 5, 6 (PL 176, 132).

[45] Cf. Peter Abelard, *Commentaria in Epistolam Pauli ad Romanos* 2 [5, 19], Corpus Christianorum: Continuatio mediaevalis 11, 169–70.

[46] Cf. *Sententiae* 2, 33, 2 (I. Brady, 1/2 [Grottaferrata, 1971], 520).

heaven for the saints, and the privation of this celestial happiness for the damned and for infants who died unbaptised. In the developments of medieval doctrine, the loss of the beatific vision (*poena damni*) was understood to be the proper punishment for original sin, whereas the "torments of perpetual hell" constituted the punishment for mortal sins actually committed.[47] In the Middle Ages, the ecclesiastical magisterium affirmed more than once that those "who die in mortal sin" and those who die "with original sin only" receive "different punishments".[48]

23. Because children below the age of reason did not commit actual sin, theologians came to the common view that these unbaptised children feel no pain at all, or even that they enjoy a full natural happiness through their union with God in all natural goods (Thomas Aquinas, Duns Scotus).[49] The contribution of this last theological thesis consists especially in its recognition of an authentic joy among children who die without sacramental Baptism: they possess a true form of union with God proportionate to their condition. The thesis relies on a certain way of conceptualising the relationship between the natural and the supernatural orders, and, in particular, the orientation to the supernatural; it must not be confused, however, with the later development of the idea of "pure nature". Thomas Aquinas, for instance, insisted that faith alone allows us to know that the supernatural end of human life consists in the glory of the saints, that is, in participation in the life of the Triune God through the beatific vision. Since this supernatural end transcends natural human knowledge, and since unbaptised children lack the sacrament that would have given them the seed of such supernatural knowledge, Aquinas concluded that infants who die without Baptism do not know what they are deprived of, and hence do not suffer from the privation of the beatific vision.[50] Even when they adopted such a view, theologians considered the privation of the beatific vision as an affliction ("punishment") within the divine economy. The theological doctrine

---

[47] Cf. Innocent III, Letter to Humbert, Archbishop of Arles, "Maiores Ecclesiae causas" (DS 780): "Poena originalis peccati est carentia visionis Dei, actualis vero poena peccati est gehennae perpetuae cruciatus." This theological tradition identified the "torments of hell" with afflictive pains both sensible and spiritual; cf. Thomas Aquinas, *IV Sent.*, d. 44, q. 3, a. 3, qla 3; d. 50, q. 2, a. 3.

[48] Council of Lyons II, *Profession of Faith for Michael Paleologus*, DS 858; John XXII, Letter to the Armenians "Nequaquam sine dolore", DS 926; Council of Florence, Decree "Laetentur Caeli", DS 1306.

[49] Thomas Aquinas, *II Sent.*, d. 33, q. 2, a. 2; *De malo*, q. 5, a. 3. John Duns Scotus, *Lectura* II, d. 33, q. un.; *Ordinatio* II, d. 33, q. un.

[50] Thomas Aquinas, *De malo*, q. 5, a. 3: "Anime puerorum ... carent supernaturali cognitione que hic in nobis per fidem plantatur, eo quod nec hic fidem habuerunt in actu, nec sacramentum fidei susceperunt.... Et ideo se privari tali bono anime puerorum non cognoscunt, et propter hoc non dolent." Cf. ibid., ad 4; Leonine edition, 23:136.

of a "natural beatitude" (and the absence of any suffering) can be understood as an attempt to account for God's justice and mercy regarding children who did not commit any actual fault, thus giving more weight to God's mercy than in Augustine's view. The theologians who held this thesis of a natural happiness for children who died without Baptism manifest a very lively sense of the gratuity of salvation and of the mystery of God's will that human thought cannot fully grasp.

24. The theologians who taught, in one form or another, that unbaptised children are deprived of the vision of God generally held at the same time a double affirmation: (a) God wills that everyone be saved, and (b) God, who wills that all be saved, wills equally the dispensations and the means that he himself has established for this salvation and that he has made known to us by his revelation. The second affirmation, of itself, does not exclude other dispositions of the divine economy (as is clear, for example, in the witness of the Holy Innocents). As for the expression "Limbo of Infants", it was forged at the turn of the twelfth to thirteenth century to name the "resting place" of such infants (the "border" of the inferior region). Theologians could discuss this question, however, without using the word "Limbo". Their doctrines should not be confused with the use of the word "Limbo".

25. The main affirmation of these doctrines is that those who were not capable of a free act by which they could consent to grace, and who died without having been regenerated by the sacrament of Baptism, are deprived of the vision of God because of original sin which they inherit through human generation.

1.5. The Modern/Post-Tridentine Era

26. Augustine's thought enjoyed a revival in the sixteenth century, and with it his theory regarding the fate of unbaptised infants, as Robert Bellarmine, for example, bears witness.[51] One consequence of this revival of Augustinianism was Jansenism. Together with Catholic theologians of the Augustinian school, the Jansenists vigorously opposed the theory of Limbo. During this period the popes (Paul III, Benedict XIV, Clement XIII)[52]

---

[51] Cf. Robert Bellarmine, *De amissione gratiae* 6, 2 and 6, 6, in *Opera*, vol. 5 (Paris: Vivès, 1873), 458, 470.

[52] Cf. Paul III, "Alias cum felicitate" (23 September 1535), in Jo. Laurentii Berti Florentini, *Opus de theologicis disciplinis* (Venetiis: Ex Typographia Remondiniana, 1760), 5:36; Paul III, "Cum alias quorumdam" (11 March 1538), in ibid., 1:167–68; Benedict XIV, "Dum praeterito mense" (31 July 1748), "Non sine magno" (30 December 1750), "Sotto il 15 di luglio" (12 May 1751), in *Benedicti XIV acta sive nondum sive sparsim edita nunc autem primum collecta cura Raphaelis de Martinis* (Neapoli, Ex Typogr. Puerorum Artificium,

defended the right of Catholics to teach Augustine's stern view that infants dying with original sin alone are damned and punished with the perpetual torment of the fire of hell, though with the "mildest pain" (Augustine) compared with what was suffered by adults who were punished for their mortal sins. On the other hand, when the Jansenist Synod of Pistoia (1786) denounced the medieval theory of "Limbo", Pius VI defended the right of the Catholic schools to teach that those who died with the guilt of original sin alone are punished with the lack of the beatific vision ("punishment of loss"), but not sensible pains (the punishment of "fire"). In the bull "Auctorem fidei" (1794), the pope condemned as "false, rash, injurious to the Catholic schools" the Jansenist teaching "which rejects as a Pelagian fable [fabula pelagiana] that place in the lower regions (which the faithful call the 'Limbo of Children') in which the souls of those departing with the sole guilt of original sin are punished with the punishment of the condemned, without the punishment of fire, just as if whoever removes the punishment of fire thereby introduces that middle place and state free of guilt and of punishment between the Kingdom of God and eternal damnation of which the Pelagians idly talk." [53] Papal interventions during this period, then, protected the freedom of the Catholic schools to wrestle with this question. They did not endorse the theory of Limbo as a doctrine of faith. Limbo, however, was the common Catholic teaching until the mid-twentieth century.

1.6. *From the Time of Vatican I to Vatican II*

27. Prior to the First Vatican Council, and again prior to the Second Vatican Council, there was a strong interest in some quarters in defining Catholic doctrine on this matter. This interest was evident in the revised schema of the dogmatic constitution, *De doctrina catholica*, prepared for the First Vatican Council (but not voted upon by the Council), which presented the destiny of children who died without Baptism as between that of the damned, on the one hand, and that of the souls in purgatory

---

1894), 1:554–57; 2:74, 412–13. For other texts and references, see G.J. Dyer, *The Denial of Limbo and the Jansenist Controversy* (Mundelein, Ill.: Saint Mary of the Lake Seminary, 1955), 139–59; see especially, on pp. 139–42, the account of the discussions under Clement XIII in 1758–1759, according to the manuscript 1485 of the *Biblioteca Corsiniana*, Rome, classification mark 41.C.15 ("Cause trattate nella S.C. del Sant'Uffizio di Roma dal 1733 al 1761").

[53] Pius VI, Bull "Auctorem fidei", DS 2626. On this question, see Dyer, *Denial of Limbo*, 159–70.

and the blessed, on the other: "Etiam qui cum solo originali peccato mortem obeunt, beata Dei visione in perpetuum carebunt." [54] In the twentieth century, however, theologians sought the right to imagine new solutions, including the possibility that Christ's full salvation reaches these infants.[55]

28. In the preparatory phase of Vatican II, there was a desire on the part of some that the Council affirm the common doctrine that unbaptised infants cannot attain the beatific vision, and thereby close the question. The Central Preparatory Commission, which was aware of many arguments against the traditional doctrine and of the need to propose a solution in better accordance with the developing *sensus fidelium*, opposed this move. Because it was thought that theological reflection on the issue was not mature enough, the question was not included in the Council's agenda; it did not enter into the Council's deliberations and was left open for further investigation.[56] The question raised a number of problems whose outcome was debated among theologians, in particular: the status of the Church's traditional teaching concerning children who die without Baptism; the absence of an explicit indication in Holy Scripture on the subject; the connection between the natural order and the supernatural vocation of human beings; original sin and the universal saving will of God; and the "substitutions" for sacramental Baptism that can be invoked for young children.

29. The Catholic Church's belief that Baptism is necessary for salvation was powerfully expressed in the Decree for the Jacobites at the Council

---

[54] *Schema reformatum constitutionis dogmaticae de doctrina catholica*, 5, 6 in *Acta et decreta sacrorum conciliorum recentiorum: Collectio lacensis*, vol. 7 (Friburgi Brisgoviae, 1890), 565.

[55] For a survey of the discussions and of some new solutions proposed before Vatican II, see Y. Congar, "Morts avant l'aurore de la raison", in *Vaste monde ma paroisse: Vérité et dimensions du salut* (Paris: Témoignage Chrétien, 1959), 174–83; G. Dyer, *Limbo: Unsettled Question* (New York: Sheed and Ward, 1964), 93–182 (with the indication of many publications on pp. 192–96); W. A. van Roo, "Infants Dying without Baptism: A Survey of Recent Literature and Determination of the State of the Question", *Gregorianum* 35 (1954): 406–73; A. Michel, *Enfants morts sans baptême* (Paris: Téqui, 1954); C. Journet, *La volonté divine salvifique sur les petits enfants* (Paris: Desclée de Brouwer, 1958); L. Renwart, "Le baptême des enfants et les limbes", *Nouvelle Revue Théologique* 80 (1958): 449–67; H. de Lavalette, "Autour de la question des enfants morts sans baptême", *Nouvelle Revue Théologique* 82 (1960): 56–69; P. Gumpel, "Unbaptized Infants: May They Be Saved?", *Downside Review* 72 (1954): 342–458; P. Gumpel, "Unbaptized Infants: A Further Report", *Downside Review* 73 (1955): 317–46; V. Wilkin, *From Limbo to Heaven: An Essay on the Economy of Redemption* (New York: Sheed and Ward, 1961). After Vatican II: E. Boissard, *Réflexions sur le sort des enfants morts sans baptême* (Paris: Éditions de la Source, 1974).

[56] For the references, see G. Alberigo and J. A. Komonchak, eds., *History of Vatican II*, vol. 1 (Maryknoll: Orbis and Leuven: Peeters, 1995), 236–45; 308–10.

of Florence in 1442: "There is no other way to come to the aid [of little children] than the sacrament of Baptism by which they are snatched from the power of the devil and adopted as children of God." [57] This teaching implies a very vivid perception of the divine favour displayed in the sacramental economy instituted by Christ; the Church does not know of any other means which would certainly give little children access to eternal life. However, the Church has also traditionally recognised some substitutions for Baptism of water (which is the sacramental incorporation into the mystery of Christ dead and risen), namely, Baptism of blood (incorporation into Christ by witness of martyrdom for Christ) and Baptism of desire (incorporation into Christ by the desire or longing for sacramental Baptism). During the twentieth century, some theologians, developing certain more ancient theological theses, proposed to recognise for little children either some kind of Baptism of blood (by taking into consideration the suffering and death of these infants), or some kind of Baptism of desire (by invoking an "unconscious desire" for Baptism in these infants oriented toward justification, or the desire of the Church).[58] The proposals invoking some kind of Baptism of desire or Baptism of blood, however, involved certain difficulties. On the one hand, the adult's act of desire for Baptism can hardly be attributed to children. The little child is scarcely capable of supplying the fully free and responsible personal act which would constitute a substitution for sacramental Baptism; such a fully free and responsible act is rooted in a judgement of reason and cannot be properly achieved before the human person has reached a sufficient or appropriate use of reason (*aetas discretionis*: "age of discretion"). On the other hand, it is difficult to understand how the Church could properly "supply" for unbaptised infants. The case of sacramental Baptism, instead, is quite different because sacramental Baptism, administered to infants, obtains grace in virtue of that which is specifically proper to the sacrament as such, that is, the certain gift of regeneration by the power of Christ himself. That is why Pope Pius XII, recalling the importance of sacramental Baptism, explained in the "Allocution to Italian Midwives" in 1951: "The state of grace is absolutely necessary for salvation: without it supernatural happiness, the beatific vision of God, cannot be attained. In an adult an act of love may suffice to obtain him sanctifying grace and so supply for the lack of Baptism; to the child still unborn, or newly born, this way is not open." [59] This gave rise among theologians to a renewed reflection on the dispositions of infants with respect to the

[57] DS 1349.

[58] On these propositions and the questions they raised, see Dyer, *Denial of Limbo*, 102–22.

[59] Pius XII, "Allocution to Italian Midwives", *AAS* 43 (1951): 841.

reception of divine grace, on the possibility of an extra-sacramental con-figuration to Christ, and on the maternal mediation of the Church.

30. It is equally necessary to note, among the debated questions with a bearing on this matter, that of the gratuity of the supernatural order. Before the Second Vatican Council, in other circumstances and regarding other questions, Pius XII had vigorously brought this to the conscious-ness of the Church by explaining that one destroys the gratuity of the supernatural order if one asserts that God could not create intelligent beings without ordaining and calling them to the beatific vision.[60] The goodness and justice of God do not imply that grace is necessarily or "automatically" given. Among theologians, then, reflection on the des-tiny of unbaptised infants involved from that time onwards a renewed consideration of the absolute gratuity of grace, and of the ordination of all human beings to Christ and to the redemption that he won for us.

31. Without responding directly to the question of the destiny of unbap-tised infants, the Second Vatican Council marked out many paths to guide theological reflection. The Council recalled many times the universality of God's saving will which extends to all people (1 Tim 2:4).[61] All "share a common destiny, namely God. His providence, evident goodness, and saving designs extend to all humankind" (NA 1, cf. LG 16). In a more particular vein, presenting a conception of human life founded on the dignity of the human being created in the image of God, the constitution *Gaudium et spes* recalls that "[h]uman dignity rests above all on the fact that humanity is called to communion with God", specifying that "[t]he invitation to converse with God is addressed to men and women as soon as they are born" (GS 19). This same constitution proclaims with vigour that only in the mystery of the Incarnate Word does the mystery of the human being take on light. Furthermore, there is the renowned state-ment of the Council which asserted: "Since Christ died for all, and since all are in fact called to one and the same destiny, which is divine, we must hold that the Holy Spirit offers to all the possibility of being made partners, in a way known to God, in the paschal mystery" (GS 22). Although the Council did not expressly apply this teaching to children who die without Baptism, these passages open a way to account for hope in their favour.[62]

---

[60] Cf. Pius XII, Encyclical Letter "Humani generis", *AAS* 42 (1950): 570: "Alii veram 'gratuitatem' ordinis supernaturalis corrumpunt, cum autument Deum entia intellectu praed-ita condere non posse, quin eadem ad beatificam visionem ordinet et vocet."

[61] Cf. *LG* 15–16; *NA* 1; *DH* 11; *AG* 7.

[62] See for instance—among other authors—the observations of K. Rahner. "Die bleibende Bedeutung des II Vatikanischen Konzils", in *Schriften zur Theologie*, band 14 (Zürich, Köln, Einsiedeln: Benziger Verlag, 1980), 314–16. With other nuances: J.-H. Nicolas, *Synthèse*

1.7 *Issues of a Hermeneutical Nature*

32. The study of history shows an evolution and a development of Catholic teaching concerning the destiny of infants who die without Baptism. This progress engages some foundational doctrinal principles which remain permanent, and some secondary elements of unequal value. In effect, revelation does not communicate directly in an explicit fashion knowledge of God's plan for unbaptised children, but it enlightens the Church regarding the principles of faith which must guide her thought and her practice. A theological reading of the history of Catholic teaching up to Vatican II shows in particular that three main affirmations which belong to the faith of the Church appear at the core of the problem of the fate of unbaptised infants. (i) God wants all human beings to be saved. (ii) This salvation is given only through participation in Christ's paschal mystery, that is, through Baptism for the forgiveness of sins, either sacramental or in some other way. Human beings, including infants, cannot be saved apart from the grace of Christ poured out by the Holy Spirit. (iii) Infants will not enter the Kingdom of God without being freed from original sin by redemptive grace.

33. The history of theology and of magisterial teaching show in particular a development concerning the manner of understanding the universal saving will of God. The theological tradition of the past (antiquity, the Middle Ages, the beginning of modern times), in particular the Augustinian tradition, often presents what by comparison with modern theological developments would seem to be a "restrictive" conception of the universality of God's saving will.[63] In theological research, the perception of the divine will to save as "quantitatively" universal is relatively recent. At the level of the magisterium, this larger perception was progressively affirmed. Without trying to date it exactly, one can observe that it appeared very clearly in the nineteenth century, especially in the teaching of Pius IX on the possible salvation of those who, without fault on their part, were unaware of the Catholic faith: those who "lead a virtuous and just life, can, with the aid of divine light and grace, attain eternal life; for God, who understands perfectly, scrutinizes and knows the minds, souls, thoughts and habits of all, in his very great goodness and patience, will not permit anyone who is not guilty of a voluntary fault to be punished with eternal

---

dogmatique: De la Trinité à la Trinité (Fribourg: Editions Universitaires; Paris: Beauchesne, 1985), 848–53. See also the observations of J. Ratzinger speaking as a private theologian in Vittorio Messori a colloquio con il cardinale Joseph Ratzinger, *Rapporto sulla fede* (Cinisello Balsamo: Edizioni Paoline, 1985), 154–55. [English edition: *The Ratzinger Report: An Exclusive Interview on the State of the Church* (San Francisco: Ignatius Press, 1985), 147–48.]

[63] See above, note 38.

torments."[64] This integration and maturation in Catholic doctrine meanwhile gave rise to a renewed reflection on the possible ways of salvation for unbaptised infants.

34. In the Church's tradition, the affirmation that children who died unbaptised are deprived of the beatific vision has for a long time been "common doctrine". This common doctrine followed upon a certain way of reconciling the received principles of revelation, but it did not possess the certitude of a statement of faith, or the same certitude as other affirmations whose rejection would entail the denial of a divinely revealed dogma or of a teaching proclaimed by a definitive act of the magisterium. The study of the history of the Church's reflection on this subject shows that it is necessary to make distinctions. In this summary we distinguish first, statements of faith and what pertains to the faith; second, common doctrine; and third, theological opinion.

35. a. The Pelagian understanding of the access of unbaptised infants to "eternal life" must be considered as contrary to Catholic faith.

36. b. The affirmation that "the punishment for original sin is the loss of the beatific vision", formulated by Innocent III,[65] pertains to the faith: original sin is of itself an impediment to the beatific vision. Grace is necessary in order to be purified of original sin and to be raised to communion with God so as to be able to enter into eternal life and enjoy the vision of God. Historically, the common doctrine applied this affirmation to the fate of unbaptised infants and concluded that these infants lack the beatific vision. But Pope Innocent's teaching, in its content of faith, does not necessarily imply that infants who die without sacramental Baptism are deprived of grace and condemned to the loss of the beatific vision; it allows us to hope that God who wants all to be saved, provides some merciful remedy for their purification from original sin and their access to the beatific vision.

37. c. In the documents of the magisterium in the Middle Ages, the mention of "different punishments" for those who die in actual mortal sin or with original sin only ("[a]s for the souls of those who die in mortal sin or with original sin only, they go down immediately to hell, to be punished, however, with different punishments")[66] must be interpreted according to the common teaching of the time. Historically, these affirmations have certainly been applied to unbaptised infants, with the

---

[64] Pius IX, Encyclical Letter "Quanto conficiamur", 10 August 1863 (DS 2866): "Qui ... honestam rectamque vitam agunt, posse, divinae lucis et gratiae operante virtute, aeternam consequi vitam, cum Deus, qui omnium mentes, animos, cogitationes habitusque plane intuetur, scrutatur et noscit, pro summa sua bonitate et clementia minime patiatur, quempiam aeternis puniri suppliciis, qui voluntarie culpae reatum non habeat."

[65] Cf. Innocent III, "Maiores Ecclesiae causas", DS 780.

[66] Council of Lyons II, *Profession for Michael Paleologus*, DS 858; see above, note 48.

conclusion that these infants suffer punishment for original sin. It must be observed however that, in a general way, the focus of these Church pronouncements was not on the lack of salvation for unbaptised infants, but on the immediacy of the particular judgment after death and the assignment of souls to heaven or hell. These magisterial statements do not oblige us to think that these infants necessarily die with original sin, so that there would be no way of salvation for them.

38. d. The Bull "Auctorem fidei" of Pope Pius VI is not a dogmatic definition of the existence of Limbo: the papal Bull confines itself to rejecting the Jansenist charge that the "Limbo" taught by scholastic theologians is identical with the "eternal life" promised to unbaptised infants by the ancient Pelagians. Pius VI did not condemn the Jansenists because they denied Limbo, but because they held that the defenders of Limbo were guilty of the heresy of Pelagius. By maintaining the freedom of the Catholic schools to propose different solutions to the problem of the fate of unbaptised infants, the Holy See defended the common teaching as an acceptable and legitimate option, without endorsing it.

39. e. Pius XII's "Allocution to Italian Midwives",[67] which states that apart from Baptism "there is no other means of communicating [supernatural] life to the child who has not yet the use of reason", expressed the Church's faith regarding the necessity of grace to attain the beatific vision and the necessity of Baptism as the means to receive such grace.[68] The specification that little children (unlike adults) are unable to act on their own behalf, that is, are incapable of an act of reason and freedom that could "supply for Baptism", did not constitute a pronouncement on the content of current theological theories and did not prohibit the theological search for other ways of salvation. Pius XII rather recalled the limits within which the debate must take place and reasserted firmly the moral obligation to provide Baptism to infants in danger of death.

40. In summary: the affirmation that infants who die without Baptism suffer the privation of the beatific vision has long been the common doctrine of the Church, which must be distinguished from the faith of the Church. As for the theory that the privation of the beatific vision is their sole punishment, to the exclusion of any other pain, this is a theological opinion, despite its long acceptance in the West. The particular theological thesis concerning a "natural happiness" sometimes ascribed to these infants likewise constitutes a theological opinion.

41. Therefore, besides the theory of Limbo (which remains a possible theological opinion), there can be other ways to integrate and safeguard

---

[67] AAS 43 (1951): 841.
[68] See above, 1.6 and below, 2.4.

the principles of the faith grounded in Scripture: the creation of the human being in Christ and his vocation to communion with God; the universal salvific will of God; the transmission and the consequences of original sin; the necessity of grace in order to enter into the Kingdom of God and attain the vision of God; the uniqueness and universality of the saving mediation of Christ Jesus; and the necessity of Baptism for salvation. These other ways are not achieved by modifying the principles of the faith, or by elaborating hypothetical theories; rather, they seek an integration and coherent reconciliation of the principles of the faith under the guidance of the ecclesial magisterium, by giving more weight to God's universal salvific will and to solidarity in Christ (cf. GS 22) in order to account for the hope that infants dying without Baptism could enjoy eternal life in the beatific vision. In keeping with a methodological principle that what is less known must be investigated by way of what is better known, it appears that the point of departure for considering the destiny of these children should be the salvific will of God, the mediation of Christ and the gift of the Holy Spirit, and a consideration of the condition of children who receive Baptism and are saved through the action of the Church in the name of Christ. The destiny of unbaptised infants remains, however, a limit-case as regards theological inquiry: theologians should keep in mind the apophatic perspective of the Greek Fathers.

2. *INQUIRERE VIAS DOMINI*: SEEKING TO DISCERN GOD'S WAYS— THEOLOGICAL PRINCIPLES

42. Since the theme under consideration concerns a topic for which no explicit answer is directly forthcoming from revelation as embodied in Sacred Scripture and Tradition, the Catholic believer must have recourse to certain underlying theological principles which the Church, and specifically the magisterium, the guardian of the deposit of the faith, has articulated with the assistance of the Holy Spirit. As Vatican II affirms: "In Catholic doctrine there exists an order or 'hierarchy' of truths since they vary in their relation to the foundation of the Christian faith" (*UR* 11). No human being can ultimately save himself or herself. Salvation comes only from God the Father through Jesus Christ in the Holy Spirit. This fundamental truth (of the "absolute necessity" of God's saving act towards human beings) is unfolded in history through the mediation of the Church and its sacramental ministry. The *ordo tractandi* we will adopt here follows the *ordo salutis*, with one exception: we have put the anthropological dimension between the trinitarian and the ecclesiological-sacramental dimensions.

2.1. *The Universal Salvific Will of God as Realized through the Unique Mediation of Jesus Christ in the Holy Spirit*

43. In the context of the discussion on the destiny of those infants who die without Baptism, the mystery of the universal salvific will of God is a fundamental and central principle. The depth of this mystery is reflected in the paradox of divine love which is manifested as both universal and preferential.

44. In the Old Testament, God is called the Saviour of the nation of Israel (cf. Ex 6:6; Deut 7:8; 13:5; 32:15; 33:29; Is 41:14; 43:14; 44:24; Ps 78; 1 Mac 4:30). But his preferential love for Israel has a universal scope, which extends to individuals (cf. 2 Sam 22:18, 44, 49; Ps 25:5; 27:1), and all human beings: "Thou lovest all things that exist, and hast loathing for none of the things which thou hast made, for thou wouldst not have made anything if thou hast hated it" (Wis 11:24). Through Israel the gentile nations will find salvation (cf. Is 2:1–4; 42:1; 60:1–14). "I will give you as a light to the nations, that my salvation may reach to the end of the earth" (Is 49:6).

45. This preferential and universal love of God is intertwined and realized in a unique and exemplary fashion in Jesus Christ, who is the unique Saviour of all (cf. Acts 4:12), but particularly of whoever becomes low or humble (*tapeinôsei*) like the "little ones". Indeed, as one who is gentle or humble in heart (cf. Mt 11:29), Jesus maintains a mysterious affinity and solidarity with them (cf. Mt 18:3–5; 10:40–42; 25:40, 45). Jesus asserts that the care of these little ones is entrusted to the angels of God (cf. Mt 18:10). "So it is not the will of my Father who is in heaven that one of these little ones should perish" (Mt 18:14). This mystery of his will, according to the good pleasure of the Father,[69] is revealed through the Son[70] and dispensed by the gift of the Holy Spirit.[71]

46. The universality of the saving will of God the Father as realized through the unique and universal mediation of his Son, Jesus Christ, is forcefully expressed in the first letter to Timothy: "This is good, and it is acceptable in the sight of God our Saviour, who wills [*thelei*] all men to be saved and to come to the knowledge of the truth. For there is one God, and there is one mediator between God and men, the man Christ Jesus, who gave himself as a ransom for all, the testimony to which was borne at the proper time" (1 Tim 2:3–6). The emphatic

---

[69] Cf. Eph 1:6, 9: "the purpose [*eudokía*] of his will".

[70] Cf. Lk 10:22: "the one to whom the Son chooses [*bouletai*] to reveal him".

[71] Cf. 1 Cor 12:11: "who apportions to each one individually as he wills [*bouletai*]".

reiteration of "all" (vv. 1, 4, 6), and the justification of this universality on the basis of the uniqueness of God and of his mediator who himself is a man, suggests that nobody is excluded from this salvific will. Insofar as it is the object of prayer (cf. 1 Tim 2:1), this salvific will (*thelèma*) refers to a will which is sincere on the part of God, but, at times, is resisted by human beings.[72] Therefore we need to pray to Our Father in heaven that his will (*thelèma*) may be done on earth as it is in heaven (cf. Mt 6:10).

47. The mystery of this will, revealed to Paul as "the very least of all the saints" (Eph 3:8f.), has its roots in the Father's purpose to make his only Son not just "the first-born among many brethren" (Rom 8:29), but also "the first-born of all creation ... [and] from the dead" (Col 1:15, 18). This revelation allows one to discover in the mediation of the Son universal and cosmic dimensions, which overcome all divisions (cf. *GS* 13). With respect to the universality of humankind, the mediation of the Son surmounts (i) the various cultural, social and gender divisions: "[T]here is neither Jew nor Greek ... neither slave nor free ... neither male nor female" (Gal 3:28); and (ii) the divisions caused by sin, internal (cf. Rom 7) as well as interpersonal (cf. Eph 2:14): "For as by one man's disobedience many were made sinners, so by one man's obedience many will be made righteous" (Rom 5:19). With respect to cosmic divisions, Paul explains that "[f]or in him all the fulness of God was pleased to dwell, and through him to reconcile to himself all things, whether on earth or in heaven, making peace by the blood of his cross" (Col 1:19–20). Both dimensions are brought together in the letter to the Ephesians (1:7–10): "In him we have redemption through his blood, the forgiveness of our trespasses ... according to his purpose which he set forth in Christ ... to unite all things in [Christ], things in heaven and things on earth."

48. Certainly we do not see yet the fulfilment of this mystery of salvation, "for in this hope we were saved" (Rom 8:24). The Holy Spirit indeed testifies that it is not yet realised, and at the same time encourages Christians to pray and to hope for the final resurrection: "We know that the whole creation has been groaning in travail together until now; and not only the creation, but we ourselves, who have the first fruits of the Spirit, groan inwardly as we wait for adoption as sons, the redemption of our bodies.... Likewise the Spirit helps us in our weakness; for we do not know how to pray as we ought, but the Spirit himself intercedes for us with sighs too deep for words" (Rom 8:22f., 26). So the groaning of the Spirit not only helps our prayers but

---

[72] Cf. for instance Mt 23:37.

encompasses so to speak the pains of all adults, of all children, of the whole of creation.[73]

49. The Synod of Quiercy (853) asserts: "Almighty God wishes all men without exception to be saved [1 Tim 2:4], although not all are saved. The fact that some are saved, however, is a gift of the Saviour, while the fact that others perish is the fault of those who perish."[74] Spelling out the positive implications of this statement as regards the universal solidarity of all in the mystery of Jesus Christ, the synod further asserts: "As there is no man who was, is or will be, whose nature was not assumed in him [the Lord Jesus Christ], likewise there is no one who was, is or will be, for whom he did not suffer, even though not everyone [factually] is redeemed by his passion."[75]

50. This Christocentric conviction has found expression all through Catholic tradition. Saint Irenaeus, for instance, quotes the Pauline text asserting that Christ will return "to unite all things in him" (Eph 1:10) and that every knee should bow to him in heaven and on earth and under the earth and every tongue confess that Jesus Christ is Lord.[76] On his part, Saint Thomas Aquinas, once again basing himself on the Pauline text, has this to say: "Christ is the perfect mediator of God and men by reason of his having reconciled through his death the human race with God."[77]

51. The documents of Vatican II, not only quote the Pauline text in its entirety (cf. LG 60; AG 7), but also refer to it (cf. LG 49), and furthermore repeatedly use the designation Unicus Mediator Christus (LG 8, 14, 62). This core affirmation of Christological faith also finds expression in the post-Conciliar papal magisterium: "'And there is salvation in no one else, for there is no other name under heaven given among men by which we must be saved' (Acts 4:12). This statement ... has a universal value, since for all people ... salvation can only come from Jesus Christ."[78]

52. The declaration Dominus Iesus succinctly sums up the Catholic conviction and attitude: "It must therefore be firmly believed as a truth of Catholic faith that the universal salvific will of the One and Triune God is offered and accomplished once for all in the mystery of the incarnation, death, and resurrection of the Son of God."[79]

[73] Cf. CCC 307.
[74] DS 623.
[75] DS 624.
[76] See Irenaeus, Adv. Haer. 1, 10, 1 (PG 7, 550).
[77] Thomas Aquinas, STh III, q. 26, art. 1, corpus.
[78] John Paul II, Encyclical Redemptoris missio, 5.
[79] Congregation for the Doctrine of the Faith, Declaration Dominus Iesus, 14.

2.2. *The Universality of Sin and the Universal Need of Salvation*

53. The universal salvific will of God through Jesus Christ, in a mysterious relationship with the Church, is directed to all humans, who, according to the faith of the Church, are sinners in need of salvation. Already in the Old Testament, the all-pervading nature of human sin is mentioned in almost every book. The book of Genesis affirms that sin did not find its origin with God but with human beings, because God created everything and saw that it was good (cf. Gen 1:31). From the moment the human race began to increase on the earth, God had to reckon with the sinfulness of human-kind: "The Lord saw that the wickedness of man was great in the earth, and that every imagination of the thoughts of his heart was only evil contin-ually." He was even "sorry that he had made man on the earth", and ordered a flood to destroy every living thing, except Noah who found favour in his eyes (cf. Gen 6:5–7). But even the flood did not change the human incli-nation to sin: "I will never again curse the ground because of man, for the imagination of man's heart is evil from his youth" (Gen 8:21). The Old Tes-tament writers are convinced that sin is deeply rooted and pervasive in human-ity (cf. Prov 20:9; Eccl 7:20, 29). Hence the frequent petitions for God's indulgence, as in Psalm 143:2: "Enter not into judgment with thy servant; for no man living is righteous before thee", or in the prayer of Solomon: "If they sin against thee—for there is no man who does not sin—. . . if they repent with all their mind and with all their heart . . . then hear thou in heaven thy dwelling place their prayer . . . and forgive thy people who have sinned against thee" (1 Kings 8:46ff.). There are some texts which speak of the sin-fulness from birth. The psalmist affirms: "Behold, I was brought forth in iniq-uity, and in sin did my mother conceive me" (Ps 51:5). And the statement of Eliphaz: "What is man, that he can be clean? Or he that is born of a woman, that he can be righteous?" (Job 15:14; cf. 25:4), is in agreement with Job's own convictions (cf. Job 14:1, 4) and those of other biblical writers (cf. Ps 58:3; Is 48:8). In Wisdom Literature there is even a beginning of reflection on the effects of the sin of the ancestors, Adam and Eve, on the whole of humankind: "But through the devil's envy death entered the world, and those who belong to his party experience it" (Wis 2:24); "From a woman sin had its beginning, and because of her we all die" (Sir 25:24).[80]

54. For Paul, the universality of the redemption brought by Jesus Christ finds its counterpart in the universality of sin. When Paul in his letter to

---

[80] Other attestations of the Jewish belief about Adam's influence in the time of Paul are: 2 Apoc. Bar. 17:3; 23:4; 48:42; 54:15; 4 Ezra 3:7; 7:118: "O Adam, what have you done? Though it was you who sinned, the fall was not yours alone, but ours too who are your descendants."

the Romans asserts "that all men, both Jews and Greeks, are under the power of sin" (Rom 3:9)[81] and that no one can be excluded from this universal verdict, he naturally bases this on Scripture: "As it is written: 'None is righteous, no, not one; no one understands, no one seeks for God. All have turned aside, together they have gone wrong; no one does good, not even one'" (Rom 3:10–12, quoting Eccl 7:20 and Ps 14:1–3 which is identical to Ps 53:1–3). On the one side, all human beings are sinners and need to be delivered through the redemptive death and resurrection of Jesus Christ, the new Adam. Not the works of the Law, but only faith in Jesus Christ can save humanity, Jews and Gentiles alike. On the other side, the sinful condition of humankind is linked to the sin of the first man, Adam. This solidarity with the first man, Adam, is expressed in two Pauline texts: First Corinthians 15:21 and especially Romans 5:12: "Therefore as sin came into the world through one man and death through sin, and so death spread to all men because [Gr. *eph'hô*: other possible translations 'on the basis of which' or 'with the result that'][82] all men sinned ..." In this anacolouthon, the primary causality for the sinful and mortal condition of humankind is ascribed to Adam, no matter how one understands the phrase *eph'hô*. The universal causality of Adam's sin is presupposed in Romans 5:15a, 16a, 17a, and 18a and clearly expressed in 5:19a: "by one man's disobedience many were made sinners". However, Paul never explains how Adam's sin is transmitted. Against Pelagius, who thought that Adam influenced humanity by giving it a bad example, Augustine objected that Adam's sin was transmitted by propagation or heredity, and so brought the doctrine of "original sin" to its classical expression.[83]

---

[81] Cf. Rom 3:23: "All have sinned and fall short of the glory of God".

[82] In the Western Church, the Greek phrase *eph'hô* was understood as a relative clause with a masculine pronoun referring to Adam or a neuter pronoun referring to sin (*peccatum*) (cf. Vetus Latina and Vulgate *in quo*). Augustine at first accepted both interpretations, but when he realized that the Greek word for sin was feminine (*hamartia*) he opted for the first interpretation, which would imply the notion of incorporation of all human beings in Adam. He was followed by many Latin theologians, either "sive in Adamo, sive in peccato", or "in Adamo". The latter interpretation was not known in the Eastern Church before John Damascene. Several Greek Fathers understood *eph'hô* as "because of whom", i.e. Adam, "all sinned". The phrase *eph'hô* has also been understood as a conjunction and translated as "since, because", "on condition that", or "with the result that, so that". J. Fitzmyer (*Romans*, Anchor Bible 33 [New York, 1992], 413–16) discusses eleven different interpretations and opts for the latter possibility of a consecutive meaning: "*Eph' hô*, then, would mean that Paul is expressing a result, the sequel to Adam's baleful influence on humanity by the ratification of his sin in the sins of all individuals" (p. 416).

[83] *De nuptiis et concupiscentia* 2, 12, 15 (PL 44, 450): "Non ego finxi originale peccatum quod catholica fides credit antiquitus."

Under Augustine's influence, the Western Church almost unanimously interpreted Romans 5:12 in the sense of hereditary "sin".[84]

55. Following this, the Council of Trent in its Fifth Session (1546), defined: "If anyone asserts that Adam's sin harmed only him and not his descendants and that the holiness and justice received from God which he lost was lost only for him and not for us also; or that, stained by the sin of disobedience, he transmitted to all humankind only death and the sufferings of the body but not sin as well which is the death of the soul, *anathema sit.* For, he contradicts the words of the apostle: "Sin came into the world through one man and death through sin, and so [death] spread to all as all men sinned in him" [Rom 5:12 *Vulg.*].[85]

56. As the *Catechism of the Catholic Church* puts it: "The doctrine of original sin is, so to speak, the 'reverse side' of the Good News that Jesus is the Saviour of all men, that all need salvation, and that salvation is offered to all through Christ. The Church, which has the mind of Christ, knows very well that we cannot tamper with the revelation of original sin without undermining the mystery of Christ." [86]

2.3. The Need for the Church

57. Catholic tradition has constantly affirmed that the Church is necessary for salvation as the historical mediation of the redemptive work of Jesus Christ. This conviction found its classical expression in the adage of Saint Cyprian: "*Salus extra Ecclesiam non est.*" [87] The Second Vatican Council has reiterated this faith conviction: "Basing itself on Scripture and tradition, it [the Council] teaches that the Church, a pilgrim now on earth,

---

[84] *CCC* 404 speaks of "a sin which will be transmitted by propagation to all mankind, that is, by the transmission of a human nature deprived of original holiness and justice." And it adds: "And that is why original sin is called 'sin' only in an analogical sense: it is a sin 'contracted' and not 'committed'—a state and not an act."

[85] Council of Trent, Fifth Session, Decree on Original Sin, DS 1512; ND 509. The decree of Trent echoes the second canon of the Second Council of Orange (529).

[86] *CCC* 389.

[87] Cyprian, *Epistola ad Iubaianum* 73, 21 (PL 3, 1123); see also Council of Florence, Bull "Cantate Domino", DS 1351; ND 810: "The holy Roman Church ... firmly believes, professes and preaches that 'no one remaining outside the Catholic Church, not only pagans', but also Jews, heretics or schismatics, can become partakers of eternal life; but they will go to the 'eternal fire prepared for the devil and his angels' [Mt 25:41], unless before the end of their life they are joined to [*aggregati*] it. ... 'And no one can be saved, no matter how much alms one has given, even if shedding one's blood for the name of Christ, unless one remains in the bosom and unity of the Catholic Church.'" (Fulgentius of Ruspe, *De fide ad Petrum*, 1, 38, 79 and 1, 39, 80).

is necessary for salvation: the one Christ is mediator and the way of salvation; he is present to us in his body which is the Church. He himself explicitly asserted the necessity of faith and Baptism (cf. Mk 16:16; Jn 3:5), and thereby affirmed at the same time the necessity of the Church which men enter through Baptism as through a door. Hence they could not be saved who, knowing that the Catholic Church was founded as necessary by God through Christ, would refuse either to enter it, or to remain in it" (*LG* 14). The Council expounded the mystery of the Church at length: "The Church, in Christ, is in the nature of [a] sacrament—a sign and instrument, that is, of communion with God and of the unity among all men" (*LG* 1); "Just as Christ carried out the work of redemption in poverty and oppression, so the Church is called to follow the same path if she is to communicate the fruits of salvation to men" (*LG* 8); "Rising from the dead (cf. Rom 6:9) he [Christ] sent his life-giving Spirit upon his disciples and through him set up his Body which is the Church as the universal sacrament of salvation" (*LG* 48). What is striking in these quotations is the universal extent of the Church's mediating role in ministering God's salvation: "the unity among *all men*", "salvation of [all] *men*", "*universal* sacrament of salvation".

58. In the face of new problems and situations and of an exclusive interpretation of the adage: "*salus extra Ecclesiam non est*",[88] the magisterium, in recent times, has articulated a more nuanced understanding as to the manner in which a saving relationship with the Church can be realized. The Allocution of Pope Pius IX, *Singulari quadam* (1854) clearly states the issues involved: "It must, of course, be held as a matter of faith that outside the apostolic Roman Church no one can be saved, that the Church is the only ark of salvation, and that whoever does not enter it, will perish in the flood. On the other hand, it must likewise be held as certain that those who live in ignorance of the true religion, if such ignorance be invincible, are not subject to any guilt in this matter before the eyes of the Lord."[89]

59. The Letter of the Holy Office to the Archbishop of Boston (1949) offers further specifications. "To gain eternal salvation, it is not always required that a person be incorporated in reality [*reapse*] as a member of the Church, but it is necessary that one belong to it at least in desire and longing [*voto et desiderio*]. It is not always necessary that this desire be explicit as it is with catechumens. When one is invincibly ignorant, God

---

[88] Cf. Boniface VIII, Bull "Unam sanctam": "Porro subesse Romano Pontifici omni humanae creaturae declaramus, dicimus, diffinimus omnino esse de necessitate salutis", DS 875; cf. DS 1351; ND 875: "Furthermore we declare, state and define that it is absolutely necessary for the salvation of all human beings that they submit to the Roman Pontiff."

[89] Pius IX, Allocution "Singulari quadam", DS 2865i; ND 813.

also accepts an implicit desire, so called because it is contained in the good disposition of soul by which a person wants his or her will to be conformed to God's will." [90]

60. The universal salvific will of God, realized through Jesus Christ, in the Holy Spirit, which includes the Church as the universal sacrament of salvation, finds expression in Vatican II: "All men are called to this Catholic unity which prefigures and promotes universal peace. And in different ways to it belong, or are related: all the Catholic faithful, others who believe in Christ and finally all mankind called by God's grace to salvation" (LG 13). That the unique and universal mediation of Jesus Christ is realized in the context of a relationship with the Church is further reiterated by the post-Conciliar papal magisterium. Speaking of those who have not had the opportunity to come to know or accept Gospel revelation—even in their case, the encyclical Redemptoris missio has this to say: "Salvation in Christ is accessible by virtue of a grace which [has] a mysterious relationship to the Church".[91]

2.4. The Necessity of Sacramental Baptism

61. God the Father intends to configure all human beings to Christ by the Holy Spirit, who transforms and empowers them by his grace. Ordinarily, this configuration to Jesus Christ takes place through sacramental Baptism, whereby one is conformed to Christ, receives the Holy Spirit, is liberated from sin and becomes a member of the Church.

62. The numerous baptismal statements in the New Testament, in their variety, articulate the different dimensions of the significance of Baptism as understood by the early Christian community. In the first place, Baptism is designated as the forgiveness of sins, as cleansing (cf. Eph 5:26), or as a sprinkling which cleanses the heart from an evil conscience (cf. Heb 10:22; 1 Pet 3:21). "Repent, and be baptised every one of you in the name of Jesus Christ for the forgiveness of your sins; and you shall receive the gift of the Holy Spirit" (Acts 2:38; cf. Acts 22:16). The baptised are thus configured to Jesus Christ: "We were buried therefore with him by baptism into death, so that as Christ was raised from the dead by the glory of the Father, we too might walk in newness of life" (Rom 6:4).

63. Furthermore, the activity of the Holy Spirit in connection with Baptism is repeatedly referred to (cf. Tit 3:5). It is the belief of the Church that the Holy Spirit is imparted with Baptism (cf. 1 Cor 6:11; Tit 3:5).

---

[90] Letter of the Holy Office to the Archbishop of Boston, DS 3870; ND 855.

[91] John Paul II, Redemptoris missio, 10.

The Risen Christ is active through his Spirit, who makes us children of God (cf. Rom 8:14), confident to call God Father (cf. Gal 4:6).

64. Finally, there are the statements about being "added" to the People of God in the context of Baptism, of being baptised "into one body" (Acts 2:41). Baptism results in the incorporation of the human person into the People of God, the Body of Christ and the spiritual temple. Paul speaks of "being baptised into one body" (1 Cor 12:13). Luke, instead, of "being added" to the Church through Baptism (Acts 2:41). Through Baptism, the believer is not only an individual, but becomes a member of the People of God. He or she becomes a member of the Church which Peter calls "a chosen race, a royal priesthood, a holy nation, God's own people" (1 Pet 2:9).

65. The tradition of conferring sacramental Baptism is extended to all, even to infants. Among the New Testament testimonies of Christian Baptism in the book of the Acts of the Apostles, there are instances of "household baptisms" (cf. Acts 16:15; 16:33; 18:8), which possibly included children. The ancient praxis of baptising children,[92] endorsed by the Fathers and the magisterium of the Church, is accepted as an essential part of the faith understanding of the Catholic Church. The Council of Trent will affirm: "In accordance with apostolic tradition, even children who of themselves cannot have yet committed any sin are truly baptised for the remission of sins, so that by regeneration they may be cleansed from what they contracted through generation. For 'unless one is born of water and the Spirit, one cannot enter the Kingdom of God [Jn 3:5].'"[93]

66. The necessity of the sacrament of Baptism is proclaimed and professed as integral to the Christian faith understanding. On the basis of the command as found in Matthew 28:19ff. and Mark 16:15, and of the prescription laid down in John 3:5,[94] the Christian community has from the

---

[92] Polycarp may be an indirect witness to this, since he declares before the proconsul: "For eighty-six years I have been serving Him [the Christ]", *Martyrium Polycarpi* 9, 3. Polycarp's martyrdom probably occurred during the final years of the reign of Antoninus Pius (156–160).

[93] Council of Trent, Fifth Session, Decree on Original Sin, DS 1514; ND 511. The canon echoes the second canon of the Council of Carthage (418), DS 23.

[94] Taking into account the Old Testament texts regarding the outpouring of the Spirit by God, the principal idea in Jn 3:5 seems to refer to God's gift of the Spirit. If natural life is attributable to the fact of God giving the spirit to human beings, analogously eternal life begins when God gives his Holy Spirit to human beings. Cf. R. E. Brown, *The Gospel according to John (I–XII)*, Anchor Bible 29 (New York: Doubleday, 1966), 140. In this regard, Brown observes: "The baptismal motif that is woven into the text of the whole scene is secondary; the phrase 'of water' in which the baptismal motif expresses itself most clearly may have been always part of the scene, although originally not having a specific reference to Christian Baptism; or the phrase may have been added to the tradition later in order to

earliest time, believed in the necessity of Baptism for salvation. While considering sacramental Baptism necessary inasmuch as it is the ordinary way established by Jesus Christ to configure human beings to himself, the Church has never taught the "absolute necessity" of sacramental Baptism for salvation; there are other avenues whereby the configuration with Christ can be realized. Already in the early Christian community, it was accepted that martyrdom, the "Baptism of blood", was a substitute for sacramental Baptism. Furthermore, there was the acknowledgement of the Baptism of desire. In this regard, the words of Thomas Aquinas are pertinent: "The sacrament of Baptism may be wanting to someone in two ways. First, both in reality and in desire; as is the case with those who neither are baptised, nor wish to be baptised.... Secondly, the sacrament of Baptism may be wanting to anyone in reality but not in desire.... Such a man can obtain salvation without being actually baptised on account of his desire for Baptism." [95] The Council of Trent acknowledges "Baptism of desire" as a way whereby one can be justified without the actual reception of the sacrament of Baptism: "After the promulgation of the Gospel, this transition [from sin to justice] cannot take place without the bath of regeneration or the desire for it for as it is written: 'Unless one is born of water and the Spirit, one cannot enter the kingdom of God (Jn 3:5).'" [96]

67. The Christian faith affirmation of the necessity of sacramental Baptism for salvation cannot be depleted of its existential significance by being reduced to a merely theoretical affirmation. On the other hand, God's freedom over the saving means given by him must be equally respected. Consequently, one must avoid any attempt to oppose sacramental Baptism, the Baptism of desire and Baptism of blood as antithetical. They are but expressions of the creative polarities within the realization of God's universal salvific will on behalf of humanity, which include both a real possibility of salvation, and a salvific dialogue in freedom with the human person. It is precisely this dynamism which impels the Church, as the universal sacrament of salvation, to summon everyone to repentance, to faith and to sacramental Baptism. This dialogue in grace is elicited only when the human person is existentially capable of a response in the

---

bring out the baptismal motif" (143). The Lord stresses the necessity of a birth "of water and spirit" to enter into the Kingdom of God. In Christian Tradition, this has been understood as pointing to the "sacrament of Baptism", although the "sacramental" reading is a limitation of the pneumatological meaning. Read in this way, the issue can be raised as to whether the text expresses here a general principle without exception. One should be aware of the slight shift in interpretation.

[95] Thomas Aquinas, *STh* III, q. 68, art. 2, *corpus*.

[96] Council of Trent, Sixth Session, Decree on Justification, DS 1524; ND 1928.

concrete—which is not the case with infants. Hence the need for parents and godparents to speak on behalf of infants who are baptised. But what of infants who die without Baptism?

2.5 *Hope and Prayer for Universal Salvation*

68. Christians are people of hope. They have set their hope "on the living God, who is the saviour of all, especially of those who believe" (1 Tim 4:10). They ardently desire that all human beings, unbaptised children included, may share in God's glory and live with Christ (cf. 1 Thess 5:9–11; Rom 8:2–5, 23–35), in keeping with the recommendation of Theophylactus: "If he [our God] wants all men to be saved, you should also want it, and imitate God."[97] This Christian hope is a "hope ... against hope" (Rom 4:18), going far beyond any form of human hope. It takes its example from Abraham, our father in faith. Abraham put great trust in the promises that God had given him. He trusted ("hoped") in God against all human evidence or odds ("against hope"). So Christians, even when they do not see how unbaptised children can be saved, nevertheless dare to hope that God will embrace them in his saving mercy. They are also prepared to make a defence to anyone who calls them to account for the hope that is in them (cf. 1 Pet 3:15). When they meet mothers and parents in distress because their children died before or after birth, without being baptised, they feel urged to explain to them why their own hope for salvation can also extend to those infants or children.[98]

69. Christians are people of prayer. They take to heart the admonition of Paul: "First of all, then, I urge that supplications, prayers, intercessions, and thanksgivings be made for all" (1 Tim 2:1). This universal prayer is acceptable to God who "desires all men to be saved and to come to the knowledge of truth" (1 Tim 2:4), and to whose creative power "nothing is impossible" (Job 42:2; Mk 10:27; 12:24–27; Lk 1:37). It is based on the hope that the whole creation will finally share in the glory of God (cf. Rom 8:22–27). Such a prayer is in line with Saint John Chrysostom's

---

[97] Theophylactus, *In 1 Tim 2:4* (PG 125, 32): "Ei pantas anthrôpous thelè sôthènai ekeinos, thele kai su, kai mimou ton theon."

[98] It is notable that the *editio typica* of the encyclical of Pope John Paul II, *Evangelium vitae*, has replaced paragraph 99 which read: "You will come to understand that nothing is definitively lost and you will also be able to ask forgiveness from your child, who is now living in the Lord" (a phrasing which was susceptible to a faulty interpretation), by this definitive text: "Infantem autem vestrum potestis Eidem Patri Eiusque misericordiae cum spe committere" (cf. *AAS* 87 [1995]: 515), which may be translated as follows: "You can entrust your child to the same Father and to his mercy with hope."

admonition: "Imitate God. If he wants all to be saved, then it is reasonable that one should pray for all."[99]

3. *SPES ORANS:*
REASONS FOR HOPE

3.1. *The New Context*

70. The two preceding chapters, considering the history of Christian reflection on the destiny of unbaptised infants[100] and the theological principles that bear upon this issue,[101] respectively, have presented a chiaroscuro. On the one hand, in many ways, the underpinning Christian theological principles seem to favour the salvation of unbaptised infants in accordance with God's universal salvific will. On the other hand, however, it cannot be denied that there has been a rather longstanding doctrinal tradition (whose theological value is doubtless not definitive), which, in its concern to safeguard and not compromise other truths of the Christian theological edifice, has expressed either a certain reticence in this regard, or even a clear refusal to envisage the salvation of these infants. There is a fundamental continuity in the Church's reflection upon the mystery of salvation from generation to generation under the guidance of the Holy Spirit. Within that mystery, the question of the eternal destiny of infants who die unbaptised is "one of the most difficult to solve in the structure of theology".[102] It is a "limit-case" where vital tenets of faith, especially the need of Baptism for salvation and the universal salvific will of God, can easily appear to be in tension. With respect for the wisdom and fidelity of those who have investigated this difficult matter before, but also with a keen awareness that the magisterium of the Church has specifically and perhaps providentially opted, at key moments in the history of doctrine,[103] not to define that these infants are deprived of the beatific vision but to keep the question open, we have considered how the Spirit may be guiding the Church at this

---

[99] John Chrysostom, *In 1 Tim. homil.* 7, 2 (PG 62, 536): "Mimou Theon. Ei pantas anthrôpous thelei sôthènai, eikotôs huper hapantôn dei euchesthai."

[100] See above, Chapter 1.

[101] See above, Chapter 2.

[102] Congar, *Vaste monde ma paroisse*, 169: "un de ceux dont la solution est la plus difficile ensynthèse théologique".

[103] See above, 1.5 and 1.6.

point in history to reflect anew on this exceptionally delicate issue (cf. *DV* 8).

71. The Second Vatican Council called the Church to read the signs of the times and to interpret them in the light of the Gospel (cf. *GS* 4, 11), "in order that the revealed truth may be more deeply penetrated, better understood, and more suitably presented" (*GS* 44). In other words, engagement with the world for which Christ suffered, died and rose again, is always for the Church, which is the body of Christ, an occasion to deepen her understanding of the Lord himself and of his love, and indeed of herself, an occasion to penetrate more deeply the message of salvation entrusted to her. It is possible to identify various signs of our modern times that prompt a renewed awareness of aspects of the Gospel which particularly bear upon the question under consideration. In some ways, they provide a new context for its consideration at the start of the twenty-first century.

72. a. The warfare and turmoil of the twentieth century, and the yearning of humanity for peace and unity, shown by the founding of, e.g., the United Nations organization, the European Union, and the African Union, have helped the Church to understand more deeply the importance of the theme of communion in the Gospel message and so to develop an ecclesiology of communion (cf. *LG* 4, 9; *UR* 2; *GS* 12, 24).

73. b. Many people today grapple with the temptation to despair. The crisis of hope in the contemporary world leads the Church to a deeper appreciation of the hope that is central to the Christian Gospel. "There is one body and one Spirit, just as you were called to the one hope that belongs to your call" (Eph 4:4). Christians are particularly called today to be witnesses to hope and ministers of hope in the world (cf. *LG* 48, 49; *GS* 1). The Church in its universality and catholicity is the bearer of a hope that extends to all humankind, and Christians have a mission to offer that hope to everyone.

74. c. The development of global communications, graphically highlighting all the suffering in the world, has been an occasion for the Church to understand God's love, mercy and compassion more profoundly, and to appreciate the primacy of charity. God is merciful, and, faced with the enormity of the world's pain, we learn to trust and glorify God "who by the power at work within us is able to do far more abundantly than all that we ask or think" (Eph 3:20).

75. d. People everywhere are scandalised by the suffering of children and want to enable children to achieve their potential.[104] In such a setting, the Church naturally recalls and ponders anew various New Testament texts

---

[104] Cf. events such as Live Aid (1985) and Live 8 (2005).

expressing the preferential love of Jesus: "Let the children come to me ...
for to such belongs the kingdom of heaven" (Mt 19:14; cf. Lk 18:15–16,
"infants"); "Whoever receives one such in my name receives me" (Mk
9:37); "[U]nless you turn and become like children, you will never enter
the kingdom of heaven" (Mt 18:3); "Whoever humbles himself like this
child, he is the greatest in the kingdom of heaven" (Mt 18:4); "[W]ho-
ever causes one of these little ones who believe in me to sin, it would be
better for him to have a great millstone fastened around his neck and to
be drowned in the depth of the sea" (Mt 18:6); "See that you do not
despise one of these little ones; for I tell you that in heaven their angels
always behold the face of my Father who is in heaven" (Mt 18:10). So
the Church renews her commitment to show Christ's own love and care
for children (cf. *LG* 11; *GS* 48, 50).

76. e. Increased travel and contact among people of different faiths and
the great increase of dialogue between people of different religions have
encouraged the Church to develop a greater awareness of the manifold
and mysterious ways of God (cf. *NA* 1, 2), and of her own mission in
this context.

77. The development of an ecclesiology of communion, a theology of
hope, an appreciation of divine mercy, together with a renewed concern
for the welfare of infants and an ever-increasing awareness that the Holy
Spirit works in the lives of all "in a way known to God" (*GS* 22), all of
these features of our modern age constitute a new context for the examination of our question. This may be a providential moment for its reconsideration. By the grace of the Holy Spirit, the Church in its engagement
with the world of our time has gained deeper insights into God's revelation that can cast new light on our question.

78. Hope is the all-embracing context of our reflections and report.
The Church of today responds to the signs of our own times with
renewed hope for the world at large and, with particular regard to our
question, for unbaptised infants who die.[105] We must here and now
give an account of that hope (cf. 1 Pet 3:15). In the last fifty years or
so, the magisterium of the Church has shown an increasing openness to
the possibility of the salvation of unbaptised infants, and the *sensus fidelium* seems to have been developing in the same direction. Christians
constantly experience, most powerfully in the liturgy, Christ's victory
over sin and death,[106] God's infinite mercy, and the loving communion
of the saints in heaven, all of which increases our hope. There the hope

---

[105] Cf. *CCC* 1261.

[106] "Christ is risen from the dead. By death He conquered death, and to those in the
grave he granted life" (Easter troparion of the Byzantine liturgy). This paschal verse is

that is in us, that we must proclaim and explain, is regularly renewed, and it is from that experience of hope that various considerations can now be offered.

79. It must be clearly acknowledged that the Church does not have sure knowledge about the salvation of unbaptised infants who die. She knows and celebrates the glory of the Holy Innocents, but the destiny of the generality of infants who die without Baptism has not been revealed to us, and the Church teaches and judges only with regard to what has been revealed. What we do positively know of God, Christ and the Church gives us grounds to hope for their salvation, as must now be explained.

3.2. God's Merciful Philanthropy

80. God is rich in mercy, *dives in misericordia* (Eph 2:4). The Byzantine liturgy frequently praises God's philanthropy; God is the "lover of man".[107] Moreover, God's loving purpose, now revealed through the Spirit, is beyond our imagining: "what God has prepared for those who love him" is something "no eye has seen, nor ear heard, nor the heart of man conceived" (1 Cor 2:9–10, quoting Is 64:4). Those who grieve over the fate of infants who die unbaptised, especially their parents, are often themselves people who love God, people whom these words should console. In particular, the following observations can be made:

81. a. God's grace reaches all people and his providence embraces all. The Second Vatican Council teaches that God does not deny "the assistance necessary for salvation" to those who, without any fault of their own, have not yet arrived at an explicit knowledge of God, but who, with the help of grace, "strive to lead a good life". God enlightens all people "that they may at length have life" (cf. *LG* 16). Again it teaches that grace is "active invisibly" in the hearts of all people of good will (*GS* 22). These words apply directly to those above the age of reason, who are making responsible decisions, but it is difficult to deny their applicability also to those below the age of reason. The following words, in particular, seem truly universal in their scope. "For since Christ died for all, and since all are in fact called to one and the same destiny, which is divine [*cumque vocatio hominis ultima revera una sit, scilicet divina*], we must hold

---

sung many times on each of the forty days of the Easter season in the Byzantine tradition. It is, thus, the principal Easter hymn.

[107] In all its ceremonies and celebrations, the Byzantine liturgy praises God's merciful love: "For You are a merciful God who loves mankind, and we glorify You, Father, Son, and Holy Spirit, now and ever and forever."

that the Holy Spirit offers to all the possibility of being made partners, in a way known to God, in the paschal mystery" (*GS* 22). This profound sentence of Vatican II takes us into the heart of the loving purpose of the blessed Trinity and stresses that God's purpose exceeds our understanding.

82. b. God does not demand the impossible of us.[108] Furthermore, God's power is not restricted to the sacraments: "Deus virtutem suam non alligavit sacramentis quin possit sine sacramentis effectum sacramentorum conferre" (God did not bind his power to the sacraments, so as to be unable to bestow the sacramental effect without conferring the sacrament).[109] God can therefore give the grace of Baptism without the sacrament being conferred, and this fact should particularly be recalled when the conferring of Baptism would be impossible. The need for the sacrament is not absolute. What is absolute is humanity's need for the *Ursakrament* which is Christ himself. All salvation comes from him and therefore, in some way, through the Church.[110]

83. c. At all times and in all circumstances, God provides a remedy of salvation for humanity.[111] This was the teaching of Aquinas,[112] and already before him of Augustine[113] and Leo the Great.[114] It is also found in Cajetan.[115] Pope Innocent III specifically focused on the situation of children: "Far from us the thought that all the small children, of whom such a great multitude dies every day, should perish without the merciful

---

[108] Cf. Augustine, *De natura et gratia* 43, 50 (PL 44, 271).

[109] Thomas Aquinas, *STh* III, 64, 7; cf. III, 64, 3; III, 66, 6; III, 68, 2.

[110] See below, 3.4. and 3.5.

[111] Cf. Thomas Aquinas, *In IV Sent.* d. 1, q. 2, a. 4, q. 1, a. 2: "In quolibet statu post peccatum fuit aliquod remedium per quod originale peccatum ex virtute passionis Christi tolleretur."

[112] Cf. also note 109, above.

[113] Cf. Augustine, *Ep.* 102, 2, 12.

[114] Cf. Leo the Great, *In nat. Domini* 4, 1 (PL 54, 203): "Sacramentum salutis humanae nulla umquam antiquitate cessavit.... Semper quidem, dilectissimi, diversis modis multisque mensuris humano generi bonitas divina consuluit. Et plurima providentiae suae munera omnibus retro saeculis clementer impertuit."

[115] Cf. Cajetan, *In IIIam Part.*, q. 68, a. 11: "Rationabile esse ut divina misericordia provideret homini in quocumque naturali statu de aliquo remedio salutis" (It is reasonable that God's mercy should provide man, in whatever natural state [he be], with some remedy of salvation). Cajetan was actually looking to the time before Christ when there was a kind of *sacramentum naturae*, e.g. offering a sacrifice, which was the occasion (but not the cause) of grace. He understood the situation of human beings prior to Christ to be "in the time of the law of nature" and understood the situation of unbaptised infants similarly. He therefore applied his principle in favour of the idea of Limbo as the destiny of such infants. His fundamental point, however, is very important and does not necessarily lead to the conclusion of Limbo: namely, that at all times in history and in all circumstances God cares for the human situation and offers appropriate opportunities for salvation.

God, who wishes no one to perish, having provided for them also some means of salvation. . . . We say that two kinds of sin must be distinguished, original and actual: original which is contracted without consent and actual which is committed with consent. Thus original sin, which is contracted without consent is remitted without consent by the power of the sacrament [of Baptism]."[116] Innocent was defending infant Baptism as the means provided by God for the salvation of the many infants who die each day. We may ask, however, on the basis of a more searching application of the same principle, whether God also provides some remedy for those infants who die without Baptism. There is no question of denying Innocent's teaching that those who die in original sin are deprived of the beatific vision.[117] What we may ask and are asking is whether infants who die without Baptism necessarily die in original sin, without a divine remedy.

84. With confidence that in all circumstances God provides, how might we imagine such a remedy? The following are ways by which unbaptised infants who die may perhaps be united to Christ.

85. a. Broadly, we may discern in those infants who themselves suffer and die a saving conformity to Christ in his own death, and a companionship with him. Christ himself on the Cross bore the weight of all of humanity's sin and death, and all suffering and death thereafter is an engagement with his own enemy (cf. 1 Cor 15:26), a participation in his own battle, in the midst of which we can find him alongside us (cf. Dan 3:24–25 [91–92]; Rom 8:31–39; 2 Tim 4:17). His resurrection is the source of humanity's hope (cf. 1 Cor 15:20); in him alone is there life in abundance (cf. Jn 10:10); and the Holy Spirit offers to all a participation in his paschal mystery (cf. GS 22).

86. b. Some of the infants who suffer and die do so as victims of violence. In their case, we may readily refer to the example of the Holy Innocents and discern an analogy in the case of these infants to the Baptism of blood which brings salvation. Albeit unknowingly, the Holy Innocents suffered and died on account of Christ; their murderers were seeking to kill the infant Jesus. Just as those who took the lives of the Holy Innocents were motivated by fear and selfishness, so the lives

---

[116] Innocent III, Letter to Humbert, Archbishop of Arles, ND 1409, 506; DS 780 ("Absit enim, ut universi parvuli pereant, quorum quotidie tanta multitudo moritur, quin et ipse misericors Deus, qui neminem vult perire, aliquod remedium procuraverit ad salutem. . . . Dicimus distinguendum, quod peccatum est duplex: originale scilicet et actuale: originale, quod absque consensu contrahitur, et actuale, quod committitur cum consensu. Originale igitur, quod sine consensu contrahitur, sine consensu per vim remittitur sacramenti").

[117] Cf. DS 780.

particularly of unborn babies today are often endangered by the fear or selfishness of others. In that sense, they are in solidarity with the Holy Innocents. Moreover, they are in solidarity with the Christ who said: "Truly, I say to you, as you did it to one of the least of these my brethren, you did it to me" (Mt 25:40). How vital it is for the Church to proclaim the hope and generosity that are intrinsic to the Gospel and essential for the protection of life.

87. c. It is also possible that God simply acts to give the gift of salvation to unbaptised infants by analogy with the gift of salvation given sacramentally to baptised infants.[118] We may perhaps compare this to God's unmerited gift to Mary at her Immaculate Conception, by which he simply acted to give her in advance the grace of salvation in Christ.

3.3. Solidarity with Christ

88. There is a fundamental unity and solidarity between Christ and the whole human race. By his Incarnation, the Son of God has united himself, in some way ("*quodammodo*"), with every human being (GS 22).[119] There is, therefore, no one who is untouched by the mystery of the Word made flesh. Humanity, and indeed all creation, has been objectively changed by the very fact of the Incarnation and objectively saved by the suffering, death and resurrection of Christ.[120] However, that objective salvation must be subjectively appropriated (cf. Acts 2:37–38; 3:19), ordinarily by the personal exercise of free will in favour of grace in adults, with or without sacramental Baptism, or by infants' reception of sacramental Baptism. The situation of unbaptised infants is problematic precisely because of their presumed lack of free will.[121] Their situation acutely raises the question of the relationship between the objective salvation won by Christ and

---

[118] The situation of unbaptised infants may be considered by analogy with that of baptised infants, as here. More problematically, it may also perhaps be considered by analogy with the situation of unbaptised adults; see below, note 127.

[119] The Fathers of the Church delight in reflecting on the assumption by Christ of the whole of humanity; e.g. Irenaeus, *Adv. Haer.* 3, 19, 3 (SCh 211, 380), *Epideixis* 33 (SCh 406, 130–31); Hilary of Poitiers, *In Mt.* 4, 8 (SCh 254, 130); 18, 6 (SCh 258, 80); *Trin.* 2, 24 (CCL 62, 60); *Tr. Ps.* 51, 17; 54, 9 (CCL 61, 104; 146); etc.; Gregory of Nyssa, *In Cant.* Or. 2 (*Opera*, ed. Jaeger, 6:61); *Adv. Apoll.* (*Opera* 3/1:152); Cyril of Alexandria, *In Joh. Evang.* 1, 9 (PG 73, 161–64); Leo the Great, *Tract.* 64, 3; 72, 2 (CCL 138A, 392; 442f.).

[120] Some Fathers had a salvific understanding of the Incarnation itself; e.g. Cyril of Alexandria, *Comm. in Joh.* 5 (PG 73, 753).

[121] See below, note 127.

original sin, and the question also of the exact import of the Conciliar word, "*quodammodo*".

89. Christ lived, died and rose again for all. Pauline teaching is that "at the name of Jesus every knee should bow, ... and every tongue confess that Jesus Christ is Lord" (Phil 2:10–11); "to this end Christ died and lived again, that he might be Lord both of the dead and of the living"; "we shall all stand before the judgement seat of God" (Rom 14:9–11). Likewise Johannine teaching stresses that "the Father judges no one, but has given all judgement to the Son, that all may honour the Son, even as they honour the Father" (Jn 5:22–23); "I heard every creature in heaven and on earth and under the earth and in the sea, and all therein, saying: 'To him who sits upon the throne and to the Lamb be blessing and honour and glory and might for ever and ever!'" (Rev 5:13).

90. The Scriptures relate all humanity without exception to Christ. A major weakness of the traditional view of Limbo is that it is unclear whether the souls there have any relationship to Christ; the Christocentricity of the doctrine seems deficient. In some accounts, the souls in Limbo seem to have a natural happiness that belongs to a different order from the supernatural order in which people choose for or against Christ. This appears to be a feature of Aquinas' account, though Suarez and the later scholastics emphasised that Christ restores human nature (his grace is *gratia sanans*, healing of human nature) and thereby enables the very natural happiness that Aquinas attributed to the souls in Limbo. The grace of Christ was therefore implicit in Aquinas' account, though not developed. The later scholastics thereby envisaged three possible destinies (at least in practice, though in principle they might have accepted only two destinies: heaven and hell), and understood, against Augustine, that it was by the grace of Christ that the numerous infants in Limbo were there and not in hell!

91. Where sin abounded, grace superabounded! That is the emphatic teaching of Scripture, but the idea of Limbo seems to constrain that superabundance. "[T]he free gift is not like the trespass. For if many died through one man's trespass, much more have the grace of God and the free gift in the grace of that one man Jesus Christ abounded for many"; "as one man's trespass led to condemnation for all men, so one man's act of righteousness leads to acquittal and life for all men"; "where sin increased, grace abounded all the more" (Rom 5:15, 18, 20). "For as in Adam all die, so also in Christ shall all be made alive" (1 Cor 15:22). Scripture teaches of our sinful solidarity in Adam, yes, but it does so as the backdrop to teaching our salvific solidarity in Christ. "The doctrine of original sin is, so to speak, the 'reverse side' of the Good News that Jesus is the Saviour of all men, that all need salvation and that salvation is offered

to all through Christ." [122] Many traditional accounts of sin and salvation (and of Limbo) have stressed solidarity with Adam more than solidarity with Christ or at least such accounts have had a restrictive conception of the ways by which human beings benefit from solidarity with Christ. This would seem to have been a characteristic of Augustine's thought in particular: [123] Christ saves a select few from the mass who are damned in Adam. The teaching of Saint Paul would urge us to redress the balance and to centre humanity on Christ the Saviour, to whom all, in some way, are united. [124] "He who is the 'image of the invisible God' [125] is himself the perfect man who has restored in the children of Adam that likeness to God which had been disfigured ever since the first sin. Human nature, by the very fact that it was assumed, not absorbed, in him, has been raised in us also to a dignity beyond compare" (GS 22). We wish to stress that humanity's solidarity with Christ (or, more properly, Christ's solidarity with all of humanity) must have priority over the solidarity of human beings with Adam, and that the question of the destiny of unbaptised infants who die must be addressed in that light.

92. "He is the image of the invisible God, the first-born of all creation; for in him all things were created, in heaven and on earth, visible and invisible, . . . all things were created through him and for him. He is before all things, and in him all things hold together. He is the head of the body, the church; he is the beginning, the first-born from the dead, that in everything he might be pre-eminent" (Col 1:15–18). God's plan is "to unite all things in him, things in heaven and things on earth" (Eph 1:10). There is a renewed appreciation of the great cosmic mystery of communion in Christ. This, in fact, is the fundamental context for our question.

93. Nevertheless, human beings are blessed with freedom, and a free acceptance of Christ is the ordinary means of salvation; we are not saved without our acceptance and certainly not against our will. All adults either explicitly or implicitly make a decision vis-à-vis Christ who has united himself with them (cf. GS 22). Some modern theologians see the option for or against Christ as implicated in all choices. However, it is precisely

---

[122] CCC 389.

[123] E.g. Augustine, Enarr. in Ps. 70, 2, 1 (PL 36, 891): "Omnis autem homo Adam; sicut in his qui crediderunt, omnis homo Christus, quia membra sunt Christi." This text shows Augustine's difficulty in regarding solidarity with Christ as universally as solidarity with Adam. All have solidarity with Adam; those who believe have solidarity with Christ. Irenaeus is more even-handed in his doctrine of recapitulation; cf. Adv. Haer. 3, 21, 10; 5, 12, 3; 5, 14, 2; 5, 15, 4; 5, 34, 2.

[124] By the fact of the Incarnation; cf. GS 22.

[125] Col 1:15; cf. 2 Cor 4:4.

the lack of free will and responsible choice on the part of infants that leads to the query as to how they stand vis-à-vis Christ if they die unbaptised. The fact that infants can enjoy the vision of God is recognised in the practice of baptizing infants. The traditional view is that it is only through sacramental Baptism that infants have solidarity with Christ and hence access to the vision of God. Otherwise, solidarity with Adam has priority. We may ask, however, how that view might be changed if priority were restored to our solidarity with Christ (i.e. Christ's solidarity with us).

94. Baptism for salvation can be received either *in re* or *in voto*. It is traditionally understood that the implicit choice for Christ that adults who are not actually baptised can make constitutes a *votum* for Baptism and is salvific. In the traditional view, such an option is not open to infants who have not attained the use of free will. The supposed impossibility of Baptism *in voto* for infants is central to the whole question. Hence, many, many attempts have been made in modern times to explore the possibility of a *votum* in the case of an unbaptised infant, either a *votum* exercised on behalf of the infant by its parents or by the Church,[126] or perhaps a *votum* exercised by the infant in some way.[127] The Church has never ruled out such a solution, and attempts to get Vatican II to do so significantly failed, because of a widespread sense that investigation of this matter was still ongoing and a widespread desire to entrust such infants to the mercy of God.

95. It is important to recognise a "double gratuity" which calls us into being and simultaneously calls us to eternal life. Though a purely natural order is conceivable, no human life is actually lived in such an order. The actual order is supernatural; channels of grace are open from the very beginning of each human life. All are born with that humanity which was assumed by Christ himself and all live in some kind of relation to him, with different degrees of explicitness (cf. *LG* 16) and acceptance, at

[126] See below, 3.4.

[127] With regard to the possibility of a *votum* on the part of the infant, growth towards free will might perhaps be imagined as a continuum which unfolds towards maturity from the first moment of existence, rather than there being a sudden qualitative jump to the exercise of mature, responsible decision. The existence of the unborn is a continuum of human life and growth; it does not suddenly become human at some point. Consequently, infants may actually be capable of exercising some kind of rudimentary *votum* by analogy with that of unbaptised adults. Some theologians have understood the mother's smile to mediate the love of God to the infant, and have therefore seen the infant's response to that smile as a response to God himself. Some modern psychologists and neurologists are convinced that the infant in the womb is already in some way conscious and has some use of freedom. Cf. V. Frankl, *Der unbewusste Gott: Psychotherapie und Religion* (München, 1979); D. Amen, *Healing the Hardware of the Soul* (New York, 2002).

every moment. There are two possible ends for a human being in such an order: either the vision of God or hell (cf. *GS* 22). Though some medieval theologians maintained the possibility of an intermediate, natural, destiny, gained by the grace of Christ (*gratia sanans*), namely Limbo,[128] we consider such a solution problematic and wish to indicate that other approaches are possible, based on hope for a redemptive grace given to unbaptised infants who die which opens for them the way to heaven. We believe that, in the development of doctrine, the solution in terms of Limbo can be surpassed in view of a greater theological hope.

3.4. *The Church and the Communion of Saints*

96. Because all people live in some kind of relation to Christ (cf. *GS* 22), and the Church is the body of Christ, all people live also in some kind of relation to the Church at every moment. The Church has a profound solidarity or communion with the whole of humanity (cf. *GS* 1). She lives with a dynamic orientation to the fulness of life with God in Christ (cf. *LG*, chap. 7), and wills to draw all people into that fulness of life. The Church is, in fact, "the universal sacrament of salvation" (*LG* 48; cf. 1, 9). Salvation is social (cf. *GS* 12), and the Church already lives the graced life of the communion of saints to which all are called, and embraces all people in all circumstances in her prayer, most especially when she celebrates the Eucharist. The Church includes in her prayer non-Christian adults and non-baptised infants who die. Very significantly, the pre–Vatican II lack of liturgical prayers for unbaptised infants who die, has been remedied since the Council.[129] Bound in a common *sensus fidei* (cf. *LG* 12), the Church reaches out to all, knowing them to be loved by God. An important reason for the failure of attempts to get Vatican II to teach that unbaptised infants are definitely deprived of the vision of God[130] was the testimony of bishops that that was not the faith of their people; it did not correspond to the *sensus fidelium*.

97. Saint Paul teaches that the unbelieving husband or wife of a Christian believer is "consecrated" through their wife or husband, respectively, and moreover that their children too are "holy" (1 Cor 7:14). This is a remarkable indication that the holiness that resides in the Church reaches out to people outside the visible bounds of the Church by means of the bonds of human communion, in this case the family bonds between

---

[128] See above, paragraph 90.
[129] See below, 3.5.
[130] See above, 1.6.

husband and wife in marriage and parents and children. Saint Paul implies that the spouse and the child of a believing Christian have by that very fact at least a connection to membership of the Church and to salvation; their family situation "involves a certain introduction to the Covenant".[131] His words give no assurance of salvation for the unbaptised spouse (cf. 1 Cor 7:16) or child, but surely, once again, grounds for hope.

98. When an infant is baptised, he or she cannot personally make a profession of faith. Rather, at that moment, the parents and the Church as a whole provide a context of faith for the sacramental action. Indeed, Saint Augustine teaches that it is the Church that presents a child for baptism.[132] The Church professes her faith and intercedes powerfully for the infant, supplying the act of faith that the infant is unable to make; again the bonds of communion, both natural and supernatural, are operative and manifest. If an unbaptised infant is incapable of a *votum baptismi*, then by the same bonds of communion the Church might be able to intercede for the infant and express a *votum baptismi* on his or her behalf that is effective before God. Moreover, the Church effectively does express in her liturgy just such a *votum* by the very charity towards all that is renewed in her in every celebration of the Eucharist.

99. Jesus taught: "Unless one is born of water and the Spirit, he cannot enter the kingdom of God" (Jn 3:5), from which we understand the need for sacramental Baptism.[133] Likewise, he said: "[U]nless you eat the flesh of the Son of man and drink his blood, you have no life in you" (Jn 6:53), from which we understand the (closely related) need for participation in the Eucharist. However, just as we do not conclude from the latter words that someone who has not received the sacrament of the Eucharist cannot be saved, so we should not deduce from the former words that someone who has not received the sacrament of Baptism cannot be saved. What we should conclude is that no one is saved without some relation to Baptism and Eucharist, and therefore to the Church which is defined by these sacraments. All salvation has some relation to Baptism, Eucharist and the Church. The principle that there is "no salvation outside the Church" means that there is no salvation which is not from Christ and ecclesial by its very nature. Likewise, the scriptural teaching that "without faith it is impossible to please [God]" (Heb 11:6) indicates the intrinsic role of the Church, the communion of faith, in the work of salvation. It is especially in the liturgy of the Church that this role becomes

---

[131] Congar, *Vaste monde ma paroisse*, 171.
[132] Cf. Augustine, *First Letter to Boniface* 22, 40 (PL 44, 570).
[133] Cf. note 94 above.

manifest, as the Church prays and intercedes for all, including unbaptised infants who die.

3.5. *Lex Orandi, Lex Credendi*

100. Before Vatican II, in the Latin Church, there was no Christian funeral rite for unbaptised infants and such infants were buried in unconsecrated ground. Strictly speaking, there was no funeral rite for baptised infants either, but in their case a Mass of the Angels was celebrated and of course they were given a Christian burial. Thanks to the liturgical reform after the Council, the *Roman Missal* now has a funeral Mass for a child who died before Baptism, and there are also special prayers for such a situation in the *Ordo exsequiarum*. Though the tone of the prayers in both instances is noticeably cautious, it is now the case that the Church liturgically expresses hope in the mercy of God, to whose loving care the infant is entrusted. This liturgical prayer both reflects and shapes the *sensus fidei* of the Latin Church regarding the fate of unbaptised infants who die: *lex orandi, lex credendi*. Significantly, in the Greek Catholic Church there is only one funeral rite for infants whether baptised or not yet baptised, and the Church prays for all deceased infants that they may be received into the bosom of Abraham where there is no sorrow or anguish but only eternal life.

101. "As regards children who have died without Baptism, the Church can only entrust them to the mercy of God, as she does in her funeral rites for them. Indeed, the great mercy of God who desires that all men should be saved, and Jesus' tenderness toward children which caused him to say: 'Let the children come to me, do not hinder them' (Mk 10:14; cf. 1 Tim 2:4), allow us to hope that there is a way of salvation for children who have died without Baptism. All the more urgent is the Church's call not to prevent little children coming to Christ through the gift of holy Baptism."[134]

3.6. *Hope*

102. Within the hope that the Church bears for the whole of humanity and wants to proclaim afresh to the world of today, is there a hope for the salvation of infants who die without Baptism? We have carefully re-considered this complex question, with gratitude and respect for the responses that have been given through the history of the Church, but

---

[134] *CCC* 1261.

also with an awareness that it falls to us to give a coherent response for today. Reflecting within the one tradition of faith that unites the Church through the ages, and relying utterly on the guidance of the Holy Spirit whom Jesus promised would lead his followers "into all the truth" (Jn 16:13), we have sought to read the signs of the times and to interpret them in the light of the Gospel. Our conclusion is that the many factors that we have considered above give serious theological and liturgical grounds for hope that unbaptised infants who die will be saved and enjoy the beatific vision. We emphasise that these are reasons for prayerful *hope*, rather than grounds for sure knowledge. There is much that simply has not been revealed to us (cf. Jn 16:12). We live by faith and hope in the God of mercy and love who has been revealed to us in Christ, and the Spirit moves us to pray in constant thankfulness and joy (cf. 1 Thess 5:18).

103. What has been revealed to us is that the ordinary way of salvation is by the sacrament of Baptism. None of the above considerations should be taken as qualifying the necessity of Baptism or justifying delay in administering the sacrament.[135] Rather, as we want to reaffirm in conclusion, they provide strong grounds for hope that God will save infants when we have not been able to do for them what we would have wished to do, namely, to baptise them into the faith and life of the Church.

---

[135] Cf. *CCC* 1257.

MEMBERS OF THE
INTERNATIONAL THEOLOGICAL
COMMISSION

First Five Years

Appointments of May 1, 1969; cf. DC 66 (1969), 495

Rev. Barnabas Ahern, C.P. (United States)
Rev. Hans Urs von Balthasar (Switzerland)
Rev. Louis Bouyer of the Oratory (France)
Rev. Walter Burghardt, SJ. (United States)
Msgr. Carlo Colombo (Italy)
Rev. Yves Congar, O.P. (France)
Msgr. Philippe Delhaye (Belgium)
Rev. Johannes Feiner (Switzerland)
Rev. André Feuillet, P.S.S. (France)
Rev. Lucio Gera (Argentina)
Rev. Olegario Gonzalez de Cardedal (Spain)
Rev. Ignace Abdo Khalife, S.J. (Lebanon)
Rev. Franz Lakner, S.J. (Austria)
Rev. Marie-Joseph Le Guillou, O.P. (France)
Rev. Joseph Lescrauwaet, M.S.C. (Holland)
Rev. Bernard Lonergan, S.J. (Japan)
Rev. Henri de Lubac, S.J. (France)
Rev. Andreas H. Maltha, O.P. (Holland)
Msgr. Jorge Medina Este vez (Chile)
Rev. Peter Nemeshegyi, S.J. (Japan)
Msgr. Stanislaw Olejnik (Poland)
Msgr. Gérard Philips (Belgium)
Rev. Karl Rahner, S.J. (West Germany)
Rev. Joseph Ratzinger (West Germany)
Msgr. Roberto Mascarenhas Roxo (Brazil)
Rev. Tomislaw Sagi-Bunic, O.F.M. Cap. (Yugoslavia)
Msgr. Rudolf Schnackenburg (West Germany)
Rev. Heinz Schürmann (East Germany)
Msgr. Tharcisius Tshibangu (Zaire)

Rev. Cipriano Vagaggini, O.S.B. (Italy)

Second Five Years

Appointments of August 1, 1974; cf. *AAS* 66 (1974), 520–21; DC 71 (1974), 759

Rev. Barnabas Ahern*
Rev. Juan Alfaro, S.J. (Spain)
Rev. Catalino G. Arevalo, S.J. (Philippines)
Rev. Hans Urs von Balthasar*
Rev. Carlos José Boaventura Kloppenburg, O.F.M. (Brazil)
Rev. Louis Bouyer*[1]
Rev. Walter Burghardt*
Msgr. Carlo Caffarra (Italy)
Rev. Raniero Cantalamessa, O.F.M. Cap. (Italy)
Rev. Yves Congar*
Msgr. Philippe Delhaye*
Rev. Edouard Dhanis, S.J. (Belgium)
Rev. Wilhelm Ernst (East Germany)
Rev. Olegario Gonzalez de Cardedal*
Rev. Edouard Hamel, S.J. (Canada)
Rev. Boguslaw Inlender (Poland)
Rev. Marie-Joseph Le Guillou*
Rev. Karl Lehmann (West Germany)
Rev. Joseph Lescrauwaet*
Rev. John Mahoney, S.J. (U.K.)
Rev. Gustave Martelet, S.J. (France)
Msgr. Jorge Medina Estevez*
Rev. Vincent Mulago (Zaire)
Msgr. Joseph Ratzinger*
Rev. Georges Saber, O.L.M. (Lebanon)
Rev. Heinz Schürmann*
Rev. Otto Semmelroth, S.J. (West Germany)
Rev. Anton Strlé (Yugoslavia)
Rev. Jean-Marie Tillard, O.P. (Canada)
Rev. Cipriano Vagaggini*
Rev. Jan Walgrave, O.P. (Belgium)

---

*The asterisk refers to previous lists.

[1] Father Bouyer did not accept the appointment for personal reasons and was replaced by Fr. Dhanis (cf. *AAS* 67 (1975), 286).

Third Five Years

Nominations of August 12, 1980; cf. *AAS* 72 (1980), 977–78; DC 77 (1980), 112

Rev. Barnabas Ahern*
Rev. Juan Alfaro*
Rev. Catalino G. Arevalo*
Rev. Hans Urs von Balthasar*
Msgr. Carlos José Boaventura Kloppenburg*
Msgr. Carlo Caffarra*
Msgr. Giuseppe Colombo (Italy)
Rev. Yves Congar*
Msgr. Philippe Delhaye*
Msgr. Wilhelm Ernst*
Msgr. Pierre Eyt (France)
Rev. Ivan Fucek (Yugoslavia)
Rev. Ferenc Gal (Hungary)
Rev. Edouard Hamel*
Rev.'Walter Kasper (West Germany)
Rev. Elie Khalife Hachem, O.L.M. (Lebanon)
Msgr. Michael Ledwith (Ireland)
Msgr. Karl Lehmann*
Msgr. Jorge Medina Estevez*
Msgr. John Onaiyekan (Nigeria)
Rev. Carl Peter (United States)
Rev. Candido Pozo, S.J. (Spain)
Rev. Walter Principe, C.S.B. (Canada)
Msgr. Ignacy Rózycki (Poland)
Rev. Christophe von Schonborn, O.P. (Switzerland)
Msgr. Heinz Schürmann*
Rev. Bernard Sesboüé, S.J. (France)
Rev. John Thornhill, S.M. (Australia)
Rev. Cipriano Vagaggini*
Rev. Jan Walgrave, O.P.*

Fourth Five Years

Appointments of May 23, 1986; cf. *AAS* 78 (1986) 804

Rev. Barthélémy Adoukonou (Benin, Africa)
Rev. Jan Ambaum (Holland)
Rev. Hans Urs von Balthasar*
Bishop Carlos José Boaventura Kloppenburg, O.F.M.*

Rev. Jean-Louis Bruguès O.P. (France)
Msgr. Carlo Caffarra*
Msgr. Giuseppe Colombo*
Rev. Jean Corbon (France)
Rev. George Cottier, O.P. (Switzerland)
Msgr. Philippe Delhaye*
Msgr. Wilhelm Ernst*
Prof. John Finnis (U.K.)
Rev. Joachim Gnilka (Germany)
Rev. José Miguel Ibáñez Langlois (Chile)
Rev. Walter Kasper*
Rev. Gilles Langevin, S.J. (Canada)
Msgr. Michael Ledwith*
Prof. William May (U.S.A.)
Bishop Jorge Medina Estévez*
Rev. Peter Miyakawa (Japan)
Rev. Francis Moloney, S.D.B. (Australia)
Rev. Stanislaw Nagy, S.C.I. (Poland)
Rev. Henrique de Noronha Galvão (Portugal)
Rev. James Okoye, C.S.Sp. (Nigeria)
Rev. Franc Perko (Yugoslavia)
Rev. Carl Peter*
Rev. Cándido Pozo*
Rev. Christoph Schönborn*
Rev. Jan Walgrave, O.P.*
Rev. Felix Wilfred (India)

Fifth Five Years

Appointments of July 3, 1992; cf. *AAS* 84 (1992) 1096

Rev. Charles Acton (U.K.)
Rev. Barthélémy Adoukonou*
Rev. Jan Ambaum*
Rev. Jean-Louis Bruguès, O.P.*
Msgr. Giuseppe Colombo*
Rev. Jean Corbon*
Rev. George Cottier, O.P.*
Rev. Joseph Doré P.S.S. (France)
Rev. Mario de França Miranda, S.J. (Brazil)
Rev. Adolphe Gesché (Belgium)
Rev. Joachim Gnilka*
Rev. Ivan Golub (Croatia)

Prof. Gösta Hallosten (Suecia)
Rev. Tadahiko Iwashima, S.J. (Japan)
Rev. Sebastian Karotemprel, S.D.B. (India)
Rev. Luis F. Ladaria, S.J. (Spain)
Rev. Gilles Langevin, S.J.*
Msgr. Michael Ledwith*
Prof. William May*
Rev. Francis Moloney, S.D.B.*
Rev. Stanislaw Nagy, S.C.I.*
Rev. Henrique de Noronha Galvão*
Rev. Joseph Osei-Bonsu (Ghana)
Rev. Cándido Pozo*
Rev. Christoph Schönborn*
Rev. Norbert Strotmann, M.S.C. (Peru)
Rev. Andrzej Szoztek, M.I.C.[2] (Poland)
Msgr. Max Thurian (Switzerland)
Rev. Lászlo Vanyo (Hungary

Sixth Five Years

Appointments of October 10, 1997; cf. *AAS* 89 (1997) 878–79

Rev. Charles Acton*
Rev. Christopher Begg (U.S.A.)
Rev. Jean-Louis Bruguès O.P.*
Rev. Tanios Bou Mansour, O.L.M. (Lebanon)
Rev. George Cottier, O.P.*
Rev. Santiago del Cura Elena (Spain)
Rev. Joseph Augustine Di Noia, O.P. (U.S.A.)
Rev. Willem Jacobus Eijk (Holland)
Rev. Bruno Forte (Italy)
Rev. Mario de França Miranda, S.J.*
Rev. Pierre Gaudette (Canada)
Rev. Adolphe Gesché*
Prof. Gösta Hallosten*
Rev. George Karakkunnel (India)
Rev. Sebastian Karotemprel, S.D.B.*
Msgr. Roland Minnerath (France)
Rev. Francis Moloney, S.D.B.*
Rev. Gerhard Ludwig Müller (Germany)
Rev. Henrique de Noronha Galvão*

[2]Appointment of November 19, 1992; cf. *AAS* 84 (1992) 1197.

Rev. Thomas Norris (Ireland)
Rev. Adewale Anthony Ojo (Nigeria)
Rev. Hermann Joseph Pottmeyer*
Rev. Rafael Salazar Cardenas, M.Sp.S. (Mexico)
Rev. Fadel Sidarouss, S.J. (Egypt)
Msgr. Anton Strukelj (Slovenia)
Rev. Louis Tagle (Philippines)
Rev. Shun'ichi Takayanagi, S.J. (Japan)
Rev. Lászlo Vanyo*
Rev. Tomasz Weclawski (Poland)
Rev. Sergio Zañartu Undurraga, S.J. (Chile)

Seventh Five Years

Appointments of February 9, 2004; cf. *AAS* 96 (2004) 246–47

Rev. Peter Damien Akpunonu (Nigeria)
Rev. Serge Thomas Bonino, O.P. (France)
Rev. Geraldo Luis Borges Hackmann (Brazil)
Sr. Sara Butler M.S.B.T. (U.S.A.)
Rev. Antonio Castellano (Chile)
Rev. Basil Cho Kyu-Man (South Korea)
Rev. Santiago del Cura Elena*
Rev. Adelbert Denaux (Belgium)
Rev. Gilles P. Emery, O.P. (Switzerland)
Msgr. Ricardo Antonio Ferrara (Argentina)
Archbishop Bruno Forte*
Rev. Pierre Gaudette*
Prof. Barbara Hallensleben (Switzerland)
Rev. Savio Hon Tai-Fai, S.D.B. (China, Hong King)
Rev. Tomislav Ivančić (Croatia)
Rev. István Ivancsó (Hungary)
Rev. Tony Kelly, C.S.S.R. (Australia)
Rev. Luis Ladaria, S.J.*
Rev. Jan W. M. Leisen (Holland)
Rev. John Michael McDermott, S.J. (U.S.A.)
Rev. Paul McPartland (U.K.)
Archbishop Roland Minnerath*
Rev. Thomas Norris*
Rev. Johannes Reiter (Germany)
Rev. Paul Rouhana (Lebanon)
Msgr. Ignazio Sanna (Italy)
Rev. Leonard Santedi Kinkupu (Democratic Republic of Congo)

Prof. Thomas Soeding (Germany)
Rev. Jerzy Szymik (Poland)
Rev. Dominic Veliath, S.D.B. (India)

Presidents of the Commission

His Eminence Franjo Cardinal Seper (1969–1981)
His Eminence Joseph Cardinal Ratzinger (from 1981)

Secretary of the Commission

Secretary General: Msgr. Philippe Delhaye (from 1972)
Assistant Secretaries: Msgr. Jozef Tomko (1969–1971), Msgr. Jozef Zlant-
    nansky (1971–1974), Msgr. Pierre Jarry (1974–1985), Rev. Adriano
    Garuti, O.F.M. (1985).

ABBREVIATIONS

AA   *Apostolicam actuositatem*

AAS   *Acta Apostolicae Sedis*

AG   *Ad gentes*

AS   *Acta Synodalia Sacrosancti Concilii Oecumenici Vaticani II*

CA   *Constitiones Apostolorum*

CCC   *Catechism of the Catholic Church*

CCE   *Catechismus Catholicae Ecclesia* (1992, 1997)

CCL   *Corpus Christianorum, Series Latina*

CD   *Christus Dominus*

CIC   *Codex Iuris Canonici* (1983)

CSEL   *Corpus Scriptorum Ecclesiasticorum Latinorum*

DA   *Didascalia Apostolorum*

DH   *Dignitatis humanae*

DS   H. Denzinger and A. Schönmetzer, eds., *Enchiridion symbolorum, definitionum et declarationem de rebus fidei et morum*

DV   *Dei Verbum*

GCS   *Dei Grieschischen Christlichen Schriftsteller der ersten drei Johrhunderte*

GS   *Gaudium et spes*

ITC   International Theological Commission *Documenta* (Latin Edition)

LG   *Lumen gentium*

NA   *Nostra aetate*

OE   *Orientalium Ecclesiarum*

410

OT	*Optatam Totius*
PG	Patrologia Graeca
PL	Patrologia Latina
PO	Patrologia Orientalis
PO	*Presbyterorum Ordinis*
SC	*Sacrosanctum concilium*
SCh	Sources Chrétiènes
STh	*Summa theologiae*
UR	*Unitatis redintegratio*

INDEX OF COUNCILS AND
ECCLESIASTICAL DOCUMENTS

PARTICULAR COUNCILS AND SYNODS

INDEX OF CODE OF CANON LAW

SCRIPTURE INDEX

INDEX OF PROPER NAMES

INDEX OF SUBJECTS